APULEIUS OF MADAUROS

THE ISIS-BOOK

(METAMORPHOSES, BOOK XI)

ÉTUDES PRÉLIMINAIRES
AUX RELIGIONS ORIENTALES
DANS L'EMPIRE ROMAIN

PUBLIÉES PAR

M. J. VERMASEREN

TOME TRENTE-NEUVIÈME

J. GWYN GRIFFITHS

APULEIUS OF MADAUROS

THE ISIS-BOOK

(METAMORPHOSES, BOOK XI)

LEIDEN
E. J. BRILL
1975

Bronze figure of Osiris with *atef*-crown and
uraei surmounted by sun-disks (height 0.272).
Now in the Ashmolean Museum, Oxford, 1962.614: Radford Gift.
Courtesy Ashmolean Museum, Oxford

APULEIUS OF MADAUROS

THE ISIS-BOOK

(METAMORPHOSES, BOOK XI)

EDITED WITH AN INTRODUCTION, TRANSLATION
AND COMMENTARY

BY

J. GWYN GRIFFITHS

WITH A FRONTISPIECE

LEIDEN
E. J. BRILL
1975

ISBN 90 04 04270 9

(My dear) brother, delight your heart with Isis,
for she is more splendid than millions of soldiers.

Cleopatra II or III in Philae to her husband Ptolemy VIII. A text
on the main gate of the second pylon in Philae, Berlin Photograph
1293, quoted by Erich Winter, *Untersuchungen zu den ägyptischen*
Tempelreliefs der griechisch-römischen Zeit (Denkschr. Wien,
98, 1968), 101.

LÁSZLÓ KÁKOSY

Amico Docto

CONTENTS

PREFACE

I am grateful to Prof. M. J. Vermaseren for his kind invitation to contribute this work to the present series, and to Mr T. A. Edridge for his patience.

The Leverhulme Trust has aided my work, enabling me in particular to spend some time in Alexandria. Dr Henry Riad was then Director of the Graeco-Roman Museum there, and he extended every facility to me with unfailing courtesy. The late Prof. Hanns Stock enabled me to use the Library of the German Archaeological Institute in Cairo, and Prof. A. M. Bakir has helped me in various ways. At a later stage I was indebted to Professors H. Erbse and Elmar Edel for allowing my wife and me to use the libraries of the Classical and Egyptological Seminars of the University of Bonn during a very happy sabbatical term which we spent there. To the Librarians of the University College of Swansea and of the Ashmolean Museum, Oxford, including the Griffith Institute, I am constantly indebted, as also to the staff of the Bodleian Library, Oxford.

My study of the codices has been kindly facilitated by the Librarians of the Laurentian Library, Florence; of the Ambrosian Library, Milan; of the Landesbibliothek, Dresden; of the Bodleian Library, Oxford; of the University of Illinois Library; of the Bibliothèque Publique, St Omer; of the Library of Eton College; and similar facilities were extended by the Keeper of Manuscripts in the British Museum. For the most part I have used photostats, but I have consulted the original manuscripts in Florence, Milan, Oxford and London.

An invitation to lecture at the Eötvös Loránd University, Budapest resulted in an extended visit sponsored by the British Council. This enabled me to study the Iseum at Savaria and to visit museums and sites elsewhere in Hungary; it also brought me the pleasure and privilege of *colloquia* with a number of Hungarian scholars who are interested in Graeco-Egyptian religion and its Roman counterpart. To one of these, Dr László Kákosy, I dedicate the volume gratefully. I am indebted also to the others, as my Commentary makes clear, especially for light on Isis Pelagia. I have thus become happily exposed to an *interpretatio*

Hungarica. Fortunately it is not a unified system, but a series of independent contributions.

My wife and I have also been able to study other European sites and objects, including those in Athens, Piraeus, Cenchreae, Delos and Gortyn; Rome, Tivoli, Pompeii, Naples and Turin; Cologne and Trier. I am obliged to Mr Stephen Ryle, of the University of Liverpool, for graciously allowing me to cite opinions expressed in his unpublished Oxford thesis, which is a Commentary on Apuleius, *Metam.* XI. I have profited from discussions on some points of Latinity with my colleague at Swansea, Mr W. R. Smyth. My wife, as always, has shared my interest in the work and has guided me on several matters of archaeological import. My brother, the Rev. D. R. Griffiths, of the University College, Cardiff, has helped me with the parallels in early Christian literature. I am indebted also to many others who have written on this subject or related themes, but I trust that I have made full acknowledgements in the body of the work. For what has resulted I am alone responsible.

In conclusion I should like to renew my thanks to Professor Vermaseren. He has given me valuable help in the final stages, especially in matters of bibliography. I am also very grateful to his scholarly aides, Mme M. E. C. Vermaseren - van Haaren and Mlle Margaretta B. de Boer.

University College, Swansea   JOHN GWYN GRIFFITHS
6 March 1973

ABBREVIATED REFERENCES

See also the *Oxford Classical Dictionary* (2nd ed., 1970)
and the *Annual Egyptological Bibliography* (Leiden)

Acta Ant. Hung. = *Acta Antiqua Academiae Scientiarum Hungaricae.*
Acta Arch. Hung. = *Acta Archaeologica Academiae Scientiarum Hungaricae.*
Acta Orient. Hung. = *Acta Orientalia* (Budapest).
Adriani, *Rep. d'Arte* = A. Adriani, *Reportorio d'Arte dell'Egitto Greco-Romano*
(Palermo, 1961-66).
Alföldi, 'Die alexandrinischen Götter' = Andreas Alföldi, 'Die alexandrinischen
Götter und die "Vota Publica" ', *Jahrbuch für Antike und Christentum* 8/9
(1965-66), 53-87.
Alföldi, *Festival of Isis* = Andreas Alföldi, *A festival of Isis in Rome under the Christian
emperors of the IVth century*. Dissertationes Pannonicae, II, 7. (Budapest, 1937).
Annuaire = *Annuaire du Musée Gréco-Romain. Municipalité d'Alexandria.*
von Arnim, *Stoic. Vet. Fr.* = H. von Arnim, *Stoicorum Veterum Fragmenta* (Leipzig,
1905 et postea).

Bernhard, *Stil* = Max Bernhard, *Der Stil des Apuleius von Madaura*. Tübinger Beiträge zur Altertumswissenschaft, 11. (Stuttgart, 1927; repr. Amsterdam, 1965).
Berreth = Joseph Berreth, *Studien zum Isisbuch Apuleius' Metamorphosen* (Ellwangen,
1931).
Bevan, *Hist. Ptol. Eg.* = Edwyn Bevan, *A History of Egypt under the Ptolemaic
Dynasty* (London, 1927).
von Bissing, *Ägypt. Kultbilder* = F. W. von Bissing, *Ägyptische Kultbilder der Ptolo-
maier- und Römerzeit. Der alte Orient* 34 (1936).
von Bissing, 'Paintings from Pompeii' = F. W. von Bissing, 'Notes on Some Paintings
from Pompeii referring to the Cult of Isis', *Transactions of the 3rd International
Congress for the History of Religions* I (Oxford, 1908), 225-8.
Boeken, *Adnot.* = H. J. Boeken, *Adnotationes ad Apuleii Metamorphoseon Librum XI*
(Amsterdam, 1899).
Bonner, *Stud. Mag. Am.* = Campbell Bonner, *Studies in Magical Amulets, chiefly
Graeco-Egyptian* (Ann Arbor, 1950).
Bonnet, *Bilderatlas* = Hans Bonnet, *Bilderatlas zur Religionsgeschichte*, ed. D. Hans
Haas. 2-4. *Ägyptische Religion* (Leipzig, 1924).
Bonnet, *Reallexikon* = Hans Bonnet, *Reallexikon der ägyptischen Religionsgeschichte*
(Berlin, 1952).

Boyce, *Lararia of Pompeii* = George K. Boyce, *Corpus of the Lararia of Pompeii* (Memoirs of the American Academy in Rome, 1937).

Brady, *Rec. Egn. Cults* = T. A. Brady, *The Reception of the Egyptian Cults by the Greeks (330-30 B.C.)* (Missouri, 1935).

Breccia, *Alex.* = Evaristo Breccia, *Alexandrea ad Aegyptum* (Bergamo, 1914).

Breccia, *Iscr.* = Evaristo Breccia, *Iscrizioni greche e latine. Musée gréco-romain, Alexandria. Cat. général. Nos. 1-568* (Cairo, 1911).

Breccia, *Monuments*, I = Evaristo Breccia, *Monuments de l'Égypte Gréco-Romaine*, I (Bergamo, 1926).

Breccia, *Terr.* 1 and 2 = Evaristo Brecchia, *Terrecotte Figurate Greche e Greco-Egizie del Museo di Alessandria* (= *Monuments de l'Égypte Gréco-Romaine* II, i and ii; Bergamo, 1930 and 1934).

CCG = Cairo Museum, *Catalogue Général*.

Callebat, *Sermo Cotid.* = Louis Callebat, *Sermo Cotidianus dans les Métamorphoses d'Apulée* (Caen, 1968).

Castiglione, 'Isis Pharia' = László Castiglione, 'Isis Pharia : Remarque sur la statue de Budapest', *Bulletin du Musée Hongrois des beaux-Arts*, nos. 34-35, pp. 37-55 (Budapest, 1970).

Castiglione, 'Kunst' = László Castiglione, 'Kunst und Gesellschaft im römischen Ägypten', *Acta Ant. Hung.* 15 (1967), 107-152.

Clemen, *Einfluss der Mysterienrel.* = Carl Clemen, *Der Einfluss der Mysterienreligionen auf das älteste Christentum*. RGVV 13. 1. (Giessen, 1913).

Corp. Herm. = *Corpus Hermeticum*, ed. A. D. Nock and A.-J. Festugière, 4 Vols. (Paris, 1945-54; also entitled *Hermès Trismégiste*). Cited by no. of treatise and chapter, followed by vol. and page.

Cumont, *Or. Rel.* = Franz Cumont, *Die orientalischen Religionen im römischen Heidentum*, rev. August Burckhardt-Brandenberg (Darmstadt, 1959).

Cumont, *Rel. Or.* = Franz Cumont, *Les religions orientales dans le paganisme romain.* (Ed. 4, Paris, 1929).

Delatte and Derchain, *Intailles Magiques* = A. Delatte and Ph. Derchain, *Les intailles magiques gréco-égyptiennes*. Bibliothèque Nationale. Cabinet des médailles et antiques. (Paris, 1964).

Derchain, *P. Salt 825* = Philippe Derchain, *Le Papyrus Salt 825 (B.M. 10051), rituel pour la conservation de la vie en Égypte*. Acad. de Belgique, Mém. 58. (Brussels, 1965).

Derchain, ed. *Rel. en Égypte* = Philippe Derchain, ed., *Religions en Égypte hellénistique et romaine*. Colloque de Strasbourg, 18-18 mai 1967. (Bibliothèque des Centres d'Études supérieures spécialisés; Paris, 1969).

Dibelius, 'Isisweihe' = Martin Dibelius, 'Die Isisweihe bei Apuleius und verwandte Initiations-Riten' (Sitzb. Heidelberg, 1917), repr. in Martin Dibelius, *Botschaft und Geschichte*, II (Tübingen, 1956), 30-79.

Edgar, *Graeco-Egyptian Coffins* = C. C. Edgar, *Graeco-Egyptian Coffins, Masks and Portraits* (*CCG*, Cairo, 1905).

Erman - Ranke, *Ägypten* = Adolf Erman and Hermann Ranke, *Aegypten und aegyptisches Leben im Altertum* (Tübingen, 1923).

Fernhout, *Metam*. V = J. M. H. Fernhout, *Ad Apulei Madaurensis Metamorphoseon Librum Quintum Commentarius Exegeticus* (Medioburgi, 1949).

Festugière, 'Lucius and Isis' = André-Jean Festugière, *Personal Religion among the Greeks*. Sather Classical Lectures, 1954. (Berkeley, repr. 1960).

Frankfort, *Rel.* = Henri Frankfort, *Ancient Egyptian Religion* (New York, 1961).

Fraser, 'Two Studies' = P. M. Fraser, 'Two Studies on the Cult of Sarapis in the Hellenistic World', *Opuscula Atheniensia* 3 (1960), 1-54.

Friedländer, *Sittengeschichte Roms* = L. Friedländer, *Darstellungen aus der Sittengeschichte Roms* (Ed. 10, rev. Georg Wissowa; 3 Vols., Leipzig, 1922-23).

Fugier, *L'Expression du Sacré* = Huguette Fugier, *Recherches sur l'Expression du Sacré dans la Langue Latine* (Paris, 1963).

Gabra and Drioton, *Touna el-Gebel* = Sami Gabra and Étienne Drioton, *Peintures à Fresques et Scènes Peintes à Hermoupolis-Ouest* [*Touna el-Gebel*] (Cairo, 1954).

J. von Geisau, *De Apul. Synt.* = Johannes von Geisau, *De Apulei Syntaxi Poetica et Graecanica* (Münster, 1912).

V. von Gonzenbach, *Knabenweihen* = Victorine von Gonzenbach, *Untersuchungen zu den Knabenweihen im Isiskult der römischen Kaiserzeit*. Abhandlungen zur alten Geschichte, 4. (Bonn, 1957).

Grant, *Hellenistic Rel.* = Frederick C. Grant, *Hellenistic Religions. The Age of Syncretism* (New York, 1953).

Gressmann, *Orient. Rel.* = Hugo Gressmann, *Die orientalischen Religionen im hellenistisch-römischen Zeitalter* (Berlin, 1930).

Gressmann, *Osiris* = Hugo Gressmann, *Tod und Auferstehung des Osiris. Der Alte Orient* 23, 3. (Leipzig, 1923).

Griffiths, *Conflict* = J. Gwyn Griffiths, *The Conflict of Horus and Seth*. Liverpool Monographs in Archaeology and Oriental Studies. (Liverpool, 1960).

Griffiths, *Plut. De Is. et Os.* = J. Gwyn Griffiths, *Plutarch's De Iside et Osiride* (Cardiff, 1970).

Grimm, *Ägypt. Rel. im röm. Deutschland* = Günter Grimm, *Die Zeugnisse ägyptischer Religion und Kunstelemente im römischen Deutschland*. ÉPRO, 12, (Leiden, 1969).

Helck and Otto, *Kl. Wb.* = Wolfgang Helck and Eberhard Otto, *Kleines Wörterbuch der Aegyptologie* (Ed. 2, Wiesbaden, 1970).

Hepding, *Attis* = H. Hepding, *Attis : seine Mythen und sein Kult*. RGVV 1. (Giessen, 1903).

Hofmann and Szantyr, *Lat. Syntax* = J.B. Hofmann, rev. A. Szantyr, *Lateinische Syntax und Stilistik* (Munich, 1965) = Bd 2 of Leumann, Hofmann and Szantyr, *Lateinische Grammatik* (*Handbuch der Altertumswissenschaft*, 2, 2).

Hopfner, *Fontes* = Theodor Hopfner, *Fontes Historiae Religionis Aegyptiacae.* Fontes Historiae Religionum, ed. C. Clemen. (Bonn, 1922-25).

Index Apul. = W. A. Oldfather, H. V. Canter, B. E. Perry, K. M. Abbott, *Index Apuleianus.* Philological Monographs of the American Philological Assoc. no. 3. (Middletown, Conn. 1934).

de Jong, *De Apul.* = K. H. E. de Jong, *De Apuleio Isiacorum Mysteriorum Teste* (Leiden, 1900).

de Jong, *Myst.* = K. H. E. de Jong, *Das antike Mysterienwesen* (Leiden, 1909).

Junghanns, *Erzählungstechnik* = Paul Junghanns, *Die Erzählungstechnik von Apuleius' Metamorphosen und ihrer Vorlage.* Philologus Suppl. 24. 1 (Leipzig, 1952).

Junker, *Der grosse Pylon* = Hermann Junker, *Der grosse Pylon des Tempels der Isis in Philä* (Denkschr. Wien, 1958).

Junker and Winter, *Geburtshaus* = Hermann Junker and Erich Winter, *Das Geburtshaus des Tempels der Isis in Philä* (Denkschr. Wien, 1965).

Kerényi, *Rel.* = Carl Kerényi, *The Religion of the Greeks and Romans* (London, 1962).

Koziol, *Stil* = Heinrich Koziol, *Der Stil des L. Apuleius* (Vienna, 1872).

Kühner and Holzweissig, *Gramm. Lat.²* = Raphael Kühner and Friedrich Holzweissig, *Ausführliche Grammatik der Lateinischen Sprache. I. Elementar-, Formen-, und Wortlehre.* (Ed. 2, Hanover, 1912, repr. 1966).

Kühner and Stegmann, *Gramm. Lat.²* = Raphael Kühner, rev. Carl Stegmann, *Ausführliche Grammatik der Lateinischen Sprache. II. Satzlehre* (Ed. 2, Hanover, 1912 and 1914, in two parts).

Lafaye, *Hist. du culte* = Georges Lafaye, *Histoire du culte des divinités d'Alexandrie, Sérapis, Isis, Harpocrate et Anubis, hors de l'Égypte* (Paris, 1884).

Latte, *Röm. Rel.* = Kurt Latte, *Römische Religionsgeschichte* (Munich, 1960).

Leclant, *Mons. Thébains* = Jean Leclant, *Recherches sur les monuments Thébains de la XXVᵉ dynastie dite éthiopienne.* IFAO, BE 36 (Cairo, 1965).

Leipoldt, *Bilderatlas* = *Bilderatlas zur Religionsgeschichte*, ed. D. Hans Haas, 9-11. *Die Religionen in der Umwelt des Christentums.* (Leipzig, 1926).
In square brackets afterwards is cited the corresponding figure (when it occurs) in Leipoldt (ed. Grundmann), *Umwelt des Urchristentums*, III (Ed. 2, Berlin, 1967).

Leipoldt, *Umwelt*, III = Johannes Leipoldt, *Umwelt des Urchristentums*, III (ed. Walter Grundmann, Ed. 2, Berlin, 1967).

Médan. *Lat.* = Pierre Médan, *La Latinité d'Apulée dans les Métamorphoses. Étude de Grammaire et de Stylistique* (Paris, 1926).

M Molt, *Metam. I* = Margaretha Molt, *Ad Apulei Madaurensis Metamorphoseon Librum Primum Commentarius Exegeticus* (Groningen, 1938).

Morenz, 'Problem des Werdens zu Osiris' = Siegfried Morenz, 'Das Problem des Werdens zu Osiris in der griechisch-römischen Zeit Ägyptens' in Ph. Derchain (ed.), *Religions en Égypte hellénistique et romaine* (Paris, 1969), 75-91.

D. Müller, *Isis-Aret.* = Dieter Müller, *Ägypten und die griechischen Isis-Aretalogien.* Abh. Leipzig, 53, 1. (Berlin, 1961).

H. W. Müller, *Sammling München* = Staatliche Sammlung Ägyptischer Kunst (Munich, 1972).

H. W. Müller 'Isis mit dem Horuskinde' = the study with this title, subtitled 'Ein Beitrag zur Ikonographie der stillenden Gottesmutter im hellenistischen und römischen Ägypten', *Münchener Jahrbuch der Bildenden Kunst* 14 (1963), 7-38.

M. Münster, *Isis* = Maria Münster, *Untersuchungen zur Göttin Isis.* MÄS 11. (Berlin, 1968).

Neuenschwander, *Der bildliche Ausdruck* = Paul Neuenschwander, *Der bildliche Ausdruck des Apuleius von Madaura* (Diss. Zürich, 1913).

Nilsson, *Dionysiac Mysteries* = Martin P. Nilsson, *The Dionysiac Mysteries of the Hellenistic and Roman Age.* Acta Inst. Atheniens. Regni Sueciae, 8° V (Lund, 1957).

Nilsson, *Gesch. Gr. Rel.* = Martin P. Nilsson, *Geschichte der Griechischen Religion.* I (Ed. 3, Munich, 1967). II (Ed. 2, Munich, 1961).

Nock. *Essays* = Arthur Darby Nock, *Essays on Religion and the Ancient World,* ed. Zeph Stewart. 2 vols, (Oxford, 1972).

Oldfather et al., *Index Apul.* = W. A. Oldfather, H. V. Canter, B. E. Perry, K. M. Abbott, *Index Apuleianus.* PAPA 3. (Middletown, 1934).

E. Otto, *Gott und Mensch* = Eberhard Otto, *Gott und Mensch nach den ägyptischen Tempelinschriften der griechisch-römischen Zeit* (Heidelberg, 1964).

E. Otto, *Osiris and Amon* = Eberhard Otto, *Egyptian Art and the Cults of Osiris and Amon* (tr. K. B. Griffiths, London, 1968).

W. Otto, *Priester und Tempel* = Walter Otto, *Priester und Tempel im hellenistischen Ägypten.* 2 vols. (Leipzig, 1905 and 1908).

PGM = *Papyri Graecae Magicae* ed. Karl Preisendanz. (Leipzig, 1928-1931).

PW = Pauly, Wissowa, Kroll, and Mittelhaus, *Real-Encyclopädie der classischen Altertumswissenschaft.* (Stuttgart, 1893-   ).

van der Paardt, *Metam. III* = R. T. van der Paardt, *L. Apuleius Madaurensis, The Metamorphoses : A commentary on book III with text and introduction* (Amsterdam, 1971).

Parlasca, *Mumienporträts* = Klaus Parlasca, *Mumienporträts und verwandte Denkmäler* (Wiesbaden, 1966).

Peek, *Isishymnus* = Werner Peek, *Der Isishymnus von Andros* (Berlin, 1930).

Perdrizet, *Bronzes* = Paul Perdrizet, *Bronzes Grecs d'Égypte de la Collection Fouquet* (Paris, 1911).

Perdrizet, *Terr.* = Paul Perdrizet, *Les terres cuites grecques d'Égypte de la collection Fouquet.* 2 vols. (Nancy, 1921).

Plutarch, *De Is. et Os.* = *De Iside et Osiride.*

Purser, *Cupid and Psyche* = Louis C. Purser, *The Story of Cupid and Psyche as related by Apuleius* (London, 1910).

Reitzenstein, *Hellenist. Myst.* = R. Reitzenstein, *Die hellenistischen Mysterien-religionen* (Ed. 3, Leipzig, 1927).

Rel. = *Religion.*

Roeder, *Bronzefiguren* = Günther Roeder, *Ägyptische Bronzefiguren.* Staatliche Museen zu Berlin. Mitt. aus der ägyptischen Sammlung. VI (Berlin, 1956).

Roeder, *Rel.* = Günther Roeder, *Die ägyptische Religion in Text und Bild.* 4 vols. (Zürich, 1959-61).

Roeder, *Urk. Rel.* = Günther Roeder, *Urkunden zur Religion des alten Ägypten* (Jena, 1923).

Roscher, *Lex. Myth.* = W. H. Roscher, *Ausführliches Lexikon der Griechischen und Römischen Mythologie* (Leipzig, 1884-1937).

Rose, *Hdbk. Gr. Myth.* = H. J. Rose, *A Handbook of Greek Mythology* (London, 1928, Ed. 6, 1958).

Anne Roullet, *Rome* = Anne Roullet, *The Egyptian and Egyptianizing Monuments of Imperial Rome.* ÉPRO 20, (Leiden, 1972).

Roussel, *CED* = Pierre Roussel, *Les cultes égyptiens à Delos du IIIᵉ au Iᵉʳ siècle av. J.-C.* Annales de l'Est, Université de Nancy, 29-30. (Paris, 1915-1916).

Ryle = Stephen Francis Ryle, 'A Commentary on Apuleius, *Metamorphoses*, XI' (Unpublished B. Litt. Thesis, Oxford, 1968).

R. Salditt-Trappmann, *Tempel* = *Tempel der ägyptischen Götter in Griechenland und an der Westküste Kleinasiens.* ÉPRO 15. (Leiden 1970).

Salem, *Cult* = M. S. Salem, 'The Cult of Isis in Italy, (unpublished Diss., Liverpool, 1936).

Sauneron, *Priests* = Serge Sauneron, *The Priests of Ancient Egypt* (tr. Ann Morrissett, London, 1960).

Schäfer, 'Das Gewand der Isis' = Heinrich Schäfer, 'Das Gewand der Isis — ein Beitrag zur Kunst-, Kultur- und Religionsgeschichte des Hellenismus', *FS. C. F. Lehmann-Haupt* (Vienna, 1921), 194-205 (= *Janus*, Heft 1, ed. K. Regling and H. Reich).

Schanz, Hosius and Krüger, *Röm. Litt.* = Martin Schanz, rev. Carl Hosius and Gustav Krüger, *Geschichte der römischen Litteratur*, III (Ed. 3, Munich, 1922).

Schober, *Comp. num.* = Ernestus Schober, *De Apulei Metamorphoseon compositione numerosa* (Diss. Halle, 1904).

J. E. Stambaugh, *Sarapis* = *Sarapis under the Early Ptolemies.* ÉPRO 25. (Leiden, 1972).

Stolz and Schmalz, *Lat. Gramm.*⁵ = Fr. Stolz and J. H. Schmalz, *Lateinische Grammatik*, Ed. 5, rev. M. Leumann and J. B. Hofmann (Munich, 1928).

Thes. L.L. = *Thesaurus Linguae Latinae* (Leipzig, 1900-   ).

Tran Tam Tinh, *Herculanum* = V. Tran Tam Tinh, *Le culte des divinités orientales à Herculanum.* ÉPRO 17. (Leiden, 1971).

Tran Tam Tinh, *Isis à Pompéi* = V. Tran Tam Tinh, *Essai sur le culte d'Isis à Pompéi* (Paris, 1964).

Turchi, *Fontes Hist. Myst.* = Nicolaus Turchi, *Fontes Historiae Mysteriorum Aevi Hellenistici* (Rome, 1930).

Vandebeek, *Isisfiguur* = G. Vandebeek, *De Interpretatio Graeca van de Isisfiguur.* Studia Hellenistica, 4. (Louvain, 1946).

Vermaseren, *CIM Rel. Mithr.* = M.J. Vermaseren, *Corpus Inscriptionum et Monumentorum Religionis Mithriacae* (2 vols., The Hague, 1956 and 1960).

Vermaseren and van Essen, *Santa Prisca* = M. J. Vermaseren and C. C. van Essen, *The Excavations in the Mithraeum of the Church of Santa Prisca in Rome* (Leiden, 1965).

Vidman, *Isis und Sarapis* = Ladislav Vidman, *Isis und Sarapis bei den Griechen und Römern.* RGVV 29. (Berlin, 1970).

Vidman , *SIRIS* = Ladislaus Vidman, *Sylloge inscriptionum religionis Isiacae et Sarapiacae.* RGVV 28. (Berlin, 1969).

Vogt, *Terr.* = Joseph Vogt, *Die griechisch-ägyptische Sammlung Ernst von Sieglin.* 2. *Terrakotten.* Expedition Ernst von Sieglin. Ausgrabungen in Alexandria. Bd. II, 2. (Leipzig, 1924).

Volten, 'Testi Demotici' = Aksel Volten, 'I testi demotici quali fonti della storia della religione egiziana', *Le fonti indirette della storia egiziana* ed. S. Donadoni (Rome, 1963).

G. Wagner, *Problem* = Günter Wagner, *Das religionsgeschichtliche Problem von Römer 6, 1-11* (Stuttgart, 1962). See also the translation by J. P. Smith entitled *Pauline Baptism and the Pagan Mysteries* (Edinburgh, 1967).

Weber, *Terr.* = Wilhelm Weber, *Die ägyptisch-griechischen Terrakotten.* 2 vols. Königliche Museen zu Berlin. Mitt. aus der ägyptischen Sammlung, Bd. II. (Berlin, 1914).

Weinreich, *Neue Urkunden* = Otto Weinreich, *Neue Urkunden zur Sarapisreligion* (Tübingen, 1919), repr. in his *Ausgewählte Schriften,* I (Amsterdam, 1969), 410-442.

Wessetzky, *Ägypt. Kulte in Ungarn* = Vilmos Wessetzky, *Die ägyptischen Kulte zur Römerzeit in Ungarn.* ÉPRO 1. (Leiden, 1961).

Westendorf, *Egn. Art* = Wolfhart Westendorf, *Painting, Sculpture, and Architecture of Ancient Egypt.* Panorama of World Art. (New York, 1968).

R. E. Witt, *Isis. Gr.-R.* = *Isis in the Graeco-Roman World* (London, 1971) .

R. E. Witt, 'Isis-Hellas' = 'Isis-Hellas', *Proc. Cambridge Phil. Soc.* 12 (1966), 48-69.

R. E. Witt, 'Macedonia' = 'The Egyptian Cults in Ancient Macedonia', *Ancient Macedonia* (Symposium Thessaloniki, 1970), 324-333.

Wittmann = Willi Wittmann, *Das Isisbuch des Apuleius. Untersuchungen zur Geistesgeschichte des 2. Jahrhunderts.* Forschungen zur Kirchen- und Geistesgeschichte, 12 (Diss. Berlin, Stuttgart, 1938).

Woldering, *Art : Egypt* = Irmgard Woldering, *Egypt : The Art of the Pharaohs.* Art of the World, 12. (London, 1963).

Zimmermann, *Rel.* = Friedrich Zimmermann, *Die ägyptische Religion nach der Dar-*

stellung der Kirchenschriftsteller und die ägyptischen Denkmäler. Studien zur Geschichte und Kultur des Altertums, 5. (Paderborn, 1912).

Note

All references to the works of Apuleius involve the Teubner editions. Chapters are cited with the number of page and line in brackets. The same system applies to allusions to the present book, save that the page references of the Teubner edition are now given in the margin, whereas the line references are to the lines of the new edition.

INTRODUCTION

I. THE AUTOBIOGRAPHICAL ELEMENT

It is generally agreed that the *Metamorphoses* of Apuleius is a work based on a lost Greek work of which *Lucius or Ass* (Λούκιος ἢ "Ονος) is the epitome. In the ninth century A.D. the patriarch Photius (*Bibl.* 129 p. 103 f. R. Henry [1960]) assigned the lost Greek *Metamorphoses* to a writer called Lucius of Patrae, and this too is the name of the person who tells the story, in the first person, of *Lucius or Ass*. The text is usually printed with Lucian's works : v. C. Iacobitz, *Luciani ... Opera*, II (Leipzig, Teubner, 1897), 303 ff.; M. D. Macleod, *Lucian*, 8 (London, Loeb C. L., 1967), 47 ff. Macleod presents also an English translation, and a German translation is appended, together with the Greek text, at the end of Edward Brandt's *Der goldene Esel*, where the Latin text of Apuleius, with a German translation, is the main subject (ed. 2, Stuttgart, 1963). Ben Edwin Perry [1] has urged, following Pauly, that Lucian was the author of the lost *Metamorphoses* in Greek; if so, one would expect to find traces of Lucian's satire and humour in *Lucius or Ass*. This is unhappily not so, although there is linguistic affinity. Perhaps a Lucianic imitator is implied.

When *Lucius or Ass* is compared with the Apuleian work, the difference is seen to be immense, even if we allow for the fact that the former is only an epitome. Nor is it merely a stylistic difference — that between chalk and cheese, between penny plain and twopence coloured; [2] in Apuleius the artistic intent is so much deeper and richer. The broad

---

[1] *The Metamorphoses Ascribed to Lucius of Patrae* (Lancaster, Pa., 1920); id. *The Ancient Romances* (Berkeley, 1967), 211 ff. See also, for the whole problem, W. S. *Teuffels Geschichte der römischen Lit.*[6] rev. W. Kroll (Leipzig, 1913), 106; Schanz, Hosius and Krüger, *Röm. Litt.* III[3] (1922), 106 ff.; M. D. Macleod, *Lucian*, 8 (Loeb), 47 ff.; P. G. Walsh, *The Roman Novel* (Cambridge, 1970), 145 ff.

[2] H. E. Butler (translation, Vol. I, 10), after admitting this contrast, says : 'And yet the style of the author of *Lucius or the Ass*, whoever he may have been, is far from being bad, and has certainly fewer positive defects than the style of Apuleius.' This verdict can be based only on a foolishly narrow standard of correctness.

outline of the story is common to the two narratives; they also share
the hero's name, Lucius, and the use of the First Person. Apuleius
himself suggests a debt to Greek writers when he speaks of writing
'in the well-known Milesian style' (*sermone isto Milesio*, 1. 1 *init.*), by
which is meant the humorous and lascivious manner used by Aristides
in the second century B.C. and introduced to Rome in the following
century by Sisenna; cf. M. Molt's commentary *ad loc.*, pp. 21 f. The
genre attracted the kind of attention given later to the *Decameron* of
Boccaccio; cf. P. Vallette, *Introd.* (Budé), xxii and Walsh, *The Roman
Novel*, 10 f. Probably what Aristides presented was a series of short
stories [1] and Apuleius may be referring to stories inserted into his
Metamorphoses rather than to the main theme, [2] although Reitzenstein [3]
tried to trace even the story of the man who became an ass to Sisenna
and Aristides. It is a little surprising to find Apuleius referring to the
story of 'Cupid and Psyche' as a Milesian tale (4.32, p. 100, 19, *propter
Milesiae conditorem*), for in spite of its humorous touches and the basic
theme of love, the Milesian stamp is hard to see; although Grimal's
remarks *ad loc.* (1963, p. 42 n. 6) tend otherwise, the description may apply
to Apuleius in a more general sense; [4] cf. *inter Milesias Punicas Apulei*
(J. Capitolinus, *Vit. Alb.* 12.12, on which see Vallette, *Introd.* xxii).
The term *fabula Graecanica*, which Apuleius also uses of the *Metamorphoses* in general (1.1, p. 2, 3), confirms his sense of debt to the Greek
tradition.

How can a possible autobiographical element enter, it may be asked,
into a self-confessed framework of borrowed material? [5] Clearly this

---

[1] Perry, *The Ancient Romances*, 94. J. P. Sullivan, *The 'Satyricon' of Petronius*
(London, 1968), 232-4 surveys 'The Pornographic Tradition' without a mention,
strangely, of either Aristides or Sisenna.

[2] Cf. A. Scobie, *Aspects of the Ancient Romance and its Heritage* (Meisenheim am
Glan, 1969), 32 f.; Walsh, *The Roman Novel*, 11.

[3] *Das Märchen von Amor und Psyche bei Apuleius* (Leipzig, 1912), 59 ff.; now in
Binder and Merkelbach, *Amor und Psyche* (Darmstadt, 1968), 133 ff. The attempt
is not wholly successful; cf. Sophie Trenkner, *The Greek Novella in the Classical
Period* (Cambridge, 1958), 173; A. Scobie, op. cit. 33 f.; Walsh, op. cit. 17.

[4] Cf. Purser *ad loc.* p. 13 and Scobie, op. cit. 33.

[5] There are good discussions in Nock, *Conversion*, 138 ff. and Festugière, 'Lucius
and Isis', 72 ff.

may happen in those parts of the work where there is a marked deviation from the prototype. Here a slight embarrassment accompanies the enquiry in that the prototype is not known to us in full. Can we be sure that the apparent differences introduced by Apuleius were not simply omitted in the epitome? On this matter the careful investigation conducted by Junghanns in his *Die Erzählungstechnik von Apuleius' Metamorphosen und ihrer Vorlage* (Leipzig, 1932) is helpful; his conclusion is that the epitome is shorter only by about one-tenth than its original. It follows that the major deviations—the story of 'Cupid and Psyche' and Book XI—were probably not present in any form in the prototype; Walsh, *The Roman Novel*, 148, after presenting a useful comparative table of the material, sees these two episodes as 'wholly independent of the Greek original'.

It does not follow, of course, that these episodes are necessarily autobiographical in content. The story of 'Cupid and Psyche' has been shown to be based on a folk-tale, and any personal imprint it bears seems to be due to its relationship to Book XI. That this book has a strong element of autobiography is suggested, first of all, by the contrast between it and the end of *Lucius or Ass*. In both narratives Lucius in his asinine form faces an act of sexual union with a woman in an amphitheatre. *Lucius or Ass* describes how a man passing by was carrying flowers, including roses, and how Lucius achieves immediate restoration to human form by eating the rose-leaves. Afterwards he returns to the woman with whom he had previously had intercourse, but she despises him because he no longer possesses the mighty sexual organ of an ass. Then he sails away home with his brother. Roses are also the medium of restoration in the *Metamorphoses*, but they seem to belong to a different world—they form the garland of a priest of Isis. The following narrative of conversion and initiation has very few points of contact with the other story. Lucius returns home for a short interval, but Rome and further initiations are then described. The whole atmosphere is one of spiritual expectation and tension, and it is hard to avoid the impression that a personal experience is being portrayed. At Rome the success of Lucius as an advocate is a concomitant of his progress as an initiate. Our main source for the life of Apuleius is the *Apologia*, and it confirms the experience of initiation. He states (55, p. 62, 20), 'I have taken part in a number of initiation ceremonies in Greece' (*sacrorum pleraque initia*

in Graecia participavi)[1], and goes on to say that he has carefully preserved
certain *signa et monumenta* given to him by the priests. He then claims that
his incentive was 'desire to know the truth and a sense of duty towards
the gods' (*studio veri et officio erga deos*); because of this he learned
'holy procedures of many kinds, a great number of rites, and diverse
ceremonies' (*multiiuga sacra et plurimos ritus et varias cerimonias*).
We may confidently infer that the Isiac rites were among these.[2] The only
slight inconsistency is the exclusive claim that Isis appears to make on
the initiate, as in ch. 6. It is well known, in fact, that one person could
combine various mysteries in his adherence, as Clea is said to do in
Plutarch's *De Iside et Osiride* and as Apuleius himself implies in the
Apologia.

As for his career at Rome, allusion is made in the *Apologia* (23, p. 27,
5) to lengthy travels and protracted studies, and in the *Florida* (17,
p. 31, 8 ff.), in a piece addressed to Scipio Orfitus, Apuleius claims that
he has always cultivated *bonas artes* and that both in Africa and 'among
your friends in Rome' (*Romae penes amicos tuos*) he has tried to win a
good reputation for his character and studies. There is some stress in
Metam. 11.28 *fin.* on the ability of Lucius to use Latin in his speeches
in the courts; Apuleius, however, must have known Latin before going
to Rome : [3] see n. *ad loc.* citing *Apol.* 4. Here, then, the element of autobiography is atrophied somewhat in favour of the Corinthian Lucius
who is said in 1.1 to have tackled Latin only after studying it in Rome
(*in urbe Latia*) as a language that was strange to him. At the end of ch.
27 the priest Asinius Marcellus is said to be given divine information
about the future of Lucius; by the gods' providence he is destined to
'glory of learning' (*studiorum gloriam*). Since Lucius in *Lucius or Ass*,
55, also makes a literary claim which can be compared with this and

---

[1] Cf. *Metam.* 3.15 (63, 8 f.) : Photis tells Lucius that he has been 'initiated into many
sacred rites' (*sacris pluribus initiatus*).

[2] A. Abt, *Die Apologie des Apuleius*, 288, points out that knowledge of the rites
of the Dea Syria is shown in *Metam.* 8.24 ff. and 9.3 ff. although external activities
only are involved; also that *Metam.* 6.2 describes the Eleusinian rites, to which likewise the words *unius Liberi patris mystae* in *Apol.* 55 (p. 62, 23) probably refer. Apuleius counts himself, it seems, among the Eleusinian initiates.

[3] On the other hand, his African accent may have caused embarrassment; cf.
M. Hicter, *Ant. Class.* 13 (1945), 105.

with *Metam.* 2.12 *fin.* (the prophecy of Diophanes the Chaldaean about Lucius), the allusion in ch. 27 is partly an echo of the Greek original; it is partly autobiographical at the same time, since the emphasis on learning agrees with claims made elsewhere by Apuleius : see n. *ad* ch. 27 *fin.*

It is in this passage in ch. 27 that Lucius is referred to as a poor man from Madauros (*Madaurensem, sed admodum pauperem*), and the consensus of opinion has rightly seen Apuleius here in the act of dropping the mask and openly identifying himself with the Lucius of the story. The attempts to emend *Madaurensem* are unconvincing. Nor is it likely that this is an unwitting *lapsus calami*; it may well accord with the practice of providing a kind of signature in this kind of work,[1] but it goes further in that the religious experience described is by implication avowed by Apuleius himself. Walsh [2] has argued that this position is one assumed in reaction to the spread of Christianity in Africa : '... *Madaurensis* is inserted here to connect the conversion to Isis with that African backcloth which is being transformed through the advance of Christianity.' The focussing of such a feeling on Madauros is hard to accept. It is true that tradition connects Madauros with the appearance of Africa's first Christian martyrs in A.D. 180, but Walsh [3] himself dismisses the evidence as 'fragile'. That an anti-Christian purpose is linked with the autobiographical element in a more general sense is a thesis presented more cogently by Walsh. He makes the attractive suggestion that the ass-theme is linked with the belief, attested for Africa by Tertullian, *Apol.* 16, that Christians worshipped an ass's head; they were, in Tertullian's language, *asinarii.* [4] A difficulty in this interpretation is that the abuse of the ass in Apuleius (e.g. the words of Isis in ch. 6) is based firmly on the Egyptian view of the ass as an animal pre-eminently associated with Seth-Typhon. This, at any rate,

---

[1] Cf. H. Werner, *Hermes* 53 (1918), 242, cited by Scobie, *Aspects of the Ancient Romance etc.* 82 (Scobie himself rejects the explanation); Paratore, *La novella in Apuleio²*, 65; Walsh, *The Roman Novel*, 184; Paul Veyne, *Rev. Phil.* 39 (1965), 241.

[2] *Phoenix* 22 (1968), 151 ff., this dictum on p. 154; cf. id. *The Roman Novel*, 186 ff.

[3] *Phoenix* 22 (1968), 154.

[4] The best study of the development of this Sethian concept is that of B. H. Stricker, 'Asinarii', in *OMRO* 46 (1965), 52-75.

is the first emphasis; an undertone may simultaneously involve the extension to Christian contexts.

With certain minor reservations, therefore, which concern consistency in the presentation of the main character, Apuleius may be regarded as conveying in Book XI his own experience as an Isiac initiate. This means that his testimony is of inestimable value as evidence for the cult of Isis at a Greek centre. Earlier in the century Plutarch also wrote his study, and personal experience likewise enters into this, possibly, as well as the active participation in the cult of his friend Clea. Yet Plutarch for various reasons is often looking back to the history of the cult in Egypt itself, and when he is using good sources his work is of capital importance in a wider sense than can apply to the book of Apuleius.[1] The latter is concerned for the most part with a particular rite in a particular place. Within this limitation his work has an immediacy and an elaboration of detail that are quite rare in our sources for ancient religion. Such qualities may naturally derive from personal experience, and the existence of the Eleventh Book, suggesting a compulsive accretion, itself points in the same direction.[2] Jack Lindsay[3] calls attention to the doubt expressed by St Augustine as to whether the whole of the *Golden Ass* was genuine autobiography or mere fiction. In *De civ. Dei*, 18.18 Augustine is talking of transformations wrought by drugs; men can be changed into animals, he says, but their minds remain human. He goes on : 'That is what Apuleius, in the work entitled *The Golden Ass*, reported or pretended had happened to him; having taken a potion he became an ass, without losing his human intelligence.'[4] (... *sicut Apuleius in libris quos asini aurei titulo inscripsit sibi ipsi accidisse, ut accepto veneno humano animo permanente asinus fieret, aut indicavit aut finxit.*) That the work in general had an autobiographical purpose is, of course, out of the question in view of the statements by Apuleius himself about its derivation and in

---

[1] For a more detailed comparison see J. Gwyn Griffiths, *Plutarch's De Iside et Osiride* (Cardiff, 1970), 49-51.

[2] Cf. Berreth, 115; Wittmann, 123, referring to 'die reine Biographie des Apuleius' in which every illusion is renounced from ch. 26 on.

[3] *The Golden Ass by Apuleius*. Translated. (New York, 1932), vi.

[4] Tr. by Sandford and Green (Loeb, 1965), vol. 5, 423. Cf. the error into which Adlington finely falls in his heading to Bk. XI : 'How Apuleius by Roses and praier returned to his humane shape.' (ed. of 1596, p. 190).

view of the extant *Lucius or Ass*. Occasionally, it is true, autobiography may coincide with facets of the prototype, and the very choice of the tale may indicate an inner attraction. We have seen that a coincidence of fact and story may apply to a reference to literary fame. A more important coincidence of this type, since it involves the basic theme, is that Apuleius himself was undoubtedly interested profoundly in magic, as the *Apologia* proves—the very trait that caused the misfortune of Lucius. [1] If Book XI is largely a record of personal experience, [2] it is enabled to cohere organically with what precedes through this significant connection. The fact that the book is not introduced as a separate unit does not argue against its special position. Apuleius occasionally makes a self-conscious allusion to the stories with which he digresses. 'Cupid and Psyche' is introduced by the old woman who tells the tale as one typical of 'pretty stories and old wives' tales' (4.27 *fin.*); and when it is over the asinine Lucius regrets that he cannot write down 'so fine a story' (*tam bellam fabellam*; 6.25 *init.*). The story which begins in 10.2 is introduced with a flourish of serious intent : 'Know, therefore, excellent reader, that you are now reading a tragedy and no mere comedy, and that you shall rise from the comic sock to the tragic buskin' (*iam ergo, lector optime, scito te tragoediam, non fabulam legere et a socco ad coturnum ascendere*). [3] Book XI, however, is not a digression. It carries on the narrative smoothly, providing at once a culmination and a spiritual ordering of the whole.

II. Date and Place of Composition

A firm date in the literary career of Apuleius is provided by the fact that his *Apologia* was delivered before the proconsul Claudius Maximus. This proconsulate is to be dated to A. D. 158/9 [4]. The philosophical works are agreed to have been written later, otherwise they would doubt-

---

[1] Cf. Jack Lindsay, op. cit. v.

[2] Conveyed, to be sure, rather deviously. Cf. the remarks by L. von Schwabe in *PW* s.v. Apuleius von Madaura (1896), 250 : Apuleius plays hide-and-seek with the reader.

[3] Cf. the discussion by M. Kawczyński in *Rozprawy Akad. Umiejetnosci*, II, 16 (Krakow, 1900), 201.

[4] R. Syme, 'Proconsuls d'Afrique sous Antonin le Pieux', *Rev. Ét. Anc.* 61 (1959), 310-319, this point pp. 316 f.

less have been mentioned in a speech primed with a good deal of self-preening. [1] The *Florida* are also later, for they show a greater degree of rhetorical experience, and some are precisely datable. [2]

More debate has gathered round the *Metamorphoses*, and Bernhard (*Stil*, 360), while he concludes his discussion with a *non liquet*, is attracted to Rohde's view that it is a creation of the youth of Apuleius. Bernhard sees a possible sign of this in the apologetic allusion made by Lucius (*Metam.* 1.1.) to his inexperience in a language at which he has laboured hard; he describes himself as 'an uncouth speaker of a foreign tongue and of the jargon of the forum' (*exotici ac forensis sermonis rudis locutor*). This, of course, applies to Lucius and not to Apuleius; and yet, argues Bernhard, it must refer in some sense to the style of what follows, [3] and it can reflect the shyness of a young writer in tackling what was not his mother tongue—a shyness actually confirmed by the host of vulgarisms and neologisms embedded in his language. A somewhat harsh judgement is implied here. Unorthodox and bizarre as it may at times appear, the style of the work is in fact a glittering success.

A further argument advanced is that the large number of metaphors derived from Roman legal procedure suggests that the work was written at Rome, where Apuleius spent some time as a young man in the role of legal adviser. The *Apologia*, as we have noted above, refers to his travels and studies and also to his initiations in Greece. A period in Rome is probably covered by these references, so that the autobiography included could revert to a quite early phase. But there is clearly no need to assume an instantaneous recording of such impressions; and the rebuttal of the argument does not depend on attempts such as Helm's (praef. XIV) to explain away the juridical function. A time-lag often accompanies the reflection of personal experience in literature.

The argument relating to content and style may seem more imposing. Bernhard suggests that the many obscenities, the crazy new word-

---

[1] Cf. Bernhard, *Stil*, 357.

[2] See Butler and Owen, *Apol.* xvii.

[3] Purser, *Cupid and Psyche*, xvi n. 0, cites E. Norden's view that 'this request in the preface for indulgence was a stock procedure'; cf. Tacitus, *Agr.* 3, *incondita ac rudi voce*. But Purser himself believes that 'the reference is rather to the efforts Apuleius made to acquire the specially Roman idiom (*Quiritium indigenam sermonem*).'

formations and the dallying diminutives point to a young author. [1] The stylistic points are hardly valid since Apuleius, as Bernhard himself makes clear (pp. 353 ff.), deliberately adopted different modes in essaying different themes and forms. More worth pondering is the obscene element. There is manifestly a riot of pleasure in the portrayal of sexual experiences, particularly those of Lucius and Photis. The similar episode in *Lucius or Ass* is not without metaphorical elaboration, which relates partly to the name Palaestra; she provides Lucius with an *initiamentum Veneris* which is fairly realistically recounted. Apuleius, in contrast, makes the episode more of an end in itself—to him it is not merely a means of furthering the quest of magical secrets; the affair is altogether more passionate and personal, and it is skilfully graded to a lyrical climax; an element, moreover, in the livelier presentation is the snappier, briefer dialogue. [2] The latter element also enlivens the elaborate account of the copulation of ass and woman as given by Apuleius (10.21 f.) although *Lucius or Ass*, 50 f., contains a few of the embellishments, such as the allusion to Pasiphaë. Does this interest in sexual experience and extravaganza point necessarily to the writing of a young author? It would be hard to sustain such a criterion in any literature. In modern terms one can think of the lifelong literary interest of Alberto Moravia and Henry Miller, but they are writers whose main preoccupation is with this theme. A very different writer is Thomas Mann. He wrote *Buddenbrooks* when he was twenty-five; it was not till he was sixty-three that his picaresque novel about Felix Krull was published, though a fragment had appeared when he was forty-seven. The sexual *mores* of the *bourgeoisie* were the theme of an early novel of the Welsh writer Saunders Lewis; he was thirty-seven when he published *Monica*; his later work does not show this preoccupation save that adultery is a theme in several of his plays. In all these cases it is the literary interest that is being discussed. Naturally it bears some relation to the author's actual experiences, although

---

[1] Cf. Jack Lindsay, *The Golden Ass by Apuleius*. Translated. (Indiana U.P., 1962), 14 : 'The tale has a youthful effervescence which suits better the enthusiast convert of Rome than the worldly-wise and flowering orator of Carthage.'

[2] See the admirable comparison by Junghanns, *Erzählungstechnik*, 33 ff.; also Scobie, *Aspects of the Ancient Romance etc.* 56 ff. Merkelbach, *Maia* 5 (1952), 239, urges that an epitome cannot give an idea of the style of its original; if the easy method of selection and omission is followed, then the style will not be wholly lost.

the link may be far from simple. Thus Freud's sexual activity was over, it seems, soon after he was forty, [1] but this did not prevent him giving a key role to this activity in his psychology.

Apuleius probably wrote the *Metamorphoses* during the later part of his literary career after he had returned from his travels and settled down in Carthage. If he was writing *c.* A.D. 170, this would make him about forty-six on the assumption, which is generally accepted, that he was born about 124. [2] It was hardly an age, especially in North Africa, for a cessation of erotic interest. In any case the novel, it might be argued, does not eventually and finally give primacy to such an interest, but rejects it in favour of the spiritual joys of the Isis-cult. Concerned as we are here, in the main, with this exalted *dénouement*, we are entitled to emphasize that its message is to some extent anticipated in the exquisite 'Cupid and Psyche', as Merkelbach has shown, even if all the details of his *exposé* are not equally acceptable. Here is an episode, like Book XI, which was not present in the prototype. Yet one must admit, as far as the preponderant weight of the content is concerned, that the work as a whole gives more attention to magical themes and to erotic adventures. Thus the designation by H. J. Rose [3] is not unfair : 'a picaresque romance enlisted in the service of mystical religion, a sort of *Pilgrim's Progress* whose Christian spends most of the book enjoying himself heartily at Vanity Fair'. He goes on to stress (p. 522) that 'the story is meant to convey a religious lesson' since 'Isis saves Lucius from the vanities of this world, which make men of no more worth than beasts, to a life of blissful service, here and hereafter.'

The prominence of the magical theme is relevant to a crucial point of chronology. If the book was written before A.D. 158/9, when Apuleius faced a charge, *inter alia*, of using magic as a means to make the rich widow Aemilia Pudentilla his wife, then why on earth did his accusers not adduce the *Metamorphoses* as evidence against him? While admitting that this is the strongest argument for a later date, Bernhard (*Stil*, 358) attempts to play it down. It is an *argumentum ex silentio*, he urges,

---

[1] Erich Fromm, *Sigmund Freuds Sendung* (Berlin, 1961), 51 f.

[2] Schanz, Hosius and Krüger, *Röm. Litt.* 101; Butler and Owen, *Apol.* viii; Walsh, *The Roman Novel*, 248.

[3] *A Handbook of Latin Literature* (London, 1936), 521.

which loses some force if the view is taken that the novel originated in
Rome and that the enemies of Apuleius in Africa will therefore not necessarily have known about it. But Apuleius was writing in Latin for the
Roman world, and the province of Africa was a part of this world.[1]
Bernhard shifts his ground in his next point : the novel was written,
following a Greek model, for the purpose of entertainment, and the
accusers could well have neglected, therefore, to take it seriously and to
make it a reason for reproaching the author with magic. The imitation
of a Greek model is, of course, admitted by Apuleius; but accusers who
were keen to use any and every avenue of abuse would surely not have
refrained from pressing the point that the choice of this tale reflected
the author's own magical pursuits. [2] We have seen that more than two
centuries later Augustine (*De civ. Dei*, 18.18) was taking it more seriously
even than that.

   Also in favour of a later date is the fact that in two passages of the
Florida—9 (13, 17 ff.) and 20 (41, 2 ff.)—Apuleius mentions his versatility
as a writer, but does not refer to the novel, although he names many
genres. He can scarcely be using the term *historiae* to refer to novels; [3]
he uses, in the first passage, the term *historiae variae rerum*, where the last
word suggests history (*rerum gestarum*); in the second passage he names
Xenophon as an author of *historiae*. *Fabula* is the term he uses for fiction
in *Metam.* 1.1 and 6.25. Now the *Florida* are later than the *Apologia*;
the novel must be later than both, unless we accept Bernhard's argument
that the silence of the *Florida* is due to the refusal of the aging mellow
philosopher to recognize the shallow work of his youth which was replete
with obscenities. Perhaps the novel, he suggests, had put him in bad

---

   [1] A way out of this objection is to assume that the novel was at first published
anonymously; thus Rohde and C. Bürger, for whom see Helm, praef. X; cf. Purser.
Cupid and Psyche, xvii.

   [2] As well as his lascivious nature; cf. Helm, praef. IX.

   [3] Cf. Purser, *Cupid and Psyche*, xxiii, refuting Bürger; also p. 126. In *Lucius or
Ass*, 55, Lucius says that he is the author of ἱστορίαι. M. D. Macleod translates as
'histories', but in a note (p. 141 n. 2) states that the word can also mean 'treatises'or
'novels or other narrative works'. A reference to fiction is clearly possible in the sense
that historical romances or fantastic accounts of travels or records of miraculous
happenings developed from the original concept of fact as opposed to fiction. Cf.
Reitzenstein, *Hellenistische Wundererzählungen*, 33, where the pseudo-Lucianic word
is taken as 'tales of marvels'; and Perry, *The Ancient Romances*, 38.

odour. Evidence for this low estimate of the *Golden Ass* is not forthcoming in spite of Perry's remarks in *The Ancient Romances*, 372 n. 11.
The statement in Capitolinus, *Vit. Alb.* 12.12 admittedly classifies it as
amusing literature with a touch of rebuke from Severus; but it is a
tribute, nonetheless, to its popularity in high circles. Since Albinus died
in 197 and the reference is to his old age, he might be reading the work
during the previous decade.

Other points raised in the debate over chronology seem less decisive.
In *Metam.* 1.2 (2, 5 ff.) Lucius claims to be descended on his mother's
side from Plutarch and from his nephew, the philosopher Sextus; cf.
2.3 (26, 12 ff.). If this means that the author whom Apuleius followed
was the son of Plutarch's nephew, then a date before A.D. 165 is hard to
accept since Plutarch probably died soon after A.D. 120. The detail
may apply to Apuleius himself, [1] in which case a slightly earlier date
would be possible. But since Sextus was teaching philosophy to Marcus
Aurelius about A.D. 161, [2] it seems doubtful whether kinship could
have been claimed, at that time, between a rather scandalous character
of fiction and a celebrated living philosopher. Again, knowledge of the
topography of Rome is shown in the allusion to the *metae Murtiae* in
6.8 (133, 20 f.), but no more than Roman colouring is implied; [3] nor
does the use of *Tullianum* for 'prison' in 9.10 (210, 9 f.) indicate at all that
the work was composed in Rome. Some legal terms used are more revealing. The allusion in 1.6 (5, 20 f.) to guardians appointed 'by order of the
chief justice of the province' (*iuridici provincialis decreto*) has been
explained by Hesky, *Wiener St.* 26 (1904), 71 ff. as pointing to a date after
163/4 since these officers were then instituted, it is claimed, by Marcus
Aurelius. [4] Vallette, however, *ad loc.* (pp. 7 ff. of 2nd ed., 1956) points
out that in the case of Italy, at any rate, these offices were not created,
but re-established by Marcus Aurelius. [5] Richard G. Summers, *Historia*
21 (1972), 120-126, has successfully re-opened this question by showing

---

[1] Bowersock, *Rhein. Mus.* 108 (1965), 288 f. shows that this is quite likely.

[2] Helm, praef. IX and p. 46.

[3] Cf. Grimal (Paris, 1963), *ad loc.* p. 108.

[4] Hesky also argues that since the book refers to 'Caesar' and not 'Caesares', it
involves the later years of Marcus Aurelius, after A. D. 169, when his co-rule with
Verus was over. It is unlikely that such nicety of allusion was aimed at.

[5] Cf. Purser, *Cupid and Psyche*, xvii n. 0.

that the Greeks sometimes used the term δικαιοδότης to denote the *legatus Augusti pro praetore*; he suggests that Apuleius has loosely used the Latin equivalent *iuridicus* with reference to the same officer. His further suggestion that an inscription of A.D. 147 involving Titianus, imperial governor of Achaea under Antoninus Pius, points actually to the *iuridicus* meant by Apuleius (the latter being then a student in Athens) is attractive if speculative. If this is accepted it means that 'if any terminus *a quo* for the novel is to be set, it must now be set at *ca* A.D. 147.' This argument, of course, does not exclude a much later date of writing. Details about Thessaly have been ably interpreted by G. W. Bowersock,[1] who shows that the *praeses provinciae* in 1.26 (24, 7 f.) and his *auxilia* in 2.18 (40, 2) correspond to historical reality; so does the importance of Hypata, cf. below *ad* ch. 20 (282, 3). After the middle of the second century Thessaly was a part of Macedonia—even from A.D. 67 if Bowersock is right (p. 288); and this is doubtless assumed in the query of Milo about the governor in 1.26. Bowersock (p. 282 n. 31) also compares the end of 6.4, where Juno refers to the 'laws that forbid protection to others' runaway slaves, except with the consent of their masters', with the *Digest*, 11.4.1.2 (cf. Grimal, *ad loc.* pp. 103 f.). The latter decree is by Marcus Aurelius and Commodus and compels the giving up of runaway slaves; previously twenty days' grace had been allowed.[2] Bowersock urges that the sterner regulation of A.D. 177 is involved, thus giving this date as a *terminus post quem*. There is, however, a shadow of a doubt, for he cites also 6.2 *ad fin.* where Psyche pleads, 'Allow me to lie hid, if only for a few days' (*patere vel pauculos dies delitescam*), with a possible suggestion that this might be legal.

Walsh[3] points out that nothing is heard of Apuleius after about A. D. 170. If the evidence is admitted to be in favour of a late date at Carthage, then this date or one near it is likely. A double date, one early and one late, has seemed probable to some scholars who believe that an original which was purely Milesian was afterwards adapted to a more serious

---

[1] 'Zur Geschichte des römischen Thessaliens', *Rhein. Mus.* 108 (1965), 277-289, esp. 279 and 282.

[2] Cf. Walsh, *The Roman Novel*, 250.

[3] Op. cit. 249 and 251.

purpose. Perry [1] finds a dichotomy between the first ten books and the last one, arguing that the closing book was added 'to redeem his book from the appearance of complete frivolity'; he does not suggest, however, an earlier publication of the first ten books. It was Carl Dilthey in his *Festrede* (Göttingen, 1879) who made the interesting suggestion that Apuleius was the author of the original Greek romance to which Photius refers and that he published it anonymously in his youth, only to republish it later in Latin, but with many changes and a more serious purpose. This thesis was revived by E. Cocchia, [2] and its speculative nature is obvious.

III. THE SETTING IN CENCHREAE

In *Lucius or Ass* the hero is from Patrae in Achaea, and the amphitheatre where he is to display, though still an ass, a feat of sexual union with a woman is in Thessalonica (ch. 49). His restoration to human form occurs there and he then takes a ship back to Patrae. Apuleius derives his Lucius from Corinth or its vicinity : see n. *ad* ch. 26 (287, 15), *patrium larem*. It is at Corinth that the show is to take place (10.19) and Thiasus, who is arranging the show, is himself a native of Corinth, being currently a *duumvir quinquennalis* of the city (10.18). He has gone to Thessaly merely to fetch wild beasts and gladiators, whereas his opposite number in Pseudo-Lucian is Menecles, a native of Thessalonica. Apuleius makes Lucius flee from Corinth to Cenchreae, six full miles swiftly covered (10.35). [3] This town, it is stressed, is regarded as part of the most splendid colony of the Corinthians (*nobilissimae coloniae Corinthien-*

---

[1] *The Ancient Romances*, 244. On p. 234 he is palpably wrong in stating of Book XI that there is 'no real connection with the ten books which precede it.' The priest's address to Lucius in ch. 15 of the last book aspires to, and achieves, a profound connection.

[2] Cf. Schanz, Hosius and Krüger, *Röm. Litt.* 107.

[3] From the Cenchreaean Gate of Corinth to the ruins of Cenchreae is eight good kilometres as the crow flies according to Veyne, *Rev. Phil.* 39 (1965), 246 n. 1 ('Apulée à Cenchrées'). So Apuleius is not far out. Butler, *Apol.* X n. 4, says of Lucius and Corinth that 'he never shows any interest in it', but this is hardly correct in view of the details cited above. Certainly he shows no joy in returning to it, and Butler may be right in suggesting that his home is regarded as being outside the city itself.

sium).[1] But it is not precisely correct to aver, as Paul Veyne [2] has done, that the birth and rebirth (cf. *renatus* in chs. 16 and 21) of Lucius occur in the same place. Yet Veyne's study is a valuable one, and he raises the question as to why Apuleius has changed the main scene of the end of the novel. After quoting Lesky's [3] view that Cenchreae was chosen because it was an important cult-centre for Isis, Veyne argues that Thessalonica would have done equally well from this point of view; so would Athens or Corinth itself. At Thessalonica [4] indeed, the closing scene of *Lucius or Ass*, the cult of Sarapis had been established in the third century B. C. and is attested up to the late imperial era. Isis is herself more prominent in Corinth and Cenchreae. But Veyne is doubtless right in his main point : it was a religious experience which came to Apuleius himself in Cenchreae that decided his choice of venue. He wisely demurs to an identification of everything described in Book XI with this personal experience. Clearly it is very likely, though, that Apuleius witnessed the ceremonies of the *Isidis Navigium* in Cenchreae. He did not, it seems, make any lasting commitment to the Isis-cult, for during his later life at Carthage he was given the chief-priesthood of the province (*Flor.* 16, p. 29, 10 f., *suscepti sacerdotii*), and there is no allusion to any other allegiance. In Book XI he has recorded, then, an earlier experience. There was a strong element of the showman, as Perry stresses, in his literary conduct; but in this case the attitude does not preclude the narration of initiations which he had undergone. Indeed he took a pride in being able to.

What is not so clear, is whether Apuleius wished, in making Lucius

---

[1] Helm suggests restoring <*emporium*> before *nobilissimae*.

[2] Op. cit. 242.

[3] *Hermes* 76 (1941), 45.

[4] See Vidman, *SIRIS* 108-111 *d*; id. *Isis und Sarapis*, 44 and 56 f. There was a Serapeum there, but Isis is mentioned in inscriptions, and the material includes a fragmentary aretalogy of Isis. Cf. P. M. Fraser, 'Two Studies', 38-40; R. E. Witt in 'Macedonia', 324-33, esp. 330 ff.; R. Salditt-Trappmann, *Tempel der ägyptischen Götter usw.* (Leiden, 1970), 47-52, including a description of a statue of Isis (with fig. 44). Mazzarino, *La Milesia e Apuleio*, 152, misleads on this matter. To encounter the cult Apuleius would not have had to leave Africa; see St. Gsell, *Rev. Hist. Rel.* 30 (1909), 149-59, who shows that the cult-centres included Carthage; cf. Vidman, *SIRIS* 325-9; J. Leclant, *Orientalia* 35 (1966), 174 with fig. 72; Gisèle Clerc, *Rev. d'Egypt.* 22 (1970), 241. See further Addenda.

a Corinthian in origin, to avow that he himself was spiritually a Corinthian (in Veyne's phrase, p. 249, 'voulant confesser à mi-voix qu'il est
devenu corinthien de cœur'). Veyne does not pursue this suggestion except
to say that the circuitous ways employed to indicate Lucius' Corinthian
origin may be explained by supposing that the novel was published
anonymously under the title *Lucii Corinthiensis metamorphoseis*. Of
more significance would be an attempt to interpret the Corinthian guise
of Apuleius, if this indeed is the author's purpose. H. J. Mason [1] has
argued that the choice of Corinth reflects a more impersonal aim : the
dissolute reputation of the city is contrasted with the life of the devotee
of Isis. One must agree that the Corinthian tradition suggested 'cruelty,
sexuality in its many and often perverse aspects, murder, and the desire
for wealth—which the devotee of Isis shunned'. What is not so clear is
whether Apuleius has deliberately focussed attention on the contrast.
Certainly the show at the end of Book X is lusciously described, and the
flight of Lucius with its peaceful sequel on the shore of Cenchreae is a
telling antithesis. Later, however, there is an element of sportive ostent-
ation in the colourful account of the burlesque which precedes the Isiac
procession (11.8) and the procession itself is not without a facet of pomp
and circumstance, albeit more reverently treated. The people are said to
delight in the playful prelude (11.9 *init.*), but when the restoration of
Lucius to human form has occurred, they marvel (ch. 13, p. 276, 10,
populi mirantur). In ch. 16 it is still more pointedly said that the whole
community (*tota civitas*) knew about the event and all the people (*omnes
... populi*) talked about Lucius. The *macarismos* which follows is assigned
to the people in general. At the end of the same chapter the ceremonies
of the *Isidis Navigium* are described and it is stated that everyone, both
those who were adherents of the faith and those who were not (*cuncti
populi tam religiosi quam profani*) took part. Similarly in ch. 17 (280, 2 ff.)
the people are overcome with joy (*gaudio delibuti populares*) when they
bring offerings and kiss the feet of the goddess. In ch. 18 friends and
relatives, presumably from Corinth or near, are said to come to express
their joy. After this the converse of Lucius, both in Cenchreae and in
Rome, is with those of the faith; others are excluded; cf. ch. 23 (285,4),
semotis procul profanis. Apart, then, from the contrast of the initial

---

[1] 'Lucius at Corinth', *Phoenix* 25 (1971), 160-65.

situation Apuleius is hardly intent on showing a lurid Corinthian *milieu* as a background to the initiations.

Apuleius tells us (10.35) that the harbour of Cenchreae was thronged with a great mass of people, but that the asinine Lucius chose a deserted part of the shore to rest his tired body. Topographical allusions are afterwards very scanty. When Isis informs Lucius in ch. 5 of the festival of dedicating a new ship to her, she omits any mention of the place. We are told in ch. 7 that Lucius finds all the streets full of people (*turbulae complent totas plateas*), and this agrees with the detail proffered in 10.35 about Cenchreae. At the end of the same chapter it is said that the sea is now calmer—an indication of the same place. The trumpeters dedicated to Sarapis are said in ch. 9 *ad fin.* to play a melody traditional to the temple and the god (*familiarem templi deique modulum*). Does this mean that there was a temple of Sarapis close by? Not necessarily, it seems; see n. *ad loc.* If it did, there might be here an argument in favour of Berreth's view that the ceremonies are to be envisaged as taking place not in Cenchreae but in Corinth, for Pausanias (2.2.3) states that there was a temple of Isis in Cenchreae with those of other deities, while Corinth, according to him (2.4.6), contained, on the way up to Acrocorinth, two sanctuaries of Isis (one of Isis Pelagia, the other of Egyptian Isis) and also two sanctuaries of Sarapis (one of which was called the sanctuary of Sarapis in Canopus). [1] In ch. 16 Apuleius renews our assurance that Cenchreae is the scene, for he says that the procession which the transformed Lucius had joined gradually approached the sea-shore and came to the very place where Lucius had rested on the previous day (278, 12 ff.). If this procession had started from a temple in Corinth, it would have had the very unlikely task of trudging over six miles. The new ship is launched on the sea (ch. 16), so that this too must be Cenchreae; and a return is made to the sanctuary (*ad fanum reditum capessunt*, ch. 16, *fin.*). No further indication is given. In ch. 23 the phrases *ad proximas balneas* and *rursumque ad templum* do not reveal anything tangible.

Berreth (pp. 47-9) approaches the question after examining the account

---

[1] Castiglione, 'Isis Pharia', 47 f. propounds, with some cogency, the view that two sanctuaries are really meant in all, in which the pairs Egyptian Isis and Sarapis, on the one hand, and Isis Pelagia and Sarapis of Canopus (= Osiris), on the other, were worshipped.

of the image of the goddess in chs. 3 and 4. This image is clearly of a
fairly representative type, and whether an actual local cult-image is implied is doubtful. He refers to a bronze coin of Antoninus Pius (now in
Berlin) with C L I CDR (*colonia Laus Iulia Corinthus...*) on its reverse;
see Leipoldt and Regling in *Angelos* 1 (1925), 130 and pl. 5, 3. The harbour
of Cenchreae is also shown on the reverse as a semi-circle fronted by
three ships; in the centre Isis Pharia is shown in her traditional form with
extended sail; cf. M. Bernhart, *Handbuch zur Münzkunde der römischen
Kaiserzeit* (Halle, 1926), 64 and pl. 22, 5; Drexler, 'Isis', 389 f.; and Castiglione, 'Isis Pharia', figs. 33-8. Berreth proceeds to identify this form
with the Isis of Cenchreae and links it with the temple mentioned by
Pausanias (not 2.4.6 as printed, but 2.2.3). The latter, be it noted, does
not use the term Isis Pelagia in this connection, although it is obvious
that she must have had some place in the cult at Cenchreae. After rejecting a possible association with the form of Isis Campensis, Berreth
adduces a coin of Hadrian from Corinth, on which Isis is shown with
sistrum and situla as in the description given by Apuleius : see F.
Imhoof-Blumer and P. Gardner, *A Numismatic Comm. on Pausanias*
(repr. from *JHS*, 1885-7), pl. F, 119; on p. 25, no. 31, the authors cite the
reference to sanctuaries of Isis in Corinth (Pausanias, 2.4.6), but without
indicating which Isis is here signified. It is, of course, his Isis Aegyptia.
Wittmann (p. 94 and n. 518) adduces the same coin as referring to Isis in
Cenchreae, since the figure resembles the image of the goddess which
appears to Lucius on the sea-shore there. The truth is that the figure
on the coin could apply to either. Where Berreth errs is in his facile identification of cult and coinage. Isis Pelagia was undoubtedly worshipped
in Cenchreae as she was too in one of the Corinthian sanctuaries. But
many other attributes and forms of the goddess were probably included
in the cult, as Isis is made to suggest in her epiphany from the sea (ch. 5).
Apart from the uncertain reference to a temple of Sarapis, the internal
evidence implies that Cenchreae is the scene throughout, that is, up to the
departure of Lucius for his home and then for Rome.

Recently the excavations conducted at Cenchreae by the Universities
of Chicago and Indiana have contributed data which are of great interest
and relevance, although they do not add up to a decisive verdict on the
question raised. [1] A sanctuary or 'temple-like structure' was discovered,

---

[1] See in general John G. Hawthorne, 'Cenchreae Port of Corinth', *Archaeology*
18 (1965), 191-200; Robert L. Scranton and Edwin S. Ramage, 'Investigations at

and various Egyptian motifs have been noted in the *opus sectile* associated with it : there is an ibis in a marsh where lotus and papyrus plants are shown, together with Nilotic scenes involving a crocodile, a group of fishermen and a cow. [1] These scenes have obviously no direct religious significance, and at first sight one might be disposed to query the confidence with which the temple of Isis in Cenchreae mentioned by Pausanias has been identified with this site. [2] Such scepticism would be ill-advised. Not only is the site roughly in the area which Pausanias had in mind; there is evidence also in sanctuaries of the Egyptian cults outside Egypt that a religious aura was imparted to various objects not strictly connected with the cult. A good example is the Iseum in the Campus Martius, where sphinxes, fragments of obelisks and statues, together with a sculptured lion and crocodile, [3] mingle with objects that are more truly Isiac in significance. The same applies to the sphinxes, ibises and Bes-figures depicted in the Iseum of Pompeii. Erman [4] expressed the matter thus : 'Daher hat man in Pompeji, in Benevent, in Rom and gewiss überall, wo man Isistempel baute, sich irgendwelche alten Opfersteine, Sphinxe, Statuen und andere Skulpturen aus dem unerschöpflichen Bestande der ägyptischen Tempel und Gräber verschafft und sie zur Freude der Isis aufgestellt.' The 'Canopus' of Hadrian in Tivoli had a wider purpose but it was adjacent to a Serapeum, and various Egyptian objects were displayed there. [5] In Cenchreae the scenes of harbour acti-

---

Corinthian Kenchreai', *Hesperia* 36 (1967), 124-86; Scranton, 'Glass Pictures from the Sea', *Archaeology* 20 (1967), 163-73; J. Leclant, *Orientalia* 36 (1967), 219; 37 (1968), 131; 38 (1969), 299; Miriam Ervin, *AJA* 71 (1967), 298 and 73 (1969), 345-6; also the refs, given by Leclant, locis cit.; F. Dunand, *Le culte d'Isis en Grèce* (1973), 18.

[1] Scranton and Ramage, *Hesperia* 36 (1967), figs. 7-8 and pp. 141 ff.; also pls. 39-41. There is a colour photograph in *Archaeology* 18 (1965), 198.

[2] J. G. Hawthorne, *Archaeology* 18 (1965), 197-99, with a dating to the second century A. D.; cf. his title, 'Preserving and Removing the *Opus Sectile* from the Sanctuary of Isis at Kenchreai', referred to in *AJA* 71 (1967), 189. R. E. Witt, *Isis Gr.-R.* 177 accepts the association and on p. 309 n. 24 rightly lauds the skill of the excavators in dealing with material under water.

[3] Bosticco, *Mus. Capitol. : monumenti egizi ed egittizzanti* (Rome, 1952), 13-31; P. F. Tschudin, *Isis in Rom* (Aarau, 1962), 26.

[4] *Die Religion der Ägypter* (Berlin, 1934), 431. On Beneventum see now H. W. Müller, *Der Isiskult im antiken Benevent* (MÄR 16, Berlin, 1969).

[5] On the site itself, where there has been some restoration, classical themes are more in evidence, as the present writer has noted. Cf. *Ill. Lond. News* 231 (1957), 552 f.

vity are naturally germane both to the place itself and to the role of
Isis as patroness of sea-faring. Scranton refers to one depiction of 'a
child (perhaps winged) among water birds, apparently holding a duck'.
It is a pity that the wings are in doubt. Clearly their presence would imply
a figure from mythology. The concomitants are, however, naturalistic,
and it seems wiser to interpret the scene as one of the popular hunting,
fowling and fishing motifs so frequent in Egypt and in imitations of
Egyptian art. [1] If the *sacra* of the temple itself have not been revealed,
it must be conceded that the works of art which have been recovered
constitute, at the very least, what would have formed most appropriate
embellishments of such a temple, with an emphasis on the association
with the sea.

IV. THE EGYPTIAN ELEMENTS

Viewed as a phenomenon in the history of literature, the *Metamorphoses* can be described as a successful Latin adaptation of a Greek
romance. In the early centuries of our era the Greek romance was
itself a form that gained recognition and respectability only tardily by
the extension of the concept of *historia* to include an account of what
was claimed to be personal experience. An ironic expression of the scepticism engendered by the claim is seen in Lucian's title *Vera Historia*,
applied to a work that is obviously fictional. Rohde had emphasized
the contribution made to this development by travel tales and by the

---

A statue of the Nile was there, and probably a colossal bust of Isis together with other
Egyptian items of more general import which are now in the Egyptian Mus. of the
Vatican : see *The Pontifical Monuments, Museums and Galleries : A Short General
Guide* (Vatican, 1950), 100 f. From this site too comes a black granite statue of a
Ptolemaic Pharaoh which the writer encountered in the Egyptian Coll. of the National
Mus. in Stockholm (no. 67). Cf. Tschudin, *Isis in Rom*, 25; Vidman, *Isis und Sarapis*,
170; G. Mancini, *Hadrian's Villa and Villa d'Este* (Rome, 1950), 9 f.; S. Aurigemma,
Villa Adriana (Rome, 1961), 100 ff.; Anne Roullet, *Rome*, 49 ff.

[1] Cf. the great Nile mosaic from the temple of Fortuna Primigeneia at Praeneste,
on which see G. Gullini, *I Mosaici di Palestrina* (Roma, 1956). This form of Fortuna
seems to have been equated with Isis-Tychê, as Schefold, *Vergessenes Pompeji* (Bern,
1962), 32, has shown; cf. Merkelbach, *Isisfeste*, 18; Tschudin, *Isis in Rom*, 15; R. E.
Witt, *Isis Gr.-R*, pls. 8-11 and 45 with pp. 34-5. The Nilotic scenes are accompanied
by some of directly ritual import : v. Castiglione, 'Isis Pharia', 44 f. Cf. n. *ad* ch. 30
(291, 14), *Syllae temporibus*.

Alexandrian love-elegy; Schwartz stressed the role of the decadence of Hellenistic historiography; Lavagnini has invoked the importance of the popular local legends such as the Alexandrian poets used in their elegies; and Giangrande [1] has opined that 'the origin of the Greek love-romance must reside in prose paraphrases of Alexandrian love-elegies and epyllia.' Although there is a strong erotic element in the *Metamorphoses*, it is by no means a typical love-romance.

One of the early books of the Hungarian scholar Kerényi—and perhaps one of his best—attempted an approach that transcended the development of form in an external sense. In his *Die Griechisch-Orientalische Romanliteratur* (Tübingen, 1927) he showed a readiness, as his title indicates, to recognize the presence of oriental source-material. He also appreciated the religious aspects of several of the Greek romances. Doubtless the Osirian theme is traced too ubiquitously in the recurrent stories of lovers who are separated to be reunited. But the religious element is sometimes explicit in the plots of Chariton, Xenophon of Ephesus and Heliodorus, as is admitted in a critical review by Nock in *Gnomon* 4 (1928), 489. The latter is hardly justified in rejecting the echo of Mystery-formulae in a collocation like τέθνηκα ἀνέζησα (*Chaer.* 3.8.9); his rejection is purely stylistic and ignores the obvious conceptual similarity. Perhaps such similarities—and many have been further suggested by Merkelbach—are unconscious rather than deliberate. In his *Roman und Mysterium in der Antike* (Munich, 1962) Merkelbach has elaborated both facets of Kerényi's construction, and the reaction has been varied. Ben Edwin Perry, a scholar who was thoroughly versed in the classical material, adopted a trenchantly negative attitude. To him Merkelbach's interpretations amounted to 'nonsense'. [2] On the question of oriental origins his reaction was certainly ill-advised, although typical perhaps of the older school of classical philologists. Happily it is now widely recognized that no single *genre* of Greek literature emerged fully-fledged with sudden radiance like Aphrodite from the waves. On the question

---

[1] 'On the origins of the Greek romance', *Eranos* 60 (1962), 132-59, this on p. 155. Scobie, *Aspects of the Ancient Romance*, 43 ff, shows the significance of the Alexandrian pursuit of surprising curiosities, *paradoxa*.

[2] *The Ancient Romances*, 336 n. 17 : 'This is all nonsense to me.' Kerényi, Merkelbach and Altheim are included in the condemnation. Cf. the detailed criticisms of R. Turcan, *Rev. Hist. Rel.* 163 (1963), 149-99.

of religious significance there is more room for debate. Are the undoubted religious elements a part of the author's serious purpose or are they features accidentally embodied in the material he has inherited? Perry acknowledges the manifestly serious purpose of the 'Isis-Book' of Apuleius, but rejects its presence in earlier books. The story of 'Cupid and Psyche' is a test-case. Merkelbach's over-subtle explanations may not always be acceptable, but he has amply vindicated a deeper artistic intent than desultory entertainment. It seems to me that P. G. Walsh in *The Roman Novel* (Cambridge, 1970) has treated the complexities of 'Cupid and Psyche' with a combination of good sense and imaginative sensitivity. He rightly accepts some of the broad lines of Merkelbach's approach, while rejecting its extravagances. Above all he establishes clearly the serious purpose which links the story with the novel as a whole.

Just as 'Cupid and Psyche' is in origin a folk-tale that was popular in north-west Africa, so was the story of *Lucius or Ass*, in spite of its Greek setting, originally a folk-tale that arose, very probably, in Egypt. A change of setting has also occurred with 'Cupid and Psyche'. In this connection a striking contrast is provided by comparative literature. At a time when the Greek romance was struggling for recognition as a literary form, the tradition of the romance in Egypt could boast a high antiquity. In such a situation the influence of the older tradition would have been naturally exerted. The literature of Ancient Egypt contains several romances of great charm, some of which, like 'Sinuhe' and the stories of the Westcar Papyrus, derive from the early part of the second millennium B.C. John Barns [1] has pointed out that the earliest piece of prose fiction in Greek is the 'Dream of Nectanebus', which is manifestly a translation from the Egyptian (demotic). It was in part a love story; Barns notes that 'the scribe breaks off at the point where his hero, the hieroglyphic sculptor Petesis, has just met the prettiest girl he has ever seen.' The element of travel which involves strange adventures is exemplified in the Egyptian tradition by 'The Shipwrecked Sailor' and the demotic fragment 'Amasis and the Sea-captain'; and in 'The Doomed Prince' this element is combined, as Barns goes on to indicate, with a

---

[1] 'Egypt and the Greek Romance', Acta of the Eighth Congress for Papyrology (Vienna, 1956), 29-36.

love-story, which goes some way to contradict Giangrande's [1] claim that Egypt possessed historical romances, but not a "Liebesroman", centred upon a couple of human lovers'. It is true that the Egyptian instances are not as thematically sustained as the Greek love-romances, although they do contain other variations on the subject of love, especially its unhappy and jealous aspects, as in 'The Tale of the Two Brothers' and the first story of Setne Kha'emwese. Miracle and magic abound in the Egyptian tales as they do in the later classical romances; but the historical element is prominent too, as in the Coptic 'Cambyses Romance' and several prototypes. Barns is careful to note that other oriental sources were sometimes used by the classical writers; Ctesias, for instance, used Persian material. He also produces firm evidence for the Greek habit of translating or imitating Egyptian originals. As well as the 'Dream of Nectanebus' there is the story of Tefnut [2] and probably the 'Dialogue of Dogs' by Eudoxus. [3]

For 'Sinuhe' a still larger claim has been advanced by Alfred Hermann. [4] He believes it should be recognized as the first instance of the picaresque novel in world literature. Certainly, as he shows, it has several of the elements which became traditional : it is narrated in the First Person, it depicts wandering in foreign lands and various adventures, it incorporates several types of writing, such as conversations, letters, songs and hymns; and there is a happy ending although the hero has a certain roguish quality. This romance, which probably developed as a form in Egyptian from the funerary autobiography, [5] is not unjustly hailed as the modest precursor in the series in which Parzival, Simplicius Simplicissimus, and Gil Blas eventually figured, as well as Felix Krull and Tom Jones. The *Metamorphoses* clearly belongs to an early phase of the same evolution, as Hermann recognizes (p. 108). 'Wenamûn', an

---

[1] *Eranos* 60 (1962), 143.

[2] See now Stephanie West, 'The Greek Version of the Legend of Tefnut', *JEA* 55 (1969), 161-183.

[3] J. Gwyn Griffiths, 'A Translation from the Egyptian by Eudoxus', *CQ* 15 (1965), 75-8.

[4] 'Sinuhe—ein ägyptischer Schelmenroman?', *OLZ* 48 (1953), 101-9.

[5] Cf. H. Brunner, *Grundzüge einer Geschichte der altägyptischen Literatur* (Darmstadt, 1966), 65. In the valuable discussion that follows Brunner denies that 'Sinuhe' is a 'psychological novel', but remarks on the humour, irony, and self-portrayal of the story.

Egyptian story which is about a thousand years later than 'Sinuhe', has some affinities; it is an autobiographical account of travels in Syria, and in spite of its historical framework conveys a frequent sense of playful irony. Whereas Kerényi and others have realized the influence of Egyptian source-material, it is equally important to recognize the existence in a rich Egyptian tradition of the literary form which must have made some impact on Greek writing.

As for the basic folk-tale of the 'Eselmensch', it is to the Egyptian fables and *Märchen* that one turns for a likely source. That it is in essence a folk-tale and not a myth has been long since recognized.[1] Emma Brunner-Traut provides an attractive selection of Egyptian folk-tales in her *Altägyptische Märchen* (Düsseldorf, 1963). In these the theme of metamorphosis is not uncommon. In the 'Tale of the Two Brothers' Bata changes into a bull, and drops of blood from the bull become two persea-trees. In 'The Contendings of Horus and Seth' these two gods, during one episode, change into hippopotami. In the 'Myth of the Eye of the Sun', Tefnut, the sun-god's daughter, becomes a wild cat. In P. Jumilhac 3, 1 ff. Isis takes the form of a bitch, and Seth changes into a bull.[2] In all this the animal-forms of many gods are a potent factor; myth is often the matrix of *Märchen*. At the same time the idea of metamorphosis is common to many mythologies. It is the significance of the ass as a Sethian animal that points, in the story of Apuleius and his predecessor, to an Egyptian source. This was realized already by Kerényi.[3] The ass is an animal abhorrent to Isis (ch. 6, p. 270, 14 f.); and this attitude cannot, it seems, be paralleled in other ancient traditions. In the fables of Sumeria, for instance, the ass is treated good-humouredly as a 'slow-moving, and frequently foolish, creature',[4] and

---

[1] Cf. K. Weinhold, 'Über das Märchen vom Eselmenschen', *Sitzb. Berlin* 26 (1893), 475-488, who cites many parallels, including some from India, and concludes (p. 485) that it was a widespread tale, a *novellina popolare*. Helmut van Thiel, *Der Eselsroman. I. Untersuchungen.* (Zetemata, 54.1. Munich, 1971), 184 ff. considers 'Fabel und Tiergeschichte' which may be parallel to *Lucius or Ass*.

[2] See the edition by J. Vandier (Paris, 1962). Cf. J. Gwyn Griffiths, *CQ* 15 (1965), 76 f.

[3] Op. cit. 196, citing the Pyramid Texts. Cf. U. Bianchi, *Rev. Hist. Rel.* 179 (1971), 125 f., who notes that the ass symbolizes in the *Metam.* the fatalistic power of *Saeva* or *Nefaria Fortuna*, as opposed to the divine Pronoia which is Isis.

[4] S. N. Kramer, *History Begins at Sumer*[2] (London, 1961), 189.

perhaps there is an allusion to its lustful nature in the proverb, 'My youthful vigour has quit my thighs like a runaway donkey.'[1] Whereas the modern world sees obstinacy as the ass's prime quality, its sexual excess was more apparent to the ancients, as the Apuleian tale makes clear. The priest's address in ch. 15 castigates the sins of lust and *curiositas*; and while they characterized Lucius before his change into an ass, they continue in the ass-form, which becomes in a way symbolic of them. In origin the god Seth was canine in form, but the ass was prominently associated with him in his later phase of degradation. It is true that he is equated with an ass who carries corn (which symbolizes Osiris) in the very early Dramatic Ramesseum Papyrus. [2] In later developments his connection with the ass is sometimes sexual. Thus a demotic magical papyrus [3] recommends, as a preparation for making a woman love a man, a compound including the 'blood of a male ass' and an 'ass's skin', where a Sethian association is probably present; the god is also figured on gems as an ass with sexual powers that are not entirely beneficent. [4] The climax of the folk-tale is the copulation of ass and woman, and a Berlin statuette (no. 7948) figures exactly this : see E. Brunner-Traut, *Die altägyptischen Scherbenbilder* (Wiesbaden, 1956), 60, fig. 17; cf. Keimer, *Études d'Égyptologie*, III (Cairo, 1941), 7 n. 1 : '... je constate avoir déjà vu deux statuettes de faïence [ramessides ou saïtes] représentant une femme et un âne dans l'attitude libertine dont parlent les textes.' For such texts see Wiedemann, *Das alte Ägypten* (Heidelberg, 1920), 102, quoting a curse-formula which avows that an ass shall have intercourse with a man's wife. Wiedemann also cites F. Wieseler in *Bonner Jb.* 41 (1866), 56, on a terra cotta lamp, apparently of Roman origin, which represents the copulation of a woman and a crocodile. Ass and woman are shown on two intaglios reproduced by A. A. Barb, *JWCI* 22 (1959), pl. 38, f and g, as well as on an Indian stela (pl. 38, h). [5]

---

[1] Ibid. 190.

[2] J. Gwyn Griffiths, *The Origins of Osiris*, 50 f.

[3] P. Demot. Lond. Leid, 25, 23 ff.

[4] J. Gwyn Griffiths and A. A. Barb, 'Seth or Anubis?' *JWCI* 22 (1959), 367 ff. For Greek depictions of an ithyphallic ass see Bruneau, *BCH* 87 (1963), 512 and figs. 4-6.

[5] Cf. Hornblower, *Man* 26 (1926), 83; Bonnet, *Reallexikon*, 172. Greek lamps from the second century A.D. and later represent a similar scene : see Bruneau, *BCH* 89 (1965), 351 f.

Barb (p. 370) states that 'it has, I think rightly, been suggested, that the familiar story in Apuleius' *Golden Ass* may ultimately have been derived from such Old-Egyptian imagery.' Moreover, it is relevant to the whole concept of the 'Eselmensch' that Seth-Typhon occasionally appears in Greek magical papyri as an ass-headed man.[1]

An Egyptian version of the story is not actually attested, and scholars have adduced many later parallels. One of these, invoked by E. Brunner-Traut,[2] may conceivably go back to a Pharaonic source : it concerns the Egyptian Ali, who in the *Thousand and One Nights* is said to have been changed into an ass and used to carry water, in which role he sexually assaults the wife of his master. Walter Anderson [3] has amassed a plethora of European parallels from the seventeeth century and later, some of which include even the detail that restoration to human form can only follow the eating of a garland in a priest's hand. Such parallels must derive eventually from the Apuleian form rather than its Greek precursor, as H. van Thiel [4] points out, since the latter version has no religious finale. Less tangible are the affinities invoked by Trencsényi-Waldapfel [5] between the Apuleian tale and the apocryphal *Acts of Thomas* or the Christophorus legend or between it and the mediaeval French *festus asinorum*. An Arabic legend cited by him (p. 452) represents, perhaps, an echo in Christian tradition : it states that the Holy Family during its flight into Egypt came across an ass which had formerly been a young man whom evil women had transformed, but that by carrying the child Jesus it had reverted to human form. From Hungary comes a later version which can be linked with the material adduced by Anderson :

---

[1] Preisendanz, *Akephalos* (Leipzig, 1926), 54 and pl. 3, 2 = *PGM* 3, 70 with pl. 2, 3; cf. Hopfner, *Tierkult*, 103. There is a precursor in Lanzone, *Diz. Mit.* pl. 378, 3, from a demotic papyrus. Cf. also E. Brunner-Traut, *Altägyptische Tiergeschichte und Fabel* (Darmstadt, 1968), 61.

[2] Ibid. 61 n. 342 a.

[3] 'Das sogenannte Märchen vom Eselmenschen', *Zeitschrift für Volkskunde* 51 (1954), 215-36; also 54 (1958), 121-5.

[4] *Der Eselsroman*, I, 188.

[5] *Untersuchungen zur Religionsgeschichte* (Amsterdam, 1966), 449. On p. 552 n. 127 he cites bowls from Aquincum on which Isis and an ass are said to be figured. I have not been able to see these. Whereas the ass may well be Sethian, one may question whether a love-relationship is suggested, according to the view ascribed to Dobrovits. Cf. Wessetzky, *Ägypt. Kulte in Ungarn*, 14.

it concerns the restoration to human form, in a religious festival (that of Corpus Christi), after a young man had been changed into an ass by the mother of the girl whom he was courting. [1]

A prominent feature in the development of the 'Eselmensch' is the ability of the ass to do things like a man. This is not surprising within the context of the story, for Lucius tells us in 3.26 *init*. that he still kept his human intelligence (*sensum tamen retinebam humanum*). The ass emulates a man in eating and drinking, boxing and dancing (10.17; cf. *Lucius or Ass*, 47 f.) This is also a conspicuous trait of animals in the fables mirrored on the Egyptian ostraca : animals are there shown behaving like men.[2] Thus a lion and a gazelle are depicted playing draughts : v. E. Brunner-Traut, *Altägyptische Tiergeschichte und Fabel*, fig. 6; and an ass is shown playing a harp : v. ibid. fig. 4 and p. 9. On the other hand, an interpretation of *asellus* as *cinaedus*, illustrated in the association of the ass with catamites (8.26, with the priests of Dea Syria, cf. *Lucius or Ass*, 36; cf. 7.21, his readiness to violate a *tener puellus*), is illuminated from Greek sources : v. L. A. Moritz, *Grain-Mills and Flour in Classical Antiquity* (Oxford, 1958), 16 and fig. 1 (p. 13). [3]

Clearly, in pressing the claims of a basic Egyptian folk-tale, we should be wise to allow for various non-Egyptian accretions. In his first chapter Apuleius refers to the Milesian mode and to a *fabula Graecanica*. He also alludes, in his very first sentence, to 'an Egyptian papyrus inscribed with the clever clarity of a Nilotic reed' (*papyrum Aegyptiam argutia Nilotici calami inscriptam*), suggesting that here are tales which record the transformations of men's shapes and fortunes into other forms and their subsequent restoration to human state. This, it may be argued, is sufficient confirmation of the idea that behind the Greek form is an Egyptian source. The summarized prototype contains no such allusion, but the possibility that a mere convention is being followed should not be overlooked. Scobie, *Aspects of the Ancient Romance* etc. 31 n. 10 compares Martial, 13.1.3 f. :

---

[1] Trencsényi-Waldapfel, 'Das Rosenmotiv ausserhalb des Eselromans' in *Beiträge zur Alten Geschichte und deren Nachleben* (FS. F. Altheim, Berlin, 1969), 512-17, this on p. 517. The story was recorded in 1936.

[2] H. van Thiel, *Der Eselsroman*, I, 186, discusses the theme without mentioning Egyptian parallels.

[3] Cf. H. van Thiel, ibid. 185.

perdite Niliacas, Musae, mea damna, papyros :
postulat, ecce, novas ebria bruma sales.

Here the 'papyri of the Nile' are clearly contrasted with 'new pleasantries',
the hoary with the brand new; *ebria bruma* refers to the Saturnalia (cf.
H. J. Izaac [Budé, 1961], p. 293). There is little to compare; and still less
in Pliny, *NH* 13.22.71 ff., also cited by Scobie, where we are told all
about papyrus and where it grows. Ciaffi's [1] opinion that the Apuleian
allusion is really to Book XI only is rightly rejected by Scobie. R.
Thibau [2] has propounded the view that Apuleius is using a metaphor
through which he is appealing to the reader to apply an intelligent
allegorical approach; one must listen spiritually and examine the superimposed sense which the author is giving to these Milesian tales. Thibau
(p. 93) argues that an Egyptian papyrus needs to be deciphered; its text
is written with all the subtlety and ambiguity (*argutia*) of a Nilotic reed.
So too the story of Apuleius : it is a hermetic text whose symbolism will
need to be unravelled. One must agree with Thibau [3] that to explain the
allusion, in the manner of some commentators, as a mere description
of the materials with which the text of Apuleius has been written down
shows an unpardonable naïveté. However, Thibau himself does not give
due weight to the words that follow; these imply that the Egyptian
papyrus deals with the theme of metamorphosis.

Whereas the allusion may have occurred in the lost Greek source,
its precise pointer to the theme of metamorphosis in Egyptian literature
may be taken seriously. Hildebrand appositely refers to the exalted view
of the Egyptians held by Apuleius; he compares 11.5 (269, 20 f.), *priscaque
doctrina pollentes Aegyptii* and *Flor.* 6 (6, 5 f.), *Aegyptios eruditos*. Could
not Apuleius, he asks, be referring to his own origin as an African though
not an Egyptian? He is more probably vouching for the ancient source
of his story in Egypt. We have seen above that the theme, in a general
sense, often occurs in Egyptian tales, so that the statement is abundantly
valid.

---

[1] *Petronio in Apuleio* (Turin, 1960), 4.

[2] 'Les Métamorphoses d'Apulée et la Théorie Platonicienne de l'Erôs', *Studia
Philosophica Gandensia* 3 (Gent, 1965), 89-144. For the Egyptian allegorical approach
and its possible impact on the Greeks, see my remarks in *JEA* 53 (1967), 79-102.

[3] Cf. the sympathetic mention of his exegesis by H. van Thiel, *Der Eselsroman*, I,
44 n. 3.

In spite of the mainly Greek scene which was allotted to the story, various Egyptian elements are well described even before Book XI is reached. The episode of the fish in 1.24-26 can be explained in relation to Egyptian ideas. The fish are bought by Lucius from an exorbitant dealer and are trodden underfoot by way of punishing the fishmonger; it is an odd punishment since it is poor Lucius, as he himself remarks, who has lost his money and his fish. Ph. Derchain and J. Hubaux, *Ant. Class.* 27 (1958), 100-104, have cogently suggested that the Egyptian rite of trampling fish is here reflected, the fish being identified with the god's enemies. Pythias is therefore punishing the fishmonger in a serious way, for he is identifying him magically with the fish that are being trampled on. [1] If we ask why this episode, which does not occur in *Lucius or Ass*, should be displaying an Egyptian belief in Thessaly, the answer must be that it has been transposed from its original locale.

There is an authentic portrait in 2.28 of Zatchlas, the Egyptian *propheta primarius*; he is signally successful in his work since he is said to raise a dead man to life. A. Souter in *JTS* 37 (1936), 80 wanted to identify this august gentleman with a demon called Saclas mentioned in authors of the fourth century A.D. and associated with 'peritia Aegyptiaca'. [2] It is more likely that the name is close to the form $\Sigma\omega\tau\alpha\lambda\tilde{\alpha}\varsigma$ which occurs in Egypt : see G. Möller, *Demotische Texte*, I (Leipzig, 1913), n. 86, Inv. no. 10543. Spiegelberg, *Aegyptische und Griechische Eigennamen usw.* (Leipzig, 1901), 47* no. 325 equates the first syllable with the adjective $\sigma\tilde{\omega}\varsigma$, 'safe, healthy', comparing the Egyptian name ʿ$A\rho\nu\tilde{\omega}\tau\eta\varsigma$, 'Horus ist heil (gesund).'

The account of the priests of the Dea Syria in 8.25 ff. (cf. *Lucius or Ass*, 35 ff.) has traits of contempt that suggest the attitude of a writer more interested in a superior religion—that of Isis. This religion is adumbrated in some ways before Book XI begins. Riefstahl, *Der Roman des Apuleius*, 67 f., notes the rather pointed premonition about *curiositas* and its punishment in 2.4, where Lucius sees, in the house of Byrrena, a piece of statuary figuring Actaeon turned into a stag because of his determination to view Diana with curious gaze. The chaste Isis can share

---

[1] For a different approach see M. Hicter, *Ant. Class.* 13 (1945), 106-111.

[2] There is no suggestion that this is the meaning of the name, although Walsh, *The Roman Novel*, 179, puts it thus.

spiritually in this rebuke. If she is mistress of magic, yet she punishes the prying pursuit of magic without her sanction. Scobie [1] well remarks that a shrine of Isis in a villa at Pompeii contained a wall-painting which depicted Actaeon and Diana. This brief touch is eloquent about the method employed by Apuleius. If he seems desultory and inconsequential, as Perry liked to stress, if there are a number of loose ends and inconsistencies in his novel, [2] yet one is impressed by a cohesion of purpose and an elaboration of symbolism.

This is exquisitely clear in the story of 'Cupid and Psyche'. Here the African folk-tale is subtly used, for all its apparent digression, to enlarge on the theme of *curiositas*. It is not just a replica of the sacred story of Isis and Osiris, although there are reminiscences of it, perhaps unconscious, in Psyche's quest and suffering. It points forward, rather, to the happiness which is to be secured for Lucius through divine intervention, and this is itself a part of the teaching of the Isis-religion.

It is not necessary here to examine the Egyptian elements in Book XI, since this is attempted at length in the Commentary. The books of Berreth and Wittmann, together with some more recent studies, have shown, on the whole, a due appreciation of the role of ancient tradition in the cult. It is true that Apuleius chooses to use language that will be clear, in a conventional sense, to the Latin reader of his day. I am not referring here to his style, which is often unconventional, but to his terminology, as in words like *Elysium, Acheron, venia, salus, servitium,* and *sacramentum.* A few scholars, notably Nilsson, [3] have been misled by this into believing that the Egyptian background of the cult has been more or less abandoned in its Greek form. Such a conclusion is a grave error. Greek elements have certainly entered into the cult, but its basic appeal, especially that concerned with immortality, remains Egyptian. This is particularly clear in several of the doctrinal emphases of chs. 6 and 15 and in the impressive details of the First Initiation given in chs. 23-24. The elaborate portrayal in chs. 9-11 of the Isiac procession, once the *anteludia* are done with, contains lucid pointers in the same direction.

---

[1] *Aspects of the Ancient Romance* etc., 73, citing Tran Tam Tinh, *Isis à Pompéi,* 83.
[2] Cf. Helm, praef. XV ff.
[3] *Gesch. Gr. Rel.* II, 632.

The cult objects and personnel are for the most part unmistakably Egyptian in origin.

In some respects, on the other hand, the influence of the Dionysiac and Eleusinian cults is evident. This is true of the ears of corn in the iconography of Isis in ch. 3 (268, 10) and perhaps of the *aurea vannus* in ch. 10 (274, 12); of the serpents emerging from the *cista mystica* (not specifically referred to by Apuleius, but prominent in representations : see n. *ad* ch. 11 (274, 20), *cista*); while the thyrsus and ivy in ch. 27 (288, 12) are in origin Dionysiac. The laurel twigs of ch. 10 (274, 12 f.) are probably those of Apollo. Of the non-Egyptian ideas that seem to have penetrated the cult, the most important is perhaps the theme of spiritual regeneration in the present life. Yet this may have developed in the Hellenistic era in Egypt as a development and projection of a very ancient funerary tradition.

V. THE LAUNCHING OF THE SHIP OF ISIS

In ch. 16 is described the launching of a new ship called the *Isis* and dedicated to the goddess. It is said to be decorated with wonderful Egyptian paintings, and when it has been put out to sea with elaborate ceremonies, the priestly officiants are said to return to the sanctuary. Here, according to ch. 17, the chief priest proclaims before the temple gates the 'Launching of the Ships' in Greek and according to the Greek rite, after a prayer for the Roman emperor and people. The term πλοιαφέσια, a certain emendation by Mommsen, is used, and it is made clear that the ship of Isis, ceremonially inaugurated, is a means of securing prosperous navigation in the new season's sailing. The rite is called πλοιαφέσια and ὁ πλοῦς τῆς Ἴσιδος by Joannes Lydus in the sixth century (*De mensibus*, 4.45 = Hopfner, *Fontes*, 698); and the calendar of Philocalus in the middle of the fourth century refers to the rite as *Isidis navigium*, a festival held on March 5th (Hopfner, *Fontes*, 523). [1] A hymn to Isis by Claudian was probably intended to be sung in the course of the festival (Hopfner, *Fontes*, 595). [2] Apuleius gives a prospective allusion to the rite at the end of ch. 5, where Isis tells Lucius that on the following

---

[1] Cf. Merkelbach, *Isisfeste*, 39 with other refs.; M. Malaise, *Les Conditions de pénétration et de diffusion des cultes égyptiens en Italie* (Leiden, 1972), 217 ff.

[2] Cf. M. S. Salem, 'The Cult of Isis in Italy' (unpubl. diss. Liverpool 1937), 5.

day her priests will dedicate to the sea, now navigable once more, a new ship which will symbolize the reassumption of navigation.

Apart from chs. 16 and 17 there is very little about this ceremony in the book. The initiations of Lucius have no connection with it, and they are the central religious theme. Allusions are made, admittedly, to the role of Isis as mistress of the sea : see ch. 5 (269, 12 f.), *maris salubria flamina ... nutibus meis dispenso* and ch. 25 (286, 20 ff.), *mari terraque protegas homines* etc. Before the rite on the sea-shore and in front of the temple there is a procession of priests and initiates, but neither this nor the fancy-dress carnival that precedes it appears to be connected in any significant way with the rite of dedicating the ship. In the *anteludia* the only item which could at all be associated with the sea is the fisherman (ch. 8, p. 272, 11). Among the objects carried in the sacred procession is a lantern which is described as having the shape of a golden boat (*aureum cymbium*) : see ch. 10, p. 274, 3. This may certainly allude to the sovereignty of Isis over the sea. In the main, however, the procession displays the objects and divinities which are associated with the cult of the goddess in the most general sense. The whole processional show is a prelude to the *Isidis Navigium*, but not an integral part of it. Presumably it could have introduced any other particular festive rite of the goddess. Wittmann, therefore, misleads when he gives the heading *Isidis Navigium* to the *anteludia* and the procession as well as to 'Die Feier am Meer und im Tempel'; strictly speaking it concerns only the last item, and Berreth (pp. 85 ff.) rightly locates the title thus.

Until fairly recently it has been assumed that the rite of dedicating the ship was of Greek origin and that the function of Isis as Pelagia, Pharia or Euploia was an accretion contributed by the Hellenistic cult to the tradition inherited from Egypt. [1] The distinction made by Pausanias with regard to the two sanctuaries of Isis in Corinth could be invoked in support of this view. But of late there has been a tendency to look for antecedents in the Egyptian cult for the nautical function of Isis. The admirable discussion by D. Müller in *Isis-Aret.* 61 ff. brings out the point that Isis-Sothis was assigned power over the Nile, and that the Nile was regarded as part of Nun, the primal ocean; but he stresses the fact that

---

[1] Cf. Vandebeek, *Isisfiguur*, 50 ff.; Wittmann, 93, sees a likely origin in the Alexandrian cult. Witt, *Isis Gr-R.* 299 n. 2 suggests that Artemis Pelagia may have been influential. The Greeks also associated the sea-born Aphrodite with the function.

Amûn was more often connected with the sea as a help to sailors. Isis, he argues, could scarcely have inherited the role from Amûn. Bergman, *Ich bin Isis*, 202 n. 6 has interesting references to the role of Isis at the prow of the ship of Horus in Edfu (cf. Roeder, *Mythen und Legenden*, 129, fig. 25), but suggests that an identification with Neïth and Bastet, goddesses of the Delta, played a part.

It is on coins that the Graeco-Roman Isis Pelagia is mainly represented and those of the fourth century A.D. have been interpreted by Andreas Alföldi [1] as evidence that the *vota publica* of January 3rd were also connected with the festival of the ship of Isis in order to highlight the cult of the Alexandrian gods. In a more recent study [2] he has modifed his claim about the detailed imitation of the rites of the *Navigium* in the festival of the *vota publica*, and acknowledged the importance of Serapis in this latter connection. The New Year ceremonies are shown to have given prominence to the Alexandrian gods, but there is no need to assume that the *Isidis Navigium* was enacted in any sense on January 3rd, since the main point of the ceremony would be lacking on such an early date. In his second study (p. 64) Alföldi points to a marble relief from Delos as the earliest known example (i B.C.) of Isis Pelagia in sculpture; see Ph. Bruneau, 'Isis Pelagia à Delos', *BCH* 85 (1961), 435-46 and his further remarks in *BCH* 87 (1963), 301-308. In 1969, however, Jean-Georges Szilágyi [3] published the results of a clever piece of detection on his part : he has proved that a now headless statue in the Budapest Museum of Fine Arts is not one of Niobe, as previously thought, but of Isis Pelagia.

Another Hungarian scholar, L. Castiglione, [4] making Szilágyi's discovery his starting-point, has advanced our knowledge of the whole theme. What is clear, to start with, is that the figure of Isis holding an extended sail on the prow of a ship [5] has no exact prototype in Greek

---

[1] *A Festival of Isis in Rome under the Christian Emperors of the Fourth Century* (Budapest, 1937).

[2] 'Die alexandrinischen Götter und die Vota Publica am Jahresbeginn', *Jb. für Antike und Christentum* 8-9 (1965-6), 53-87.

[3] 'Un problème iconographiqe (*sic*)', *Bull. de Musée Hungrois des Beaux-Arts* 32-33 (1969), 19-30.

[4] 'Isis Pharia : remarque sur la statue de Budapest', ibid. 34-35 (1970), 37-55.

[5] Miss Susan Handler, of Rutgers University, U.S.A., is the author of a doctoral thesis on 'Architecture of the Roman Coins of Alexandria', where she has given special

art. It is Nikê and Aphrodite that come closest, but hardly close enough. [1]
Are there precedents in Egyptian art? Castiglione shows that Isis standing
in a boat was a frequent theme in Egypt. He reproduces (his fig. 27)
a representation of Isis and Nephthys in a boat which has Horus [2] as its
central figure; also one of Isis leading the company on the prow of the
sun-god's solar barque. The latter role of the goddess is of some significance : see Hornung, *Das Amduat*, figs. 150 (with Nephthys, both as
serpents) and 505 (seventh hour, middle register); cf. the Papyrus of Nu,
BD 100 and 129 (the vignette in Budge, *Book of the Dead* [London, 1909,
repr. 1956], 302), [3] and the tomb of Onurkh'awy (Ramesside era), which
shows Isis in front of the solar barque, with Thoth, Khepri, and Ḥu
behind her; cf. H. te Velde, *JEOL* 21 (1970), 184 and pl. 27 B. It is not
unreasonable to link with this the Graeco-Roman role of Isis as figured
on both sides of the prow of a ship, as in Lucian, *Ploion*, 5 (cf. Geneviève
Husson *ad. loc.* Paris, 1970, II, 15 f.). Ph. Derchain, *Rev. d'égyptol.* 21
(1969), 22 f. points, however, to allusions to Hathor on the prow of the
solar barque, citing Davies and Gardiner, *Antefoker*, pl. 29, 5-6, as the
earliest example known to him. [4] In the First Hour of Amduat (Hornung,
no. 45, text p. 20 f.) the 'Mistress of the Barque' (*nbt wiɜ*) is named, and
with the exception of the Seventh Hour, where she is replaced by Isis,
it is she that consistently appears as the sun-god's pilot; cf. Jéquier, *Le
livre de ce qu'il y a dans l'Hadès* (Paris, 1894), 21. Hornung (p. 21)
points out that this goddess is usually represented as Hathor, with cow-
horns and sun-disk, and Hathor's function in this respect is attested by
S. Allam, *Beiträge zum Hathorkult* (MÄS 4, 1963), 116 ff. who cites
Pyr. 490*b* (Hathor is *she who is at the head of the ship of Rēʿ*).

Whereas Castiglione has not remarked on this importance of Hathor
(save for his final remarks on Hathor and Byblos), he notes that a sacral
boat figures in Osirian rites as early as the Stela of Ikhernofret (12th

---

attention to Isis Pharia. She tells me (15 Nov. 1969) that in her view 'this Isis of the
coins is exactly like the marble Isis, headless, in the Budapest Museum.' She adds that
'it may, I feel, represent a cult statue originally set up on Pharos island.'

  [1] Cf. Bruneau, *BCH* 85 (1961), 442; Castiglione, op. cit. 19 f.

  [2] The falcon may, however, represent Sokar or Osiris-Sokar.

  [3] Cf. Naville, pl. 113 (Kap. 100), *P, b.* and *P. c.*

  [4] Cf. Derchain, *Elkab I* (Brussels, 1971), 55; and id. *Hathor Quadrifrons* (Istanbul,
1972), 36-44.

Dynasty). It is the *neshmet*-barque and is the ship of Osiris—*his great ship of eternity and everlasting*. The first rite described by Ikhernofret is one in which the *neshmet*-barque is the centre of a ritual combat :

> I enacted the procession of Wepwawet when he went to help his father. I smote those who attacked the *neshmet*-barque and overthrew the enemies of Osiris.

Here the mention of Wepwawet suggests that Horus as the living king is the central figure of the procession; [1] the combat is essentially that of Horus and Seth. Afterwards, however, the *neshmet*-barque is concerned with the passion, death and burial of Osiris. There is a second ritual combat, but in this context the slaying of Osiris in Nedyet is referred to :

> I directed the Great Procession and followed the god to his journeyings. I caused the god's ship to sail and Thoth ordered the voyage. I equipped *The Lord of Abydos Appears in Truth* with a shrine ... I led the god's way to his tomb in Peker. I saved Onnophris on the day of the great contest and overthrew all his enemies on the ridges of Nedyet. I caused him to embark on the great ship which carried his beauty ... It came to land in Abydos and brought Osiris, Foremost of the Westerners, to his palace.

Some of these rites may reflect, as Helck [2] has argued, the early burial ceremonies of the Thinite kings. It should be noted that Isis is not mentioned in this inscription. The tradition relating to the *neshmet*-barque persisted vigorously, [3] and J.-C. Goyon, 'Textes mythologiques : Le livre de protéger la barque du dieu' (*Kêmi* 19 [1969], 23-65), has edited three Ptolemaic versions of a text which he rightly describes as a 'rituel osirien dirigé contre Seth'. Nor is it surprising that the *neshmet*-barque is given a funerary application : in the Theban tomb of Ramose (temp. Ramesses II) the text is inscribed on a wall of the funerary chapel and Ramose is depicted being rowed in the boat. [4] On the other hand, the

---

[1] Cf. J. Gwyn Griffiths, *Conflict*, 66 n. 2.

[2] 'Die Herkunft des abydenischen Osirisrituals', *Archiv Orientální* 20 (1952), 72-85. On p. 77 he suggests that the 'enemies' were originally the king's court and harîm, buried with him, but this is very unlikely. Why should the king's intimates be so regarded? For the text see Schäfer, *Die Mysterien des Osiris in Abydos* (Leipzig, 1904).

[3] Cf. Schott (tr. E. B. Hauser), *Wall Scenes from the Mortuary Chapel of the Mayor Paser at Medinet Habu* (Studies in Ancient Oriental Civilization, 30, Chicago, 1957), 1; 8 f.

[4] J.-C. Goyon, *Kêmi* 19 (1969), 25.

version from Denderah which Goyon has edited states (col. 33, p. 65) that the text is to be recited in the festivals of Osiris; an interchange of purely Osirian and general funerary usage is, at the same time, natural, since the deceased was identified with Osiris. The anti-Sethian stress of the Ptolemaic versions does not preclude a prominence to Isis. In the final chant, for instance (L 35, pp. 60 f.), it is said that 'Isis the great, the mother of the god, is made triumphant over the wretched Seth and his accomplices.' It is noteworthy that the *neshmet*-barque in this text is sometimes confused or equated with the boat of Rē', whose enemy is Apopis (cf. NY 11, pp. 60 f. and D 34, pp. 64 f., 'the *neshmet*-barque of Rē").

A god closely associated with Osiris was Sokar, [1] who is often depicted in the form of a falcon and has his distinctive barque, usually the *ḥnw*-barque. A festival concerned with Sokar is presented in texts of the Ptolemaic era : see R. O. Faulkner, *JEA* 23 (1937), 12-16 and J.-C. Goyon, *Rev. d'égyptol.* 20 (1968), 63-96. A feature of the second part of the liturgy is an address by Isis in which she greets Hathor as a deity embodied in the barque of Sokar. The prominence of Hathor in this connection, and also with regard to her own barques in the procession of Sokar, has been well analysed by Gaballa and Kitchen, op. cit. 62 ff., who note (p. 63) that 'her boat leads the others (in the Sokar scenes at Medinet Habu), she has a full litany in Bremner-Rhind and parallels, and in those documents the other goddesses are largely considered as forms of her.' They point also to an early association of Hathor and Sokar. While this may be taken to confirm the boat-connections of Hathor, one must be wary of pressing it, since divine boats are ubiquitous in Egyptian processions. Gressmann [2] was clearly unaware of this when he argued that Osiris began as a tree-god, then became a house-god and a boat-god, and could hardly be thought of without a boat. For processional purposes gods are generally carried in barques; this was because a part of the journey would be on the Nile. Such barques pre-

---

[1] Cf. G. A. Gaballa and K. A. Kitchen, 'The Festival of Sokar', *Orientalia* 38 (1969), 1-76. On p. 36 they state that 'after the New Kingdom Sokar was increasingly little more than a name or aspect of Osiris.'

[2] *Orient. Rel.* 25 f.

serve ancient forms, and the boats actually used would of course be larger. [1]

A boat in which Isis frequently figures with a specific purpose is the funerary boat that ferries the dead to the West. She and Nephthys are the 'Two Kites' who bewail the dead, and they appear as wailing women close to the body of the deceased : see J. Settgast, *Untersuchungen zu alt-ägyptischen Bestattungsdarstellungen* (*ADAIK* 3, 1963), pls. 7 and 11 and pp. 26, 58 ff., 76); cf. J. Gwyn Griffiths, *Origins of Osiris*, 28 f. and Maria Münster, *Isis.*, 61 and 201 (in the latter instance Isis appears as a falcon on the bow of the funerary boat). The *Book of the Dead* preserves the same tradition : v. Naville, Kap. 1, pl. 3 (several examples); Barguet, *Livre des morts*, 40. Variety is shown in the position of the goddesses: Isis is sometimes at the prow, sometimes at the stern. In Tylor and Griffith, *The Tomb of Paheri* (1894), pl. 5, Isis is at the prow. Related to this concept is her presence with the mummy of Osiris : see Budge, *Osiris*, I, 12 and 14 (Isis and Nephthys are shown, in reliefs from Denderah, separately); also II, 73. These are from the Graeco-Roman era; and from the Roman era too there is a painted mummy-covering showing Isis and Nephthys flanking a figure of the sun-disk which encloses Harpocrates : v. Castiglione, *Acta Ant. Hung.* 15 (1967), 147, pl. 13, 1 and p. 124; cf. a clay sealing from Edfu, of the middle Ptolemaic era, figuring Isis and the infant Horus 'enthroned in the cabin of a sacred barque', according to M. A. Murray, 'Ptolemaic Clay-sealings', *ZÄS* 44 (1907), 67, no. 25 (also pl. 4). A stela of the Ptolemaic era shows Isis on the prow of a boat which includes also Thoth and Horus; the deities are being worshipped by the deceased (Inaros) : v. Otto Koefoed-Petersen, *Les stèles égyptiennes* (Copenhagen, 1948), pl. 63 and p. 49. A more specific motive attaches to a figure of Isis in a shrine on a boat which occurs in Philae (Junker, *Abaton*, 56, fig. 19) : she is represented here as visiting the grave of Osiris in Bigeh.

There are thus several possible antecedents for the association of Isis with a boat. But for a goddess who is a patron of shipping we must look primarily to Hathor, although Isis may have inherited the function from her. Derchain, *Rev. d'égyptol.* 21 (1969), 19-25, has shown how Hathor

---

[1] Cf. A. M. Blackman, tr. Roeder, *Das hundert-torige Theben* (Leipzig, 1926), 57 f. and pl. 17.

in this role is involved in P. Westcar, 5, 7 ff., where the twenty rowing girls are described with epithets used of Hathor. [1] Egypt had early maritime contact with Byblos, and Hathor's title, Mistress of Byblos, clearly reflects this association with the sea; cf. Allam, *Beiträge zum Hathorkult*, 142, quoting from Spell 61 of the Coffin Texts ('Hathor, the Mistress of Byblos, will steer your boat'). We may compare, further, the scenes in the Hathor-chapel of Deir el-Bahari in which an oar is offered to Hathor : v. Naville, *The Temple of Deir el Bahari*, IV (London, 1901), pls. 92-93; in pl. 93 the oar is adorned with two *wedjat*-eyes indicative of safe voyaging.[2] Tuthmosis III, who is bringing the oar in pl. 92, has many ships depicted behind him—a fact not apparent in the plates, but noted by the present writer *in situ*. Pls. 90-91 show ships which have bows ending in bovine Hathor-heads, and in one case (pl. 104) the Hathor-cow is figured in her sacred boat; cf. the early Egyptian ships in Emery, *Archaic Egypt*, 39, fig. 1 = Westendorf, *Egn. Art.*, 21. Hathor is also Mistress of Pwenet : v. Allam, *op. cit.* 132 et al. In Deir el-Baḥari, it is true, Amûn presides over the Pwenet-scenes.

With these varied antecedents the data of the Graeco-Roman era are not always easy to relate. In the Canopus Decree (Sethe, *Urk.* II, 142 ff.) it is said that the deceased Berenice is to rest with the god Osiris in the temple of Canopus, and allusion is made to the entry of Osiris into the temple in the Sektet-boat on the 29th day of Khoiak. [3] Later, mention is made of a boat -procession for Berenice in the month of Tybi; and of the Festival of the Cicellia it is stated (Sethe, 149 f.) that 'when the Cicellia are celebrated in the month of Khoiak before the voyage of Osiris, the maidens and priests are to prepare another image of Berenice, Lady of Virgins.' Clearly the association of the dead Princess Berenice and Osiris is intended, and her boat-procession will be Osirian. But it is not easy to distinguish the two Osirian voyages; they may indeed be one. In

---

[1] Cf. W. K. Simpson in *The Literature of Ancient Egypt* (Yale, 1972), 20.

[2] Cf. the four larger rudders attached to crowned uraei in the tomb of Ramesses III. The connection there is perhaps with Wedjoyet, the goddess of Buto. In the tomb of Sethos I the King is seen holding a rudder in his right hand and a flail in his left. Perhaps the symbolism there is different.

[3] Cf. Bevan, *Hist. Ptol. Eg.* 208 ff.

Demotic the Cicellia are called the 'Rites of Isis.'[1] According to Epiphanius (ed. Dindorf, II, 482) the Cicellia were to the Alexandrians what the Saturnalia were to the Romans and the Cronia to the Egyptians, and these festivals were all on December 25th. E. Chassinat, *Le mystère d'Osiris*, II (Cairo, 1968), 614 f. compares the thirty-four boats which form a nautical procession in the Osirian rites of Khoiak described in the texts of Denderah. A voyage of Osiris occurs on Khoiak 29th according to the first mention of it in the Canopus Decree, and it seems unlikely that there was a second; the Decree uses the expression 'before the voyage of Osiris' to denote the Cicellia, and Holl (cited by Bilabel, *Die gräko-ägyptischen Feste*, 42 n. 3) suggests that the Cicellia therefore preceded Khoiak 29th. Bilabel cogently connects the two rites, adducing the Demotic reference to Isis; he also cites a voyage of Osiris on Khoiak 26th from the Festival Calendar of Saïs : see P. Hibeh 27, 60-62 ('Osiris voyages around and a golden boat is taken out'). Grenfell and Hunt *ad loc.* (p. 153) skilfully reconcile the boat-ceremonies of this calendar and of the Canopus Decree : they invoke Plutarch, *De Is. et Os.* 13, where the death of Osiris is dated to Athyr 17th; and Plutarch, ch. 39, says that special Osirian rites last for four days from Athyr 17th. In spite of the discrepancy in the name of the month, Plutarch's festival is clearly the same as that described in the Denderah texts as relating to Khoiak. Thus if the voyage of Osiris is on Khoiak 26th in the Calendar of Saïs and on Khoiak 29th in the Canopus Decree, this may well denote the beginning and end of the voyage in a festival known to last for four days.

Merkelbach, *Isisfeste*, 35 ff., accepts and elaborates these identifications, and also seeks to correlate the boat-ceremonies with Plutarch's mythology. The body of Osiris, according to ch. 13, goes out to sea in a chest by way of the Tanitic mouth. 'Ihn zu suchen, ist dann Isis zum erstenmal aufs Meer hinausgefahren, wie wir bald sehen werden', says Merkelbach (p. 35). There is no mention of this in Plutarch's ch. 13, but Merkelbach refers to the seeking and finding of Osiris described in ch. 39, where the priests are said to go down to the sea. Isis is here represented as a gilded cow with a black garment, but there is no allusion to any boat-

---

[1] Spiegelberg, *Der demotische Text der Priesterdekrete von Kanopus und Memphis* (Heidelberg, 1922), 75—'die Tage der Isis-Riten (?)'—and 91; F. Daumas, *Les moyens d'expression du Grec et de l'Égyptien* (Cairo, 1952), 176.

ceremony. In ch. 50, however, as Merkelbach afterwards remarks (p. 36), Plutarch mentions a festival on Tybi 7th when the return of Isis from Phoenicia was celebrated. Since Tybi follows Khoiak Merkelbach is able to suggest, 'Diese Rückkehr der Isis hängt vielleicht mit ihrer Ausfahrt am 29. Choiach zusammen.' But the trouble is that this initial voyage of hers is not specifically mentioned. An Osirian voyage fits the date of Khoiak 29th, and Isis may naturally be involved. Her voyage to Byblos may be assumed, suggests Merkelbach (p. 36 n. 36), as happening between this date and Tybi 7th. The idea involves little over a week for a journey to Byblos and back—an impossible proposition; cf. Lucian, *De Syr. dea*, 7 (from Egypt to Byblos takes seven days). In ch. 16 Plutarch tells us how Isis set out in a boat from Byblos; in ch. 18 he describes Isis sailing through the marshes of the Delta in a papyrus boat in her quest for the mutilated body of Osiris. He is silent about her voyage *to* Byblos except for his curt statement that she arrived there (εἰς Βύβλον ἀφικέσθαι, 15, 357 A) when she heard that the chest was there.

If there are good reasons for equating the Cicellia with the Osirian ceremonies at the end of Khoiak, can the rites of the *Isidis Navigium* also be identified with these festivals? Merkelbach, pp. 39-41, is confident about the identification, and Castiglione, 'Isis Pharia', 41f., cheerfully accepts it. Yet it is noteworthy that Merkelbach's account is concerned more with the *anteludia* than with the *Ploiaphesia* proper. The latter rite he connects (p. 41) with the ship of Isis that seeks Osiris, and this indeed seems the only possible interpretation if the rite and the myth are to be linked. It is the ship that set out for Phoenicia and returned therefrom with the body of Osiris (cf. Plutarch, 16, 357 D : 'placing the coffin in a boat, she set sail.') It is also, therefore, the funerary boat of the age-long tradition which makes Isis accompany the dead Osiris or the Osirian dead. It is to be identified too with the *neshmet*-boat of Osiris in which the god, finally, is taken to his burial-place. In this sense it is the same boat as that involved in the 'voyage of Osiris' mentioned in the Canopus Decree and the Calender of Saïs. Admittedly, Apuleius does not supply this ritual and mythical background to the *Ploiaphesia*; what he stresses is the function of the rite as an act of renewing navigation.

There is, nonetheless, a fatal objection to the equation of *Isidis Navigium* and the ceremonies at the end of Khoiak : the former rite was held on March 5th, and this Julianic date can only correspond to Khoiak

29th if it is projected back to 304 B.C. Such is precisely the procedure adopted by Merkelbach (pp. 57-60) in his ingenious attempt at equation. Why should this date in 304 B.C. have determined the time of the festival throughout the Hellenistic and Roman era (p. 59)? Merkelbach has stressed, before this, the importance of Athyr 1st (= Jan. 6th) 304 as the coronation date of Ptolemy Soter, but with equal stress on Tybi 1st (= March 7th) as the traditional ideal coronation date. It would have been reasonable, he argues, for Ptolemy to have arranged a repeated ceremony on Tybi 1st, and he finds evidence of this in the fact that the Canopus Decree in 238 B.C. ordered the celebration of the Cicellia and then, on Tybi 17th (= March 7th), proclaimed the decree with honours for the divine pair and the calendar-reform. There is a good deal of assumption and speculation in all this, and evidence from the Roman era prompts one to reject the theory firmly. The Calendar of Philocalus (A.D.iv) assigns *Isia* to Oct. 28th - Nov. 1st, and these dates undoubtedly represent those involved in the Khoiak festival; the same calendar puts *Isidis Navigium* down for March 5th. Youtie [1] has well remarked that 'both the Isia and Ploiaphesia were universal festivals and their names were not so unfamiliar that they would be readily confused.'

Whereas Castiglione, 'Isis Pharia', 41, unwisely accepts Merkelbach's equation (and with no discussion at all), he proceeds to invoke some relevant Graeco-Roman representations where the ship of Isis may be figured. Although the Cicellia and the *Isidis Navigium* must be distinguished as separate festivals, the Isiac ship involved is the same one—the ship in which she sought and found Osiris. Castiglione refers first to a mural painting from the sanctuary of Isis in Pompeii : see his fig. 29 and Tran Tam Tinh, *Isis à Pompéi*, pl. 10, 1 and pp. 65 f., also pp. 143 f. The latter entitles the picture 'Découverte d'Osiris'. [2] Two boats are depicted in one of which stands a feminine figure with a sash hanging down from her left shoulder; cf. the note below on ch. 4, p. 268, 17-18 (a feature of the dress of Isis). She is very probably Isis and she is shown pulling towards her another boat in the centre of which is

---

[1] In *Studies in Roman Economic and Social History* (FS. A. C. Johnson, Princeton, 1951), 195. Cf. Tran Tam Tinh, *Herculanum*, 49.

[2] Cf. the interpretation by Olga Elia, discussed below in n. *ad* ch. 16 (277, 14 f.), *navem faberrime factam*.

a chest enclosing a falcon. Tran Tam Tinh, p. 65, interprets this falcon as Horus (and in this he is followed by Castiglione), quoting in support *BD* 77 ('I am risen as a great falcon...'). Certainly the Osirian dead there proclaims his identification with the sacred falcon who joins the day and night barques of the sun-god. But a much more directly Osirian falcon is that of Sokar, and its encasement in a chest is a rough approximation to the traditional usage; the freer form, like that of Isis, can be expected in a Pompeian context. The scene is doubtless the Nile or a sacred lake. Volten, 'Testi Demotici', 102, quotes the Magical Pap. of London and Leiden, 21, 2 ff, for the idea that Osiris is a falcon like Horus; but even here it is Sokar who is probably implied.

In the setting of Canopus this ceremony might well be on the sea, although Castiglione's argument (following Merkelbach) that the Canopic vase depicting Osiris Hydreios supports the association is quite unconvincing. In origin this type of vase has nothing to do with Canopus, still less with the sea. It does denote an association of Osiris with water and with the Nile : see n. *ad.* ch. 11 (275, 6), *urnula.* When Castiglione, 'Isis Pharia', 43, cites Plutarch, *De Is. et Os.* 13 for a connection with Canopus, he is certainly straining the evidence; Plutarch there remarks that the chest containing the dead Osiris went out to sea, but he names the Tanitic mouth, and this was far from the Canopic mouth. In *Acta Ant. Hung.* 5 (1957), 209-227 Castiglione was able to show that the mosaic of Praeneste includes a depiction of four priests with a vase figuring Osiris Hydreios; cf. R. E. Witt, *Isis Gr.-R.* pl. 8 (right). (Gullini has shown there is restoration; but it may be on ancient lines.) The ship here represented might well suggest Canopus, although Alexandria itself could be even liklier as the inspiration. In spite of the well-known account in Rufinus, these vases figuring Osiris Hydreios do not necessarily derive from Canopus; compare the two fine examples in the Alexandria Graeco-Roman Museum from a sanctuary of Isis in Ras es-Soda (P. 443 and 444); cf. n. *ad* ch. 11 (275, 6), *urnula.* Strangely enough, only one instance [1] is recorded by Breccia, *Monuments* I (1926), 63 as coming from

---

[1] Tran Tam Tinh, *Herculanum* 33 n. 3 wrongly states that there are two. He cites the same locus in Breccia, but the latter refers to the solitary instance with some emphasis; his pl. 29, 6 is from Alexandria, though grouped by Tran Tam Tinh with the example from Canopus.

Abukir (Canopus, near the modern Fort Tewfik), although a number derive from Alexandria. An inscription from Delos connects Sarapis with Canopus : v. Roussel, *CED* 275; cf. Pausanias, 2.4.7; and Plutarch's allusion to an oracle of Pluto in Canopus occurs in a context where he cites the belief that Pluto and Sarapis are identical (*De Is. et Os.* 27, 361 E). [1] In a general sense Alexandria is the probable source of a Ptolemaic development of the association of Isis or Hathor with the sea; Canopus of course was also on the sea and only 23 kilometres from the centre of Alexandria, but while it preserved its religious significance, it had yielded its trading importance to Alexandria; nor are the Canopic connections of Osiris (or Sarapis) Hydreios, such as they are, a sufficient reason for locating the beginnings of the *Isidis Navigium* there. Whereas Castiglione gives undue prominence to Canopus in his theory of origins, he rightly stresses the crucial role of Alexandria : v. 'Isis Pharia', 45 ff.; his stress, in particular, on the likely function played by the sanctuary of Isis on Pharos is quite convincing, even if the sanctuary itself is not attested archaeologically.

The typology of the forms assumed by Isis Pharia in sculpture and coins has been well studied by both Bruneau and Castiglione. The former, in his first study (*BCH* 85, 435 ff.), after discussing the relief from Delos which E. Lapalus had connected with Isis and dating it to the first half of the first century B.C., surveys the whole field and distinguishes seven types. Whereas the distinctions he makes are valid, they hardly justify the sevenfold division, and Castiglione, 'Isis Pharia', 50 f., points out that the crucial difference between the forms of the imperial era and those of the Hellenistic period is that the later group shows the mantle of the goddess thrown back behind her and extended by the wind—an illogical feature, as it happens, since the swollen sail which she steadies in front of her betrays a wind blowing in the opposite direction. A Phoenician coin of the reign of Claudius is the first datable instance of the later form (cf. Bruneau, op. cit. 440), but Castiglione plausibly suggests, in view of the earlier type being last represented by the Delian relief of the first half of the first century B.C., that the destruction of Pharos during Julius Caesar's Alexandrian war caused the original statue to be destroyed

---

[1] See my Comm., pp. 377 and 392; cf. J. E. Stambaugh, *Sarapis under the Early Ptolemies* (Leiden, 1972), 29.

or damaged, thus giving rise to the fashioning of a new form. The earlier type is also first figured on a coin from Byblos from the reign of Antiochus IV Epiphanes (v. Castiglione, p. 49), 215-163 B. C., and an origin in the early third century is likely. The prominence of Byblos in the evolution of both types is striking; Castiglione (p. 54) rightly relates this to the early importance of Hathor as a patron of navigation in this connection.

Representations concerned with the actual rite of the *Isidis Navigium* would be more closely germane to our interest. They are, alas, rare and difficult of interpretation. We have already discussed a mural from Pompeii and the representations on coins. According to Doro Levi, *Antioch Mosaic Pavements*, I (Princeton, 1947), 164 ff., a section entitled 'The Navigium Isidis (?)", a fragmentary mosaic may be concerned with the theme, where a curved bay of the sea is depicted with two boats which have their sterns opposed; above are the legs of a standing figure and part of a large metallic shield; to the left are the legs of a man 'who seems to be climbing up a rock in order to enter the boat'. Here too, it is claimed, was a Victory in the air above the boat, flying with open wings. All these elements, he avers, correspond to features of the Πλοιαφέσια as figured on Roman imperial coins, and the mosaics in this house in Antioch-on-Orontes may belong to the third century A.D. Unfortunately the photograph (pl. 33b) allows little of the detail mentioned to be discerned; the two boats are perhaps to be seen, that is all. The interpretation on Isiac lines of another mosaic there is also doubtful : see n. *ad* ch. 23 (285, 11 f.), *accessi confinium mortis*; on the other hand, a figure in one panel is probably Isiac since the depiction of the moon and stars on her sash points to this : see n. *ad* ch. 4 (268, 17 f.), *stellae ... semenstris luna*.

Again, V. Tran Tam Tinh, *Herculanum*, 48 f., wishes to interpret the best known of the frescoes of Herculaneum (his pl. 27) as being concerned with the *Isidis Navigium*. He states that the rite was characterized by a great procession during which 'le grand-prêtre promena le vase sacré symbolisant Isis'. The fresco, he maintains, represents the solemn procession in its initial stages. That the rite depicted may concern the beginning of a procession (or its end) is not at all unlikely; it is noted on p. 46 that Dölger in *Antike und Christentum* 5 (1936), 164 had already made a similar suggestion. Further, Apuleius in chs. 10 and 11 mentions more than one type of vase being carried by priests; perhaps it is the *am-*

phora at the end of ch. 10 that is involved here : see n. ad loc. The basic objection, however, to the interpretation is that the procession described by Apuleius is not specifically a part of the rite of the *Isidis Navigium*, as we have shown above. A secondary objection is that there is no good evidence for saying that the vase symbolizes Isis. The *urnula* in ch. 11 symbolizes Osiris, although Isis and Nephthys might also be figured on it; the sacred water is likewise equated with Osiris.

Some questions still remain open, but what emerges is that the role of Isis in the Osirian funerary boat is important in the evolution of ideas which results in her function in this rite. Prominence has not been hitherto given to her significance in this context; indeed it has not been even mentioned, and yet it is the role that links her to the Osirian *nesh-met*-barque, whose importance persists. The barque is invoked as a deity in P. Rhind; see Volten, 'Testi Demotici', 101. On the other hand, it is from Hathor that Isis has derived her status as goddess of navigation. Bastet was also identified with Hathor, and the nearest festive date in a possible Sothic correspondence which supplies a similar motif is the fifth of the eighth month of winter (Pharmuthi); this, if Sothic, would be the Julianic Feb. 18th; for the Egyptian date Schott, *Altägyptische Fest-daten*, 101 (no. 123), records a festival from an inscription on a Saïte statue in the Louvre : 'Ich habe Bastet in ihrem Schiff erscheinen lassen an ihrem schönen Fest des 5.VIII.' A goddess and festival prominent in the Delta are obviously a likely source. Bastet and Renenutet are conspicuous in the festivals of this month, and both are identified with Hathor and Isis; cf. J. Broekhuis, *De Godin Renenwetet* (Assen, 1971), 38 (Renenutet with emblems of Hathor) and 105-109 (Renenutet and Isis). On the 28th of the month (if Sothic, it would equal Julianic March 13th) offering is made to Hathor according to a Ramesside ostracon (Schott, p. 102, no. 130). It is not unlikely, however, that in Alexandria this festival of Isis was given a date independently of the previously established rites, corresponding to the traditional end of the 'mare clausum' .[1] E. de Saint-Denis [2] quotes Vegetius, 4.39, for the dates Nov. 11th to March 10th as those applying to the cessation of navigation, but shows (pp. 203 ff.) that they were not too rigorously observed. Paul's voyage to Rome on

---

[1] For this tradition see E. de Saint-Denis, 'Mare Clausum', *REL* 25 (1947), 196-214.
[2] Op. cit. 196.

an Alexandrian ship from Myrrha in Lycia (Acts 27.5 ff.) begins in the autumn and is planned to proceed in winter. In ch. 26 Lucius himself undertakes a voyage from Corinth to Ostia which brings him to Rome on December 15th.

An interesting result of the importance in the religion of Isis of this marine ceremony is the application of nautical titles to personnel of the cult; see n. *ad* ch. 16 (278, 15), *summus sacerdos*. Inscriptions from Byzantium and Eretria reveal that persons given the title *nauarchos*, 'admiral', were responsible for the *Ploiaphesia* : see the excellent discussion of such titles by Vidman, *Isis und Sarapis*, 76 ff. A concrete result in the appurtenances of the cult was the use of boat-shaped lamps with figures of Isis and Sarapis : see n. ad. ch. 10 (274, 1), *lucernam*.

Was the *Navigium* which was launched at Cenchreae real or merely ceremonial? Berreth, pp. 85 ff., begins his discussion by comparing a rite among modern primitives in the Island of Ceram near New Guinea : a small ship is loaded with rice, tobaccco and eggs, and as it is launched, a man cries out that all diseases and evils are now leaving them, not to return evermore. The festive rite at Cenchreae, urges Berreth, is similarly apotropaic, and the ship is a purely ritual object. Whereas several commentators, including Médan and Wittmann, seem to leave the question open, Merkelbach, *Roman und Mysterium*, 95, notes that it is 'ein unbemanntes Schiff' [1] and he adds that the interpretation may well be that Isis herself went out upon it as the first voyager by sea; in this connection he cites the tradition that she invented sails. It is true that Apuleius mentions no crew; he refers only to the people who loaded the ship with spices and offerings while they also poured a libation of meal and milk on the waves. Nevertheless there are reasons for believing that this was a real ship bound for a real destination.

(1) A purification of it is carried out very solemnly. Admittedly this might apply also to a ritual vessel.

(2) The ship is dedicated to Isis, and is called the *Isis*; this latter feature is attested of several real ships : see n. *ad* ch. 16, p. 278, 16 f.

(3) A ceremonial ship might be expected to be small—a mere model. Vidman, *Isis und Sarapis*, 76, thus speaks of 'ein kleines der Isis geweihtes Schiff'. Apuleius does not suggest this. Indeed he suggests the con-

---

[1] Cf. R. E. Witt, *Isis Gr.-R.* 177, 'with no crew to guide her'.

trary when he speaks of the mast as 'lofty in its radiance' (*splendore sublimis*). His ship is, further, freed from anchor cables, like a normal vessel, and is launched with a favourable breeze.

(4) At the end of ch. 16 the ship is said to fade from sight. Clearly it is going far. But if it is just a ritual model, its fate is to sink. That may suit the kind of vessel adduced by Berreth, since it is carrying evil forces away, but it is most unfortunate in a vessel that is to symbolize the renewal of safe navigation. In *Florida*, 23, Apuleius describes, in rather similar, if more modest, terms, a *navem bonam, fabre factam*, but goes on to say that if it is guided by the storm and not by a helmsman, then it will be sunk or broken on rocks. One therefore doubts whether his silence about the crew of the *Isis* should be pressed to imply the absence of a crew.

(5) In ch. 5 Isis says that her priests 'are wont to vow a new barque to the now navigable sea and offer it as first-fruits of a new year's naviga-tion'. This reinforces (4). If the sea is now navigable, a new ship offered to it will surely prove seaworthy.

(6) If the ship were purely ritual it would doubtless have been carried in the procession in a waggon. In fact this was suggested by J. Burckhardt, *Die Zeit Konstantins des Grossen* (1852, Ed. 5, Leipzig, 1924), 194 n. 1, adding, 'Der Festzug dieses carrus navalis (Schiffwagen) ist sehr wahr-scheinlich die Grundform des neuern Karnevals...' If this were so, it is strange that Apuleius, who devotes such detail to the procession, omits to mention it; cf. Wittmann, p. 213 n. 476.

It seems likely, then, that for all its sumptuous decoration and ritual import, this was a real ship bound for a real destination, the first ship of the new season in Cenchreae. Its destination might well have been Delos, where a ship called *Isis* would have been especially welcome. [1]

VI. Magic and Miracle

It is the miraculous intervention of Isis that secures for Lucius, in this book, his transformation back into human form. This eminently suits the traditional role of Isis as the mistress of magic and miracle. In ch. 15 the priest reminds Lucius that the cause of his downfall was dual : his lustful excess and his ill-starred curiosity. Since the *curiositas* was

---

[1] Cf. Roussel, *CED* 287. Vidman, *Isis und Sarapis*, 85, unwisely takes another view.

itself concerned with magic, a contradiction appears here *prima facie*. If prying into magical secrets led to the change into an ass, what was wrong with this, since the re-transformation and the final redemption are themselves wrought by the mistress of magic? The contradiction is resolved by two dualities : magic can be benign or baleful, and *curiositas* can be good or bad.

The magical and the miraculous are combined, in the novel as a whole, with erotic and humorous elements, and the impetus behind the telling derives from the writer's moral purpose. The amalgam may seem bizarre, but Reitzenstein in his *Hellenistische Wundererzählungen* (Leipzig, 1906), 32 ff. provides parallels, including early Christian apocryphal literature. [1] It was a tradition which the Renaissance took up again. Edgar Wind, *Pagan Mysteries in the Renaissance* (London, 1958), 189, states that '*serio ludere* was a methodical maxim of Cusanus, Ficino, Pico, Calcagnini ...' He also points out that Cusanus was a teacher of Giovanni Andrea de Bussi, who in his preface to the first printed edition of the *Metamorphoses* praised Bessarion as a defender of Plato and Cusanus as a student of Proclus' Theology, thus implying a philosophical approach to an amusing story.

According to his own programmatic prelude Apuleius aims to provide delectation (*laetaberis*) and also astonishment (*ut mireris*). [2] The latter aim relates to the miraculous, and although this element is prominent in the stories about wonders experienced by travellers, in Apuleius it has the stamp not of fantasy, but of realism. [3] To Apuleius the loftier kind of magic is akin to miracle. Antonie Wlosok [4] points out that Lucius refers to magic as a *divina disciplina* (3.19) and that it is only the audacious meddling of Lucius himself that is condemned : it is a form, virtually,

---

[1] Cf. Georg Misch, *Geschichte der Autobiographie*, I, 2 (Ed. 3, Bern, 1950), 384 : 'charakteristisch für die Geistesverfassung der Zeit'. The combination of the serious and the playful is, of course attested earlier. See L. Giangrande, *The Use of Spoudaiogeloion in Greek and Roman Literature* (The Hague, 1972).

[2] Cf. F. Pfister, *Phil. Woch.* 60 (1940), 539.

[3] Cf. Ed. Schwartz, *Fünf Vorträge über den Griechischen Roman* (Ed. 2, Berlin, 1945), 144.

[4] *Phil.* 113 (1969), 72 ('Zur Einheit der Metamorphosen des Apuleius'). The phrase *divini potens* (1.8), however, is read otherwise by Robertson : *Saga ... et divina, potens caelum deponere*, which Valette renders 'Une magicienne, une divineresse...'

of *hubris*. When Isis reveals herself to him, it is as an all-powerful goddess who dominates every sphere (ch. 5). In 2.28 ff. the Egyptian Zatchlas,
a prophet of the first order (*propheta primarius*), raises a person from the
dead for a brief span of time.

According to the *Apology* Apuleius was charged with having used magic
in order to secure the rich widow Pudentilla as his wife (the initial additional charge of having murdered his step-son Pontianus was dropped),
and the first allusion to the accusation implies a charge of magical evil
deeds (*magicorum maleficiorum*, ch. 1), a phrase expanded in ch. 25 to
'terrible crimes, horrible evils, and execrable arts' (*scelera immania et
inconcessa maleficia et artis nefandas*). Apuleius then asks, What is a
magician? He proceeds to argue that *magus* is the Persian word for priest,
and that this implies knowledge of religion and ritual—the opposite
of any criminal suggestion. He then quotes Plato on the education of
Persian princes : this is said to include 'the magic of Zoroaster the son
of Oromazes, which is the worship of the gods'. Magic is therefore an
art acceptable to the immortal gods. Plato is again quoted, this time
in relation to Zalmoxis, a Thracian master of magic : thinking of him
makes Plato say that 'magical charms (ἐπῳδαί) are beautiful words.'
Apuleius, however, then turns to another view of magic : according to
popular usage (*more vulgari*) a magician is one who through converse
with the immortal gods is able to do anything he wishes by means of a
strange power of incantation (ch. 27, *ad omnia quae velit incredibili
quadam vi cantaminum polleat*). Such a faculty, he adds, is wrongly
ascribed to philosophers; and it is as a philosopher that Apuleius here
wants to be regarded. It is against the second type of magic that he then
tries to defend himself, and in ch. 28 he stresses that he is not guilty of
any evil practice. : 'Next I will show that, even if I were a supremely
skilled magician, I have never provided a reason or opportunity for them
to convict me of any evil practice (*ut me in aliquo maleficio experirentur*).'
He denies that he has bought fish for an evil purpose (*maleficio* again,
ch. 29). In Homer, he recalls (ch. 40), the blood of Ulysses is stopped by
a magical incantation (*cantamine*); 'now nothing that is done to save
life can be open to a criminal charge.' If this is beneficent magic, the kind
that is condemned by the Twelve Tables is as mysterious as it is shocking
and horrible (*occulta non minus quam tetra et horribilis*, ch. 47).

To Apuleius, then, the magic that is bad, though it has undoubted power, is reprehensible because it is wilful, merely serving the magician's desires, and because it fulfils aims that are evil. [1] The first condemnation will apply to the kind of magic sought by Lucius in the opening of the *Metamorphoses*. In an Isiac context it may well be viewed as Typhonic magic, as Merkelbach [2] aptly remarks. It could scarcely be claimed that Egyptian thought distinguishes between good and bad magic in a moral sense; the dichotomy is achieved rather by a process of association. As Seth-Typhon becomes a sort of Satan, his magical powers are regarded as evil. Isis too can rebuke and punish, sometimes with undue cruelty, as when she kills the son of the rich woman who has closed her door to her in the Metternich Stela, although the goddess later relents. By and large, however, her magic is beneficent according to the canons of Apuleius; it does not harm, but heals.

When the miracle of metamorphosis is recounted in ch. 13, the people are said to show amazement, while the believers laud the *potentia* and *magnificentia* of the goddess; they acclaim too her radiant blessing (*tam inlustre deae beneficium*). The *macarismos* in ch. 16 similarly highlights 'the splendid divinity of the all-powerful goddess', although it then, rather unexpectedly, emphasizes the merit of Lucius; v.n. ad loc. The priest himself in ch. 14 is 'deeply moved by the wondrous miracle (*insigni permotus miraculo*)'. All this accords well with the early attitude to miracle in several religions : it expresses divine power, it is a manifest sign of it : cf. 1 Cor. 1. 22 Ἰουδαῖοι σημεῖα αἰτοῦσι and the words of G. van der Leeuw, *Rel. in Essence and Manifestation*, 568 : 'But a real injury to belief in miracles is done as soon as the rarity and the amazing element in miracle outweigh its character as a sign, for then miracle entirely loses its revelatory content, and therewith its very essence.' Clearly the concept approaches the definition in Apuleius of the type of magic that is good and holy. The idea of two types of magic, the higher of which is akin to miracle, has parallels in the New Testament. It is suggested, for instance, that evil spirits *can* be exorcized in the name of Beelzebub, though it is done more effectively in the name of God (Luke 11.14 ff.); the lower type of magic is represented by Simon Magus (Acts 8.9-24),

---

[1] Cf. L. A. Mackay, 'The Sin of the Golden Ass', *Arion* 4 (1965), 477.

[2] *Eranos-Jahrbücher* 35 (1966), 164. He also notes that Isis is a goddess of marriage, so that the erotic affair with Photis is condemned. One can press the contrast still further, for Seth-Typhon is often connected with lustful excess.

and he figures conspicuously in the early debates between Christians and their opponents, where a line often followed is 'Your magic is my miracle and vice versa.' [1] The common ground is adumbrated by Augustine (*Ep.* 138) : 'The enemies of Christianity dare to set Apuleius and Apollonius of Tyana on the same level as Christ, or even higher.' [2] Here the allusion is to the reputation which Apuleius personally established as a thaumaturge.

The spiritual aspect of the metamorphosis should not be neglected. Lucius has lived the life of an ass in more senses than one. In his human nakedness he is given a cloak by the priest; it plainly betokens a new life, for the priests says (ch. 15), 'Show, then a happier face in keeping with the white cloak you have assumed.' At the end of the *macarismos* in ch. 16 the people point his blessedness by saying that he has deserved 'such a wondrous favour from heaven that he is, as it were, born again, and has at once pledged himself to service in the sacred rites.' His spiritual regeneration is the greatest miracle, and the sequel elaborates this felicitously. [3]

VII. THE NEW LIFE

The description of the initiations, and especially of the initiate's inner reactions, constitutes a religious classic. Nock, *Conversion*, 138, calls it 'the high-water mark of the piety which grew out of the mystery religions'.

Apuleius twice uses the term *renatus*—in chs. 16 (278, 9) and 21 (283, 9). The term has both physical and spiritual reference. It denotes an end and a new beginning, and the concern with a spiritual sense is borne out by the emphasis on death in the First Initiation : see notes on chs. 21 and 23. The rebirth is mentioned too in the 'birthday of the initiation' (ch. 24, p. 286, 5 f., *natalem sacrorum*). Whereas the idea of being born again is found also in the cults of Demeter at Eleusis, of Cybele and of Mithras, as

---

[1] Cf. R. M. Grant, ed. *Gnosticism* (London, 1961), 21-30; E. R. Dodds, *Pagan and Christian in an Age of Anxiety* (Cambridge, 1965), 124-6. Wittmann, pp. 69-77, writes ably on 'Das Wunder', but tends to overlook the relation to magic.

[2] Cf. G. W. Bowersock in *Philostratus, Life of Apollonius* (Harmondsworth, 1970), 13 f.

[3] Cf. Merkelbach, op. cit. 164 ff.

well as in Christianity and the Corpus Hermeticum, it is the ritual nexus of
death and rebirth as presented by Apuleius that is the most distinctive
element; and the precise parallel provided by Paul's exposition of Christ-
tian baptism in Romans 6.1-11 is very striking, particularly as the interpretation of baptism as a dying and rising with Christ is absent from the
rest of the New Testament, as G. R. Beasley-Murray rightly stresses
in *Christian Baptism*, ed. A. Gilmore (London, 1959), 131, although he
argues at the same time that Paul's source is at hand in his own citation
of the primitive *kerygma* in 1 Cor. 15.3 f.   : 'Christ died, was buried,
has been raised.' This is scarcely convincing since it gives no reason why
the *kerygma* should be embodied in the ritual in a manner not reflected
by other N.T. writers. It is true that Apuleius does not confine the two
ideas to the rite of baptism; they infiltrate rather the whole First Initiation. Wagner, *Problem*, 299 ff., presents a similar solution to that of
Beasley-Murray; he conducts an admirably thorough analysis, but scarcely
bridges the gap between the *kerygma* and the rite. Günther Bornkamm
(tr. Stalker), *Paul* (London, 1971), 190, carries more conviction when he
says 'that this idea arose in the Hellenistic churches under the influence
of pagan mystery cults in which initiates were given a share in the fortunes of their deity and, by means of a ritual dying and rising along with
him, attained salvation, deliverance from their own appointed death.' [1]
Bornkamm is careful to add how he sees Paul's thought to be contributing
something distinctive to the borrowed formulation : resurrection to him
means here the new life in Christ. To this, however, there is a parallel
in the Isiac's attitude to Osiris. In Christianity the identity was undoubtedly more personal, and it was concerned, unlike Isiacism, with
a historical person. If there is a similar formulation, the spiritual
content differs. The Isiac believer identified his death and rebirth with
those of Osiris. That the concept was applied to spiritual regeneration
in the present life is not clearly attested in the ancient tradition; perhaps
it was a development in the Graeco-Roman phase.

On three occasions Lucius is portrayed in a state of hesitancy and doubt

---

[1] In contrast A. D. Nock is remarkably non-committal. See his 'Hellenistic Mysteries and Christian Sacraments' (1952), repr. in *Early Gentile Christianity and its
Hellenistic Background* (New York, 1964), 109 ff. He discusses the material with varying
degrees of elaboration, but reaches no tangible conclusion.

before proceeding with his commitment. In the first instance the rigorous demands of the involvement hold him back. Festugière is able to cite some parallels to this attitude in reports concerning the miracles of Asclepius. Yet there is every mark of psychological truth in what Apuleius conveys; see n. *ad* ch. 19 (281, 6), *religiosa formidine retardabar*. An idea that stands out in the account is that of election and predestination. Isis has chosen Lucius beforehand to be the recipient of her special favour and grace; see n. *ad* ch. 19 (281, 5), *censebat initiari*, where a previous phrase refers to Lucius as *iam dudum destinatum*.

The devotional aspects of the initiate's progress clearly include confession : see n. *ad* ch. 19 (280, 17 f.). In ch. 23 the priest pronounces the forgiveness of the gods, *praefatus deum veniam* (284, 21) : see n. *ad loc.* and also *ad* ch. 21 (283, 11), *dignatione*. In ch. 25 *fin.* Lucius asks for the priest's forgiveness : *veniam postulabam*. The priest is indeed referred to as a spiritual father, *meum iam parentem*, ch. 25 (287, 12); cf. ch. 21 (282, 15), *ut solent parentes* and n. The idea has parallels in Mithraism and Christianity, and it stems from the concept of rebirth. Another idea shared with these religions is the equation of the religious vow and the military oath : the priest urges Lucius in ch. 15, 'Enrol your name in this holy military service, whose solemn oath you were asked to take not long ago, and vow yourself from this moment to the ministry of our religion. Accept of your own free will the yoke of service.' A concept common to many religions is the sublimation of erotic love. Here it belongs conspicuously to the general theme, for the sexual excesses of Lucius are eventually abandoned in his adoration of the goddess. Apuleius is doubtless applying the Platonic interpretation of Eros to the process, as he does too in 'Cupid and Psyche'; cf. R. Thibau, 'Les Métamorphoses d'Apulée et la Théorie Platonicienne de l'Erôs', *Studia Philosophica Gandensia* 3 (Gent, 1965), 89-144, who refers especially (pp. 132 ff.) to Plato's views in the *Symposium* and *Phaedrus*; the erotic sentiment, according to these, can prefigure the aspiration of the soul to be united with the divine. For this a guide or initiation, according to Plato, is necessary. Thibau argues too (p. 137) that Apuleius is closer to Plutarch on this matter than to the Peripatetics and Stoics in that he defends conjugal love; he also expresses horror at the homosexuality of the priests of Cybele. But the consummation of Eros, for him, is in the *unio mystica* of the believer with Isis. Such is clearly implied in the accounts of adoration.

Yet it is the identity of the believer with Osiris that secures his salvation. The dichotomy results from the changing roles of the two deities; Isis has now become dominant in the cult, but the earlier importance of Osiris has not been entirely lost. The soul thus achieves, in the Platonic sense, its ascent, freedom and return home, as Merkelbach [1] puts it : 'Wie sündige Liebe ihren Fall (i.e. der Seele) herbeiführte, so wird die wahre Liebe ihr zum Aufstieg verhelfen; wenn der Isismyste die wahre Liebe, die Liebe zur Göttin, erfasst hat, hat seine Seele begonnen, sich vom Liebe zu befreien und—mit Hilfe der Göttin—in ihre Heimat zurückzukehren.' Henry Ebel [2] feels that 'Apuleius envisions a spirituality suffused with the tangibility of *Voluptas*'; and he rightly notes (p. 174) that there is an anticipation in 'Cupid and Psyche'.[3]

The descriptions of the initiate's adoration in chs. 17, 19, 20, 22, 23, 24 and 25 are full of tender affection. The goddess's 'radiant commands in the dark night' are mentioned (ch. 22); and a revealing sentence is 'I enjoyed the ineffable pleasure of the image of the goddess' (*inexplicabili voluptate simulacri divini perfruebar*). Even before the First Initiation Lucius become a *cultor inseparabilis* (ch. 19, p. 281, 3); in Rome, prior to the Second and Third Initiations, he is a *cultor ... adsiduus* at the Iseum Campense (ch. 26, p. 287, 24). A touching prayer of praise to Isis (ch. 25) states that she brings 'the sweet love of a mother to the trials of the unfortunate.' At the same time the account of her epiphany and image in chs. 3-4 is lusciously sensuous.

C. S. Lewis has epitomised his experience of conversion in the title *Surprised by Joy* (a quotation from Wordsworth). Joy (*gaudium*) is an attractive note in the experience of Lucius : see n. *ad* ch. 30 (291, 15), *gaudens*. In this last instance the emotion is slightly tinged with a feeling of self-interest after the Osirian boons which are both spiritual and material. In the attitude to Isis, however, it is absolutely disinterested love and gratitude, a joyful adoration that has no parallel in the ancient world outside Christianity; see the fine analysis by Festugière, 'Lucius and Isis', 80 f.

---

[1] *Eranos-Jahrbücher* 35 (1966), 167.

[2] 'Apuleius and the Present Time', *Arethusa* 3 (1970), 155-176, this on p. 172.

[3] Antonie Wlosok, *Phil.* 113 (1969), 69, is hardly justified, then, in claiming, 'Nichts scheint die religiöse Lösung vorzubereiten.'

L. A. MacKay [1] is right to remind us that 'Apuleius appears to have ended his life not in pious and abstemious retirement at a convent of Isis in Rome, but in full enjoyment of the world at Carthage.' He infers from this that the *Metamorphoses* is not a spiritual autobiography, but an 'extended myth, with a rambling but real unity'. We have discussed above the extent of the autobiographical element. There can be no mistaking the stamp of truth in the religious exposition of Book XI. 'He must himself have known that spiritual condition.' [2] This is borne out by the ritual and theological detail. The ordinances of ten-day abstinence are referred to in relation to all three initiations in chs. 21, 23, 28, and 30. The shaven heads of devotees and priests are mentioned in chs. 10, 28 and 30, and sacral dresses are carefully described in chs. 23 and 24. Lucius himself joins the *pastophori* and their role is described in chs. 17, 27 and 30. The importance of the hieroglyphic sacred writings is noted in ch. 22, and the rite of the *apertio templi* is portrayed in chs. 20 and 22. In ch. 23 two rites of purification are described; the second is the baptism which inaugurates initiation. After the First Initiation comes the sacred banquet (ch. 24).

Impressive as these ritual details are, the theological content of the experience achieves a still greater impact. The address of the priest to Lucius in ch. 15 and the prayer to Isis in ch. 25 present the basic ideas. Lucius, after being buffetted by the storms of Fortune, has reached a haven of rest. Lust and curiosity had caused his downfall, but Isis now gives him victory over Fortune; unlike Fortune, Isis is not blind : she sees and protects, and Lucius now owes her his vow of service. This exacting service will nevertheless give him true freedom.

VIII. LINGUISTIC FEATURES

E. Löfstedt, *Late Latin* (Oslo, 1959), 1, has described the style of Apuleius as 'borrowing freely from poetry, deliberately archaizing, strongly influenced by Greek, and, in the *Metamorphoses*, by the realistic narrative style of the prose romances, from which it draws certain popular elements of its language.' The presence of popular speech in a more precise sense

---

[1] *Arion* 4 (1965), 479.
[2] Festugière, 'Lucius and Isis', 84.

has been variously assessed. Piechotta, *Curae Apuleianae* (Vratislava, 1882), 52, was already of the opinion that many words alleged to be archaistic or obsolete were derived from popular usage, a view which is broadly approved by Bernhard, *Stil*, 130. Bernhard justly points to the difficulty of deciding, in particular cases, whether a word has been imitated from Plautus or Terence, or whether it has continued to live in the popular speech and has been employed for this reason. If a word occurs in a number of late authors who were fond of vulgarisms, then this is useful evidence; again, the occurrence of certain endings favoured in popular speech is some indication. This leads Bernhard to an assembly of instances of archaisms and vulgarisms in which the latter group is considerably larger (his pp. 131-4); the frequency of substantives in *-ela* of adjectives in *-arius, -osus*, and *-ilis*, and of adverbs in *-im*, is adduced in support of this emphasis.

More recently Louis Callebat in his *Sermo Cotidianus dans les Métamorphoses d'Apulée* (Caen, 1968) has devoted more searching attention to the popular element. He considers contexts in detail with reference to narration or description or direct speech and also to general tone (whether precious, elaborated, serious or comic); he also adduces the evidence of earlier, later and contemporary writers (especially Fronto and Aulus Gellius) as well as that of the other works of Apuleius. He finds a good instance of the importance of context in *Ubi ducis asinum istum?* (9.39, p. 233, 9) where *ubi* for *quo* has sometimes been cited as a sign of the author's negligence or ignorance; it is a solitary instance and occurs in direct speech, so that it probably reflects popular idiom deliberately. [1] Callebat also pays more attention to syntax than has hitherto been done in this connection. He concedes that spoken, living Latin cannot be regarded as a homogeneous entity; it has variations relating to place and time and social circles. At the same time he avoids like the plague any discussion of the 'myth' of *Africitas* (p. 19); while he may justly feel thus about the theory of Semitic influence in a big way, it is obviously inconsistent of him to ignore the possibility of local variations of living Latin in the province of Africa. An example is the predilection

---

[1] Callebat would qualify the notion that all the characters in Apuleius use the same style of speaking; see his p. 549. In general, however, the notion is valid. Cf. Bernhard, *Stil*, 255 ff. Petronius differs markedly in this matter.

for *iste*; cf. n. *ad* ch. 5 (270, 5), *istis meis*. Doubtless the distinction between *sermo familiaris* and *sermo plebeius* (p. 18), applying to the speech of cultivated persons and of the people generally, is a useful one. In general Callebat is often compelled to hesitate between the options of literary and colloquial influence. His final formulation (pp. 547-52) is fairly reserved; he speaks of the 'sublimation' of *sermo cotidianus* and of a strong artistic control of this element. [1]

The content of Book XI is far removed from that of the other books. It consists mainly of narrative in a tense and exalted tone. There is occasionally description of nature as in ch. 6, where the coming of spring is lyrically conveyed to match the buoyancy in the heart of Lucius. There is but little dialogue, and what there is concerns matters of religion. Thus the priest's address to Lucius in ch. 15, although partly a personal and devotional act of guidance, is in some ways a sermon; in its second part it is directed for a time to the people in order to serve a missionary purpose. In spite of its high seriousness, Bernhard, *Stil*, 256 f., is able to compare this with the robber's speech in 4.13 and point to the essential stylistic similarity. It is Apuleius, in these and other speeches, that is really speaking. Shorter counsels addressed by the priest to Lucius appear in chs. 21 (in indirect speech), 22 and 28. Elements emanating from specific religious forms appear in the following sections :

    I. Prayers.
        1. To the moon-goddess (ch. 2).
        2. For emperor, senate, knights and people (in summary, ch. 17).
        3. To Isis, expressing praise and gratitude (ch. 25).
    II. The 'Little Aretalogy' in 'I-Style'.
        The self-proclamation of Isis (chs. 5-6).
    III. The *Macarismos*.
        The beatitude of the transformed Lucius is proclaimed (ch. 16).
    IV. The *Synthema*.
        The essence of the Mystery is conveyed in formulaic utterances (ch. 23).

There are also descriptions of divine epiphanies (Isis appears in chs. 3-4 and 26) and of visions by night (chs. 20, 27 and 30), but these owe less to traditional forms. Apuleius accepts the inherited structure in the

---

[1] A. Ernout, *Rev. Phil.* 45 (1971), 178 is unduly harsh on this work. For a more objective view see P. G. Walsh, *CR* 22 (1972), 128.

other cases noted, but aims at greater beauty of expression. Without inter-
fering with the hieratic simplicity of the form, he adds a distinctive lustre.
The content is often ancient, and the 'Little Aretalogy' (chs. 5-6) preserves also the proclamatory First Person of many Egyptian texts; there
are traces too of the cataloguish concatenation of epithets and of the
parallelismus membrorum which mark the early literature. For the most
part, however, the style is furbished with the fashionable floridity of
the 'Asianic' school; it uses triadic and tetradic structures, and consciously
handles rhyme, assonance and rhythm. Cf. Wittmann, 142 f. The prayers
follow a pattern which is traditional in Greek and Latin; see Bernhard,
Stil, 277-9.

It is not surprising that there is a goodly quota of archaisms :

adambulare 8 (272, 14)

aerumna 2 (267, 16); 15 (277, 19)

baxea 8 (272, 10)

bellule 30 (291, 5)

conradere 28 (289, 16)

domuitio 24 (286, 12)

examussim 27 (288, 21)

fabulari 16 (278, 6)

guttatim 9 (273, 4)

hilaritudo 7 (271, 13)

largitus 30 (291, 2)

oppido 29 (290, 7)

penitus adj. 6 (270, 21)

percontare 19 (281, 6 f.)

post aliquam multum temporis 26
   (287, 16)

reabse 13 (275, 22)

saepicule 28 (289, 14)

summas adj. 10 (274, 6)

totae Dat. 16 (278, 5)

utut 20 (281, 17)

What is more surprising in a book of mainly religious interest is the rich
harvest of neologisms. In the following list the words which occur in
Apuleius only are marked with an asterisk :

*adfamen 7 (271, 19); 30 (291, 8)

adluctor 12 (275, 17)

adorabilis 18 (280, 8)

*altiuscule 11 (275, 8)

*amicimen 9 (272, 19)

*antecantamentum 9 (273, 11)

*anteludium 8 (272, 3)

barbitium 8 (272, 10)

*capreolatim 22 (284, 15)

cataclista 9 (273, 8)

cheniscus 16 (279, 1)

*circumrorans 23 (284, 21)

circumsecus 16 (278, 14)

commeator 11 (274, 15)

*coronamen 9 (272, 20)

*crepides 8 (272, 5)

disseminatio 30 (291, 10)

effigiatus 11 (275, 7)

*elocutilis 3 (268, 4)

exercitius adv. 29 (290, 8)

floride adv. 24 (285, 22)

impaenitendus 28 (289, 19)

incapistrare 20 (282, 4)

incunctanter 6 (270, 11)

inextricabiliter 25 (286, 22)

*inovans 15 (277, 18)

inremunerabilis 24 (286, 10)
invinius 23 (285, 1)
luminare 25 (286, 24)
minuties 13 (276, 9)
munerabundus 18 (280, 12 f.)
nubilosus 7 (272, 1)
obauratus 8 (272, 6)
obpexus 9 (273, 3)
obsibilare 7 (271, 22)
orificium 11 (275, 7)
pator 10 (274, 4)
perfluus 8 (272, 7)
pervigilis 26 (288, 2)

praemicare 10 (274, 2)
repertus subst. 2 (267, 5); 11 (275,3)
semirutundus subst. 6 (271, 2)
silentiosus (266, 13)
sospitatrix 9 (272, 18) ; 15 (277, 18)
spondeum 20 (282, 1)
spontalis 30 (291, 1)
supplicue 24 (286, 12)
teleta 22 (284, 17); 24 (286, 8) ; 26 (288, 3); (290, 6)
turbula 6 (270, 11); 7 (271, 13)
viriculae 28 (289, 10)
volentia 6 (270, 12)

It seems likely that the traditional nature of some of the content has not inhibited his urge to indulge in new coinages. One has the impression that they figure as much in Book XI as elsewhere. A fondness for abstractions, composite verbs, diminutives, and Graecisms plays a part in the urge. How far can we assign them to a deliberate psychological attitude? Norden, *Die antike Kunstprosa*, II, 602, speaks of his assuming the right to the freest word-coinage 'with tyrannical self-satisfaction' ('mit tyrannischer Selbstgefälligkeit'), and he refers to *amicimen* and *coronamen* in ch. 9 as 'Kindereien'. This may well be the impression one gets, but Bernhard, *Stil*, 141, produces a necessary *caveat* : we cannot be certain how far the new coinages (as they appear to us) were consciously felt to be so by Apuleius himself and by his contemporaries. Some of these words very probably belonged to popular speech. But the very abundance of apparent neologisms speaks for itself, as Bernhard concedes. A desire for exuberance can be felt when Apuleius refuses to use the old *sospes* and *sospita*, producing instead *sospitator* and *sospitatrix*. A fondness for abstractions could derive from either Greek or Semitic sources. The process seems often quite natural. Since Latin before this had no abstract noun from *velle*, the coinage *volentia* came easily. Sometimes the variant from is hard to explain. Why, for instance, is *barbitium* used for *barba*? A desire for novelty may be invoked, but it should not be forgotten that the writer of an acquired language is not so sensitive to the orthodoxy of established forms.

The lush inventiveness shown by Apuleius may be assigned in part to the attitude of a writer to whom Latin was not a mother tongue. His first language was undoubtedly Punic. He was a native of Madauros, [1] today Mdaurusch in Algeria. In *Apol.* 24 he describes the town as a flourishing Roman colony (*splendidissima colonia*) which had been a town of some import before that; cf. Butler and Owen, *Apol.* vii and Vallette, *Apol.* vii. P. Romanelli, *Storia delle province romane dell' Africa* (Rome, 1959), 294, thinks it may have become a *colonia* in the time of Titus or Domitian. It became highly Romanized, but Apuleius describes himself with a flourish as *Seminumidam et Semigaetulum*, adding aggressively, *non video quid mihi sit in ea re pudendum*; [2] cf. too *Apol.* 41 (he is in the mountains of Gaetulia). Was not Cyrus the Great a half-Mede and half-Persian? His previous allusion to his *patria* being on the borders of Numidia and Gaetulia is a little exaggerated, as Paul Monceaux shows in his *Les Africains* (Paris, 1894), 266 : the desert land of Gaetulia began a good deal to the south. Yet the Musulamii of Gaetulia came close to Madauros : v. St. Gsell, *Mdaourouch*, 5. T. R. S. Broughton, *The Romanization of Africa Proconsularis* (Oxford, 1929), 104 f., suggests that the *colonia* in Madauros had a strategic purpose, perhaps 'to check a strongly indigenous area'; to the north were Thagaste and Calama, towns which had a Punic colouring, although the region in general was more strongly native Libyan. This is borne out by the common Libyan inscriptions, although Punic ones are also found; cf. Anna M. Bisi, *Le Stele Puniche* (Rome, 1967), 117 ff. That the name Madauros is Phoenician was maintained by F. C. Movers, *Die Phoenizier*, II, 2 (Berlin, 1850), 440 n. 79 c : he invokes מרר, 'Wohnung', as the root of both 'Madaura' and 'Amedara'. This is rejected by St. Gsell, *Mdaourouch*, 8, with no discussion and no alternative proposal. There is certainly a difficulty with the second consonant. H. Dessau, *PW* s.v. Madauros (1928), 201, cites a Dalmatian god, Medaurus, known in two African inscriptions. The matter must remain in doubt. One might compare Madeira, which may well have been discovered by the Phoenicians; cf. D. Harden, *The Phoenicians* (London, 1962), 178; but Madeira doubtless

---

[1] St. Gsell points out in *Khamissa, Mdaourouch, Announa*, II (= *Mdaourouch*, Alger, 1922), 8 n. 3, that the form Madaura is not attested in ancient documents; cf. Dessau, *PW* s.v. Maudauros (1928), 201.

[2] E. S. Bouchier, *Life and Letters in Roman Africa* (Oxford, 1913), 11 n. 1, cites other evidence for the pride of Africans in their native tribal connections.

derives from the Spanish *madre* used of the Madonna (cf. Madera in Mexico).

The dictum of St. Gsell (p. 13), 'Madaure a été un centre vraiment romain' is quite superficial. Certainly its archaeological remains attest a Romanized town life in its externals. The numerous Latin inscriptions, however, might be comparable to those of Roman Britain, where there are no inscriptions in Celtic although we know that in actual speech the Celtic languages were dominant. St. Gsell wisely qualifies this on pp. 23 ff., pointing out that Punic names occur among the early Christian martyrs of Madauros. The vitality of the Punic language in parts of the province is well summed up by Bouchier, op. cit. 8 f.

> In neighbouring towns (to Carthage) Punic remained the common speech of the lower orders, and in a few, such as Leptis and Oea, was used officially till about A.D. 100, if less generally than Greek in the eastern provinces. There was a distinct branch of Punic eloquence, and old Carthaginian literature was studied. Even in the fourth century, when Greek and Syriac had ousted Punic from its home in Asia, we read of a Punic-speaking bishop being needed for Fussala, and, in a sermon to his own flock at Hippo, Augustine says, 'Latine vobis dicam, quia Punice non omnes nostis.' [1]

The relevance of this is that Apuleius was himself a speaker of Punic. The term *Afer* used of him by Augustine (*De civ. Dei*, 8.12) is of course an umbrella term; the consciousness of African nationality united the Libyan, Punic, Moorish, and Roman elements. But the phrase used by Septimius Severus in *Vita Clod. Alb.* 12.12 is more precise : *inter Milesias Punicas Apulei sui*. It shows that Apuleius had come to be regarded as the outstanding writer of a Punic region; cf. A. Mazzarino, *La Milesia e Apuleio*, 36. Further, *Apol.* 98 indicates decisively that Apuleius spoke Punic. There he is referring rather contemptuously to his step-son Pudens : under the influence of Aemilianus and Rufinus the young man is becoming a complete waster. His education is being utterly neglected, and the final evidence is that he never speaks anything but Punic even if he still has some Greek through his mother's influence. Now his mother

---

[1] Cf. K. Sittl, *Die lokalen Verschiedenheiten der lateinischen Sprache usw.* (Erlangen, 1882), 92; Alex. Graham, *Roman Africa* (London, 1902), 132; St. Gsell, *Histoire ancienne de l'Afrique du Nord*, IV (Paris, 1920), 496; Donald Harden, *The Phoenicians* 178; S. Moscati, *The World of the Phoenicians* (London, 1965), 185 f.

was Pudentilla, whom Apuleius has just married. She clearly spoke some Greek, and her letters to Pontianus were in Greek. Butler and Owen duly note this, but show no interest in the more obvious fact that Pudentilla's first language was Punic, as was her son's.[1] A compelling corollary is that Apuleius too had Punic for mother-tongue, and that his linguistic development was exactly that which Pudens had been expected to follow —an acquisition, after Punic, of Greek and then of Latin. Paul Monceaux, *Les Africains*, 267, states of Apuleius, 'Comme tous ses camarades, il savait surtout la langue du pays, un patois libyque, mêlé de punique,' but he gives no evidence for connecting Apuleius with a Libyan-Punic *farrago*. Perhaps the phrase about his being half-Numidian and half-Gaetulian might suggest it. T. Sinko, *Eos* 18 (1912), 143, thinks that Apuleius spoke Latin from his boyhood and learnt Greek at Carthage; he ignores the third language which really came first.

The further interesting revelation in *Apol.* 98 is the very low, almost derisory, position occupied by Punic in the scheme. This is borne out by the other allusions made by Apuleius to his linguistic accomplishments. In *Apol.* 4 (*init.*) he quotes with relish the point made by his accusers that he is most eloquent in both Greek and Latin. In *Flor.* 9 (13, 17 ff.) he preens himself on his literary versatility, stressing the phrase *tam graece quam latine*. J. Beaujeu, "Apulée helléniste', *Rev. Ét. Lat.* 46 (1968), 11, says, 'Apulée ... était bilingue' with a reference to this passage, but the emphasis is on literary composition rather than knowledge of languages. Esteem attaches, it is true, only to Greek and Latin; cf. *Flor.* 18 (35, 16 f.), *vox mea utraque lingua iam vestris auribus... probe cognita.* Augustine's mother tongue was Punic,[2] but in a reference to Apuleius in *De civ. Dei*, 8.12, he stresses the same dual mastery without mentioning Punic : *in utraque autem lingua, id est Graeca et Latina, Apuleius Afer extitit Platonicus nobilis.* Culturally Apuleius gave precedence to Greek; cf. Schwabe *PW* s.v. Appuleius (1896), 253. Evidence of the influence of Greek culture in districts near Madauros is seen in W. Peek, *Versinschriften aus der Cyrenaica, aus Mauretanien und Numi-*

---

[1] It was so too with the sister of Septimius Severus, a lady of Leptis : the emperor blushed because she spoke almost no Latin; v. Spartian. *Sever.* 15 and cf. Monceaux, *Les Africains*, 37.

[2] Augustine was a native of Thagaste, a little to the north of Madauros.

dien (Abh. Leipzig; Berlin, 1972), esp. pp. 22 f.; cf. Rohde's claim, *Kleine Schriften*, 60, that Apuleius had learnt Greek in Africa ('wie eine Muttersprache zu eigen gemacht hatte'). The claim of Lucius in *Metam.* 1.1, that he is able to jump from the one linguistic horse to the other, certainly applies to Apuleius, whom Norden[1] described as 'der virtuoseste Wortjongleur, den es gegeben hat'. His provincial audience, moreover, expected the utmost correctness, for he states, speaking probably in Carthage, 'Which of you will pardon even one lapse on my part?' (*quis enim vestrum mihi unum soloecismum ignoverit?*) and 'Who will tolerate even one syllable pronounced with an un-Roman accent?' (*barbare*, probably 'with a Punic accent'). See *Flor.* 9 (10, 21 ff.) and cf. Koziol, *Stil*, 2.

Norden, however, quotes (p. 593) the reference to Punic in the *Apology* only as evidence of its total rejection by Apuleius; and he laughs (p. 589) at the idea of the baby Apuleius stuttering Punic at the breast of a Punic nurse. In the main he was right to insist (with Kroll and others) that Apuleius and other African writers of Latin were adherents of the 'Second Sophistic' and that their style is not distinctively African. The obliteration of Punic influence was accomplished, nevertheless, with too great zeal. If Apuleius's mother-tongue was Punic, [2] and if he yet tended to scorn Punic, [3] that is a by no means unprecedented phenomenon in the psychology of language. Material advancement or intellectual snobbery may bring people to despise their first language. [4] In the last century the Russian nobility are said to have talked Russian to their servants and dogs, but French among themselves. In Wales during the same era Welsh-

---

[1] *Die antike Kunstprosa*, II, 600 (with a misprint of the adjective). He goes on to say that in Apuleius the Roman language, formerly a worthy matron, has become a prostitute.

[2] Cf. R. Hanslik, *Lex. der alten Welt* (1965), 232, 'Apuleius ... beherrschte die punische, lateinische and griech. Sprache.'

[3] St. Gsell, *Mdaourouch*, 30, interprets the scorn as implying ignorance; at least he doubts whether Apuleius knew Libyan and Punic. He then tells us, 'En réalité, cet enfant de Madaure fut semi-Latin, semi-Grec.' It is certain, he says, that he spoke Latin from the first; cf. F. Norwood, *Phoenix* 10 (1956), 3. In fact that is highly unlikely.

[4] Cf. the attitude of some Yiddish speakers who opt for English in a community of Jewish immigrants near Santa Monica, Los Angeles : see J. R. Rayfield, *The Languages of a Bilingual Community* (The Hague, 1970), 37 f.

speaking children, with the full approval of their parents, were allowed to speak nothing but English in their schools, and were punished if they used the mother-tongue. It would be foolish to assume that in either case the native language was without influence. Even in the use of the adopted language it was influential; and there are national trends which can operate even apart from a national language. Few would deny that James Joyce, J. M. Synge and W. B. Yeats share certain well-flavoured characteristics in their use of English, although it is not the Irish language that explains the difference. The African writers Florus, Apuleius, Minucius Felix, and Tertullian may not have imported Semitisms *en masse* into their Latin. Yet the zest with which they took to the fashionably florid style of 'Asianic' oratory argues an African predisposition.[1]

In the case of Apuleius we have noted already the psychological factor that an acquired language, when used by a virtuoso, tends to be more richly treated. In more precise matters Semitic influence was present in the attitude, on occasion, to abstract nouns and to parataxis. It is true that Greek influence may sometimes colour the former; but in ch. 19 (281, 7), *castimoniorum abstinentiam* and ch. 28 (290, 3 f.), *patrocinia sermonis Romani*, there seem to be instances of the Semitic *Genitivus Inhaerentiae*. See notes *ad loc.*

The origins of his love of parataxis are not easy to demonstrate. M. Leky, *De Syntaxi Apuleiana* (Diss. Born. 1908), 41-4, argues that Apuleius is following Early Latin, and this, of course, would agree with his Plautine predilections in other ways. Greek influence was adduced by J. von Geisau : see Bernhard, *Stil*, 48. Parataxis is common, also, however, in Petronius, and the source here is popular speech. The style of letters is naturally closer to that of colloquial forms, so that parataxis is more frequent in the Letters of Cicero than elsewhere in his works : cf. Hofmann and Szantyr, *Lat. Syntax*, 527. Popular speech is the influence stressed by Bernhard, *Stil*, 48 ff. He points out that co-ordination of clauses is a feature of such speech in all languages. If Punic was the first language of Apuleius, we cannot doubt that the urge to parataxis derived initially from this source, especially as in this case, as in the other Semitic languages, it characterizes the written language too. Yet it is clear that Apuleius, as Bernhard shows, does not follow the snappy style of popular

---

[1] Cf. L. C. Purser, *Cupid and Psyche*, lxxxiv.

speech, whether Punic or Latin or Greek, in this connection : cf. E. Paratore, 'La prosa di Apuleio', *Maia* 1 (1948), 42. His sentences are often
long, in spite of the frequent co-ordination. Sometimes the particular
mode derives from a distinctive tradition relating to one form. Thus in
ch. 23 (*accessi confinium mortis etc.*) the shorter clauses echo the traditional *synthemata*. The prayer in ch. 2, on the other hand, has more hypo-
taxis, especially in relative clauses, and this too derives from a type
attested in Greek and Latin literature. An oriental origin is shiningly
clear in the magnificent titles of Osiris in ch. 30 (291, 7 ff.), which begin
deus deum magnorum potior. Bernhard, *Stil.*, 173 f., rejects any non-
classical influence here, though he does not include this remarkable
expression in his list of similar constructions. Kroll, *Rhein. Mus.* 52
(1897), 585, points to *nummorum nummos* in Petronius, 37, as being clearly
outside the Semitic sphere of influence; but the construction and concept
of *rex regum* was conspicuous in Mesopotamian, Egyptian and Hebrew
sources, and it is perverse to deny its non-classical origin. In some
possible instances of Punic influence it must be confessed that the
position remains doubtful : see notes *ad* ch. 6 (270, 20 f.), *memineris*;
ch. 6 (271, 1), *demearis* : ch. 15 (277, 18), *inovanti gradu.*

For the most part Apuleius is sedulously following classical models
and fashions, and Bernhard's admirable study probes his usages fully.
Attention may be called to instances in this book of the use of alliteration
in a triple sequence (cf. Bernhard, 221) :

 ch. 13 (276, 4), *deformis et ferina facies*
 ch. 13 (276, 5 f.), *pedum plantae per ungulas*
 ch. 13 (276, 8), *repetunt pristinam parvitatem*
 ch. 14 (276, 15 f.), *potissimum praefarer primarium*
 ch. 21 (283, 12), *cultores ceteri cibis*

In ch. 16 (278, 5 f.) we find something different, a sequence of three
consonants repeated : *nutibusque notabilis.* For a linked assonance,
see p. 171.

This book reveals better than any other the strongly poetical colouring
of the prose of Apuleius. He belonged to an age when poetry used prose
as its vehicle, and the Semitic languages made little formal distinction
between them. The new poetry was a poetry in prose. [1]

For other stylistic features see the Index and notes.

---

[1] Cf. Bowersock, *Greek Sophists in the Roman Empire* (Oxford, 1969), 116 f.

IX. THE TEXT

The excellent work done by previous scholars, notably by R. Helm, D. S. Robertson, and C. Giarratano, might be regarded as a reason for dispensing with any form of new recension. Difficulties, of course, remain, and previous editions are somewhat compendious in the type of *apparatus criticus* adopted. What has been aimed at here is a selective collation of eleven of the codices and of the *Editio Princeps*. The presence of this collation will be apparent by the more detailed references to the separate codices. Elsewhere the evidence of the editions named has been drawn upon.

No editor who tackles the time-consuming job of collating manuscripts will feel himself rewarded unless he is enabled occasionally to supplement or correct the record hitherto presented. There is a good instance in ch. 13 (276, 9 f.), *causa nusquam comparuit*, where the previous record is quite wrong in stating that *comparuit* occurs only in a much later hand in F. It occurs in fact in several other codices and also in the *Editio Princeps*.

Such an instance might prompt one to challenge the reigning dogma that F is the *fons et origo* of all other known codices. Mazzarino produced a theory that a 'gemello di F' was the archetype of the best codices : see his *La Milesia e Apuleio*, 18 ff, and also the sceptical reactions of Merkelbach in *Maia* 5 (1952), 234-41, esp. 236 ff. Clearly the question cannot be adequately examined on the basis of the text of Book XI alone, especially as the Manuscript C, discovered in 1942 (or earlier) by G. Muzzioli in the Biblioteca Comunale of Assisi, contains only fragments of the *Apology* : see D. S. Robertson, *CQ* n.s. 6 (1956), 68-80; also Carl C. Schlam, *Classical World* 64 (1971), 288 f. In *Aevum* 26 (1952), 369 Giovanni Cremaschi reports briefly on his discovery and examination of a manuscript of the *Metam.* in the Biblioteca Comunale of Bergamo. He assigns it to a family of contaminated manuscripts of the fourteenth or fifteenth century and deems it to be derived from F and ϕ.

APULEI METAMORPHOSEON
LIBER XI

SIGLA

EDITIONES ET ANIMADVERSIONES

Barth(ius), C.
Bernhard, M.
Beroald(us), P.
Bluemner, H.
Brakman, C.
Brant(ius), J.
Bursian, C.
Cast(iglioni), L.
Chodaczek, L.
Colv(ius), P.
Cornelissen, J. J.
Cuper(us) [Cuypers], G.
D'Orléans, L.
Dousa, J.
Elmenh(orst), G.
Eyssenh(ardt), F.
Giarr(atano), C.
Goldbacher, A.
Gr(iffiths), J. G.
Haupt. M.

Helm, R.
Hild(ebrand), G. F.
Hopfner, Th.
Kaibel, G.
Kiessling, A.
Koziol, H.
Kroll, W.
Kronenb(erg), A.
Leo, F.
Lipsius, J.
Loefstedt, E.
Luetj(ohann), C.
Médan, P.
Mommsen, Th.
Norden, E.
Oud(endorp), F.
Passerat, J.
Petsch(enig), M.
Philomathes, B.
Pontanus, J. J.

Pric(aeus), J.
Reinesius, T.
Rob(ertson), D. S.
Rohde, E.
Salm(asius), C.
Scaliger, J. J.
Schickerad(us), M.
Scriver(ius), P.
Stewech, G.
Sudhaus, S.
Thomas, P.
Vallette, P.
v(an) d(er) Vl(iet), J.
Vulcan(ius), B.
Walter, F.
Wolterstorff, G.
Wasse, J.
Wiman, G.
Wower, J.

LIBER XI

266   **1** Circa primam ferme noctis vigiliam experrectus pavore subito, video praemicantis lunae candore nimio completum orbem commodum marinis emergentem fluctibus; nanctusque opacae noctis silentiosa secreta, certus etiam summatem deam praecipua maiestate pollere
15 resque prorsus humanas ipsius regi providentia, nec tantum pecuina et ferina, verum inanima etiam divino eius luminis numinisque nutu vegetari, ipsa etiam corpora terra caelo marique nunc incrementis consequenter augeri, nunc detrimentis obsequenter imminui, fato scilicet iam meis tot tantisque cladibus satiato et spem salutis, licet tardam,
20 subministrante augustum specimen deae praesentis statui deprecari; confestimque discussa pigra quiete laetus et alacer exurgo meque protinus purificandi studio marino lavacro trado septiesque summerso fluctibus
267 capite, quod eum numerum praecipue religionibus aptissimum divinus ille Pythagoras prodidit, deam praepotentem lacrimoso vultu sic adprecabar :

  2 'Regina caeli — sive tu Ceres alma frugum parens originalis, quae,
5 repertu laetata filiae, vetustae glandis ferino remoto pabulo, miti commonstrato cibo nunc Eleusiniam glebam percolis, seu tu caelestis Venus, quae primis rerum exordiis sexuum diversitatem generato Amore sociasti et aeterna subole humano genere propagato nunc circumfluo Paphi sacrario coleris, seu Phoebi soror, quae partu fetarum medelis
10 lenientibus recreato populos tantos educasti praeclarisque nunc veneraris delubris Ephesi, seu nocturnis ululatibus horrenda Proserpina triformi facie larvales impetus comprimens terraeque claustra cohibens lucos diversos inerrans vario cultu propitiaris, — ista luce feminea conlustrans cuncta moenia et sudis ignibus nutriens laeta semina et solis
15 ambagibus dispensans incerta lumina, quoquo nomine, quoquo ritu,

---

266   14 summatam F*Φ* *em. v*   18 decrementis F *Φ* B3 E detrimentis O   21 <laetus et> *Helm*

267   2 laetus et alacer *ante* deam *codd. secl. Leo propter* lacrimoso *trp. Helm def. Chodaczek, Eos 34, 48*   7 generabili *Bursian, Sitzb. Munich 1881, 1, 138, cf. Asc. 14* 14 sudis *Bluemner, Mél. Nicole 38* undis F *Φ* B1 O D nudis (*in mg. al. m. Φ*) E U R udis B3 S uvidis A *cf. Pontanus* umidis *Giarr.*

BOOK XI

1 At about the first watch of night I was awakened by a sudden fright and I saw the full orb of the moon gleaming radiantly with splendid sheen and coming out just then from the waves of the sea; and aware of the mute mysteries of the dark night, I knew that now the eminent goddess was prevailing with especial power and that all human affairs were governed by her providence, while not only cattle and wild beasts, but lifeless beings too were invigorated by the divine favour of her light and majesty; further that the very bodies in earth, sea and sky were at one time blessed with growth by her favour, and at another time afflicted through her with decline. Now that fate, it seemed, had taken its fill of my many great misfortunes and was offering, though late, a hope of deliverance, I decided to address in prayer the sacred image of the goddess now present in person. So shaking off at once my torpid slumber, I gladly and eagerly arose and, anxious to purify myself, I went to bathe in the sea. Seven times I plunged my head under the waves, since the divine Pythagoras pronounced that number to be very specially suitable in sacred rites. Then with a tear-stained face I prayed to the all-powerful goddess thus :

2 'O Queen of Heaven — whether thou art Ceres, the primal and bountiful mother of crops, who, glad in the return of her daughter, removed the brutish acorn provender of old, and showed to men gentler nourishment, after which thou now honourest the soil of Eleusis; or whether thou art heavenly Venus, who didst unite the difference of the sexes in the first beginnings of nature by creating Love, and after bringing forth mankind with its unceasing offspring, art worshipped in the island shrine of Paphos; or the sister of Phoebus, who didst relieve the delivery of young ones by soothing remedies, thus rearing such teeming masses, and art now adored in the celebrated temples of Ephesus; or whether as Proserpine, dreaded in cries that pierce the night, repelling attacks of ghosts with thy threefold countenance, and keeping barred the bolts of the earth, wandering the while in groves here and there, thou art propitiated with differing rites — whoever thou art, illumining all city walls with that womanly light, nourishing with bright fires the joyous

quaqua facie te fas est invocare : tu meis iam nunc extremis aerumnis
subsiste, tu fortunam conlapsam adfirma, tu saevis exanclatis casibus
pausam pacemque tribue; sit satis laborum, sit satis periculorum. depelle
quadripedis diram faciem, redde me conspectui meorum, redde me meo
20 Lucio. ac si quod offensum numen inexorabili me saevitia premit, mori
saltem liceat, si non licet vivere.'

3 Ad istum modum fusis precibus et adstructis miseris lamentationibus
rursus mihi marcentem animum in eodem illo cubili sopor circumfusus
oppressit. necdum satis composieram, et ecce pelago medio venerandos
25 diis etiam vultus attollens emergit divina facies; ac dehinc paulatim toto
268 corpore perlucidum simulacrum excusso pelago ante me constitisse
visum est. eius mirandam speciem ad vos etiam referre conitar, si tamen
mihi disserendi tribuerit facultatem paupertas oris humani vel ipsum
numen eius dapsilem copiam elocutilis facundiae subministraverit.

5 Iam primum crines uberrimi prolixique et sensim intorti per divina
colla passive dispersi molliter defluebant. corona multiformis variis
floribus sublimem destrinxerat verticem, cuius media quidem super
frontem plana rutunditas in modum speculi vel immo argumentum lunae
candidum lumen emicabat, dextra laevaque sulcis insurgentium vipera-
10 rum cohibita, spicis etiam Cerialibus desuper porrectis ornata. tunica
multicolor, bysso tenui pertexta, nunc albo candore lucida, nunc croceo
flore lutea, nunc roseo rubore flammida et, quae longe longeque etiam
meum confutabat optutum, palla nigerrima splendescens atro nitore,
quae circumcirca remeans et sub dexterum latus ad umerum laevum
15 recurrens umbonis vicem deiecta parte laciniae multiplici contabulatione dependula ad ultimas oras nodulis fimbriarum decoriter confluc-
tuabat. **4** per intextam extremitatem et in ipsa eius planitie stellae
dispersae coruscabant earumque media semenstris luna flammeos

16 quaque F, *em. v*   tumeis F *Φ* D   21 <hominem> vivere *vdVl.*   24 composieram *Wiman* conipseram *aut* compseram F compseram *Φ* B2 B3 U O E R
corrupsiam B1 compsedam (?) S coniveram *Wower* coniexeram *Philomathes*   25 dī
isetiam(*sed is eras.*) F, *em. al. m. in Φ*   dehinc (*sed hi ex nu corr. al. m.*) F
268   4 locutilis (*eras. ut vid.* e) F e locutilis (*corr. al. m. in mg. Φ* elocutilis A B1 U E R
elocutulis S eloquutilis R loqutilis B2 D locutilis B3 O   7 distinxerat A *v*   medio
Pric. media—fronte *Wower*   8 augmentum *Pric.*   10 <ornata. sed et vestis>
Cast. <vestis tunica> *vdVl.*   17 intextam F² B2 (*om.* per) E iunctam S intectam *al.*
18 semenstris F *Φ* B3 semestris *al.*   flamineos F, *em. v*

seeds, and bestowing uncertain illumination only during digressions from thy path, by whatever name or ceremony or visage it is right to address thee, help me now in the depth of my trouble, strengthen my crushed fortune, grant respite and peace after the endurance of dire ills; regard this as enough of toil, enough of danger. Remove the cruel four-footed form, restore me to the sight of my loved ones, restore me to my own self as Lucius. And if some deity is angered so as to pursue me with implacable cruelty, at least allow me to die, if I am not allowed really to live'.

3 When I had thus poured out my prayers, adding pitiable wailings, sleep again spread over my wilting spirit and overpowered me on that same sandy bed. I had scarcely settled down when lo! from the middle of the sea a face divine arose, showing above the waves a countenance which even gods must admire; and then gradually the radiant image of the whole body, when the brine had been shaken off, seemed to stand before me. I will try to communicate to you her wonderful appearance if the poverty of human speech affords me the means of description or if the deity herself lends me her rich store of rhetorical eloquence.

First, her abundant, long hair, gently curled over her divine neck or loosely spread, streamed down softly. A crown of many designs with all kinds of flowers had girt her lofty head; in its centre a flat disk above the forehead shone with a clear light in the manner of a mirror or indeed like the moon, while on its right and left it was embraced by coils of uprising snakes; from above it was adorned also with outstretched ears of corn. Her tunic too was of many colours, woven entirely of fine linen, now bright with a white gleam, now yellow with saffron hue, now fiery with roseate ruddiness. But what most of all overwhelmed my sight further was the cloak of deepest black, resplendent with dark sheen; it went round about her, returning under the right side to the left shoulder, a part of the garment being dropped in the manner of a knot; and hanging down with many folds, the whole robe undulated gracefully with tasselled fringes to its lowest edges.

4 Along the embroidered border and in the very body of the material there gleamed stars here and there, and in their midst a half-moon

spirabat ignes. quaqua tamen insignis illius pallae perfluebat ambitus,
20 individuo nexu corona totis floribus totisque constructa pomis adhaere-
269 bat. iam gestamina longe diversa. nam dextra quidem ferebat aereum
crepitaculum, cuius per angustam lamminam in modum baltei recurvatam
traiectae mediae paucae virgulae, crispante brachio trigeminos iactus,
reddebant argutum sonorem. laevae vero cymbium dependebat aureum,
5 cuius ansulae, qua parte conspicua est, insurgebat aspis caput extollens
arduum cervicibus late tumescentibus. pedes ambroseos tegebant soleae
palmae victricis foliis intextae. talis ac tanta, spirans Arabiae felicia
germina, divina me voce dignata est :
    5 'En adsum tuis commota, Luci, precibus, rerum naturae parens,
10 elementorum omnium domina, saeculorum progenies initialis, summa
numinum, regina manium, prima caelitum, deorum dearumque facies
uniformis, quae caeli luminosa culmina, maris salubria flamina, inferum
deplorata silentia nutibus meis dispenso : cuius numen unicum multiformi specie, ritu vario, nomine multiiugo totus veneratur orbis. inde
15 primigenii Phryges Pessinuntiam deum matrem, hinc autocthones
Attici Cecropeiam Minervam, illinc fluctuantes Cyprii Paphiam Venerem, Cretes sagittiferi Dictynnam Dianam, Siculi trilingues Ortygiam
Proserpinam, Eleusinii vetustam deam Cererem, Iunonem alii, Bellonam
alii, Hecatam isti, Rhamnusiam illi, et qui nascentis dei Solis inchoan-
20 tibus inlustrantur radiis Aethiopes Afrique priscaque doctrina pol-
270 lentes Aegyptii caerimoniis me propriis percolentes appellant vero
nomine reginam Isidem. adsum tuos miserata casus, adsum favens et
propitia. mitte iam fletus et lamentationes omitte, depelle maerorem;

---

269   3 virgulae (*in mg. fort.* ungulae) F   6 solae F, *em. v*   7 arabiae felicia *indux.*
F²   8 gemina F, *em. v*   9 tui F A B1 U O S tuis *al.*   11 reginam anium F, *em.*
v regina animum *Φ* O amnium B3   deorum dearumque F² *Φ* dearum dearumque F
A U dearumque (*semel*) E S   14 totum F *Φ*, em. *Φ²* v   15 Pessinuntiam *Wower*
pessimunticam R pessinumtant(.d *in mg. addit.*) F *Φ*   16 illic F, *em. v*   phlaphi-
am F, *em. v*   17 Ortygiam *Kaibel* stigiam F stygiam *v*   18 eleusini F, *em. v*   ve-
tust<i sanct> *Cast.* vetust<i Actae>am *Rob. coll. Stat. silv. 4. 8. 50*   cererem
et F²   19 raannusiam *dein* rhannusiam F, *em. v*   illi et qui *v* illi   qui (*eras.* ec)
F illi ecqui … *ss.* et …² illi sed *Bluemner*   20 Afrique *Cuper,* arique *vel* trique F
arique … B2 R trique A B1 U omnes B3 D O utri que S utrique *Barth cf. p. 8, 17, Hom.*
Od. 1. 23
270   2 reginamisidem F *Φ corr.* F² *Φ²*   3 omitte *del. Helm ut var. lect. ad* mitte, *def.*
Bernhard omnem *Cast.*

breathed a flame of fire. But wherevever the sweep of that magnificent mantle moved, a wreath garlanded of all manner of flowers and fruits was indivisibly joined to it. The things she carried were of quite varied kind. For in her right hand she bore a bronze rattle in which a few rods in the middle, thrust across a thin sheet of metal that was curved like a belt, emitted a tinkling sound when the arm made three quivering jolts. From the left hand then there hung a golden vessel on whose handle, where it was conspicuous, there rose a serpent which reared its head high and puffed its neck thickly. Her ambrosian feet were covered by sandals woven with leaves of victorious palm. Such was the great goddess who, breathing the blessed fragrance of Arabia, deigned to address me with divine voice.

5 'Lo, I am with you, Lucius, moved by your prayers, I who am the mother of the universe, the mistress of all the elements, the first offspring of time, the highest of deities, the queen of the dead, foremost of heavenly beings, the single form that fuses all gods and goddesses; I who order by my will the starry heights of heaven, the health-giving breezes of the sea, and the awful silences of those in the underworld : my single godhead is adored by the whole world in varied forms, in differing rites and with many diverse names.

'Thus the Phrygians, earliest of races, call me Pessinuntia, Mother of the Gods; thus the Athenians, sprung from their own soil, call me Cecropeian Minerva; and the sea-tossed Cyprians call me Paphian Venus, the archer Cretans Diana Dictynna, and the trilingual Sicilians Ortygian Proserpine; to the Eleusinians I am Ceres, the ancient goddess, to others Juno, to others Bellona and Hecate and Rhamnusia. But the Ethiopians, who are illumined by the first rays of the sun-god as he is born every day, together with the Africans and the Egyptians who excel through having the original doctrine, honour me with my distinctive rites and give me my true name of Queen Isis.

'I am here taking pity on your ills; I am here to give aid and solace. Cease then from tears and wailings, set aside your sadness; there is now

iam tibi providentia mea inlucescit dies salutaris. ergo igitur imperiis
5 istis meis animum intende sollicitum. diem, qui dies ex ista nocte nascetur,
aeterna mihi nuncupavit religio, quo sedatis hibernis tempestatibus et
lenitis maris procellosis fluctibus navigabili iam pelago rudem dedicantes carinam primitias commeatus libant mei sacerdotes. id sacrum nec
sollicita nec profana mente debebis opperiri. **6** nam meo monitu
10 sacerdos in ipso procinctu pompae roseam manu dextera sistro cohaeren-
tem gestabit coronam. incunctanter ergo dimotis turbulis alacer continuare pompam mea volentia fretus et de proximo clementer velut manum
sacerdotis osculabundus rosis decerptis pessimae mihique iam dudum
detestabilis beluae istius corio te protinus exue. nec quicquam rerum
15 mearum reformides ut arduum. nam hoc eodem momento, quo tibi
venio, simul et ibi praesens, quae sunt sequentia, sacerdoti meo per
quietem facienda praecipio. meo iussu tibi constricti comitatus decedent
populi, nec inter hilares caerimonias et festiva spectacula quisquam defor-
mem istam, quam geris, faciem perhorrescet vel figuram tuam repente
20 mutatam sequius interpretatus aliquis maligne criminabitur. plane memineris et penita mente conditum semper tenebis mihi reliqua vitae
tuae curricula adusque terminos ultimi spiritus vadata. nec iniurium,
cuius beneficio redieris ad homines, ei totum debere, quod vives. vives
autem beatus, vives in mea tutela gloriosus, et cum spatium saeculi
271 tui permensus ad inferos demearis, ibi quoque in ipso subterraneo
semirutundo me, quam vides, Acherontis tenebris interlucentem Stygiis-
que penetralibus regnantem, campos Elysios incolens ipse, tibi propitiam
frequens adorabis. quodsi sedulis obsequiis et religiosis ministeriis et
5 tenacibus castimoniis numen nostrum promerueris, scies ultra statuta
fato tuo spatia vitam quoque tibi prorogare mihi tantum licere.'
     7 Sic oraculi venerabilis fine prolato numen invictum in se recessit.
nec mora, cum somno protinus absolutus pavore et gaudio ac dein
sudore nimio permixtus exurgo summeque miratus deae potentis tam

---

6 nuncupabit F Φ, *em.v*   10 noseam F Φ, *corr.* F²   10-11 coharentem F Φ,
em. v   11-12 continare *Kiessling cf. p. 22, 11*   12 meam F Φ, *em. Colv.*   violentia F² Φ² B2 B3 D O E²   13-14 iam detestabilis dudum Φ detestabilis iam dudum
al. trp. Rob. ex indiciis in F datis   14 earum *Scriver*   16 tibi F Φ, *em. Colv.*
18 hylares F Φ, *em. v*
271   2 semirotundo (*prior o ex* u *mut. ead. fort. m.*) F   3 elisios F, em Φ 7 perlato
F Φ A   8-9 dein furore divino *Bluemner, Herm. 29, 312*

dawning for you, through my providence, the day of salvation. For this reason pay careful heed to these commands of mine. The day which will follow the coming night has been dedicated to me by eternal religious sanction. Then, when the storms of winter have been calmed, and the wild waves of the sea have been stilled, my priests are wont to vow a new barque to the now navigable sea and offer it as first-fruits of a new year's navigation. You should await that sacred rite with a mind neither anxious nor profane.

6 'For at my suggestion a priest in the very midst of the moving procession will carry a crown of roses attached to the sistrum in his right hand. Without delay, therefore, push through the crowds and eagerly join the procession, relying on my favour; then get close to the priest and gently, as if you meant to kiss his hand, pluck off the roses with your mouth and forthwith cast off the hide of that vile beast that has long since been hateful to me. Nor need you fear any of my instructions as being difficult. For at this very moment when I come to you, I am there also with my priest, instructing him in his sleep as to what he must do next. At my command the dense crowds of people will make way for you, nor will anyone amid the joyous rites and festive revelries shudder at that ungainly guise you bear, or explain amiss your sudden change of form and attack you spitefully for it. But especially remember, and ever hold enshrined deep in your heart, that the remaining course of your life, even to the limit of your last breath, is dedicated to me. Nor is it wrong that you should devote to her, by whose favour you shall return to men, the rest of your life. You shall live indeed a happy man, you shall live full of glory in my protection, and when you have completed the span of your lifetime, you will pass down to the nether world, but there also, in the very midst of the subterranean hemisphere, you shall often worship me, whom you now see, as one who favours you, shining in the darkness of Acheron and ruling in the Stygian depths, when you the while shall dwell in the Elysian fields. But if with diligent service, religious tendance and constant chastity you will be worthy of my godhead, know that I alone have power to prolong your life also beyond the span determined by your destiny'.

7 Thus did the revered oracle come to an end, and the unvanquished deity withdrew into her own being. Without delay I was at once released from sleep and, steeped in fear, joy and then a surge of sweat, I arose full

10 claram praesentiam, marino rore respersus magnisque imperiis eius
intentus monitionis ordinem recolebam. nec mora, cum noctis atrae
fugato nubilo sol exurgit aureus, et ecce discursu religioso ac prorsus
triumphali turbulae complent totas plateas, tantaque hilaritudine
praeter peculiarem meam gestire mihi cuncta videbantur, ut pecua etiam
15 cuiusce modi et totas domos et ipsum diem serena facie gaudere senti-
rem. nam et pruinam pridianam dies apricus ac placidus repente fuerat
insecutus, ut canorae etiam aviculae prolectatae verno vapore concentus
suaves adsonarent, matrem siderum, parentem temporum orbisque totius
dominam blando mulcentes adfamine. quid quod arbores etiam, quae
20 pomifera subole fecundae quaeque earum tantum umbra contentae
steriles, austrinis laxatae flatibus, germine foliorum renidentes, clementi
motu brachiorum dulces strepitus obsibilabant, magnoque procellarum
sedato fragore ac turbido fluctuum tumore posito mare quietas adluvies
272 temperabat, caelum autem nubilosa caligine disiecta nudo sudoque
luminis proprii splendore candebat.

8 Ecce pompae magnae paulatim praecedunt anteludia votivis
cuiusque studiis exornata pulcherrume. hic incinctus balteo militem gere-
5 bat, illum succinctum chlamide crepides et venabula venatorem fecerant,
alius soccis obauratis inductus serica veste mundoque pretioso et adtextis
capite crinibus incessu perfluo feminam mentiebatur. porro alium ocreis,
scuto, galea ferroque insignem e ludo putares gladiatorio procedere. nec
ille deerat, qui magistratum facibus purpuraque luderet, nec qui pallio
10 baculoque et baxeis et hircino barbitio philosophum fingeret, nec qui
diversis harundinibus alter aucupem cum visco, alter piscatorem cum
hamis induceret. vidi et ursam mansuem cultu matronali, sella vehebatur,
et simiam pilleo textili crocotisque Frygiis Catamiti pastoris specie
aureum gestantem poculum et asinum pinnis adglutinatis adambulantem

---

11 nec mora, cum *ut ex p. 271, 8 repetitum dub. secl. Rob.*   15 cuiusque *Eyssenh.*
17 vapore (*ex favore aut* pavore *em.*) F   20 subolę F sobolę F²   20-21 contente
est eriles F, *em.* v contecta B2 D   21 filiorum F, *em.* v   23 adlubies F, *em.* v
272   3 praecedunt F Φ procedunt v   votibus F vocibus v *em. Vulcan* 6 occis
F, *covr.* F²   obauratis (*ex obduratis em.*) F   inductus F Φ B2 O indu-
tus *al.*   7 capiti (*dein corr.*) F   8 eludo F   9 facibus F Φ B3 D O
fascibus *al.*   10 hyrcino F, *em.* v   12 mansuem quae cultu B3 O *post*
mansuem *spatium vac.* (2 *litt.*) *habet* F, *vel* q̄ *capax ut scribit Rob. nec spatium nec*
quae *habent al.* <quae> sella *vdVl. prob. Helm, ut parenthesim vel parataxim recte def.*
Oud. prob. Giarr.   13 crocotiisque F Φ A, *em. Beroald.*   frigiis F Φ A, *em.* v

of rapt wonder at such a direct manifestation of the mighty goddess. I sprinkled myself with salt spray and, thinking on her great commands, I went over her instructions again one by one. There was no delay when the sun, after the black night's clouds had been routed, came out in golden hue, and there were the crowds filling all the streets in a religious and truly triumphal procession. Everything seemed to me to be throbbing with such a sense of joy, quite apart from my personal happiness, that I felt that all kinds of animals too and all the houses and the very day itself were rejoicing with bright faces. For the frost of yesterday had been suddenly followed by a sunny and calm day, so that the tuneful little birds too, allured by the warmth of spring, were sweetly singing together, cheering with their gracious welcome the Mother of the Stars, the Creator of the Seasons and the Mistress of the Universe. Why, the very trees, rich in their offspring of fruit or barrenly contented with their mere shade, were now regaled by southerly breezes and glistened again with their budded leaves, making sweet sounds with the soft motion of their branches. The great crash of storms had subsided and the wild swell of the waves had gone down; the sea calmed its breaking billows to a quiet lapping, and the sky, when its dark clouds had dispersed, shone with the sheer and serene radiance of its own light.

8 Now there gradually appeared the forerunners of the great procession, each finely decked out with the fancy dress of his choice. One man girded with a belt played the part of a soldier; another with cloak tucked up was shown by his boots and spears to be a huntsman, while another, wearing gilded shoes, a silk gown, and expensive ornaments, pretended to be a woman by attaching a wig to his head and walking with a wanton gait. Another again, distinguished by his greaves, shield, helmet and sword, you would think had just emerged from a gladiatorial school. Then there was one acting a magistrate, complete with torches and purple; and another with cloak, staff, woven sandals and goat-beard played a philosopher. There were two with different kinds of reed rods, one acting a fowler with bird-lime, the other a fisherman with hooks. I saw too a tame she-bear dressed like a matron and carried in a sedan-chair; a monkey with a plaited cap and clothes of Phrygian saffron carrying a gold

15 cuidam seni debili, ut illum quidem Bellerophontem, hunc autem diceres
Pegasum, tamen rideres utrumque.

9   Inter has oblectationes ludicras popularium, quae passim vagabantur, iam sospitatricis deae peculiaris pompa moliebatur. mulieres candido
splendentes amicimine, vario laetantes gestamine, verno florentes
20 coronamine, quae de gremio per viam, qua sacer incedebat comitatus, solum sternebant flosculis, aliae, quae nitentibus speculis pone
273 tergum reversis venienti deae obvium commonstrarent obsequium et
quae pectines eburnos ferentes gestu brachiorum flexuque digitorum
ornatum atque obpexum crinium regalium fingerent, illae etiam, quae
ceteris unguentis et geniali balsamo guttatim excusso conspargebant
5 plateas; magnus praeterea sexus utriusque numerus lucernis, taedis, cereis
et alio genere facticii luminis siderum caelestium stirpem propitiantes.
symphoniae dehinc suaves, fistulae tibiaeque modulis dulcissimis personabant. eas amoenus lectissimae iuventutis veste nivea et cataclista prae-
nitens sequebatur chorus, carmen venustum iterantes, quod Camenarum
10 favore sollers poeta modulatus edixerat, quod argumentum referebat interim maiorum antecantamenta votorum. ibant et dicati magno Sarapi tibicines, qui per oblicum calamum, ad aurem porrectum dexteram, familiarem templi deique modulum frequentabant, et plerique, qui facilem
sacris viam dari praedicarent.   10   tunc influunt turbae sacris divinis
15 initiatae, viri feminaeque omnis dignitatis et omnis aetatis, linteae vestis
candore puro luminosi, illae limpido tegmine crines madidos obvolutae,
hi capillum derasi funditus verticem praenitentes, aereis et argenteis,
immo vero aureis etiam sistris argutum tinnitum constrepentes, et
magnae religionis terrena sidera, antistites sacrorum proceres illi, qui
20 candido linteamine cinctum pectoralem adusque vestigia strictim iniecti
274 potentissimorum deum proferebant insignis exuvias. quorum primus

---

21 alieque F, em. v
273   6 facticii luminis *Haupt* facuum lumine (*in mg.* facti luminis) F Φ facium lumine B3
O faculum lumine D ficti luminis *al.*   syderum F, emp. Φ   7 simphoniae F, em. Φ
tybiaeque F Φ, *em.* A   7-8 personabant F Φ personabat F²   8 iuventis F, *em.* v
catha clysta F, *em.* v   9 vetustum *Wasse*   13 et plerique F praeciaeque *Dousa*
ap. Colv. coll. Fest. p. 250 L [et] plebique *Rohde*   17 hic F Φ, *em.* v   vertice D
post praenitentes *codd.* habent magnae religionis terrena sidera, *quae vdVl. ante*
antistites *trp.*   18 systris F, *em.* Φ   constrepentes ed F Φ *dein mut. in* -te
sed F, *em.* v constrepentes sed et *Oud.*
274   1 praeferebant B2 O S   exubias F Φ, *em.* v

cup like the shepherd Ganymede; an ass with wings glued on his back walking beside a decrepit old man, so that one suggested Bellerophon, the other Pegasus, but both were equally comic.

9 While these amusing delights of the people were appearing all over the place, the procession proper of the Saviour Goddess was on its way. Women radiant in white garments, rejoicing in different kinds of emblems, which they carried, and garlanded with flowers of spring, were strewing the ground with blossoms from their bosoms along the road where the sacred company proceeded. Other women had reversed shining mirrors behind their backs to show respect to the goddess as she moved after them; others carrying ivory combs represented with waving arms and bending fingers the adornment and combing of the queen's hair; others again bespattered the streets with various perfumes and a delightful balm shaken out in drops. A large number of people, besides, of both sexes were seeking the blessing of Her who is the creator of the stars of heaven with lanterns, torches, wax tapers, and other kinds of artificial light. Then came the charming music of many instruments, and the sound of pipe and flute in the sweetest melodies. They were followed by a delightful choir of the most select youths, radiant in snow-white festal tunics; they repeated a captivating song which a skilled poet had written for music with the aid of the Goddesses of Song, and the theme of this from time to time contained musical preludes to the solemn vows to come. There came also flautists dedicated to great Sarapis, who repeated through a reed, held sideways towards the right ear, a tune traditional to the temple and its deity; and there were many shouting out, 'Keep the way clear for the holy procession!'

10 Then surged on the throngs of those initiated into the divine mysteries, men and women of every rank and age, shining in the immaculate whiteness of linen raiment. The women had wrapped a transparent veil round their locks, that were moist with perfume, and the men had gleaming pates after shaving their heads completely. Together they produced a shrill tinkling noise with sistrums that were of bronze or silver, or indeed of gold. With them were the terrestrial stars of the great

lucernam claro praemicantem porrigebat lumine non adeo nostris illis
consimilem, quae vespertinas illuminant epulas, sed aureum cymbium
medio sui patore flammulam suscitans largiorem. secundus vestitum qui-
5 dem similis, sed manibus ambabus gerebat altaria, id est auxilia, quibus
nomen dedit proprium deae summatis auxiliaris providentia. ibat tertius
attollens palmam auro subtiliter foliatam nec non Mercuriale etiam
caduceum. quartus aequitatis ostendebat indicium deformatam manum
sinistram porrecta palmula, quae genuina pigritia, nulla calliditate nulla
10 sollertia praedita, videbatur aequitati magis aptior quam dextera; idem
gerebat et aureum vasculum in modum papillae rutundatum, de quo
lacte libabat. quintus auream vannum laureis congestam ramulis et
alius ferebat amphoram.

11 Nec mora, cum dei dignati pedibus humanis incedere prodeunt,
15 hic horrendus ille superum commeator et inferum, nunc atra, nunc
aurea facie sublimis, attollens canis cervices arduas, Anubis, laeva caduceum gerens, dextera palmam virentem quatiens. cuius vestigium conti-
nuum sequebatur bos in erectum levata statum, bos, omniparentis deae
fecundum simulacrum, quod residens umeris suis proferebat unus e
20 ministerio beato gressu gestuosus. ferebatur ab alio cista secretorum
275 capax penitus celans operta magnificae religionis. gerebat alius felici
suo gremio summi numinis venerandam effigiem, non pecoris, non avis,
non ferae ac ne hominis quidem ipsius consimilem, sed sollerti repertu
etiam ipsa novitate reverendam, altioris utcumque et magno silentio
5 tegendae religionis argumentum ineffabile, sed ad istum plane modum
fulgente auro figuratum : urnula faberrime cavata, fundo quam rutundo,
miris extrinsecus simulacris Aegyptiorum effigiata; eius orificium non
altiuscule levatum in canalem porrectum longo rivulo prominebat, ex

3 vespertina F, *em. v*   cybium F, *em. v*   4 vestitum *dein* vestitu F   5 altaria F
alcteria *Wiman*   id est auxilia F *del. dub. Oud.* id est auxillas *Wiman* auxillas, id est
altaria (*vel. delet.* id est altaria) *Kaibel, Hermes 35, 204*   11 rutundatum (*in mg.* d) F
rudundatum B3 D rotundatum *al.*   12 aureis *codd. def. Norden, Geburt des Kindes,
19 em. Passerat*   12 f. et sextus *Bluemner* sextus *Rob.*   15 horrendum F Φ
horrendum! *v em. D'Orléans*   17 virentem levatam. Erat et bos omniaparentis
B3 D O   huius (*in mg.* cuius) F cuius Φ *v*   18 vacca *ss.* Φ² bos *al.* erat bos² B2
<erat ea> bos *Wower*   omnia parentis F. Φ, *em. Beroald.*   20 gestuosu F Φ
gestuoso F² *v em. Petsch. cill. p 260, 21*
275   2 summi sui numinis A B1 U E S R   5 tegente F Φ, *em. Beroald.*   6 figuratum
F¹ Φ A *v* figurata F²   6 rutundo F¹ *in* rotundo *mut.* F¹ *aut* F² rotundo Φ A *v*

faith, those noble leaders, the priests of the ritual, who, clad in white linen that was fitted tightly round the breast and reached to their feet, bore forward the distinguished emblems of the mightiest gods. The first of them stretched out a lantern which gleamed out with a bright light, not indeed like those that illumine our night banquets, but a golden vessel that kindled a quite big flame in its central orifice. A second priest was dressed similarly, but with both his hands he carried a high altar, that is, a 'source of help', a distinctive name derived from the helping providence of the eminent goddess. A third walked holding up a palm-branch with leaves delicately wrought of gold, and also a herald's staff such as Mercury has. The fourth displayed an emblem of justice, a de-formed left hand with the palm outstretched; this seemed, because of its innate slowness, and lack of all cunning and skill, to represent justice better than the right hand. The same man carried too a small golden vessel rounded in the shape of a female breast, from which he poured libations of milk. A fifth priest carried a golden winnowing-basket made of laurel twigs, and another bore a two-handled pitcher.

11   There was no delay when the gods then came forward, deigning to tread with human feet. First came that dread messenger of both celestial and infernal beings, Anubis, of lofty stature and with a face now black, now golden, holding high his dog's neck; in his left hand he bore a herald's staff and with his right hand he shook a green palm-branch. Hard on his steps followed a cow in upright posture; that cow was the fertile image of the goddess who is the creator of all, and one of the blessed priesthood carried the image on his shoulders with proud steps. Another carried a box holding secret things and concealing within it the hidden attributes of the sublime faith. Another bore in his happy bosom the revered image of the highest deity, in a likeness not of an ox or bird or wild animal, nor even of a man, but inspiring reverence both through its skilled workman-ship and by its very strangeness, it was an unutterable witness to a faith ever lofty which claimed to be hidden in a vast silence. It was fashioned of gleaming gold in the following form : a small vase it was, most cunningly hollowed out, with a base finely rounded, while outside it was adorned with wondrous Egyptian figures. Its mouth was not so high and stretched to a channel, standing out in a long spout; on its other side was a handle turning well away and joined in a sweeping curve. On top of the handle

alia vero parte multum recedens spatiosa dilatione adhaerebat ansa,
10 quam contorto nodulo supersedebat aspis squameae cervicis striato
tumore sublimis.

12 Et ecce praesentissimi numinis promissa nobis accedunt beneficia
et fata salutemque ipsam meam gerens sacerdos adpropinquat, ad
ipsum praescriptum divinae promissionis ornatum dextera proferens
15 sistrum deae, mihi coronam—et hercules coronam consequenter, quod
tot ac tantis exanclatis laboribus, tot emensis periculis deae maximae
providentia adluctantem mihi saevissime Fortunam superarem. nec
tamen gaudio subitario commotus inclementi me cursu proripui, verens
scilicet, ne repentino quadripedis impetu religionis quietus turbaretur
20 ordo, sed placido ac prorsus humano gradu cunctabundus paulatim
obliquato corpore, sane divinitus decedente populo, sensim inrepo.

13 at sacerdos, ut reabse cognoscere potui, nocturni commonefactus
oraculi miratusque congruentiam mandati muneris, confestim restitit et
ultro porrecta dextera ob os ipsum meum coronam exhibuit. tunc
276 ego trepidans, adsiduo pulsu micanti corde, coronam, quae rosis amoenis
intexta fulgurabat, avido ore susceptam cupidus promissi cupidissime
devoravi. nec me fefellit caeleste promissum : protinus mihi delabitur
deformis et ferina facies. ac primo quidem squalens pilus defluit, ac
5 dehinc cutis crassa tenuatur, venter obesus residet, pedum plantae per
ungulas in digitos exeunt, manus non iam pedes sunt, sed in erecta
porriguntur officia, cervix procera cohibetur, os et caput rutundatur,
aures enormes repetunt pristinam parvitatem, dentes saxei redeunt ad
humanam minutiem, et, quae me potissimum cruciabat ante, cauda
10 nusquam comparuit! populi mirantur, religiosi venerantur tam evidentem
maximi numinis potentiam et consimilem nocturnis imaginibus magni-
ficentiam et facilitatem reformationis claraque et consona voce, caelo
manus adtendentes, testantur tam inlustre deae beneficium. **14** at ego
stupore nimio defixus tacitus haerebam, animo meo tam repentinum tam-

---

15 sistrum, <sistrum> *Kronenb.*   22 reabse F U re abse *al.*   24 exibuit F *Φ*,
em. A *v*
276   2-3 cupidus promissi devoravi (*in mg. ad* promissi *complur. vocab. eras.* F) F B3 D O
cupidissime d. *Φ* B2 cupidus cupidissime d. A B1 U E S R   5 residit *vdVl.*
5-6 pro ungulis *Oud.*   7 rotundatur *Φ*   10 *post* nusquam *add.* comparuit F² B2
B3 D O R *tantum* cauda nusquam F¹ *Φ* A B1 U E S comparet *vdVl. coll. pp. 193 15*;
248,4   venerantur re (*sed* re *induct.*) F   11 ymaginibus F, *em. Φ*

was set an asp in a coiled knot, its scaly neck rearing itself with a streaked swelling.

12 And behold! here come to me the promised blessings of the most helpful goddess and a priest approaches bringing with him my destiny and my very salvation. He was equipped as the divine promise had foretold, carrying in his right hand a sistrum intended for the goddess, and a crown for me—and assuredly the crown was most fitting, since after enduring so many and so great toils and passing through so many dangers, by the providence of the mighty goddess I was now overcoming Fortune that had buffeted me so cruelly. Yet I did not push forward impetuously disturbed by sudden joy, for I was naturally afraid that the orderly sequence of the sacred rite would be upset by the precipitous rush of a four-footed beast. But slowly with quiet steps, such as a man might make, I gradually edged my way through the crowd, that gave before me, clearly by the guidance of the goddess, and I gently crept inwards.

13 But the priest, as in fact I was able to find out, remembered his vision by night, and marvelled how well everything agreed with the instructions received. He instantly stopped, and raising his right hand without any prompting, held the crown of roses up to my very mouth. Then I in my agitation, with my heart throbbing wildly, took up with greedy mouth the crown which was bright with the bloom of lovely inwoven roses, and eagerly hoping for fulfilment of the promise, I most eagerly munched through it all. Nor was I disappointed in the heavenly promise: at once my ugly animal form left me.

First my scruffy bristles fell off, then my rough hide became thin and the fat belly subsided, while the soles of my feet now ended in toes instead of hoofs and the hands were no longer feet, doing their work now in my upright posture. My lofty neck contracted, my mouth and head became round; my huge ears regained their former slenderness and my rock-like molars returned to human scale; and my tail, my chief torment of old, was non-existent! The people marvelled; and the devotees expressed their adoration of such a manifest token of the highest deity's power and of the glory which had conformed to the visions of the night, as well as her easy skill in achieving my transformation. This they did with clear voices in unison, raising their hands to heaven and acclaiming the radiant blessing bestowed by the goddess.

14 But I was smitten with profound amazement and stood rooted to

15 que magnum non capiente gaudium, quid potissimum praefarer
   primarium, unde novae vocis exordium caperem, quo sermone nunc
   renatam linguam felicius auspicarer, quibus quantisque verbis tantae
   deae gratias agerem. sed sacerdos utcumque divino monitu cognitis ab
   origine cunctis cladibus meis, quanquam et ipse insigni permotus mira-
20 culo, nutu significato prius praecipit tegendo mihi linteam dari laciniam;
   nam me cum primum nefando tegmine despoliaverat asinus, compressis
   in artum feminibus et superstrictis accurate manibus, quantum nudo
   licebat, velamento me naturali probe muniveram. tunc e cohorte reli-
277 gionis unus inpigre superiorem exutus tunicam supertexit me celerrume.
   quo facto sacerdos vultu geniali et hercules perhumanum in aspectum
   meum attonitus sic effatur :
       15 'Multis et variis exanclatis laboribus magnisque Fortunae tem-
 5 pestatibus et maximis actus procellis ad portum Quietis et aram Misericordiae tandem, Luci, venisti. nec tibi natales ac ne dignitas quidem,
   vel ipsa, qua flores, usquam doctrina profuit, sed lubrico virentis aetatulae
   ad serviles delapsus voluptates curiositatis inprosperae sinistrum praemium reportasti. sed utcumque Fortunae caecitas, dum te pessimis
10 periculis discruciat, ad religiosam istam beatitudinem inprovida produxit
   malitia. eat nunc et summo furore saeviat et crudelitati suae materiem
   quaerat aliam; nam in eos, quorum sibi vitas deae nostrae maiestas vindicavit, non habet locum casus infestus. quid latrones, quid ferae, quid
   servitium, quid asperrimorum itinerum ambages reciprocae, quid metus
15 mortis cotidianae nefariae Fortunae profuit? in tutelam iam receptus es
   Fortunae, sed videntis, quae suae lucis splendore ceteros etiam deos illuminat. sume iam vultum laetiorem candido isto habitu tuo congruentem,
   comitare pompam deae sospitatricis inovanti gradu. videant inreligiosi,
   videant et errorem suum recognoscant : en ecce pristinis aerumnis absolu-
20 tus Isidis magnae providentia gaudens Lucius de sua Fortuna triumphat.

---

16 sermonem S B2 U D S R   17 renata lingua *codd.*, *em. vdVl.*   20 liciniam
F Φ A B2 U E S laciniam *al.*   21 mecum F¹ me cum F² *al.* me *del. vdVl.*   nefando
U (*vestigia* E) S R nefasto *al.*   22 altum *codd.*, *em. Beroald.*
277   2 inhumano F¹ Φ A B1 U S perhumano F² *al.* perhumanum *Gr.*   3 effatur
F Φ B3 D O affatur *al.*   6 Luci tandem A B1 B2 U S R   12 vitas servitium
deae *codd.* <in> servitium *Luetj.* [servitium] *ut ex proximis illat.* Oud. servitum *Walter*
13 locus F¹ Φ locum F² *al.*   18 popam F¹ *corr.* F² Φ   innovandi (*supra a parv. ras.*)
F Φ B2 D O innovanti Φ² B1 U E S R inovanti A cf. *Beroald.*   20 prudentia *codd.*,
em. Beroald.

the spot in silence, for my mind could not take in so sudden and so mighty a joy. What would be best for me to say first? How should I first use my restored voice? With what conversation could I most aptly inaugurate my reborn power of speech? In what words and at what length was I to thank so great a goddess? But the priest, who had by divine communication, as ever, become acquainted with all my misfortunes from the start, although he himself had been deeply moved by the wondrous miracle, first gave orders with a meaningful nod that a linen garment should be given to cover me; for as soon as the ass had removed its loathsome skin from me, I pressed my thighs closely together and applied my hands carefully, so that as far as my nakedness allowed, I had decently covered myself up with a veil given by nature. Then one of the band of devotees smartly took off his outer cloak and quickly put it over me. This done, the priest, with a benign expression, looked in astonishment at my form which was now indeed thoroughly human and spoke thus :

15 'After enduring many different troubles and after being driven by the wildest storms of Fortune and her heaviest gales, at last, Lucius, you have come to the haven of Rest and the altar of Mercy. Your high birth was of no avail to you nor even your position in society, nor yet the learning in which you are so rich, but on the slippery path of your hot-headed youth you fell into low pleasures and you have gained a grim reward for your ill-starred curiosity. Nevertheless the blindness of Fortune, while it tortured you with the worst of dangers, yet led you in its unforeseeing evil to your state of religious bliss. Let her quit now and rage in her wildest frenzy and seek another object for her cruelty. For hostile fate has no power over those whose lives have been claimed by the majesty of our goddess. What avail to wicked Fortune were the robbers, the wild beasts, the slavery, the hardships of journeys that winded on and back, and the daily fear of death? Now you have been received into the protection of a Fortune who is not blind, but sees, and who illumines the other gods too with the radiance of her light.

'Show, then, a happier face in keeping with the white cloak you have assumed. Follow the procession of the Saviour Goddess with triumphant step. Let the unbelievers take note, let them take note and acknowledge their mistake : behold, here is Lucius! He has been freed from his former

quo tamen tutior sis atque munitior, da nomen sanctae huic militiae,
cuius non olim sacramento etiam rogabaris, teque iam nunc obsequio
278 religionis nostrae dedica et ministerii iugum subi voluntarium. nam cum
coeperis deae servire, tunc magis senties fructum tuae libertatis.'
    16 Ad istum modum vaticinatus sacerdos egregius fatigatos anhelitus
trahens conticuit. exin permixtus agmini religioso procedens comitabar
5 sacrarium totae civitati notus ac conspicuus, digitis hominum nutibusque
notabilis. omnes in me populi fabulabantur : 'hunc omnipotentis hodie
deae numen augustum reformavit ad homines. felix hercules et ter beatus,
qui vitae scilicet praecedentis innocentia fideque meruerit tam praeclarum
de caelo patrocinum, ut renatus quodam modo statim sacrorum obse-
10 quio desponderetur.'
    Inter haec et festorum votorum tumultum paulatim progressi iam
ripam maris proximamus atque at ipsum illum locum, quo pridie meus
stabulaverat asinus, pervenimus. ibidem simulacris rite dispositis navem
faberrime factam picturis miris Aegyptiorum circumsecus varie-
15 gatam summus sacerdos taeda lucida et ovo et sulpure, sollemnissimas
preces de casto praefatus ore, quam purissime purificatam deae nuncupavit dedicavitque. huius felicis alvei nitens carbasus litteras aureas intextas progerebat : eae litterae votum instaurabant de novi commeatus
prospera navigatione. iam malus insurgit pinus rutunda, splendore
279 sublimis, insigni carchesio conspicua, et puppis intorta chenisco,
bracteis aureis vestita fulgebat omnisque prorsus carina citro limpido
perpolita florebat. tunc cuncti populi tam religiosi quam profani vannos
onustas aromatis et huiusce modi suppliciis certatim congerunt et insuper
5 fluctus libant intritum lacte confectum, donec muneribus largis et devo-
tionibus faustis completa navis, absoluta strophiis ancoralibus, peculiari

---

278   13 ibidem (*ras. supra* em) F B1 B2 B3 U D O R ibidum Φ ibi dem A ibi demum E
ibi deum *aut* dium S   14 faverrime F¹ *corr.* F²   circumsectus *codd., em. Stewech*
14-15 varie grecam *codd., em. Beroald.*   16 de <libro> *Wiman, cf. p. 279, 16 f.*
17 albei F¹ *corr.* F²   17-18 litteras aureas intextas *Giarr.* littere votum Ingestas
(*in mg.* .d F¹, *supra* a *lineol. add.* F²) F ingestans A U D O S R litteras vocum intextas
Oud. litteras ingestas proferebat, quae litterae *Wolterstorff, Gl. 8, 200 n. 1*   18 eae
(*sed in* ecce *radendo mutat.*) F ecce *al.* ecce hae *Luetj.*   19 rutunda F rotunda Φ
279   1 sublimis insignis F Φ A insigni *Salm.* insignis, sublimi *Oud.*   2 vestito *vdVl.*
coll. Luc. nav. 5 χρυσοῦν χηνίσκον ἐπικειμένη   fulgebat (*eras. supra* eb *fort.* ura)
F fulgurabat Φ A   5 intrimentum *dub. Helm coll. p. 246, 9*   6 strofiis F Φ,
em. A

sufferings and, rejoicing in the providence of mighty Isis, he is victorious over his Fortune. But to be safer and better equipped, enrol your name in this holy military service, whose solemn oath you were asked to take not long ago, and vow yourself from this moment to the ministry of our religion. Accept of your own free will the yoke of service. For when you have begun to serve the goddess, then will you better realize the result of your freedom.'

16 After prophesying in this manner the excellent priest took several gasping weary breaths and was silent. Then I mingled with the sacred procession and went forward, accompanying the shrine, so that I was plain and prominent for the whole populace to see. Men pointed to me with their fingers and nodded their heads. All the people were talking about me : 'This is the man who has been today restored to human shape through the splendid divinity of the all-powerful goddess. Happy is he, by heaven, and thrice blessed, to have clearly deserved, by the purity of his former life and his pious loyalty, such a wondrous favour from heaven that he is, as it were, born again and has at once pledged himself to service in the sacred rites.'

In the meantime, amid the clamour of vows made in festive spirit, we gradually passed onwards and now, approaching the sea-shore, we reached the very spot where my double the ass had lain the day before. When the images of the gods had been duly set down there, from reverent lips the chief priest first uttered the most exalted prayers over a ship that had been built with exquisite skill and decorated round about with wonderful Egyptian paintings. With a bright torch, with an egg and with sulphur he purified the ship so well that it was purity itself. Then he publicly named it and dedicated it to the goddess. The gleaming sail of this auspicious barque bore golden letters woven into its texture; these signified the inaugural prayer for fortunate sailing in the new year's commerce. A rounded pine rose as its mast, lofty in its radiance and with a finely resplendent top. The stern had a curving beak and shone with a covering of gold leaf. In short the whole ship was aglow with the polish of smooth citrus-wood. Thereupon all the people, both the devotees and the unattached alike, vied in loading the ship with baskets heaped with spices and similar offerings and they poured on the waves libations of meal mixed with milk, until the ship, laden full with generous gifts and

serenoque flatu pelago redderetur. quae postquam cursus spatio pros-
pectum sui nobis incertat, sacrorum geruli sumtis rursum, quae quisque
detulerant, alacres ad fanum reditum capessunt simili structu pompae
10 decori.

17 At cum ad ipsum iam templum pervenimus, sacerdos maximus
quique divinas effigies progerebant et qui venerandis penetralibus
pridem fuerant initiati, intra cubiculum deae recepti disponunt rite
simulacra spirantia. tunc ex his unus, quem cuncti grammatea dicebant,
15 pro foribus assistens coetu pastophorum—quod sacrosancti collegii
nomen est—velut in contionem vocato indidem de sublimi suggestu de
libro de litteris fausta vota praefatus principi magno senatuique et
equiti totoque Romano populo, nauticis navibus quaeque sub imperio
mundi nostratis reguntur, renuntiat sermone rituque Graeciensi πλοια-
280 φέσια. quam vocem feliciter cunctis evenire signavit populi clamor
insecutus. exin gaudio delibuti populares thallos verbenas corollas ferentes exosculatis vestigiis deae, quae gradibus haerebat argento formata,
ad suos discedunt lares. nec tamen me sinebat animus ungue latius
5 indidem digredi, sed intentus in deae specimen pristinos casus meos
recordabar.

18 Nec tamen Fama volucris pigra pinnarum tarditate cessaverat,
sed protinus in patria deae providentis adorabile beneficium meamque
ipsius fortunam memorabilem narraverat passim. confestim denique
10 familiares ac vernulae quique mihi proximo nexu sanguinis cohaerebant,
luctu deposito, quem de meae mortis falso nuntio susceperant,
repentino laetati gaudio varie quisque munerabundi ad meum festinant
ilico diurnum reducemque ab inferis conspectum. quorum desperata
ipse etiam facie recreatus oblationes honestas aequi bonique facio,
15 quippe cum mihi familiares, quo ad cultum sumptumque largiter succe-
deret, deferre prospicue curassent.

---

9 strictu FΦ B3^1 D structu B3^2 O ritu *al.*   14 grammatea F^1 grammata F^2 Φ
16-17 de libro *dub. del. Helm coll. p. 278, 16* de litteris *dub. del. Rob.*   18 navibus
quaeque *def. Giarr. coll. p. 161, 6* navibusque quae *Oud.*   19 f. Ιταασιαεφεσια F Φ
A B1 ita πλοιαφέσια *Mommsen* τὰ πλ. *vdVl.* πλ. *Haupt* τὰ οια (vel ιαω) 'Εφέσια *Sudhaus*
quam vocem F^1 Φ A B1 U S R qua voce F^2 *al.*
280   1 signavit F significavit *v*   5 intentus <in> *Wower* intuitus *Scaliger* intentus <in
praesentis> *Rob.*   specimen *del. Brakman*   15 quoad F A coad (*in mg.* quod
ad) Φ *dist. v*

votive tokens of good omen, was freed from its anchor cables and launched to sea with a favourable breeze that blew especially for it. When by
reason of its movement it had faded from our sight, the bearers of the
images took up again their respective loads and with a will made their
way back to the temple, observing the same dignified order of procession.

17 But when we had arrived at the temple itself, the chief priest and
the bearers of the divine images together with those who had already been
initiated into the mysteries of the awful sanctuary, were received into
the chamber of the goddess and there set down in order the breathing
effigies. Then one of them, whom they called the Lector, stood near the
entrance and after summoning a gathering of the *pastophori*—that is the
name of a sacred college—as though to a public meeting, in the same
place he pronounced from a high pedestal, using the writings in a book,
prayers for the prosperity of our great emperor, the senate, the knights
and the whole Roman people, as well as of sailors and ships and the
entire domain of our rule. Then he proclaimed the *Launching of the Ships*
in Greek and after the Greek ritual. That this speech brought pleasure to
to everyone was clear from the subsequent applause of the people.
Thereupon, elated with joy, members of the populace presented boughs,
greenery and garlands, kissing the while the feet of the goddess, her
silver-wrought statue being on the temple steps. After this they departed
to their homes. As for me, however, my mind did not allow me to budge
an inch from the spot; I was wrapt in my gaze on the image of the goddess
and I began to ponder my previous misfortunes.

18 Swift Rumour, however, had not tarried with inert slowness of
wing, but forthwith she had related everywhere in my country the glorious
favour of the goddess and my own notable good fortune. Then my
relatives and domestic servants, and those who were nearest of my kith
and kin, abandoning the grief which had seized them after the false
report of my death, were thrilled with sudden joy and hurried instantly
with various presents to see me there as one who had returned from the
dead to the light of day. I was refreshed also myself to see faces I had
given up hope of seeing again and I accepted their generous gifts with
glad gratitude, since my relatives had thoughtfully catered for my well-
being in providing amply for my upkeep and expenses.

19 Adfatis itaque ex officio singulis narratisque meis propere et
pristinis aerumnis et praesentibus gaudiis me rursum ad deae gratissi-
mum mihi refero conspectum aedibusque conductis intra conseptum
281 templi larem temporarium mihi constituo, deae ministeriis adhuc privatis
adpositus contuberniisque sacerdotum individuus et numinis magni
cultor inseparabilis. nec fuit nox una vel quies aliqua visu deae monituque ieiuna, sed crebris imperiis sacris suis me, iam dudum destinatum,
5 nunc saltem censebat initiari. at ego quanquam cupienti voluntate praeditus tamen religiosa formidine retardabar, quod enim sedulo percontaveram difficile religionis obsequium et castimoniorum abstinentiam
satis arduam cautoque circumspectu vitam, quae multis casibus subiacet,
esse muniendam. haec identidem mecum reputans nescio quo modo,
10 quamquam festinans, differebam.

20 Nocte quadam plenum gremium suum visus est mihi summus
sacerdos offerre ac requirenti, quid utique istud, respondisse partes illas
de Thessalia mihi missas, servum etiam meum indidem supervenisse
nomine Candidum. hanc experrectus imaginem diu diuque apud cogi-
15 tationes meas revolvebam, quid rei portenderet, praesertim cum nullum
unquam habuisse me servum isto nomine nuncupatum certus essem.
utut tamen sese praesagium somni porrigeret, lucrum certum modis
omnibus significari partium oblatione credebam. sic anxius et in proventum prosperiorem attonitus templi matutinas apertiones opperiebar.
20 ac dum, velis candentibus reductis in diversum, deae venerabilem conspectum adprecamur et, per dispositas aras circumiens sacerdos, rem
divinam procurans supplicamentis sollemnibus, deae de penetrali fontem
282 petitum spondeo libat : rebus iam rite consummatis inchoatae lucis
salutationibus religiosi primam nuntiantes horam perstrepunt. et ecce
superveniunt Hypata quos ibi reliqueram famulos. cum me Fotis malis
incapistrasset erroribus, cognitis scilicet fabulis meis, nec non et equum

---

17 adfatis F¹ affatis F²   pro F Φ *om.* pro et *al. om.* pro B2 B3 pro <pere> *Kronenb.*
pro <rsus> *Giarr.*
281   4 ejuna F ei*una Φ ei una *al. em.* O² R vaciva *Brant.*   6 retabar F¹ Φ D
corr. F² renitebar A B1 U E S R enitebar B2 vetabar B3 retrahebar O   13 servus
F¹ Φ A servum F² *v*   meus F¹ Φ A meum F² *v*   17 ut F, *em. Pric.*   18 patrium F, *em. v*   22 procurans *ut ex F se ipsum corrigente restit. Hild.* procurat Φ
A B1 B2 U   deae F, *em. v*   fonte *codd, em. Lipsius*
282   2 ece F, *em.* Φ   3 Hypata *Bursian* de patria *codd.*   fotidis F¹ Φ A B1 U, *em.*
F² *v* Fotidis <malitia> *Brakman*   4 famulis *codd., em. vdVl.*

19 Thus when I had addressed each one with the respect due to him and quickly told them of my former troubles and present joys, I betook myself again to the delectable presence of the goddess, and hiring a dwelling within the precinct of the temple I set up house for myself for the time being. Thus I attached myself to the service of the goddess in a manner so far purely personal, taking intimate part in the comradeship of the priests and worshipping the great deity without interruption. Nor did I spend a single night or indulge in any sleep without being blessed by the vision and counsel of the goddess; but in frequent sacred injunctions she opined that now, after being long since destined for the mysteries, I should at length be initiated. For my part, however, while I ardently desired this end, I was restrained by religious fear. For I had taken care to ascertain how arduous was the service of the faith, how extremely hard were the rules of chastity and abstinence, and how needful it was to fortify cautiously and carefully a life exposed to many blows of chance. Revolving such thoughts repeatedly in my mind, for some reason, in spite of my ardour, I kept delaying the matter.

20 One night the chief priest appeared to me in a visitation, showing his lap full of gifts. When I asked what then they meant, he replied that they had been sent from Thessaly to be mine, and that from there also had arrived my slave, called Candidus. When I awoke I pondered over and over in my mind what this vision might augur, especially as I was sure that I had never owned a slave of that name. But whatever the omen of the dream might come to, I believed that the presentation of the gifts portended in every way a definite gain. Being thus disturbed and overwhelmed by the notion of a happier outcome, I awaited the opening ceremonies of the temple at dawn. Then, after the shining white curtains had been drawn, we prayed to the adored image of the goddess, and the priest went around the altars set here and there, carrying out the divine service with exalted entreaties. Drawing water from within the sanctuary of the goddess, he poured a libation from a sacred pitcher. Then, when the rites had been duly performed, the faithful devotees greeted the light of dawn and with raised voices announced the first hour of the day. Who should then appear but the servants I had left behind in Hypata when Photis had entangled me with unhappy aberrations. They had naturally heard of my adventures and they even produced that horse of mine who had been sold to different people, but whom they had recovered

5 quoque illum meum reducentes, quem diverse distractum notae dorsualis
agnitione recuperaverant. quare sollertiam somni tum mirabar vel
maxime, quod praeter congruentiam lucrosae pollicitationis argumento
servi Candidi equum mihi reddidisset colore candidum.

21 Quo facto idem sollicitius sedulum colendi frequentabam mini-
10 sterium, spe futura beneficiis praesentibus pignerata. nec minus in dies
mihi magis magisque accipiendorum sacrorum cupido gliscebat sum-
misque precibus primarium sacerdotem saepissime conveneram petens,
ut me noctis sacratae tandem arcanis initiaret. at ille, vir alioquin
gravis et sobriae religionis observatione famosus, clementer ac comiter
15 et ut solent parentes inmaturis liberorum desideriis modificari, meam
differens instantiam, spei melioris solaciis alioquin anxium mihi permul-
cebat animum : nam et diem, quo quisque possit initiari, deae nutu de-
monstrari et sacerdotem, qui sacra debeat ministrare, eiusdem providentia deligi, sumptus etiam caerimoniis necessarios simili praecepto
20 destinari. quae cuncta nos quoque observabili patientia sustinere
censebat, quippe cum aviditate contumaciaque summe cavere et utram-
que culpam vitare ac neque vocatus morari nec non iussus festinare
283 deberem; nec tamen esse quemquam de suo numero tam perditae men-
tis vel immo destinatae mortis, qui, non sibi quoque seorsum iubente
domina, temerarium atque sacrilegum audeat ministerium subire noxamque
letalem contrahere; nam et inferum claustra et salutis tutelam in deae
5 manu posita ipsamque traditionem ad instar voluntariae mortis et precariae salutis celebrari, quippe cum transactis vitae temporibus iam in
ipso finitae lucis limine constitutos, quis tamen tuto possint magna
religionis committi silentia, numen deae soleat eligere et sua providentia
quodam modo renatos ad novae reponere rursus salutis curricula;
10 ergo igitur me quoque oportere caeleste sustinere praeceptum, quanquam
praecipua evidentique magni numinis dignatione iam dudum felici ministerio nuncupatum destinatumque; nec secus quam cultores ceteri cibis

9 pridem *Kroll*   sollicitus *codd., em. Pric.*   11 glissebat F, *em.* Φ   13 archanis F, *em.* Φ   21 aviditati contumaciaeque (*sed prius* aviditate F) F Φ *al.* <ab>
aviditate contumaciaque *vel* aviditatem contumaciamque *Oud.*
283   7 limine B2 S lumine *al.*   8 elicere *codd., em. Beroald.*   11 praecipua (*dein*
perspicua F)F B2 B3 D O perspicua *al.*   felicis F Φ A B1 U D E¹ R, *em.* B2 B3
O E²

by recognizing the mark on its back. This is why I then especially ad-
mired the perspicacity of the vision, because besides the accord with
reality revealed in its promise of gain, it had implied, in the reference to
a slave called Candidus (white), the return to me of a horse of white
colour.

21 When this was over I still more eagerly pursued the same assiduous service of the cult, in the hope that present blessings warranted
others to come. Nor did my desire to be admitted to the mysteries fail
to grow daily more and more ardent, and with the most urgent entreaties
had I very often confronted the high priest, begging that at last he should
initiate me into the secret rites of the holy night. But he, who was a severe
character and celebrated also for his strict interpretation of the faith,
put off my insistence kindly and courteously rather like parents restrain-
ing the precocious desires of their children; and he soothed the agitation
of my mind with the comforting hope of better things. He explained that
not only was the day of one's initiation indicated by the will of the
goddess, but that the priest who performed the rites was also chosen by
her foresight, while the sum needed for the ceremonies was likewise
designated in a similar instruction. He advised me to bear all these
ordinances with reverent endurance, since it was my duty to beware especially of overeagerness and boldness and to avoid both these faults,
neither delaying when called nor hastening when unbidden. Nor was
there anyone, he said, of his own number so abandoned in mind or indeed
so given over to death as to undergo a hazardous and sacrilegious discipline, thus incurring a sin worthy of death, unless the sovereign mistress
had expressly commanded him. For the gates of hell and the guarantee
of life were alike in the power of the goddess, and the very rite of dedication itself was performed in the manner of a voluntary death and of a
life obtained by grace. Indeed the goddess was accustomed to elect
people who stood near the close of their life-span, on the very threshold
of the end of light, but who could be safely entrusted, nevertheless, with
the mighty mysteries of the faith. By her providence she caused them in
some way to be born again and placed them once more on the course of
a new life. Therefore it was my duty also to accept the command of
heaven although I had already been appointed and destined for the blessed
service by the special and manifest favour of the great deity. In the meantime, like the other worshippers, I should abstain from unhallowed and

profanis ac nefariis iam nunc temperarem, quo rectius ad arcana puris-
simae religionis secreta pervaderem.

15   **22** Dixerat sacerdos, nec inpatientia corrumpebatur obsequium meum,
sed intentus miti quiete et probabili taciturnitate sedulum aliquot dies
obibam culturae sacrorum ministerium. nec me fefellit vel longi temporis
prolatione cruciavit deae potentis benignitas salutaris, sed noctis obscurae
non obscuris imperiis evidenter monuit advenisse diem mihi semper opta-
20 bilem, quo me maxumi voti compotiret, quantoque sumptu deberem
procurare supplicamentis, ipsumque Mithram illum suum sacerdotem
praecipuum divino quodam stellarum consortio, ut aiebat, mihi coniunc-
tum sacrorum ministrum decernit.

284 Quis et ceteris benivolis praeceptis summatis deae recreatus animi
necdum satis luce lucida, discussa quiete, protinus ad receptaculum
sacerdotis contendo atque eum cubiculo suo commodum prodeuntem
continatus saluto. solito constantius destinaveram iam velut debitum
5 sacris obsequium flagitare. at ille statim ut me conspexit, prior : 'o',
inquit, 'Luci, te felicem, te beatum, quem propitia voluntate numen
augustum tantopere dignatur'; et 'quid', inquit, 'iam nunc stas otiosus
teque ipsum demoraris? adest tibi dies votis adsiduis exoptatus, quo deae
multinominis divinis imperiis per istas meas manus piissimis sacrorum
10 arcanis insinueris' et iniecta dextera senex comissimus ducit me protinus
ad ipsas fores aedis amplissimae rituque sollemni apertionis celebrato
ministerio ac matutino peracto sacrificio de opertis adyti profert quosdam
libros litteris ignorabilibus praenotatos, partim figuris cuiusce modi
animalium concepti sermonis compendiosa verba suggerentes, partim
15 nodosis et in modum rotae tortuosis capreolatimque condensis apicibus a
curiositate profanorum lectione munita. indidem mihi praedicat, quae
forent ad usum teletae necessario praeparanda. **23** ea protinus naviter
et aliquanto liberalius partim ipse, partim per meos socios coemenda
procuro. iamque tempore, ut aiebat sacerdos, id postulante stipatum me

13 temperare *codd., em. Helm*   archana F, *em. v*   16 intentis F¹ intentas *dein*
intentus F² intentus Φ B2 B3 D O E² intentis A B1 U E¹ S R   quod F Φ B3 O
quot A *al. em. vdVl.* quinque? Eyssenh.   20 competeret (*in mg.* comperiret F) F Φ
compotiret *Lipsius*
284   5 sacris <imperiis> *vdVl.*   6 inquid F, *em.* Φ   7 iam *codd.* etiam *Kroll*
10 archanis F, *em. v*   12 aditi F, *em. v*   13 cuiuscemo F, *em.* Φ   16 curiosa
Elmenh.   17 gnaviter Φ A U

unlawful foods, so that I might the better make my way to the hidden mysteries of the purest faith.

22   Thus spoke the priest, nor was my obedience spoilt by impatience, but for some days wrapt in gentle calm and exemplary silence I followed the zealous service of the holy cult. The saving grace of the powerful goddess did not disappoint me, nor torment me with a long delay in time, but through her radiant commands in the dark night she clearly informed me that the day of my constant desire had come, when she would grant me the realization of my greatest prayer. She also divulged how much expense I should incur in preparing for the supplications, and she appointed that same Mithras himself, the high priest, to be in charge of the rites since he was linked to me, so she said, by a certain divine assotion of constellations.

Refreshed in mind by these and other kind admonitions of the supreme goddess, before day had fully dawned, I interrupted my rest and went straight to the priest's lodging, where I joined and greeted him just as he was coming out of his dormitory. I was determined to demand more earnestly than usual, as something due to me, my initiation into the sacred rites. But he, as soon as he saw me, anticipated me, saying, 'O Lucius, what a happy blessed man you are, to have been so markedly favoured by the august deity's beneficent grace.' 'Why', he went on, 'do you now stand idle and delay your own progress? The day is at hand for which you have longed with constant prayers, the day when you shall enter, in accordance with the divine behests of the goddess of many names and through these hands of mine, into the most sacred mysteries of the holy rites.' Then the very kindly old man, putting his right hand in mine, took me straight to the very doors of the spacious shrine. There, after the service of the opening of the temple had been celebrated with exalted ceremony and the morning sacrifice performed, he brought out from the hidden quarters of the shrine certain books in which the writing was in undecipherable letters. Some of them conveyed, through forms of all kinds of animals, abridged expressions of traditional sayings; others barred the possibility of being read from the curiosity of the profane, in that their extremities were knotted and curved like wheels or closely intertwined like vine-tendrils. From these writings he indicated to me the preparations necessary for the rite of initiation.

23.   With a will I at once arranged for these things to be bought on a quite liberal scale, acting partly myself and partly through my friends.

20 religiosa cohorte deducit ad proximas balneas et prius sueto lavacro tradi-
tum, praefatus deum veniam, purissime circumrorans abluit rursumque ad
templum reductum, iam duabus diei partibus transactis, ante ipsa deae
vestigia constituit secretoque mandatis quibusdam, quae voce meliora
sunt, illud plane cunctis arbitris praecipit, decem continuis illis diebus
25 cibariam voluptatem cohercerem neque ullum animal essem et essem
285 invinius. quis venerabili continentia rite servatis, iam dies aderat divino
destinatus vadimonio, et sol curvatus intrahebat vesperam. tum ecce
confluunt undique turbae sacratorum ritu vetusto variis quisque me muneribus honorantes. tunc semotis procul profanis omnibus linteo rudique me
5 contectum amicimine arrepta manu sacerdos deducit ad ipsius sacrarii
penetralia.
   Quaeras forsitan satis anxie, studiose lector, quid deinde dictum,
quid factum; dicerem, si dicere liceret, cognosceres, si liceret audire.
sed parem noxam contraherent et aures et linguae illae temerariae curio-
10 sitatis. nec te tamen desiderio forsitan religioso suspensum angore diu-
tino cruciabo. igitur audi, sed crede, quae vera sunt. accessi confinium
mortis et calcato Proserpinae limine per omnia vectus elementa remeavi,
nocte media vidi solem candido coruscantem lumine, deos inferos
et deos superos accessi coram et adoravi de proxumo. ecce tibi rettuli,
15 quae, quamvis audita, ignores tamen necesse est.
   Ergo quod solum potest sine piaculo ad profanorum intellegentias
enuntiari, referam. **24** mane factum est, et perfectis sollemnibus
processi duodecim sacratus stolis, habitu quidem religioso satis, sed
effari de eo nullo vinculo prohibeor, quippe quod tunc temporis videre
20 praesentes plurimi. namque in ipso aedis sacrae meditullio ante deae simulacrum constitutum tribunal ligneum iussus superstiti byssina quidem, sed
floride depicta veste conspicuus. et umeris dependebat pone tergum
talorum tenus pretiosa chlamida. quaqua tamen viseres, colore vario
circumnotatis insignibar animalibus; hinc dracones Indici, inde grypes

---

25 cibarias F¹ Φ cibariam F² A B1 B2 B3 U   25 f. invinius essem *codd. trp. Médan*
285   1 adherat (*postea aliquid eras.*) F, *em.* Φ   2 distinatus F, *em.* v   intrabat (*dein*
intrahebat F)F D trahebat Φ introibat B2 intrahebat *al.*   3 sacrorum *codd., em.*
Brant. cf. p. 288, 6 sacrorum ritu *coniung. Oud.*   7 curiose Φ   9 contrahente
(e *aut* -em *aut* -es *in ras.* F)F Φ A contrahentem B1 *em.* v   lingua, <ista impiae
loquacitatis> *vdVl.*   24 f. gripes yperborei *codd., em.* R

Since the occasion, as the priest said, now demanded it, he led me with an escort of the faithful to the baths at hand and first submitted me to the customary ablution. Then he prayed for the forgiveness of the gods and besprinkling me cleansed me most purely. When he had taken me back again to the temple, two thirds of the day having now passed, he set me before the feet of the goddess herself and gave me certain secret instructions too holy to be uttered. One command, however, he announced clearly for all present to hear, that for the ten following days I should curb my desire for food, abstaining from all animal flesh and from wine. After I had kept these rules with reverent restrain, now came the destined day of the divine pledge. The veering sun was bringing on the evening, when lo! from all sides surged out crowds of devotees paying tribute to me after the ancient rite with their several different gifts. Next, when all the uninitiated had been far removed, I was dressed in a hitherto unworn linen garment and the priest, taking my hand, led me to the very heart of the holy shrine.

You would perchance enquire quite eagerly, attentive reader, what was then said and done. I would tell you, if it were lawful; you would get to know all, were it lawful for you to hear. But both ear and tongue would incur equal guilt through such daring curiosity. Yet you are perchance racked by religious longing, so I shall not torture you with prolonged anguish. Listen then, but believe, for my account is true. I approached the boundary of death and treading on Proserpine's threshold, I was carried through all the elements, after which I returned. At dead of night I saw the sun flashing with bright effulgence. I approached close to the gods above and the gods below and worshipped them face to face. Behold, I have related things about which you must remain in ignorance, though you have heard them.

Therefore I shall recount only what can be communicated without guilt to the understanding of the uninitiated.

24 By morning all was over and the rites being completed I went forth after receiving the initiate's twelve robes, a mode that was indeed most exalted, but no restraint prevented my speaking of it since from that moment many bystanders saw me. For at the priest's behest I ascended a wooden dais set in the very heart of the sanctuary before the statue of the goddess, and I attracted attention by reason of my tunic; it was only of linen, but bore sumptuous decorations. Further, from my shoulders, behind my back down to my heels, there hung a precious cloak.

286 Hyperborei, quos in speciem pinnatae alitis generat mundus alter.
hanc Olympiacam stolam sacrati nuncupant. at manu dextera gerebam
flammis adultam facem et caput decore corona cinxerat palmae
candidae foliis in modum radiorum prosistentibus. sic ad instar Solis
5 exornato me et in vicem simulacri constituto, repente velis reductis, in
aspectum populus errabat. exhinc festissimum celebravi natalem sacrorum, et suaves epulae et faceta convivia. dies etiam tertius pari caeri-
moniarum ritu celebratus et ientaculum religiosum et teletae legitima
consummatio. paucis dehinc ibidem commoratus diebus inexplicabili
10 voluptate simulacri divini perfruebar, inremunerabili quippe beneficio
pigneratus. sed tandem deae monitu, licet non plene, tamen pro meo
modulo supplicue gratis persolutis, tardam satis domuitionem com-
paro, vix equidem abruptis ardentissimi desiderii retinaculis. provolutus
denique ante conspectum deae et facie mea diu detersis vestigiis eius,
15 lacrimis obortis, singultu crebro sermonem interficiens et verba devorans
aio :
    25 'Tu quidem, sancta et humani generis sospitatrix perpetua,
semper fovendis mortalibus munifica, dulcem matris adfectionem miserorum casibus tribuis. nec dies nec quies ulla ac ne momentum quidem
20 tenue tuis transcurrit beneficiis otiosum, quin mari terraque protegas homines et depulsis vitae procellis salutarem porrigas dexteram, qua fatorum
etiam inextricabiliter contorta retractas licia et Fortunae tempestates
mitigas et stellarum noxios meatus cohibes. te superi colunt, observant
inferi, tu rotas orbem, luminas solem, regis mundum, calcas Tartarum.
25 tibi respondent sidera, redeunt tempora, gaudent numina, serviunt
287 elementa. tuo nutu spirant flamina, nutriunt nubila, germinant semina,
crescunt germina. tuam maiestatem perhorrescunt aves caelo meantes,
ferae montibus errantes, serpentes solo labentes, beluae ponto natantes.

---

286   1 generati nudus Φ¹ g. mundus Φ² muldus B3 D alacer B2 alter *om.* E S   2 olimpiacam F Φ D I E² olympiacam R olim pictam A B1 U E¹ S olim piacam B2 olim pia-
cham B3 Osiriacam *Kaibel, Hermes 35, 202f. prob. Giarr.* Leonticam *Reinesius cf. Porphyr. De antro nymph. 15 (de Mithrae mysteriis)*   ad F Φ, *em. v*   manum dexteram
Φ S   5 exornatu F¹ E¹ exornato F² B2 B3 D O E² exornatum Φ A B1 U R ador-
natum S exornato <me> *Schickerad.*   6 sacrum *Rohde prob. Hopfner*   12 gratis
F¹ Φ gratiis F².   15 interficiens *codd. def. Loefstedt* intercipiens *Cornelissen*
17 <et deum> sancta *dub. Rob.*   25 resplendent *Rohde*
287   1 nutriuntur *Oud.* ingruunt *vel* coguntur *Cast.*   3 latentes *codd., em. Hild.*
veluae *dein* beluae F

Wherever you looked, I was adorned by beasts embroidered round about my garments in varied colours. Here were Indian dragons, there were griffons from the far north, animals created in the form of a winged bird by a world other than ours. The initiates call this the Olympian robe. But in my right hand I carried a torch with rearing flames and my head was garlanded gracefully by a crown of gleaming palm whose leaves stood out like rays. When I had thus been adorned like the sun and set up in the manner of a divine statue, suddenly the curtains were drawn and the people crowded to behold me. Then I celebrated the most happy birthday of my initiation, and there were welcome feasts and merry banquets.

The third day was celebrated with an equal show of rites; there was a sacred meal and my initiation was duly consummated. Having tarried there for a few days longer, I enjoyed the ineffable pleasure of the image of the goddess, to whom I was now pledged by a favour that could not be repaid.

But at length, instructed by the goddess, when I had rendered humble thanks, admittedly not in full, but according to my lowly ability, I prepared my journey home, though tardily in all conscience, for the bonds of my fervent longing had scarcely yet been broken. I laid myself down at last in obeisance before the goddess and for a long time wiped her feet with my face. Then with welling tears, breaking my speech with frequent sobs and swallowing my words, I addressed her thus :

25 'Thou in truth art the holy and eternal saviour of the human race, ever beneficent in helping mortal men, and thou bringest the sweet love of a mother to the trials of the unfortunate. No day nor any restful night, nor even the slightest moment passes by untouched by thy blessings, but ever on sea and land thou art guarding men, and when thou hast stilled the storms of life thou dost stretch out thy saving hand, with which thou unravelest even those threads of fate which are inextricably woven together; thou dost pacify the gales of Fortune and keep in check the baleful movements of the stars. Thee do the gods above honour, and thou art worshipped by those below; thou dost revolve the sphere of heaven, and illumine the sun, thou dost guide the earth, and trample Hell under thy feet. For thee the constellations move, for thee the seasons return; the divine beings rejoice for thee, and the elements are thy slaves. By thy command breezes blow and rain-clouds nourish, seeds sprout

at ego referendis laudibus tuis exilis ingenio et adhibendis sacrificiis
5 tenuis patrimonio; nec mihi vocis ubertas ad dicenda, quae de tua maiestate sentio, sufficit nec ora mille linguaeque totidem vel indefessi sermonis aeterna series. ergo quod solum potest religiosus quidem, sed
pauper alioquin, efficere curabo : divinos tuos vultus numenque sanctis-
simum intra pectoris mei secreta conditum perpetuo custodiens imagina-
10 bor.'
    Ad istum modum deprecato summo numine complexus Mithram sacer-
dotem et meum iam parentem colloque eius multis osculis inhaerens
veniam postulabam, quod eum condigne tantis beneficiis munerari
nequirem. **26** diu denique gratiarum gerendarum sermone prolixo
15 commoratus, tandem digredior et recta patrium larem revisurus meum
post aliquam multum temporis contendo paucisque post diebus deae
potentis instinctu raptim constrictis sarcinulis, nave conscensa, Romam
versus profectionem dirigo tutusque prosperitate ventorum ferentium
Augusti portum celerrime appello ac dehinc carpento pervolavi vesperaque,
20 quam dies insequebatur Iduum Decembrium, sacrosanctam istam civi-
tatem accedo. nec ullum tam praecipuum mihi exinde studium fuit
quam cotidie supplicare summo numini reginae Isidis, quae de templi
situ sumpto nomine Campensis summa cum veneratione propitiatur.
eram cultor denique adsiduus, fani quidem advena, religionis autem
25 indigena.
288   Ecce transcurso signifero circulo Sol magnus annum compleverat,
et quietem meam rursus interpellat numinis benefici cura pervigilis et rursus
teletae, rursus sacrorum commonet. mirabar, quid rei temptaret, quid
pronuntiaret futurum; quidni, plenissime iam dudum videbar initiatus.
5   **27** ac dum religiosum scrupulum partim apud meum sensum disputo,
partim sacratorum consiliis examino, novum mirumque plane comperior : deae quidem me tantum sacris inbutum, at magni dei deumque

6 *hora* dein *ora* F   12 colloque *om. S*   13 deum F Φ cum B2 E *coniec. Beroald.*
deam *Rohde*   15 patriam *vdVl.*   16 teporis F, *em.* Φ   18 iutusque *Wasse*
adiutusque *Pric.*   19 hausi R U hauxi S Augusti *al.*   appello *suppl. Helm*
<pervenio> Rohde ac F Φ B2 B3 U D O E S ad dehinc A B1 ac dehinc *al.* nactus
Oud. nactus Latium *Leo*   22 regina ei sidis F regina eisidis Φ regina ysidis *al.*
reginae Isidis R   23 compensis *codd., em. edd.*
288   1 magnum *Beroald. coll. Verg. Aen. 3. 284*   2 numini F¹ Φ A numinis F² *v*
muneri B1   3 temptarem *dein* temptaret F temptaret Φ *v*   4 quidni? <qui>
Rob.   7 at *in mg.* Φ²E² ac B2 ad F *al.*

and buds grow. Awe of thy majesty imbues the birds that move in the
sky, the wild beasts that roam the mountains, the serpents that glide
in the earth, and the monsters that swim in the sea. But I am bereft of
talent in singing thy praises, and have scarce means to offer thee fit
sacrifices. Nor have I the rich power of speech to express what I feel
about thy majesty; indeed a thousand mouths and tongues are not
enough for the task, nor an everlasting sequence of tireless talk. Therefore I shall try to do the only thing possible for one who is devoted but
indigent; I shall keep for ever, stored in my inmost heart, the memory
of thy divine countenance and most holy godhead.'

When I had prayed thus humbly to the supreme deity, I embraced
Mithras the priest, who was now as my father, and clinging to his neck
with many kisses I begged him to pardon me because I was unable to
recompense him justly for so great favours.

26 At long last, when I had lingered to give thanks in a lengthy
conversation, I parted with him and hastened by the shortest way to
visit the house of my fathers after so long an absence. Then after a few
days, with the guidance of the mighty goddess, I quickly packed my
baggage and boarded a ship which was bound for Rome. The supporting
winds being favourable, I swiftly came ashore safe and sound at the port
of Augustus. From there I sped on in a carriage, and on the following
evening, on the twelfth of December, I approached the holy and inviolate
city. Nor did I desire anything more from that time onwards than to
offer supplication daily to the supreme divinity of Queen Isis, who is
worshipped here with the warmest adoration as Isis Campensis, the name
deriving from the site of her temple. Here then I became a constant worshipper, for though I was a stranger to the temple, I was now at home
in the faith.

And lo! the great sun had now traversed through its zodiacal orb
and had finished a year, when my sleep was again disturbed by the ever-
watchful care of the kindly divinity, who warned me that I needed a further initiation and a further ritual. I wondered what her purpose was and
what she was foretelling; my feeling was natural since I seemed already
fully initiated.

27 While I was, on the one hand, debating the religious question in
my own mind, and, on the other, considering the counsels of my fellow-
initiates, I made a strange and quite wonderful discovery : I had been

summi parentis invicti Osiris necdum sacris inlustratum; quanquam enim
conexa, immo vero unita ratio numinis religionisque esset, tamen teletae
10 discrimen interesse maximum; prohinc me quoque peti magno etiam
deo famulum sentire deberem. nec diu res in ambiguo stetit. nam proxuma
nocte vidi quendam de sacratis linteis iniectum, qui thyrsos et hederas
et tacenda quaedam gerens ad ipsos meos lares collocaret et occupato
sedili meo religionis amplae denuntiaret epulas. is ut agnitionem mihi
15 scilicet certo aliquo sui signo subministraret, sinistri pedis talo paululum
reflexo cunctabundo clementer incedebat vestigio. sublata est ergo post
tam manifestam deum voluntatem ambiguitatis tota caligo et ilico deae
matutinis perfectis salutationibus summo studio percontabar singulos,
ecqui vestigum similis ut somnium. nec fides afuit. nam de pastophoris
20 unum conspexi statim praeter indicium pedis cetero etiam statu atque
habitu examussim nocturnae imagini congruentem, quem Asinium
289 Marcellum vocitari cognovi postea, reformationis meae non alienum
nomen. nec moratus, conveni protinus eum sane nec ipsum futuri sermonis ignarum, quippe iam dudum consimili praecepto sacrorum mini-
strandorum commonefactum. nam sibi visus est quiete proxima, dum
5 magno deo coronas exaptat, ... et de eius ore, quo singulorum
fata dictat, audisse mitti sibi Madaurensem, sed admodum pauperem,
cui statim sua sacra deberet ministrare; nam et illi studiorum gloriam
et ipsi grande compendium sua comparari providentia. **28** ad istum
modum desponsus sacris sumptuum tenuitate contra votum meum retar-
10 dabar. nam et viriculas patrimonii peregrinationis adtriverant impensae
et erogationes urbicae pristinis illis provincialibus antistabant plurimum.
ergo duritia paupertatis intercedente, quod ait vetus proverbium, inter
sacrum ego et saxum positus cruciabar, nec setius tamen identidem

---

9 munit artio F1 Φ A B1 E munita ratio F² D O unita ratio B2 B3 unica artio UR unica
arctio S   19 et qui *codd.*, *em. Beroald.* eccui vestigium simile sit [ut somnium]
Stewech vestigio similis sit somnii *vdVl.*   fide *codd.*, *em. Beroald.*   20 ceteros
codd., *em. v*   21 asinum *codd.*, *em. m. rec. in* Φ *cf. Beroald.*
289   1 non *suppl. Beroald.* <minime> *Rob.*   5 *lac. post* exaptat *stat.* Helm exaptat
et F Φ² exoptat Φ¹ exaptat [et] *vel* exaptaret *Luetj.*   6 facta *codd.*, *em. Beroald.*
madaurensem F A B2 B3 O maudarensem Φ D mandaurensem *al.* mane Doriensem
Goldbacher   9 responsus A B1 U S   11 peregrinationis F¹ -es F²   12 *post*
plurimum *primus dist. vdVl., post* antistabant *edd. priores*   12 aiter F ait Φ A U
ociter B2 B3 O occiter D   13 sacruetosaxum F¹ sacrumetsaxum F² sacru et osaxum
Φ A sacrum et asaxum B1 *em. v* sacrum ego et saxum *Rob.*

initiated only into the mysteries of the goddess, but had not yet been enlightened by the mysteries of the great god and supreme father of the gods, unconquered Osiris. For although the principle of the deity himself and of his faith was associated, and indeed was at one, with that of Isis, yet a very great distinction was made in the rites of initiation; accordingly I ought to feel that the great god too was seeking me for his servant. Nor was the matter long in doubt. For the following night I saw one of the initiates clad in linen who was carrying wands, ivy and certain sacred objects which must be nameless, and he placed them in my own lodging. He took my seat and announced a banquet in the name of the great faith. In order to intimate to me who he was, by means of a sure sign, the ankle of his left foot was bent upwards a little and he walked gently with a halting gait. Every dark shadow of doubt was thus removed after such an obvious show of the will of the gods, and instantly, as soon as the morning salutations to the goddess were completed, I most eagerly questioned individuals, whether any of them had a foot formed like that in my dream. Nor was confirmation far to seek. For I instantly saw one among the *pastophori* who, apart from the revealing shape of his foot, corresponded exactly in build and bearing to the form in my nocturnal vision. I learned afterwards that he was called Asinius Marcellus, a name alluding, it seemed, to my transformation. Without delay I accosted him and found him not without knowledge of what I was to say, since he had been already warned through a similar instruction that he should arrange for my initiation. For on the previous night there had appeared to him, while he was preparing crowns for the great god ... and from his lips, that pronounce the fate of each and all, he had heard that a man from Madauros was being sent to him, one who was quite poor, but one for whom he should at once prepare the god's mysteries; for by the god's providence that man was destined to glory of learning, and he himself to a great reward.

28   While I was thus pledged to the rites of initiation, I was being hindered, much against my desire, by the scarcity of my means. For not only had the expenses of travel diminished the modest sum of my fortune, but the cost of living in Rome was much higher than that I had known in the provinces. So under the hard pressure of poverty I was tormented, standing as I was, in the words of the old proverb, between the devil and the deep sea. None the less I was being repeatedly urged on by the persistence of the deity. For after being incited quite often, not without

numinis premebar instantia. iamque saepicule non sine magna turba-
15 tione stimulatus, postremo iussus, veste ipsa mea quamvis parvula distracta, sufficientem conrasi summulam. et id ipsum praeceptum fuerat
specialiter : 'an tu', inquit, 'si quam rem voluptati struendae moliris,
laciniis tuis nequaquam parceres : nunc tantas caerimonias aditurus
impaenitendae te pauperiei cunctaris committere'?
20   Ergo igitur cunctis adfatim praeparatis, decem rursus diebus inanimis
contentus cibis, insuper etiam deraso capite, principalis dei nocturnis
orgiis inlustratus, plena iam fiducia germanae religionis obsequium divi-
290 num frequentabam. quae res summum peregrinationi meae tribuebat
solacium nec minus etiam victum uberiorem subministrabat, quidni,
spiritu faventis Eventus quaesticulo forensi nutrito per patrocinia sermonis Romani.
5   **29** Et ecce post pauculum tempus inopinatis et usquequaque mirificis
imperiis deum rursus interpellor et cogor tertiam quoque teletam sustinere. nec levi cura sollicitus, sed oppido suspensus animi mecum ipse
cogitationes exercitius agitabam, quorsus nova haec et inaudita se caelestium porrigeret intentio, quid subsicivum, quamvis iteratae iam, traditioni
10 remansisset : 'nimirum perperam vel minus plene consuluerunt in me
sacerdos uterque'; et hercules iam de fide quoque eorum opinari coepta-
bam sequius. quo me cogitationis aestu fluctuantem ad instar insaniae
percitum sic instruxit nocturna divinatione clemens imago :
'Nihil est', inquit, 'quod numerosa serie religionis, quasi quicquam sit
15 prius omissum, terreare. quin adsidua ista numinum dignatione laetus
capesse gaudium et potius exulta ter futurus, quod alii vel semel vix
conceditur, teque de isto numero merito praesume semper beatum.
ceterum futura tibi sacrorum traditio pernecessaria est, si tecum nunc
saltem reputaveris exuvias deae, quas in provincia sumpsisti, in eodem
20 fano depositas perseverare nec te Romae diebus sollemnibns vel

---

17 molireris E² R   20 praeparans F¹ Φ¹ praeparatis F² Φ² A   21 deras capi F
Φ D B3 O de serapis A B1 B2 U E S R deraso capite *aut* capillo *Luetj.* *de Sarapis* *Hild.*
290   6-7 suscitare *codd., em. Helm* susceptare *Wower*   8 agitabam f (*ap. Hild.*) cogitabam *al.*   10 perpera F, *em.* Φ   consuluerunt *codd.* consuluerant *Bluemner*
14 inquid F, *em.* Φ   quisquam F Φ B1 U S *em. al.*   15 terrere F Φ A, *em. v*
laetum *aut* letum *codd.* laetus *Helm*   17 semper *codd.* ter *Leo*   19 exubias
F Φ B3 O, *em. al.*   20 funo F Φ, *em.* A B1 U E S R solo B2 B3 D O

considerable mental stress, and in the end commanded, I sold even my wardrobe, scanty as it was, and managed to scrape together an adequate little sum. This deed was the result of a particular exhortation : 'If you were arranging something for the satisfaction of your pleasure, by no means would you demur to sell your clothes; now that you are about to approach such august rites, do you hesitate to entrust yourself to a poverty you will never regret?'

Therefore I saw that all preparations were properly made. I contented myself for another ten days with meatless food and in addition shaved my head. Then I was illumined with the nocturnal ecstasies of the supreme god, and with abundant confidence now I attended the divine service of this kindred faith. This circumstance contributed the greatest comfort to my sojourn in Rome, and it also provided a more generous livelihood, naturally, since I was borne on by the breeze of favourable fortune and made some small profit in the forum through advocate's speeches in the Latin language.

29 And lo! after a brief space of time I was again disturbed by unexpected and constantly marvellous commands of the gods and compelled to undergo yet a third initiation. I was not a little anxious about it and in a state of keen agitation I asked myself very earnestly where this new and strange plan of the gods was leading. What could remain to be revealed now that two initiations had already been made? Clearly, I thought, the two priests advised me wrongly, or at least incompletely. Indeed I began to cast doubt even on their integrity. As I was thus tossed on the tide of thought, exciting myself almost to madness, a gracious form enlightened me thus in a prophetic message by night :

'There is no reason', it said, 'for you to be frightened by the long series of rituals, as though something had been previously overlooked. Be filled with gladsome joy, rather, because the gods so constantly think you worthy, and indeed rejoice that you will achieve three times a boon that is scarcely granted to others even once. From this number deservedly conclude that you will be happy forever. Further, the approaching revelation of the mysteries is most necessary for you, if you now recall to your mind that the garments of the goddess, which you took upon you in Achaea, were stored in that temple and there remain, so that you will not be able, on festival-days in Rome, either to make supplication in them, or, when the command is given, to be made radiant by that

supplicare iis vel, cum praeceptum fuerit, felici illo amictu illustrari posse.
quod felix itaque ac faustum salutareque tibi sit, animo gaudiali rursum
sacris initiare deis magnis auctoribus.'

30 Hactenus divini somnii suada maiestas, quod usus foret, pro-
25 nuntiavit. nec deinceps postposito vel in supinam procrastinationem
reiecto negotio, statim sacerdoti meo relatis quae videram, inanimae
protinus castimoniae iugum subeo et lege perpetua praescriptis illis
291 decem diebus spontali sobrietate multiplicatis instructum teletae com-
paro largitus ex studio pietatis magis quam mensura rerum collatis
sumptibus. nec hercules laborum me sumptuumque quidquam tamen
paenituit, quidni, liberali deum providentia iam stipendiis forensibus
5 bellule fotum. denique post dies admodum pauculos deus deum magnorum potior et maiorum summus et summorum maximus et maximorum
regnator Osiris non in alienam quampiam personam reformatus, sed
coram suo illo venerando me dignatus adfamine per quietem recipere
visus est : quae nunc, incunctanter gloriosa in foro redderem patro-
10 cinia nec extimescerem malevolorum disseminationes, quas studiorum
meorum laboriosa doctrina ibidem exciebat. ac ne sacris suis gregi cetero
permixtus deservirem, in collegium me pastophorum suorum, immo inter
ipsos decurionum quinquennales adlegit. rursus denique quam raso
capillo collegii vetustissimi et sub illis Syllae temporibus conditi munia,
15 non obumbrato vel obtecto calvitio, sed quoquoversus obvio, gaudens
obibam.

---

21 <in> iis *vdVl.* diis *dub. Rob.*   24 actenus F Φ, *em.* A
291   1 teletae *v* ac letae F ac lege *dein* ac lete Φ   2 largius *Elmenh.* largiter *Brakman*
post largitus *suppl.* omnibus *olim Helm*   mensura rerum *Eyssenh.* mansurarum
F Φ A mensura rebus *v* mensura <rerum mea> rum *vdVl. prob. Rob.*   collatis <sum-
ptibus> *Gr.* <stipibus> collatis *Brakman* mensura rebus collatis <necessariis>
Koziol   5 vellula F Φ A U, *em. v* bellula B1 R   6 maiorum *codd.* potiorum
Vallette   7 in R *om. codd.*   alienum F A B1, *em.* Φ alienam in *Hild.*   8 praeci-
pere *Beroald.*   9 quam *codd., em. Helm* iam *Pric.*   faro F, *em.* Φ A   11 ibidem
exciebat *P. Thomas, Ac. Belg. Bull.* 14, 221 *prob. Helm* ibi deserviebat *codd.*
ibidem serebat *Oud.*   12 pastoforum F Φ A, *em. v*   13 qua raro F Φ U, *em.*
Beroald. quam A R quaqua raso *Oud.*   14 illius *Rohde*   16 *subscriptio deest in* F
Apulei Platonici Floridorum lib. 1 Φ

blessed robe. Accept, then, this further initiation with joyful heart at the behest of the great gods, and may it turn out well for your happiness, prosperity and salvation.

30 Thus did the impressive dignity of the divine vision proclaim what would be necessary. Afterwards I did not delay with the plan nor postpone it lethargically, but at once imparted to my priest what I had seen, and straightway submitted to the rigour of a vegetarian diet; indeed I added, with a voluntary discipline, to the ten days laid down by an immemorial law and liberally procured the equipment needed for the rite, meeting the expenses more in a spirit of devotion than according to the measure of my property.

Yet by heaven I did not regret any of my toil and expenditure; why should I, now that I was rather nicely favoured by my earnings at the bar through the generous providence of the gods? Then, after the lapse of very few days, he that is mightiest of the great gods, the highest of the greatest among them, the loftiest of the highest, and the sovereign of the loftiest, Osiris himself, appeared to me while I slept at night. He had not adopted any other semblance, but deemed me worthy to be welcomed face to face with his august converse.

He told me to carry on, as now, and without hesitation, to win fame and favour in the courts; nor should I fear the slanders of spiteful people, which had been aroused by my assiduous pursuit of learning in Rome. In order to avoid my having to serve his rites as one of a throng of initiates, he admitted me to the college of his *pastophori*, even as one of the quinquennial board of officers. Once more, then, I shaved my head entirely, and without trying to cover or hide my baldness, I showed it to all onlookers, and joyfully carried out the duties of that most ancient college of priests, which was founded in the far-off days of Sulla.

COMMENTARY

CHAPTER 1

p. 266, 11 **primam ... vigiliam** : The night was divided into four watches, each of three hours' duration; cf. Mark 6.48 and Hier. *Ep.* 140.8 (ed. J. Labourt, VIII, 84).

pavore subito : Its cause is not explained. At the end of Book X Lucius, still in the form of an ass, escapes from a Corinthian show in which he was to lie publicly with a convicted murderess, and after running about six miles comes to a quiet spot on the shore near the harbour of Cenchreae.

p. 266, 12 **nimio** : See n. *ad* p. 276, 14.

completum orbem : According to Salem, 'Cult', 277, the allusion is to 'the first full moon before the spring equinox'. Certainly it was the season of spring; cf. *verno vapore* (271, 17) and the whole description of the festive preparations in ch. 7. Salem goes on to urge that the festival, the *Isidis Navigium*, was originally identical with the celebration of 'the entry of Osiris into the moon', which Plut., *De Is. et Os.* 43, 368 C assigns to the first of the month of Phamenoth, the beginning of spring. While there may be a calendrical approximation, the two festivals seem to have little in common otherwise.

p. 266, 13 **emergentem** : Adlington renders 'leaped out', but 'arise', 'break forth', is indicated by usage; the personification suggested by 'leaped out' is not present. Although *Thes. L. L.* 5, 2, 474 quotes *Metam.* 5.29 *ad init.* (where it is said of Venus, *emergit e mari*) and compares 11.3, *pelago medio ... emergit divina facies*, it refers later (474, 6) to frequent occurrences used of the rising of stars.

nanctusque : Apuleius uses the form *nanctus* rather more often than *nactus* : v. *Index Apul.* 273. It is a well authenticated form in the best manuscripts of classical authors : e.g. Cic. *De rep.* 1.10.16 (ed. Ziegler, 1960, p. 12, 2); cf. Forcellini, *Lex.* s.v. *nactus*. Here the meaning is somewhat attenuated : 'aware of' rather than 'having discovered'.

p. 266, 13-14 **silentiosa secreta** : For the pleonasm see Bernhard, *Stil*, 174 f. *Silentiosus* is a neologism.

p. 266, 14 **summatem deam** : The form *summatam* (F *Φ*) is not supported either by general usage or by that of Apuleius; v. *Index Apul.* 431; cf. ch. 10 (274, 6) with n. and 22 (284, 1).

It was only under the influence of the later syncretism that the moon-goddess assumed this dominating position. She is called θεὰ βασίλεια in *Orph. Hymn.* 9.1 (ed. G. Quandt, Berlin, 1955), and these hymns are not earlier than the second century A.D. In the Great Paris Magical Papyrus, which derives from the fourth century. Selenê is addressed as μόνη τύραννε ... τύχη θεῶν καὶ δαιμόνων (*PGM* 4, 2664-5). See further W. H. Roscher, *Nachträge zu meiner Schrift über Selene und Verwandtes* (Gymnas, Wurzen, 1895), 36; A. Dieterich, *Abraxas* (Leipzig, 1891); Schwenn, *PW* s.v. Selene (1923), 1140 f. On the other hand, the belief that the moon, by her waxing and waning, influences processes of growth in nature is both ancient and widespread; v. Roscher, *Lex. Myth.* II, 3150 ff. who quotes Cicero, *De nat. deor.* 2.119, *ut ... luna inluminata graviditates et partus adferat maturitatesque gignendi*; Pease ad loc. refers to Darwin's suggestion that menstrual periods may be vestiges of former tidal influences on our ancestors. In Plut. *De Is. et Os.* 43, 368 C the Egyptians are said to call the moon μητέρα ... τοῦ κόσμου. Nock, *Conversion*, 138 and F. C. Grant, *Hellenistic Religions*, 136 f. together with some commentators assume that Lucius is presented as conscious of addressing Isis, but this is most unlikely. Only after her epiphany in ch. 3 does Isis announce herself to him, and the prayer in ch. 2 contains no allusion to her. See further J. Gwyn Griffiths, *Class. Phil.* 63 (1968), 144 f. In general see Claire Préaux, *La lune dans la pensée grecque* (Brussels, 1973, Ac. Roy. Belgique, Mém. Lettres, S. 2, vol. 61, 4).

p. 266, 15 **providentia** : Later this concept is prominently associated with Isis : see ch. 5 (270, 4 f.); 10 (274, 5 f.); 12 (275, 17); 15 (277, 20).

p. 266, 16-17 **luminis numinisque nutu** : On the combination of rhyme and alliteration see n. *ad* ch. 7 (272, 1), *nudo sudoque*.

p. 266, 17-18 **incrementis ... detrimentis** : Helm disposes of the vulgate reading *decrementis*. *Thes. L.L.* 5, 1, 837 takes the terms as applying to *corpora* and compares Ps. Apul. *Ascl.* 3. There indeed the very same idea is found, which views the sun and the moon as bestowers of the growth and decrease of bodies : *caelum ergo, sensibilis deus, administrator est omnium corporum, quorum augmenta detrimentaque sol et luna sortiti sunt.* (ed. p. Thomas, 1921, p. 38, 20-22) Cf. Festugière ad loc. While *incrementis* and *detrimentis* are antithetical, *consequenter* and *obsequenter* are roughly synonymous. The idea has a parallel also in August. *De civ. Dei*, 5.6 (some species are increased and diminished *lunaribus incrementis atque detrimentis*), as Ryle points out.

p. 266, 19 **tot tantisque cladibus** : The initial disaster is related in the third book where Lucius is changed into an ass because Photis, a Thessalian maid-servant with whom he has a love affair promises to transform him momentarily into a bird, but uses the wrong ointment. It is the inquisitive desire to explore the secrets of magic that leads Lucius astray; he describes himself (2.1) as *nimis cupidus cognoscendi quae rara miraque sunt* and also as *curiosus* about magic art. His sensuality is also rebuked, as in ch. 15 of this book. Yet his affair with Photis is represented as a means to an end — the penetration of the secrets of her mistress. Nock, *Conversion*, 138, is rather misleading when he says that Lucius 'was led by an amour into careless dabbling in magic.' R. Graves, *Apuleius, The Golden Ass*, 12, is still more misleading when he says, 'The fault which involved Lucius in all his miseries was that, though a nobleman, he decided on a frivolous love-affair with a slave-girl.' He then proceeds, however, to describe the real cause. In the form of an ass Lucius suffers at the hands of bandits, and then becomes the property of priests of the Syrian goddess, of a miller, a gardener, and a soldier. His lot is improved by two slaves, a cook, and a baker, who then get hold of him, but their master has a plan of publicly exhibiting Lucius in the act of sexual union with a woman convicted of murder. It is from this misfortune that he flees to Cenchreae.

 p. 266, 19 **salutis** : See n. *ad* ch. 12 (275, 13), *salutemque*.

 p. 266, 21 **discussa ... quiete** : Cf. ch. 22 (284, 2).

 p. 266, 22 **septiesque summerso** : Purification by washing is the preliminary to worship; cf. Dittenberger, *Syll.*[1] 633 (an inscription of the Roman imperial era) : λουσαμένους δὲ κατακέφαλα εἰ[σπορεύ]εσθαι, where the adverb, according to *LSJ*, means 'from head to foot'; cf. also Persius, *Sat.* 2.15 f.; Hor. *Sat.* 2.3.291 f.; Juv. *Sat.* 6. 522 ff. Plut. *De superst.* 3, 166 A remarks on βάπτισον σεαυτὸν εἰς θάλασσαν as a type of superstitious injunction, but it is a striking parallel to the *marino lavacro* of Apuleius.

The magic power of the number seven was evident in Greek religion, especially in the cult of Apollo, quite apart from the special sanction given to it by Pythagoreanism : see Roscher, *Die Sieben- und Neunzahl im Kultus und Mythus der Griechen* (*Abh. Leipzig*, 1904), where it is derived from the seven and nine day phases of the moon and their observation. He points out (p. 16 n. 41) that the seven acts of lustration here mentioned are particularly apposite to this theory since the moon-goddess is being worshipped. The number seven is of course a magic number in several other ancient traditions, including those of Egypt, Israel, and Babylon, the cult of the seven planets being one feature of the Babylonian observance. One may compare the seven kisses (plus a specially luscious one) which Venus promises in *Metam.* 6.8 to him who will reveal the abode of Psyche to her; cf. O. Weinreich, 'Zu Apuleius', *Hermes* 56 (1921), 333 f., where it is suggested that Moschus is being elaborated on. Nilsson, *Gesch. Gr. Rel.* I (Ed. 2, 1955), 561 f., argues that it is only in the cult of Apollo that the number seven is prominent, and that it reflects Babylonian influence, since the seventh day of the month, the *sibutu*, was in Babylon a day of special offerings, just as almost all the festivals of Apollo are on that day. He admits that the number is sacred to many peoples, but claims that this indicates a detailed correspondence. For the use of the number in lustrations cf. 2 Kings 5.10, where Naaman is to 'wash in Jordan seven times'; Pliny, *HN* 31.3.34 : *Epigenes autem aquam, quae septies putrefacta purgata sit, ait amplius non putrescere.* The Greeks regarded flowing water, especially that of the sea, as potent in purification; cf. Eur. *IT* 1193 ('The sea washes away all the evils of man') and Rohde, *Psyche* (Ed. 10, 1925), II, 405. The Egyptians preferred the water of the Nile.

 p. 267, 1-2 **divinus ille Pythagoras** : There was a strong tradition that Pythagoras derived much of his lore from Egypt; v. Plut. *De Is. et Os.* 10, 354 E (he was instructed by Oenuphis of Heliopolis). In view of the main theme of this book Apuleius may have had such a connection in mind. The Egyptian tradition gave much prominence to seven as a sacred number : v. Kees, *Götter-*

glaube, 158 f. and the many instances cited by Sethe, *Von Zahlen und Zahl-worten bei den alten Ägyptern* (Strassburg, 1916), 33 ff., from which it is clear that to do an action seven times was a frequent injunction in Egyptian magic. On the other hand, a specific indebtedness on the part of Pythagoras and his school is hard to establish in this respect, even if Hopfner and others have been unduly sceptical of the pro-Egyptian attributions. The Pythagoreans may have been influenced on this point by the Delphic cult of Apollo; v. Roscher, *Die Hebdomadenlehren der griechischen Philosophen und Ärzte* (*Abh. Leipzig*, 1906), 24 ff.

The laudative use of *ille* here is classical, and there is no need to assume a weakening of its demonstrative force. G. Wolterstorff, *Glotta* 8 (1916), 97-226 ('Artikelbedeutung von *ille* bei Apuleius') argued otherwise, but see Löfstedt, *Syntactica*, I (Ed. 2, Lund, 1956), 361 and cf. Callebat, *Sermo Cotid.* 276.

p. 267, 2 **lacrimoso vultu** : In order to evoke the pity of the gods tears often accompanied prayer; cf. *Metam.* 6.2 (130, 4-6), *Tunc Psyche ... uberi fletu rigans ... veniam postulabat*; Lucan, *Phars.* 2.30, *Hae lacrimis sparsere deos*; see also G. Appel, *De Romanorum precationibus* (Giessen, 1909), 208; H. Schmidt, *Veteres philosophi quomodo iudicaverint de precibus* (Numburgi ad Salam, 1907), 71 n. 1, who notes that the early Christians were even fonder of tearful prayers. Of course Lucius was in an unhappy state in spite of his new hope at the sight of the goddess. His tears combine the appropriate convention and his real feelings; cf. ch. 3 *ad init.*, *adstructis miseris lamentationibus* and ch. 24, *ad fin.*, *lacrimis obortis* (before a prayer to Isis). It follows that *laetus et alacer*, which the codices read before *deam* in line 2, is out of place here, and Leo rightly removed the phrase; it fits well on p. 266, 21 before *exurgo*, as Helm proposed; cf. p. 73, 25, *spe salutis alacer et laetus* and p. 15, 18, *Emergo laetus atque alacer*. The difficulty was solved in some editions by reading *alacrissimo vultu*, but this would be inconsistent with the subsequent allusion to tears. Oudendorp defended the reading of the codices by suggesting that the joy was inwardly felt, but suppressed outwardly in favour of the conventional tearfulness. This is a possible interpretation, but the Latin as it stands offers no such reconciliation of the opposed attitudes.

p. 267, 2-3 **adprecabar** : The use of the imperfect following the present tenses *exurgo* and *trado* is a sequence often found in the *Metam.* and occurs too in Livy and Tacitus. It implies a desire to impart vividness and variety to the narrative; cf. Callebat, *Sermo Cotid.* 427.

CHAPTER 2

p. 267, 4 **Regina caeli** : A natural title for the moon-goddess in the night sky. For βασίλεια and τύραννος used of Selene see n. *ad* p. 266, 14. In *PGM* 4, 1301 ff. Selene is called θεὰ μεγίστη ἄρχουσα οὐρανοῦ. The allusion to *caeli regem* in Verg. *Georg.* 4. 152 involves Zeus, and he or Iuppiter is of course the supreme sky-god; cf. Sen. *Thy.* 1077, *summe caeli rector*. When

Horace talks of Diana as *lucidum caeli decus* (*Carm. saec.* 2), he is thinking of her as the moon. See further Bruchmann, *Epitheta Deorum*, 205 (βασίλεια and βασίλισσα) and 208 (πότνα and πότνια) s.v. Selene.

As we have already noted, some scholars assume that Lucius is here represented as being conscious of addressing Isis; thus Blümner in *Mél. Nicole* (Geneva, 1905), 38; so too Oudendorp ad loc.; H. J. Boeken, *Adnot.* 20 ff.; G. Appel, *De Romanorum precationibus*, 78; Ed. Norden, *Agnostos Theos* (Leipzig, 1923), 144; Vandebeek, *Isisfiguur*, 89 f. But the prayer opened by *Regina caeli* does not refer specifically to Isis. On the other hand, the prominent lunar connections of Isis make the situation, as it evolves later, quite feasible. Lucius is addressing a deity deemed by him to be a moon-goddess, and he applies several suitable names to her. Only later is his ignorance enlightened; before this he does not reveal that he is even aware of the existence of Isis, the first mention of her being in ch. 5. Wittmann, p. 14, urges that Lucius is at first in complete ignorance as to who the deity is. If so, it is odd that he should name four goddesses with whom Selene was identified (Ceres of Eleusis, Venus of Paphos, Diana of Ephesus, and Proserpina) and proceed to describe their qualities. The element of apparent uncertainty is confined to the particular form which the moon-goddess is now thought to have assumed. Thus, rightly, Berreth and Festugière. In fact, the clauses which suggest uncertainty were a regular feature of prayers; see further *infra* and J. Gwyn Griffiths, *Class. Phil.* 63 (1968), 144 f.

sive tu Ceres : The identification of Selene with Demeter, although not common, is clearly attested in the Roman imperial era. It is ascribed to the Stoics by Servius *ad* Verg. *Georg.* 1.5 (v. app. crit. ed. H. Hagen, Leipzig, 1902, p. 201) : [*Stoici*] *item Lunam, eandem Dianam, eandem Cererem, eandem Proserpinam dicunt.* Apuleius refers to all three equations; cf. Arnobius, 3.34 (Ed. 2, Marchesi, Milan, 1953, p. 191); *Myth. Vat.* 2 prooem. (ed. Bode, Chelles, 1834, p. 74); *Anth. Lat.* 723.9 (Ed. 2, Riese, Leipzig, 1906, p. 208), where the third name in the group *Isis, Luna, Choris, Caelestis, Iuno, Cybebe* is emended to *Ceres* by Buecheler and Haupt. Further, it is likely that Luna and Ceres are identified in Verg. *Georg.* 1.5 ff. : *vos, O clarissima mundi | lumina, labentem caelo quae ducitis annum, | Liber et alma Ceres, vestro si munere tellus | Chaoniam pingui glandem mutavit arista,* although some editors print a stop after *annum.* The Vergilian identification is expressly supported not only by Servius (v. *supra*), but also by Macrobius, *Saturn.* 1.18.23 (ed. Willis, Leipzig, 1963, p. 107) : *hinc et Virgilius sciens Liberum patrem solem esse et Cererem lunam ...* See further Roscher, *Lex. Myth.* s.v. Mondgöttin (1897), 3189 and Schwenn, *PW* s.v. Selene (1923), 1142. According to H. Le Bonniec, *Le Culte de Cérès à Rome* (Paris, 1958), 192, an agrarian association may have characterized Luna, but the Roman tradition does not identify her with Ceres. Apuleius, *Metam.* 6.2 represents a prayer being offered by Psyche to Ceres, but the moon is not mentioned there. On the other hand, in ch. 5 Isis informs Lucius that she is really the moon-goddess who has appeared to him, but that different peoples give her different names; among these, the Eleusinians call her *vetustam* *deam Cererem.* That Ceres or Demeter was responsible for replacing primitive man's diet of acorns with the gentler nourishment of corn is a view expressed by Verg. *Georg.* 1.5 ff., quoted above, and Ovid, *Fasti*, 1.675 f., on which see Sir James Frazer's Commentary, II (London, 1929), 259.

p. 267, 5 **repertu** : A neologism; see n. *ad* ch. 11 (275, 3).

p. 267. 6 **percolis** : The passages cited in the *Index Apul.* show that Apuleius uses this word in the sense either of 'cultivate, pursue' (e.g. *sapientiam*) or of 'honour, venerate' (a god). The present instance probably intends the second meaning, since the first sense is usually metaphorical; but 'inhabit, frequent' (cf. Vallette, 'qui hantes') can scarcely be derived from the sense of literal cultivation of the soil, as *LS* and Georges maintain.

caelestis Venus : The resemblance of the moon to Aphrodite is noted in Plut. *Amat.* 19, 764 D; and in the Great Paris Magical Papyrus (*PGM* 4, 2557 f.) Aphrodite is called φαέθουσα καὶ αὐγάζουσα Σελήνη; cf. Schwenn, *PW* s.v. Selene (1923), 1142. H. Usener, *Rhein. Mus.* 23 (1868), 342 f. argued that lunar qualities emerge when Aphrodite is called 'golden' or when Hecate is called 'the gold-gleaming attendant of Aphrodite'. More apposite is his reference to πασιφάεσσα as an epithet of Aphrodite. Roscher, *Lex. Myth.* I s.v., Aphrodite, 396, rightly connects this and cognate epithets with the moon and he argues too that the goddess's role in the myth of Phaethon, where she entices Phaethon from his parents, Eos and Cephalus, to make him the nocturnal overseer of her temple, points in the same direction. It is the name Urania, however, which places Aphrodite most firmly in the heaven; it is probably a translation of a Phoenician name and indicates the oriental origin of the goddess, giving rise also to the story in Hesiod, *Theog.* 188 ff. that she derived her birth from the genitals of Uranus when they had been hurled into the sea. See Roscher, *Lex. Myth.* s.v. Aphrodite, 396 f. and Nilsson, *Gesch. Gr. Rel.* I, 519 ff. Apuleius may well be thinking especially of the Phoenician Astarte, worshipped in his native metropolis Carthage as Tanit or Virgo Caelestis; she is called 'Queen of Heaven' in Jerem. 7.18 and 44.19 and is equated with Aphrodite Urania by Herodotus (1.105) and Pausanias (1.14.7). See Steuding in Roscher, *Lex. Myth.* s.v. Caelestis (1890), 844; Cumont, *PW* s.v. Caelestis (1899), 1247 ff.; L. P. Paton in Hastings, *ERE* 2 (1909), 117 f. She was the African goddess *par excellence*; cf. Tertullian. *Ad nat.* 2.8, *Caelestem Afrorum.* Wittmann, p. 14 f., asks whether Apuleius as an African may not have her initially in mind when he begins his prayer with *Regina caeli*. It is more likely that he is thinking of her in the name *caelestis Venus*, although in *Metam.* 6.4, as Wittmann points out, it is Hera who is likened to this goddess, for Hera is there said to live in lofty Carthage, where she is worshipped as the maid who came down from heaven on a lion's back.

p. 267, 8-9 **circumfluo Paphi sacrario** : The island home ascribed to Aphrodite by the Greeks was essentially a Phoenician sanctuary, as Herodotus (1.105) already recognized, and as archaeology has borne out; cf. R. E. Smith, *JHS* 9 (1888), 201 (on 'The Temple of Aphrodite') : '... we cannot look upon the building as other than a Phoenician temple.' C. Blinkenberg in *Le Temple de*

Paphos (Copenhagen, 1924) urged a Minoan affinity, but Stanley Casson, *Ancient Cyprus* (London, 1937), 161 ff., shows that neither Minoan nor Greek styles were followed in Cyprus, although he also denies a slavish adoption of Oriental architecture. The conical object associated with the goddess may be Phoenician too in origin; sometimes stars, or a star in a crescent, are shown near the cone on gems and coins. See also Johanna Schmidt, *PW* s.v. Paphos II (1949), 951-64. Sir George Hill, *A History of Cyprus*, I (Cambridge, 1940), 69 ff., is firmly opposed to the theory of Phoenician influence in Paphos, but he hardly comes to grips at all with the view that Aphrodite, as shown by her key epithet Urania, is essentially of Phoenician origin.

p. 267, 9 **seu Phoebi soror** : The moon is called the eye of Artemis (ὄμμα Λητῴας κόρης) in Aesch. *Xantriae*, Fr. 87 (ed. H. W. Smyth, Loeb, 1957, p. 437); cf. Cic. *De nat. deorum*, 2.68 : *Dianam autem et lunam eandem esse putant* and A. S. Pease ad loc.; Catull. 34.15 f. (in a hymn to Diana); Varro, *Ling.* 5.68; Hor. *Carm. saec.* 1 ff.; Plut. *Quaest. conv.* 3.10, 658 F f., where the element of moisture is regarded as being common to the moon and Artemis, and where the latter is said to be Locheia and Eileithyia, names denoting her role in childbirth in the manner of the Apuleian allusion. At the end of the Catullan ode Diana, as the moon, is regarded as the giver of fertility; cf. Fordyce ad loc. (Oxford, 1961, p. 174): and this may be the point of contact between the two goddesses, although Guthrie, *The Greeks and their Gods* (London, 1950), 103, thinks that a concern with the life of women is the link, while Rose in *OCD¹* 104 and *OCD²* 126 suggests that 'learned speculation' is the cause of the connection — an explanation which will hardly apply to the allusions in the poets; in *A Handbook of Greek Mythology* (Ed. 6, London, 1958), 113, he says of Artemis that 'her connexion with the life of women led to her identification with the moon, precisely as in the case of Hera', but adds that 'any real arguments for these identifications are wanting.' At Ephesus the goddess worshipped as Artemis was probably in origin a type of the Asiatic Great Mother goddess. In statues and on coins she is shown as a figure with many 'breasts'; cf. Minucius Felix, *Octav.* 22, *mammis multis et uberibus extructa.* Franz Miltner in *Anatolia* 3 (1958), 21-34, discusses statues of her found in 1956 and claims (p. 24 f.) that eggs are intended, as a mark of fertility; cf. his *Ephesus* : *Stadt der Artemis und des Johannes* (Vienna, 1958), 41-3. That they are not breasts had been urged by Seltman in *Num.Chron.* 12 (1952), 40 ff., but the latter's idea that 'Artemis was wearing a belly-plate made of a great cluster of dates' is not so convincing. A good conspectus of theories to date is presented by R. Fleischer, *Artemis von Ephesos und verwandte Kultstatuen aus Anatolien und Syrien* (ÉPRO, 35, Leiden, 1973), 74 ff. His own verdict is a *non liquet*, although he does not seem to think that breasts were originally intended.

p. 267, 11 **Proserpina** : It is as the goddess of the underworld that Proserpina is dreaded in nocturnal cries; thus too does she keep the bolts of the earth barred. In Homer she is the spouse of Hades and she is called 'the dreaded Persephoneia' (ἐπαινή *Il.* 9.457 and 569; *Od.* 10.491 and 534), so that *horrenda* here may be regarded as perpetuating the adjective. Although her terrifying aspect was assuaged through her association with Demeter, the corn- mother, in the popular mind she persisted as the bringer of death; cf. Verg. *Aen.* 4.698 f. and 6.138; Statius, *Silv.* 2.1.147 and *Theb.* 4.526 f. See further Leo Bloch in Roscher, *Lex. Myth.* s.v. Proserpina (1909), 1336. The 'threefold countenance' of Proserpina derives ultimately from the goddess Hecate, who is often shown in Greek art either with three bodies or with three heads on one body. Like Persephone (of which Proserpina is a Latinized form) Hecate was a chthonic deity connected with Hades, and a celebrated relief on the Pergamon frieze, which belongs to the second century B. C., shows Hecate attacking a Giant and serpents; she is represented as one figure with three heads and six arms, and carries a huge torch in one of her right hands, while in her other hands are weapons and a shield; see J. Overbeck, *Geschichte der griechischen Plastik*, II (Ed. 3, Leipzig, 1882), fig. 132 C; E. Petersen, *Die dreigestaltige Hekate* (Leipzig, 1880, repr. from *Arch-epigr. Mitt. aus Österreich*, 4); H. Kähler, *Die grosse Fries von Pergamon* (Berlin, 1948), pl. 6; Th. Kraus, *Hekate* (Heidelberg, 1960), 102 ff. and 160 f.; Eva Maria Schmidt, *Der grosse Altar zu Pergamon* (Leipzig, 1961), pls. 15 and 59 with p. 27. In Hellenistic and Roman times Hecate is often shown and described as carrying a key — another attribute of the mistress of the underworld; v. Roscher, op. cit. 1906 and Kraus, op. cit. 49. Proserpina clearly took over these attributes, and thus is the one who keeps the underworld locked. Her triple aspect, as derived from Hecate, may reflect the belief that the three well-defined phases of the moon within a month are tantamount to three different moons. Hecate was in one tradition connected also with the place where three roads cross; and an Orphic interpretation conjoined Artemis, Persephone, and Hecate as a unified trinity; v. Lobeck, *Aglaophamus* (Königsberg, 1829), 543 ff. In Roman literature the three goddesses appear as Iuno Licina, Trivia, and Luna (Catull. 34.9), the same triad being perhaps intended by Horace's *diva triformis* (*Carm.* 3.22.4), though Diana is addressed. Page explains the Horatian goddess as being 'in heaven Luna, on earth Diana, in hell Hecate'; the importance of Hecate in the concept emerges in Verg. *Aen.* 4.511 and in Ovid, *Metam.* 7.94 f. as well as Ovid, *Fasti*, 1.141, on which see Frazer and F. Bömer. Modern literature has inherited the tripartite spatial division, as in Lowell's lines

> Goddess triform, I own thy triple spell :
> Queen of my earth, Queen too of my heaven and hell.

Keune in Roscher, *Lex. Myth.* V (1915), 1108f. shows that *triformis* can apply also to Cerberus, the Chimaera, Geryones, and the Sphinx. For its application to Proserpina, when called Libera, he cites *CIL* 3, 1095 and other inscriptions; but he rightly gives first prominence to Hecate, who seems to underlie Proserpina's role in this respect. As to the latter's equation with the moon, Leo Bloch in Roscher, *Lex. Myth.* II (1897), 1288, is prepared to find etymological support for it in the second element of the name Persephone, deriving -φόνη or -φάσσα from φαίνω; but the considerable variation in the form suggests a non-Greek origin; cf. Wilamowitz-Moellendorf, *Glaube der Hellenen*, I (Berlin, 1931), 108 f. and K.-H. Roloff, *Lex. der alten Welt*, 2260. Varro, *Ling.* 5.68 ascribes an instance of the identification to Ennius : *Hinc Epicharmus Ennii Proserpinam quoque appellat (Lunam), quod solet esse sub terris*; cf. also Plut. *De fac.* 28, 943 B, ἐν τῇ σελήνῃ τῆς Φερσεφόνης and *Quaest. Rom.* 76. Roscher in his *Lex. Myth.* II (1897), 3186, suggested that the identification originated in the idea that the souls of the dead do not dwell in the underworld, the proper sphere of Persephone, but in the heaven, particularly in the sun and moon. For this idea, however, he is unable to cite early evidence, and Proserpina probably owes her lunar function to her association with Artemis and Hecate, who are occasionally represented as her sisters, as in Hdt. 2.156 and Eur. *Ion*, 1048. In the latter locus Hecate is called Einodia, and in origin Einodia was an independent goddess : see Kraus, *Hekate*, 77 ff. and, in general, G. Zuntz, *Persephone* (Oxford, 1971).

p. 267, 14 **sudis ignibus** : In defence of the vulgate reading *udis* it has been urged that some of the ancients believed fire and water to be essentially connected; cf. the view ascribed by Plutarch, *De Is. et Os.* 7, 353 E to the Egyptian priests, but probably to be derived from Greek thought : ὅλως δὲ καὶ τὴν θάλατταν ἐκ πυρὸς ἡγοῦνται, where editors have needlessly emended ἐκ πυρός. In the present passage the phrase which follows, *nutriens laeta semina*, might indeed be explained as referring to moisture. On the other hand, *udis* (or *uvidis* or *umidis*) *ignibus* involves too glaring a paradox, although *uvidis* proposed by Pontanus, is probably the reading of A, a point unobserved by previous editors. Blümner in *Mél. Nicole* (Geneva, 1905), 38, refers to Hildebrand's suggestion that *uvidis* might allude to the *hydreion* carried in the Isiac procession; but *ignibus* belies any such allusion. Blümner's own proposal, *sudis*, is convincing in every way. His case can be further buttressed by the fact that *sudus* is used several times by Apuleius in such a context; v. *Index Apul.* and cf. below ch. 7 *ad fin.* : *caelum ... nudo sudoque luminis proprii splendore candebat.*

p. 267, 16 **aerumnis** : For this archaism compare ch. 15 (277, 19); and Médan *Lat.* 164. According to Quintilian, 8.3.26 the word was then obsolete. Apuleius also uses the adjective *aerumnabilis*, as in *Metam.* 1.1 (1, 11); see M. Molt *ad loc.*

p. 267, 16-17 **tu ... subsiste** : Only now does the main burden of the prayer begin to find expression in a series of requests. In its general arrangement the whole composition is highly conventional, following a time-honoured pattern of which there is an admirable study in G. Appel's *De Romanorum precationibus*, 75 ff. The traditional prayer begins with the name of the deity invoked. Knowing his correct name is vitally important : *nomen numen*. It was then essential to specify the function of the deity which was most suited to respond to the particular request which the petitioner had in mind. Here an anxiety not to overlook the exactly relevant function often led to an expression of uncertainty which might seem to apply even to the identity of the god invoked. Thus an ancient prayer preserved in Macrobius, *Saturn.* 3.9.10 (ed. Willis, 1963, p. 185) begins with the sentence *Dis pater Veiovis Manes, sive vos quo alio nomine fas est nominare.* It will be noted that Apuleius in our chapter strikingly recalls the ancient formula in the words *quoquo nomine ... te fas est invocare.* Cf. Catull. 34.21 f. : *Sis quocumque tibi placet / sancta nomine.* Occasionally the uncertainty might seem to be more basic, as in Verg. *Aen.* 4.576 f., *Sequimur te, sancte deorum, quisquis es*; yet R. G. Austin ad loc. (Oxford, 1955, p. 170) justly observes that Aeneas 'does not doubt that the god is Mercury, but adds *quisquis es* in the usual precautionary way.' This convention is also found in Greek religion, as in Aesch. *Ag.* 160, Ζεύς, ὅστις ποτ' ἐστίν ...; see Fraenkel ad loc. and cf. Norden, *Agnostos Theos* (Leipzig, 1923), 144. Norden, however, while recognizing the ancient liturgical character of the prayer in our chapter, describes it as a prayer to Isis. We have seen that this view is no longer tenable. That Apuleius was consciously following the traditional formula is apparent in other prayers penned by him (e.g. Psyche's prayer to Hera, *Metam.* 6.4 and to Ceres, 6.2, although the latter lacks the *sive* clauses) and also by his statement in the *De deo Socratis*, 15 (153) : *Cum vero incertum est, quae cuique eorum sortitio evenerit, utrum Lar sit an Larva, nomine Manem deum nuncupant; scilicet ei honoris gratia dei vocabulum additum est.* Cf. Appel, op. cit. 79.

Stylistically our prayer is felicitously and symmetrically fashioned; and the fact that its structure follows early prototypes need not of course hinder its aesthetic effect. *Regina caeli*, the initial invocation, replaces the more specific *Luna*, but is the more impressive; then come four clauses introduced by *sive* or *seu.* with the names of Ceres, Venus, Diana, and Proserpina, whose functions are elaborated in relative clauses or participial phrases. The main goal of the prayers is expressed in two sequences of imperatives, divided by the clauses *sit satis laborum* and *sit satis periculorum.* After the renewed force of the simple, brief implorings comes the quiet end with its readiness to accept death rather than rebuttal.

Schematically the prayer is best arranged in the form adopted by Berreth (pp. 13 f.) :

A. Regina caeli —
B. 1. Sive tu Ceres alma frugum parens originalis,
   2. *quae* repertu laetatae filiae,
      vetustae glandis ferino remoto pabulo,
      miti commonstrato cibo
   3. *nunc* Eleusiniam glebam percolis,
C. 1. seu tu caelestis Venus
   2. *quae* primis rerum exordiis diversitate generato Amore sociasti
      et aeterna subole humano genere propagato
   3. *nunc* circumfluo Paphi sacrario coleris,

D. 1. seu Phoebi soror,
　2. *quae* partu fetarum medelis lenientibus populos tantos educasti
　3. praeclaris *nunc* veneraris delubris Ephesi,
E. 1. seu nocturnis ululatibus horrenda Proserpina triformi facie
　2. a) larvales inpetus comprim e n s
　　b) terraeque claustra cohib e n s
　　　lucos diversos inerr a n s
　3. 　vario cultu propitiaris,
D. 1. a) ista luce feminea conlustr a n s
　　b) c u n c t a m o e n i a
　2. a) et sudis ignibus nutri e n s
　　b) l a e t a s e m i n a
　3. a) et solis ambagibus dispens a n s
　　b) i n c e r t a l u m i n a,
G. 1. 　quoquo nomine
　2. 　quoquo ritu
　3. 　quaqua facie
　　　te fas est invocare :
H. 1. tu meis iam nunc extremis aerumnis subsiste,
　　tu fortunam conlapsam adfirma,
　　tu saevis exanclatis casibus pausam pacemque tribue;
J. 1. 　sit satis lab o r u m,
　2. 　sit satis pericul o r u m.
K. 1. depelle quadrupedis diram faciem,
　　redde me conspectui meorum,
　　redde me meo Lucio.
L. 　ac si quod offensum numen
　　inexorabili me saevitia premit.
　　mori saltem liceat
　　si non licet vivere.

Fondness for a triadic scheme is one feature which emerges forcibly and it is at its best when simplest, as in the final plea, *depelle ... redde ... redde.* Alliteration (*triformi facie, claustra cohibens, pausam pacemque, sit satis*), rhyme (see the juxtaposed participial forms and the *-orum* terminations in J; also the groups ending in *moenia, semina, lumina*) and anaphora (*sive ... seu ... seu ... seu*; the *quae* clauses; *sit satis* repeated; and especially *quoquo nomine, quoquo ritu, quaqua facie* and the three clauses beginning with *tu*, as well as the repeated *redde*) are devices skilfully used without being over-deployed. What is particularly striking is that Apuleius, an original stylist who often strives for new and strange effects, here tempers his manner to deal with ancient and traditional forms. These have been richly explored by Norden who shows (*Agnostos Theos*, 168 ff.) that the relative clauses were regularly used from Homer onwards to refer to the deity's cult-centre; originally, he thinks, such clauses were participial phrases. Such allusions are a constant feature of Egyptian and Hebrew prayers and hymns; in P. Anastasi 5, 9, 2 Thoth is *the god who longs for Hermopolis*; cf. Psalm 135.21, *Blessed be the Lord out of Zion, who dwelleth at Jerusalem*; see further A. Barucq, *L'expression de la louange divine et de la prière dans la Bible et en Egypte* (Cairo, 1962), 22 ff. et passim and cf. the present writer's review, *JEA* 50 (1964), 189-91. In *Our father which art in heaven* (Mat. 6.9) there is no relative clause in the Greek (ὁ ἐν τοῖς οὐρανοῖς) and the background is doubtless Hebraic; cf. Norden, op. cit. 257 f. Apuleius, however, is closely following the Graeco-Roman convention, even if it is now coloured by Oriental influences.

Whether the self-conscious artistry of the prayer extends to a careful choice and balance in the number of words is another matter. Wittmann, p. 13, applies a mathematical analysis to the various clauses and word-groupings and finds it significant that the clauses dealing with Ceres and Venus contain 20 words each, while those dealing with Diana and Proserpina have 14 words each. Certainly an exact symmetry thus emerges, but it is not as exact as Wittmann posits, since his count does not include the opening phrases; his own table shows that the total figures are respectively 23, 24, 17 and 19. He also finds significance in the fact that two groupings in the prayer proper (the triad of clauses beginning with *tu* and that which starts with *depelle*) have 18 words apiece; here he admits that two clauses of three words each intervene — probably to avoid monotony. Hellenistic number symbolism, thinks Wittmann, accounts for the total of words in the prayer, 166; this figure denotes heavenly light; and the half, ending with *propitiaris*, gives 83, a number denoting ἀστέρες, star-like. Wittmann, p. 197 n. 8, justifies this by referring to P. Friesenhahn, *Hellenistische Wortzahlenmystik im Neuen Testament* (Leipzig, 1935), 180 ff., but no indication is there given of the exact source of the many numerical values said to derive from Babylonian astrology, nor ideed of the extent to which they were known at large in the early centuries of our era. Such speculations, according to Wittmann, are naturally associated with the ritual of the heavenly queen; but this may be questioned. Bernhard, *Stil*, 73, rightly emphasizes the triadic structure of the prayer in the three sections beginning *ista luce*, *tu meis*, and *depelle*; he notes that these are interrupted by two short anaphoric pieces, the first of which, starting with *quoquo nomine*, is itself triadic. Three as a sacred number lies behind such a usage, as Bernhard (p. 62) shows, for it is frequent in religious contexts. Whereas the search for lines of metrical verse is mostly misconceived even in an author so devoted to poetical colouring, since lines may often emerge by accident, it cannot be fortuitous that the opening words of this prayer, *Regina caeli*, — *sive tu Ceres alma*, form a choliambus or scazon; v. Bernhard, p. 250 n. 84.

p. 267, 17 **exanclatis** : Cf. ch. 12 (275, 16), *tantis exanclatis laboribus*; 15 (277,4), *exanclatis laboribus*. This word is mostly ante-classical in occurrence; cf. Ennius, *scen.* 102 (ed. Vahlen, Leipzig, 1903, p. 133), *quantis cum aerumnis illum exanclavi diem*. Cicero uses it only when translating poetry or recalling it. A reconditely archaistic touch is clearly aimed at here; other instances show Apuleius's fondness of the word; cf. Hofmann and Szantyr, *Lat. Syntax*, 768 f.; Médan, *Lat.* 169; and Bernhard, *Stil*, 131.

p. 267, 18 **pausam pacemque** : Alliteration occurs often in archaic Latin. It figures more frequently in Plautus than Terence; cf. Bernhard, *Stil*, 219.

p. 267, 19 **redde** : Words like δός and *da* are naturally frequent in traditionial prayers; cf. Plaut. *Poen.* 1188, *da diem hunc sospitem, quaeso*; *Il.* 10.281, δὸς δὲ πάλιν ἐπὶ νῆας ἐϋκλεῖας ἀφικέσθαι; see further Appel, op. cit. 133 f. and C. Ausfeld, *De Graecorum precationibus quaestiones* (Diss. Leipzig, 1903), 515.

p. 267, 21 **vivere** : There is something to be said for van der Vliet's restoration <*hominem*> *vivere* since there are three possibilities open to Lucius—death, or life as an ass, or life as a man.

CHAPTER 3

p. 267, 22 **Ad istum modum** : Apuleius is fond of this expression; cf. ch. 16 (278, 3); 25 (287, 11); 28 (289, 8-9). The usage is classical : v. Kühner and Stegmann, *Gramm. Lat.*² II, 2, 523.

p. 267, 23 **circumfusus** : Following not so far after *fusis precibus*, the choice of this word seems infelicitous to modern taste.

p. 267, 24 **composieram** : The presence of *at commodum coniverat nec diu* in *Metam.* 4. 25 (93,22) is plausibly adduced by Helm, following Wower, in favour of *coniveram*, 'I had (scarcely) closed my eyes', for the context is fairly similar. An alternative pluperfect form for *coniveram* is *conixeram*; v. *Thes. L.L.* 4, 320, 47 f. and Robertson. *Compseram*, however, is the reading of φ, E, and other codices, and Wiman rightly suggests that this may be intended also in F, although *conipseram* or *compseram* is apparently there. Wiman cogently proceeds to propose *composieram*, 'I had settled down'.

p. 267, 25 **vultus attollens** : For the use of the plural of *vultus* with a singular meaning and for the association with this verb compare Ovid, *Metam.* 4.144 (Thisbe to Pyramus), *vultusque attolle iacentes*!

p. 268, 4 **elocutilis** : This is the only occurrence of the word, but the reading is well established as it is found in φ, A, and other codices; the initial letter is erased in F. The word is formed from *elocutus*; cf. *scriptilis*; v. *Thes. L.L.* 5, 2, 398, 80. Piechotta, *Curae Apuleianae*, 49, shows that adjectives in *-tilis* were fashionable in the Apuleian era and later; cf. *electilis*, *Metam.* 10.15 (248, 4).

p. 268, 5 **Iam primum crines** : The figure of Isis, both in its purely Egyptian and in its partly Hellenized form, displays considerable variety, and all the elements mentioned by Apuleius are well attested.

His description of the *coiffure* finds a counterpart in Weber, *Terr.* pl. 2, 24 and p. 36, save that all the hair is there thickly entwined: one has to look to

other instances, such as Weber's pl. 3, 27 and 28, to see the tresses falling
loosely on the shoulders, a point which Apuleius combines with the former
feature; cf. Tran Tam Tinh, *Isis à Pompéi*, pl. 13 and p. 156. The style in
these cases is Greek, and the whole *coiffure* is often considerable in extent;
cf. Perdrizet, *Terr.* pl. 9 and p. 7, no. 18. Isis is called 'the fair-tressed' (εὐπλόκαμος) in an inscription from Alexandria (A.D. iii), v. Milne, *Greek Inscriptions* (*CCG*), p. 35, no. 9237; cf. P. Oxy. 1380, 133 f. (A.D. ii); Adriani, *Rep.
d'Arte*, A,I, pl. 41, 121 with p. 40, no 56. The hair of Isis was venerated in the
ancient tradition and is apostrophized in De Buck, *CT* V, 188 *i* and 204 *d*
(= *BD* 99); cf, also Plut, *De Is. et Os.* 14, 356 D and J. Gwyn Griffiths ad loc.

p. 268, 6 **corona multiformis** : Her crown is *multiformis* in the sense that
it contains many elements, of which Apuleius mentions flowers, a round disk,
erect serpents, and ears of corn. Other elements often present were two horns
and high feathers, and sometimes the vulture's hood; v. Weber, *Terr.* 37 and
for the vulture's hood, Edgar, *Greek Bronzes* (*CCG*), pl. 4, 27673 and p. 11.

A lotus-flower occasionally appears on the head-dress : v. Leipoldt, *Bilderatlas*, 25 [256] and 26, but the former instance is modern according to Anne
Roullet, *Rome*, 93, no. 126.; cf. the Ptolemaic form of diadem with lotus-buds
on which see B. V. Bothmer in *Egyptian Sculpture of the Late Period* (Brooklyn,
1960), 163. A bronze figure from Karnak represents Isis suckling Horus; on
her head is a cluster of lotus-flowers; v. G. Michaïlides, 'Isis Déesse de l'Amour',
BIE 37 (1956), pl. 21 and cf. Daressy, *Statues de Divinités*, I (*CCG* 1906),
234, no. 38925 and II, pl. 47 (he calls her Merit-quemât or Shem'at). A crown
of flowers or of palm-leaves is represented in Breccia, *Terr.* 1, pl. 48, 10, cf.
p. 32; two vertical palm-branches form the crown in Breccia, ibid. 2, pl. 7,
24, cf. p. 19, and in this case crowns of flowers adorn a shoulder-belt; a garland
of five flowers adorns the hair in Tran Tam Tinh, *Isis à Pompéi*, pl. 13 and p. 156.
In other instances a flower is held in the hand; v. Edgar, *Greek Sculpture* (*CCG*),
pl. 9, no. 27471 and p. 18 (Isis or a queen); ibid. pl. 9, no. 27473 and p. 19;
Edgar, *Greek Bronzes* (*CCG*), pl. 4, no. 27669 and p. 10. Vogt, *Terr.* pl. 6, 4
and 6 includes two cases of Isis as a mother-goddess emerging from a flower-
bud — a conceit distinctively Egyptian, as Vogt, p. 6, points out. Indeed the
flower theme in the Isis image is entirely of Egyptian origin. On the other hand,
its earlier tradition is not specifically Isiac or divine; flowers are shown adorning
the heads of women, often in banqueting scenes; cf. Woldering, *Art : Egypt*,
145-8; Westendorf, *Egn. Art*, 114-19. In the Andrian Hymn, 17 f. Isis is 'weighed
down by the proud flowers of my tresses'; cf. W. Peek ad loc. p. 36.

p. 268, 8 **rutunditas** : The round disk is originally that of the sun, and Isis
derives this element in her head-dress, together with the cow-horns which
often flank the sun-disk, from the goddess Hathor. Cf. H. W. Müller, 'Isis
mit dem Horuskinde', 10 and fig. 2. Tran Tam Tinh, *Isis à Pompéi*, 72, appears
to date the assumption of the emblem, as well as the identification with Hathor,
to the Alexandrian epoch, but both processes are certainly earlier. Thus Isis
bears the sun-disk and horns on her head in a Nineteenth-Dynasty relief from

Abydos : v. Bonnet, *Bilderatlas*, 61 and *Reallexikon*, 329 (referring to the New Kingdom). It is the *interpretatio Graeca* that has imposed a lunar attribute on Isis. Plutarch, *De Is. et Os.* 43, 368 C and 52, 372 D exemplifies the approach, and in the second passage he refers to the explanation of the horns as being imitations of the crescent moon; cf. Diod. Sic. 1.11.2. A transformation of the horns into stylized feathers appears in a bronze statuette in the von Bissing collection : v. R. Pagenstecher, *Malerei und Plastik* (Sammlung Ernst von Sieglin, IA), 77, fig. 78. A bronze figure published by Michaïlides, *BIE* 37 (1956), fig. 14 (facing pl. 13) shows the bust of the goddess above the shape of a crescent moon (unless it be a floral bud). See further Roeder, *Bronzefiguren*, 236 ff. and esp. 261-64 (Isis in Greek style); id. *Rel.* IV, pl. 30; Leipoldt, *Bilderatlas*, 37-8 and *Umwelt*, III, 270.

p. 268, 9-10 **viperarum** : The serpents mentioned by Apuleius are the uraei which often appear in a double form on the head-dress of queens and sometimes in the form of a chaplet of uraei; a single uraeus is also found. All three variants appear with representations of Isis. When she is also shown wearing the cow-horns and disk, the uraeus motif is spatially constricted, but it is sometimes combined with the horns as in Junker and Winter, *Geburtshaus*, fig. 461 et saepe: cf. Michaïlides, *BIE* 37 (1956), pl. 1 (where uraei are below the horns and one is on the solar disk). At other times the horns are replaced by uraei; in C. M. Kaufmann, *Ägyptische Terrakotten der griechisch-römischen und koptischen Epoche* (Cairo, 1913), fig. 22, p. 40 (a head of the Ptolemaic era) a uraeus appears in the middle of the head-dress, and the two horns are also shown as uraei; cf. A. Scharff, *Götter Ägyptens* (Berlin, 1923), pl. 8 and p. 14, where a small crown of horns with sun-disk is fused with an entwining uraeus which projects on the two sides. Since Apuleius does not mention the cow-horns, the type envisaged by him may well be that in which the horns are treated in a way that suggests uraei; cf. the synthetic drawing by C. Michaud at the beginning of Médan's edition. Examples can be seen in two bronzes of the Ptolemaic era reproduced by Roeder, *Bronzefiguren*, pl. 38 g and m : here the horns which flank the disk are figured in a wavy style suggestive of snakes. Roeder, p. 261, § 317 b and c, while he does not mention this idea, admits (in the preceding paragraph) that they are hard to recognize as cow-horns. In these instances there is a uraeus within the disk. It is possible that Apuleius has misinterpreted the horns as snakes. Sometimes Isis is depicted grasping a uraeus in her hand or with a uraeus twisted around her forearm; again, a serpent is represented as rising from the mystic Isiac casket; but these are different in function although they all doubtless derive from the uraeus of Wedjoyet which adorns the royal head-dress; cf. J. Gwyn Griffiths, *JEA* 47 (1961), 117 ff.

p. 268, 10 **spicis** : Ears of corn often appear in representations of the Hellenized Isis; see Edgar, *Greek Bronzes* (*CCG*), pl. 4, no. 27671 and p. 11; Perdrizet, *Terr.* I, 25 f. and II, pl. 19, entitled 'Isis-Déméter' by Perdrizet, while he gives 'Isis déesse agraire' as title to the section; Breccia, *Terr.* 1, pl. 24, 1 and 4 with p. 52; ibid. 2, pl. 47, 235 and p. 31; Drexler, 'Isis', 448 f. with references to statuary and coinage; Tassie and Raspe, *A Descriptive Cat. of ... Gems etc.* (London, 1791), 2, pl. 24, no. 1446; Head, *A Cat. of the Greek Coins in the B.M.* : *Sicily*, pl. 14, 7 and p. 228, nos. 704 and 705; Matz and Duhn, *Antike Bildwerke in Rom*, I (Leipzig, 1881), 451, no. 1581; Roeder, *Bronzefiguren*, pl. 38 g and m, beneath the horns and disk, although Roeder, p. 261, interprets them as feathers which project sideways like bull-horns; ibid. pl. 38 e and k, recognized with some hesitancy on pp. 261 and 264; Roeder, *Rel.* IV, pl. 30 and p. 415 (Berlin, 7502) = Leipoldt, *Bilderatlas*, 31; Grimm, *Äg. Rel. im röm. Deutschland*, pl. 24, 4 and p. 182, no. 83; H. W. Müller, 'Isis mit dem Horuskinde', 29, fig. 27 (both with Isis-Thermuthis and with Isis the mother); Tran Tam Tinh. *Herculanum*, pl. 8, figs. 11 and 12 with pp. 61 ff.; Aurigemma, *Villa Adriana*, 50, fig. 25 = Anne Roullet, *Rome*, fig. 124 and p. 93. The Canopus Decree, 31 f., ordained that the crown of Berenice should include two ears of corn with an asp-shaped diadem between them; cf. Mahaffy, *A Hist. of Egypt under the Ptolemaic Dynasty* (London, 1899), 117 with fig. 33; Spiegelberg, *ZÄS* 43 (1906), 156 f.: Weber, *Terr.* 37; Bevan, *A Hist. of Egypt under the Ptolemaic Dynasty* (London, 1927), 212 f., surprisingly omits Spiegelberg's attempt to explain the reference of the symbols according to the script, as the Decree states. What the Decree also makes plain, as Weber remarks, is the carefully deliberate planning of such designs. Weber, p. 38, goes on to suggest that the ears of corn borne aloft by Isis are derived from the constellation Parthenos mentioned by an early Hellenistic writer (Ps. Eratosthenes, *Cataster.* no. 9). The iconography of Demeter, however, is a much more likely source; she is often represented with corn in her hair or with a wreath of corn ears : v. Leo Bloch, in Roscher, *Lex. Myth.* s.v. Demeter (1897), 1344 ff.; M. Rat, *Mythologie* (Paris, 1950), 22; F. Guirand, *Greek Mythology* (London 1963), fig. on p. 108; G. Lippold, *Gemmen und Kameen* (Stuttgart, n.d.) pl. 118, 7, The idea that she is to be equated with Isis is conspicuously present already in Herodotus. Watzinger, *Sammlung Ernst von Sieglin : Malerei und Plastik*, 79, propounds the view that figures of Isis with stalks of corn in her hand derive rather from Korê, since the large torch shown in the other hand is characteristic of her in Greek tradition. This seems true of the torch, but Watzinger agrees that the ears of corn in the hair are typical of Demeter. Isis claims in the Aretalogies to have discovered corn (M 7, v. D. Müller, 31 ff.), but Egyptian texts, as Müller shows, tend to ascribe the function to Osiris; cf. my comments in *Plut. De Is. et Os.* 57 f.

No single figure or representation appears to combine all the elements of the head-dress described by Apuleius. One which comes close is a white marble statue in Berlin (no. 12440, *Ausführliches Verzeichnis*, 1899, pp. 325 f. with fig. 63 = Scharff, *Götter Ägyptens*, pl. 8 and p. 14).

tunica : The subsequent contradistinctive mention of the black *palla* favours Robertson's restoration of *tunica*, following van der Vliet in part, rather than the *vestis* of Castiglioni and others. According to Plut. *De Is. et Os.* 77, 368 C, 'the robes of Isis are variegated in colour', whereas that of Osiris is uniformly bright. Plutarch, ibid. 3, 352 B, also states that the keepers of the Sacred Vestments (of Isis) are concerned with different kinds of clothes, some of which are dark and shadowy, others bright and shining. In Egyptian paintings the goddess is indeed depicted with robes of varying colours; thus in the Papyrus of Ani, her robes are green (pl. 4), red (pl. 20) and white (pl. 33): see further my comments on Plut. ch. 77 (p. 562). Schäfer discussed the dress of Isis in his 'Das Gewand der Isis — ein Beitrag zur Kunst-,kultur- and Religionsgeschichte des Hellenismus', in *FS. C. F. Lehmann-Haupt* (Vienna, 1921), 194-206; there he showed how the dress of Isis in the classical Egyptian tradition did not differ essentially from that of other goddesses or indeed from that of queens or of ordinary mortals. The more elaborate costume assigned to her in Hellenistic and Roman times argues a conscious contribution by religious artists, and some Greek influence is clear, as in Demeter's ears of corn. A new un-Egyptian creation is rightly denied by C. C. Edgar, *Greek Bronzes (CCG)*, p. v : 'M. S. Reinach's theory that there was a statue by Bryaxis in the Sarapeion at Alexandria, originally a Kore, but transformed into an Isis by some slight alterations, is an extremely improbable conjecture. The Greek conceptions of the goddess were certainly founded on Egyptian forms.' The case is rather different, of course, with the iconography of Sarapis, on which see a recent discussion by J. E. Stambaugh, *Sarapis*, ch. 2, pp. 14 ff. Apuleius clearly assumes that two garments are involved in the accoutrement of the divine statue — the close-fitting tunic beneath and the looser cloak above. In describing the tunic as being of the finest linen, with hues of white, yellow and red, Apuleius is reproducing the traditional Egyptian mode which was doubtless followed also in other countries where the cult prevailed. The general effect of the terracotta figures of the goddess often corresponds, according to Weber, *Terr.* 36, to the norm of beauty sanctioned by early Hellenism; it is the type of a young, elegant woman of Alexandria. But this in turn reflected a contemporary Egyptian fashion whose origins are in the New Kingdom. H. W. Müller, 'Isis mit dem Horuskinde', 13 with notes, points out that owing to the archaizing tendencies of Egyptian art in its later phases, it is only occasionally that the contemporary female fashion is represented; he cites one instance in Bothmer, *Egyptian Sculpture of the Late Period*, no. 82, fig. 203 ('Hap-iu's Lady Musicians', dated to 'about 360 B.C.); cf. no. 87, fig. 217, also a group of lady musicians, dated to 'about 350 B.C.' E. Breccia, *Terr.* 2, 19, states the view that the Isiac dress became fashionable among Egyptian women through the influence of the cult. Joseph Vogt, *Expedition Ernst von Sieglin*, II, 2, 4, more wisely accepts Schäfer's point that the Isis-dress was previously worn by Egyptian women, but argues that its application to the goddess was the work of a Greek artist in the time of Alexander the Great or shortly before that. See further, Vandebeek, *Isisfiguur*, 17-20; Grimm, *Äg. Rel. im röm. Deutschland*, 146; Castiglione, 'Kunst', 128 ff.

　　p. 268, 12 **longe longeque** : E. Wölfflin, *Arch. Lat. Lex.* 6 (1889), 1-7 ('Die ersten Spuren des afrikanischen Lateins') states that this phrase is found only occasionally in classical and silver Latin, and that both Florus and Fronto use it. He suggests, then, that it is a token of Africanism and he compares *diu diuque*, ch. 20 (281, 14). Several other cases, however, occur in Latin of repeated adverbs : see n. *ad* loc. cit. *diu diuque*,

p. 268, 13 **palla nigerrima** : According to Plut. *De Is. et Os.* 52, 372 D some statues of Isis were accoutred in black garments; compare the gilded cow with black linen in 39, 366 E, where mourning is the motive of the colour. Apuleius states in ch. 10 that both the initiates and the priests were in white, so that the cloak of Isis, as here described, may indicate a contrast. But her tunic is colourful, and a similar variation is suggested by Plut. 3, 352 B with respect to priestly dress. In Delos some priests of Isis wore black; cf. the epithet μελανηφόρος which applied probably to special groups of priests and believers : v. Roussel, *CED* 288 f., who refers also (p. 296) to a mention in Eretria of a synod of *melanêphoroi* and hypostolists; cf. Vidman, *SIRIS* 37, no. 75, who dates the Eretrian inscription to iii B.C., and 208-9, nos. 426-7 (inscriptions from Rome which mention a *melaneporus* and *melanephorus*); also id. *Isis und Sarapis*, 69-74 : the *melanêphoroi* are often mentioned with the *therapeutai*, another association of believers, but they had greater ritual importance, and developed into an exclusive *synodos*. In the Hymns of Isidorus 3,34 (*SEG* 8, 550) Thermuthis-Isis is addressed as μελανηφόρε; cf. Vanderlip ad loc., p. 62; and the term μελανόστολος is used by Plut. *De Is. et Os.* 52, 372 D of statues of Isis which have black clothes. That black was used in an Isiac context before Isis was Hellenized seems unlikely, for it was the Greek and not the Egyptian tradition that regarded black as the colour of mourning. It is hardly to be expected that figures or statues of Isis will embody the colours described by Apuleius, although Berreth, p. 39, points to a statue of Isis now in Vienna, in which two types of marble are used, white for the body, and black for the dress : see Leipoldt, *Bilderatlas*, 27 [257]; cf. an Isiac statue found near Naples, which is said to have a black dress on a white-coloured body : v. J. Gwyn Griffiths, *Plut. De Is. et Os.* 451. A fresco shows Isermuthis with a dark robe : sec Vanderlip, *Hymns of Isidorus*, pl. 14. The marble statue of Isis presented to the Pompeian temple of the goddess by L. Caecilius Phoebus was richly gilded and painted, the outer garment being depicted as partly red and partly golden : v. J. Overbeck and A. Mau, *Pompeji* (Leipzig, 1884), 106 and 536; Tran Tam Tinh, *Isis à Pompéi*, pl. 13 and p. 156 (no. 81). The Greek and Egyptian elements in this statue are well discriminated by F. W. F. von Bissing, *Ägyptische Kultbilder der Ptolomaier- und Römerzeit = Der alte Orient* 34 (1936), 14 f. But the colouring here has little special significance since marble statues were commonly painted in the ancient world, and other goddesses were similarly treated in Pompeii. A statue of Isis at Alexandria in white marble, which is dated to the second half of the second century A.D. and therefore approximates in date to the composition of the *Metam.* shows no trace of polychromy apart from the red colouring of the small crocodile under the left foot of the goddess; the statue is from Ras es-Soda : v. A. Adriani, *Annuaire du Musée Gréco-Romain* 1935-39, (Alexandria, 1940), 139 f. and *Rep. d'Arte*, A, II, pl. 73, 242 with pp. 39 f. The redness of the crocodile is probably Typhonic. The dress of the goddess as represented here is even more elaborate than Apuleius suggests, for it has three constituents as opposed to his two—a tunic, mantle and flowing veil. But cf. p. 268, 17 f.

p. 268, 15 **umbonis vicem** : Since *umbo* can be used of the full part or swelling of a garment (as in Tert. *Pall.* 5.1; cf. Persius, 5.33, where *candidus umbo* refers by synecdoche to the whole toga), a metaphorical extension of its first meaning of 'boss' or 'knob', it is natural to understand it here of the 'knot' between the breasts which was a prominent feature of the Isiac dress. The phrase in Persius, loc. cit. has admittedly been variously explained : J. Conington (Oxford, 1893, p. 93) rendered it 'the yet unsullied shield of my gown'; A. Pretor (Cambridge, 1907, p. 66) takes *umbo* as 'the "knot" into which the folds of the toga were gathered after passing the left shoulder'; cf. N. Scivoletto (Florence, 1956, p. 105); but F. Villeneuve (Paris, 1918, p. 118) more convincingly argues that 'ce n'est ici qu'une métonymie pour *toga*;' cf. L. Herrmann (Brussels, 1962, p. 3). If 'knot' is the meaning here, Schäfer, 'Das Gewand der Isis', 197, is not quite correct when he says that Apuleius does not mention the breast-knot. H. W. Müller, 'Isis mit dem Horuskinde', 14, after describing the formation of the knot, points out that it occurs also on statues of Ptolemaic queens. Slight variations in the precise position of the knot appear in statuary : see, for instance, Edgar, *Greek Sculpture* (*CCG*), pl. 9, nos. 27470, 27471 and 27473 with pp. 18 f. and p. x; cf. Ibrahim Noshy, *The Arts in Ptolemaic Egypt* (Oxford, 1937), 126 f. When Apuleius speaks of the *palla* going 'round about her, returning under the right side to the left shoulder, a part of the garment being dropped in the manner of a knot', it is the incompleteness of his account that causes difficulty. For the ends of the garment have to emerge frontwards over both shoulders to make the knot possible; cf. Schäfer, op. cit. 198. This is how a symmetrical effect in relation to the breasts is achieved in the style that was often followed; cf. Wittmann, p. 189 n. 32. One of the breasts is often shown bare (sometimes the two) because the goddess is the one who suckles Horus.

p. 268, 15-16 **contabulatione** : The word is first used of the joining together of boards in flooring. Applied metaphorically to clothes (Apuleius alone develops this usage), it will refer to folds or tucks.

p. 268, 16 **nodulis fimbriarum** : 'Tasselled fringes' are shown in many instances; e.g. Edgar, *Greek Sculpture* (*CCG*), pl. 9, no. 27470 with p. 18; no. 27471 with p. 18; Breccia *La Necropoli di Sciatbi*, II, pl. 81, no. 276; Pietrangeli, *Mus. Cap.* : *I Monumenti dei Culti Orientali*, pl. 12 and p. 50 = Leipoldt, *Bilderatlas*, 25 [256]; Schäfer, *Die Kunst Ägyptens*, pl. 430 (upper bronze figure); Edgar, *Greek Moulds* (*CCG*), pl. 24, no. 32049 with p. 15; pl. 10, no. 32058 with p. 17. Sometimes no such fringes appear (e.g. Edgar, *Greek Sculpture* (*CCG*), pl. 9, no. 27473 with p. 19) and in any case it is only on one narrow end of the garment that they are normally found — one of the ends involved in the knot; cf. H. W. Müller, 'Isis mit dem Horuskinde', 14. In some instances the mantle is shown with a fringed border on its long side, but with no added tassels; v. Edgar, *Greek Bronzes (CCG)*, pl. 4, no 27669 with p. 10 and no. 27671 with p. 11. In other cases the tassels are added to a sash or belt which is superimposed on the *palla* : see note *ad* p. 268, 17, *intextam*.

CHAPTER 4

p. 268, 17 **intextam** : F's reading *intectam* is hesitantly respected by Robertson in *CQ* 18 (1924), 95 ('I doubt if *intectam* is defensible, but it has been defended; as F's reading, it deserves to be considered.'). The meaning suggested by Hildebrand in support of this reading (cf. Beroaldus, 'oculis obviam et apertum') is that the stars were gleaming 'through the flimsy border', the material being so thin that the stars on the body of the material could be seen through it; he compares *Metam.* 10.31 (*Venus ... nudo et intecto corpore perfectam formositatem professa*). While this is a possible interpretation of the Latin (with *intectam*) and while the reading has been supported by Eyssenhardt and Giarratano, the archaeological evidence hardly favours it, since a number of representations show stars and a crescent moon affixed to the stoles or sashes as they hang over the chest, suggesting that they were thrown over this part of the material. *Intextam* itself, of course, implies embroidery, and it could possibly refer to embroidered stars and moon. The separation of stole and cloak is not made clear, and if *iniunctam* is the reading of S (cf. Hildebrand). it has some attraction in its expression of this idea.

p. 268, 17-18 **stellae ... semenstris luna** : There are three instances where sashes on the Isiac dress are represented with these emblems : (1) on a marble statue from Hermopolis in Middle Egypt, following depictions of Egyptian crowns; it is now in Berlin and belongs perhaps to the first century A.D. : see F. Zucker, *Archäologischer Anzeiger* 1910, 254 f. and Leipoldt, *Bilderatlas*, 51 [263]; (2) on a marble funerary relief of the Isis-priestess Galatea, of the early second century A.D., where the stole twice shows two lunar crescents and one star between them : see W. Amelung, *Die Sculpturen des Vaticanischen Museums*, II (Plates, Berlin, 1908), pl. 82, no. 19 and text vol. II, 4, 738 ff.; cf. Vidman, SIRIS 218 no. 453; with Galatea, who appears as a young woman, is sculptured an elderly man whom Amelung describes as her husband; Altmann regarded him, according to Amelung, as a priest, but probably he is her father, who had dedicated her to the Isiac priesthood; (3) a mosaic from Antioch on the Orontes, perhaps of the third century A.D., represents Isis or an Isiac priestess with a lunar crescent on a vertical sash and two stars on a sash that crosses the chest diagonally : see Doro Levi, *Antioch Mosaic Pavements* (Princeton, 1947), II, pl. 8 *b* and I, 50; cf. id. *Berytus* 7 (1942), pl. 3,1 and p. 30; also R. E. Witt, *Isis Gr.-R.* pl. 35. Levi describes the garment in the first-mentioned work as a 'scarf'; in the article in *Berytus* he calls it a 'stole'. For other examples of the garment see Weber, *Terr.* 41 n. 55; R. E. Witt, 'Macedonia', 331; Leipoldt, *Angelos* 1 (1925), 127 with pl. 1 = id. *Bilderatlas* 53 [294] = Tran Tam Tinh, *Herculanum*, pl. 27, fig. 40 with p. 84; Alda Levi, *Mon. Antichi* 28 (1922), col. 163, fig. 5 ('L'Iside Barberini'); Tran Tam Tinh, *Isis à Pompéi*, pl. 10,1 (Isis in a boat). On p. 74 f. of the last-named work Tran Tam Tinh suggests that the Isiac *palla* was basically always the same. In some instances, however, the fringed band in a loose addition, whereas it is mostly an extension of the *palla*. On p. 75 n. 2 the same author states that only two examples exist of the *palla* with astral symbols; the example from Hermopolis is ignored.

Stars occur in other ways in the funerary symbolism of the Egyptian cults in the Graeco-Roman era; thus a fresco at Pompeii depicts Isis-Fortuna with a cavalier Harpocrates and Helius (?), and the goddess wears on her head a lunar crescent which embraces a star; furthermore, the whole background is studded with stars; see Tran Tam Tinh, op. cit. pl. 17 with pp. 79 f. and 86 (correcting the catalogue ref. from 29 to 59) and also 148. One is instantly reminded of the role of Nut, the sky-goddess, in Egyptian religion, for the dead person who receives her protection has the ceiling of his tomb-chamber or the cover of his coffin adored with stars in exactly this way; cf. Bonnet, *Reallexikon*, 538. The presence of one star only might invoke the connection of Isis with Sirius-Sothis; cf. Drexler, 'Isis', 435. Drexler also refers to gems where several stars are shown with the goddess; cf. Delatte and Derchain, *Intailles Magiques* (Paris, 1964), nos. 106 and *107; on the other hand, a lunar crescent and star occur with Bes (*103) and the child on the lotus (*141). Their occurrence with Serapis can naturally be linked with the Isiac tradition; see A. H. Smith, *Cat. of Engraved Gems in the B.M.* (London, 1888), nos. 1208, 1212 and G. M. Richter, *Cat. of Engraved Gems of the Classical* Style (MMA, New York, 1920), no. 347. When more than one star appears with Isis, Nut's funerary sovereignty over the stars, to which the dead is elevated, is probably the association, and it will apply to the representations to which Apuleius refers. Cf. the row of white stars on a black band above a funerary scene featuring Isis, Osiris and Horus on the back of a mummy mask reproduced by Edgar, *Graeco-Egyptian Coffins*, no. 33130, pl. 11 with p. 22; also by L. Castiglione, 'Kunst und Gesellschaft im Römischen Ägypten', *Acta Ant. Hung.* 15 (1967), pl. 13,4 with p. 132. In a different category, perhaps, are the golden star-emblems found in the mummy-portraits; cf. Parlasca, *Mumienporträts*, 90 and Shore, *Portrait Painting from Roman Egypt*, sub pl. 8. See also Parlasca, *Rep. d'arte*, Ser. B. col. I (Palermo, 1969), pl. 39, fig. 2, N. 163; pl. 42, fig. 6, N, 177; pl. 51, fig. 2, N. 206. A depiction of stars in connection with Osiris is unusual, but see J. G. Milne, *Hist. of Egypt under Roman Rule* (Ed. 3, 1924), 212, fig. 113 (from Coptos). In the Aretalogies Isis claims to have 'shown the way of the stars' (D. Müller, *Isis-Aret.* 39 f.), and a number of Egyptian allusions describe her as 'mistress of the stars', although

Hathor, Satis, and Sothis bear the same title : see D. Müller, loc. cit. An Arabic legend translated from Coptic in A. D. 840 (the 'Surid legend') includes a feminine figure who represents the sky and moon and probably reflects Isis; v. A. Fodor, 'The Origins of the Arabic Legends of the Pyramids',*Acta Orient. Hung.* 23 (1970), 335-63, esp. 355.

Semenstris is an authentic form, as Hildebrand is able to show, although most of the MSS. here give *semestris*. The formation must be from *semi* and *mensis* (Forcellini's other alternative, *sex* and *mensis* would yield no sense here); yet the moon at mid-month is the full moon, whereas all the representations show a half-moon. Ryle points out that in Amm. Marc. 20.3.1 *semenstris* means 'with half its surface showing', i.e. 'like a half-moon' (though the allusion there is to the sun; see the note by W. Seyfarth ad loc. Berlin, 1968, II, 194 f. n. 14, where the present passage, however, is taken to refer to the full moon).

p. 268, 20 **totis floribus** etc. : Apuleius has previously mentioned, in ch. 3, as being on her head, 'a crown of many designs with all kinds of flowers' (*corona multiformis variis floribus*). The use of garlands of flowers was very common in Egypt as a means of decorating both secular and religious scenes. With divinities it is the head-dress that is most often treated in this way. The placing of a garland on a garment is not often attested. Weber, *Terr.* (Tafelband) 3, 28, shows Isis with such a garland on the sash or stole which is attached to the mantle; cf. his Textband, 49; and also Vogt, *Terr.* (Textband) 5, fig. 3 with his comment on p. 6 n. 1. These two instances are cited by Wittmann; add Breccia, *Terr.* 2, pl. 7, 24 with p. 19; 2, pl. 6, nos. 18 and 21. That the practice is rarely illustrated in representations is clearly due to the fact that these garlands or wreaths were not a constant or static part of the goddess's dress; they were expressions of devotion resulting from particular occasions of worship. G. Roeder, 'Die Blumen der Isis von Philä', *ZÄS* 48 (1910), 115-22, shows how flowers were often presented to gods and he refers to different types of flower-bouquets presented to Isis in Philae. See also, for instances of these, Junker, *Der grosse Pylon*, fig. 26 and p. 53 (Ptolemy XIII presents flowers to Isis, and the goddess says, 'I give thee the Nile, verdant with flowers'); Junker and Winter, *Geburtshaus*, 338 f. (Tiberius presents flowers to Isis). For the use of crowns of flowers, with varied significance, see Derchain, *Ant. Class.* 25 (1956), 408 ff. and *CdE* 30 (1955), 225 ff. Isis was sometimes regarded as the creator of the verdant land; cf. the claim in the Aretalogies (D. Müller, *Isis-Aret.* M 7, pp. 31 ff.) ἐγώ εἰμι ἡ καρπὸν ἀνθρώποις εὑροῦσα, and the Egyptian parallels cited by Müller, loc. cit. and pp. 89 f., as well as that cited by Bergman, *Ich bin Isis*, 227 and 304 from a text in Esna (Sauneron, *Esna III* (1968), 223, 1 ff.); cf. Tran Tam Tinh, *Isis à Pompéi*, pl. 14, 2, where Isis is shown standing on land teeming with flowers. This is not, at the same time, an early attribute of the goddess. Nor is it strictly apposite to apply it here, as Berreth does, since the presentation of garlands was a mark of veneration applied to many deities.

p. 269, 1-2 **aereum crepitaculum** ; There were two main types of sistrum, one with the centre portion in the shape of a loop, the other with this part in the form of a naos. Like Plutarch, *De Is. et Os.* 63, 376 C ff. (cf. my remarks ad loc., pp. 525 ff.), Apuleius has the former type in mind. Since the number of rattle-rods was sometimes three, some translators have seen an allusion to this in *trigeminos iactus*, but the 'three shakings' will obviously involve all the rods at the same time; of their number Apuleius simply says *paucae*. Cf. Tib. 1.3.23 f. *quid mihi prosunt | illa tua totiens aera repulsa manu* ...? Plutarch, loc. cit. wants to connect σεῖστρον and σείω, 'shake'. Since Apuleius does not use the word *sistrum*, he is not suggesting a connection with, say, *sisto* (which would be unsuitable in any case), although *crepitaculum* does link similarly with *crepitare*. The Egyptian word was *sššt* (*Wb.* III, 486 f.) and it may derive from *sšš*, used of plucking papyrus. Hathor was the goddess originally concerned, and Isis here has taken over one of several attributes from Hathor, who is the goddess of music. The goddess Bastet is often shown too with this instrument. The sistrum could be apotropaic in intent, in the sense of repelling Typhon or other enemies; it could also express mourning or joy. It is suggested in Juvenal, 13.93 (*irato feriat mea lumina sistro*), that Isis could use it to inflict blindness. The words *argutum sonorem* imply that Apuleius is thinking of the more joyous effect of the sistrum, such as in the 'Festival Songs of Isis and Nephthys', where Osiris is called upon in a spirit of love. Isis and her devotees are often represented with the sistrum and also with the water-pitcher afterwards mentioned, and many sistra have been found in European cult-centres; see Grimm, *Ägypt. Rel. im röm. Deutschland*, 182-4, with refs. to other regions too; Tran Tam Tinh, *Herculanum*, 80 f.

p. 269, 3 **crispante brachio trigeminos iactus** : Cf. n. *ad* ch. 29 (290, 8), *cogitationes ... agitabam.*

p. 269, 4 **laevae** : The Dative is not common with *dependere*, but *Thes. L.L.* cites several other examples.

cymbium ... aureum : *Cymbium* is from κυμβίον, with a suggestion of boat-like shape. All the instances in *Thes. L.L.* s.v., with the exception of the two in this book, refer to cups or bowls used as drinking vessels. Something bigger must be implied in the present allusion, since a handle is mentioned on which a snake is climbing. Probably the water-pitcher is meant, such as is shown in the left hand of Isis in Leipoldt, *Bilderatlas* 27 [257]; in the 'Capitoline Isis', *ibid.* 26 [256] it has been restored; see C. Pietrangeli, *I Monumenti dei Culti Orientali* (Rome, 1951), 50. See also Leipoldt, op. cit. 39 (not in his second collection) and the discussion by G. E. Rizzo, 'Vasi del culto d'Iside', in his *Le Pitture dell' Aula Isiaca di Caligola* (Rome, E.F. 14 = 1936), 32 ff. A different type is the long-beaked pitcher, apparently intended as a sprinkler, which is depicted in a painting from Stabiae : see Leipoldt, op. cit. 55 [286]; Rizzo, op. cit. 33; Tran Tam Tinh, *Herculanum*, 32, who follows Vercoutter in deriving this from a type which is attested in Egypt in the New Kingdom.

In his choice of the word *cymbium* Apuleius is clearly deviating from normal linguistic usage; still more so when he uses it, in ch. 10, of a lantern (*lucerna*).

In the present case Wittmann may be right in suggesting the influence of Vergil, *Aen.* 3.66 (*spumantia cymbia lacte*), although R. D. Williams ad loc. takes *cymbia* here to have the normal meaning of 'cups', as in *Aen.* 5. 267 (small drinking cups). H. Merguet, *Lex. Verg.* 159 gives the non-commital 'Schale, Napf' for *cymbium*.

p. 269, 5 **aspis** : An example of a serpent on an Isiac vessel is found in the large rounded pitcher (doubtless different from the present one) carried by the third figure in a procession which a marble relief in the Vatican figures : see Amelung, *Die Sculpturen des Vaticanischen Museums*, II (plates), pl. 7, no. 55 and Textband II, 1, pp. 142 ff., where it is stated that the head of the serpent which forms the handle has been restored. See also Leipoldt, *Bilderatlas*, 56 [292]. A serpent similarly forms the handle of a broad-bottomed vessel in Weber, *Terr.* pl. 3, no. 28 (Textband, p. 49). Dattari, *Numi Augg. Alexandrini*, pl. 28, no. 1977, shows a vase of the oenochoë type with the handle in the form of a serpent; ibid. no. 287 for a similar vessel with five uraei on top of its cover. The former of these will correspond to the type envisaged here. The broad-based vessels, on the other hand, will be parallel to the *urnula* mentioned at the end of ch. 11, which has a handle surmounted by an asp. A situla from the 'Aula Isiaca' on the Palatine shows two uraei projecting from the base of the handle : see Rizzo, *Le Pitture dell'Aula Isiaca*, 32, fig. 33. The *cista mystica* and the sprinklers also reveal the serpentine theme : see Leipoldt, *Bilderatlas*, 57 [279] and 55 [286]. The serpent was appended, then to many types of Isiac vessels.

It is clearly the uraeus-serpent and its role in the Isis-cult was a varied one : see J. Gwyn Griffiths, *JEA* 47 (1961), 113 f., where the appearance of the goddess herself as a uraeus should be given an earlier date, for Isis and Nephthys occur in this form in Maystre and Piankoff, *Le Livre des Portes*, III (*MIFAO* 90, Cairo, 1962), 163 f. (in the 12th Division there, two uraei appear behind the door, bearing the names of Isis and Nephthys; cf. Piankoff and Rambova, *The Tomb of Ramesses* VI (New York, 1954), 222, fig. 73). It seems that this double uraeus is a duplication, applying to Upper as well as Lower Egypt, of the uraeus-goddess of Buto, Wedjoyet; so much is strongly suggested by the texts addressed to the royal crown on which Wedjoyet figures; cf. Erman, *Hymnen an das Diadem der Pharaonen* (Abh. Berlin, 1911), 34 ff. Another serpent-goddess, Renenutet (Thermuthis), exerts an influence on this form of Isis, expecially as she is also a uraeus : see J. Broekhuis, *De godin Renenwetet* (Assen, 1971), 10 ff. But when Wittmann states (p. 20), 'Im Isiskult ist die Uräus die weibliche Schlange, Isis selbst', he is indulging in a misleading generalization. On p. 191 n. 69 he states that already in the New Kingdom Isis is followed by the uraeus as determinative; but this applied also to the names of other goddesses. He correctly points out, before this, that the uraeus is a destroyer of enemies; what he omits to point out is that this role belonged originally to Wedjoyet and that it appears in several royal and divine connections. A multiplication of uraei on the royal crown and on the top façade of shrines meant that its extension to the adornment of vessels would not have been difficult. Here the uraeus is still, however, the attribute of Wedjoyet. Indeed, there would be a slight conceptual embarrassment to have Isis herself holding, or being associated with, a uraeus which connoted Isis. The description in Apuleius here makes no doubt that the cobra, either the *Naja haje* or the *Naja nigricollis* (cf. *JEA* 47 [1961], 113 n. 2) is meant. The serpents shown in the Isiac procession on the relief in the Vatican (Leipoldt, *Bilderatlas*, 56 [292]) are clearly uraei; so too is the snake held up by a bronze figure of Isis on her right arm in Roeder, *Bronzefiguren*, pl. 38 *i* with p. 262, § 321. In the other instances cited above, the swollen neck of the uraeus is not always indicated. In fact the serpent emerging from the *cista* (Leipoldt, 57 [279]) reminds one more of Eleusinian contexts; cf. n. below *ad* ch. 11 (274, 20), *cista*. Gressmann, 'Die Umwandlung der orientalischen Religionen unter dem Einfluss hellenischen Geistes', *Vorträge Bibl. Warburg 1923-4*, 170-95, has argued (pp. 187 ff.) for the Greek origin of the belief that Isis and Osiris could be represented by uraei, Certainly we find, as he says, serpents in Greek religion guarding the dead as benign creatures, ἀγαθοδαίμονες; cf. Leipoldt, *Umwelt*, III, 18 ('Totenmahl'). Yet the Egyptian symbolism of the uraeus provides a better explanation of its use in the cases here discussed. The one exception is the serpent emerging from the *cista*. Wedjoyet is the source of the other instances, and it would be unfortunate to identify Isis herself with what is, in the present allusion, an ancillary attribute.

p. 269, 6 **ambroseos** : Elsewhere Apuleius uses this adjective of the colour of a Venus-like woman (*Metam.* 10.31 [261, 25]), of a man's body (8.9 [184, 16]), of hair (5.22 [120, 14]), and of dew on a woman's lips (10.22 [253, 16]). According to *Thes. L.L.* s.v. it is a poetical word which Apuleius alone uses in prose. Neuenschwander, *Der bildliche Ausdruck des Apul.* 47, notes how the adjective is applied vaguely, as in modern usage.

p. 269, 6-7 **soleae palmae victricis foliis intextae** : The accepted view that the symbolism of the palm as a mark of victory derives from the Greek athletic games has been indirectly challenged by the researches of Ingrid Wallert in her book, *Die Palmen im alten Ägypten* (*MÄS* 1, Berlin, 1962). Discussing the date-palm in relation to Thoth as 'Lord of Time' (pp. 101 ff.), she shows how this god holds a palm-branch as a symbol of length of life, a concept which continued into Coptic times, though not in connection with Thoth. In a funerary context the palm-branch denoted continued life after death; it occurs thus on the breast of a mummy, or when it is carried in the funeral procession. The limestone bust of a young woman from Sheikh-Abâde (A.D. iv) shows her holding a palm-branch in her hand as a sign of eternal life, thus indicating that the Copts had maintained the symbolism in a Christian context. Dr Wallert seems reluctant, however, to gainsay the traditional view that the palm-branch, as a sign of victory, was Graeco-Roman in origin. Victory and eternal life, she suggests, are different concepts. When death is the theme, nevertheless, victory and eternal life are synonymous, and the occurrence of the palm-branch (or its leaves, as here) in connection with both Isis and Anubis must surely be assigned to the ancient tradition of Egypt.

In *Metam.* 2.28 Apuleius describes Zatchlas, an Egyptian high priest (*Aegyptius propheta primarius*). He occurs in Thessalian Larissa, in the story of Thelyphron; no high dignitary of an Egyptian cult, that is, in Egypt, can be imagined as being so far afield; one of the cult-centres of Thessaly can be rather invoked. (For his name see Introd. IV, end.) He is said to be wearing clothes and sandals of palm-leaves (*pedesque palmeis baxeis inductum*). According to Herodotus, 2.37, however, Egyptian priests wore sandals of papyrus. It was the bark of papyrus that was used for this purpose : see Wiedemann, *Herodots Zweites Buch*, 168 and id. *Das alte Ägypten*, 125 f. Two fragmentary statements of accounts were found written on parts of papyrus sandals, deriving probably from the second century B.C. : see Wilcken, *UPZ* I, no. 150, pp. 641 f. Many sandals of the Roman era were found by Petrie at Hawara; they were mostly of papyrus, but some were of leather or string; see Petrie, *Hawara, Biahmu and Arsinoe* (London, 1889), pls. 19 and 21 with pp. 12 and 13. In the Old Kingdom sandals were of leather : see E. Staehelin, *Unters. zur ägyptischen Tracht im Alten Reich* (*MÄS* 8, Berlin, 1966), 94 ff., but from the Middle and New Kingdoms there are several examples of sandals made of palm-fibre or of palm-leaves; they are recorded in *Berlin Mus. Ausführliches Verzeichnis* (Berlin, 1894), 77 and 140 f. (of the N.K. instances : 'Zumeist aus Palmblättern geflochten'); no examples of this material are recorded here from the Graeco-Roman era. For further instances of sandals of palm-fibre or palm-leaves see Wm. C. Hayes, *The Scepter of Egypt*, II (Cambridge, Mass., 1959), 188; V. Täckholm and M. Drar, *Flora of Egypt*, II (Cairo, 1950), 227; Wallert, *Die Palmen im Alten Ägypten*, 26, who also cites in n. 8 Passalacqua, *Cat. ... des Antiquités découvertes en Égypte* (Paris, 1826 [not 1926]), 24, nos. 474-77, where four sandals of palm-leaves are mentioned. From early times sandals were left in graves or depicted on the bottom of the coffin, the idea doubtless being, as Staehelin, op. cit. 98 f., suggests, to allow the deceased freedom of movement from the tomb. It is remarkable that the custom persisted into the Roman era and is exemplified in a mummified burial at Aquincum in Hungary : see V. Wessetzky, *Ägypt. Kulte in Ungarn* (Leiden, 1961), 11 f.; here the sandals were so small (18 cms. long) that Wessetzky rightly urges a symbolical meaning — the power, perhaps, to wander in the celestial fields. Gunn's theory that the ʿnḫ-sign represents a sandal-string would support the exceptional potency assigned to sandals in funerary connections. Staehelin, op. cit. 96, rejects the theory, however, and apparently with good reasons, although she admits the force of the early writing 𓏏𓋹𓊪𓈖 (p. 96 n. 3). Isis is in origin a funerary goddess, and the victory associated with her sandals is that over death. In the Hellenic athletic tradition crowns of various leaves, such as laurel or olive, were used to indicate triumph, but a palm-branch was used also in all of them with a similar meaning according to Plutarch, *Quaest. conv.* 8.4, 723 A ff. When the Romans took over the custom, they awarded crowns of palm-leaves as well as a palm-branch to the winner, and from 293 B.C. victorious generals were given crowns of this kind, and the *toga palmata* was also decorated with palm-leaves; see Steier, *PW* s.v. Phoinix (1941), 402, where it is also shown how *palma* was used by metonymy for victory; Apuleius himself uses it thus in *Metam.* 2.4. (27, 4f.) of Nikê (*palmaris deae facies*). The symbolism thus widely known in the Roman world may well have produced, coincidentally, a conflation here with Egyptian ideas. But the fact that sandals of palm-leaves, twice mentioned by Apuleius in an Egyptian religious connection, are unknown otherwise to the Roman world, points to the primacy of the Egyptian concept.

p. 269, 7 **talis ac tanta** : Alliteration often derives from popular speech and proverbs, and its cultivation in authors such as Tacitus, Fronto and Apuleius may be due to a desire to preserve old expressions thus sanctioned; cf. Bernhard, *Stil*, 219 ff. The alliterative nexus of two elements, as here, is the most common form.

p. 269, 7-8 **Arabiae felicia germina** : The reading *felicis* in some codices results from a natural misreading, for the stylistic purpose may be to suggest a reference to Arabia Felix, famed for perfumes and riches (Pliny, *HN* 5.12.65), a name which is 'oddly extended to nearly the whole mass of the peninsula, Petraea and Deserta being confined to the northern fringe' (J. O. Thomson, *History of Ancient Geography* [Cambridge, 1948], 297). Technically there is hypallage here for *Arabiae Felicis germina*, but a richer meaning is achieved by the transference; cf. Bernhard, *Stil*, 215.

The vivid description of the statue impelled Berreth, pp. 47 ff., to argue that a particular statue in a particular cult is being portrayed. A natural procedure, we might think, to one recording what is undoubtedly a personal experience. Berreth proceeds to argue that, since neither Isis Tychê nor Isis Pharia is being described, Apuleius here has in mind the Isis Aegyptia worshipped in one of the Isiac temples of Corinth; cf. the discussion above, Introd. III. It is noteworthy that no known statue or reflief or painting of Isis combines all the details mentioned here. Isis as corn-mother with situla and sistrum or with pitcher and sistrum may have been portrayed in Cenchreae; but the profusion of other detail suggests that Apuleius has conflated more than one type seen by him in various cult-centres.

CHAPTER 5

p. 269, 9 **'En adsum ...** : Whereas Reitzenstein, *Hellenist. Myst.* 240 rightly compares, for the whole of this statement, the form of prayers used in the magical papyri and in the 'Isis-Litany' of P. Oxy. 1380, it is in the Aretalogies of Isis, with their self-predication in the form of Ἐγώ εἰμι, that the close parallel is to be found. On the self-predication see D. Müller, *Isis-Aret.* 15 ff. and J. Bergman, *Ich bin Isis*, 23 ff.

The first part of the statement, up to *veneratur orbis*, has been well analysed by Berreth, Wittmann and Bernhard (*Stil*, 73). Like the prayer of Lucius to the moon-goddess in ch. 2, it shows a four-fold triadic arrangement intersected in three cases by short units which stand on their own :

En adsum tuis commota, Luci, precibus,

A. 1. rerum naturae parens,
   2. elementorum omnium domina,
   3. saeculorum progenies initialis,
B. 1. summa numinum,
   2. regina manium,
   3. prima caelitum,
   deorum dearumque facies uniformis, quae
C. 1. caeli luminosa culmina,
   2. maris salubria flamina,
   3. inferum deplorata silentia
   nutibus meis dispenso : cuius numen unicum
D. 1. multiformi specie,
   2. ritu   vario,
   3. nomine   multiiugo
   totus veneratur orbis.

Bernhard, *Stil*, 73 f., who ignores the last triad, points out that the tricolon is not a stranger to the ancient language of cult, and he cites the Song of the Arval Brothers. A slight difference is apparent, however : there the same phrase is repeated thrice (e.g. *Enos Lases iuvate!*) and the repetition seems due to a three-step rhythm (cf. *tripodaverunt*) : see W. Henzen, *Acta Fratrum Arvalium* (Berlin, 1874), 26 f.; F. C. Grant, *Ancient Roman Religion*, 17 f. Triadic formulation in a manner closer to that seen in Apuleius is common in Cicero, as Bernhard, *Stil*, 64 f., shows, citing e.g. *Pro Mil.* 10. There is no need, therefore, to adduce as an explanation the frequency of the triadic scheme in Egyptian (see O. Firchow, *Grundzüge der Stilistik in den altägyptischen Pyramidentexten* [Berlin, 1954], 147 ff., 'Das Dreierschema'; cf. the two examples, substantival and verbal, in G. Fecht, *Literarische Zeugnisse zur 'Persönlichen Frömmigkeit' in Ägypten* [*Abh. Heidelberg*, 1965], 39 et al.); nor to refer to the custom in Hebrew, where *parallelismus membrorum*, though normally concerned with two units, can sometimes produce three or more (see W. H. Cobb, *A Criticism of Systems of Hebrew Metre* [Oxford, 1905], 67 f.). Clearly the tricolon is not a very distinctive stylistic mark. What is distinctive in the present composition is the Ἐγώ εἰμι formulation, which Norden has shown to be Oriental in origin; see his *Agnostos Theos*, 178 ff. and cf. Ed. Schweizer, *Ego Eimi* (Göttingen, 1939), 43; also un-Greek and un-Latin in origin is the accumulation of divine attributes in the self-predication (see Norden, loc. cit, who quotes a Coptic hymn of A.D. iii which Bernhard in turn (p. 74) regards as offering a parallel to chs. 2 and 5 of Apuleius). In the Psalms and in Egyptian hymns this accumulation is common in the second person; see A. Barucq, *L'expression de la louange divine et la prière dans la Bible et en Égypte* (Cairo, 1962), 290 ff. From such sources the influence on Apuleius must be indirect, that is, through Greek or Latin writings tinged by Egyptian or Semitic style. The most obvious example would be the corpus of Isiac Aretalogies. Apuleius makes considerable use of rhyme here, particularly in the second and third triads, with their sequence of rhymed couplets. In these two sections the order of words follows a regular pattern; by way of contrast the fourth triad indulges in chiasmus (*multiformi specie, ritu vario*).

   p. 269, 9 **tuis commota ... precibus** : After his prayer to the moon-goddess (ch. 2) Lucius is said to have fallen asleep (ch. 3 *ad init.*). Isis therefore has appeared and spoken to him in a dream or trance; cf. ch. 19 (281, 3-4), *nec fuit nox una vel quies aliqua visu deae monituque ieiuna.* Since Lucius has been thinking of the moon-goddess, Berreth points to examples of Selenê sending dreams (e.g. *PGM* 4, 2624 ὀνειροπομπεῖ). But it is Isis who is really at work here, and like other Egyptian deities she was credited with this power, the dreams inspired by her being mantic or healing or both, so that a deliberate *incubatio* by worshippers aimed at receiving them; cf. *SIG* 1133 (Delos, ii B.C.) and Roussel, *CED* 269; Diod. Sic. 1.25; Josephus, *C. Ap.* 1.32; Tib. 1.3.27 f.; Juv. 6. 530; Wilcken, *UPZ* I, 68 f. (of Sarapis); W. Otto, *Priester und Tempel*, I, 14 f. (of Sarapis). The interpretation of dreams was long since known in Egypt : see Morenz, *Die Begegnung Europas mit Ägypten* (*Sitzb. Leipzig*, 1968), 85 f. with refs. Sauneron, *Les Songes et leur Interprétation* (*Sources Orientales*, II, Paris, 1959), 20, points out that the Egyptians gave special regard to the premonitory vision and that elaborate collections of interpretations were prepared (p. 38); see especially his discussion of the role of Isis in dreams (p. 47). Bonnet, *Reallexikon*, 837, believes that Isis probably achieved her role as a healing goddess in this connection through her association with Sarapis; cf. Ilse Becher, 'Antike Heilgötter und die römische Staatsreligion', *Philol.* 114 (1970), 228 ff., esp. 230 n. 115. Yet Isis is invoked before this in magico-medical papyri as the healer of Horus, who becomes the divine prototype of patients; cf. J. Gwyn Griffiths, *Conflict*, 35; R. E. Witt, *Isis Gr.-R.* 185 ff. The tradition appears too in the Metternich Stela and related texts. In the second century A.D. the most famous incubation oracles were the sanctuary of Asclepius in Pergamon and that of Sarapis in Alexandria; cf. Martin Kaiser, *Artemidor von Daldis : Traumbuch* (Basel, 1965), 10. According to Pausanias, 10.32.9 = Hopfner, *Fontes*, 339 no one could enter the temple of Isis in Tithorea, Phocis, unless Isis had invited him in a dream. The function of dreams in the early Greek novels is well discussed by Kerényi, *Die Griechisch-Orientalische Roman-literatur*, 165 ff.; he notes that simultaneous double dream-epiphanies occur in chs. 22 and 27; one may add ch. 6. Heliodorus and Longus also use this phenomenon. See also n. *ad* ch. 6 (270, 9), *meo monitu; ad* ch. 6 (270, 16-17, *per quietem*; and *ad* ch. 21 (282, 17), *deae nutu.* For the importance of the idea in Mithraism see Vermaseren, *CIM Rel. Mithr.* II, Index s.v. *monitus.*

p. 269, 9 **rerum naturae parens** : In the traditional Graeco-Roman mythology
it was Aphrodite or Venus who occupied this position; according to *Hom.
Hymn.* 5.1-5 Aphrodite has instilled the passion of love in gods, men and all
creatures; Lucretius, I, *init.* extends this idea to make Venus the creator of the
universe. Apuleius himself in *Metam.* 4.30 (*init.*) puts similar words into the
mouth of Venus : *en rerum naturae prisca parens, en elementorum origo initialis,
en orbis totius alma Venus* ... Tschudin, *Isis in Rom*, 15, points out that the
Venus of Lucretius (and here he is including the whole presentation, not merely
the initial invocation) possesses, as universal goddess, all the qualities of Isis;
and it is urged by Schefold, *Vergessenes Pompeji*, 30, that the concept of the
universal goddess, which was associated with Venus in the first century B. C.,
was not an achievement of the Rome of the late Republic; behind it was really
the theology of Alexandria. Isis Panthea may well be the prototype. At the
same time the influence of Stoicism must not be forgotten; it doubtless played
its part in the evolution of Isis Panthea herself. Apuleius relates the concept
of pantheism in *Apol.* 64 to the Platonic ruler of the universe; there (72, 20)
he is described as *totius rerum naturae causa et ratio et origo initialis*. In ch. 2
of the present book the moon-goddess is addressed as *Ceres alma frugum parens
originalis*; she is not, then, the creator of all. As far as Isis is concerned, the
claim that she created the universe seems to exceed what is stated elsewhere
in the Graeco-Roman material. Plutarch, *De Is. et Os.* 43, 368 C and 53,
372 E, explains Isis as the female and creative principle that has union with
Osiris; cf. 32, 363 D where Osiris is the Nile and Isis the earth. The Aretalogies
come nearer to Apuleius : Isis is the ruler of every land (M 3 a), but is only
the eldest daughter of Cronus (Geb, the earth-god), hence hardly the First
Cause (M 5); she is the discoverer of corn (M 7) and she has power over stars,
sun, moon and sea (M 13 ff.) as well as over thunder and rain (M 42 and 54).

Pantheism, then, is ascribed to her, but she is not *expressis verbis* the creator
of the universe. P. Oxy. 1380, 121 hardly comes nearer to that : Isis is addressed
as 'ruler of the world' (ἄνασσα τῆς οἰκουμένης), but cf. M 3 a ('ruler of every
land'). Athenagoras, *Pro Christ.* 112 (ed. E. Schwartz, p. 28) is a real parallel,
for Isis is said to be regarded as the 'nature of Aion (Time, Eternity), by which
all have been created and through which all exist.' This is the Iranian Aion,
the cosmic creator-god, and the doctrine concerning him may have influenced
Apuleius here : v. E. Norden, *Geburt des Kindes*, 30, who cites also (n. 2)
Diod. Sic. 1.11.5. L. Kákosy has shown in 'Osiris-Aion', *Oriens Ant.* 3 (1967),
15-25, that Osiris was likewise associated with Aion. In the early Egyptian
tradition Isis is certainly a mother-goddess, that is, the mother of Horus and
of the King, and even of the gods : see Maria Münster, *Unters. zur Göttin
Isis*, 191 f.; 205. Allusions to her as an 'Urgöttin' who is the mother of creation
are neither frequent nor clear. M. Münster, op. cit. 208, quotes a phrase which
seems to mean 'Great One who initiated existence'; cf. Bergman, *Ich bin Isis*,
132 ff. and 282 f. More apposite is the fact that Isis has now assimilated,
as Bergman, 133, points out, the cosmic qualities of Nut, Neïth, and Hathor.

Even so, Apuleius here, familiar as he doubtless was with writings similar to the Aretalogies known to us, has gone further in explicitly applying to Isis the concept applied previously to Venus-Aphrodite, a concept that is itself indebted to Isis Panthea as evolved under Stoic influence.

p. 269, 10 **elementorum** : Cf. ch. 23 (285, 12), *per omnia vectus elementa* and n. As we have seen, Venus is the *elementorum origo initialis* in *Metam.* 4.30; in 3.15 *serviunt elementa* is used of the magic secrets of the mistress of Photis, and the same expression is applied to Isis in ch. 25 below. Isis is said in P. Oxy. 1380, 183 f. to be the discoverer of the moist, dry and cold (the hot, θερμῶν, should probably be restored). But Apuleius may well be thinking of the four elements which had become traditional since Empedocles — earth, water, air and fire. Wittmann raises the pertinent question of whether an Egyptian doctrine of elements may not be involved. Certainly the doctrine of Hermopolis ascribed four basic qualities to the *Urgötter*, and to their feminine counterparts : water, infinity, darkness, and invisibility. Diog. Laert. prooem. 10 = Jacoby, *FGrH* 264 F 1 states that in 'the philosophy of the Egyptians' matter was the first principle, and that the four elements were derived from it. Hecataeus of Abdera, *On the Philosophy of the Egyptians*, is then cited, with Manetho, *Epitome of Physical Doctrines.* Cf. Diod. Sic. 1.11.6, but five elements are there ascribed to the Egyptians, *pneuma* being added to fire, air, earth and water; see Jacoby, *FGrH* III Komm. (1954), 39 and Spoerri, *Späthellenistische Berichte über Welt, Kultur und Götter* (Basel, 1959), 186 ff.; also (on the relation between Hecataeus and Diodorus) Oswyn Murray, *JEA* 56 (1970), 169 f. None of these sources reproduces the Egyptian doctrine as clearly as Seneca, *Nat. quaest.* 3.12.2 (ed. Gercke, p. 105) : *Aegyptii quattuor elementa fecerunt, deinde ex singulis bina maria et feminea* (reading the last two words with E; P. Oltramare, Budé text 1961, p. 129, omits them). See further, for the Egyptian teaching, Sethe, *Amun und die Acbt Urgötter von Hermopolis* (*Abh. Berlin,* 1929) and cf. Iamblichus, *De Myst.* 8.3 (ed. E. des Places, Budé, p. 197). If Apuleius was familiar with any of these ideas, he does not reveal that in any of his allusions to *elementa*.

domina : Cf. ch. 7 (271, 18-19), *orbisque totius dominam*; ch. 21 (283, 2-3), *iubente domina.* Cf. παντοκράτειρα, Hymns of Isidorus, I, 2. = *SEG* 8, 548, 2; see Vanderlip, *ad. loc.* p. 21.

initialis : The two other occurrences of this word in Apuleius are in similar contexts : *Metam.* 4.30 (Venus as *origo initialis*) and *Apol.* 64. (72, 20), where a similar phrase is used of Plato's cosmic ruler. *Thes. L.L.* s.v. lists only two doubtful occurrences before Apuleius. The idea is applied to Isis in the collocation ῏Ισις Τύχη Πρωτογένεια found in Delos (ii B.C.) = *SIG* 1133. The idea of sovereignty over time was prominent in the Isis-cult of the Roman era, as L. Kákosy shows in 'Zu einer Etymologie von Philä : die "Insel der Zeit" ', *Acta Ant. Hung.* 16 (1968), 39-48. The etymology cited, although not a valid one (the name is probably Nubian), is one mark of this concept, which is shown to apply especially to Osiris (cf. Kákosy's 'Osiris-Aion', cited

above p. 140). Yet Isis shares in it too; cf. Diod. Sic. 1.11.4 on the name of
Isis as meaning 'the ancient one', perhaps invoking the Egn. *is*, 'old'. In Plut.
De Is. et Os. 9, 354 C Athena (= Neïth), identified with Isis, is said to incor-
porate the past, present and future; v. my Comm. *ad loc.* p. 284.

  p. 269, 10-11 **summa numinum** : Cf. Εἶσις θεὰ μεγίστη, *OGIS* 704; *SEG*
8, 657; Breccia, *Iscr.* 103 (of Isis Pharia); μ[ε]γίστη θεῶν, P. Oxy, 1380,
142; βασίλεια θεῶν, Hymns of Isidorus, 1.1 = *SEG* 8, 548, 1; μήτηρ θεῶν
CIG 4919 (cited *SB* III, 389); and for similar locutions in Egn. v. Junker and
Winter, *Geburtshaus*, 9, 13 ff. 'sovereign of the gods of heaven, governor of
the gods of earth, kite-goddess of the gods of the underworld'; Isis is 'the
great one' (*wrt*) in Leclant, *Enquêtes*, 108 and 'sovereign of the gods' (*ḥnwt
nṯrw*) in Leclant, *Mons. Thébains*, 287; cf. *Wb.* II, 332, 9 (of 'Hathor-Isis');
'mistress of the gods' (*nbt nṯrw*) and 'mistress of all the gods', refs in M. Münster,
Unters. zur Göttin Isis, 204; v. also Bergman, *Ich bin Isis*, 169 f. Both Greek and
Egyptian epithets here should be taken with a pinch of salt in view of the
lavishing of similar phrases on other deities. Thus in *SEG* 8, 654 Aphrodite and
Isis are coupled as μέγισται; and in Egn. claims of uniqueness are made by
many gods : v. E. Otto, *Gott und Mensch*, 11 ff.

  p. 269, 11 **regina manium** : Other readings include *regina animarum* (as
animum) and *regina amnium*; and conceptually support can be adduced for
any of the three. Like Osiris, Isis has a strong funerary association, and in
Plut. *De Is. et Os.* 27, 361 E (v. my Comm. 392 f.) she is equated with Persephassa (Persephone), while Osiris is often identified with Hades or Pluto and
described, in a priestly view, as king of the dead (78, 382 E). In ch. 23 Apuleius
gives special prominence to the experience of Lucius as an initiate in respect
of his visit to the realm of death : *accessi confinium mortis etc.* Representations
on mummy-coverings in the Graeco-Roman era sometimes depict the deceased
woman as Isis : v. Parlasca, *Mumienporträts*, pl. 20, 1 and p. 66 (both sistrum
and Isis-knot appear; perhaps a priestess of Isis is implied); pl. 31, 4 and p. 72;
p. 112 with refs.; Edgar, *Graeco-Egyptian Coffins*, pl. 44 and pp. 110, 112
(nos. 33270 and 33271), where Edgar notes that the mantle is knotted between
the breasts, but without further discussion; cf. V. Schmidt, *Levende og Døde
i det Gamle Aegypten* (Copenhagen, 1919), fig. 1353; Erman, *Rel.²* 254 (Berlin,
13, 462) and Schäfer, 'Das Gewand der Isis', 198 n. 2. Four examples from the
Roman era of funerary statues of women in Athens which show the Isiac
knot are noted by S. Dow, *Harv. Theol. Rev.* 30 (1937), 227. In all these cases
except the first the Isis-knot is the feature which prompted Schäfer to propound
his convincing theory about the origin of the Isiac dress. Since he posits basically that the Greek Isis-garment imitated a form of dress found in Egypt in
the Late Era, it may be questioned whether the mummy-paintings themselves
are imitating a contemporary fashion; presumably Schäfer's view was that
by the Roman period, at any rate, the breast-knot had become distinctively
Isiac in spite of its origin in the life of the people. If dead women are sometimes

represented as Isis, it is a striking fact, nevertheless, that the identification of the dead with Osiris, when it was varied in respect of women in the Graeco-Roman era, led to the introduction, not of Isis, but of Hathor : v. G. Lefebvre, *ASAE* 23 (1923), 239, citing seven cases in *Le livre que mon nom fleurisse* and one instance (published by him) where 'Osiris-Hathor' is placed before the woman's name; cf. Bonnet, *Reallexikon*, 280; Erman (tr. Wild), *Rel.* 466; Morenz, 'Das Problem des Werdens zu Osiris usw.' in Derchain, ed. *Rel. en Egypte*, 81. Wittmann thinks that the sovereignty of Isis over the dead involves her part in the judgement of the dead, and he invokes the phrase 'fire of Hades' ($\pi\tilde{\upsilon}\rho$ "$A\ddot{\iota}\delta\sigma$s) used of Isis in the hymn by Mesomedes, line 9 : v. Peek, *Isishymnus*, 145 and J. U. Powell, *Collect. Alexandrina*, 198. Peek himself (p. 146) was unable to explain the phrase, and the part of Isis in the judgement, ancillary as it is, scarcely justifies such a hell-fiery epitome. Not that the Egyptians refrained from believing in hell-fire and other tortures of the damned; far from it : v. Zandee, *Death as an Enemy*, 285 and my remarks in *JEA* 48 (1962), 168. But Isis was not seen as an instrument of this fury; in the vignettes she benignly accompanies her husband Osiris, who is the judge. The phrase $\tau\dot{\eta}\nu$ $\dot{\epsilon}\nu$ $\varLambda[\dot{\eta}]\theta\eta$ $\dot{\iota}\lambda\alpha\rho\dot{\alpha}\nu$ $\ddot{\sigma}\psi\iota\nu$ (P. Oxy. 1380, 127), on the other hand, is apposite to her role. The reading *regina animorum*, 'queen of souls', might be justified with reference to Plutarch, *De Is. et Os.* 27, 361 E, where Isis is said to give to men and women a 'pattern of piety' ($\dot{\epsilon}\dot{\upsilon}\sigma\epsilon\beta\epsilon\dot{\iota}\alpha s$ ... $\delta\dot{\iota}\delta\alpha\gamma\mu\alpha$); cf. 78, 382 F f., where her husband Osiris is said to be a 'leader' of the souls of men. *Regina amnium* could also be supported, for the Aretalogies refer to the sway of Isis over rivers (M 39; D. Müller, pp. 61 ff.). Apuleius is really providing a shortened Aretalogy, so that much is omitted. The connection of the goddess with seas (and indirectly with rivers) is mentioned in the next line (*maris salubria flamina*), and an allusion to her power over the underworld follows. If avoidance of repetition is the criterion, then *regina animorum* might be the preferred reading; but it would be unwise to assume so fastidious an approach to details of content.

p. 269, 11 **prima caelitum** : Cf. ch. 7 (271, 18), *matrem siderum*; ch. 25 (286, 25), *tibi respondent sidera*. The Aretalogies confirm this in that Isis is said to order the course of the sun and moon (M 14, D. Müller, 40 f.); cf. *PGM* 13, 62 ff. and 571 ff. (of Hermes) and Reitzenstein, *Poimandres*, 22 ff. Isis also orders the stars (M 13) and is herself identified with Selenè and with Sirius, the latter being an ancient equation. Cf. also Hymns of Isidorus, 3, 1 = *SEG* 8, 550, 1, and Vanderlip *ad. loc.*, p. 51.

p. 269, 11-12 **deorum dearumque facies uniformis** : Since no gods, but only goddesses, are mentioned in the identifications that follow, Beroaldus deleted *deorum*, and some of the manuscript readings support this. The trouble then arises, however, as Hildebrand shows, that the phrase would begin with *dearumque*, where the conjunction would mar the pattern of uniform asyndeton in the passage. Similar claims made for Isis elsewhere suggest that she combines the nature of all deities; and Apuleius repeats the idea at the end of the sentence (*cuius numen unicum etc.*). The phrases *facies uniformis* and *nomen unicum* reveal the monotheistic trend in the concept, but with it goes a recognition of other gods subsumed in the godhead. Thus E. Peterson, *Εἷς Θεός*, 253 f., rightly discusses the idea under the heading 'Die synkretistische Einheits- formel'; cf. Weinreich, *Neue Urkunden zur Sarapis-Religion*, 17 and 28. An inscription from Capua (*CIL* X, 3800 = Dessau, *Inscr. Sel.* 4362 = Vidman, *SIRIS* 234, no. 502) sums up this approach : *Te tibi / una quae / es omnia / dea Isis* ... A factor in such an attitude, as D. Müller, *Isis-Aret.* 86, points out, is the universalism engendered by widening political horizons in the Hell- enistic era. By the second and third centuries of our era a number of religions in the Roman Empire, including the cults of Mithras, Isis, the Great Mother, the Carthaginian Dea Caelestis, the Phrygian Sabazios, Hecate, Attis, and Orphic Dionysus, were claiming that ultimate truth was theirs and that other gods were merely manifestations of the deity of the cult in question; v. G. Wissowa, *Rel. und Kultus der Römer*[2] (Munich, 1912), 91, who instances the use of the epithet Pantheus with several of these gods. Berreth notes a spirit of tolerance in the Apuleian passage; admittedly, this is so, as with the Aretalogies, but it is a condescending tolerance, a henotheism which does not leave in doubt which deity is superior. Berreth also notes the possibility of Egyptian influence on the universalist concept; this is discussed below in relation to the list of deities equated. In a study of the development of Sarapis Ugo Bianchi, in *Mythos : FS. M. Untersteiner* (Genoa, 1970), 97-106, makes a good case for applying the term 'cosmopolitan' rather than 'universalist' to the god, reserving the latter term for the strictly monotheistic religions which reject syncretism with other cults. A good deal of what he says about Sarapis can be applied to Isis (cf. his p. 106); they both have cosmic functions and achieve a position of widely-acknowledged supremacy. The big difference is that in the case of Isis one can trace a long development within Egypt of her assumption of the attributes of other deities.

p. 269, 12 **caeli ... maris ... inferum** : Heaven, earth, and the underworld are the three divisions intented, although the sea rather oddly represents the earth; this is why Meursius suggested *aeris* for *maris*. But in the Aretalogies Isis is explicitly associated with seas, rivers, and winds : 'I have discovered the activities of seamanship' (M 15); 'I am mistress of rivers and winds and sea' (M 39); 'I calm and swell the sea' (M 43, Peek, *Isishymnus*, 124, cf. Roussel, *Rev. Ét. Grec.* 42 [1929], 155); 'I am mistress of shipping, I make the navigable unnavigable whenever I decide' (M 49-50); according to P. Oxy. 1380, 125 and 223 ff. the Eleutheros in Tripoli and the Ganges in India are equally favoured by Isis. See Dieter Mueller, *OLZ* 67 (1972), 126 and above, Introd. V. for the earlier roles of Isis in this connection. Compare the figure of Isis Pharia on coins, gems and reliefs, steadying a wind-swollen sail in front of her; v. J.-G. Szilágyi in *Bull. du musée hongrois des beaux-arts nos.* 32-33 (1969), 19-30 and L. Castiglione, 'Isis Pharia'. The division into heaven, earth and the underworld is amplified into further categories in ch. 25 (*te superi* *colunt, observant inferi* etc.). *Inferum* is an instance of the fondness of Apuleius for the shortened form of the genitive plural; commentators cite *nummum*, *denarium, servulum, pastophorum* (the last in chs. 17 and 30); in this book he varies *deorum* and *deum*. Bernhard, *Stil*, 215, regards *inferum deplorata silentia* as an instance of hypallage; this may be questioned, since *deploratus* as a participle used adjectivally with the sense of *miserabilis* is used more often with abstract nouns than with persons; v. *Thes. L.L.* s.v. (5, 575, 43 ff.).

flamina : The reading *flumina* is recorded by Hildebrand for his M; it would agree with the reference to rivers in the Aretalogies, but hardly goes with *maris*; further, winds are mentioned too in the Aretalogies : see above.

p. 269, 13 **numen unicum** : The name Thiouis, said to be used of Isis by the Egyptians in Hymns of Isidorus, 1, 23 = *SEG* 8, 548, 23 really means 'The Only One', Egn *t3 wʿt*, 'unica'; cf. Hondius and Vanderlip ad loc.; cf. too P. Oxy. 1380, 6, μίαν; also the Aretalogy from Cyrene, 4 Εἶσις αἰῶνος μόνη (Peek, *Isishymnus*, 129). Another expression which applies the concept to Isis is 'there exists not her like'; it is used of other gods too, and probably derives from the biographical literature of the Middle Kingdom : see E. Otto, *Gott und Mensch*, 11 f.

p. 269, 14 **nomine multiiugo** : Cf. ch. 22 (284, 10 f.), *deae multinominis*; μυριώνυμος, Plut. *De Is. et Os.* 53, 372 E and my remarks ad loc. citing examples in inscriptions and papyri; πολυώνυμος, Anubis-hymn from Cius (Peek, *Isishymnus*, 139, 5); P. Oxy. 1380, 97 and 101 f. with B. A. van Groningen's Comm. *ad* 97. Demeter has the latter epithet too in P. Berol. Inv. 11793, 1 and it is used of Hades in *Homer. Hymn* 2. 18 (see Allen, Halliday, and Sikes ad loc. and cf. C. H. Roberts, *Aegyptus* 14 [1934], 448). For its application to other gods see Paul Collart, *Rev. égyptol.* 1 (1919), 5, who cites several instances from the Orphic Hymns. Médan, *Lat.* 252, points out that *speciʃe ritu vario, nomine multiiugo* constitutes a pentameter.

Similar epithets applied to Isis are πολύμορφος (P.Oxy. 1380, 9) and μυριό-μορφος (*Anth. Graec.* 16.264). Πολυώνυμος is paralleled in Egn. by 'š3 rnw, 'with many names', used of several gods, though no instance is extant of its application to Isis.

p. 269, 14-15 **inde primigenii etc.** : The remainder of the general self-predication of the goddess may be considered as forming this pattern :

A. 1. Inde primigenii Phryges Pessinuntiam deum matrem,
   2. hinc autocthones Attici Cecropeiam Minervam,
   3. illinc fluctuantes Cyprii Paphiam Venerem,
B. 1. Cretes sagittiferi Dictynnam Dianam,
   2. Siculi trilingues Stygiam Proserpinam,
   3. Eleusinii vetustam deam Cererem,
C. 1. Iunonem   alii,
   2. Bellonam   alii,

    3. Hecatam   isti,
    4. Rhamnusiam   illi,
D. 1. et qui nascentis dei Solis
    2. inchoantibus illustrantur radiis
    3. Aethiopes Afrique
    4. priscaque doctrina pollentis Aegyptii
    5. caerimoniis me propriis percolentes
    6. appellant vero nomine
    7.   reginam Isidem.

The 'true name' is well located in the skilfully emphatic ending, and its location
contrasts with the method of the Aretalogies which begin Εἶσις ἐγώ εἰμι
or the like (M 3a, D. Müller, 19), thus proclaiming the name *tout d'abord*.
There are two triadic sections followed by a tetrad; within these three sections
there is a good deal of rhyme, and a regular scheme of word-order is presented
except for the studied variation in the location of the adjectives; also the tetrad
relates chiastically to the order of the triads (e.g. *Eleusinii vetustam deam
Cererem, Iunonem alii*). The last section is more amorphous, suggesting an
ending in prose, with a sense of unwinding. Wittmann rightly argues that
a cult-hymn is being imitated, but his suggestion that it was divided into two
parts, to be sung by two choirs (he compares the two groups in one of the paintings from Herculaneum which shows an Isiac rite : v. Leipoldt, *Bilderatlas*,
53 [294] and Tran Tam Tinh, *Herculanum*, pl. 27) is somewhat fanciful. So
is his arithmology. Leaving *reginam Isidem* out of the count, he finds the four
parts yielding 13 + 12 + 8 + 21 words, a total of 56; the first three sections
together give 35, and the relation 56 : 35 : 21 is said to agree with 'dem ureigent-
lichen Prinzip der Harmonie, dem goldenen Schnitt' (8 : 5 : 3). The sequence,
be it noted, is achieved in an arbitrary way : the total and the first three sections
and the fourth section; why should such an odd pattern be elicited? Further,
he argues, the whole hymn has a total of 108 words, which is 27 quadrupled;
27 itself is the 'third potency' of the sacred number three. Number-symbolism
in the ancient world may often seem bizarre to the modern mind; the question
here is what evidence there is for its conscious use in literary composition
in this way. It may be doubted whether there is any. In poetry, of course, the
number of syllables in a line is often dictated by the metre; a prose imitation
of a hymn may show signs of a regular pattern, but syllables rather than
words would be involved.
    One may also question Berreth's suggestion that special significance attaches
to the fact that the Egyptians are thirteenth in the list of peoples named; he
cites Weinreich, *Triskaidekadische Studien* (RGVV 16, 1, Giessen, 1916).
What is more obviously significant is that the Egyptians are last in the list;
the last here is clearly the most important, just as Isis herself commandingly
ends the whole hymn. One must agree, on the other hand, with both Berreth
and Wittmann that the musical effect of the hymn is enhanced by its richly

varied vocalisation. Also there is a skilful achievement of variety in dealing with material which invites uniformity and monotony, especially, for instance, the list of venerating peoples; cf. Bernhard, *Stil*, 87.

It is with P. Oxy. 1380 that this part of the hymn invites comparison, although the papyrus hymn is on a much bigger scale : it refers to more than fifty names of compared deities; v. B. A. van Groningen, *De Papyro Oxy*. 1380, 72; Berreth reckoned that the papyrus mentions 67 places in Lower Egypt and 55 places outside Egypt (with many places only adjectival attributes are given, without naming a deity). Apuleius, on the other hand, names only thirteen peoples. In spite of this he seems to be following the approach of the papyrus, which dates probably from the early second century A. D., its composition deriving, it seems likely, from the first century. The Egyptian equivalences in the papyrus are of at least three kinds : first, a genuine cult-assimilation is indicated, as in line 30, where Isis is said to be Athena in Saïs (a complication in the whole of this part is that Greek names may conceal Egyptian originals, in this case Athena standing for Neïth); secondly, an assimilation is maintained though no known syncretism lies behind it, as in line 72, where Isis is said to be Korê in the Metelite nome (Korê probably conceals the name of an Egyptian funerary goddess); thirdly, general attributes of Isis are freely allotted to different cult-centres without being necessarily distinctive to them, as in line 51. where Isis is said to be Good Fortune ($T\acute{v}\chi\eta$ $\,{}^{\prime}A\gamma a\theta\acute{\eta}$) in Busiris. Clearly the second and third categories have some affinity. Documents relating to Osiris show that an assimilation of deities in all the forty-two nomes of Egypt was proclaimed on his behalf, and that in many cases there was no process of syncretism such as occurred with Osiris-Sokar or Osiris-Ptaḥ, though these are included : v. *Book of the Dead*, 142 (Lepsius, *Todtenbuch* ... *P. Turin*, pl. 59; this, the Saïte recension, gives a longer list than that in the Papyrus of Nu, and Budge gives both in his translation). The formula most often followed is 'Osiris in Saïs' (1, 23 = Budge, p. 323), i.e. Osiris + a place- name; sometimes a general epithet follows, such as 'Osiris Lord of Eternity' (3, 4); cf. the expressions 'Osiris in all his places' (6, 13) and 'Osiris in all his names' (6, 19), and especially, from our point of view, the small section beginning 'Isis, the goddess in all her names' (5, 15). Parts of B.M.P. 10569 are rather similar : v. R. O. Faulkner, *An Ancient Egyptian Book of Hours* (Oxford, 1958). The extension of the cult-power of Osiris as proclaimed in *BD* 142 is a thorough-going process, and is comparable to the procedure of P. Oxy. 1380 and of Apuleius here. Cf. my review of Faulkner's book in *JEA* 46 (1960), 123 f.; it will be seen, however, that I now regard the spell in *BD* as differing from Faulkner's text in this matter. In P. Oxy. 1380 the question arises whether the equivalences claimed in places outside Egypt have any validity in cult. B. A. van Groningen, op. cit. 75 ff., denies this, maintaining that the idea is that the goddesses in all these places are merely forms of Isis. In lines 83 ff. people are said to call Isis $\tau\rho\iota\phi v\acute{\eta}v$ in the Cyclades; van Groningen, 27 f., takes the reference to be to Delos and to Hecate or Artemis Hecate, and holds to the meaning that she is interpreted as a form of Isis. He admits, however (p. 28), that the evidence of the Egyptian cults in Delos shows that Artemis and Hecate were closely associated with Isis there : v. Roussel, *CED* 151, nos. 127 and 128. Further, several true attributes of the goddess occur in the list, such as ταυρῶπις 107 (for βοῶπις); πολυώνυμος 97, 101; δεσπότις 108; σώτειρα 91; μεγίστη 92, even if their validity in the local cults referred to cannot be demonstrated. By and large, nonetheless, van Groningen's approach seems to be sound, and he rightly compares (p. 79) the prototypes in Egyptian texts, such as a list of the names of Hathor (Mariette, *Dendérah*, I, 39 e, cf. Brugsch, *Dict. Géog.* 1158 f.); what he omits to point out is that this list embodies some genuine syncretisms, e.g. Hathor is Bastet in Bubastis and Neïth in Saïs. Certainly, the list in Apuleius invites comparison, as van Groningen, 74 f., remarks. It is striking that it omits many places in Greek lands where the cult of Isis is known to have flourished; as for the places it does mention, it is an open question whether the cult was established in some of them, so that one is tempted to explain them, for the most part, as foreign goddesses interpreted in an arbitrary fashion as forms of Isis; cf. Stephanie West, *JTS* 18 (1967), 142 f. on P. Oxy. 1380; she compares the first Hymn of Isidorus, *SEG* 8, 548, 14-23, where the principle is plainly stated; v also. ead. *JTS* 20 (1969), 228-30.

p. 269, 15 **primigenii Phryges** : The tradition which Herodotus, 2.2, records about the Phrygians as the oldest race had clearly won wide acceptance. Cf. Hippolytus, *Refut.* 7.7.22 = Hopfner, *Fontes*, 435 : Αἰγύπτια, πάντων ἀνθρώπων μετὰ τοὺς Φρύγας ἀρχαιότεροι καθεστῶτες (from a text which was admittedly intended for a Phrygian-Jewish audience, v. Reitzenstein, *Hellenist. Myst.* 12 and 240 ff., and which claims that Osiris and other gods were forms of Attis, v. K. Latte, *Lesebuch* : *Rel. der Römer*, 80). Apuleius, while reserving for the Egyptians the role of guardians of the authentic religion, assigns the greatest antiquity to the Phrygians.

Pessinuntiam : The evidence of the codices suggests that scribes were in difficulties with the name. Herodian, 1,11. refers to τὴν Πεσσινουντίαν θεόν; cf. Cic. *Pro Sest.* 26, 56, *Matris Magnae Pessinuntius ille sacerdos.* Cybele or the Great Mother is meant, and the city of Pessinus was the earliest and most important centre of her cult, in which she was closely associated with the god Attis; cf. W. Ruge, *PW* s.v. Pessinus (1938), 1109, where the forms Πεσσινουντίς (Strabo, 10, 469) and Πεσσινέ(ι)α (on a coin) are noted. The origins of Cybele's cult in Pessinus probably precede the immigration of the Phrygians into the area : v. Ruge, 1106 and P. Lambrechts, 'Excavations at Pessinus' (Memo from Belgium, Feb. 1968), 5; cf. Hdt. 7.73. Coins of Augustus and Tiberius (probably from Pessinus) showed the portraits of the emperors with an image of the Great Mother and the legend Μήτηρ Θεῶν : v. D. Magie, *Roman Rule in Asia Minor* (Princeton, 1950), II, 455 n. 11. Cybele had a black meteoric stone as her symbol in the temple of Pessinus, and Attalus I arranged for this to be taken to Rome (Magie, I, 25). Eisler's theory that the name Pessinus derives from πεσσός or πεσσόν, 'dice-stone', 'cube'

(v. *Philol.* 68 [1909], 125 f.) is rejected by Ruge, op. cit. 1105 f. Among the many foreign deities whose worship at Pessinus is attested by coins are Isis, Sarapis, and Harpocrates : v. Ruge, op. cit. 1110; so that a development in cult-syncretism might possibly lie behind this equivalence.

p. 269, 15-16 **autocthones Attici Cecropeiam Minervam** : The first adjective presents one of the claims of the Athenians to be second in the list; for the principle of precedence in lists see S. Dow, *Harv. Theol. Rev.* 20 (1937), 192 ff.; 210. Apuleius shared the general esteem of Athens in the cultured world, and the fact that he had studied philosophy there probably confirmed his attitude. Cecrops symbolized, of course, the autochthonous claim of the Athenians; he was, for them, 'a sort of Adam' (Rose, *Hbk. Gr. Myth.*[6] [1958], 261); as such he was represented as a serpent below the waist. In one myth he aided Pallas Athene (here Minerva) in her struggle against Poseidon for control of the city : v. Apollodorus, 3.14.1 and J. G. Frazer ad loc. The adjective *Cecropeia* might refer to the aid given by Cecrops as judge or witness; cf. Ovid, *Metam.* 6.70 (*Cecropia Pallas*); but probably its meaning is vaguer. Both Berreth and Wittmann dwell on the reference to Athena in Saïs in Plut. *De Is. et Os.* 9, 354 C and 32, 363 F, but since Neïth is really involved there, no real parallel emerges, any more than in P. Oxy. 1380, 30 with its similar allusion. Nor is it likely that the allusion should be connected with the tradition that Cecrops came from Egypt, although this appears by the time of Diodorus Siculus (1.28.6-7, where Cecrops is clearly implied in spite of the lacuna); cf. Immisch in Roscher, *Lex. Myth.* s.v. Kekrops (1892), 1017 and Gruppe, *Griech. Myth.* I (Munich, 1906), 16. The cult of Isis in Athens dates from 333/332 B.C.; by the second century B.C. the cult had achieved great popularity : v. Sterling Dow, 'The Egyptian Cults in Athens', *Harv. Theol. Rev.* 30 (1937), 183-232. There is no trace, however, of assimilation to Athena or her attributes; Isis is called Dikaiosynê (Dow, p. 226), but this represents the Egyptian Ma'at.

p. 269, 16-17 **fluctuantes Cyprii ... Venerem** : For *fluctuantes* cf. *Homer. Hymn* 10.5, εἰναλίης τε Κύπρου and Musaeus, *Hero et Leander*, 46. Aphrodite, as Wittmann shows, is often identified with Isis, and in Egypt the identification is palpably expressed in cult statuettes. In P. Oxy. 1380, 86 Isis is said to bear in Paphos the epithets ἀγνή, δία, and ἠπία. There was a shrine of Sarapis in Soloi in Cyprus probably as early as the third century B.C.; v. P. M. Fraser, 'Two Studies', 46, referring to private dedications; A. Westholm, *The Swedish Cyprus Expedition* 3 (Stockholm, 1937), 544 ff. on later temples of Isis and Sarapis; also id. *Temples of Soli* (Stockholm, 1936), 17, citing Strabo's allusion (14, 683) to a temple of Aphrodite and Isis, and pp. 152 f. and 196 ff., where he argues that a limestone sculpture (pl. 9, 1-2) represents a Ptolemaic queen as Isis. A priest of Isis Aphrodite is attested early in Perinthus, perhaps as early as the fourth century B.C. : v. Vidman, *Isis und Sarapis*, 32 f., who also points to Isis Aphrodite in Delos (somewhat later); cf. Roussel, *CED* 276. Grimm, *Ägypt. Rel. im röm. Deutschland*, 144, no. 25, records a statuette of Isis-Hathor-Aphrodite found near Cologne, a naked figure with a diadem (now broken); he is sceptical as to whether it was really discovered in this region (cf. p. 12 n. 3), but there seems no valid cause for doubt. Cf. Leipoldt, *Bilderatlas*, 30; id. *Umwelt III*, 267 (two instances); D. Müller, *Isis-Aret.* 35 f. and 44 f.; my *Plut. De Is. et Os.* 501 f. How much Apuleius knew of all, or any, of this is problematic. He may well have been familiar with the Alexandrian nude statuettes of Isis Aphrodite in which the head-dress usually includes Egyptian features; cf. Roeder, *Bronzefiguren*, 259 f. For *Paphiam Venerem* see n. *ad* ch. 2 (267, 10), *Paphi sacrario*.

p. 269, 17 **Cretes sagittiferi** : *Sagittifer* is used of the Parthians in Catull. 11.6, but Vergil, *Aen.* 8.725 uses it of the Geloni in Sicily; cf. Hor. *Carm.* 3.4.35. H. L. Lorimer, *Homer and the Monuments* (London, 1950), 277 ff., shows that the archaeological evidence provides rather more examples of the bow in Crete than elsewhere in the Mycenaean world; cf. R. W. Hutchinson, *Prehistoric Crete* (Pelican, 1962), 251 f.; J. D. S. Pendlebury, *The Archaeology of Crete* (London, 1939), 272. Among the classical Greeks detachments of archers were not formed, but Cretans and others, who had maintained the skill, were employed. The Romans found that among their Oriental enemies, such as the Parthians, archery was much used, and the result was that it became important again among the Romans themselves, who, however, often recruited archers from other nations; v. H. Hommel, *PW* s.v. τοξόται (1937), 1854 f.

Dictynnam Dianam : Dictynna was worshipped in western Crete as a virgin goddess connected with hunting; she was parallel to Britomartis in the East of the island, and both were associated with Artemis; v. Nilsson, *The Minoan-Mycenaean Rel.*[2] (Lund, 1950), 510 ff.; for the continued cult of Britomartis, Dictynna and Artemis in Crete in the early Christian centuries see R. F. Willetts, *Cretan Cults and Festivals* (London, 1962), 188 ff. P. Oxy. 1380, 82 says that Isis was called Dictynnis in Crete, the intention in this case being probably identical with that of Apuleius, that is, to identify Isis with the most prominent Cretan goddess. At the same time the cult of Isis in Crete goes back to the third or second century B.C.; v. G. Oliverio, *Ann. della regia scuola arch. di Atene* 1 (1914), 376 f. (a sanctuary at Gortyn dedicated to Isis and Sarapis and θεοὶ σύνναοι); cf. Brady, *Rec. Egn. Cults*, 44 f. and 63 f. (Cretan names in the cults). Cf. too the prayer of the Cretan Iphis to Isis in Ovid, *Metam.* 9.773 ff. on which see F. Arnaldi in *Atti del Convegno Internazionale Ovidiano*, II (Rome, 1959), 371-5. For the Isiac sanctuary at Gortyna see S. G. Spanakis, *Crete* (Iraklion, n.d.), 110 and R. Salditt-Trappmann, *Tempel*, 20 ff.

Siculi trilingues : By Roman times Latin as well as Greek would be assigned linguistically to the Sicilians. The third language envisaged by Apuleius is more enigmatic. If 'Siculi' is meant to apply strictly to the ancient people of East Sicily, their language is recognized now as being probably Indo-European : v. U. Schmoll, *Die vorgriechischen Sprachen Siziliens* (Wiesbaden, 1958), 102 ff.; E. Pulgram, *The Tongues of Italy* (Cambridge, Mass., 1958), 176 f. The languages of the Elymi and Sicani in the West of the island are problematic in their affinities, but in the West also there was Punic or

Neo-Punic; cf. S. Moscati, *The World of the Phoenicians* (1965, tr. London, 1968), 185 f. Since Apuleius was himself trilingual, speaking Punic, Greek and Latin, he may well be thinking of the Sicilians who spoke Punic (or at least a native language) in addition to the classical tongues. Ovid, *Metam.* 13.724 is adduced by some commentators; it is there said of Sicania : *Tribus haec excurrit in aequora pinnis*, but *linguis* appears in some MSS. (v. D. A. Slater ad loc.). The reference, however, is to three promontories.

   p. 269, 17-18 **Ortygiam Proserpinam** : Isis is identified with Proserpina (Persephassa) in Plut. *De Is. et Os.* 27, 361 E and P. Oxy. 1380, 71 f., cf. 127 f.; also Porphyry, *De imag.* ap. Euseb. *Praep. evang.* 3.11.50. In the later tradition Sicily was regarded as especially sacred to Demeter and Korê, and the rape of Persephone was located there, although various other places figure in earlier accounts : v. Allen, Halliday and Sykes ad *Homer. Hymn.* 2, pp. 131 f.; L. Bloch in Roscher, *Lex .Myth.* s.v. Kora (1890 f.), 1313; Book I of G. Zuntz, *Persephone* (Oxford, 1971). where attention is given also to the prehistoric goddess of Sicily whose role was taken over by Persephone. The younger Carcinus (fl. 375 B.C.) seems to be the first to locate the story in Sicily; v. Diod. Sic. 5.5.1. Kaibel's proposal in *Hermes* 35 (1900), 203 to read *Ortygiam* instead of *Stygiam* has the virtue of appending a geographical adjective on the pattern of the previous groups For the worship of Demeter in Syracuse and Ortygia see Pindar, *Ol.* 6.92 ff. Admittedly Juno (= Proserpina) is called *Stygia* in Statius, *Theb.* 4.526 f., as Ryle points out, and the epithet would not be unsuitable were it not for the geographical allusions in the others. There are plentiful allusions to the cult of Sarapis and Isis in Sicily from the second century B.C. onwards, notably at Tauromenion and Syracuse; Cicero, *In Verr.* 2.2.66, describes the Serapeum in Syracuse as being the *celeberrimus et religiosissimus locus* of the city; there were probably cult-centres too at Catana and Menaenum; cf. P. M. Fraser, 'Two Studies', 47 n. 3. (correcting his paragraph-ref. to Cic. *In Verr.*).

   p. 269, 18 **Eleusinii vetustam deam Cererem** : The Eleusinian Demeter was identified with Isis already by Herodotus (2.59). For the association of Isis with corn see ch. 3 (268, 10), *spicis Cerialibus* and n. Demeter was explained as 'earth' ($\gamma\hat{\eta}$) and in Plut. *De Is. et Os.* 38 the body of Isis is thus interpreted; cf. $\tau\grave{\eta}\nu$ $\gamma\hat{\eta}\nu$ $\sigma\pi o\rho\acute{\iota}\mu\eta\nu$ in P. Oxy. 1380, 170; Firm. Mat. *Err. prof. rel.* 2.6 (*Isim terram*); *Isis frugifera*, *CIL* VI, 351; Drexler, 'Isis', 412 ff. The ears of corn, flowers and cornucopia in the iconography point also to the connection. In the Aretalogies (M 7, D. Müller 31 ff.) Isis claims to have discovered corn, although the Egyptian tradition ascribes this rather to Osiris. Yet Isis was identified with the corn-goddess Thermuthis. Further, there was a conscious assimilation, in Egypt, of Isis and Demeter. This was doubtless familiar to Apuleius, but his point is that the Eleusinian cult of Demeter was but a form of the Isis-cult. P. Foucart put forward a theory, in a more special way, in his *Les Mystères d'Éleusis*, 47 ff., that qualities of Demeter in this cult derive historically from those of Isis, but his thesis is not acceptable because the correspondences claimed are not valid (e.g. the transference of the idea of *mꜣꜥ ḫrw*); nor is the attempt by A. A. Barb in *The Legacy of Egypt* (ed. J. R. Harris, Oxford, 1971), 151 f. to revive the connection at all convincing.

The emendation of *vetustam* to *vetusti* (Castiglioni) has some attraction; the Eleusinians could indeed lay claim to an antiquity, both in habitation and in cult, which reached to the middle of the second millennium B.C.; v. G. E. Mylonas, *Eleusis and the Eleusinian Mysteries* (Princeton, 1961), 14 ff. and 29 ff. The insipidity of *deam Cererem* is a possible problem; and Castiglioni's *sanctam* is not a big improvement. Robertson's *Actaeam* neatly — perhaps too neatly — restores an appellative, for which he compares Statius, *Silv.* 4.8.50 (*tuque, Actaea Ceres*).

p. 269, 18 **Iunonem** : The dominating position of Hera-Juno is the source of the equation, which is often found; cf. Diod. Sic. 1.25.1; P. Oxy. 1380, 32; 34; 60; 68; Hymns of Isidorus, 1, 21 = *SEG* 8, 548, 21, on which see Bergman, *Ich bin Isis*, 131, showing the Egyptian antecedents of the appended μεγαλόθρονος; cf. Vanderlip *ad loc.*, p. 30. Drexler, 'Isis', 513 ff. gives examples from later iconography where Isis has attributes of a celestial goddess befitting her role of the wife of Zeus Helius Sarapis.

Bellonam : In *Metam.* 8.25 Bellona is named after *dea Syria* and *sanctus Sabadius*. She was equated in Roman syncretism with the Greek Enyo and Mâ of Cappadocia; cf. A. García y Bellido, *Les religions orientales dans l'Espagne romaine*, ch. 16. Isis in the Aretalogies (M 41, D. Müller, 72) claims that she is 'mistress of war'; cf. P. Oxy. 1380, 83, where Isis at Rome is 'warlike', but the reading στρατία is uncertain. D. Müller points out, loc. cit., that Isis in Egyptian texts is often the giver of victory, an attribute which she shares, however, with several other deities; cf. Vandebeek, *Isisfiguur*, 71 f., on Isis-Nikê. In myth her most aggressive role is her aid to her battling son Horus in his form Harendotes; cf. Bergman, *Ich bin Isis*, 103. The *Hermetica* know of a wrathful Isis : *Isin vero Osiridis quam multa bona praestare propitiam, quantis obesse scimus iratam!* (Asclepius, 37, ed. Nock, but reading *Osiridis* for *Osiris* with W. Scott). In the late imperial period Bellona was closely connected with the Magna Mater, and Alföldi, *Die Trojanischen Urahner der Römer* (Basel, 1957), 6, would trace the connection back to the first century B.C., a view contested by Weinstock in *JRS* 49 (1959), 170.

p. 269, 19 **Hecatam** : The association of Isis with Persephone made one with Hecate easy, not only through the affinities of all three with the under-world, but also, in the case of Hecate and Isis, because of the special power in magic ascribed to them. Artemis and Hecate were closely allied too, and when P. Oxy. 1380, 84 f. calls Isis 'Artemis of three-fold nature', Hecate may well be involved as τρίμορφος, as Grenfell and Hunt suggest; see also van Groningen ad loc. In spite of this it is hard to see what possible connection with Isis is present in a group showing Artemis and Actaeon in the sanctuary of Isis belonging to the Pompeian house of Loreius Tiburtinus (Tran Tam Tinh, *Isis à Pompéi*, 83); Schefold, *Vergessenes Pompeji*, 33, claims that details of the decoration show that Isis is meant by Artemis; he also refers to Juv. 12.28 (*Pictores quis nescit ab Iside pasci?*), but Juvenal is alluding to the *ex-voto* paintings which persons rescued from shipwreck dedicated to Isis. In *Ancient Egypt*, 1915, 108 J. G. Milne finds 'Isis-Hecate' in figures on leaden tokens from Memphis; each has a triple face and is crowned with horns and disk. Cf. Vandebeek, *Isisfiguur*, 130. Here, then, an equation favoured by syncretism has been chosen.

p. 269, 19 **Rhamnusiam** : The same is true of this form of Nemesis worshipped at Rhamnus in Attica, a little north of Marathon. For a description of her temple see W. H. Plommer, *BSA* 45 (1950), 94-109. Whether another temple there was dedicated to Nemesis or to Themis has been the subject of debate; v. J. Pouilloux, *La Forteresse de Rhamnonte* (Paris, 1954), 151; cf. Strabo, 9.396; Pliny, *HN* 36.17; Pausanias, 1.33.2 with J. G. Frazer's note ad loc. (pp. 451 ff.) and that of Peter Levi (I, p. 95); Hesychius, Photius, the Suda, s.v. ῾Ραμνουσία Νέμεσις. The celebrated statue of Nemesis there was probably by Agoracritus, a pupil of Pheidias. On the cult of Nemesis at Rhamnus see O. Rossbach in Roscher, *Lex. Myth.* II (1897), 124-8; 147-55. Rossbach also shows how Nemesis was identified with Tychê, Hygieia, Nikê and Isis (pp, 163 f.). Apuleius was undoubtedly aware of the equation of Isis and Nemesis, for it was vigorously entrenched in the cult by the second century A.D. An inscription from Delos (110-109 B.C.) records the dedication of a chapel and statue to Isis Nemesis; v. Roussel, *CED* 158, no. 138; cf. the dedications to Isis Nemesis in nos. 139 and 140, p. 159. Vandebeek, *Isisfiguur*, 104-6, rightly compares with this concept the statements in the Aretalogies (Cyme. 20; 34; 35; Ios, 17 = M 34 and 35, D. Müller, 60) : 'I have given over him who plots unjustly against others into the hands of him he plotted against; I mete out punishment to those who act unjustly.' P. Perdrizet, *BCH* 36 (1912), 256, justly suggests that the identification of Isis and Nemesis began not in Delos but in Alexandria, but does not convince in his further suggestion that the prior assimilation of both goddesses to Tychê was the prompting factor. In Egyptian tradition Isis-Ma'at was an important concept, and it may be regarded as the theological origin of both Isis-Dikaiosynê and Isis-Nemesis, since Ma'at as a goddess of justice represented these ideas; Isis-Thesmophoros, too, will derive from Ma'at; cf. Bergman, *Ich bin Isis*, 209. It is surprising that neither D. Müller nor Bergman has realized the antecedent role, in relation to Nemesis (though she is not actually named in the Aretalogies), of Isis-Ma'at, though Bergman in particular gives much prominence to the latter figure. In a magical papyrus of A.D. iii-iv a charm seeking protection addresses 'Isis, Nemesis, Adrasteia' (Adrasteia being 'the one you cannot run away from', a separate deity); v. *PGM* 7, 502. In ch. 26 Apuleius refers to an epithet *Campensis* used of Isis in the Campus Martius. Hildebrand ventures, no doubt rightly, to see Isis therefore in the name *Nemesis sancta campestris* (*CIL* VI, 1, 533); cf. Drexler, 'Isis', 544; the words *somnio admonitus* at the end of the inscription would seem to confirm the idea. From the examples cited by Drexler, 'Isis', 544 f. (esp. J. T.

Bent, *Athenaeum* 1887, no. 3113, p. 839 on a relief at Thasos, cf. H. Posnansky, *Nemesis und Adrasteia* (Breslau, 1890), 123; and C. W. King, *Arch. Journal* 24 (1867), 306 on a green jasper gem), it may be questioned whether a *Mischtypus* was firmly established iconographically for Isis-Nemesis. Wings, a gryphon, a uraeus and a balance appear; the last two are Egyptian elements, the others not so, and there is not much consistency. Even so an amalgam is indicated, and Bonner, *Stud. Mag. Am.* 43, seems hardly justified in stating of Nemesis, 'The cult was introduced into Egypt, but remained distinctly Greek'. For an association of Nemesis and the Egyptian goddess Bastet see H. Posnansky, op. cit. 57 f., citing Phot. Bibl. 144 B; on p. 167 he refers to examples of Nemesis-Hygieia-Isis. On Isis-Nemesis see also K. Herbert, *Greek and Latin Inscriptions in the Brooklyn Museum* (Brooklyn, 1972), 46 f.

p. 269, 20 **Aethiopes** ; The preceding clause, which refers only to the Ethiopians, reflects the mythical view, found as early as Homer (*Il.* 1.423; 23.205), that they were a people living on the edge of the world, near Oceanus; they were in the furthest East where Helius began his morning journey. Yet Apuleius is regarding them simultaneously as a people whose land, the ancient Nubia or Kush, bordered on that of Egypt. As such they were a people who received Egyptian culture and religion; cf. Hdt. 2.30; Diod. Sic. 2.15.1 (they embalmed the dead, but with some distinctive methods); Strabo, 17.822 (the inhabitants of Meroë worshipped Heracles, Pan and Isis). On the worship of Isis in Gematen (Kawa) see Macadam, *Temples of Kawa* (London, 1949), 7; 28; 47; 56; 126 n. 1; in several cases Isis is identified there with the Queen Mother. Cf. Frank M. Snowden, Jr., 'Ethiopians and the Isiac Worship', *Ant. Class.* 25 (1956), 112-6. For the general impact of Egypt on this region see T. Säve-Söderbergh, *Ägypten und Nubien* (Lund, 1941); W. B. Emery, *Egypt in Nubia* (London, 1965); F. und U. Hintze, *Alte Kulturen im Sudan* (Leipzig, 1966); and P. L. Shinnie, *Meroe* (London, 1967). The geographical concepts of Greek and Egyptians on this matter are discussed by Jozef M. A. Janssen, *Bibl. Orient.* 8 (1951), 213 f.

Afrique : Accepting the reading *Ariique*, Médan explains them as an African people mentioned by Livy, 33.18.3; he also cites Xenophon of Ephesus, 5.66 f. (= 5.2.4) for a κόμη Ἄρεια near the Ethiopians. *Arei* is indeed read by one Ms. in the Livy locus; another reading is *Trahi*, and McDonald (Oxford, 1965) prints Robert's emendation *Theraei*. In Xen. Ephes. 5.2.4 (ed. G. Dalmeyda, Budé, p. 60) a village of Egypt (κώμην ... τῆς Αἰγύπτου, Ἀρείαν καλουμένην) is referred to; there is no clear indication of its position. Wittmann, accepting the same reading, refers to Arrian, *Anab. Alex.* 3.25 where the Ἄρειοι are mentioned who belonged to the Persian satrapy of Areia; it is hard to see a connection with the Ethiopians save in terms of the Homeric polarity. Barth's proposal *utrique* found favour with both Robertson and Giarratano; cf. Metam. 1.8 (8, 17 f.), *Indi vel Aethiopes utrique vel ipsi Antichthones*. The two kinds of Ethiopians, according to Homer, *Od.* 1.23 ff., will be those of East and West, where the divisions, however, will be far apart, corresponding to sunrise and sunset. The tradition developed into a distinction

between Asiatic and African Ethiopians, or in other terms; v. Hdt. 7.70; cf.
Strabo, 1.2.24 ff.; Pliny, *HN* 5.8.43 (*duas Aethiopias*); A. Lesky, *Hermes* 87
(1959), 37; D. Herminghausen, *Herodots Angaben über Äthiopien* (Hamburg,
1964), 7. In favour of *utrique*, then, there is a tradition of duality in this matter,
and an actual occurrence of a similar phrase in Apuleius himself. Cuper's
proposal, *Afrique*, is still more attractive, for it would imply that neighbouring
peoples in Africa, apart from the Ethiopians, had a share in the glory of Egypt's
heritage, and that Apuleius personally could therefore claim a connection.
The name seems to occur only once elsewhere in Apuleius (*Apol.* 66, p. 75, 12).

p. 270, 1 **Aegyptii** : This name is the last and most important in the list of
the names of peoples, just as Isis is the last and the climax in the sequence of
deities. Three religious privileges are ascribed to the Egyptians : first, they hold
the ancient and authentic doctrine; secondly, they employ the correct ritual;
thirdly, they know the true name of the deity. Veneration for the antiquity
of Egypt was often a part of the Greek attitude, and this may colour the present
emphasis, although the Egyptians were manifestly, for other reasons, the authorities on Isiac doctrine. In the Greek cult-centres of the religion the earliest
priests tended to be of Egyptian origin; later they were replaced by Greeks who
also followed the Greek custom of taking the priesthood on an annual basis;
v. Vidman, *Isis und Sarapis*, 48 ff.

p. 270, 1-2 **vero nomine** : Egyptian tradition perhaps supplies more examples
than any of the importance and magical power of the right name. 'One works
magic for a man through his name' is a dictum from the Turin Papyrus, where
Seth is bitten and Horus tries to help him, but cannot until he knows Seth's
real name, which turns out to be 'Evil Day'; v. J. Gwyn Griffiths, *Conflict*,
51 f. In the story of Isis and Rē' (P. Turin 131, 14 ff.; cf. Roeder, *Urk. Rel.*
138 ff.) it is Isis who is the magician, and she heals Rē' by getting him to reveal
his true name; cf. Morenz, *Rel.* 22. A most instructive example in the Greek
magical papyri, as Wittmann points out, is *PGM* 8 (A.D. iv or v), in which
Hermes is addressed. After citing his 'foreign names' (τὰ βαρβαρικὰ ὀνόματα)
the magician goes on to stress that he knows his 'true name' (τὸ ἀλη-
θινὸν ὄνομα), claiming also that the god's name is his own and vice versa
(τὸ σὸν ὄνομα ἐμὸν καὶ τὸ ἐμὸν σόν). The latter point does not enter
into the self-revelation of the goddess as given by Apuleius, since no magical
adjuration is here involved; but there is a similar contrast between foreign
names and the true name; cf, Iamblichus, *De myst.* 7.4 (the Assyrians [= Chald-
aeans] and Egyptians are regarded as 'holy peoples', so that their names have
special authenticity.) In ch. 2, where Lucius prays to the moon-goddess, many
divine names are mentioned; we saw that this follows a tradition in Latin
prayers, the worshipper being anxious not to omit the real or most apposite
appellation. The purpose of the many names in the self-revelation of Isis is
quite different : they emphasize her all-pervasive presence and also her superio-
rity over other deities who are but subordinate expressions of her own essence.
Reviewing the list of divine names, one notes that in the cases of Pessinuntia,

Minerva, Venus, Diana, and Proserpina there are Isiac cult connections in the localities concerned; but Apuleius was probably not thinking of such connections since his purpose was to represent these great goddesses as forms of Isis. It is hard to know in the case of Ceres whether he was not thinking of the ancient and well-known equation of the two goddesses. With the others —Juno, Bellona, Hecate, and Rhamnusia—geographical associations are not supplied, and the close correspondence, with the exception of Bellona, to aspects of Isis compels one to believe that these are deliberately chosen because of accepted affinities.

p. 270, 2 **reginam Isidem** : The Anubis-Hymn from Cius, 9, (Peek, p. 139), describes Isis as 'the divine ruler of the whole earth and the sea'; cf. P. Oxy. 1380, 120, 'first ruler of the world'. Isis is queen, then, not merely of Egypt, but of the whole world; cf. the phrase in the Aretalogies (M 3 a, D. Müller, p. 19), τύραννος πάσης χώρας, where Diod. Sic. has βασίλισσα; the Andros Aretal. 7-9 alludes to her rule as one which includes all that the sun embraces, and D. Müller, loc. cit., well compares an Egyptian phrase in the inscriptions from the temple of Opet, Karnak; here Isis is 'mistress of all that the sun goes round'. With reference to τύραννος πάσης χώρας Bergman, *Ich bin Isis*, 150 n. 0, argues that an allusion to Egypt remains possible since Egypt was a combination of 'Two Lands' and since the nomes are sometimes referred to as χῶραι. The other statements in the Aretalogies surely compel us to adopt the wider meaning, especially as there are excellent parallels, as Bergman admits, in the Egyptian texts of the Late Era. *Isidi Reginae* is a dedication in several inscriptions : CIL VI, 354 (= Dessau, *ILS* 2218 and Vidman, *SIRIS* 189, no. 370); VI, 574; XI, 1577 (= *SIRIS* 261, no. 566); XI, 1581-2 (= *SIRIS* 262, nos. 570-71); XI, 1584-5 (= *SIRIS* 362, nos. 573-4). Priests of Isis Regina are named in CIL VI, 32463 (= *SIRIS* 204, no. 410) and IX, 1153 (= *SIRIS* 222, no. 469). In one case, CIL XIV, 352 (= *SIRIS* 249, no. 536) *Sancta Regina* is the phrase used, and Wittmann aptly compares βασ[ί]λεισ[σαν ἀγε]ίαν in P. Oxy. 1380, 36. Vidman, *Isis und Sarapis*, 115, cites further instances of *regina* from Rome and the provinces. After suggesting that Juno as queen is the prototype, since the Greek parallels are few (yet those cited above should be borne in mind, and Vidman seems to ignore them), he justly invokes 'Roman (or Egyptian)' influence. His parenthesis is vital, for there are plentiful parallels, as we have already noted, in Egyptian sources. The term *nswyt* is very often used in the Graeco-Roman era of Hathor-Isis as queen of the gods; v. *Wb.* II, 332, 9. Words such as *nbt*, 'mistress', *ḥnwt*, 'ruling lady', and *ḥkȝt*, 'governor' are used of Isis in similar phrases; v. D. Müller, *Isis-Aret.* 20; J. Bergman, *Ich bin Isis* 152 f. The Isis-hymns from Aswân (D. Müller, 89 f.) express her sovereignty over the universe; she is 'mistress of heaven'. The phrase 'The Two Lands', used of Egypt, normally refers to Upper and Lower Egypt, and J. Bergman, op. cit. 149, follows Moret and Thierry in the rather doubtful idea that heaven and earth are sometimes meant, thereby conferring a cosmic notion on the phrase. Yet Bergman, 150 ff., has every right to stress that the concept of the sovereignty of Isis, however comprehensive it eventually became, has its origin in the Egyptian kingship; cf. Aretal. Andros, 1, Αἰγύπτου βασίλεια and the similar phrases collected by Drexler, 'Isis', 513. Isis is the sister-wife of Osiris, who is equated with the deceased King; of almost equal importance is her role as the mother of Horus, who is equated with the living King. Furthermore, several of the Ptolemaic queens identified themselves with Isis in a special way; v. Vandebeek, *Isisfiguur*, 66 ff.; Visser, *Götter und Kulte*, 16; and my remarks in *JEA* 47 (1961), 113 f. At Pompeii an interesting variation of the title is Isis Augusta, found on an altar in the second Iseum; v. Tran Tam Tinh, *Isis à Pompéi*, 69; cf. Vidman, *Isis und Sarapis*, 115. R. E. Witt, *Isis Gr.-R.* 126, speaks of the Alexandrian theologians 'converting Hera as the queen of the Olympian pantheon into Isis' and 'granting Isis in addition the omnipotence of Poseidon over the ocean and ultimate responsibility for the deliverance of sailors by her agents, the Dioscuri.' The process was not so simple, for at each point there is an Egyptian antecedent. For a depiction of an enthroned Isis see Olga Elia, *Le Pitture del Tempio di Iside*, 21, fig. 25; Tran Tam Tinh, op. cit. 145, no. 51, 'Isis et Sérapis', referring to pl. 8, 1, (without the Isis-figure).

p. 270, 2-3 **favens et propitia** : Médan sees here an instance of the 'abondance de style' found in Apuleius. It is evidence rather of his familiarity with the traditional language of liturgy in Latin, in which such couplings were common; cf. E. Diehl, *Rhein. Mus.* 83 (1934), 358, citing *vos quaeso precorque*, and 362, citing *estote fitote volentes propitiae*. with which he compares Plautus, *Curc.* 89, *fite mihi volentes propitiae.* See also E. Norden, *Aus altrömischen Priesterbüchern* (Lund, 1939), 19 n. 1, citing Servius *ad Aen.* 1.731 f. (733, *volens propitiusque sis* was a traditional Etruscan expression).

p. 270, 4 **providentia** : Cf. ch. 10 (274, 6); 12 (275, 17); and 15 (277, 20) with n.

dies salutaris : The adjective, as Médan says, approaches the sense familiar in the usage of the Church, as in *O salutaris hostia.* The day will bring a double 'salvation' to Lucius : it will save him from his animal form and it will also bring spiritual salvation. The first meaning appears in *Metam.* 3.25 (70, 18), *salutis inopia*, of Lucius becoming an ass. For the developed meaning see n. *ad* ch. 12 (275, 13), *salutemque* and *ad* ch. 21 (283, 5-6), *precariae salutis.*

ergo igitur : Cf. ch. 21 (283, 10); 28 (289, 20); also *ergo idcirco*, Cic. *S. Rosc.* 39 (112) and similar pleonastic collocations cited by *Thes. L.L.* 5, 774, 68 ff. The expression occurs seventeen times in Apuleius according to *Thes. L.L.* loc. cit. Oldfather et al. *Index Apul.* rather woodenly cite all the occurrences of each word separately, with no guide to the combination. Apuleius seems to have taken the usage from Plautus; v. *Most.* 847 and *Trin.* 756. Bernhard, *Stil*, 173, follows Löfstedt in regarding such pleonasms as the product of popular speech.

p. 270, 5 **istis meis** : Hofmann and Szantyr, *Lat. Syntax*, 183 f., show that *iste* was connected from its earliest usage with the second person; they quote

Plaut. *Most.* 47, *tu tibi istos habeas turtures*; hence the common nexus *iste tuus.* A tendency is then noted for *iste* to encroach on the field of *hic* or *ille* and for its association with the first person, as in Catull. 17.21, *iste meus stupor* (= *iste meus homo stupidus*), where Fordyce, however, regards *iste meus as* 'a very surprising combination' and doubts the reading. The use of *iste meus* and *iste noster* in Apuleius and Fronto (another African) is without the nuance of contempt sometimes found in other applications of *iste.* Bernhard, *Stil,* 171, ascribes the development to a weakening of the pronoun's deictic force, and on p. 115, citing a statistical analysis by Wolterstorff, he agrees with Hoppe in his view that the relative frequency of *iste* in Apuleius and other African writers constitutes an African provincialism. Callebat, *Sermo Cotid.* 270, denies this; but the fact that Seneca and Lucan were fond of *iste* is a rather vague rebuttal.

p. 270, 5 **diem, qui dies** : *Dies* seems superfluous, but such a repetition of the antecedent in agreement with the relative pronoun clearly aims at greater emphasis and has a touch of juridical pomp about it. In juridical expressions it seeks to remove any possible ambiguity. Hofmann and Szantyr, *Lat. Syntax,* 563, quote *Lex agr.* 4 as an instance : *quei ager publicus ... fuit, extra eum agrum.* It is curious that the usage is found also in Comedy; e.g. Ter. *Haut.* 20, *exemplum, quo exemplo*; a desire for emphasis and clarity explains it. With Apuleius, as with Gellius, Fronto and Arnobius, it is doubtless a hankering after archaisms that prompts it; so Hofmann and Szantyr, loc. cit. Cf. M. Leky, *De Syntaxi Apul.* 48, who cites *Metam.* 2.4, (27, 11 f.), *canes, ... qui canes ...*

p. 270, 7 **navigabili iam pelago** : A clear statement of the basic aim of the festival called the *Isidis Navigium*, which celebrated, under the patronage of the goddess, the renewal of navigation after the winter. See further Introd. V.

p. 270, 8 **carinam primitias commeatus** : The new ship is regarded as the 'first fruits' of revived navigation. Homer describes the sea as 'unharvested' (*Od.* 13.419 with Stanford's n.), but Apuleius boldly applies the metaphor of harvest to the sea's undertakings.

CHAPTER 6

p. 270, 9 **meo monitu** : Cf. n. *ad* ch. 5 (269, 9), *tuis commota ... precibus*: ch. 6 (270, 16-17), *per quietem*; and ch. 21 (282, 17), *deae nutu.* The noun is that constantly used of divine instructions which come through dreams; cf. ch. 14 (276, 18), *sed sacerdos utcumque divino monitu etc.*; ch. 19 (281, 3-4), *nec fuit nox una vel quies aliqua visu deae monituque ieiuna*; ch. 24 (286, 11), *deae monitu*; and the verb *monuit* in ch. 22 (283, 19). Cf. too Cic. *De divin.* 2.86 (*Fortunae monitu*); Ovid, *Metam.* 13.216; and see further *Thes. L.L.* 8, 1421, 64 ff. H. Fugier, *L'Expression du Sacré*, 302 f., shows how the word emphasizes, in Apuleius, the initiative of the goddess and the domination of her majestic personality.

p. 270, 10-11 **roseam** ... **coronam** : Garlands were often used in religious rites in Egypt; cf. n. *ad* ch. 4 (268, 20), *totis floribus*. Indeed a garland carried by a priest would mostly be intended for a purpose such as that mentioned there: it would ultimately adorn the statue of a deity. When Lucius becomes an ass (3.25), Photis tells him that only by eating roses (*rosis tantum demorsicatis*) will he get rid of the animal form, but there is no mention of a ritual context. Naturally there are tantalizing glimpses of roses in the course of the subsequent story : see 3.29; 4.2; 7.15 (a hope of roses); 10.29. The promised fulfilment comes in ch. 12 f.; and in ch. 12 a symbolism of victory over Fortune is indicated. It is Derchain that has illumined the religious origin of this crown of roses : v. his study of 'La couronne de la justification', *CdÉ* 30 (1955), 225-87. Spell 19 of the *Book of Dead* is entitled 'Spell of the crown of justification' (or, 'of triumph, victory'; cf. Derchain, 231 n. 2), the basic idea being that the deceased person who is identified with Osiris will receive, like him, the crown which signifies his triumph in the judgement after death. This triumph was originally the achievement of Horus, but it was early transferred to Osiris; and although an association with the sun-god Rē' appears also, Derchain shows that in the Ptolemaic era, when the concept became very popular (the rite of presenting the crown is represented twenty times in the temple of Edfu alone), the main emphasis was Osirian. In non-funerary contexts triumph over all enemies and apotropaic security are stressed.

The rose was not known in earliest Egypt, and was imported perhaps from Greece or perhaps from Ethiopia; v. F. Woenig, *Die Pflanzen im alten Aegypten* (Leipzig, 1886), 244 and V. Loret, *La flore Pharaonique*[2] (Paris, 1882), 82, § 136. L. Keimer, 'La rose égyptienne', in his *Études d'Égyptologie* 5 (Cairo, 1943), 23, leaves the place of origin open, but notes that the rose grew wild in Syria and Palestine. Derchain points out, op. cit. 250 ff., apropos of our passage, that crowns of roses are known from Egypt in the Late Era, and he refers to some real examples in the Berlin Museum (Inv. 19538-44); cf. also those cited in *Ausführliches Verzeichnis*, Berlin (1899), 453. Such crowns are represented on the head of a deceased person in the Roman era; v. G. Daressy, *ASAE* 18 (1919), 186 and Spiegelberg, *Die demotische Denkmäler*, III (1932), fig. on p. 20; A. Rowe, *ASAE* 40 (1940), 17; cf. Parlasca, *Mumienporträts*, 145. Sometimes garlands were placed on the coffin, as in the case of Tut'ankhamûn's second coffin; v. Carter and Mace, *The Tomb of Tut-Ankh-Amen*, II (London, 1927), 72 and pl. 22; in this case too there was a wreath of flowers on the head; v. Carter and Mace, II, 52 and pl. 67 (i.e. the head of the effigy on the first coffin). On the arrangement of rose petals found at Hawara by Petrie (of the Roman era) see L. Keimer, 'Egyptian Formal Bouquets', *AJSL* 41 (1925), 145 ff., esp. 156-7. The mummy-portraits of the Graeco-Roman era often represent wreaths of flowers either on the head or in a hand of the deceased, and sometimes in both places; v. Parlasca, *Mumienporträts*, 144 ff., who shows that roses are sometimes involved and who accepts Derchain's interpretation that it is the Osirian 'crown of justification' that is figured, whether it is on the head or in the hand. Keimer in his 'La rose égyptienne' (see above) gives a full documentation of the evidence for the rose in Egypt. No archaeological testimony prior to the Roman era was known to him. The first literary allusion to the rose in Egypt is apparently Theophrastus, *Hist. plant.* 6.8.5 (Keimer, p. 21 n. 1, but with wrong ref.) about the beginning of the third century B. C. Keimer, p. 23, thinks that the rose probably became known in Egypt during the 26th Dynasty, i.e. during the seventh or sixth centuries. Derchain, op. cit. 251, points out that when Apuleius, both here and in ch. 13, states that the crown of roses is held in the priest's hand, this corresponds to several of the painted representations on mummies. He cites Coche de la Ferté, *Portraits romano-égyptiens* (Paris. 1952), 17; Perdrizet, *Mon. Piot.* 34 (1934), 115, fig. 6; Guimet, *Les Portraits d'Antinoé* (Paris, n. d.), 19 and figs. 58, 59, 64, 73. Cf. too Morenz, 'Das Werden zu Osiris', *Forschungen und Berichte* 1 (Berlin, 1957), 58. But it is a Greek tradition that seems to be followed in scenes from Herculaneum where a garland of flowers appears on a temple gate; v. Leipoldt, *Angelos* 1 (1925), 126. The Egyptian tradition is implied by the crown of roses held in the hand of a boy on a mummy-portrait now in Detroit : see von Gonzenbach, *Knabenweihen*, pl. 1 with pp. 120 ff. and 162. The crown in Apuleius must doubtless be regarded as destined for a statue of Isis, although a figure of Osiris could equally well be the recipient; cf. the roseate pattern at the base of the Canopic Osiris.

A festival of 'bearing roses' (*Rhodophoria*) is mentioned in three Greek papyri of the second century A.D. : P. Ross.-Georg. II, 41, 9 (cf. line 14); P. Heidelberg 1818, *vs.* 11; and S.P.P. XXII, 183, 76. Bilabel, *Die gräko-ägyptischen Feste* (Heidelberg, 1929), 48, suggested a connection with the cult of Horus in Dendera or of Isis or Hathor-Isis in Edfu. A detailed correspondence is lacking, and Eitrem, *Symb. Oslo.* 17 (1937), 46 f., vehemently denied an Egyptian connection; his statement that the wreath of roses mentioned by Apuleius here 'does not signify more than, e.g., the purely poetic Isis ῥοδόστερνος in an inscription from Nubia (*CIG* 5115 and *LS* s.v.)' is wide of the mark. There is obviously a difference between a festival in which a wreath or roses plays an incidental part and one in which carrying roses is the main thing. Eitrem identifies the *Rhodophoria* of the papyri with the *Rosalia*, a spring or summer festival of rejoicing in which roses symbolized the rebirth of nature; he is supported in this by Youtie in *Studies in Roman Economic and Social History*, ed. Coleman-Norton (Princeton, 1951), 193. The *Rosalia* originated in Italy in the first century A.D. and spread to the Balkans and Asia Minor; v. P. Perdrizet, 'Les Rosalies', *BCH* 24 (1900), 299 ff.; M. P. Nilsson, *PW* s.v. Rosalia (1920), 1111-15; A. S. Hoey, *Harv. Theol. Rev.* 30 (1937), 15-35; J. Lindsay, *Leisure and Pleasure in Roman Egypt* (London, 1965), 11 ff. It is certainly tempting to equate the *Rhodophoria* with this festival, although Bilabel, op. cit. 48, makes the strong point that the festival calendar of Socnopaiou Nesos is mainly concerned with festivals of Socnopaios and Isis Nepherses, so that the concomitant rites might also be expected to be Egyptian. But there is no necessary connection between the *Rosalia* and the Isiac wreath of roses, even if one need not exclude a measure of syncretism in the symbolic interpretation. Cf. Mme. N. Fick, *Latomus* 30 (1971), 339-43, especially her discussion of the non-Isiac function of the rose, pp. 340 f.; she notes that in the *Vinalia* courtesans offered roses to Venus. Heinrich Junker, *Vorträge Bibl. Warburg* 1921-22 (Leipzig, 1923), 153, says the rose, since its petals are five, a number sacred to the Iranian Aiôn, became an image of eternal life and resurrection; cf. E. Norden, *Geburt des Kindes*, 30 ff.; Reitzenstein, *Hellenist. Myst.* 50; 80; Festugière, *Rev. d'Égyptol.* 8 (1951), 65; Delatte and Derchain, *Intailles Magiques*, 109. In a festival of Isis, however, the idea of resurrection must be primarily connected with Osiris, and it is to Wittmann's credit (p. 73 with n. 405) that he recognized the Osirian crown of victory in the *rosea corona* even before Derchain's study appeared in *CdÉ* 30 (1955); the Egyptian tradition was of course broadly known before then : cf. Drioton's remarks, *Bull. S. A. Copte* 6 (1940), 259 and Keimer, op. cit. 7 as well as in *AJSL* 41 (1925), 145. It is strange that Karl Baus in his *Der Kranz in Antike und Christentum* (Bonn, 1940), while he knows of the Egyptian tradition (p. 3 n. 10), seems to ignore the 'crown of justification' (or 'victory') in his discussion of the 'Siegeskranz' (pp. 143 ff.).

For the subsequent transformation of Lucius see n *ad* ch. 13 (276, 1 f. *coronam ... devoravi*).

p. 270, 11 **incunctanter** : While *cunctanter* appears in Livy and Tacitus, Apuleius seems to be the first to use the negative form, which occurs several times in the *Metam.* Cf. *Thes. L.L.* 7, 1079, 12. It is a less adventurous neologism than the adverbs listed by Bernhard, *Stil*, 140.

turbulis : Cf. ch. 7 (271, 13). This noun occurs only in Apuleius. His special fondness for diminutives both old and new is examined by Koziol, *Stil*, 260-66 and Bernhard, *Stil*, 135 ff.

p. 270, 11-12 **continuare** : In *Metam.* 1.24 (22, 11) Robertson reports F as reading *continatur* : v. his critical n. *ad loc.* and *Thes. L.L.* 4, 720, 64. Cf. ch. 22 (284, 3-4), and Kiessling's proposal here.

p. 270, 12 **volentia** : While several of the codices read *violentia*, the other reading is better suited to the quality of the aid provided by the goddess. *Volentia* will have its first occurrence here, as a synonym of *voluntas* in ch. 22 (284, 6) and ch. 27 (288, 17), where it is used, in each case, of divine favour.

p. 270, 13 **osculabundus** : The fondness of Apuleius for this type of formation is shown by his new coinages *imaginabundus*, *munerabundus*, *murmurabundus*, and *periclitabundus*, cited by Bernhard, *Stil*, 139. For the present instance compare *Apol.* 94 (105, 7 f.), *manus nostras osculabundus*. This type of verbal adjective strengthens the idea of the present participle; cf. Kühner and Holzweissig, *Gr.*² 995; it often governs an accusative; cf. A. S. Owen *ad Apol.* 72, pp. 138 f. In *Apol.* 94 hands are kissed in a personal plea for forgiveness; kissing the hands and feet of statues of the gods was a part of the act of *supplicatio*; cf. K. Latte, *Röm. Rel.* 245. Here the pretended gesture would imply reverence for the priest and for the religion.

p. 270, 13-14 **mihique... detestabilis** : The ass was hateful to Isis as an animal prominently connected with Seth-Typhon. While the Seth-animal itself is canine rather than asinine, Seth is represented by an ass as early as the Dramatic Ramesseum Papyrus in the Old Kingdom (33); and in the Graeco-Roman era he is often referred to as an ass : v. Schott, *Urk. Myth.* I, 37; Chassinat, *Edfou*, VI, 219-23 (Seth as a red ass fights Horus in the form of a youth); Plut. *De Is. et Os.* 30, 362 E-F with my comment *ad loc.*, pp. 409 f.; *PGM* 3, 70 (Preisendanz, Taf. II, 3, Seth depicted as an ass-headed man). The Egyptian word for 'ass' was '3, and sometimes it was written with the Seth-animal as determinative; v. *Wb.* I, 165 and cf. the refs. in I, 165, 11. See further my *Origins of Osiris*, 50 f.; H. te Velde, *Seth, God of Confusion*, 14; 109; pl. 12, 2; B. H. Stricker, 'Asinarii', *OMRO*, 46 (1965), 52-75. In *Metam.* 3.24, where the transformation into an ass is described in horrific detail, there is admittedly no hint of the connection with Seth-Typhon.

p. 270, 14. **istius corio te protinus exue** : Médan, *Lat.* 254, remarks on a dactylic series. E. Schober, *Comp. num.* 12, rightly treats it as a *clausula*. But it may be accidental rather than deliberate; cf. Bernhard, *Stil*, 250 n. 1.

p. 270, 14-15 **nec ... reformides** : in Early Latin prohibition was thus expressed, with *ne* and the Present Subjunctive, along with the constructions *ne fac*, *ne faxis* and *ne feceris*. In the classical era it became a poetical usage only, apart from its employment in the Letters of Cicero. Then it reappeared, in prose, in Seneca and Apuleius. See Hofmann and Szantyr, *Lat. Syntax*, 336; C. E. Bennett, *Syntax of Early Latin*, I (Boston, 1910), 167 ff.; Callebat, *Sermo Cotid.* 101. Médan refuses to regard this as a subjunctive of prohibition; it is rather, he argues, the subjunctive of obligation : 'tu ne dois pas craindre'. The distinction is hardly a valid one.

p. 270, 16 **quae sunt sequentia** : Another instance of the archaistic tendency in Apuleius, for the periphrasis in which the present participle is combined with the verb *sum* is often found in Early Latin; v. C. E. Bennett, *Syntax of Early Latin*, I, 458 f. Hofmann and Szantyr, *Lat. Syntax*, 388, find the construction which is thus attested in the popular speech to be expressive of the continuous and lasting nature of the action. In the present instance a future reference is implied, but this derives perhaps from the meaning of the verb *sequor*.

p. 270, 16-17 **per quietem** : It is in a dream that Isis will appear to the priest; cf. n. *ad* ch. 5 (269, 9), *En adsum*. The phrase is used again in ch. 30 (291, 8); cf. too 9.31 (226, 15); see also n. *ad* ch. 5 (269, 9), *tuis commota ... precibus*; *ad* ch. 6 (270, 9), *meo monitu*; and *ad* ch. 21 (282, 17), *deae nutu*.

p. 270, 18 **hilares** : The present rites were joyous in that they were concerned with the renewal of navigation in the spring. An Isiac festival at Rome was called the *Hilaria* : v. Hopfner, *Fontes*, 526; cf. the *Charmosyna*, Plut. *De Is. et Os.* 29, 362 D. The *Hilaria* were on Nov. 3rd; cf. R. E. Witt *Isis Gr.-R.* 162; 180. Most Isiac rites were marked with both sorrow and joy deriving from the sufferings and triumph of Osiris.

p. 270, 19 **perhorrescet** : In ch. 12 *ad fin.* the people are said to give way on his approach (*sane divinitus decedente populo*).

p. 270, 20 **sequius interpretatus** : The comparative form of *secus* seems to have true comparative force in *Apol.* 99 (110, 3 : *enim longe sequius ratus fuerat*) and in *Metam.* 9.29 (225,5), but here a strengthening of the positive is involved; cf. ch. 29 (290, 12). In ch. 13 the impression made on the people by the transformation is said to be admiration for a miracle which reveals the manifest power of the highest deity (*populi mirantur etc.*) The possibility of a bad interpretation probably lay in the amenable suggestion that evil magic had been resorted to, an accusation which Apuleius had personally faced.

p. 270, 20-21 **memineris ... tenebis** : The use of the Future Indicative with an imperative meaning was common in Early Latin; v. C. E. Bennett, *Syntax of Early Latin*, I, 39. It continued to be thus used (in the second and third persons), according to Hofmann and Szantyr, *Lat. Syntax*, 311, and the psychological basis of its use is mostly the speaker's sure expectation that the command will be carried out. It perhaps arises from colloquial usage, although it occurs in legal and technical contexts too; cf. Callebat, *Sermo Cotid.* 100. In view of this, Médan's interesting suggestion that the usage passed from Punic into the Latin of Apuleius is untenable. He says that 'en hebreu, en effet, le futur, répresenté par l'aoriste, exprime un ordre et s'appelle aoriste jussif; cf. la Bible : *unum Deum ADORABIS ... non MOECHABERIS.*' He adds that 'on sait que le punique était très proche parent de l'hebreu.' His parallel has some force in that לֹא תִנְאָף in Ex. 20.14 uses a tense (the imperfect) which often refers to the future. Cf. Gesenius and Kautzsch, rev. Cowley, *Hebrew Gr.* (Oxford, 1910), 317, § 107 *o* : 'The imperfect with לֹא represents a more emphatic form of prohibition than the jussive with אַל ..., and corresponds to our *thou shalt not do it*! with the strongest expectation of obedience ...' However, the well attested, and early, use of the Future Indicative in Latin with an imperative sense renders the invocation of a Semitic usage unnecessary.

p. 270, 21 **penita** : Whereas Apuleius here, and in at least two other instances, uses *penitus* as an adjective, following a Plautine mode, he more often treats the word as an adverb, as in classical usage. Cf. Hofmann and Szantyr, *Lat. Syntax*, 173.

p. 270, 21-22 **mihi ... vadata** : Only here does Apuleius use the perfect passive participle of this verb; the participial use is attested, characteristically, in ante- and post-classical literature. What is involved is that a legal term referring to bail or surety (*vadimonium*) is given a sacral sense; cf. H. Fugier, *L'Expression du Sacré*, 305, comparing *patrocinium* in ch. 16 (278, 12). So the meaning 'bound, pledged, dedicated' is here given a religious application and the sentence thus conveys the extent of the involvement to which Lucius has now to commit himself. His whole future life will belong to her in return for the restoration to human form conferred by her. The spiritual conversion thus implied entails an exclusive and total claim by Isis. Cf. *mihi tantum licere* at the end of the chapter; and the words of the priest at the end of ch. 15 : '...

vow yourself from this moment to the ministry of our religion; accept of your own free will the yoke of service.' This exclusiveness is hardly borne out by what is known of the cult. Plutarch's Clea has no difficulty in combining a priesthood of Isis and Osiris with her role as leader of the Dionysiac Thyiads at Delphi, and Plutarch's own attitude is similar in that he is passionately devoted to the Isiac cult, but maintains his belief in the Greek pantheon. A constant syncretism marks the attitude of intelligent believers and is particularly clear in the association of Demeter and Isis. Here, perhaps, we see a means of reconciling the exclusive claim of the goddess with the tolerant approach to other deities and cults : Apuleius represents Isis as uniquely sovereign, but her godhead absorbs the qualities of others. Cf. Nock, *Conversion*, 155 : 'Lucius is not forbidden to take part in other cults, and formal public observances he would no doubt make, but any other worship must to him appear tame and inferior.' See also Introd. I, p. 4.

p. 270, 23-24 **vives autem beatus ... gloriosus** : Cf. ch. 6 (278, 7), *felix hercules et ter beatus*, of Lucius when restored to human form. One is tempted, in view of the verb, to take *beatus* in its most general sense of happiness, as in Martial's famous epigram, *Vitam quae faciant beatiorem ...* (10.47); cf. *Thes. L.L.* I, 1909, 32 ff. *Beatitudo* and *dignitas gloriosa* are mentioned together in *Metam.* 6.29 (150, 18 f.). Yet the second adjective impels one to invoke a religious meaning, quite unlike *vivebat gloriosus* in 9.35 (229, 13); for Lucius is surely not going to be 'famous' or 'renowned' in the wordly sense, in spite of his remarkable experience. His success at the Roman bar (ch. 28, p. 290, 2-4 and ch. 30, p. 291, 4-5) scarcely merits such splendid terms. Wittmann (p. 195 n. 150) must therefore be right in suggesting that the beatitude and glory are conferred by the Mysteries. For *beatus* in this sense compare Verg. *Aen.* 6.639, *Fortunatorum nemorum, sedesque beatas* and Cic. *Rep.* 6.13, *ubi beati aevo sempiterno fruantur*. These allusions are, of course, to the blessed dead : v. *Thes. L.L.* 4, 1913, 72 ff. and cf. μάκαρ. Apuleius is transferring the blessedness and glory to this life, to begin with. Perhaps there are Egyptian prototypes here, for *nfr* and *mꜣꜥ ḫrw* are used with the specialized meanings of *beatus* and *gloriosus* here suggested. For *nfr* see Naville, *BD* 172, 4 ('How happy!' will the deceased be); see further *Wb.* II, 254, 22 and 256, 5. *Mꜣꜥ ḫrw* is, of course, the frequent term for the triumph or justification of the deceased identified with Osiris. The concept of glory is linked with Isis (and Horus), as Wittmann points out, in *PGM* 7, 504 (A.D. iv) where Isis Nemesis Adrasteia is asked, 'Glorify me as I glorified the name of your son Horus.' Reitzenstein, *Hellenist. Myst.* 344 and 359, finds a related idea of glory, linked with strength, in 1 Cor. 15.41.

p. 271, 1 **demearis** : Cf. Hor. *Carm.* 4.7.14 f., *Nos, ubi decidimus, | Quo pater Aeneas, quo dives Tullus et Ancus, | Pulvis et umbra sumus*. Cf. *Metam.* 9.31 (226, 18), *ad inferos demeasset*. First used by Fronto, then by Apuleius, and afterwards by Martianus Capella — three African writers — the word was possibly a part of 'African Latin', according to Médan, and was formed on the pattern of *commeo*. It does not seem likely that it was a feature of collo-quial language in Africa, but having been coined there, perhaps by Fronto, it might have been imitated by the other African authors. Partiality for each others' works may well have characterized their writings.

p. 271, 1-2 **subterraneo semirutundo etc.** : In *Metam.* 5.3 (105, 6) Apuleius uses *semirotundus* in its expected adjectival sense; the word is found only in these two instances. Giving the adjective a substantival meaning is a poetical tendency; cf. Médan, *Lat.* 249; Bernhard, *Stil*, 105 ff. It is *subterraneo*, however, that Médan regards as the substantive. Cumont, *CRAIBL* (1920), 282 n. 2, states that these words translate ἐν ὑπογείῳ ἡμισφαιρίῳ in the pseudo-Platonic *Axiochus*; certainly the correspondence is striking. The prepositional phrase reinforces the adverb of place (*ibi*); cf. Callebat, *Sermo Cotid.* 532 f.; it is probably imitation of Plautus and Terence. Cf. ch. 17 (279, 16).

The terms used here of the promised happy afterlife are those traditional in the classical languages; cf. *Metam.* 6.16 (140, 17 f.), *ad inferos et ipsius Orci ferales penates te derigo*. To the Homeric Hades belong the concepts of the netherworld, the subterranean hemisphere, the darkness of Acheron, and the Stygian depths. Homer and Hesiod place Elysium or the Isles of the Blest at the ends of the earth, but later tradition accommodated the brighter hereafter within the netherworld, as Vergil did in the sixth book of the *Aeneid*; cf. E. Norden *ad* 637 ff. (p. 295). It is Isis, however, that is promising to Lucius the joys of a blessed eschatology, so that behind the allusions to Elysium and to the goddess shining in the darkness of Acheron it is legitimate to seek, as Wittmann does, Egyptian doctrine. The Osirian dead were certainly pro-mised the equivalent of Elysium, for the celestial heaven is often portrayed as a region where the justified dead will enjoy a blissful life in fertile fields and islands; v. J. Gwyn Griffiths, 'In Search of the Isles of the Blest', *Greece and Rome* 16 (1947), 122-26. A further relevant point, although it cannot be ascribed to the approach of Apuleius, is that the Greeks probably derived the idea of Elysium from the Minoans, who in turn borrowed it from Egypt; this was argued in the article just cited; cf. Martin P. Nilsson, *The Minoan-Mycenaean Religion and its Survival in Greek Religion*[2] (Lund, 1950), 621. The Egyptians also had their concept of an underworld, called Dat or Dewat, but it is the sun-god Rē' who originally illumines this region and indeed proffers new life to the dead who accompany him in the solar barque. It is true that Dat was in a special sense the domain of Osiris; see my *Origins of Osiris*, 99. It is the abode of the dead, and Osiris is the king of the dead. At night, however, the sun-god is believed to visit the region and illumine it. In this context Rē''s qualities were sometimes transferred to other gods; cf. E. Otto, *Gott und Mensch*, 47 f. 'What exists lives when she shines' is a sentence applied to Isis in Chassinat, *Dendara*, II, 189, 13 f.; cf. E. Otto, op. cit. 109, no. 7. Apuleius may be thinking of Isis shining as the moon; cf. Plut. *De Is. et Os.* 44, 368 D and my remarks *ad loc.* p. 465. Wittmann compares πῦρ Ἄϊδος, used of Isis in the Hymn of Mesomedes, 9, and P. Oxy. 1380, 127, where Isis is 'the glad face in Lethe', the latter place being opposed to Olympus and Isis being associated in Olympus and Lethe with the sun in these allusions, as lines 157 ff. in the same papyrus show; cf. van Groningen *ad* 127 (p. 46).

p. 271, 5 **castimoniis** : The regimen is described in ch. 23, on which see notes *ad loc.*; cf. ch. 19 (281,7), *castimoniorum abstinentiam*; ch. 21 (283, 12-13), *cibis profanis.*

p. 271, 5-6 **ultra statuta fato tuo spatia** : The Egyptians regarded longevity as bestowed by the gods, and their ideal space for a full lifetime was 110 years; v. Josef M. A. Janssen, *OMRO* 31 (1950), 33-43, where (p. 41) Gen. 50, 26 is compared (Joseph reached this age), Cf. too Ex. 20, 12; Ps. 91.16 ('With long life will I satisfy him'). In a Leiden Hymn to Amûn, 3, 17 f. (ed. Zandee, Leiden, 1947, pp. 58 ff.) it is said of Amûn, 'He lengthens the space of life, and he shortens it'. Zandee, *loc. cit.* supplies a number of parallels; cf. Volten, 'Testi Demotici', 92 n. 33, citing *Wenamun*, 257 ff. Many other deities were regarded as bestowers of life, and Isis was among them. Isis is 'the mistress of life, who commands life ... everyone lives when he [hears] her name' : E. Otto, *Gott und Mensch*, 110, no. 17; cf. nos 18 and 19 *ibid.*, p. 121, nos. 19-22; 'she who gives life to him who is devoted to her', *ibid.* 137, nos. 18-20; cf. 145, nos. 21 ff. In the Hymns of Isidorus, 2.8 (*SEG* 8, 549) it is said of those in the grip of death, 'if they pray to you (Isis), they quickly attain your life' (i.e. renewal of life), though the idea here may concern life after death. According to a text in Philae (Junker, *Der grosse Pylon*, 76, 4-6) Isis is 'Mistress of jubilees with a long reign, who increases the years for him who obeys her and makes his office last for ever.' Cf. J. Bergman, 'I Overcome Fate' in H. Ringgren, ed., *Fatalistic Beliefs* (Stockholm, 1967), 37 f.

The Hymn to Amûn cited above also says of the god, 'He frees from destiny' (3, 16, Zandee p. 56), and this claim was often made for Isis in the Graeco-Roman era; e.g. the Aretalogies M 55, 'I conquer Destiny': M 56, 'Destiny obeys me'; v. D. Müller, 74 ff. Cumont in *Rev. d'hist. et de litt. religieuses* 3 (1912), 539, argues that the meaning here is that Isis will prolong the life of Lucius beyond the term appointed by Destiny, that is, the hour of death, in the sense of assuring him an immortality of bliss; cf. Cumont, *Astrology and Religion among the Greeks and Romans* (New York, 1912), 160 f.; 182. Such an idea is indeed present in other words of Isis. But it is much more likely that at this point Isis is promising a prolongation of life on earth beyond the limit which astrological prognosis has fixed for him; cf. W. Gundel, *PW* s.v. Hei-, marmene (1912), 2639; Weinreich, *Neue Urk. zur Sarapisrel.* 13; D. Müller *Isis-Aret.* 79. In his other works Apuleius shows considerable interest in astrology, and in *Apol.* 97 he refers to a correct prophecy by astrologers of the early death of a bridegroom; cf. Frederick H. Cramer, *Astrology in Roman Law and Politics* (Philadelphia, 1954), 217 ff.; W. Gundel and H. G. Gundel, *Astrologumena* (Sudhoffs Archiv, Beiheft 6, 1966), 297 f. In *Metam.* 2.12 and 3.1 an astrologer Diophanes is referred to with little respect. Apuleius returns to the theme of Destiny in chs. 15 and 25. Nilsson, *Gesch. Gr. Rel.* II¹ 612 f.

and G. Wagner, *Problem*, 120 f., seem to put all the emphasis on the present statement, arguing that the blessings of Isis concern this life only. The preceding allusions to the afterworld, especially to Elysium, belie such an interpretation.

p. 271, 6 **mihi tantum licere** : The exclusive demand made by Isis on the remaining years of the life of Lucius is matched by her absolute claim that she alone can prolong his life contrary to the limit imposed by Destiny. The μόνος-formula studied by E. Peterson in *Εἷς Θεός*, 196, has a different emphasis in its implication of monotheism. An epithet of Isis in Egyptian was 'the only one', *w't*; v. Junker, *Stundenwachen*, 59, no. 51 and 117, no. 66; cf. J. Bergman, *Ich bin Isis*, 225, who compares Θιοῦιν in the Hymns of Isidorus, I, 23 f. (*SEG* 8, 548) : Αἰγύπτιοι δὲ Θιοῦιν, ὅτι μούνη εἶ σὺ ἅπασαι/ αἱ ὑπὸ τῶν ἐθνῶν ὀνομαζόμεναι θεαὶ ἄλλαι. The Greek here, however, approaches the μόνος -formula, whereas the Egyptian originally implies 'the only one (who exists)'; cf. the phrases implying uniqueness compiled by E. Otto, *Gott und Mensch*, 11 ff., where the curious paradox emerges that they were used of many deities.

CHAPTER 7

p. 271, 7 **fine prolato** : Cf. *Metam.* 3.13 (61, 24) and 10.14 (247, 23), *sermone prolato*.

numen invictum : Cf. ch. 27 (288, 8), *invicti Osiris*. The term *invictus* was used of several deities, especially of Mithras, Iuppiter Dolichenus, and various African deities; v. K. Latte, *Röm. Rel.*, 352, who shows that in these cases, as in those of Isis and Sarapis, it is an epithet indicating omnipotence rather than one literally applied; the literal application may well apply to the earlier instances relating to Hercules or Mars. In the case of Isis the earliest occurrence belongs to the reign of Claudius in an inscription by one of the freedmen of Servilia, wife of M'. Acilius Aviola, who was consul in A.D. 54 : v. *CIL* VI, 353 and 30747 = Vidman, *SIRIS* 202, no. 402. The date involved (A.D. 51) seems to preclude the idea that Mithraic influence was responsible for the application of the epithet *invictus* to Isis, for, according to Vermaseren, *Mithras, the Secret God* (London, 1963), 29, 'no Mithraic monument can be dated earlier than the end of the first century A.D.' Cf. Vidman, *Isis und Sarapis*, 140; and Grimm, *Ägypt. Rel. im röm. Deutschland*, 132 n. 2, relating to an example of *Isidi invict(a)e* on a statue of Isis at Cologne (no. 14 of his Catalogue: see also no. 15, and cf. my remarks in *CdÉ* 39 [1964], 67 f.). Isis was also called *triumphalis* : v. *CIL* VI, 355 = Vidman, *SIRIS* 205, no. 413; and also *victrix* : v. *CIL* IX, 3144 = *SIRIS* 224, no. 474; see further Drexler, 'Isis', 521, and n. *ad* ch. 6 (269, 18), *Bellonam*, where Egyptian antecedents are discussed. On the equation of Nikê with Isis see Weinreich, *Neue Urk. zur Sarapis-Rel.* 34.

in se recessit : Cf. *Metam.* 8.8 (182, 16 f.), *in sese ... lassesceret luctus*. Yet there is no exact parallel, it seems, to this expression, although there is some similarity in Ovid, *Metam.* 2.302 f. (of Tellus), *suumque / rettulit os in se.* Price suggests that *in se recedere* here means *se in nubem condere.* This would suit the circumstances of the appearance of Isis as the moon rising from the sea. The phrase can nonetheless be independent of this, and as such has a pleasantly metaphysical touch.

p. 271, 8 **nec mora, cum** : Cf. ch. 11 *init.* The construction *nec mora (fuit)*, *cum* occurs in Propertius, 4.8.51 : *nec mora, cum totas resupinat Cynthia valvas*; cf. Callebat, *Sermo Cotid.* 445 f., accepting its literary origin. See further *Thes. L.L.* 8, 1471, 55 ff; Apuleius is said to use the expression seventeen times.

p. 271, 8-9 **pavore et gaudio ac dein sudore nimio permixtus** : Cf. *Metam.* 9.39 (233, 2 f.), *maerore permixtus*, an application of the participle apparently found only in Apuleius. The nexus of abstract and concrete in *gaudio ac dein sudore* provides a happy instance of zeugma of the type 'I swallowed my beer and my pride'; cf. Cic. *Phil.* 13.24, *cum in gremiis mimarum mentum mentemque deponeres* and see further Hofmann and Szantyr, *Lat. Syntax*, 832. Bernhard, *Stil*, 161, finds little use of zeugma generally in Apuleius. E. A. Lussky, 'Misapplications of the Term Zeugma', *Class. J.* 48 (1953), 285-90, argues for a narrow interpretation of the term 'zeugma' which would exclude the above examples.

p. 271, 10 **marino rore respersus** : The alliteration here involves five *r*-sounds, and the use of the adjective, instead of the simple *maris rore*, is poetical. Men visited in sleep by visions washed themselves ritually on waking; cf. Aesch. *Pers.* 201 f. with the notes by P. Groeneboom and H. D. Broadhead *ad loc.*; Aristoph. *Ran.* 1340; Prop. 3.10, 13, *ad quem loc.* Butler and Barber boldly state that 'night itself was a pollution, and washing had a ritual significance'; their first statement might seem confirmed by Persius, 2.16 (*noctem flumine purgas*), but Otto Jahn *ad loc.* points out that the action there precedes an act of prayer and that night might be a source of pollution in two ways, from sexual intercourse and from dreams. To the ancient Egyptians morning dew was the life-giving creation of the sun : v. J. de Savignac, 'La rosée solaire d'ancienne Égypte', *La Nouvelle Clio* 6 (Mél. Roger Goossens, 1954), 345-53, where it is shown too (pp. 349 ff.)) that the sun-god was sometimes regarded as the source of revivifying waters in general. Here the expression 'dew of the sea' is, of course, a poetical way of saying 'sea water' or 'sea spray'. *Ros marinus* can also mean 'rosemary', as in Hor. *Carm.* 3.23.15 f., a term which is likewise poetical in origin.

p. 271, 11 **nec mora, cum** : Robertson hesitantly suggested the deletion of these words, since they repeat the very same phrase as occurs in line 8 and since it is never followed elsewhere in Apuleius by *et ecce*. Ryle makes the valid point that simple deletion results in an awkwardly terse opening of the sentence, and he suggests replacing *cum* (after deleting *nec mora*) with *tum* or *tunc*. Allowance should be made, however, for a different attitude in ancient style. Just as late Latin prose writers overdid the use of anaphora to the point of monotony (cf. Hofmann and Szantyr, *Lat. Syntax*, 694), thus too were they not so fastidious about the avoidance of inelegant repetition; and this point applies to classical Latin as well.

p. 271, 12 **et ecce** : Médan suggests an archaism, citing the instance in Varro *ap.* Nonius Marcellus (4, p. 364 ed. Lindsay). But the expression occurs in a wide range of authors : v. *Thes. L.L.* 2, 31, 36 ff.

p. 271, 13 **turbulae** : See n. *ad* ch. 6 (270, 11).

totas plateas : The use of *toti* with the sense of *omnes* probably originated in popular speech; cf. Plautus, *Mil.* 212, *totis horis occubant*. *Totae copiae* with the sense of *omnes copiae* occurs in Caesar, though the translation ' the whole forces' is possible. The usage appears in Seneca and the Elder Pliny, but Apuleius is the first author to employ it frequently. See E. Wölfflin, *Rhein. Mus.* 37 (1882), 107 f., who would ascribe, however, the usual meaning to *tota laniavit armenta* in *Metam.* 3.18 (65,23); E. Löfstedt, *Phil. Komm. zur Peregrinatio Aetheriae* (Uppsala, 1911, repr. 1936), 69; Hofmann and Szantyr, *Lat. Syntax*, 293.

hilaritudine : Only here does Apuleius use *hilaritudo*: elsewhere (e.g. *Apol.* 25, p. 29, 5) he uses *hilaritas*. Previously Plautus provides the only occurrences of *hilaritudo*; e.g. *Mil.* 677. See further *Thes. L.L.* 6, 2786, 9 ff.

p. 271, 14 **gestire mihi cuncta videbantur** : A similar personification occurs in Aesch. fr. 28 (58); cf. Eur. *Bacch.* 726 f. with the n. by E. R. Dodds; Theocritus, 7.74 and Gow *ad loc.*; Cic. *In Pis.* 21 and Nisbet *ad loc.*; 'Longinus', *De subl.* 15.6 and D. A. Russell *ad loc.* Here and in what follows Apuleius finds in the joy of spring and in the beauty of trees and the songs of birds something responding to the new-found happiness of Lucius. This approach to nature, which Ruskin called the '*Pathetic Fallacy*', had already been apparent in Latin poetry. Discussing 'Landscape as Symbol', Charles Paul Segal in his *Landscape in Ovid's Metamorphoses* (Wiesbaden, 1969), 4, says that 'after Virgil no Latin poet could be unaware of the possibilities of using the physical setting to evoke an atmosphere which might itself symbolically reflect major themes in the work.' Here is another important instance, then, of poetical influence on Apuleius.

p. 271, 15 **cuiusce** : For *ce* = *que* cf. some of the cognates of *que* (esp. *ca*) in Kühner and Holzweissig, *Gr. Lat.*[2] I (1912), 621, § 5. According to Stolz and Schmalz, *Lat. Gr.*[5] (1928), 126, an interchange of *qu* and *c* is sometimes caused by analogy; thus *huiusque* follows *cuiusque*; and conversely *cuiusque-modi* and *usce ad* are found for *huiuscemodi* and *usque ad*. This *ce* is a deictic particle; v. ibid. 286.

totas : See n. *ad* line 13, *totas plateas*.

p. 271, 16 **pruinam pridianam** : Events of the previous day begin to be described in *Metam.* 10.29, where the coming of spring is mentioned and there is no allusion to frost. *Pridianus* is a word used three times by Apuleius; before him it occurs only in Suetonius and the Elder Pliny.

p. 271, 16-17 **fuerat insecutus** : The use of *fui* for *eram* in this passive tense became common in *Late Latin*, although it occurs often enough before this, especially in poetry; cf. Hofmann and Szantyr, *Lat. Syntax*, 321.

p. 271, 18 **adsonarent** : Four occurrences of this verb in other authors, three of them before Apuleius, involve an intransitive use; v. *Thes. L.L.* 2, 906, 1 ff. Here it is used transitively, a bold extension characteristic of a poetic approach.

matrem siderum : Cf. ch. 5 (269, 11), *prima caelitum* and n.; ch. 25 (286, 25), *tibi respondent sidera* and n.

parentem temporum : Cf. ch. 5 ad init., *saeculorum progenies initialis*; ch. 25 (286, 25), *tibi ... redeunt tempora*. In Plut. *De Is. et Os.* 9, 354 C an inscription of Athena-Isis in Saïs is said to read; 'I am all that has been and is and will be ...' See my remarks *ad loc.*, where Egyptian antecedents relating to other deities are cited. But in Junker, *Der grosse Pylon*, 13, 4, it is Isis who is described as 'the one who was in the beginning, the one who first came into existence on earth.' Diod. Sic. 1.11.4 says that the name Isis is explained by some as 'ancient' because 'her birth was from everlasting and ancient'. Cf. Athenagoras, *Pro Christ.* 112, where Isis is regarded as 'the nature of Aion (Time, Eternity);' see further n. *ad.* ch. 5 (269, 9), *rerum naturae parens* and the phrase that follows, *saeculorum progenies initialis*. In his impressive study 'Osiris-Aion' (*Oriens Antiquus* 3 [1964], 15-25) L. Kákosy shows that the idea of time is more often linked with Osiris; see however his p. 24 for the occasional association with Isis.

p. 271, 18-19 **orbisque totius dominam** : Cf. ch. 5 (269, 10), *elementorum omnium domina*; ch. 21 (283, 2-3), *iubente domina*; Juv. 6.530 (of a believer in Isis, *Credit enim ipsius dominae favore moneri*). Vidman, *SIRIS* nos. 397, 510, 564, 588, 608, 752, 754, provides instances, several of which begin *Isidi dominae*. The term was used of other goddesses, especially of Cybele. This phrase confirms the accepted interpretation of ἡ τύραννος πάσης χώρας in *Aretal.* M 3 a : v. D. Müller, 19. Bergman, *Ich bin Isis*, 149 n. 4 offers a less convincing explanation grammatically and conceptually ('of the whole land', i.e. Egypt).

For the use of a conjunction connecting the second and third element in a group of three, although the first and second have no conjunction, see Bernhard *Stil*, 84 f. In classical usage thers is no such mixture of Syndeton and Asyndeton; Plautus has an occasional instance, and it returns in Livy to become more common from Tacitus onwards, until it becomes fully accepted in the second century. Apuleius is very fond of the usage, enabled as he thus is to achieve greater *variatio*. Cf. ch. 1 (266, 17), *terra caelo marique*; ch. 9 (273, 5-6), *lucernis, taedis cereis et alio genere facticii luminis*.

p. 271, 19 **adfamine** : Cf. ch. 30 (291, 8). An Apuleian neologism for the usual *adfatus*; v. *Thes. L.L.* 1, 1172, 8 ff.

p. 271, 20 **earum** : This genitive, occurring as it does after the relative, is probably a rhetorical pleonasm; cf. Callebat, *Sermo Cotid.* 291.

umbra contentae : The reading *contecta* is hard to follow. *Contectae*, reported by Hildebrand, would have some force if *umbra* is explained as 'foliage' : these trees, unlike the fruit-bearing ones, are 'barren, being covered only with foliage'. *Umbra*, however, can scarcely bear this meaning, although Médan strangely finds it in Vergil, *Georg.* 1.191, *At si luxuria foliorum exuberat umbra*; the word can admittedly refer to the shade caused by leaves or by the tree itself. Cf. Hildebrand *ad loc.* The reading *contentae* allows *umbra* to bear its normal meaning.

p. 271, 21 **austrinis laxatae flatibus** : Ryle compares Vergil, *Georg.* 2.239 (also in a description of spring), *et hibernis parcebant flatibus Euri*.

renidentes : In its early occurrences the word is confined to poetry, but it becomes fairly common in Silver Latin prose; it is used by Quintilian, 12.10.38 of *oratio* (*hilarior protinus renidet oratio*).

p. 271, 22 **obsibilabant** : A new coinage by Apuleius, made by prefixing *ob* to *sibilare*; the word is also a *hapax leg.* The idea that trees can whisper or speak is found in Aristoph. *Nub.* 1008; Theocritus, *Id.* 1.1; Petronius, *Satyr.* 120 (73), *virgulta loquuntur*.

p. 271, 23 f. **quietas adluvies temperabat** : *Quietas* is proleptic. No parallel seems to occur for *adluvies* with the sense of 'waves', although it means 'over-flow' in Livy, 1.4. The calm of the sea is a detail in the serenity of this particular spring day; Apuleius probably wishes to suggest, at the same time, that the sea usually becomes less turbulent in the spring, thus enabling the renewal of navigation which the *Isidis Navigium* celebrated. The happy change is doubt-less ascribed to Isis; cf. *Aretal. Cym.* 43, 'I calm and swell the sea.'

p. 272, 1 **nubilosa** : An Apuleian neologism,

nudo sudoque : Apuleius is fond of rhyming two words which are directly connected; v. Bernhard, *Stil*, 224, on what he calls 'Die reimende Verbin-dung'. He shows that whereas classical literature contains few examples of the usage, it is common in Plautus and probably derives from common speech. Cf. ch. 11 (286, 19), *nec dies nec quies*. In ch. 1 (266, 16-17), *luminis numinisque nutu*, there is a comparable rhyme but an added subtlety in the allit-eration of the second and third words; cf. Lucret, 1.73, *flammantia moenia mundi*. The pattern was later established in the Welsh strict metres as 'Cyn-ghanedd Sain', as in *Carwn y dywell bell bau* (T. Gwynn Jones). Dylan Thomas imitates the pattern in 'Fern Hill' : 'Oh as I was young and easy in the mercy of his means' and in the line 'To the burn and turn of time'. His source was apparently Gerard Manley Hopkins.

CHAPTER 8

p. 272, 3 **pompae magnae paulatim praecedunt** : The long syllables suggest the majesty of the procession itself although it is only the gay preludes that are here to be mentioned. The combination of rhyme and triple alliteration is noteworthy; for the latter see below *ad* ch. 13 (276, 4; 5; 8) and ch. 14 (276, 15-16).

anteludia : A coinage by Apuleius which does not occur elsewhere. Some antecedents of these shows are present in the *pompa circensis* as described by Q. Fabius Pictor (*Hist. Rom. Rel.*² fr. 16, pp. 29 ff. ed. H. Peter) at the end of the third century B.C. : although this was mainly a military display, a secondary element was provided by buffoons who were dressed as Satyrs and Sileni. In the imperial era, if not earlier, some young men dressed up as girls and wore feminine wigs, and Nilsson, *Opusc. Sel.* I (Lund, 1951), 252, believed this element in the *Soldatenkarneval* to be of oriental origin. Etruscan and Greek influences on this and other features are adduced by A. Alföldi, 'Die alexandrinischen Götter', 75, and he also points out that the Romans were fond, in their shows, of games with animals. According to Herodian, 1.10.5, the spring festival of the *Magna Mater* was one in which anyone acted any part he wished (ἕκαστός τε ὃ βούλεται σχῆμα ὑποκρίνεται). Some of the Roman festivals also provided rather similar features. There was an element of license in both the *Lupercalia* and the *Bacchanalia*; and the *Saturnalia*, celebrated on December 17th, certainly exuded a spirit of carnival in the temporary obliteration of the master-slave distinction. Again, there were scenic episodes and circus games attached to the *Ludi Saeculares* : v. Jean Gagé, *Recherches sur les jeux séculaires* (Paris, 1934), 67 and 70 f. The Isiac *anteludia* precede a festival which concerns the launching of a ship, and Alföldi in *A Festival of Isis*, 57 f. and 'Die alexandrinischen Götter', 76 ff. is firmly of the opinion that the mediaeval carnival in Italy, France, and the Rhineland derives from the Isiac festival. The derivation of *carnival* from *currus navalis* (Romance *car navale*) is certainly preferable on both phonetic and conceptual grounds to that from *carnelevarium* (<*carnem levare, 'the putting away of flesh (as food)'; so the Shorter Oxford English Dict. and Ernest Weekley) or that from *carne, vale*, 'O flesh, farewell!' (Ernst Klein). The ship is a common factor, although Apuleius does not tell us that the Isiac ship was drawn in procession; a lamp in the form of a ship is mentioned in ch. 10, but it is not until ch. 16 that the ship which is to be launched is described; it is said to be on the sea-shore when the procession arrives there. C. Rademacher, *ERE* 3 (1932), 226, refers to the Dionysiac ship on wheels in Athens and also to a similar feature, perhaps, in the procession of the Teutonic Earth-Mother Nerthus as described by Tacitus, *Germ.* 40. Rademacher goes on to suggest that the Isis-cult, when it was diffused among the Greek and Romans, and when it reached Gaul and Germany, found a form of ship-cart already in ritual use. Certainly more than one element is involved, but Nilsson, *Gesch. Gr. Rel.* II² (1951), 625 n. 6, seems unduly sceptical of the Isiac legacy when he stresses that more than half a millennium lies between the late imperial evidence and the first mediaeval attestation of a ship-ceremony. What is unconvincing in Alföldi's theory is the calendrical transposition. Although in his second thoughts ('Die alexandrinischen Götter', 54) he retracts the one-sided emphasis on the *Isidis Navigium* in relation to the *vota publica*, he still urges that this ceremony had a place in the rites on January 3rd. T. A. Brady, *JRS* 28 (1938), 89 f., recalls that several other Egyptian motifs appear on the relevant coins, and Alföldi now admits (loc. cit.) that he had unduly neglected the role of Serapis here. The *Isidis Navigium* was, however, celebrated on March 5th, and the natural thing in any theory of its subsequent influence is to see it emerging again in the mummery and revelry of the mediaeval carnival of the day (or week) immediately preceding Lent.

A question that concerns us more urgently here is whether the *anteludia* described by Apuleius have any religious significance. Were they a gay prelude to the serious rite, intended to attract the attention of onlookers initially, so that they would be drawn on to interest themselves in the claims of Isis? Or did they shadow forth themselves some features of the faith? In favour of the first interpretation is *rideres* at the end of the chapter; and the possible artistic motive of an ἔκφρασις designed to increase the reader's tension by postponing the climax — thus Bernhard, *Stil*, 282 f., who cites the judgement of Paris in *Metam.* 10.29 ff. as a similar episode, postponing as it does the climactic event of the ass's public intercourse with a woman. This view would regard the metamorphosis of Lucius back into human shape as the climax. But Berreth rightly points to the intrinsic interest of both masquerade and procession; they were something witnessed (*vidi*, line 12) by Lucius and the author. An absence of religious symbolism is suggested by Carlesi, p. 291 n. 2 : 'Forse queste mascherate erano indipendenti dal rito e costituivano una specie di sfogo concesso alla fantasia popolare senza alcun simbolismo religioso.' Merkelbach, *Isisfeste*, 39 f., on the other hand, believes that for the informed onlooker several elements in the masquerade had a serious religious meaning. The ingenious explanations advanced by him will be discussed *ad singula*. On the whole I am not convinced that a deeper level is present here.

p. 272, 3 **votivis** : There can be little doubt about the soundness of the emendation, since Apuleius several times uses *votivus* in the sense of 'agreeable'; e.g. *Metam.* 5.20 (119, 2), *votivis nuptiis*; 7.13 (163, 21 f.), *ad votivum conspectum*. This is Médan's view, but he adds 'avec un zèle agréable (à la déesse) ; 'agreeable in each case to himself' is rather the meaning. We have seen (Introd. IV, p. 44) that Wittmann regards the *anteludia* and the procession as belonging in a strict sense to the *Isidis Navigium*, and this is not acceptable. On p. 41 he expresses the view that the phrase *votivis studiis* shows that the masquerade had, originally, a religious meaning. If the above interpretation is correct, Wittmann's view will be seen to have no linguistic support.

p. 272, 4-5 **militem gerebat** : *Gerere* here implies 'to play the part of, to represent'; in *Metam.* 1.24 (22, 20), *aedilem gerimus*, the emphasis is on actual conduct since Pythias is really the aedile; cf. M. Molt *ad loc.* (Groningen, 1938). The *balteus* is singled out as the distinguishing mark of a soldier because various arms hung from it; Price aptly quotes Servius *ad Aen.* 5.313 : *Balteus dicitur, non tantum quo cingimur, sed etiam a quo arma dependent*. Wittmann, p. 42, suggests that the ancient Egyptian god Wepwawet is represented by the soldier, but the only point of affinity seems to be the fact that Wepwawet ('opener of the ways') was depicted as leading a procession. His form was canine; a warrior Horus would suit better. Nor is Berreth's proposal (p. 53) that the soldier should be related to the Mithras-cult any more acceptable. Certainly Mithras is well supplied with military attributes, and his followers undertake a *militia*, as Vermaseren, *Mithras : Geschichte eines Kultes* (Stuttgart, 1959), 117 f., shows; but there is no suggestion here of a precise connection with the god. Indeed, if a religious meaning must be pressed, it is at hand in the Isis-cult itself, for in ch. 15 the priest tells Lucius, 'Enrol your name in this holy military service' (*da nomen sanctae huic militiae*). Merkelbach, *Isisfeste*, 40, therefore says, 'Soldat (miles) ist jeder Myste im Dienst der Göttin.' One might question, in that case, whether the devotee is here in good company.

p. 272, 5 **crepides** : A form found only here, instead of the usual *crepidae*. Apuleius has followed the Greek original more closely; v. *Thes. L.L.* 4, 1166, 70 ff. and 1168, 59 ff.

venatorem : Hunting was a popular feature of Roman public shows, and in the Augustan *Acta* the *ludi honorarii* had an elaborate *venatio* at the end, in which the people took part in hunting deer under specially favourable conditions : see J. Gagé, *Recherches sur les jeux séculaires*, 70 f. We can assume that at Corinth in the Roman era such shows would be modestly imitated, and this solitary huntsman would represent the interest. Berreth, pp. 50 f., urges a Dionysiac association : the huntsman appears in the Dionysiac procession, since the Maenads are the hunters of Dionysus Zagreus. Certainly the original Dionysiac mysteries included the eating of raw animal-flesh after the beasts had been captured, and Dionysus himself was regarded as a hunter; cf. Walter F. Otto, *Dionysus : Mythus und Kultus* (Frankfurt, 1960), 100. In the Hellenistic and Roman eras there was often an attenuation of the old savagery, but sometimes it continued, and now men also took part in the *orgia* : v. Nilsson, *Dionysiac Mysteries*, 7 f. Hunting scenes are sometimes depicted in late Dionysiac contexts; cf. R. Eisler, *Orphisch-Dionysische Mysteriengedanken in der Christlichen Antike* (Vortrâge Bibl. Warburg 2 [1922-3], Leipzig, 1925), 165 ff., esp. 167, where it is suggested that an allegorical meaning was present, with the sense that wild passions are to be tamed. But the Dionysiac huntsman would be out of place in these *anteludia* where nothing else has such an affinity. An Isiac association could be argued in the sense that the huntsman represents Horus. One of his best known forms, especially in the temple of Edfu, is that of a hunter who pursues and captures the enemy Seth, the latter being usually a crocodile or a hippopotamus. Horus is here equipped with a spear, but not with the Greek *chlamys* and boots; cf. also the 'Cippi of Horus', where the god strangles scorpions or snakes and tramples on crocodiles. Merkelbach, *Isisfeste*, 40, refers to an inscription concerning a hunter called Oresius (*CIL* V, 2044 = *IG* XIV, 2381 = Vidman, *SIRIS* 276, no. 620), a name which may well be compounded with Horus; cf. Preisigke, *Nb.* 46, Ἀρεσίας. Rudolf Egger, *MDAI* 4 (1951), 62 ('Zwei oberitalienische Mystensarkophage') rather daringly suggests that in a fresco from Herculaneum the words GENIUS

HUIUS LOCI MONTIS, accompanying a crowned Harpocrates (v. *CIL* IV, 1176 = Dessau, *Inscr. Sel.* II. i. 3649) involve an interpretation of Horus as 'he of the mountain' (ὄρος) and that Oresius in the sarcophagus from Belluno has a similar significance. Tran Tam Tinh, *Herculanum*, publishes the picture as his frontispiece and discusses it on p. 82 without a reference to Egger's explanation. In each case a rather subtle speculation is involved. It may also be objected that if any form of Horus were present, it would not be as an item in the masquerade, but as a solemn member of the religious procession.

p. 272, 6 **soccis** : Governed by *inductus*, this noun denotes half-shoes or slippers which were worn in the imperial era exclusively by comic actors and women. Thus Suetonius, *Calig.* 52 observes, as a mark of Caligula's effeminacy, that he wore the *soccus muliebris*. They were often richly decorated with gold and pearls; cf. Seneca, *De benef.* 2.12.1; Pliny, *HN* 9.56.14; and Friedländer, *Sittengeschichte Roms*, II, 326. A. Hug, *PW* s.v. Soccus (1927), 771, points out that the Edict of Diocletian refers to *socci viriles et muliebres*, thus implying that men as well as women wore them by that time.

obauratis : For the meaning see previous n. The word is a neologism and a *hapax leg.* It belongs to the fairly large group of participial forms involving compound verbs which were coined by Apuleius : v. Bernhard, *Stil*, 120 f.

p. 272, 6-7 **adtextis capite crinibus** : Cf. Ovid, *Ars. Am.* 3.165, *crinibus emptis*; Tertull. *De cult. fem.* 2.7, *affigitis praeterea nescio quas enormitates subtilium atque textilium capillamentorum* and William Kok's n. *ad loc.* (Dokkum, 1934); also J. Carcopino, *La vie quotidienne à Rome* (Paris, 1939), 199. Here is evidence that women wore wigs, as commentators have striven to show. But Apuleius points to something else : a man impersonating a woman is sporting a female wig, as Caligula is said to have done by Joseph. *Ant. Iud.* 19.30 in order to participate in mysteries (those of Isis are undoubtedly meant). In spite of the Isiac connection in the latter context, there is no hint of it here. That wigs were sometimes worn also by men is shown by Steiniger, *PW* s.v. Haartracht und Haarschmuck, Rom (1912), 2147 f., who cites, *inter alios*, Martial, 6.57, *mentiris fictos unguento, Phoebe, capillos*. The feminine style, however, was more abundant and easily recognizable.

p. 272, 7 **perfluo** : Cf. Seneca, *De tranq. an.* 17.4, *ut nunc mos est etiam incessu ipso ultra muliebrem mollitiam fluentibus*. The adjective is a neologism and also a *hapax leg.*; cf. Koziol, *Stil*, 276 f., who notes that among the new adjectival coinages compounds with *in*, *per*, *omnis* and *multus* are prominent.

feminam mentiebatur : A ritual including exchange of clothes by the sexes is mentioned by Plut. *V. Lyc.* 15; cf. my *Plut. De Is. et Os.* 464. But no ritual origin is discernible here; each character is presented for the sake of amusement, probably in the theatrical style. Wittmann, p. 43, compares the type of the μαλακός, as played by Antony (Dio Cassius, 50.27), but the reference there is to general behaviour (γυναικίζει). The Galli in the rites of Attis wore some feminine accoutrements — pectorals and images — (cf. Polybius, 21.37 and Hepding, *Attis*, 128), and Berreth, p. 53, would like to see this exemplified here. These priests, however, were not dressed as women in other ways, unless *passis cum crinibus* (Arnobius, *Adv. nat.* 5.16) be interpreted thus. The kind of show described by Apuleius is closer, probably, to the account given by Petrus Chrysologus, a North Italian Christian writer of the fifth century who attacks a pagan show produced at the Calends : *praeterea vestiuntur homines in pecudes, et in feminas viros vertunt* ... See Nilsson in *Arch. Rel.* 19 (1916-19), 81 f. and Berreth, p. 54. Weber, *Terr*, 154 n. 4, compares an allusion in P. Hibeh 54, 15 ff. to an effeminate musician who is told to wear 'as fine clothes as possible'.

p. 272, 8 **e ludo ... gladiatorio** : A good pointer to the predominant Roman influence in the *anteludia*, even if the gladiatorial business eventually derives from the Etruscans.

p. 272, 9 **facibus** : No doubt *fasces* and purple were obvious symbols of a magistrate; but the reading of the best codices can be defended, as Helm notes, by the custom elaborated by Mommsen in his *Römisches Staatsrecht*[4] (Tübingen, 1951, repr. of ed. 3, 1887), 423 f., whereby a magistrate's nocturnal appearances were illuminated by torches; and the fire-container, from which torches were kindled, was carried as a constant symbol. Mommsen compares *prunaeque vatillum* ('pan of coals'), ascribed to a praetor in Hor. *Sat.* 1.5.36; according to Palmer *ad loc.* the purpose of this was to further a sacrifice, and according to G. Kirchner, 'um Weihrauch darauf zu streuen'. Mommsen can refer also, however, to Cic. *De sen.* 33.44 (reading *cereo funali*); and especially to ch. 62 of the Lex. Colon. Genetivae (*togas praetextas funalia cereos habere*).

p. 272, 10 **baxeis** : in *Metam.* 2.28 (48, 9) the term is used of the sandals made of palm-leaves worn by an Egyptian priest; cf. *Flor.* 9 (13, 12). According to *Thes. L.L.* 2, 1792, 50 ff. the word occurs previously only in Plautus, *Men.* 391. In Egypt sandals of this type were commonly made of papyrus; cf. Hdt. 2.37 and Wiedemann *ad loc.* (p. 168); Mau, *PW* s.v. Baxeae (1897), 176 f. and Suppl. I (1903), 245.

barbitio : Cf. *Metam.* 5.8 (109, 14). These are the only two occurrences of the word; v. *Thes. L.L.* 2, 1747, 8 ff. The use of *barbitium* for *barba* is probably due simply to a desire to produce a refinement of the word commonly employed. Plutarch, *De Is. et Os.* 3, 352 B, also mentions the idea that a beard was regarded as the hall-mark of a philosopher, and Merkelbach, *Isisfeste*, 39 f., suggests that even if a figure such as this had a purely jocular meaning for the average onlooker, a serious sense offered itself to the informed observer, namely that 'die wahren Philosophen sind die platonisierenden und pythagoreisierenden Isispriester.' In general this interpretation, as we have seen, is open to question, particularly in view of the sharp contrast drawn by Apuleius between the *anteludia* and the procession of the goddess. In relation to a specific point, too, the interpretation is doubtful here, since the Isiac priests, unlike the philosophers, had their heads clean-shaven, a fact of which Apuleius was well aware : v. ch. 10 (273, 17); 30 (291, 15).

p. 272, 11 **aucupem ... piscatorem** : The fowler is very frequently represented in Egyptian art; cf. Kees, *Kulturgeschichte : Ägypten*, 25 ff.; Erman and Ranke, *Ägypten*, 19. Weapons used were the net, the sling, and the throw-stick, of which the last-named might be one of the *harundines* mentioned by Apuleius; cf. A. D. Touny and S. Wenig, *Der Sport im alten Ägypten* (Leipzig, 1969), pls. 50, 51 and p. 67. Bird-lime was not, however, used by the Egyptians. For the *harundo* as a cane smeared with bird-lime, which Apuleius more probably intends, see Martial, 9.54.3; 14.218.2; Petronius, *Sat.* 109 (*viscatis ... viminibus*); A. Reinach, *Dar.-Sag.* s.v. Venatio (1919), 694 (but on p. 685 he seems to mislead in explaining these allusions to the *harundo* as involving a blow-pipe of the pea-shooter type used with balls of clay or lead).

Berreth, p. 51, recalls, in relation to the fisherman, the Dionysiac hunting-scenes where fishers with hooks are represented : v. Eisler, *Orphisch-Dionysische Mysteriengedanken*, 189, for fishing-scenes dedicated to Dionysus Halieus; for the latter epithet of the god see Kern, *PW* s.v. Dionysus (1903), 1027. But Berreth is keener to find an Isiac association with fishing. Although something has gone amiss with his reference here (p. 51 n. 114), it could be argued that the Aretalogies (M 15 : 'I discovered activities connected with the sea') support this idea; cf. D. Müller 41 f. whose interpretation is more convincing than that of J. Bergman, *Ich bin Isis*, 98, who argues for a cosmic allusion to Isis as the Year and as the Inundation. Merkelbach, on the other hand, wishes to regard the fowler and the fisher in the metaphorical sense of Isis priests who fish from the sea of their sins those men who have not yet been won for the service of the great goddess or who catch their souls as birds and butterflies are caught with lime-twigs (*Isisfeste*, 39 f.). This is, of course, a Christian symbol : 'ye shall be fishers of men'. A second meaning is certainly present in much of the Egyptian material which deals with hunting, but this meaning relates to the role of the living Pharaoh as Horus, while the beings hunted are equated with his enemy Seth. Cf. J. Gwyn Griffiths, *Conflict*, 47 f. with the reference to the study by T. Säve-Söderbergh. It is more likely that allegorical interpretations are to be eschewed here, for hunters of various kinds, as we have noted above, were prominent in the Roman shows of the imperial era in amphitheatres; cf. Lafaye, *Dar.-Sag.* s.v. Venatio (1919), 700 ff. For fishing with various techniques in ancient Egypt see Touny and Wenig, op. cit. 69 ff.

p. 272, 12 **ursam mansuem** : Very divergent origins are again suggested. Berreth, p. 51, follows Bachofen (*Der Bär in der Religion des Altertums*, Basel, 1863, 12 f.) in taking the she-bear and monkey together. Since Apuleius gives the monkey a Phrygian association, the bear is placed in Phrygia too : Bachofen identifies her as the Mother of the Gods and the monkey as Attis. It is urged that the choice of the ape, which had a connection with the moon, points to Attis; and an assocation of Isis with the Mother of the Gods is found confirmed in ch. 5 (*Me primigenii Phryges Pessinuntiam vocant deum matrem*). A radical objection to this theory is that Apuleius does not really suggest any coupling of bear and monkey. All his items are separate until he reaches the ass and the old man. It is also hard to see how terracottas found in Salzburg, in which a bear and a monkey are figured together, necessarily relate to a Phrygian background. Bachofen's further suggestion that the she-bear's exalted position in the sedan-chair reflects the power of 'mother-right' in early antiquity merely reflects his involvement in an attractive theory. That Cybele and Attis were commonly shown as bear and ape is evidently not true : see M. J. Vermaseren, *The Legend of Attis in Greek and Roman Art* (*ÉPRO* 9, Leiden, 1966); nor do the literary sources suggest this : see Hugo Hepding, *Attis, seine Mythen und sein Kult* (Giessen, 1903), 141 ff. In the Roman rites the idol of the goddess was carried in a cart drawn by cows, as Ovid, *Fasti*, 4.337 ff., relates (see also J. G. Frazer *ad loc.*, III, 246 ff.), but this too is rather different from the episode in Apuleius. Admittedly Livy, 29.14.10 ff., lays stress on the fact that the goddess was received by P. Cornelius 'with all the matrons' (*cum omnibus matronis*) and that again in Rome the *matronae primores civitatis* received her. Apuleius uses the word *matronalis*. It is doubtful, though, whether the goddess herself was thought of as a *matrona*. An Egyptian derivation is sought by Wittmann, p. 42, who points out that Seth-Typhon was identified with the constellation of the Great Bear, as Plutarch, *De Is. et Os.* 21, 359 D, observes. The Egyptians themselves, however, used the term 'Bull's Foreleg' for this constellation, so that a fusion with Greek ideas will be present if this allusion is admitted. A link with the rite in Apuleius is found by Wittmann in that the 'late rising of Arcturus' coincides with March 5th, the date of the *Isidis Navigium*. Ingenuity impresses one here, but the allusion remains rather too recondite to be convincing. A more immediate liaison would seem to offer itself with the rich Egyptian artistic tradition of animals acting as men and women. Thus Emma Brunner-Traut, *Die altägyptischen Scherbenbilder* (Wiesbaden, 1956), no. 95 (pl. 2 and pp. 94 ff.) reproduces an ostracon with a mouse sitting as a woman on a folding-chair; or, more relevant still is no. 96 (pl. 34 and pp. 96 f.) : 'Eine Maus sitzt als Dame auf einem mit Fell überzogenen Sessel.' The tradition is expressed also in representations on papyri and in literature : see E. Brunner-Traut, *Altägyptische Tiergeschichte und Fabel* (Darmstadt, 1968); cf. J. Gwyn Griffiths, *JEA* 53 (1967), 92 ff. and *Bibl. Orient.* 26 (1969), 203. A papyrus in London shows a lion and gazelle playing draughts (Brunner-Traut, op. cit. fig. 6). Sometimes the concept of a *mundus inversus* appears, as when a cat, equipped as a shepherd, is seen leading a flock of geese (ibid. fig. 7). The honouring of an animal in a manner befitting gods, which is what the figure in Apuleius suggests, is exemplified in the picture of a crocodile playing a lute before an enthroned mouse (ibid. fig. 31) or in the representation of jackal-priests carrying a mouse (?)-god in procession (ibid. fig. 14), where the small shrine suggests the *sella* of Apuleius.

A bear, however, does not appear in these figures or fables, although, according to Otto Keller, *Die antike Tierwelt* (1909, repr. Hildesheim 1963), I, 180, the Abyssinian bear appears on Egyptian monuments. Keller, op. cit., I,

176, shows how Arcadia in the Peloponnese was famous for bears zoologically and religiously. Arcadia itself may mean 'Bear-land', and its eponymous hero, Arcas, is represented as a passionate bear-hunter; further, his mother Callisto was said to have been changed into a she-bear; compare the suckling of Atalanta by the same animal. The she-bear in Apuleius is probably Callisto, for Cenchreae could easily reflect an Arcadian cult. At the same time we must assume the religious allusion here to have been attenuated. The matron-bear has become a figure of fun, and a man may be regarded as performing, although Price argued for a real bear. We know that nets and ropes were used to capture bears : v. George Jennison, *Animals for Show and Pleasure in Ancient Rome* (Manchester, 1937), 144. The suggestion of W. C. McDermott, *The Ape in Antiquity* (Baltimore, 1938), 138 f., that the 'bear in female clothing may be Isis' must be firmly rejected. On bears in the amphitheatre see Jack Lindsay, *Leisure and Pleasure in Roman Egypt*, 179 and 180 f. (expounding P. Oxy. 2470 with its drawing of an animal spectacle).

p. 272, 12 **sella vehebatur** : There is no need to supply <*quae*> before *sella*. The parataxis conveys vivacity; cf. Callebat, *Sermo Cotid.* 442.

p. 272, 13 **simiam** : What Apuleius sees here is a monkey playing the part of Ganymede. He is not suggesting that the latter is ever represented in art or myth by a monkey, although one instance is noted below. Berreth, as we have seen, follows Bachofen in seeing here a form of Attis. Several other commentators, from Hildebrand onwards, suggest that Apuleius has misconstrued the appearance of the Egyptian cynocephalus, that is, the god Thoth, who is connected with the moon in Iamblichus, *De myst.* 5.8 and Horapollo, *Hierogl.* 1.14; cf. the *tabula Bembina*. Wittmann expatiates on the role of Thoth in Isiac mythology. Certainly he is prominent in the Horus-Seth legend as one who tries to reconcile the warring gods and also as one who defends Horus in the trial scene; cf. J. Gwyn Griffiths, *Conflict*, 81-4. Wittmann can even cite terracottas showing Thoth with a cap that recalls the plaited cap mentioned by Apuleius; a saffron-garment is also found in the Isis-cult, though not in connection with Thoth; cf. Plut. *De Is. et Os.* 51, 371 F and 77, 382 C ff. But Ganymede's cup is an insuperable difficulty, and Wittmann himself feels uncomfortable about his attempt to suggest that the ape, as guardian of the Great Bear, holds the Cup; a small boy is said to hold the Cup : v. Boll, *Sphaera*, 143 and 224. Clearly there can be no connection with the vessel which Harpocrates is sometimes shown carrying under his left arm : v. Bonnet, *Reallexikon*, 274 with fig. 69 (= Berlin 9109); cf. perhaps von Gonzenbach, *Knabenweihen*, pl. 1 with pp. 118 ff.; Nock, *AJA* 64 (1960), 197. It is better to accept this episode at its face value : a monkey has been trained to act the part of Ganymede. Cf. Josephus, *Bell. Iud.* 7. 136, where it is said that many kinds of animals were shown in the triumph of Vespasian, all decked with appropriate trappings. W. C. McDermott, *The Ape in Antiquity*, 139 and pl. 10, points to a valuable parallel in ancient art : a Roman clay lamp now in the Louvre figures Ganymede in the form of an ape being carried away by an eagle; on p. 314, no. 561, he says, 'That the ape is a parody of Ganymede is emphasized by the fact that it wears a Phrygian cap and cloak.' On p. 299 he refers to the baboons on the marble relief from Ariccia; v. Leipoldt, *Bilderatlas* 17 [251] and Anne Roullet, *Rome*, pl. 13 with pp. 27 f. These, of course are entirely sacral. But, Graeco-Roman Egypt certainly knew of trained apes; v. McDermott, p. 48, citing Lucian, *Pisc.* 36 on an Egyptian king who taught some monkeys to dance the sword-dance, but whose show was disrupted when someone threw nuts on to the stage, causing the monkeys to fight for the nuts.

p. 272, 13 **Catamiti** : The form is attested since the time of Plautus as a derivation from Γανυμήδης, apparently through the medium of the Etruscan *Catmite* : v. P. Friedländer, *PW* s.v. Ganymedes (1910), 741 f.

p. 272, 14 **asinum** : This ass must be firmly distinguished from the central character of the narrative, although Wittmann, p. 41, adduces, even in this connection, many representations of Seth-Typhon as an ass. Not one of these, it should be noted, shows a winged ass. In general the winged fabulous animals of antiquity come from Asia Minor and Mesopotamia; but see p. 313. The winged ass is a caricature of Pegasus, the magic steed given to Bellerophon; cf. Homer, *Il.* 6.152 ff. Both are intimately associated with Corinth. Coinage reveals Pegasus as an established emblem of the city from the seventh century onwards; cf. Pindar, *Ol.* 13.90 ff. and L. R. Farnell, *ad loc.* (Comm. 97 f.).

p. 272, 14 **adambulantem** : A Plautine word revived; cf. *Thes. L.L.* 1, 566, 70 ff.

p. 272, 15 **Bellerophontem** : He is the youthful hero much endeared to the Corinthians for his fight against the Chimaera with the aid of Pegasus, and also for his attempt to fly to heaven; cf. Euripides in Nauck and Snell, *Trag. Gr. Fr.* 443 f.; Rose, *Gr. Myth.* 270 f. Discussing the evidence in art for the Bellerophon theme, T. J. Dunbabin in *Studies presented to D. M. Robinson*, II (Saint Louis, Missouri, 1953), 1176, says that 'the evidence of the early monuments is concentrated in and near Corinth, the scene of Bellerophon's capture of Pegasus, the only place in Greece where Bellerophon had a cult.' Here the youthful hero has become a decrepit old man; both steed and hero are thus a laughing-stock, but highly appreciated, nevertheless, in the harbour of Corinth. Neuenschwander, *Der bildliche Ausdruck*, 60, points out that in *Metam.* 7.26 (174, 10 f.) Lucius the ass refers to his rider as 'my Bellerophon', while in 7.30 (152, 9 f.) he is rebuked for his slowness with a reminder that a little before that he had surpassed the winged speed of Pegasus; still more elaborate in 8.16 (189, 22 ff.) is the way Lucius compares himself, spurred on by fear, with Pegasus becoming winged through fear of the Chimaera. In the present context, however, there is more than a humorous metaphor.

CHAPTER 9

p. 272, 17-18 **passim vagabantur** : Price shows how frequent is this, or a similar, collocation, citing Cic. *De invent.* 1.2; Catull. 64.278, *Ad se quisque* *vago passim pede discedebant*; Pliny, *HN* 7.2.11; Seneca, *De benef.* 4.6. In several instances the aimless wandering of animals is compared.

p. 272, 18 **sospitatricis** : A neologism which occurs only here and in ch. 15 (277, 18, also of Isis). Elsewhere Apuleius uses *sospitator*; cf. Arnobius, *Adv. nat.* 2.74, *sospitator nostri generis* (of Christ). The traditional epithet appears in the prayer in *Metam.* 6.4 (131, 14) : *sis meis extremis casibus Iuno Sospita.* For the Greek σωτήρ the Romans used *conservator*, and for σώτειρα they used *conservatrix*, which was applied to Caelestis, Diana, Fortuna, Juno, Luna, Magna Mater, and Minerva as well as to Isis; v. F. Dornseiff, *PW* s.v. Σωτήρ (1927), 1219 f., who points out that the Christian coinage *salvator* appears first in Tertullian.

deae peculiaris pompa : The *anteludia*, one may therefore infer, were not hers.

moliebatur : This verb can be used absolutely with the meaning *viam ingredi, proficisci*; v. *Thes. L.L.* 8, 1362, 43 ff. and Médan *ad loc.*

mulieres : They come first here, but they are members of the general populace who are fervent admirers of the cult rather than initiates. In fact, the order of importance is the reverse of the order of appearance; the most important priests come last. It is later that the initiates come (cf. 10, *init.* : *turbae sacris divinis initiatae, viri feminaeque*). Both groups are dressed in white. The prominence of women in the cult is suggested by the Aretalogies, M 10 : 'I am she who is called God by women'; D. Müller, 35, recalls the title 'mistress of women', ascribed to Isis, Hathor, Neïth and Hecet in Egyptian texts. Whereas P. Oxy. 1380, 214 ff., 'Thou didst make the power of women equal to that of men', is doubtless a propagandist exaggeration as applied both to the cult and to its general influence, women were clearly very welcome in the ranks of the initiates. According to Plutarch, *De Is. et Os.* 27, 361 E, Isis is a pattern and encouragement to men and women alike; cf. my comments *ad loc.* and also p. 73. Nevertheless it was men who assumed the main priestly roles, although women are sometimes mentioned as stolists : cf. *CIL* XII, 3061 (A.D. ii, an *ornatrix* in Gaul) = Vidman, *SIRIS* 312, no. 731. Roeder, *PW* s.v. Isis (1916), 2131, maintains that the *kanêphoroi*, carriers of the sacred baskets, were always women; cf. Roussel, *CED* 269; in Delos women were also torch-bearers (λαμπτηροφόροι) in the nocturnal processions : v. Roussel, ibid. 270. References to women as initiates, but not as priestesses, are made by Ovid, *Am.* 1.8.74; Tibullus, 1.3.23 f.; Propertius, 2.33.15 ff. and 4.5.34; and Juv. 6.526. According to Josephus, *Ant. Iud.* 19.30, Caligula, in order to take part in (Isiac) mysteries dressed up in women's robes and wore feminine wigs. Many tomb reliefs represent women dressed as Isis, and it is assumed that they had been priestesses. An inscription from Eretria of the first century B.C. records the names of 50 men and 45 women who acted as Isiac *nauarchs* : v. Vidman, *SIRIS* 38, no. 80; the office probably implied membership of a cult-association of worshippers : v. Vidman, *Isis und Sarapis*, 87. Women occur also in connection with *Isidis sacrorum* (ibid. 88) and as *Bubastiacae* (ibid. 92), both suggesting priestly service; cf. the term *Isiaca*, plausibly interpreted by

Vidman (ibid. 93) as implying a high grade of initiate. Plutarch's Clea is a well-known instance of a priestess. It is strange that Apuleius does not mention a single priestess. In one of the frescoes from Herculaneum showing an Isiac service, a priestess stands on the right of the presiding priest; she is holding a sistrum in her right hand and a situla in her left, and she wears a flowing Isiac stole or shawl. Among the devotees shown in the temple court below women are more numerous than men, although the priestly figures in the centre are male. See J. Leipoldt, *Angelos* 1 (1925), pl. 1 with p. 127; id. *Bilderatlas*, 53 [294]; Tran Tam Tinh, *Herculanum*, pl. 27, fig. 40, with pp. 83 ff. Women (and children) are also prominent in the fresco of the dancing Bes-figure : v. *Angelos* 1 (1925), pl. 3; *Bilderatlas*, 54 [295]; *Herculanum*, pl. 28, fig. 41 with pp. 85 ff. The oriental religions offered women a higher status than the traditional cults of the West; cf. Leipoldt, *Die Frau in der antiken Welt und im Urchristentum* (Ed. 2, Leipzig, 1955), 156; Ilse Becher, *ZÄS* 96 (1970), 82 f. As far as Egypt was concerned, this corresponded to a higher status (as compared with Greece and Rome), although not in official and political life; v. S. Allam, 'Zur Stellung der Frau im alten Ägypten', *Bibl. Orient.* 26 (1969), 155-9 and St. Wenig (tr. B. Fischer), *The Woman in Egyptian Art* (Leipzig, 1969).

p. 272, 19 **amicimine** : Coined by Apuleius from *amicire* to replace the usual *amictus*. It occurs only here and in ch. 23 (285, 5). Cf. *Thes. L.L.* 1, 1890, 43 ff.

p. 272, 20 **coronamine** : Similarly coined from *coronare* to replace *corona*, the word occurs only here. A variant which occurs several times, though not in Apuleius, is *coronamentum* : v. *Thes. L.L.* 4, 988, 64 ff.

per viam : Cf. the statement later in the chapter that other women bespattered the streets (273, 4, *conspargebant plateas*) with perfumes and balm. Such attentions were reserved for gods and their representatives. Thus in *Metam.* 4.29 (98, 1 ff.) Psyche is treated as a goddess and when she wanders through the streets (*plateas commeantem*) people pray to her with flowers made into bouquets or strewn separately (*floribus sertis et solutis*); the Hours greet Venus similarly in *Metam.* 10.32 (263, 9 ff.) Cf. Ovid, *Tristia*, 4.2.50.; Mark 11.8 ff. on Christ's Messianic entry into Jerusalem. In East Germany it is still customary in weddings to throw flowers on the path of the approaching bridal couple.

p. 272, 21 **nitentibus speculis** : Cf. the mirror held before Venus in *Metam.* 4.31 (99, 22); cf. too Seneca, *Epist.* 95.47. Recent commentators rightly agree in connecting the mirrors with what follows, that is, with the adornment of the goddess. Personal attention to the statue of a god was an important part of the Egyptian daily temple liturgy. Cf. E. Hornung, *Der Eine und die Vielen* (Darmstadt, 1971), 192, with the ref. to Moret's *Le rituel du culte divin etc.* (Paris, 1902).

p. 273, 1 **commonstrarent** : Cf. n. *ad* line 14, *praedicarent*; and *ad* ch. 27 (288, 13-14). The subjunctive is used here, and also in line 3 (*fingerent*), with no apparent distinction in meaning from the indicatives which precede (*sterne-*

bant) and follow (*conspargebant*). It is popular speech that has probably produced this atrophy; cf. Kühner and Stegmann, *Gr. Lat.*² II, 309 n. 17; Callebat, *Sermo Cotid.* 343, sees a literary purpose.

p. 273, 3 **ornatum** : Cf. the *ornatrix* of *CIL* XII, 3061 = Vidman, *SIRIS* 312, no. 731, and the stolists mentioned by Plut. *De Is. et Os.* 39, 366 F, as well as the hierostolists, ibid. 3, 352 B. In each case the meaning is wider than the present allusion suggests : these officials took charge of the general adornment of the statue of the goddess, especially of the clothes. Cf. Tran Tam Tinh, *Isis à Pompéi*, 91 and 92; Vidman, *Isis und Sarapis*, 62 f.

obpexum : A new coinage found only here. Cf. Koziol, *Stil*, 271. The verb *oppecto*, however, is found in Plautus, *Pers.* 111, where it is used metaphorically. Dionysia, as priestess of Isis at Megalepolis in Arcadia, is described as tending to the ablutions and toilet of a statue of the goddess in a funerary inscription of the second or third century A.D. : πλεξαμένη δὲ / τοὺς ἱεροὺς πλοκάμους. See F. Dunand, *ZEP* 1 (1967), 219-224, esp. p. 221, and W. Peek, *Griechische Grabgedichte* (Berlin, 1960), 186 f., no 317 (where, however, the toilet of the priestess herself is given as the interpretation).

p. 273, 4 **geniali** : Apuleius is apparently the only prose author to use this adjective in its extended sense of 'pleasing, agreeable'; v. *Thes. L.L.* 6, 1807, 36 ff. He is especially fond of it, using it of an old man's white hair in *Metam.* 2.27 (47, 11), of a flower in 4.2 (75, 15), and of the countenance of a priest in ch. 14 (277, 2). He uses it three times, in spite of this, in its more basic sense, applying it to the nuptial couch — 2.6 (30, 3); 9.26 (222, 15); 10.34 (265, 11); cf. *Thes. L.L.* 6, 1806, 59 ff. (*ad Genium deum pertinens*).

guttatim : The only previous occurrence of this adverb, according to *Thes. L.L.* 6, 2373, 64 ff., is in Ennius. Cf. *Metam.* 3.3 (54, 1).

p. 273, 4-5 **conspargebant plateas** : See n. *ad* p. 272, 20, *per viam*.

p. 273, 6 **et** : Cf. n. *ad* ch. 7 (271, 18), *orbisque*.

facticii luminis : The variety of readings indicates a deep-seated corruption, and Haupt's emendation is the most satisfying. Since there is no suggestion that the procession took place at night, we must assume that these lanterns, torches and tapers had not been kindled. Lamps were prominent in the Osirian rites in the month of Khoiak according to the texts of the temple of Denderah; on the 22nd day of the month 365 lamps were kindled; v. Blackman in *Myth and Ritual* (ed. S. H. Hooke), 20 and Chassinat, *Le Mystère d'Osiris*, 64. The Pithom Decree celebrating the Battle of Raphia (217 B.C.) mentions a festival of lamps on the birthday of Horus; v. Bevan, *Hist. Ptol. Eg.* 391 (Spiegelberg's translation); cf. Merkelbach, *Isisfeste*, 30. Lamps found at Delos had an Isiac connection : v. Roussel, *CED* 238 and 270, where female officiants called λαμπτηροφόροι are shown to be attested; Roussel (p. 270 n. 5) also refers to inscriptions pointing to a λαμπαδεία or λυχναπτρία at Priene as well as Delos, but one has to remember that the use of torches and lamps was not an exclusively Isiac feature. On the other hand, the torch rather than the lamp characterized the Demeter cult. A woman attached to the Isiac cult

in Athens (A.D. ii) had the double office of lamp-lighter and dream-interpreter :
v. Vidman, *SIRIS* 11 f., no. 16. The Calendar of Philocalus contains a rite
called *Lychnapsia* on August 12th; v. Hopfner, *Fontes*, 525. Since lamp festivals
were frequent in Egypt, this has generally been explained as an Isiac rite, and
M. S. Salem, *JRS* 27 (1937), 165-7, equates it with the Egyptian festival of the
birthday of Isis on the fourth epagomenal day. A difficulty here is that the
Egyptian records do not attest a lamp-festival on the birthday of Isis; v. Schott,
Festdaten, 112 f.; admittedly torches were lit in the New Year Festival and
during the epagomenal days, but in tombs and for the dead; v. Schott, ibid.
68 and 71. Herodotus, 2.62, describes a lamp-festival in Saïs; cf. Wiedemann
al loc., pp. 258 ff.; there the goddess venerated is Neïth. See also n. *ad* ch. 10
(274, 1), *lucernam*.

  p. 273, 6 **siderum caelestium stirpem propitiantes** : Cf. n. *ad* ch. 5 (269, 11),
prima caelitum. Berreth, p. 56, takes *propitiantes* as suggesting the apotropaic
function of the torches. Such a function was certainly present, with a precise
reference to Seth, in temple rites of lighting a fire or torch : v. J. Gwyn Griffiths,
Aegyptus 38 (1958), 3 ff. ('The Horus-Seth Motif in the Daily Temple Liturgy').
In an early Coffin Text (I, 216 *h* ff.) the gods are called on to light lamps for
the Osiris-Mysteries with the exhortation 'Protect your Lord!' Cf. Schott,
Festdaten, 23 n. 1. The 365 illuminations in the Khoiak rites, on the other hand,
allude to the 365 days of the Egyptian year, though they may simultaneously
have a protective significance in relation to the 34 divine figures in boats.

  p. 273, 7 **symphoniae** : Instrumental music was much used in the rites of
Isis and Osiris in Egypt, as it was in religious ceremonies generally, Thus in
Junker and Winter, *Geburtshaus*, 358, Isis is shown receiving sistra from the
King (Tiberius), whom she identifies (359, 19 ff.) with Iehy, the youthful musi-
cian-son of Hathor; cf. 386 and 387, 7 ff.; also 268 and 326 where Meret, goddess
of song, is shown playing the harp before Isis and Hathor respectively; in
220 ff. the seven Hathors beat tambourines before Isis. It was Hathor herself who
was pre-eminently the goddess of music; v. H. Hickmann, *Dieux et déesses
de la musique* (Cairo, 1954), 39 ff. Isis inherits some of her attributes, and in
the Aretalogy from Chalcis the claim is made by Carpocrates that he produced
the sistrum 'for Isis'; v. Harder, *Karpokrates*, line 5 and cf. my *Plut. De Is. et Os.*
525 ff. Both *fistulae* and *tibiae* can mean the composite instrument with several
pipes of graded length, and Apuleius may be using them as synonyms. Such
an instrument was known in Egypt in the Graeco-Roman era; v. Hickmann
in Helck and Otto, *Kleines Wb.* 263 and 'La flûte de Pan dans l'Égypte ancienne'
CdÉ 30 (1955), 217-24. It may, however, have been an imitation of a Greek
model, and a rite in Cenchreae may well have deployed local musical usages.
Corinth possessed a theatre and Odeion and not far away the Isthmian
Games were held. The Graeco-Roman material does not, strangely enough,
provide many instances of the depiction of musical instruments; see, for
one example, the sacral dancing-scene on the relief from Ariccia (Leipoldt,
Bilderatlas, 17 [251] = Anne Roullet, *Rome*, pl. 13). Two flute-players are

represented in an Egyptian rite on a relief on a pillar-base in the Vatican Museum : v. G. Lippold, *Die Skulpturen des Vaticanischen Museums*, III, 2, Tafeln (Berlin, 1956), pl. 59 with pp. 270 ff. of text-volume. Lippold is rightly sceptical of the earlier interpretation of Lafaye, *Hist. du culte*, 139 n. 7 and Cat. no. 108 (p. 296), where a dancing Osiris is seen in the main figure; the presence of a winged sphinx argues an Egyptian ceremony, but the main figure is not Osirian nor is he dancing. On the other hand, the well-known fresco from Herculaneum which shows an Isiac service (Leipoldt, *Bilderatlas*, 53 [294] = Tran Tam Tinh, *Herculanum*, pl. 27) clearly puts in the right foreground a seated figure playing a long single-reed flute. Its equally well-known companion piece (Leipoldt, 54 [295] = Tran Tam Tinh, pl. 28), which has a dancing dark figure in the centre, shows this figure to be accompanied by a man who is also blowing a flute or perhaps a trumpet; the latter was the suggestion of Helbig, *Wandgemälde ... Campaniens*, I, 223. The sistrum, of course, is ubiquitous, and sometimes it was dedicated to the gods; v. Vidman, *SIRIS* 241, no. 524 and 307, no. 716; cf. his 'Index archaeologicus' s.v. sistrum; also Grimm, *Ägypt. Rel. im röm Deutschland*, 182 ff. According to Roussel, *CED* 287 there was a large harp ($\psi\alpha\lambda\tau\dot{\eta}\rho\iota o\nu$) in the temple of Anubis in Delos. In P. Hibeh 54, 10-13 = Wilcken, *Chrest.* 477 (c. 245 B.C.) the tympanum, cymbals and castanets are said to be needed by female participators in a religious rite; so is a flute-player 'with both the Phrygian flutes and the rest'; cf. Weber, *Terr.* 154 n. 4 together with his whole discussion there of divine figures with tambourines or drums (see his pl. 24). Hildebrand raises the problem posed by a passage such as Strabo, 17.1.44, who says that at Abydos in the temple of Osiris no singer or flute-player or harp-player is allowed to begin the divine rites, suggesting that Osirian practice differed herein from the cult of the other gods.

What seems to have intruded here is the tradition that the tomb of Osiris was to be honoured by reverent silence; cf. Plut. *De Is. et Os.* 20, 359 E and my notes *ad loc*. As for the statement in Diod. Sic. 1.81.1 ff. about the education of Egyptian priests, it is certainly credible that music was missing (in 1.81.7 it is said to have played no part even in the general educational system of Egyptians), since it was only priests of the lower orders, including women, who were entrusted with the musical side of religious ceremonies. Cf. W. Otto, *Priester und Tempel*, II, 209 ff.; Sauneron, *The Priests of Ancient Egypt* (London, 1960), 67-70. Music was naturally a concomitant of other Egyptian rites; see, e.g., E. Otto, *Osiris and Amon*, pl. 35 (lower part), where lute players accompany a festival procession. Nor is this distinctively Egyptian; Greek and Roman ceremonies were similarly enhanced with sacred music; see a sacrificial scene before the Capitoline temple, where a flautist plays in front of Marcus Aurelius, shown in W. Goetz et al. *Hellas und Rom*, (Berlin, 1931), 413. Egyptian music was probably more emotional and at times orgiastic, and Hickmann in *Kleines Wb.* 233, rejects the theory that this was due to influence from Asia Minor.

p. 273, 8-9 **lectissimae iuventutis ... chorus** : Singing was equally important in the Egyptian tradition. In the *Songs of Isis and Nephthys* two virgins who

use tambourines sing solos and duets; v. Faulkner, *JEA* 22 (1936), 121 ff.
Thus too in the *Lamentations of Isis and Nephthys*, also edited by Faulkner,
in *Mél. Maspero*, I (Cairo, 1934), 337-48. According to Clemens Alex. *Strom.*
6.4.35.3 = Hopfner, *Fontes*, 372, a singer (ᾠδός) leads the procession; the
description here, admittedly, is not of a specifically Isiac rite. It is likely that
the groups shown in the two frescoes from Herculaneum must be regarded
as singing. Chanting was also frequent in Egyptian rites; cf. 'Chanting, this
is what they do for Osiris' in P. Louvre I. 3079, col. 110, 5 (the word is *nis*) and
J.-C. Goyon *ad loc.* in 'Le cérémonial de glorification d'Osiris etc.', *BIFAO* 65
(1967), 65-156, this *locus* p. 95. The allusion by Apuleius to a choir of select
youths confirms the idea that children were consecrated to Isis and Osiris
at an early age. In Plut. *De Is. et Os.* 35, 364 E it is said that Clea was consecrated 'in the Osirian rites' by her father and mother; see my remarks *ad loc.*,
pp. 430 f. Victorine von Gonzenbach, *Untersuchungen zu den Knabenweihen
im Isiskult* (Bonn, 1957), 113 (cf. 15), connects this with evidence she finds in
the art of the imperial era for the practice of dedicating boys to Isis. A good
example is her pl. 15 (K 18), a funerary relief from Ostia, where the Horus-lock
is clearly depicted and where the *palla contabulata* may also be an Isiac feature.

Her pl. 18 (K 20), a glass object from Rome, is, however, unconvincing;
the Horus-lock is missing and there is nothing distinctively Isiac about anything
else. When the hair-style of these figured boys follows the Egyptian trait, then
it must be allowed that a practice of dedication is implied. But it can hardly
be accepted that the Horus-lock at an early stage involved such a practice;
Parlasca rightly points out in *OLZ* 54 (1959), 475, that the sidelock of the
Horus-child is at first a mere mark of childhood. Von Gonzenbach, pp. 66 ff.,
thinks it was the token of the Pharaoh's destined successor, and was understood
generally too as referring to succession — a very doubtful theory. We must assume that in the Graeco-Roman era, with the increased veneration of Harpocrates, a somewhat different interpretation was put on it, as was done also
with the finger-to-mouth gesture of the same god. Such indeed is the position
taken by Von Gonzenbach (pp. 105 ff., esp. 123 f.); and Nock, *AJA* 64 (1960),
196 f., accepted the interpretation as applying outside Egypt. A difficulty arises
from the fact that the evidence belongs to the second century A.D. up to the
fourth, so that it begins to emerge, as Castiglione points out in *Gnomon* 31
(1959), 540, as late as four centuries after the beginning of the dissemination
of the cult outside Egypt. Still it is a striking feature of the evidence that the
literary confirmation also comes from this era; and here Castiglione adduces,
in addition to Plutarch and Apuleius, the allusions in Xenophon, *Ephesiaca*,
3.11.4 and Ammianus Marcellinus, 22.11.9. The latter refers to the curls of
boys as a pagan fashion, but the reference to the Horus-lock is not indubitable.
Thus in a procession of Apollo in Acarnania in the second century B.C. some
participants are to leave their hair uncut : v. Christian Habicht. *Hermes* 85
(1957), 86 ff. (end of line 12 of the inscription). Habicht, p. 104, connects it
with the Greek practice of hair-offerings. Nock, to whom I owe this reference,

(*AJA* 64 [1960], 197 n. 3), cites also F. Sokolowski, *Harv. Theol. Rev.* 52 (1959). Castiglione, op. cit. 542 f., makes the valuable suggestion that the dedication of boys in the Isis-religion probably derived from the Dionysiac Mysteries; he cites Nilsson, *Dionysiac Mysteries*, 106 ff., for the prominent place of the practice in those rites. Certainly Nilsson shows that children had a central place in the Hellenistic cult of Dionysus, unlike the cult in preceding ages; but when he says (p. 110) that children were not 'initiated' into the 'Oriental mysteries', he has clearly overlooked the evidence for the Isiac cult, where the case of Clea is irrefutable, although, of course, 'consecration' or 'dedication' would perhaps be a better designation. Nilsson says, ibid., that 'the child Dionysus may have been considered as a prototype of the human child initiate'. The same thing may be true of the Horus-child, and it is hard to say which development occurred first. Leipoldt points out in *Angelos* 1 (1925), 128, that one of the frescoes from Herculaneum (his pl. 3 = *Bilderatlas* 54 [295]) shows children taking part in an Isiac service; some are depicted both above and below the temple steps. Leipoldt invokes the sentimental regard for children in the Hellenistic and Roman eras, and also, in the Isis-cult, the important role of the Horus-child. See also Tran Tam Tinh, *Herculanum*, pl. 28, fig. 41, with pp. 39 and 85 f.; he states that one of the children above is holding a sistrum and situla, while the other is carrying a vase.

p. 273, 8 **cataclista** : The word does not appear in Latin before Apuleius; then in Tertull. *De pall.* 3.1 (ed. V. Bulhart, p. 110); see *Thes. L.L.* 3, 587, 15. Since it is taken from the Greek κατάκλειστος, it presumably has similar meanings — 'shut up', 'precious'. Strabo, 13.1.54, uses it of books, Sextus Empiricus, 1.143, of gold. It seems unlikely, therefore, that it can mean 'closed' in the sense of a one-piece Egyptian dress without an opening or join — the interesting suggestion of Beroaldus. The meaning 'shut up' implies here 'kept under lock and key for the festival'.

p. 273, 9 **venustum** : If one could assume that the song was Egyptian, Wasse's emendation *vetustum* would be attractive. Probably the song is to be regarded as composed in Greek; the only clear mention of the use of Egyptian in the rites is in ch. 22 (284, 12-17).

iterantes : The plural, referring to *chorus*, is a *constructio ad sensum* involving syllepsis; cf. Callebat, *Sermo Cotid.* 336. There are two possible meanings : they repeated the whole hymn, or just the refrain. We do not possess any festival hymns to Isis in the strict sense. Peek called his book *Der Isishymnus von Andros*, but he rightly says on p. 25 n. 1 : ' "Evangelium" wäre richtiger.' None of the Aretalogies is a hymn. The composition of Isidorus (*SEG* 8, 548 ff.) is technically a hymn, as it is addressed to the goddess, but its literary sophistication prevents our regarding it as a hymn which was actually sung; it has metrical faults and other infelicities, yet it is a personal expression of faith; cf. É. Bernand, *Inscriptions Métriques de l'Égypte Gréco-Romaine* (Paris, 1969), 650 ff.; Nicola Turchi, 'I quattro inni di Isidoro' in *Studi e materiali di storia delle religioni* 22 (1949-50), 139-148, with a brief note on the metres on p. 142;

Vera Vanderlip discusses features of language and style on pp. 86 ff. On the other hand, the *Songs of Isis and Nephthys* do contain refrains in the sense that several lines are repeated in the solos; e.g. 1, 10, 'O fair Stripling, come to thine house' is repeated in 9, 14, and the line 'Come to thine house without fear' occurs several times. (Faulkner's translation has been quoted.) Since Apuleius, however, explicitly says *carmen ... iterantes*, the whole song must be taken to be repeated. This is still done in festive processions, as in that of St Martin in the Rhineland, as I observed in Bonn on November 11, 1969. Ryle suggests that 'the chorus repeats each stanza or each sentence, if the hymn is in dactylic verse, when the poet has given it out (*edixerat*).' Elsewhere Apuleius, like other authors, uses *edico* of the public proclamation of laws, oracles and the like; see *Metam.* 2.12 (35, 4); 4.33 (101, 16); 6.7 (133, 10); *Flor.* 7 (8, 18). It is a very slight extension of meaning to imply the making public of a poem by the action of the composer in making it available for use. Ryle's interpretation is nonetheless favoured by *Thes. L.L.* 5, 2, 67, 43 ff., where *recitare* is the meaning applied here and also to *Anth.* 285.2 (*Non audet quisquam dignos edicere versus*, preceded by *Inter 'eils' goticum 'scapia matzia ia drincan'*, which implies recitation rather than publication). One might doubt, at the same time, whether a poet would be expected to sing in a procession.

p. 273, 11 **antecantamenta** : The word does not occur elsewhere, but its meaning is clear, and no other term apparently existed with this meaning. The *Oxford Latin Dict.* (1968) translates 'a prelude, preliminary'; here the second word is obviously inadequate since songs are meant. How can songs be preludes to vows? Probably in the sense that they contained words that were later to be recited by the initiates in their solemn vows, or at least words that enshrined the significance of these vows.

p. 273, 11-12 **dicati magno Sarapi tibicines** : When Sarapis appears in the cult of Isis, he usually replaces Osiris; and his own cult was, of course, partly Osirian in origin and partly derived from the Apis-cult, a Greek type of iconography being superimposed. In Greek centres of the Isiac religion, whether on the mainland or in the Aegean islands or in Asia Minor, Sarapis is usually found on a par with Isis instead of Osiris in the Hellenistic era; cf. Bell, *Cults and Creeds*, 66; P. M. Fraser, 'Two Studies', 24 ff.; my *Plut. De Is. et Os.* 44. Osiris tends to re-emerge, however, in the Roman era, as in the Egyptian cults in Athens; v. Sterling Dow, *Harv. Theol. Rev.* 30 (1937), 224 f. At the same time Dow appears to record only one reference to Osiris even then. The account of the festival by Apuleius assigns some importance to Osiris in chs. 27 and 30, but this is the only reference to Sarapis. Apuleius follows the spelling found in Greek writings; in Latin texts *Serapis* is more common.

p. 273, 12 **per oblicum calamum** : What is meant is probably the bombyx-flute, called also the πλαγίαυλος and *tibia obliqua*, a transverse flute with a special, inclined tube attached as a mouthpiece; v. H. Hickmann, 'The antique cross-flute', *Acta Musicologica* 24 (1952), 108-12, esp. p. 12, where reference is made to a representation of one in an Alexandrian terracotta (Breccia, *Terr.*

2, pl. 58, no 286). It is a pity that Tran Tam Tinh, in his 'Le "Tibicen Magno
Sarapi" ', *Rev. Arch.* 1967, 101-112, had not apparently seen Hickmann's study.
He argues that *obliquus* can mean 'curved', and occasionally it certainly does, as
when used of rivers. He goes on to urge that a curved flute is meant here, and
finds it illustrated in two terracotta objects in the Louvre which are perhaps of
Etruscan origin, but which are given Alexandrian affinities by him. On p. 104
n. 1 he cites Dr W. Ehlers, General Editor of the *Thesaurus*, who says that in 300
instances much the most usual meaning of *obliquus* is 'transverse', but that sometimes the meaning 'curved' is present. Hickmann has established the application
of the first meaning, and his citation of an Alexandrian representation is
decisive.

p. 273, 12-13 **familiarem templi deique modulum** : The use of the flute in
Dionysiac (= Osirian) ceremonies in Egypt is noted as early as Herodotus,
2.48. Rites connected with Sarapis probably inherited Osirian traits, although
distinctive qualities are hard to trace. Ch. A. Christos in *Arch. Eph.* 1956,
34-72 publishes an inscription from Tanagra of c. 95 B. C. in which a kind of
Eisteddfod of Sarapis-worshippers is recorded, with references to competitions
for trumpeters, flautists and lyre-players. Here, one supposes, the music would
have no necessary affinity with that used in the religious rites, although a
sacrifice to Sarapis and Isis is mentioned at the end. 'A tune traditional to the
temple and its deity' probably implies a particular melody. Pausanian, 2.4.6,
refers to two sanctuaries of Sarapis in Corinth, but it is not clear whether the
reference is specifically to one of these. Trumpeters from one of these sanctuaries
could, of couse, have been taking part in a rite at Cenchreae, over six miles
away. Cf. Introd. III, pp. 17 ff.

p. 273, 14 **sacris** : Holy objects or rites are usually meant; these are incorporated in the procession.

praedicarent : The subjunctive conveys obligation : 'many ... whose task
it was to shout out.' It differs then, in sense from the preceding indicative
frequentabant, and there is not a true parallel to the subjunctives *commonstrarent* and *fingerent* (lines 1 and 3), on which see n. Callebat, *Sermo Cotid.*
343, couples the passages, invoking merely a desire for variation.

CHAPTER 10

p. 273, 14-15 **sacris divinis initiatae** : For the Dative cf. Cic. *Leg.* 2.15.37,
initienturque eo ritu Cereri; Liv. 39.14.8, *initiari Bacchis*. Although initiation
in the original Egyptian mysteries was confined to priests, the word *bs* was
certainly used in this sense; cf. my remarks in *Plut. De Is. et Os.* 391. Among
those condemned as evil-doers in *Edfou*, V, 334, 1 ff. is 'he who initiates (*bs*)
wrongfully'; v. Fairman, *MDAIK* 16 (FS. Junker, 1958), 87.

p. 273, 15 **viri feminaeque** : The order indicates the position fairly. Men and
women were equally welcome in the cult, but the important priesthoods were
occupied by men; cf. n. *ad* ch. 9 (272, 18), *mulieres*.

p. 273, 15 **omnis dignitatis et omnis aetatis** : Price compares *Metam.* 7.13
(163, 23 f.), *pompam cerneres omnis sexus et omnis aetatis* (of a procession that
greets the rescued Charité). In ch. 15, *init.* Lucius himself is described as an
educated person of noble blood and rank. There is no reason to doubt that by
the time of Apuleius all social ranks were represented in the cult, the seal of imperial sanction having been granted in A.D. 58 when Caligula built a temple for
Isis in the Campus Martius; after this it continued to enjoy the favour of emperors. A.D. Nock observes in *CAH* 12 (1939), 412, that 'Egyptian cults were acceptable not only to the demi-monde of Rome and the men of Pompeii, but also
to farmers in Italy', his reference in the last phrase being to the mention of the
cults in the rustic calendars. For the second century, which is the era of Apuleius,
there is evidence for the patronage of the Egyptian cults by Hadrian, Antoninus
Pius, and Marcus Aurelius. The cults in Delos revert in origin to the third
century B.C., and Roussel, *CED* 283 f., shows how important the commercial
element was in their personnel. But economically there is a considerable variety :
people of lowly condition, and probably even slaves, are named side by side
with the rich. Whereas Brady, *Rec. Egn Cults*, 23, argued that during the first
century of Ptolemaic rule the Egyptian cults were spread in the Greek world by
'officers and representatives' of the political rulers. P. M. Fraser in his 'Two
Studies' was able to show that it was the private action of traders, mercenaries,
priests and travellers that was responsible for the diffusion of the cult of Sarapis
(see esp. his p. 49). The appeal of the cults, after their initial establishment,
would inevitably widen their social intake. When a cult was a public, rather than
a private one, we can assume that its adherents would include very respectable
citizens; and for instances of public cults see D. Magie, *AJA* 57 (1953), 165
(Chalcedon in Bithynia and Mitylene in Lesbos) and Sterling Dow, *Harv.
Theol. Rev.* 30 (1937), 198 ff. By the first and second centuries A.D. there is
evidence that persons of all classes, as Apuleius says, were attached to the cult.

The adherence of higher class people, as we have noted, was facilitated by
the favour of the emperors. R. E. Witt, 'Isis-Hellas', 62, although he strangely
refers to Domitian as the first emperor to have recognized the Egyptian cults
officially on Italian soil (Caligula had already taken this step : v. supra),
rightly stresses the number of intellectuals who worshipped Isis; he includes
Chaeremon, the Egyptian priest who was Librarian ad Alexandria and afterwards tutor to Nero; Lucius Julius Vestinus, another Egyptian priest who
had been President of the Museum and tutor to Hadrian; and of course
Plutarch, who could be described as the most representative Greek intellectual
of his age. We have seen above that women were very welcome in the ranks
of the initiates and in some priestly offices. The note of catholicity reminds
one of the 'great multitude' of Rev. 7.9. R. E. Witt, loc. cit., states that in
the cult of Isis 'fellow slaves could band themselves together and feel free,
coloured Africans could join with Romans, and women could claim the same
power as men.' If by 'coloured Africans' he means the people of Egypt,
Libya and Nubia, this is clearly so; in a footnote he refers to the possibility

that the dancing figure in the fresco from Herculaneum represents a negro. Others had explained the figure as that of a Nile-god. It was F. W. von Bissing in 'Paintings from Pompeii', 227 f. that first put forward the very probable view that it is a figure of the god Bes; cf. his 'Eine hellenistische Bronzefigur des Gottes Bes' in *Athenische Mitteilungen* 50 (1925), 123-32. He did not explain why the figure is dark; this is doubtless because of the Nubian derivation of Bes; v. Bonnet, *Reallexikon*, 102. F. M. Snowden, *Ant. Class.* 25 (1956), 115, rightly sees some negroid figures on the marble relief from Ariccia, where an Isiac dance is portrayed. In general the available evidence confirms the Apuleian claim. The people in the Greek world of non-Egyptian stock who became adherents before 30 B.C. are listed by Brady, *Rec. Egn. Cults*, 47 ff. and also, where possible, classified as between (a) soldiers and men of lower official rank; (b) artists, craftsmen; (c) upper classes (scholars, statesmen, generals, courtiers, priests, ambassadors; (d) lower classes. In this list the lower classes are less strongly represented than the others, but in a large number of cases no indication is possible. Vidman in his *SIRIS* (Berlin, 1969) has unhappily not indexed *nomina* and *cognomina* of adherents, arguing (p. XII) that their significance is limited. The evidence from Pompeii is earlier by a century and more than Apuleius. After a valuable survey, Tran Tam Tinh, *Isis à Pompéi*, 60, concludes that from a population of some 20,000 about 2,000 were probably Isiacs, and that these included people of all classes; certainly civic dignitaries were among them as well as members of professional corporations and of the *Sodales Iuventutis Pompeianæ*; for these last see Matteo Della Corte, *Iuventus* (Arpino, 1924), who first suggested (p. 76) that the Isiacs formed a tenth of the population. According to A. M. Duff, *Freedmen in the Early Roman Empire* (Oxford, 1928), 129, freedmen could become priests of Isis or of the Great Mother or of Mithras, and G. E. F. Chilver, *Cisalpine Gaul* (Oxford, 1941), 193 f., after noting the popularity of the Isis-cult in this region, says that most of the worshippers were freedmen, many of whom had Greek *cognomina*. Men of the highest social standing, on the other hand, among the Greek population in Egypt attended sacrifices on the birthday of Isis according to an allusion in a papyrus now in Bremen; cf. M. S. Salem, *JRS* 27 (1937), 166 n. 17, citing Wilcken, *Die Bremer Papyri*, 15, 33 ff.

The Iseum in the Roman colony of Savaria in Pannonia was founded towards the end of the second century A.D. and its founders included Roman officials and merchants : v. V. Wessetzky, *Ägypt. Kulte in Ungarn*, 22 ff. and 56, where the presence of the lower classes as cult-leaders is said to have been likely, though not clearly attested; cf. T. Szentléleky, *Das Isis-Heiligtum von Szombathely* (Szombathely, 1965), 48; id. 'Die Bedeutung des Iseums in Savaria', *Savaria Mus. Bull.* 3 (1965), 156 (stressing the presence of rich and distinguished families). For Cenchreae in the second century we have little tangible evidence. Robert L. Scranton, 'Glass Pictures from the Sea', *Archaeology* 20 (1967), 163-773, esp, 171 ff., points out that the room in which the Egyptianizing panels were found is a modest one, but that other foundations of rooms may bc associated; cf. above, INTROD. III, pp. 18 ff. The sociology of the cult is not illumined here, nor does much emerge from the dedications to Isis and Sarapis in Corinth : v. Vidman, *SIRIS*, 20, nos. 34 f.

p. 273, 15 **linteae vestis** : Cf. ch. 3 (268, 11), *bysso tenui*; 2.28 (48,8); *Apol.* 56 (63, 15 f.), *lineo texto..., quod purissimum est rebus divinis velamentum*; wool, on the other hand, is described there as *segnissimi corporis excrementum*; and in ch. 23 (285, 4-5) Lucius tells us that he himself took on a linen dress. Cf. Plut. *De Is. et Os.* 4 and also 3, 352 C, where wearing linen clothes is mentioned as the mark of an Isiac initiate. Isis herself is described as 'clad in linen' (λινόστολος) in the first line of the Aretalogy from Andros; cf. W. Peek *ad loc.*, pp. 26 f. and Cumont, *L'Égypte des Astrologues*, 118 f. Outside Egypt the linen tunic was regarded, then, as distinctively Isiac; within Egypt, however, as Herodotus, 2.37, pointed out, linen was the material used for clothes generally. Certain types of priests, and occasionally others too, wore animal skins as well; cf. J. Gwyn Griffiths, *JEA* 22 (1936), 222. Linen was produced in various colours; the suggestion here is that the Isiac initiates used only white; cf. ch. 9 (273, 18), *veste nivea*, of the youths' choir, and lines 19-20, *candido linteamine*, of the priests; also ch. 14 (276, 20), *linteam dari laciniam* and n. *ad loc.*; and ch. 15 (277, 17), *candido isto habitu tuo*.

p. 273, 16 **limpido tegmine** : Médan seems to be right, as against Hildebrand ('shining with the whiteness of linen') in taking the adjective to mean 'transparent'. In figures of the Graeco-Roman era, as indeed earlier, Egyptian females are shown wearing a ribbon or band which ties the hair together; cf. Gabra and Drioton, *Touna el-Gebel*, pl. 28 (a deceased woman), pl. 29 (Isis), and pls. 25-27 (other goddesses); cf. the band, lower on the head, which Isis or a priestess of hers is wearing in a statue in the Cyrene Museum; v. N. Turchi, *La Religione di Roma Antica* (Bologna, 1939), pl. 19, 2. Rather different is the flowing head-dress which comes down on both sides in some Graeco-Roman statues of Isis; v. Leipoldt, *Bilderatlas*, 26 [256], 27 [257], and 39. Female votaries in the frescoes from Herculaneum seem to be wearing some covering on their hair (Leipoldt, 53 [294] and 54 [295] = Tran Tam Tinh, *Herculanum*, pls. 27 and 28), but reproductions are indistinct. Priestesses figured in a relief in the Vatican (Leipoldt, 56 [292]) appear to be without a hair-covering; yet its transparency may account for this impression. Adriani, *Rep. d'Arte* A 1, pl. 41, 121 (cf. p. 40, no. 56) reproduces a head of Isis or of a priestess with a crown or wreath (it had been previously explained as the head of a queen, v. Lawrence, *JEA* 11 [1925], 187); cf. Breccia, *Terr.* 2, pl. 7, 26 (p. 19, no. 32); but Apuleius cannot be thinking of anything as elaborate as this.

madidos : Moist through the use of sweet unguents.

p. 273, 17 **capillum derasi funditus** : Lucius tells us at the end of ch. 30 that he himself had his head shaved a second time and freely showed his baldness when joining the college of *pastophori* at Rome. Complete shaving of the head was another mark of the male Isiac votary and priest; cf. Plut. *De Is. et Os.*

3, 352 C and my remarks ad loc. pp. 268 f.; Hdt. 2.36 and 37 on Egyptian priests. In Egypt most men shaved the whole head, the distinction between them and the priests being that they wore a wig on the bald pate whereas the priests did not. Cf. the figures from Pompeii in Tran Tam Tinh, *Isis à Pompéi*, pls. 4-5; the priest who enacted Anubis wore a canine mask, otherwise only the bald head is visible. In a few instances votaries who are also priests are shown with beards : v. Leipoldt, *Bilderatlas*, 55 [286]. Von Bissing discusses these instances in 'Paintings from Pompeii', 226; the depiction comes from Herculaneum and appears also in Guimet, *L'Isis romaine*, p. 17 and Moret, *Rois et Dieux d'Égypte*, pl. 15. Von Bissing is able to adduce a few other cases from Hellenistic or Roman times; cf. P. Grimal (ed.), *Hellenism and the Rise of Rome* (London, 1968), pl. 36. Greek and Roman priests are occasionally shown as bearded; v. Kerényi, *Rel.* pls. 95, 119; the Egyptian custom has been modified, it seems, from this direction. But these instances are a small minority. Juvenal, 6. 533, refers to the Isiacs as a *grex calvus*, Martial, 12.28.19, as *linigeri calvi*. Cf. W. Dennison, *AJA* 9 (1905), 28-32 and Cumont, *Rel. Or.* 240 n. 76. According to Plut. *De Is. et Os.* 4 the priestly habit of shaving had a religious cause in the desire for purity; it is more likely that in a hot climate the custom was engendered, both for priests and others, by reasons of comfort and hygiene.

p. 273, 17 **verticem praenitentes** : The Accusative imitates the Greek construction; cf. J. von Geisau, *Syntaktische Gräzismen bei Apulejus*, 86, who notes the comparable poetic use of the present participles *nigrans, flavens, tumens* and *fulgens*; cf. Kühner and Stegmann, *Gr. Lat.*² 286. See also n. *ad* ch. 10 (274, 4), *vestitum*.

aereis : See n. *ad* ch. 4 (269, 1-2), *aereum crepitaculum*.

p. 273, 18 **constrepentes** : Apuleius uses the verb transitively also in *Metam.* 4.26 (95, 4 f.), *domus tota ... constrepebat hymenaeum*, but not elsewhere. After Fronto he is the first writer to use the compound; v. *Thes. L.L.* 4, 540, 40 ff.

p. 273, 19 **terrena sidera** : Colvius cites, for the metaphorical use, Columella, 10.96, *terrestria sidera, flores*, and Hildebrand compares Ovid, *Ep. ex Ponto*, 3.2, *O sidus Fabiae, Maxime, gentis*. Horace, *Carm.* 3.9.21 f., uses the noun in a comparison (*sidere pulchrior / ille*) and in 1.12.47 speaks of *Iulium sidus*; such an application of the term to persons is nearer to the Apuleian usage here than when Propertius, 2.3.14, describes the eyes as two torches, *sidera nostra*; cf. Ovid, *Am.* 2.16.44; 3.3.9; nearer still is the expression in Curtius, 9.6.8, used of Alexander, *Macedoniae columen ac sidus*. The transposition of this phrase to its present location by van der Vliet is unanswerable; the description suits the select band of priests much better than the whole throng of male initiates. Yet editors after Helm have perversely not deigned even to record the proposal. The attitude later displayed towards the priests is uniformly respectful. Lucius himself becomes an initiate, but his humility would be far from arrogating to himself this magniloquent phrase, even though he prides himself in ch. 30 on being admitted to the college of *pastophori*.

p. 273, 19 **antistites sacrorum** : Cf. Juv. 2.113, *sacrorum antistes*, of a priest of Cybele.

proceres illi : Price argues cogently yhat *proceres*, unlike *antistites sacrorum*, will refer to their position in society; these priests will have derived, not from the plebs of Corinth, but from its nobility. This certainly accords with the general usage of the word. Price aptly cites Macrobius, *Saturn.* 1.23.13 (of a rite in Syrian Heliopolis), *et subeunt plerumque provinciae proceres raso capite*.

p. 273, 20 **cinctum pectoralem** : The upper part of the chest and the shoulders are left bare in this mode, and some figures depicted at Pompeii and Herculaneum correspond to the description : v. Tran Tam Tinh, *Isis à Pompéi*, pl. 4, 2; pl. 23 (= Leipoldt, *Bilderatlas*, 53 [294]), where three of the male figures are thus accoutred, but where others, including the central vase-bearing figure in the background, wear a dress which covers the shoulder; cf. ibid. pl. 24 (= Leipoldt, 54 [295]; the two scenes are also given in Tran Tam Tinh. *Herculanum*, pls. 27-8) : here two priests are dressed in this same way, while others have a fuller garment; cf. Olga Elia, *Le Pitture del Tempio di Iside*, 6 f., figs. 6 and 7 (with the cult of Harpocrates). Most of the priestly representations show the fuller type; cf. Tran Tam Tinh, *Isis à Pompéi*, pl. 4, 1; pl. 5, 2 and 3; pl. 7,4; pl. 11; Schefold, *Vergessenes Pompeji*, pl. 82 (house of Loreius Tiburtinus); Leipoldt, *Bilderatlas*, 48 [283], 55 [286], 56 [292], 57 [277], 59-61 [288-290]. In the relief from Ariccia (Leipoldt, 17 [251] = Anne Roullet, *Rome*, pl. 13) some of the dancing figures are naked, while others have their dress girded ro.nd the waist in a way that recalls the *cinctus Gabinus*, save that a part of the toga was thrown over the left shoulder in this mode (cf. Dar.-Sag. s.v. Toga, 352, fig. 7005), whereas the Ariccia dancers in question are naked to the waist. Apuleius, then, is describing a fashion attested in a minority only of the instances known to us. In the Egyptian tradition the priest wore, with various additions, a long linen tunic which covered the shoulders; often, however, this garment did not reach much beyond the knees. Occasionally an approach is made to the bare-shouldered dress mentioned by Apuleius; cf. Leipoldt, *Bilderatlas*, 6 (from a coffin of the Roman era); Sauneron, *The Priests of Ancient Egypt*, 41, 50, 75, 106-7, 142.

p. 274, 1 **potentissimorum** : Like Fronto and Aulus Gellius, Apuleius is fond of the intensive superlative forms, although he does not present as many new coinages as they do in this respect; cf. Callebat, *Sermo Cotid.* 398 ff. This superlative is classical. On the decline of superlative forms in later Latin see van der Paardt, *Metam. III*, 121.

proferebant : This is the reading of the majority of the codices, and also of the earliest. Cf. ch. 11 (274, 19) and ch. 22 (284, 12), used also of priests carrying sacred objects.

quorum primus : According to Plut. *De Is. et Os.* 36, 365 B the Osirian hydreion leads the Isiac procession. It is the singer ($\dot{\omega}\delta\acute{o}s$), carrying a suitable symbol, who leads the religious procession described by Clem. Alex. *Strom.*

6.4.35.3. While the leading figure doubtless had some importance, the most significant member came last.

p.274, 2 **lucernam** : A good example, probably, of the form is a lamp now in the British Museum and found in the sea off Pozzuoli : v. H.B. Walters, *Cat. of the Greek and Roman Lamps in the B.M.* (London, 1914), pl. 10 and pp. 55 f. It is of pottery, not gold, but the shape is that of a ship. Isis and Sarapis are figured at the prow (or stern, as Walters thinks), the former holding a cornucopia and the latter a steering oar; in the middle part is shown one of the Dioscuri and a potter, with the word Εὔπλοια ('good voyaging') inscribed between them. On the other side is written λαβέ με τὸν Ἡλιοσέραπιν ('Take me Helio-Serapis'), the allusion in the name being clearly to the deity who steers the ship. For other reproductions see Gressmann, *Orient. Rel.* 38, fig. 13 and *Osiris*, fig. 2; Leipoldt, *Bilderatlas*, 19 (298]. Walters, op. cit. 56 f., nos. 391-5, records five other lamps in the form of a boat; three are from Egypt, and one from Pozzuoli, the provenance of the fifth being not stated. Pozzuoli or Puteoli had, of course, a Serapeum, so that this instance also is probably connected with the Egyptian cult. Boat-shaped lamps of bronze or terracotta have also been found in Pompeii; v. Tran Tam Tinh, *Isis à Pompéi*, 93 f. and 136 f.

The scepticism of Bruneau, *Rev. Ét. Grec.* 78 (1965), 441 and of Vidman, *Isis und Sarapis*, 7, is unwarranted in cases such as this where a local cult is prominent, although an *ex-voto* offering to Isis by a sailor, which is proffered by Bruneau as an interpetation, is also possible. One could be similarly confident about the religious significance of an example from Köln, since the cult is well attested there, but Grimm, *Ägypt. Rel. im röm. Deutschland*, 166, no. <57 A>, is uncertain about the true provenance; in his comment he cites an instance from Badalona, N. E. Spain. Inscriptions at Delos, as we have seen above, mention female ministrants called λαμπτηροφόροι : v. Roussel, *CED* 270. These are probably lesser dignitaries than our priest, and they perhaps carried torches rather than elaborate lamps; a different role is played too by the 'lamplighters' (λυχνάπται) of P. Oxy. 1453, 4-6 (30-29 B.C.) attached to temples of Sarapis and Isis; others mentioned later belong to a temple of Thoëris. A similarly shaped lamp of Egyptian origin is published by Weber, *Terr.* pl. 1, 12 a, b and p. 31, no. 12; this one, which Weber would date (p. 17) to the first or second century A.D., has a figure of Sarapis on the prow and of Isis on the stern. These gods, together with Harpocrates, are likewise figured on a boat-shaped lamp from Ostia : v. Maria Squarciapino, *I Culti Orientali ad Ostia*, frontispiece, and R. Meiggs, *Roman Ostia*, 370. The specially shaped lamp carried by this priest must clearly be distinguished from the lanterns mentioned with torches and wax tapers in ch. 9; they too are in honour of Isis (as creator of the stars), but the boat shape invites a particular link with the rite at Cenchreae — the *Isidis Navigium*. This is borne out by the inscription Εὔπλοια, noted in one instance above, and further by the inscription on the lamp in Berlin : θεοῖς λαβέ εὐχαριστήριον ('take as a votive thank-offering to the gods'). Sarapis, it should be noted, shares with Isis the function of ruling the sea. Weber, *Terr.* 28 n. 24, well quotes *B.G.U.* 423, 6 : 'I give (this) as a votive offering to the Lord Sarapis, because when 1 was in danger on the sea, he brought me instantly to safety.' The ship form was not used in the pre-Hellenistic lamps of Egypt, on which see Hayes, *The Scepter of Egypt*, I (N. York, 1953), 260 f.; Erman and Ranke, *Aegypten*, 217; Boreux, *Guide-Cat. du Louvre* (1932), 265 f. For figures of Isis Pelagia on lamps (but not with a boat shape) see Bruneau, *BCH* 85 (1961), 436, fig. 1 and 87 (1963), 302, fig. 2, the former from Delos and the latter from Egypt; they are both of the second century A.D. Seneca, *De vita beata*, 26.8, mentions a 'linen-clad old man' (*linteatus senex*) who carries a lamp (*lucernam*) in broad daylight; the allusion may well be to a priest of Isis; cf. R. Turcan, *Sénèque et les religions orientales* (Brussels, 1967), 50. An Isiac inscription from *Pratum novum* near Cordova in Spain (A.D. i-ii) mentions a 'guild of lamp-makers' (*collegium Illychiniarorum*) : see García y Bellido in *Hommages à Waldemar Deonna* (Coll. Latomus, 28, Brussels, 1957), 238-44. Cf. n. *ad* ch. 9 (273, 6), *facticii luminis*.

p. 274, 3 **aureum** : Since this lamp was to be carried, the bowl was attached to a vertical shaft which the priest grasped; cf. the ladle in Gressmann, *Orient. Rel.* 41, fig. 16 and Leipoldt, *Bilderatlas*, 56 [292]. The adjective is intended to apply, probably, only to the lower part. No such lamps have survived, limestone, pottery and bronze being the material used in those that have. A lamp of pottery might well be gilded.

cymbium : See n. *ad* line 1, *lucernam*.

p. 274, 4 **sui** : The reflexive genitive may stem from Greek influence or from popular usage; cf. Callebat, *Sermo Cotid.* 262 f.

patore : A. F. Shore in *B.M. Guide* (1964), 197, describes the clay lamps of the Roman era. There were usually at least two openings, a central one for filling with oil and a hole for a wick of twisted flax or papyrus. *Patore* clearly refers to the orifice used as a burner.

vestitum : An Accusative used under Greek influence; cf. ch. 27 (288, 19), *vestigium similis*. Kühner and Stegmann, *Gr. Lat.*² 286 quote Vergil, *Aen.* 1.589, *os umerosque deo similis*, and J. von Geisau, *Syntaktische Gräzismen bei Apul.* 86, cogently argues that since this treatment of *similis* occurs in no other prose author, Apuleius may well have directly followed the Vergilian usage.

p. 274, 5 **altaria** : According to *Thes. L.L.* 1, 1725, 18 f. usage permits a singular meaning. This seems very likely here, otherwise one priest is envisaged as carrying one of these objects in each hand. If a small censer is what is meant by *altaria*, as Berreth (followed by Wittmann) argued, then that would be physically possible. Something bigger, however, is implied by *altaria*; a high altar, more exalted in meaning than *ara*. Egyptian priests did not carry altars in the literal sense, but they often carried shrines or stelae which were roughly similar to altars in their rectangular shape; cf. the shrine carried by four priests in Tran Tam Tinh, *Isis à Pompéi*, pl. 11. A shrine or stela frequently bore or represented a divine figure, and in an Isiac context a figure of Horus or of

Osiris would equally suggest the beneficent and saving power of the goddess, since both these gods were said to have been succoured by her. Many statues of the Late Era represent an Osiris-figure within a shrine being carried by a standing or kneeling man; v. K. Bosse, *Die menschliche Figur in der Rundplastik der ägyptischen Spätzeit* (Glückstadt, 1936), pl. 4, no. 84 (and p. 37); pl. 5, no. 92 (and p. 40); pl. 6, nos. 110, 112, 116, 121 and 125 (and pp. 46, 47, 49); in each case the man's two hands are touching the shrine or figure. A well-known example in the Vatican Museum which derives from the early Persian period is a statuette in green basalt of a priest who is standing and holding in front of him a naos in which a figure of Osiris occurs; v. O. Marucchi, *Museo Egizio Vaticano*, pls. 1-2, no. 113; H, Marucchi, *Guide du Musée Égyptien du Vatican* (Rome, 1927), 22, fig. 3, no. 158; K. Bosse, op. cit. 39, no. 89. A relief in the temple of Denderah shows three priests carrying rectangular shrines and each using both hands; v. Sauneron, *The Priests of Ancient Egypt*, fig. on p. 75. The deity involved is often Horus. Thus a black granite statue from Abukîr in the Alexandria Museum (no. 20723, studied by the writer) represents a *pastophorus* holding a shrine which bears a figure of Horus in warrior form. Berlin, no. 12417, reproduced by Erman, *Rel.* (1934, tr. H. Wild, 1952), 457, fig. 171 and by Leipoldt, *Bilderatlas*, 42, shows priests carrying a statue of Harpocrates; this, however, is not an exact parallel, since two priests are involved, not one; further, although the stretcher on which the statue is carried might recall an altar in shape, the statue above does not.

Harpocrates is being similarly carried in Breccia, *Terr.* 2, pl. 51, 254 (p. 39); cf. no. 251 there and also *Terr.* 1, pl. 25, 8 (p. 59, no. 281). Cf. C.M. Kaufmann, *Graeco-Ägyptische Koroplastik* (Leipzig and Cairo, 1915), 118 f. and pl. 38; the house-altars shown in the same plate were hardly portable, although some were small; cf. p. 120. Perhaps it is the stelae of 'Horus on the Crocodiles' that suit the context best. These have been studied by Daressy, *Textes et Dessins Magiques* (Cairo, 1903), and the sympathetic magic implied in all of them is that just as Horus was helped by Isis to overcome the attacks of scorpions, snakes and crocodiles, so will the stricken human who is identified with Horus achieve the same result. Sauneron, *The Priests of Ancient Egypt*, 167, reproduces a standing statue from the Louvre where such a 'saving stela' is being carried, and E. Jelinková-Reymond has studied a well-known instance in the Cairo Museum in *Les inscriptions de la statue guérisseuse Djed-Ḥer-le-Sauveur* (Cairo, 1956). In this case the person is a priest, a 'guardian of the gates of the temple of Athribis'; he is also a leading magician, and he calls himself *pꜣ šdw*, 'the saviour', in this sense, arrogating the title to himself after the pattern of Horus; v. op. cit. 123. That Horus is the recipient of protection and relief from Isis is shown by the episodes in the Metternich Stela and the parallel texts edited by Klasens in *A Magical Statue Base* (*Socle Behague*) (Leiden, 1952). The epithed *nḏ*, 'he who saves', is also used of Horus, especially in relation to his father Osiris; v. J. Gwyn Griffiths, *JEA* 37 (1951), 34 f. But it is the former situation, reflecting the saving aid given by Isis to Horus, and so to all believers, that is probably indicated in the object carried by the priest in Apuleius, since he expressly refers then to the helping providence of the goddess. This priest is manifestly a *pastophorus*, and H.J. Boeken's remark (*Adnotationes*, 77) that no *pastophori* can be recognized in the procession 'nam nullae aediculae circumferebantur', is thereby invalidated. Finally, the explanation here suggested fits so well into an Isiac religious context that the attempts to emend the text seem unnecessary.

p. 274, 6 **deae summatis** : Cf. ch. 1 (266, 14) and 22 (284, 1), also of the goddess; in *Metam.* 4.23 (92, 18) Apuleius describes an attractive girl as *summatem regionis*, 'the choicest of her district'. Frequent in Plautus, the adjective was first revived afterwards by Apuleius; cf. Desertine, *De Apulei studiis Plautinis*, 15. It gives a true indication of the position now enjoyed by Isis. Cf. Hymns of Isidorus, 1,3 (*SEG* 8, 548), ὑψίστη. An inscription from Delos calls her μήτηρ μεγάλη ἡ πάντων κρατοῦσα (Roussel, *CED* no. 50 a = Vidman, *SIRIS*, 67). She and Sarapis are called θεοὶ μέγιστοι in a papyrus in Strassburg : v. F. Dunand, *CdÉ* 44 (1969), 302, line 21 and her note on p. 309 n. 3, where θεὰ μεγίστη is cited for Isis in many inscriptions.

providentia : Cf. ch. 5 (270, 4) and 15 (277, 20) with n.

p. 274, 7-8 **palmam ... caduceum** : The third priest is clearly a priest of Anubis, and at the beginning of ch. 11 the god himself is said to walk in the procession bearing the same attributes, that is, a palm-branch and a *caduceus*. Priests would, of course, have played both these roles, and the main distinguishing feature of the Anubis-figure was the canine head-mask. Another distinction pointed to in the description is that the priest's palm-branch has its leaves wrought of gold whereas Anubis carries a green bough. Neither of these attributes is found specifically with Anubis in the Pharaonic cult, although the palm-branch appears in various contexts. The herald's staff derives from the identification of Anubis with Hermes; certainly Anubis, like Hermes, was a guide of souls in the sense that the process of embalming after death and of general tendance was in his care. Also he is sometimes depicted leading the deceased and taking him by the hand; e.g. Budge, *P. of Hunefer*, pl. 4; but in *P. of Anhai*, pls. 2 and 4, Horus is leading her; Anubis leads in the scene reproduced by Morenz, *Wissenschaftliche Z. der Karl-Marx-Univ. Leipzig* 3 (1953-4), 127, fig. 1 and 128, fig. 2;. cf. his discussion there; in Budge, *P. of Ḳersher*, pl. 1, Anubis shares the function with Ma'at. Two instances of Anubis as leader occur in Morenz, 'Das Problem des Werdens zu Osiris', in Derchain (ed.), *Rel. en Égypte*, pl. 4, 1 and 2 (facing p. 81); cf. Parlasca, *Mumienporträts*, pls. 35, 1 and 61, 2. One of the clearest depictions of Anubis with palm-branch and *caduceus* comes from the Iseum in Savaria : v. Wessetzky, *Ägypt. Kulte in Ungarn*, pl. 2, fig. 4 with pp. 30 f., where the palm-branch is in the raised right hand, and the *caduceus* in the left. Cf. the silver statuette of Anubis from Salona in Dalmatia (the camp of Diocletian) mentioned by W. Drexler, *Der Cultus der aegyptischen Gottheiten in den Donauländern* (Leipzig, 1890), 43 d and a coin from Perinthus in Thrace, ibid. 106; the former shows the two attributes, the latter the palm-branch only. For other instances see Leipoldt, *Bilderatlas*, 57 [277], 68, 69, though the two objects are not shown with equal clarity in all these cases. A good example of the palm-branch, on a column from the Iseum Campense in Rome, appears in S. Bosticco, *Musei Capitolini : I Monumenti Egizi ed Egitizzanti* (Rome, 1952), pl. 7 (right) = Anne Roullet, *Rome*, pl. 28 with p. 58 (where, however, the statement that the iconography of these reliefs has 'no parallels in Egyptian art' is quite wrong). Palm-trees are shown flanking the centre scene in the Isiac ritual frescoes from Hercula-neum; see Leipoldt, *Bilderatlas* 53 [294] and 54 [295]; cf. Tran Tam Tinh, *Herculanum*, pls. 27 and 28 with pp. 83 and 85; N. Fick, *Latomus*. 30 (1971), 337. Here, one feels, it is a question of a suitable Egyptian background.

A militarized form of Anubis, perhaps influenced by the development of Horus, not unnaturally shows a spear rather than a palm-branch : v. G. Botti in Th. Schreiber, *Die Nekropole von Kôm-esch-Schukâfa* (Exp. Sieglin, I, 1908), 356 and cf. Edgar, *Greek Bronzes*, pl. 4, 27.693 and 27.694 with p. 16 (the left hand is raised in each case, but the spear has not been preserved). Yet the palm-branch is clearly shown in a number of amulets, including that in Leipoldt, *Bilderatlas*, 79, on which see Bonner's remarks, *Stud. Mag. Am.* 31, where a purse is said to be in the other hand; two amulets published by Bonner himself (his D. 40 and 42 with pl. 2 and p. 259) show both palm-branch and *caduceus* held by Anubis (for the god's elongated head cf. Budge, *P. of Ḳersher*, pl. 1); Bonner's D. 39 (pl. 2 with p. 259) shows the god with a *caduceus*, the other object held being uncertain. Two Anubis figures equipped with both palm-branch and *caduceus* appear in Delatte and Derchain, *Intailles Magiques*, no. 161, pp. 122 f.; the god holds the palm-branch also in no. 117, p. 96; no. 126, p. 101; no. 127, p. 102; cf. no. 294, pp. 215 f. Examples of the Apuleian combination are not frequent among the Graeco-Egyptian terracottas, but there is a good one in Vogt, *Terr.* pl. 4, 8 with p. 14. In this connection Carl Watzinger in *Malerei und Plastik* (Sammlung Sieglin I, B), 121, argues that the Greek form Hermanubis is really involved as it appeared in the god's temple in Alexandria, and that its first known attestation is in the coinage of Domitian : here the god is a youthful figure with a *calathus* and lotus-leaf on his head and with the jackal of Anubis sitting to his right; in his right hand is the *caduceus*, in his left a palm-branch. The *caduceus* is present in the statue of Anubis or Hermanubis in the Vatican Museum, the object in the other hand being uncertain; see the photograph in Th. Schreiber, *Exp. Sieglin*, I, 137, fig. 82 and the remarks by O. Marruchi, *Museo Egizio Vaticano* (Rome, 1899), 312, no. 49; cf. Leipoldt, *Bilderatlas*, 48 [283]. For the Alexandrian cult of Anubis or Hermanubis see Visser, *Götter und Kulte*, 24 and 71 f., and for Hermanubis in the coinage see J. Vogt, *Die alexandrinischen Münzen* (Stuttgart, 1924), I, 91 and II, 182, where it is stated (I, 91) that the Alexandrian temple of the god is figured on coins of Trajan and Pius; cf. Adriani, *Rep. d'Arte*, C, Text, 250. Hermanubis appears often only in bust form, as in a coin of Hadrian which shows a palm-branch (or leaf) upright in front of the god : v. J.G. Milne, *Cat. of Alexandrian Coins* (Oxford, 1933), pl. 3, no. 1206; his list on p. 140 shows that the palm-branch is not a constant feature of the representations included here, whereas the *caduceus* appears more often. Drexler discusses these coins in Roscher, *Lex. Myth.* I, 2311 f. in a long article entitled 'Hermanubis' which is mainly devoted to Anubis. Sometimes the palm-branch and *caduceus* are combined in one : v. R.S. Poole, *Cat. of the Greek Coins in the B.M.; Alexandria and the Nomes* (London, 1892), lxix, where, however, the now discarded derivation of Hermanubis from Ḥr-m-'Inp is put forward; cf. the remarks in my *Plut. De Is. et Os.* 518. This misleading derivation appears also in the otherwise valuable discussion by Perdrizet, 'Les représentations d'Anoubis dans l'imagerie gréco-égyptienne' in *Revue Égyptologique* n.s. 1 (1919), 185-90. Perdrizet here maintains (p. 189) that the most ancient specimen of the type described by Apuleius is the Anubis of Delos, a statue which survives in three pieces and which is discussed (with drawings) by Perdrizet elsewhere (*Terr.* 60). One of the pieces is a hand which was obviously grasping something. What, we do not know: and the other hand is missing. Perdrizet also fails to discern that the type, on Alexandrian coins, since it often includes both palm-branch and *caduceus*, is close to that portrayed by Apuleius. The earliest surviving instance of this in art is perhaps the relief on the Isiac altar from the Campus Martius, which dates from the reign of Caligula; the two attributes appear here clearly : v. H. Stuart Jones, *Cat. of Sculptures, Mus. Capitol.* 359, no. 12 and pl. 91 and Gressmann, *Orient. Rel.* 39 f.; cf. Leipoldt, *Bilderatlas*, 57 [277] and Gressmann, *Osiris*, fig. 9. According to O. Marrucchi in *Annali dell'instituto di corrispondenza archeologica* 51 (1879), 158-72 and pl. I, a sepulchral monument of one Aemilius Cresces (Crescens), which includes a marble relief of Anubis with canine head and with *caduceus* and palm-branch in his hands, probably derives too from the Iseum in the Campus Martius; it was found in Rome near the Via Flaminia, and shows the deceased as a shaven Isiac priest. Cf. Lafaye, *Hist. du culte*, 297, no. 112. The best example extant from the age of Apuleius is undoubtedly the white marble statue of Hermanubis discovered in Ras es-Soda in 1936; only a part of the caduceus, admittedly, is preserved; otherwise the type conforms to the one found on coins, with the added detail that at the base of the palm-branch a disk appears with a uraeus in relief; v. Adriani, *Annuaire 1935-39*, pl. 55 and pp. 142 f. On Hermanubis in art see further O. Rubensohn, *Arch. Anzeiger* 20 (1905), 68 f. and 21 (1906), 143 with fig. 13 (col. 141-2); T. Schreiber, *Studien über das Bildniss Alexanders des Grossen* (Leipzig, 1903), 145, fig. 12 (a bronze from the Sinadino Collection, Alexandria, there explained as representing Alexander the Great); A. Furtwängler *Bonner Jb.* 114 (1906), 195; Perdrizet, *Bronzes Fouquet*, 29 f.

Apuleius uses the phrase *Mercuriale ... caduceum*, and the assumption of this attribute by Anubis or his priest comes from the fusion with Hermes. But what of the palm-branch? In the purely Egyptian tradition the standing figure of Anubis, if he bears anything at all, bears only a sceptre; v. Lanzone,

Diz. Mit. I, pl. 29; Erman. *Rel.* (tr. Wild), 65, fig. 31. Ingrid Wallert, *Die Palmen im Alten Ägypten* (*MÄS* 1, 1962) has shown that the gods specially connected with the date-palm (and this is the species shown with the figures of Anubis) were Thoth, Hathor, Min and Rē'; it was also conspicuous in the funerary cult. Now Thoth as a god of writing was also identified with Hermes; cf. von Bissing, *Ägypt. Kultbilder*, 24 ff.; and he holds a palm-branch as an attribute in his function of 'Lord of Time' and 'Reckoner of the Years'; v. Wallert, op. cit. 101 and cf. Junker und Winter, *Geburtshaus*, 380. Dr Wallert further shows, as we have seen above, that the palm-branch developed, from this connection with time, a significance of future life in a funerary context (see p. 102). Anubis was a funerary god *par excellence*, and whereas he probably took over this attribute from Thoth, partly because they were both identified with Hermes, it was as a promise of future life that he carried the palm-branch. In one instance it is noteworthy that he presents it to the mummy : v. Delatte and Derchain, *Intailles Magiques*, no. 126, p. 101. These two authors (p. 90) rightly ask whether the attribute may not have an Egyptian origin, but at the same time they show surprising respect to the dictum of Perdrizet, who described the palm-branch as derived from Hermes because it was a 'symbole des concours de gymnastique, auquel présidait Hermès' (*Rev. Égyptol.* 1 (1919), 189). In fact the two most common attributes of Hermes in the fourth century B.C. and afterwards are the *caduceus* and the purse; see Chr. Scherer in Roscher, *Lex. Myth.* I, 2420 and the fig. on 2428; cf. Preisendanz, *PGM* 4, 2361 f. (A.D. iv). Scherer, op. cit. 2368 f., discusses Hermes as a god of gymnastics, but without mention of a palm-branch as attribute. Graindor, it is true, in *BCH* 39 (1915), 241-401, published a relief of Greek ephebes of the Roman imperial era (v. his p. 252, fig. 1) and two of these young men are shown carrying palm-branches. As a parallel, however, Graindor cited (p. 256) the statue of 'Alexander' published by Schreibner (*Studien über das Bildnis Alexanders des Grossen*, 145, fig. 12) which is now known, as we have seen above, to represent Hermanubis. Strangely enough, although Schreibner explained it as involving Alexander, he interpreted the palm-branch not as the 'symbol of victory' as Graindor does, but as a token of time-reckoning derived from the god Thoth (Schreibner, op. cit. 147). Here, at any rate, Schreibner seems to have been right. Graindor seeks to buttress his case by reproducing a small unpublished bronze figure which he ascribes to the influence of Lysippus and which shows Alexander (?) bearing a palm-branch.

But even an attribute of Alexander could, in a particular case, have been of Egyptian origin. The palm-branch of the ephebes in an Attic context is, of course, another matter. Yet no instance of an athletic Hermes thus equipped seems to have been forthcoming. According to W.R. Halliday, *CAH* 2 (1931), 637, an image of Hermes stood in every palaestra. He does not describe any such images, and Farnell, *Cults*, V, 28-30, expatiates on Hermes and athletics without referring to them; nor do his numerous plates representing the god include this attribute. Wittmann was able to show (pp. 50 f.) that the palm-branch appears also in the Graeco-Roman era with Osiris, Sarapis, Isis, Harpocrates, Thoth, Asclepius, Tychê, Hygieia and Alexandreia. Here he is relying mostly on the coins of Alexandria, but he rightly points out that these gods are mostly in the Osirian cycle, and that the occurrences with Anubis or Hermanubis are more numerous. According to Pietschmann in *PW* s.v. Anubis (1894), 2649, the god sometimes holds, in Egyptian representations, the Osirian flail and crook; these, he suggests, were later erroneously interpreted as *caduceus* and palm-branch. This view makes too much of the occasional assumption by Anubis of Osirian *insignia*; it also fails to take account of the conscious syncretism which is clearly behind the Alexandrian Hermanubis. According to Clem. Alex. *Strom.* 6.3.35.3 f. a 'palm of astrology' was carried in an Egyptian religious procession by a priest whom he calls a *horoscopos*; cf. W. Otto, *Priester und Tempel*, I, 89 f. Berreth, p. 63, unconvincingly tries to connect this palm-branch with that of Anubis; Zimmermann, *Rel.* 150, also discusses the astrological palm-branch, but without positing such a connection, although Wittmann, p. 201 n. 262, seems to think he did.

An interesting point is made by Berreth, p. 63, about the Apuleian phrase *auro ... foliatam*; he compares the 'golden bough' which opened the underworld to Aeneas in Book VI of the *Aeneid*. A connection with the underworld and with the future life is probably present in the attribute of Anubis likewise; but in its gilded form it was similar, very likely, to other sacred paraphernalia. Vergil's *aureus ramus* has, of course, been the subject of much debate. Its symbolism is more complex. The Greek word βάϊς occurs with the meaning 'palm-leaf' or 'palm-branch', and Wittmann, p. 201 n. 265, records Grapow's conjecture that it may be a loan-word from the Coptic ΒΑ or ΒΑΙ; the idea is firmly accepted by B. van de Walle and J. Vergote, *CdÉ* 18 (1943), 43. Wittmann, p. 51, goes on to adduce Horapollo's etymology in *Hierogl.* 1.7, where the Egyptian βαϊ 'soul' is invoked to explain the term βαϊήθ, the falcon (Horus) as the soul; Horapollo then invokes a second genuinely Egyptian word, on which see F. Sbordone *ad loc.* pp. 14 f. and B. van de Walle with J. Vergote, op. cit. 45 f. In the same way, argues Wittmann, the attribution of βάϊς, 'palm-branch', to Anubis means that the Greeks explained the symbol as the immortal soul, thus suitably placing it in the hand of the *psychopompos*. This is an ingenious theory, but it lacks any support beyond what is here cited. More apposite is Wittmann's quotation (p. 52) from a Leiden papyrus of perhaps the second century A.D. : 'I am the plant with the name palm-branch (*baïs*). I am the efflux of the blood of the palm-branches from the tomb of the Great One (Osiris).' It is not, however, the sarcophagus that is being here identified with Osiris, as Wittmann suggests; the palm-branches are those of trees shading and protecting the tomb; cf. Bonnet, *Bilderatlas*, 151 (= Mariette, *Dendérah*, IV, 66, the sarcophagus of Osiris enveloped by a tree), and on the funerary use of trees in general see my *Plut. De Is. et Os.* 323 f. In such a context Anubis as a funerary deity is a suitable bearer of the palm, although he is certainly not a fertility-god as Wittmann maintains on his p. 117. What is problematic is how far the *palma victrix* of the Greek tradition, as taken over by the Romans, may have influenced the Alexandrian mode, especially in the coinage. Thus R.S. Poole, *Cat. of the Greek Coins, B.M.* : *Alexandria*, lxxxv, points out that when the palm occurs on these coins with the eagle, the sense must always relate to Roman militarism. In Egypt, on the other hand, there are instances of the palm-branch being carried by gods as a sceptre; v. R.R. Moftah, *Die heiligen Bäume im Alten Ägypten* (duplicated diss. Göttingen, 1959), 49 f., who refers to gods in the ninth hour of Amduat holding an 'ankh-sign in one hand and a palm-branch in the other; according to the relevant text they are field-gods who cause all trees and plants to grow; cf. Piankoff, *Tomb of Ramesses* VI (N. York, 1954), text vol. p. 298 and fig. 83 (facing p. 293). Piankoff rightly refers to 'palm scepters'; E. Hornung, *Das Amduat* (Wiesbaden, 1963), II, 159, uses the odd expression 'Neun Götter mit gewellten Stäben'. In the second hour of Amduat six gods carry other forms of the palm-branch which approximates to the hieroglyph depicting the object : v. Piankoff, op. cit. fig. 75 with pp. 240 ff. and Hornung, op. cit. I, appended plans, and II, 53; here the palm-branches are symbols of the year or of time. In S. Gabra, *Rapport sur les fouilles d'Hermopolis Ouest [Touna el-Gebel]* (Cairo, 1941), pl. 12, Nephthys and Isis are depicted carrying palm-branch sceptres; in Gabra and Drioton, *Touna el-Gebel*, pl. 26, the goddess Ma'at is shown carrying one in each hand. Thoth is shown carrying and presenting a palm-branch in C. De Wit, *Opet*, II, pl. 7 (top), and he is doing this 'in order that you (Osiris) may achieve millions of years' : v. *Opet*, I, 167 and III, 95. The role of palm-trees as a concomitant of graves is rather different, but the symbolism of vegetation in relation to renewed life is probably present, especially in an Osirian context. In the region of Buto there was a sacred grove of date-palms originally connected with Rē', but an association with Osiris supervened; cf. Ingrid Wallert, *Die Palmen im Alten Ägypten*, 128. The palm-branch of Anubis, then, may well derive from Egypt.

   p. 274, 8-9 **deformatam manum sinistram** : In cf. 25 Lucius speaks of Isis as stretching out 'the right hand of deliverance' (*salutarem porrigas dexteram*, 286, 21) On the meaning of the left hand here mentioned, previous commentators have little to offer that is both apposite and valid. Berreth's adduction of the title of the Theban 'Wife of Amûn', called the 'God's Hand', involves a stimulating excursion into Egyptian mythology, but has no relevance here. Wittmann has some apposite allusions to Isis as Justice; he cites Diod. Sic. 1.27.4 and might have added 1.14.3-4 as well as Plut. *De Is. et Os.* 3, 352 A-B. This idea, however, he does not connect with a hand. Happily there has since been published the admirable discussion by L. Kákosy in *Antik Tanyl-mányok* 15 (1968), 243-5 entitled 'Pythagorean Influence in Apuleius, Metamor-phoses XI?' (I translate his Hungarian.) Dr Kákosy begins by referring to the use of hand-amulets in ancient Egypt as early as the Fifth Dynasty with an apotropaic purpose; he cites Petrie, *Deshasheh*, pl. 26 (cf. p. 16) and Erman, *Zaubersprüche für Mutter und Kind*, 39; here we might add Petrie, *Amulets* *and Superstitions* (London, 1930), 467, with its allusion to the '*Great Hand*' which holds the chain that fetters the serpent Apopis; actually it is the 'Hidden Hand' (*ḏrt 'imnt*), see Bonomi and Sharpe, *The Alabaster Sarcophagus of Oimenepthah I* (London, 1864), pl. 11 (top right); for the hand as an amulet see also Bonnet, *Bilderatlas*, 164, no. 16. Kákosy refers also to the reliquary of the 'hands of Horus' kept at Hieraconpolis and he cites Bonnet, *Reallexikon*, 637 f. More problematic is the use of the hand symbol on Roman imperial standards. A.J. Reinach in Dar.-Sag. s.v. Signa (1909), 1313, suggests oriental, and specifically Egyptian, influence. Graham Webster, *The Roman Imperial Army* (London, 1969), 139, is uncertain as to its meaning. But it is to the connection in Egyptian between 'hand' and the number five that Kákosy turns for an explanation of our context. He shows that Sethe in his *Von Zahlen und Zahlworten bei den alten Ägyptern* (1916), 22, had long since demonstrated the etymological link between the two Egyptian words. The Pythagoreans would naturally have shown a great interest in such an idea, and their arithmo-logical speculations were discussed by Nichomachus of Gerasa (*fl, c.* A.D. 100) and by the Neo-Platonist Iamblichus. It is in the *Theologumena Arithme-ticae* of Iamblichus (*fl. c.* A.D. 300) that Kákosy finds a statement strikingly relevant to our theme. It is there posited (27, ed. Falco p. 35) that 'the pentad is (the unit) most expressive of justice (δικαιοσύνη), and justice is the most comprehensive of the virtues.' In another section (31, p. 41), where the pentad is still being discussed, it is said that 'because it makes the unequals equal they call it foresight and justice or division (δίκην οἷον δίχησιν) and Buba-steia because she is worshipped in Bubastis in Egypt, and Aphrodite because a male and female number are being mingled with one another.'

Kákosy is also able to cite Nicomachus of Gerasa *ap.* Photius, *Bibl.* 144 a, where the pentad is identified with a number of concepts including Justice, Nemesis and Bubastia. Now Isis and Bubastis (i.e. Bastet) were sometimes equated, and Isis herself is equated with Dikaiosynê (Ma'at) in Plut. *De Is. et Os.* 3, 352 A-B; so that an Isiac connection with the number five as Justice now emer-ges. Kákosy cites evidence for the belief that Pythagoras was genuinely acquaint-ed with Egyptian ideas, and he notes the fact that Pythagoreanism was actively revived in Alexandria under the Ptolemies. He points out that in the Graeco-Roman era the hieroglyph for a star (✶, Gardiner N 14) was used to express 'five'; the same sign could occasionally mean 'god', and Osiris is called 'the great god among the five gods' (*Urk.* IV, 545, 1; cf. Sethe, *Amun*, 40), the five here being apparently the children of Geb, among whom are both Isis and Osiris. In the Platonic theory, on the other hand, which Plutarch follows in *De Is. et Os.* 56, it is Horus that represents 'five' or the hypotenuse in the most beautiful triangle. Osiris is 'three' or the vertical, and Isis is 'four' or the base. Kákosy has, finally, little difficulty in showing that Apuleius was interested in both Plato and Pythagoras; cf. *Flor.* 15 (on Pythagoras and Egyptian lore) and the allusion in our ch. 1 to the seven immersions of the head by Lucius — a number sanctioned, as it is expressly said, by *divinus ille Pythagoras.*

All this is both attractive and instructive. If it fails to convince, it is because it relates to theory and speculation rather than to cult. What Apuleius has told us is that a hand, that is, the image of a hand, was carried by a priest in the procession, and that it was a symbol of justice. The Pythagoreans connected the pentad with justice, but did they use a hand as a symbol of this? Kákosy's emphasis on the link between Isis and Ma'at is apposite, and it may be suggested with some confidence that the image of a hand was connected with the important ceremony of presenting an image of the goddess Ma'at or Isis-Ma'at.

It is a striking fact that in a great majority of the instances noted by the present writer, the hand that offers the figure of Ma'at in representations is the left hand; e.g. Junker, *Der grosse Pylon*, figs. 18, 23, 77, 107, 117, 118; Junker and Winter, *Geburtshaus*, pp. 58, 152, 292, 330 (but in pp. 68, 84, 138, 178 the figure is held in the right hand); S. Gabra, *Rapport sur les les fouilles d'Hermoupolis Ouest* (*Touna el-Gebel*), pl. 13; Gabra and Drioton, *Touna el-Gebel*, pl. 26; Mariette, *Abydos*, I, pl. 5; Petrie, *Six Temples at Thebes, 1896*, pl. 10; E. Otto, *Cults of Osiris and Amon*, pl. 52; Chassinat, *Edfou*, XIII, pl. 447; XIV, pl. 645 (in pl. 643 it is in the right hand); Sauneron, *Esna II* (Cairo, 1963), no. 11, p. 26 (but no. 25, p. 64 shows it in the right hand); Chassinat, *Dendara*, V (Cairo, 1947), pls. 404, 406, 410, 444; De Wit, *Opet*, II, shows two instances in the left hand (pls. 2 e, top, and 8, bottom) and two in the right (pls. 1 a and 4, bottom); Winter, *Unters. zu den Ägyptischen Tempelreliefs der griechisch-römischen Zeit* (Vienna, 1968), pl. 11, top, reproduces one from Medinet Habu (Ramesses III); G. Grimm, *Jb. des römisch-germanischen Zentralmuseums Mainz* 10 (1963), 209 f. reproduces three instances from Kom Ombo, Denderah and Karnak, one of which features the right hand; cf. Roeder, *Rel.* IV, 371, fig. 40 (in the left) and 393, fig. 42 (in the right). It seems that unless both hands were occupied, the left hand was the favourite hand for carrying objects to be offered. Thus in G. Lefebvre, *Petosiris*, III, pl. 28, five persons are shown bringing various objects, and they are all carried in the left hand. Plutarch, *De Is. et Os.* 68, 378 B, refers to the ceremony of offering Ma'at in connection with Thoth; see my remarks, pp. 533 f. The figure of Ma'at was presented to many gods, and according to Anthes, *Die Maat des Echnaton von Amarna* (1952), the only depiction of the ceremony before the Amarna period is that recorded in Petrie, *Six Temples*, pl. 10 (Amenophis III). She was a goddess of truth or justice or cosmic order; and she combines human, cosmic and ethical qualities, as Zandee shows in his *Het ongedifferentieerde denken der oude Egyptenaren* (Leiden, 1966), 9.

Yet the figure of a left hand with a statuette of Ma'at was not, as far as we can see, carried by priests in procession. What *was* frequently carried was an object also shaped as a left hand, but which was really a censer or thurible. Chassinat gives a good photograph of one of these in the large frontispiece of his *Le Mystère d'Osiris*, I (Cairo, 1966) : this example clearly represents a left hand and forearm, with the upper end mounted with a falcon-head; the outstretched hand is the location of the burning of incense; above the hand is a receptacle for the keeping of incense with a small figure of a Pharaoh overlooking it. On p. 212 n. 6 Chassinat sees the 'left hand' of Apuleius's account being carried by priests who have a situla in the other hand as depicted in Moret, *Rois et Dieux d'Égypte*, pl. 15 (= Leipoldt, *Bilderatlas*, 55 [286], a painting from Herculaneum); Moret calls the object a sprinkler, but in shape it looks like a lotus bud on a stalk. The censer in the form of a forearm is often depicted, and its normal shape is less elaborate than the example featured by Chassinat; see Bonnet, *Reallexikon*, figs. 64 (p. 261) and 105 (p. 428); Sauneron, *Esna*, III, no. 236, p. 101 and *The Priests of Ancient Egypt*, 142; J. Viau, 'Egyptian Mythology' (Larousse), 9 (top); Junker and Winter, *Geburtshaus*, 308 (Tiberius before Osiris; here the falcon has a disk on its head); De Wit, *Opet*, II, pls. 2 f., 10 b, 12 b; Bonnet, *Bilderatlas*, 88; W.B. Emery, *JEA* 57 (1971), pl. 9, 5 and pl. 10, 2-4. Usually this type of censer is held in the left hand and itself looks like a left hand, as the position of the thumb shows. Further, the hand is normally represented with a lack of detail which corresponds to the type used in hieroglyphs depicting the forearm that holds various objects; cf. Gardiner's Sign-List D 37-45 as well as D 46-49 (with the hand alone). A misunderstanding of this tradition might well explain the word *deformata*. It also seems likely that the forearm type of censer has been identified with the left arm which presents the figure of Ma'at. Certainly no association emerges between incense-offering and the idea of justice; texts connected with this rite speak of a release from evil, the pleasure of the 'scents of Punt', and the presence of the god thus honoured : v. Bonnet, *ZÄS* 67 (1931), 20-28 and *Reallexikon*, 625 f.; cf. my *Plut. De Is. et Os.* 567. It is through Ma'at that the idea of justice is associated with an offering hand; a transference of symbolism has therefore occurred. That Apuleius is really describing the censer shaped like a forearm is confirmed by the reference in Clem. Alex. *Strom.* 6.4.36.2 (= Hopfner, *Fontes*, 373) to a stolist who is carrying 'the cubit (πῆχυν) of justice and the offering-bowl'. Cf. Zimmermann, *Rel.* 147, where, however, the 'cubit of justice' is strangely identified with a hieroglyph used in the writing of *mȝʿt* : v. Gardiner, Aa 11 (perhaps a pedestal).

Clearly, then, the association of the censer with Ma'at is not due to a confusion in the mind of Apuleius; it is an interpretation shared by others. Perhaps it arose because a censer was used concomitantly in the ceremony of presenting Ma'at. Such a ceremony, of course, would presumably occur only in the temple of Isis after the procession was over, and the figurine of Ma'at would not itself be on view in the procession. But it can be regarded as almost certain that the reference to *aequitatis ... indicium* is to such a ceremony. O. Marucchi in *Annali dell'instituto di correspondenza archeologica* 51 (1879), 170 f., was able to see the resemblance here between the Apuleian description and that in Clement of Alexandria; he went on to argue that the priest, Aemulius Crescens, with whose monument he was concerned, since he is shown with a *patera* in his left hand, must have the figure of a *manus sinistra* in the other hand. In fact the latter object seems to be a bag or purse; cf. Lafaye, *Hist.*

du culte, 297, no. 112. Nor does the *patera* correspond to our *aureum vasculum*. The phrase *porrecta palmula* is an admirable index to the part of the arm-censer which holds the incense in use, and a small vessel is sometimes seen to stand on the outstretched palm.

As for the explanation which Apuleius adds as to why the left hand should be so honoured in relation to the concept of justice, it appears to bear no relation to Egyptian ideas in any phase of the cult. In Egypt the left hand and side was less honourable than the right, and after judgement the guilty were assigned to the left; cf. J. Gwyn Griffiths, *ASAE* 53 (1955), 146-9; Siegfried Morenz, *ZÄS* 82 (1957), 62-71, shows how the same idea was followed, probably through Egyptian influence, by the Orphics, Plato, Vergil and the New Testament. For the relation of right and left to West and East in Egyptian thought see the remarks in my *Plut. De Is. et Os.* 421. The Greeks regarded the left as unlucky; cf. Krall, *Wien. Sitzb.* 116 (1888), 701 f. A similar approach is found among the Romans; in particular the left hand is sometimes viewed as the hand prone to thieving, as in Plaut. *Pers.* 226 and Ovid. *Metam.* 13.111; cf. Catull. 12.1 and 47.1. The association of the left hand with justice must derive from some exceptional sphere where the left is regarded as favourable. Roman augury, taken from the Etruscans, seems to provide the answer; cf. Cic. *De div.* 2.39.82, *ita nobis sinistra videntur, Graiis et barbaris dextra, meliora*; Livy, 1.18.7 f.; Vergil, *Aen.* 2.693 and 9.631 (*intonuit laevum*); Pliny, *HN* 2.55.142. A precise link with justice is, however, lacking. There is probably no connection with the opened hand figured on a rectangular monument of white limestone from Quintanilla de Somoza in N.W. Spain inscribed with Εἷς Ζεὺς Σέραπις, the hand itself bearing the name Ἰαώ : see A. García y Bellido, *El Culto a Sárapis en la Peninsula Ibérica* (Madrid, 1956), pl. 4; on p. 39 he assigns to the hand a prophylactic purpose, comparing an inscription on a sarcophagus in Trier : *Martiniani manus vi(nc)at*. See also id. *Les Religions Orientales dans l'Espagne Romaine* (Leiden, 1967), 130-32. Hardly comparable is the hand which appears in the art of the Northern Bronze Age and which may derive from belief in a one-handed god : v. Hilda E. Davidson in *The Chariot of the Sun* (London, 1969), 158 f. More relevant, indeed impressively so at first sight, is the large gilded bronze hand, with open palm, which the writer saw carried in a procession to the Church of S. Andrea at Iseo near Brescia on Sept. 24th 1972; the reliquary of a local saint was also carried here; this open raised hand, however, is doubtless that known in the Christian tradition as 'symbolical of the blessing of God' (George Ferguson, *Signs and Symbols in Christian Art* [N. York, 1966, first publ. 1954], 48).

p. 274, 10 **magis aptior** : The double comparative element obviously derives from popular speech; cf. the use of μᾶλλον in Greek. Bernhard, *Stil*, 109, cites *Metam.* 9.36 (230, 27 f.), *magis inritatiores*; cf. Callebat, *Sermo Cotid.* 253 f. Since the usage is frequent in Plautus, it may have a colour of sophistication in Apuleius : although coming ultimately from common speech, it may here be a conscious archaism. Desertine, *De Apulei studiis Plautinis*, 99 f., after citing the present phrase, notes that in some cases Apuleius follows Plautus in using *multo tanto* with the comparative adjective. Hofmann and Szantyr, *Lat. Syntax*, 166, wish to deny the comparative force of *magis* in the Plautine instances apart from certain cases where affected overstatement is involved. The latter is a subjective criterion, however, and the usage is well established by *Capt.* 644, *Men.* 987, and *Mil.* 613.

p. 274, 11 **aureum vasculum in modum papillae rutundatum** : An Osirian text from Denderah which describes what was done at Busiris on Khoiak 12th refers to a 'situla of gold' : v. Chassinat, *Mystère d'Osiris*, 204, col. 19. The determinative in the Denderah text certainly suggests the form mentioned by Apuleius, although the nipple-like protuberance at the base is not present in all the actual examples of situlae which have been recovered; see the instances in Chassinat's frontispiece. In the Egyptian concept it is the life-giving water of libation that is usually involved, but Chassinat (p. 213) is able to quote texts of the Ptolemaic era which envisage libation-vases as breasts; he dates the origin of this form of situla to the Saïte era, but a vase of rather similar shape appears in the 18th Dynasty : v. B. de Rachewiltz, *Introd. to Egyptian Art* (London, 1966, repr. 1967), pl. 102; cf. pl. 101 (Late Era); also Petrie, *Stone and Metal Vases* (London, 1937), 28 f., where the earliest example of 'pendant situlae' is dated ('probably') to the 19th Dynasty; von Bissing, *Metall-gefässe* (*CCG*, 1901), xii, cf. 37, nos. 3488 f. and 19, no. 3453 (with figure of Osiris); Roeder, *Ägyptische Bronzewerke* (Glückstadt, 1937), 72, § 303. The type seems not to occur in Europe; v. J. Kastelic, *Situla Art. Ceremonial Bronzes of Ancient Europe* (London, 1965), although his pl. 30 (the 'Capodaglio situla', now in Este) shows a tapering base. Two very ornate examples of bronze situlae from the end of the Late Era were found by Emery in Saqqâra near the mausoleum of Isis Mother of Apis : v. *JEA* 55 (1969), pl. 6, 5 and 7. One of these (pl. 6, 7) represents the Hathor-cow in a papyrus-clump before Nefer-tem on the lotus, so that the theme of suckling and rearing is present in accordance with Apuleius's *in modum papillae*. On the other bronze situla (pl. 6, 5) a child is shown under a large lotus-flower while the Nile-god Ḥ'apy stands near him. An ithyphallic Min appears on a situla of the Late Era reproduced by de Rachewiltz, op. cit. pl. 101, as also on one of Emery's examples (pl. 6, 7). For earlier reliefs on situlae see Roeder, *Bronzefiguren*, 481. A lotus design appears on the base of the instances cited above; cf. too Emery, *JEA* 53 (1967), pl. 25, 2. M.G. Michaïlidès, *BIE* 32 (1951), 291-324, discusses cinerary urns and situlae (the latter esp. pp. 304 ff.) and urges that in the situlae of the Late Era three symbolisms are conjoined : solar renewal, refreshment through water, and sexual power. The last element is clear in an instance described by him ('une situle à forme phallique'). Cf. B. de Rachewiltz, 'Le Situle e la rigenera-zione cosmica in Egitto e in Mesopotamia', *Archivio Internazionale di Etno-grafia e Preistoria* 1 (1958), 69-95, esp. 72 ff., where the cosmic importance of Nut and Hathor is shown in this connection; his pl. 15, 19 reproduces a situla from the B.M. which represents an Osirian *djed*-pillar.

There are many representations of situlae in the Graeco-Roman sources. A young assistant is depicted carrying one at Pompeii; see Tran Tam Tinh, *Isis à Pompéi*, pl. 4, 3 and pp. 94, 137 (since he has abundant hair, he is probably not a fully ordained priest). Chassinat is perhaps right in seeing a schematized form of a situla in the left hand of the statue of Isis from Pompeii; v. his *Le Mystère d'Osiris*, 212, and cf. Moret, *Rois et Dieux d'Égypte*, fig. 9 and Tran Tam Tinh, op. cit. pl. 13 and p. 156; the two last-named authors regard it as an '*ankh*-emblem. For other instances at Pompeii see Tran Tam Tinh, pl. 12,4 and p. 174; Schefold, *Vergessenes Pompeji*, 192 (*c.* 20 B.C.). A priestess in the ritual scene from Herculaneum is carrying a situla; she is one of the three figures in front of the temple, but in the background of the fresco : v. Leipoldt, *Bilderatlas*, 53 [294] and Tran Tam Tinh, *Herculanum*, pl. 27; cf. three very clear instances in another picture from Herculaneum in Leipoldt, 55 [286] and the vessel carried in her right hand by the first officiant (a priestess) in the Isiac procession shown on a relief at the Vatican (Leipoldt, 56 [292]) and by the priestess in a relief at Athens (ibid. 50; another similar one in Leipoldt, *Umwelt*, III, 291), in this case in the left hand. The rounded type of situla occurs in an apparently non-Isiac context in W. Amelung, *Die Sculpturen des Vaticanischen Museums*, I, pl. 22, 56 c-d, cf. id. I (Text), 206.

The breast shape is not invariably present; cf. a priestess of Isis on a gem in Delatte and Derchain, *Intailles Magiques*, 89, no. 112. Anubis is also shown sometimes carrying the situla, and a rounded type appears in Delatte and Derchain, op. cit. 94, no. 113 and 102, no. 128 (with a double breast-like swelling); cf. Bonner, *Stud. Mag. Am.* pl. 2, 36; 37; 41 and p. 259, only the last of which, however, has a rounded base. A dead woman portrayed in Parlasca, *Mumienporträts*, pl. 60, 3, is carrying the Apuleian type; see Parlasca, p. 163, and cf. Weber, *Terr.* pl. 3, 28 and 30 (in each case the small vessel in the left hand); Weber's pl. 42, 474 also resembles it in shape, although he takes it as the knob of an implement; to be viewed as a situla it must be put upside down (i.e. as against Weber's photograph). The symbolism is that of motherhood, and Barb, *JWCI* 16 (1953), 224, remarks that 'teats and womb are complementary symbols in the description of blessed motherhood' for which idea he cites Gen. 49.25 and Luke 11.27. (He finds the womb in the *urnula* which follows the *cista* in ch. 11.) The precise application, in the first place, is to Isis as the mother of Horus or Harpocrates. In the earliest sources Horus is known as the son of the cow-goddess Hathor, a relationship probably embodied in the Narmer Palette, and Berreth, p. 67, rightly invokes the tradition that the Pharaoh as Horus was suckled by Hathor. Isis has now, of course, subsumed this role of Hathor. Further, her particular function as mother of Horus has been universalized; she is the cosmic mother, *rerum naturae parens* (ch. 5), but Hathor anticipated this in her association with the sky and with the celestial cow; cf. de Rachewiltz, op. cit. 218, who also invokes the goddess Nut. It is possible that vases called μαστοί in certain inventories involve the type of vessel mentioned by Apuleius; thus Roussel, *CED* 286, citing *IG* XI,

1307, 9 (?) and 21 (where the reading is very doubtful in 9; in 21 μασστόν is the form); also 1308, 2 (μασ[θ]ίον). See further Roussel, *CED* 209-10; Vidman, *SIRIS* 83. The word στρόφιον used of a band worn by women round the breast or by priests round the head, is found in another inscription from Delos, and Roussel, p. 227, seems rather bold in his suggestion that it is here equivalent to μαστίον; at least a ritual meaning is already present in other occurrences, with the second meaning above : v. *LSJ* s.v. Cf. Vidman, *SIRIS* 85. We have seen that Clem. Alex. *Strom.* 6.4.36.2 (= Hopfner, *Fontes*, 373) used the word σπονδεῖον of an object which assumes a parallel place to that of the breast-shaped vessel. Since the word means a 'cup' or 'bowl', the correspondence here is not exact, although Boeken, p. 65, cites *CIG* II 2983 (Ephesus) where a σπονδαύλης is mentioned; apparently he was a flute-player who accompanied a libation. Another inscription at Ephesus (Vidman, *SIRIS* 155, no. 302) mentions a φιάλην καὶ σπονδεῖον. For the general idea Berreth, p. 69, compares Brugsch, *Hieroglyphisch-Demotisches Wb.* 380, who cites texts relating to festivals of Hathor in which the breasts of women were exposed; cf. Hdt. 2.60 on female exposure in the festival of Bubastis. In these cases, however, the motive is clearly erotic, as often happens with Hathor; with Isis benign maternity is expressed; cf. the contrast well pointed by Derchain, *Bibl Orient.* 27 (1970), 22. A type of vessel in which a mother is sometimes figured pressing her bared breast to give milk has been studied by Emma Brunner-Traut, 'Das Muttermilchkrüglein; *Die Welt des Orients* 5 (1970), 145-64 and 6 (1971), 4-6. This, of course, is a different idea from that in Apuleius; it was intended to provide mother's milk for medicinal purposes. Quite different, too, in spite of Berreth's view (p. 69), was the adoration of the two breasts of Bona Dea in Catana, Sicily; he compares the modern festival of St. Agatha in the same place, when the saint's breast (and foot and veil) are elevated at the high altar; v. J. J. Blunt, *Vestiges of Ancient Manners and Customs discoverable in Modern Italy and Sicily* (London, 1823), 73; cf. W. Menzel, *Christliche Symbolik* (Regensburg, 1854), 158 f.

p. 274, 12 **lacte** : Apuleius uses an Accusative *lactem* in *Metam.* 8.19 (192,1) and 8.28 (*bis* : 199, 23 and 200, 4), so that *lacte* is probably an Ablative here; cf. *Metam.* 4.22 (91, 10), *vino mero libant*; 8.12 (186, 24), *tuo luminum cruore libabo*, although an Accusative follows the verb in ch. 5 (270, 8), *primitias commeatus libant mei sacerdotes* and in ch. 16 (279, 5.).

A minor problem emerges in that the Egyptian situla (*wšb*) is usually connected with libations of water; cf. Chassinat, *Le Mystère d'Osiris*, 212 ff. and Yoyotte in Posener, *Dict. Egn. Civ.* 295 a. There are plentiful allusions, on the other hand, to the use of milk both as a drink-offering and for purposes of libation. In Junker, *Der große Pylon*, fig. 103, Harpocrates is offered two jugs of milk by the King, and the text (p. 180, 3-4) assigns these words to the King : 'May you have abundance of milk from what is in the udders of the Ḥesat-cow.' If fig. 20 of the same work the King offers milk to Osiris and he says (p. 42, 2-7) : 'This is the sweet milk from the udders of the Akhet-cow, this white (liquid) gleaming in appearance. The cows of Hathor reach their breasts to you; suck them (and be) free from evil. Osiris Onnophris, blessed one, milk them, the milk of the mother of Min.' Isis was sometimes regarded in Coptos as the mother of Min (here equated with Horus); cf. Kees, *Götterglaube*, 338 f. Similar texts are not unnaturally prominent in Junker and Winter, *Geburtshaus*, a corpus which also emanates from Philae. Of the King, offering milk to Osiris, it is said (64 and 65, 12-15) : 'The good god, the son of the Ḥesat-cow, nurtured in the Delta, who gives milk to his father and refreshes his body.' In such a context the relationship of the King as Horus and as son of the divine cow is naturally emphasized. When he offers milk to Harpocrates, he is called 'the son of the Ḥesat-cow, living image of Horus' (ibid. 265, 11; cf. Daumas, *Les mammisis*, 188 f.). In the Isiac rites the place of Horus was transferred to the initiate, just as in the magical stelae the sufferer is promised the release vouchsafed to Horus. The shape of the milk-carrying situla might suggest a ceremonial drinking of milk, but Apuleius adds *de quo lacte libabat*. Libations of milk were conspicuous in the rites connected with the Abaton on the Island of Bigeh; daily libations of milk were there decreed; see Junker, *Abaton*, 9, line 31; cf. Diod. Sic. 1.22.3 ff. and my note in *C.R.* 23 (1973), 9. Junker gives a detailed analysis of the use of milk in these rites and shows that the libations included those poured on offerings and on sacred trees near the grave of Osiris; the constant symbolism attached is the conferment of life and renewed vigour; every ten days Isis herself is responsible for the libation in a special visit. F. Daumas, 'Les objets sacrés d'Hathor au temple de Dendara', *BSFE* 57 (1970), 7-18, discusses (pp. 14 f.) the offering of milk to the goddesses of the mammisis (Isis in Philae, Hathor in Denderah, the 'Perfect Sister' in Kom Ombo) and notes that the milk was equated with that of the primordial celestial cows, among which was Iḥet. According to B. de Rachewiltz in *Archivio Internaz. di Etnografia e Prestoria* 1 (1958), 70 ff. milk and water are equally important in the use and meaning of the situla, the connection with Hathor as cow suggesting milk, and that with Nut, the primal ocean, implying water,

p. 274, 12 **auream vannum** : The winnowing-basket is the same as the *liknon*. In its first use it acted as a kind of sieve or fan in the process of winnowing, but it served also as a basket for carrying fruit and sacred objects : v. Dar.-Sag. s.v. Vannus with fig. 7248 on p. 627; Jane E. Harrison, 'Mystica Vannus Iacchi', *JHS* 23 (1903), 292-324. The latter suggests (p. 323) that the *liknon* by the first century A.D. was used in the rites of several religions. Its first association was with the Dionysiac cult, and Plutarch, *De Is. et Os.* 35, 365 A, has a vivid allusion to the 'secret sacrifice' offered in the temple of Apollo in Delphi when the god of the sacred basket (*Liknitês*) was awakened; ideas of fertility and immortality enter into this rite; see my remarks *ad loc.* p. 534. Jane Harrison suggested (op. cit. 323) that the equation of Dionysus and Osiris was by now influential, and that in the cult of the Orphic Zagreus the *liknon* implied a connection with the god who was dismembered and then reborn

in the *liknon*, interpreted as a cradle. 'Thus', she continues, 'to the old symbolism of the basket of fresh fruits and the winnowing of grain from chaff
[fertility and purification are involved here] was added the new, and perhaps
Egyptian, mysticism of the *palingenesia*, "the death unto sin and the new
birth unto righteousness".' Such an idea enters into some facets of the Osirian
cult, but it is hard to connect it with the *liknon*. Conversely, it does seem that
the *aurea vannus* or *liknon* mentioned here may have come into an Isiac context
from a Dionysiac or Eleusinian source. Firm evidence is admittedly lacking.

In *Georg.* 1.166 (*mystica vannus Iacchi*) Vergil combines a reference to Ceres
and Dionysus, and Servius, writing in the fourth century A.D., finds a meaning
of purification and then a secondary association with the tradition that Isis
placed the dismembered limbs of Osiris in a *cribrum* ('sieve'); cf. Gressmann,
Osiris, 21. A more likely origin is the use of the *liknon* in the Eleusinian rites
of Demeter. We have the testimony of Callimachus in his Hymn to Demeter,
126, that in Alexandria a festival of the goddess included the carrying of
likna by girls. Nilsson, *Dionysiac Mysteries*, 30, commenting on this line,
says that 'it is a little surprising that the *likna* are said to be full of gold,' and
this recalls the *auream vannum* of our text. Further, as Emile Cahen points
out in his *Les Hymnes de Callimaque* (Paris, 1930), 276, the scholiast to Aristoph.
Ach. 242 refers to baskets of gold carried in Dionysiac rites (ἦν δὲ ἐκ χρυσοῦ
πεποιημένα τὰ κανᾶ); Cahen thinks that what is really referred to is the
quality of the cult-objects and of the ribbons which bound them. On the other
hand, Apuleius freely applies the adjective *aureus* to the sacred objects mentioned
by him : some of the sistra are thus described, also the boat-shaped lantern,
and the leaves of the palm-branch; also the *urnula* at the end of ch. 11. In
all cases the objects were probably gilded. Hildebrand notes that a χρυσοῦν
κιβώτιον is mentioned by Plut. *De Is. et Os.* 39, 366 F as being inside the
'sacred box'; Plutarch refers to water being put into the κιβώτιον; and Apuleius
too follows with the mention of an amphora. Hildebrand proposes, therefore,
to identify the χρυσοῦν κιβώτιον and the *aurea vannus*. The two nouns
can hardly mean the same thing. In his search for a possible Egyptian origin,
Berreth cites a bronze figure (Perdrizet, *Terr.* (text), 45) showing the god Bes
with a winnowing-fan; cf. too, in his pls. 43-44, terracottas of Beset sitting
on a basket. A more likely source in Egypt is the background of the corn-
goddess Renenutet, who was equated with Isis in the Ptolemaic era as Thermuthis. On a stela from Denderah she was called Isis-Thermuthis : v. N.
Aimé-Giron, *ASAE* 26 (1926), 150 f. Conceived of originally as a snake-
goddess, she was also a mother-goddess, as indeed her name probably implies
(from *rnn* 'nurture a child'; cf. A. Hermann, *MDAIK* 8 [1939], 173 and J.
Broekhuis, *De Godin Renenwetet* [Assen, 1971], 4-9, concluding that the name
is best rendered by 'nurse'). This was one reason for her equation with Isis;
cf. my *Plut. De Is. et Os.* 446; Maria Münster, *Isis*, 155; J. Broekhuis, op. cit.
105 ff. Terracotta figures of Thermuthis are often serpentine in form, as in
Breccia, *Terr.* 2, pls. 8-9, but an agrarian goddess seated on a basket probably

involves Isis-Thermuthis with the influence of Demeter also present; v. Breccia, *Terr.* 1, pl. 48, 8 with p. 53, no. 243 (he calls her 'Iside Agraria' and suggests a relation to Bubastis); Vogt, *Terr.* pl. 8, 4 with p. 6 ('Frau auf Korb') and pl. 9, 2 with p. 7; in Weber, *Terr.* pl. 2, 25 with p. 49 the goddess nurses a child on the basket, and on p. 39 Weber argues, rather unconvincingly, that Isis is not really involved, while in a note (p. 39 n. 40) he has instructive references to Sarapis with a basket. That Isis is involved in Perdrizet, *Terr.* 26, no. 80 ('Isis agraire') is beyond question since she has a sistrum in her right hand; she is shown emerging from a large basket. For a depiction of a *vannus mystica* associated with the worship of Athena see Christopher M. Dawson, 'Romano-Campanian Mythological Landscape Painting' in *Yale Classical Studies* 9 (1944), pl. 8 with p. 90.

p. 274, 12 **laureis congestam ramulis** : Norden, *Geburt des Kindes*, 19 n. 2, defends the reading of the codices, *aureis*, against *laureis*, the emendation of Passeratius in the 16th century. In this highly mannered prose, he rightly argues, there is no stylistic objection to the repetition of the adjective. He would connect the idea with the *ramus aureus* of *Aeneid* VI, where he finds the mistletoe branch endowed with a magical quality because of its association with a very special point of time — the Winter Solstice. Such a connotation is doubtful here; but the further point he makes, that *congerere* can mean 'to construct', is certainly acceptable. Cf. *Thes. L.L.* 4, 278, 73 ff. (*congerendo efficere*), where Verg. *Aen.* 6.177 f. is cited (*aramque ... congerere arboribus*) It would be quite foolish to suggest that the basket was loaded with twigs; it is *made* of twigs. In ch. 16 (279, 4) *congerere* is admittedly used with the meaning of 'heap, load' : *vannos onustas aromatis ... congerunt* : 'they load (the ship) with baskets heaped with spices', but it is interesting that *onustas* is there used to mean 'heaped (with)'; see also *Metam.* 5.2 (104, 16 f.) and 6.13 (138,1). 'Made of laurel twigs' can be supported by Seneca, *De vita beata*, 27, *laurum et lucernam tenens*, although the laurel was scarcely conspicuous in the Isis-cult. Probably it is Apollo's laurel, present here because of the association of Isis and Artemis. Berreth, p. 71, interprets the allusion (reading *laureis*) as being to laurel *leaves*, and cites the superstitious man in Theophrastus who has a laurel leaf in his mouth the whole day long because of its alleged purificatory potency. Mme. N. Fick, *Latomus* 30 (1971), 335 f., makes the point that *ramulis* and not *ramis* occurs here; they are the young shoots of laurel, symbols of the continuity of vegetation and recall the lyrical description of spring in ch. 7, especially *germine foliorum renidentes* (271, 21), of the trees.

p. 274, 13 **amphoram** : Unlike the situla, the amphora was held with both hands; cf. the third officiant in the procession figured on the relief in the Vatican, Leipoldt, *Bilderatlas*, 56 [292] (it is not strictly an amphora, having only one handle, but its size probably corresponded); the central priestly figure in the service portrayed at Herculaneum is perhaps holding one; v. Leipoldt, 53 [294] = Tran Tam Tinh. *Herculanum*, pl. 27 (on p. 83 it is called 'un vase d'or posé sur une couronne de fleurs'); Tran Tam Tinh earlier (p. 37) identifies this vase with the *urnula* described by Apuleius at the end of the next chapter, and its obvious importance in both contexts is an argument in favour of the equation. The *amphora* is perhaps intended by the vase carried by last figure on the relief at Potsdam published by Martin Schede in *Angelos* 2 (1926), 60 f. and pl. 4 = Leipoldt, *Umwelt*, III, 293. = Nilsson, *Gesch. Gr. Rel.* II, pl. 11, 1. Grimm, *Ägypt. Rel. im röm. Deutschland*, 14, points out that this piece was very probably acquired in Italy; cf. Anne Roullet, *Rome*, 64 f., no. 51. Terracottas sometimes show Harpocrates carrying an amphora : v. Weber, *Terr.* 59 n. 78 with references; other types of vessel occur with him too. The Harpocratean sidelock is found likewise with two figures holding an amphora in Vogt, *Terr.* pl. 75, though neither Vogt, p. 165, nor Wittmann, p. 203, mentions Harpocrates in discussing them. 'Temple-servants' is Vogt's phrase for them. Wittmann also cites the use of the amphora in funerary lustrations, but this would not apply here unless a specifically Osirian episode was enacted. Types of amphora are attested in Egypt from the 18th Dynasty; v. Petrie, *Arts and Crafts of Ancient Egypt* (London, 1909), fig. 120 (amphora in glazed ware) and p. 121 (two types); B. M. Guide (1930), 134, fig. 62; *The Art of Ancient Egypt* (Phaidon, Vienna, 1936), pl. 286 (in the shape of a double duck); Birgit Nolte, *Die Glasgefässe im alten Ägypten* (Berlin, 1968), 163 ff. Not all of these, it is true, correspond to the Greek type of amphora (ἀμφορεύς) which is a jar with a narrow neck and with the two handles flanking the neck, but many instances derive from Egypt in the Graeco-Roman era; v. Breccia, *Necropoli di Sciatbi* (CCG, 1912), II, pl. 47, 71; 48, 73; 53, 103; 54, five examples; Edgar, *Greek Vases*, (CCG, 1911), pl. 4, 26, 171; pl. 19, 26,250; pl. 20, 26,256; 26,258; id. *Graeco-Egyptian Glass* (CCG, 1905), pl. 5, four instances. Another type has two handles on the top of the vessel's body : v. Edgar, *Greek Vases*, pls. 15 and 16 ('cinerary hydria' is the term applied by him): cf. Breccia, *Necropoli di Sciatbi*, II, pl. 35, 43; pl. 36, 44 and 45, which he describes as cinerary urns. In all, Apuleius mentions three types of vase being borne in procession : the breast-shaped vessel and the amphora in the present chapter; then the *urnula* of ch. 11. The first of the three is used, according to him, for libations of milk; the use of the third is not specified. Probably the amphora was used to carry holy water intended for libations or lustrations.

Egyptian religion, like most others, used water for many purificatory purposes as well as for ritual drink-offerings in the funerary cult, and originally the preponderant symbolism derived from the Heliopolitan worship of Rē', as Blackman shows in his article 'Purification (Egyptian)' in Hastings, *ERE* and elsewhere. Some of this symbolism was Osirianized, especially in a funerary context, Nile-water being now regarded as an exudation of Osiris; see Blackman's articles in *JEA* 5 (1918), 117-24 and 148-65; also Gardiner, *JEA* 36 (1950), 3-12 and my *Conflict*, 122 f. If we assume that the Isiac procession ended in the temple of Isis, there the water in the amphora would be used to wash the hands of the chief officiant, and also, probably, to wash ceremonially the cult-statue of the goddess which was kept in the temple.

Sacred objects were sprinkled in the temple service, and sprinklers sometimes appear in Isiac scenes; in Leipoldt, *Bilderatlas* 55 [286] (from Herculaneum) these vessels have one long curved handle and a longish spout too; obviously they are not amphorae. In offering rites, again, water served a double purpose : it could be a part of the offering itself or it could be used in a rite of purifying the altar; cf. Weber, *Terr.* 126. Plutarch, *De Is. et Os.* 36 *init.* mentions the processional carrying of the hydreion, and the term could apply to the situla, the amphora or the sprinkler; cf. my remarks *ad loc.* pp. 437 f. Other commentators have given a specifically Osirian role to the amphora, but with little firm support. Berreth, p. 72, argues for a close correspondence between the sacred objects of ch. 10 and the divine symbols of ch. 11. The following is a summary of the order :

Ch. 10	*Ch. 11*
1. Lantern	1. Anubis
2. Altar	2. Cow
3. Palm-branch and *caduceus*	3. *Cista*
4. Left Hand	4. *Urnula*
5. Breast-shaped vessel	
6. Winnowing-basket	
7. Amphora	

In ch. 11 the cow undoubtedly represents Isis, and the *urnula* very probably figures Osiris Hydreios or the Canopic Osiris. Berreth rightly connects the palm-branch and *caduceus* with Anubis; then the left hand and the breast-shaped vessel with Isis, but with the hand this is not so obvious, although Isis-Ma'at is involved; finally, the amphora, he argues, is the counterpart of the *urnula* and must be Osirian. The sequence leaves out, be it noted, the lantern, altar, and winnowing-basket. Further, the amphora has too general an application in rites of libation and lustration to be connected specifically here with Osiris.

CHAPTER 11

p. 274, 14 **nec mora** : Cf. ch. 7 *ad init.* and n.

pedibus humanis : Two senses are perhaps combined : the gods themselves now appear on earth; they do this by allowing their manifestations to be carried by human beings, that is, by the priests who bear their images. Médan well cites ch. 17, *init.*, *sacerdos maximus quique divinas effigies progerebant.* There is the further point also that in the case of Anubis and the cow, animal forms are borne on human feet.

p. 274, 15 **hic horrendus ille** : On the whole the emendation of L. D'Orléans is convincing, although the reading of the codices (*hic, horrendum! ille*) has

the merit of distinguishing more easily between the adverbial *hic* and the pronominal *ille*. Robertson's *horrendus* <*deum*> has some plausibility in that it
would explain the corruption of *horrendus* through attraction of ending.
Anubis, however, deals not only with the gods of the upper and lower worlds,
but with all their denizens.

   p.274, 15 **superum commeator et inferum** : *Commeator* is found only in Apuleius. He uses the same expression in *Apol.* 64 (72, 3 f.) of Mercury. Ryle compares Hor. *Carm.* 1.10.19 f., *superis deorum / gratus et imis.* According to Plut.
De Is. et Os. 44, 368 E Anubis is 'chthonic and Olympian at the same time'; in
the same chapter he is said to be the horizon which is common to things both
above and below the earth. Anubis was pre-eminently a funerary god entrusted
with embalming; he also escorted the dead, and he could thus be regarded
as in contact with the upper world of the living and the lower world of the dead;
cf. the remarks in my *Plut. De Is. et Os.* 466 f. and 517 f. The division between
superi and *inferi* is basically Greek, however, in origin, and Apuleius is appar-
rently thinking of Anubis as messenger of the gods and conductor of the dead,
the dual role of Hermes and Mercury; hence the *caduceus*, topped sometimes
by a serpent; cf. C. Picard, *Studi in Onore di A. Calderini e R. Paribeni*, III
(Milan, 1956), 173 and fig. 1 on p. 172. The Egyptians viewed their dead as
present not only in the underworld but also in the blessed West and in heaven.
Anubis is here the first member of the divine part of the procession, and in
the relief at Potsdam (*Angelos* 2 [1926], pl. 4 = Leipoldt, *Umwelt*, III, 293)
he seems to be leading the whole procession, although only six figures are
there taking part in all. Berreth, p. 75, cites Diod. Sic. 78 (actually 1.87.3) and
Ovid, *Metam.* 9.689 as confirming the precedence of Anubis in the procession;
the former passage says that 'dogs' came first; the second allusion says simply
that Anubis came with Isis (*cum qua latrator Anubis*). Both Berreth and Wittmann stress as a parallel the role of Wepwawet, the leader of the royal procession in Egypt; he was a jackal-god of Abydos and Asyut, and one feels that in
general the parallel is strained, since Anubis after all did not, according to
Apuleius, lead the entire Isiac procession. The role of Wepwawet in the Stela
of Ikhernofret, which describes an Osirian rite at Abydos in the Twelfth
Dynasty, might seem more relevant; the wolf-god is said to have gone forth to'
save his father Osiris; cf. Roeder, in Roscher, *Lex. Myth.* VI, 507. In Diod.
Sic. 1.18.1 two sons of Osiris are given the names Anubis and Macedon; the
latter seems to represent Wepwawet.

   p. 274, 15-16 **nunc atra, nunc aurea facie** : Hopfner, *Plutarch über Isis und
Osiris*, II, II, 198, suggests that the two hemispheres are involved. He cites
Clem. Alex. *Strom.* 5.7.43.1-3, where four golden images are said to be used
in Egyptian sacred processions, two of dogs, one of a hawk, and one of an
ibis. The dogs are explained as symbols of the two hemispheres, the hawk
as a symbol of the sun, and the ibis as that of the moon. Others, notes Clement,
explain the dogs as symbols of the tropics. Albert Deiber, *Clément d'Alexandrie
et l'Égypte* (Cairo, 1904), 61, connects the idea of hemispheres and tropics

with the Upper and Lower Egyptian forms of Wepwawet. In Clement, however, both dogs have golden images. The contrast between black and gold in the Apuleian phrase recalls rather what both Clement and Plutarch (*De Is. et Os.* 75, 381 D) have to say about the ibis; both see an association with the moon, and Clement finds the black feathers symbolizing the shadowed part, the white feathers the shining part. In Egyptian sources Anubis is sometimes shown rolling the disk of the moon; v. Naville, *The Temple of Deir el Bahari*, II, pl. 55; Junker and Winter, *Geburtshaus*, fig. 930 and p. 105, 10. It is therefore natural to suggest that although Anubis is in no sense a moon-god, he is regarded as exercising some influence on the moon, usually in a context of male fertility. For his link with celestial matters cf. Plut. *De Is. et Os.* 61, 375 E : Anubis is 'he who brings to light matters relating to the heavens' (ἀναφαίνων τὰ οὐράνια); also the Cius Hymn to Anubis, 2 : οὐρανίων πάντων βασιλεῦ (Peek, *Isishymnus*, 139). Perhaps by the time of Apuleius the process had gone a step further and the god's face is itself given the dark and bright aspects of the moon. A statue of Anubis or his priest in Rome has a disk between horns on the head; v. Leipoldt, *Bilderatlas*, 48 [283]; the disk is in origin that of the sun, but might have been interpreted now as that of the moon. A simpler explanation of the whole statement is to relate the golden part of the face to the upper world and the black part to the lower world to which Apuleius has already referred; in this case there will be a reflection simply of ideas relating to Hermes–Mercury. In Egyptian art Anubis was usually depicted black, as in the well-known instance from the tomb of Tut'ankhamûn. Perdrizet, *Terr.* 60, refers to traces of gilding on fragments of a statue of Anubis at Delos as evidence of a celestial connotation. Many sacred objects, however, were so treated, as we have observed already. Not much credence can naturally be put on the fulsome exaggeration of Lucian, *Iup. Trag.* 8 when he says that Bendis, Anubis, Attis and others are all 'of solid gold'.

p. 274, 16 **attollens** : An inscription of the Roman era from Athens, which is dedicated to Isis and Sarapis, describes a person 'carrying aloft the leader' (βαστάζων τὸν ἡγεμόνα). J. J. Pollitt, *Hesperia* 34 (1965), 125-30, justly interprets 'the leader' as referring to Anubis-Hermes in his role of leader of souls, and he aptly compares βαστάζων with *attollens* here.

canis cervices: The best known example of an actual Anubis-mask which must have been worn by a priest on such an occasion or in a funerary episode is that at the Pelizaeus-Museum, Hildesheim : v. A. Ippel and G. Roeder, *Die Denkmäler des Pelizaeus-Museums zu Hildesheim* (1921), 127, no. 1585 and 128, fig. 49 = Leipoldt, *Umwelt*, III, 284. It is of painted pottery and has cut-out curves to fit the shoulders as well as two holes (on top of the canine neck) for the user's eyes. What such a priest eventually looked like is well suggested by a statue in the Vatican Museum : v. Leipoldt, *Bilderatlas*, 48 [283] and cf. id. *Umwelt*, III, 241; Perdrizet, *Terr.* pl. 51 (middle, top) with pp. 57 f.; an example from Savaria is part of a relief : v. Wessetzky, *Ägypt. Kulte in Ungarn*, pl. 2, fig. 4 with pp. 29 f. and cf. too p. 27. On the other

hand, Perdrizet's pl. 1 represents two priests putting on show a large statue
of Anubis. They are not, he thinks, carrying the statue, although he refers
to *CIL* XII, 1919 (= Vidman, *SIRIS* 314, no. 742), *memoriae aeternae Lepidi
Rufi anubofori*, as well as to the allusions to the Emperor Commodus being
wont to 'carry the Anubis' (*ut Anubim portaret*) in Isiac rites : v. *SHA Commodus*, 9.4 and 6; *Caracalla*, 9.11; *Pescennius Niger*, 6.9 (they all relate to
Commodus). It seems likely that carrying the mask of Anubis is nevertheless
implied in these allusions. It is stated in *Commodus*, 9.6, that the Emperor
used to hit the heads of the Isiacs *ore simulacri*; D. Magie (Loeb, 1922, p. 289)
translates 'with the face of the statue'; 'with the snout of the mask' would be
preferable, alluding to the canine form; cf. Perdrizet, *Terr.* 58. *Simulacrum*
will probably be the mask which was 'carried' on the head and shoulders; to
hit the devotees with it would not be a difficult operation — it could easily
be removed for such a purpose. Further, as it was made of hard substance
(pottery), it would certainly hurt as the account suggests.

It is not surprising that Anubis appears in this chapter as one of the three
foremost gods of the cult, with Isis and Osiris. In the Greek world he figures
often in dedications with Sarapis and Isis; and P. M. Fraser, 'Two Studies',
6 n. 5, notes 'how rare joint dedications to Sarapis, Isis and Anubis are in
Egypt, while in the Mediterranean generally (especially Delos) they are the
normal type of dedication to "Egyptian" deities.' Lucian, a contemporary
of Apuleius, stresses the importance of the cult of Anubis in Egypt in *Vitarum
auctio*, 16 and *Icaromenippus*, 24. Vidman, *Isis und Sarapis*, 16, points out
that, even if the Greeks identified Anubis with Hermes, they did not succeed
in obliterating his theriomorphic aspect. Cf. R. E. Witt, *Isis Gr.-R.* 199 ff.
As early as the Pyramid Texts Anubis appears as the embalmer of Osiris in
Abydos, but it is noteworthy that at this stage he plays no part in the myth
of Osiris as such; see my *Origins of Osiris*, 19. Indeed he is at first on a par
with Osiris, and even more important than he for some time, as a funerary
god. Gradually he is subordinated to the Osirian framework of things. He
becomes, for instance, an assistant with Thoth in the judgement before Osiris,
and eventually is said to be a son of Osiris (Brugsch, *Thes.* 768, 3; P. Demot.
Mag. Lond. Leid. 2, 19; other refs. in my *Plut. De Is. et Os.* 318). Isis is sometimes named as his mother (P. Jumilhac, 6, 2-3; Anubis Hymn from Cius,
Peek, *Isishymnus*, 139), but Plutarch, *De Is. et Os.* 14, 356 E-F, says that
Anubis was the offspring of an illicit union of Osiris and Nephthys; he also
says there that Isis was helped by dogs to find the child Nephthys had exposed
and that Anubis in time became her guard and attendant. According to Diod.
Sic. 1.87.3, on the other hand, it was in her search for Osiris that Nephthys
was thus aided. Gressmann, *Osiris*, 5-7 ('Die Spürhunde') shows a little too
much respect for the variants in Minucius Felix, *Oct.* 22.1 (= Hopfner, *Fontes*,
295) and Lactantius, *Div. inst.* 1.21 (ibid. 488 f.). The canine or jackal form of
Anubis is prominent from early times (neither the Egyptians nor the classical
writers made careful distinctions here). The jackal was the dreaded ravager

of graves, and his conversion into a special protector of the dead is an instance of the transforming power of fear in religious psychology.

p. 274, 17 **palmam virentem** : On the symbolism of the palm-branch see n. *ad* ch. 10 (274, 7), *palmam*. The branch carried there by the third priest is apparently an artificial one, for its leaves are 'delicately wrought of gold'. In spite of the gold, a living verdant branch was doubtless the more powerful symbol. In *PGM* 12, 227 f. (a papyrus at Leiden, perhaps of the second century A.D.) the palm-branch is connected with Osiris : 'I am the plant with the name Palm-branch. I am the efflux of the blood of the palm-branches from the tomb of the Great One (Osiris).' Médan emends the word-order to *palmam quatiens virentem*, urging that the regularity of the metrical prose is thus re-restablished. His order is slightly more pleasing, but when he says that it also has the advantage of varying the construction, his claim is of doubtful validity. The balancing of *laeva caduceum gerens* by *dextera palmam virentem quatiens* may look too rigidly symmetrical, but chs. 2 and 5 provide similar patterns. Apuleius sometimes prefers this to a chiastic arrangement.

Since the writer of F corrected *huius* himself and since no other codex known to me reads anything other than *cuius* (some codices omit this and other words), this must be the true reading.

p. 274, 18 **bos** : The best parallel to the ritual role of Isis as a cow is the account in Plut. *De Is. et Os.* 39, 366 E, which concerns a ceremony in the month of Athyr. Osiris, it is said, has disappeared with the recession of the Nile, and the priests 'envelop a gilded cow with a black linen garment and show it as a mark of mourning on the part of the goddess.' Plutarch adds that 'they consider the cow to be an image of Isis and of the earth.' There follows the rite of pouring drinking water into a golden casket, which is itself inside a sacred box; the people then shout 'Osiris has been found' A similar ceremony seems to be mentioned by Plutarch in 52, 372 B-C : 'At the time of the winter solstice they lead the cow seven times around the temple of the sun, and the circumvention is called the Search for Osiris.' Cf. too the allusion to Hermes giving Isis a cow-headed helmet when her crown had been removed by Horus (19, 358 D). It is from Hathor that Isis derives her form as a cow, and she is often shown with this head-dress from the New Kingdom onwards; cf. Maria Münster, *Isis*, 119 f.; Hopfner, *Tierkult*, 68 ff.; one incidental result of the process was the identification of Isis and Io. While Isis remains, in spite of this, predominantly anthropomorphic in iconography (a combined human and bovine head appears in Leipoldt, *Bilderatlas*, 25, but perhaps it is a male figure : see added n. in Gressmann, *Orient. Rel.* 20 n. 1; cf. Anne Roullet, *Rome*, pl. 107 with p. 93, no. 126), there are contexts in which her form as a cow is conspicuous. A related form is undoubtedly that recorded by Herodotus, 2.129 f., who says that Mycerinus buried his daughter in a hollow cow-figure of gilded wood at Saïs. Whereas it was the goddess Neïth who was principally worshipped in this town, Herodotus (ch. 132) mentions the annual carrying abroad of the image in connection with the lamentation of Osiris, a god whom Herodotus refuses to name here, but who must be implied. Comparable is Remenet, the Isiac cow in the Denderah texts relating to the festival in Khoiak : it is said to carry inside it the mummy of Osiris (Remenet probably means 'the bearer'); and Diodorus Siculus, 1.85.5, also mentions a wooden cow covered with fine linen into which Isis placed the recovered body of Osiris; cf. Gressmann, *Osiris*, 19. The name Shentayet ('The Widow') was applied to Isis as a mourning cow-goddess in relation to Osiris; see *Wb.* IV, 518; Bonnet, *Reallexikon*, 404 f.; Maria Münster, *Isis*, 154; my *Plut. De Is. et Os.* 450 f. A stela of the early Ptolemaic era records the death of the Isis-cow called Ḥesat, so that she herself is here the object of the mourning rites : v. Spiegelberg, 'Ein Denkstein auf den Tod einer heiligen Isiskuh', *ZÄS* 43 (1906), 129-35. A syncretism of cow-cults is apparent, and Bonnet, loc. cit. is doubtless right in finding the tradition relating to Nut present in rites which use the cow-form as a protection for the dead.

From early times the sky-goddess Nut was regarded as a guardian of the dead, and her image, human in form, but sometimes with wings, was often depicted on the lids of sarcophagi; cf. my *Origins of Osiris*, 27; V. Ions, *Egn. Mythology*, 137 (fig.). Equated with the celestial cow, Nut is still protective in this sense, and on the couch of Tut'ankhamûn which has the forms of two cows holding it up (Piankoff, *The Shrines of Tut-Ankh-Amon*, pl. 14, 'The Couch of the Divine Cow'), an inscription between the two cow-heads refers to the King as 'beloved of Isis-Meḥet'; since Meḥet (Weret) was a name of the celestial cow meaning '(Great) Flood', the primaeval water which was regarded as the source of all life, Isis is here identified with the cow of heaven as Hathor is elsewhere; cf. C. Desroches-Noblecourt, *Toutankhamon et son temps [Petit Palais]* (Ed. 2, Paris, 1967), 128; cf. B. de Rachewiltz, *Egyptian Art*, 195, who misleads, however, when he speaks of this symbolism as 'the goddess Nut in twofold aspect as the celestial cow'. There is yet another connection in which Isis has the form of a cow : the worshippers of the Apis bull naturally paid special honour to the mother of each bull selected to be Apis, and this venerated cow was identified with Isis. In 1967 Emery discovered in North Saqqâra the first traces of a large structure dedicated to 'Isis, Mother of Apis' in the form of blocks of demotic graffiti in black ink with prayers and invocations to this goddess : v. *JEA* 53 (1967), 142 ff. Emery later describes the structure as a temple built by Nectanebo II (360-343 B.C.); v. *JEA* 55 (1969), 34. While Isis figures in a number of the objects found (v. ibid. pl. 24,5 and 6; pl. 25, 3 and 4) here no form as a cow is implied, unless the 'dummy mummy of a cow or bull' (*JEA* 55 [1969], 33 and pl. 8, 1-4) relates to Isis; cf. pl. 9, 2, a relief showing offerings made to Apis and perhaps his mother — certainly a cow-headed goddess. Many cattle burials were found near the site, and a mausoleum connected with Isis seems to be involved; in *JEA* 57 (1971), 12, Emery opted to call the building an 'Iseum' as a brief designation of the ancient title 'Resting-places of Isis, Mother of the Apis'. Cf. Strabo, 17.1.31; Mariette, *Mémoire sur la mère d'Apis* (Paris, 1856); Bonnet, *Reallexikon*, 50; Herodotus,

2.153, where the equation of Apis and Epaphus is mentioned; that of Isis and Io is of course connected; cf. Bergman, *Ich bin Isis*, 251 ff., who also points (p. 251 n. 5) to the cow-shaped Isis-Sothis, on which see Bonnet, *Reallexikon*, 744. In spite of this role of Isis as a cow which has recently been illumined, the basic affinity in the Apuleian symbol is different : here it is the Isis that mourns for Osiris, although she subsumes also the protective functions of Nut and Meḥet.

p. 274, 18 **levata** : The perfect passive participle, as Médan observes, is here used with a middle sense. A figure of a cow in a standing posture is indicated; cf. Drexler, 'Isis', 363; Bonnet, *Bilderatlas*, 30. Weber, *Terr*. pl. 37, 413, shows a figure of a seated sacred cow with the sun-disk between its horns; on p. 235 he cites others of this type. A small gilded bronze figure from San el-Hagar also belongs to the same category; v. *Cat. of Egn. Antiquities in the possession of F. G. Hilton Price* (London, 1897), I, 318, no. 2679; cf. p. 395, no. 3279, from Bubastis (a terracotta). A standing bovine figure, again with sun-disk between the horns, is to be seen in the Carlsberg Glyptothek : v. V. Schmidt, *De Graesk-Aegyptiske Terr*. pl. 61, 181; this may, however, be the Apis-bull, cf. Schmidt, p. 88. None of the figures referred to would have been suitable for what Apuleius describes since they are all too small. But the Remenet-cow of the Denderah text is said to be about a cubit in length : v. Chassinat, *Le Mystère d'Osiris*, 65; this would be portable without being absurdly minute. For a standing cow figured on an altar from Scarbantia see Wessetzky, *Ägypt. Kulte in Ungarn*, pl. 8 and p. 40, explained as Isis-Bubastis or Isis-Hathor-Bubastis.

bos [2] : Wower's emendation in 1606, <*erat ea*> *bos*, would seem at first to have some support from the fact that some codices (B3 D 0) read *Erat et bos*. These, however, have omitted the first part of the sentence with the first occurrence of *bos*, and they have *levatam* agreeing with *palmam* (... *palmam virentem levatam. Erat et bos omnia parentis*). The repetition of *bos* is not contrary to the Apuleian manner. Helm compares the repetition of *corona* in ch. 12 (275, 15), admittedly a more consciously emphasized locution.

p. 274, 18-19 **deae fecundum simulacrum** : Enallage for *deae fecundae simulacrum*; cf. Hofmann and Szantyr, *Lat. Syntax*, 159 f. and Bernhard, *Stil*, 215. The idea may be present, at the same time, that the image of the goddess was itself an influence on creativity; certainly her immanence in the image was assumed.

p. 274, 19 **residens umeris** : If the cow-image were in the form of a mask like that of Anubis, it would consist only of the head and neck and would rest on the priest's shoulders, in which case the plural *umeris* would be literally applicable. It would also be so applicable if two priests were carrying a large statue; cf. the statue of Harpocrates in Leipoldt, *Bilderatlas*, 42 and Perdrizet, *Terr*. 112; also Diod. Sic. 17.50 (= Hopfner, *Fontes*, 145) on the priests of Ammon carrying the god 'on their shoulders'. But we are expressly told here that one priest was carrying the image (*proferebat unus*) and that the cow was figured standing upright. It must therefore have been a statue, doubtless standing on a plinth and not too large for one priest to carry on his shoulder. *Umeris* will accordingly represent a factual singular, the usage being probably poetic (cf. Hofmann and Szantyr, *Lat. Syntax*, 16 f.) as also is the omission of *in* before *umeris*.

p. 274, 20 **beato** : Médan wishes to construe the adjective with *ministerio* : 'du clergé saint'; so too P. Vallette and J. Lindsay. On the whole this seems preferable to the application, in effect, of a double epithet to *gressu*, even if *gestuosus* is read.

cista : This is mentioned by Plutarch, *De Is. et Os.* 39, 366 F, as 'the sacred box which has inside a golden casket'; into the casket drinking water is poured, and the people shout. 'Osiris has been found!' In the Khoiak rites of Denderah this seems to be represented by the basket of rushes called *inšw* or *inšwty*; v. *Wb.* I, 100, 17 and Chassinat, *Le Mystère d'Osiris*, 65. It was a reliquary said to derive from the temple of Abydos and to contain the head of Osiris; v. Chassinat, op. cit. 121, col. 66; on p. 213 he seeks to identify Plutarch's 'casket' (κιβώτιον) with the *Wšb* or situla, but this is unlikely even though Plutarch says that water was poured into it; it could have been poured as a libation on to the image of the divine head. Cf. D. Bonneau, *La Crue du Nil*, 284. In his commentary on the locus in the second part of his book (1968, pp. 587 ff.) Chassinat makes no reference to the situla; indeed the word used for the vase here is quite different (col. 66, *krḥt*). Chassinat shows (pp. 590 f.) that there are three elements in the object described in the Denderah texts. First is the basket of rushes (*inšwty*), said to contain the head of the god; it is then said, however, that the head is 'within the secret box' (*ḥn stꜣy*)' which is described as made of reeds (*mrw*) and as a receptacle (*kꜣr*) of which 'no one knows what is inside it'. In spite of this the text goes on, engagingly, to tell us that 'the august head, adorned with the Upper Egyptian crown, in a vase (*krḥt*) is inside it.' So then we have a basket of rushes, a secret box, and a vase. The whole thing is said to bear designs which include a *djed*-pillar with crook and flail, as well as two falcons (Isis and Nephthys), the children of Horus, and Thoth. The Osirian reference is emphasized right through.

Perhaps some of the complexities have been shed in the Apuleian rite; his *cista* will doubtless refer to the enveloping box or basket. The kind of object described in the texts in Denderah is probably represented, as Chassinat, op. cit. 592, points out, in Bénédite, *Le temple de Philae* (*MIFAO* 13, 1893), pl. 40 (top register) and pl. 41 (middle register). In Graeco-Roman representations the clearest instance is perhaps on the relief which adorns an altar dedicated to Isis (ISIDI SACR(um)) which is now in the Capitoline Museum in Rome : v. H. Stuart Jones, *The Sculptures of the Museo Capitolino* (Oxford, 1912), pl. 91, 12 with p. 539 of the text volume, where the object is dated to the second century A.D.; cf. Leipoldt, *Bilderatlas*, 57 [279]; Gressmann, *Osiris*, fig. 9 (centre). The casket here figured has a cover on which a serpent is coiled, raising its head; the crescent moon (with ears of corn above it) which embellishes the body of the casket recalls Plutarch's statement, *De Is. et Os.* 39 *ad fin.* A serpent (perhaps two) rises from a similar object figured on the gravestone of a priestess of Isis which is now in the Museo Nazionale, Rome; v. Gressmann, *Osiris*, fig. 7 and p. 31, where he notes that the cover is raised and serpents are coming up from within; the same object is shown in Leipoldt, *Bilderatlas*, 58 ('Grabaltar der Cantinea Procla'); also comparable is the gravestone of another priestess of Isis in Leipoldt, *Umwelt*, III, 280, figuring a basket with a serpent coiled round it. A beautiful representation in red porphyry from Beneventum shows a serpent rising from the *cista*; it has recently been published by the expert hand of H. W. Müller (*Der Isiskult im antiken Benevent*, Berlin, 1969, pl. 32, 2) and he points out (p. 107) that this figure, like others, marks the object as originally made of wickerwork.

The half-moon is shown here, but not on the example mentioned by Lafaye, *Hist. du culte*, 298, no. 113, which has a rising serpent. For a lid of a *cista* found in Cologne see Grimm, *Ägypt. Rel. im röm. Deutschland*, 153, no. 34 A and pl. 27. It is hard to estimate the actual size of such an object. Could it have been carried by one priest as the Apuleian account indicates? A basket-like object reproduced by Leipoldt, *Bilderatlas*, 59 [297] from Edgar, *Graeco-Egyptian Coffins*, 70 (and pl. 31, 33.215), is shown in the covered hands of two priests, and Leipoldt boldly captions it 'Mystischer Korb mit verhüllten Händen gehalten'. An amphora is carried, however, in this manner by a priest in the Isiac procession of a Vatican relief (Leipoldt, 56 [292]); at the same time the general shape of the object in Leipoldt's no. 59 [297] certainly justifies his caption, although Edgar, loc .cit. is content with the vague expression 'a large object'. Comparable with the instance figured in the Capitoline Museum is a *cista* depicted in the 'Casa degli Amorini dorati' in Pompeii (XVI, VI, 7) and briefly described by A. Sogliano in *Not. Scavi* 1907, 556 (fig. 6 on p. 555). This house contained a shrine devoted to the Isiac cult and its paintings include figures of Isis and Anubis; another panel contains the *cista* referred to, which George Boyce, *Pompeian Lararia*, Rome, 1937, 57, describes as 'a large cylindrical cista with conical cover, apparently woven of reeds like wickerwork and adorned on the front with two slender wands crossed in the form of an X, and a crescent moon'. It is striking that this representation includes clear elements of the receptacle described in the Denderah texts : it is woven of reeds, and its crossed wands manifestly recall the crossed crook and flail of Osiris; the crescent moon occurs elsewhere too, as we have seen. A smaller chest depicted in the same Pompeian panel is without the crescent moon, but has the crossed wands. See further M. Della Corte, *Historia : Studi Storici* 8 (1934), 367, fig. 7 (the caption includes 'ciste sacre'); Schefold, *Vergessenes Pompeji*, pl. 149, 1; Tran Tam Tinh, *Isis à Pompéi*, pl. 15, 2 with pp. 107, 130; on p. 144 he points to another example, from the Pompeian temple of Isis (pl. 10, 1, lower register), where large snakes flank the box. A further example which Tran Tam Tinh notes on p. 153 as deriving from the 'villa rustica' of N. Popidius Florus is referred to in a report of the excavation by

Giovanna Zurlo-Pulzella in *Not. Scavi* 1921, 456, who states that it was accompanied by other Isiac symbols (a hydria, a mask of the goddess and a winged sphinx); unhappily no photograph is added, but a uraeus is said to rise from the *cista*.

Apuleius emphasizes that the box holds secret things and conceals within it the hidden attributes of the sublime faith; the idea of secrecy is three times pointed : in *secretorum capax*, in *penitus celans*, and in *operta*; cf. *Metam.* 6.2 (130, 8), *per tacita secreta cistarum*. Translators have often rendered *operta* with 'mysteries' or the like, but here a distinction needs to be drawn. The words 'mystic' and 'mystery' have originally to do with matters pertaining to the initiate, the μύστης, but since these matters were generally regarded as secret, the notion of secrecy in time coloured the meanings of the words. This has not happened in the classical terms, and so it is desirable that the meanings should be separated. That the sacred box contained secret objects is often stressed elsewhere. Tibullus, 1.7.48, speaks of the 'light box that shared the secrets of its holy objects' (*et levis occultis conscia cista sacris*), and this is in an Osirian context. It will be recalled that a 'secret box' is mentioned in the Denderah texts. A 'secret chest' (*'fdt štзt*) is a conspicuous object in funerary associations, and in his inaugural lecture, *Een Mysteriekist Ontsluierd* (Leiden, 1969), M. Heerma van Voss showed that this box, entrusted to Anubis as 'guardian of the secret' (*ḥry sštз*), held the canopic jars in which the entrails of the dead were kept. Anubis is usually shown couchant on this box, and so it cannot be identical, as Heerma van Voss shows (pp. 4-5), with the 'secret chest' (*'fdt štзt*) mentioned in cols. 81-2 of the Denderah text: this is applied to a shrine (*ỉtrt*, see *Wb.* I, 148, 11) in which, placed on a barque, the effigy of Sokar is taken to the necropolis; although Anubis is said in the text to be upon it, the representation in Mariette, *Dendérah*, IV, pls. 65 and 67, show a falcon there; see Chassinat, *Le Mystère d'Osiris*, II, 632. There is, it is true, a common funerary purpose uniting all the 'secret boxes' of the Egyptian funerary tradition. The Apuleian *cista* must, however, be derived from the *ḥn štзy* of the Denderah text, which describes it as holding a vase which contained the 'august head' of Osiris; serpents were perhaps an additional element. Plutarch's mention of water being poured into this vase suggests a connection with the hollow effigies of the god which, according to the Denderah text, were to be filled with barley and earth, so that the resulting verdure symbolized the life warranted by the god; see my remarks in *Plut. De Is. et Os.* 452 f.

It was Hildebrand *ad loc.* who first suggested that the *cista* contained a phallus, although he was content to quote Clem. Alex. *Protr.* 16 (actually 2.22.4, ed. Stählin p. 17), a passage which does not deal specifically with the Egyptian *cista* : αἱ κίσται αἱ μυστικαί, the locution used, suggests the usage of the Dionysiac and Eleusinian mysteries, and Dionysus is indeed mentioned. The gist of the passage is that the sacred objects include cake. poppies, ivy and the like, but more important is the female member. De Jong, *De Apuleio Isiacorum Myst. Teste*, 45 ff., supports Hildebrand's suggestion with a quotation from Hippolytus, *Ref. omn. haer.* 5.7.23 (= Hopfner, *Fontes*, 435) which sums up the rites of Isis as being merely the seizure of the phallus of Osiris and the quest for it by Isis. De Jong then quotes the allusion made by Plutarch, *De Is. et Os.* 18, 358 B, to the loss of the phallus in the myth. It is by no means invariable, however, for myth to be reflected in ritual; cf. G. S. Kirk, *Myth : Its Meaning and Functions in Ancient and Other Cultures* (Cambridge, 1970), 12 ff. De Jong's quotation from Diod. Sic. 1.22.6 is more to the point, since Isis is there said to have made the phallus of Osiris a venerated object in her rites. The *cista* is not mentioned, and it may be that the occasional representation of Osiris as being ithyphallic is meant; cf. Plut. *De Is. et Os.* 51, 371 E, although even this was more characteristic of Min. Gressmann, *Osiris*, 31 (cf. his *Orient. Rel.* 39 f.) propounds a synthetic view of the contents of the *cista*, suggesting that live snakes and an image of Osiris as a corn mummy or relic were in it, as well as a figure of his phallus; for the last item he compares Plut. *De Is. et Os.* 18 (see above) and 36 (the phallic rites of the Pamylia are mentioned and also the construction by Isis of an image of the phallus of Osiris for veneration in phallic processions); but neither passage refers to the *cista*. A phallus is possibly depicted on one of the two *cistae* shown on a gravestone from Ostia relating to a man who was priest of both Isis Ostiensis and of the Mater Deum : v. Benndorf and Schöne, *Die antiken Bildwerke des Lateranensischen Museums* (Leipzig, 1867), pl. 17, 2; if it is a phallus, it should be referred to the cult of the Mater Deum, as the authors state on p. 54; cf. *CIL* XIV, 429 = Vidman, *SIRIS* 252, no. 543; Squarciapino, *Culti Orientali ad Ostia*, 15; H. Graillot, *Culte de Cybèle*, 179. A revealing point about these two *cistae* is that they plainly show a vase enclosed in a box or basket and so recall Plutarch's account. That a phallus was among the sacred objects contained in the *cista* is a view that must therefore be rejected, as H. Herter rightly does in *PW* s.v. Phallos (1938), 1715, after noting evidence (Clem. Alex. *Protr.* 2.19.4 ed. Stählin p. 15) that such an object (the phallus of Dionysus) was contained in the *cista mystica* of the cult of the Cabiri. Still less can one credit the view of Rech and Saint-Croix (cited by De Jong, op. cit. 5) that a phallus was hidden in the *urnula*, the next object mentioned by Apuleius. A strong sexual element is certainly present in the attitude to Osiris reflected in the ancient tradition; it receives warm expression in the *Festival Songs of Isis and Nephthys* and in the iconographic representation of the renewal of life in the dead Osiris, where Isis is shown as a falcon settling over his phallus; cf. E. Otto, *Osiris and Amon*, pls. 17-20. Nevertheless it is hardly right to say, as R. E. Witt does (*Isis Gr.-R.* 85), that 'the Egyptian tradition has phallic worship as its core'; the evidence he there produces is weak.

The possible influence of the other mystic rites upon the symbolism of the Isiac cult must of course be considered, but in its essence, as Wittmann justly urged, the significance of the Isiac *cista* can best be explained by the detailed description of the Denderah texts. The Eleusinian *cista* contained ears of corn and the image of a vulva; for the latter see Nilsson, *Gesch. Gr. Rel.* I,

658 f. and Deubner, *Attische Feste*, 79 ff. Of these two symbols the first, the ears of corn, may well have been received from the rite of Demeter into that of Isis; this is suggested in representations both of the Isiac *cista* and of Isis herself; cf. n. *ad* ch. 3 (268, 10), *spicis etiam Cerialibus*; also Drexler, 'Isis', 443 f., though a too facile assumption is made there that the *cistae* of Demeter and Isis are practically identical. More problematic are the serpents depicted on several of the Graeco-Roman *cistae* of Isis. Wittmann, p. 64, reminds us that such serpents are seen on Bacchic *cistae* as figured on coins of Asia Minor of the second and first centuries B.C. See e.g. Fr. Lenormant s.v. Cista Mystica in Dar.-Sag. (1887), fig. 1545 on p. 1205 (a *cistophorus* of Adramyttium); cf. O. Jahn, *Hermes* 3 (1869), 317-34, esp. 323; Mau, *PW* s.v. Cista (1889), 2591 f.; H. B. Walters, *Class. Dict.* (Cambridge, 1916), 239, fig. 135; S. W. Stevenson, *Dict. of Roman Coins* (London, 1899, repr. 1964), 204 f. When these representations are compared with those of the Isiac *cistae* in Graeco-Roman sources, the similarity is so manifest that one is compelled to believe that the Egyptian cult has taken over the emerging serpents from the Dionysiac cult. It is true that Egyptian religion provides a variety of important divine serpents; cf. n. *ad* ch. 3 (268, 9-10.), *sulcis insurgentium viperarum cohibita*; and Isis herself as well as Osiris becomes intimately associated, if not identified with a serpent form. That she was so associated with a serpent emerging from a box or basket is very doubtful; it is the precise pictorial *milieu* that is lacking in the Egyptian tradition. Wittmann, p. 65, proposes a derivation from the serpent which, according to him, crosses the Osirian reliquary-shrine in the nome-sign of Abydos; this is certainly true of forms of the sign in the Graeco-Roman era (v. *Wb.* V, 222 and Steindorff, *Die ägyptische Gaue* [Abh. Leipzig, 1909], 4, a list of Ptolemaic origin); the earlier forms were different in this respect, and Edel has shown that the sign for a sail was present at first : v. *Ägyptologische Studien* (FS. Grapow, ed. O. Firchow), 73-5. Even so there is only a slight resemblance in a part of the developed nome-sign to a box or basket; cf. Steindorff, op. cit. 14; and the serpent does not emerge. At the same time Wittmann admits the influence of the Bacchic *cista*. H. W. Müller, *Der Isiskult im antiken Benevent*, 107, on the other hand, denies that 'der Korb als kultisches Requisit' is attested in the Egyptian Isis-cult, believing rather that it was taken over from the Hellenistic Bacchic Mysteries; he refers to similarly shaped baskets in the Mysteries of Cybele and Attis. At the same time he thinks that the serpent on the basket lid points plainly to the Egyptian cult. The converse of these two views seems more acceptable : a 'secret box' in the tradition of the Osirian Denderah texts is confirmed to some extent by Plutarch and is surely the true source of the Apuleian *cista*. But the serpentine concomitant seems to come from the Greek rites. Perhaps an Egyptian interpretation was then added; certainly it would not be difficult to connect the serpent with Isis. This would involve a rare procedure — an *interpretatio Aegyptiaca* of a symbolism borrowed from Greece.

p. 275, 2 **summi numinis** : The reference is to Osiris, who is regarded as incorporated in the vessel on which such loving detail is now lavished. On this kind of vessel, the 'Canopic Osiris' which figures Osiris Hydreios, the image of the god is prominently represented, so that the subsequent denial of a likeness to the form of an animal, bird or even man might seem to be contradicted in the allusion to human form, since Osiris is always anthropomorphic. Some examples, it is true, do not depict the god at all; in two instances from Beneventum the main motif is the sun-disk with flanking uraei : v. H. W. Müller, *Der Isiskult im antiken Benevent*, pl. 30 with pp. 96 f. When Osiris is represented, the top of the vessel is usually shaped to figure his head; v. von Bissing, *Ägypt. Kultbilder*, pls. 4 (three examples), 5 (11b), 8 (fig. 18) with p. 29; Bonnet, *Reallexikon*, 369, fig. 93; Anne Roullet, *Rome*, pls. 50, fig. 66, 118. figs, 164-5 with pp. 97 ff. Apuleius is clearly thinking of the vase itself, as opposed to figures carved on it; he regards it as an embodiment of the god. See further on line 6, *urnula*. De Jong, *De Apuleio Isiacorum Myst. Teste*, 5, rightly rejects, as we have already noted, the view that *summi numinis ... effigiem* will refer to a phallus hidden in the vessel.

p. 275, 2-3 **non pecoris, ... avis, ... ferae ... hominis** : A. A. Barb, 'Diva Matrix', 224 n. 119, makes the intriguing suggestion that 'this fourfold negation seems to refer to some important and very old conception.' He continues thus : 'If we substitute for the three kinds of animals their generally accepted "kings" (bull, lion, eagle) we have (including man) the four faces of the cherubims according to the vision of Ezekiel 1.5-10, reappearing in Revel. 4.7 and as the well-known symbols of the four Evangelists.' The parallel would be more convincing if Apuleius elsewhere revealed knowledge of the Jewish apocalyptic tradition. Nor is the symbolism of Roman tombstones, which Barb then invokes, a relevant system : there, we are told, 'the Lion represents the Fire, the Eagle the Air, the Dolphin (as "king" of the "fish" ...) the [sea-] Water.' More attractive is the association pointed by Barb when he then notes that 'the lids of the four "Canopic Jars" ... show the heads of a man, a dog, a jackal and a hawk.' Here, at any rate, we are line with the historical origin of the object discussed. The correspondence, however, is not exact, though Barb suggests that this group represents 'the four animated kinds of beings : man, bird, domestic quadruped (dog) and wild quadruped (jackal).' Perhaps there is no system at all behind the four categories, at least not in any esoteric sense.

p. 275, 3 **repertu** : This word occurs in ch. 2 (267, 5) and in *Flor.* 3 (3,12), but in no other author.

p. 275, 4 **novitate** : The word conveys the subjective impression of novelty or strangeness. Obviously the object had been well-known for centuries in the cult.

p. 275, 5 **ineffabile** : Pliny, *HN* 5.5.1, is the first attested user of this word, which occurs three times in Apuleius; v. Oldfather et al. *Index Apul.* 209.

p. 275, 6 **urnula** : The vessel here described is, in the main, a representation of Osiris Hydreios or 'Canopic Osiris'; but it also has the qualities of a hydreion

used as a sprinkler, and no example can be cited which combines these proper-
ties. Its role as an emblem of the highest deity (Osiris), its rounded base, and
its embellishment with Egyptian figures are features which point to Osiris
Hydreios : see Perdrizet, *Terr.* 75 ff.; Erman, *Rel.* (1934), 433, fig. 184 = Bonnet, *Reallexikon*, 369, fig. 93; von Bissing, *Ägypt. Kultbilder*, 28 f., who points
out that the first appearance on coins is in the fifth year of Claudius; Roeder,
Bronzefiguren, § 657; Hopfner in Bonnet, *Reallexikon*, 369; Grimm, *Ägypt.
Rel. im röm. Deutschland*, 36 f. with fig. 8; Tran Tam Tinh, *Herculanum*,
33 ff.; Anne Roullet, *Rome*, 97 ff. A fine example of the second century A.D.
is one from Ras es-Soda in the Alexandria Graeco-Roman Museum (P. 444,
Inv. no. 25787); the god's head is surmounted by the double plume with
sun-disk and horns, while among the gods figured in the relief below are Harpocrates, Isis and Nephthys; cf. Adriani, *Annuaire*, 1935-39, 143 f. For an
example in terracotta relating to Roman Britain see Eve and John Harris,
The Oriental Cults in Roman Britain, 89. But the long spout and handle with
large curve are characteristics of the sprinkler; so is the serpent on the handle,
although the uraeus is also figured on vases of the Osiris Hydreios type. In
view of this, the vagueness of some comments is understandable. Thus Danielle
Bonneau, *La Crue du Nil* (Paris, 1964), 283, opines that it is not a well-deter-
mined form; she cites Frankfort, *Kingship and the Gods*, 391 n. 39, who scarcely
faces up to the details; she cites the account by Clem. Alex. (= Hopfner,
Fontes, 372 f.), but two vessels are mentioned by him, the *spondeion* and the
hydreion, the former of which probably corresponds to the situla of ch. 10.

It was Weber in his *Drei Untersuchungen zur ägyptisch-griechischen Religion*
(Heidelberg, 1911). 29-48, who first showed in detail that the so-called Canopic
vessels derive from the ancient Egyptian tradition of the jars which held the
viscera of the dead; they have no original connection with Canopus. He
also showed that the god involved in the later tradition is Osiris, associated
with water and the Nile. Although these Osirian vessels are not attested for
any time before the first century A.D., it is the old funerary tradition that is
reflected in them, with Osiris, the leader of the beatified dead, used as the
reigning symbol. In a subsequent discussion (*Terr.* 19 ff.) Weber stresses the
mummiform aspect of the Canopic vessel, calling it 'Osiris als mumienformiges
Gefäss' (p. 21). The type is well represented in coins of the imperial era, and
sometimes a male vessel has a female counterpart, which Weber (*Drei Untersuchungen*, 33) would call Isis-Thermuthis or Euthenia. There can be no doubt,
then, of the Osirian nature of this cult. But the application of the word *deus*
to Canopus by Rufinus (*Hist. eccles.* 11.26 = Hopfner, *Fontes*, 629 f.) in the
fourth century A.D. led to curious misconceptions, as Erwin Panofsky shows
in his study ' "Canopus Deus" : the Iconography of a Non-Existent God',
Gazette des Beaux-Arts 57 (1961), 193-216; cf. J. Baltrušaitis, *La Quête d'Isis*
(Paris, 1967), 33, fig. 3 (after A. Kircher). Panofsky justly emphasizes the time-
gap between the last era of a flourishing use of visceral jars at the end of the
New Kingdom and the emergence of the Canopic images in the imperial era;

he stresses too some of the differences between the earlier and later phenomena :
the later vessel was an image rather than a receptacle, it had a new rose-em-
broidered base (or one with a crown of uraei, see Breccia, *Monuments*, I
[1926], pl. 29, fig. 86), and it carried figured designs on it as opposed to the
earlier hieroglyphs. Certainly there are still unsolved problems in the origin
and development of the Graeco-Roman form, and Stricker in *OMRO* 24
(1943), 1-10, has pointed to affinities in the aniconic forms of Amûn, following
a suggestion of Eduard Meyer recorded by Weber, *Terr.* 24 n. 40; for this
form and its similarity, sometimes, to an omphalos, see Daressy, *ASAE* 9
(1908), 64-9 and Wainwright, *ASAE* 28 (1928), 175-89. Be that as it may,
the vessel which can be justly called the Osiris Hydreios is clearly represented
in the hands of priests in scenes relating to Isiac processions. There is a good
example in the relief in Potsdam published by M. Schede in *Angelos* 2 (1926),
60 f. and pl. 4 and by Leipoldt in *Umwelt*, III, 392 (cf. Nilsson, *Gesch. Gr. Rel.*
II² 626 and pl. 11, 1); it is the last figure but one who is carrying the rounded
human-headed vessel in her hands — apparently the bearer is a woman, as
Schede notes on p. 61. We have observed above *ad* ch. 10 (274, 13) *amphoram*,
that the last of these figures is carrying an amphora. Several instances appear
in the procession figured on columns of the Iseum Campense, Rome, now in
the Capitoline Museum : see H. Stuart Jones, *Cat.* pl. 92, 14 and 15 with p. 360
and Leipoldt, *Bilderatlas* 60, 61 [288]; they are also given by Bosticco, *Musei
Capitol.*; *I Monumenti Egizi etc.* pl. 6, A c, pl. 7 A d and pl. 8, C a and by Anne
Roullet, *Rome*, pls. 28, 30, 32, and 33. These show Osiris-heads, but one figures
a crowned jackal-head much in the fashion of one of the early Canopic jars;
it is stated by Stuart Jones, op. cit. 360, to be the head of Anubis; perhaps it
reverts rather to Duamutef, although the figures on these vases suggest on the
whole that Osiris, Isis, Harpocrates and Anubis have replaced the Four Sons
of Horus. Anne Roullet, *Rome*, 99, states that 'on most if not all these reliefs,
the so-called Osiris Canopus are (sic) in fact often confused with canopic
jars'; she does not go into detail, and perhaps she is thinking especially of the
jackal-headed vase. The others are quite different from the early types, although
the whole idea is one which is based on them. In the Museum of the Depart-
ment of Egyptology at Uppsala University there is a charming terracotta
figure of a priest carring an Osiris Hydreios; it was examined by the writer
in August 1970 and is comparable to that shown in Vogt, *Terr.* pl. 1, 3; cf. his
text, p. 2.

Equally there are clear instances on the monuments of the long-spouted
vessel with curved handle being used in Isiac rites. The third officiant in the
processional group on the relief in the Vatican (Leipoldt, *Bilderatlas*, 56 [292])
is carrying a vessel of this type, and a uraeus rises out of it; two figures in a
fresco from Herculaneum (Leipoldt, 55 [286]) carry a vessel roughly similar,
except that the spout is much longer and more like that described by Apuleius.
Isis or an Isis-priestess has a similar object in her right hand in Weber, *Terr.*
pl. 3, 28, and a serpent is present here too; Weber, p. 49, thinks that the serpent

constitutes the handle. In discussing a vase which is missing from a priestly figure in bronze in the Fouquet collection, Perdrizet, *Bronzes*, 49, thinks that it was probably like that portrayed by Apuleius, and he compares the vase in the ritual fresco from Herculaneum (Leipoldt, 53 [294] = Tran Tam Tinh, *Herculanum*, pl. 27). This we hesitantly grouped under the evidence for the amphora mentioned at the end of ch. 10. It certainly lacks the Osirian top, but its base of flowers supports the idea that it is an Osiris Hydreios; cf. Weber, *Drei Untersuchungen*, 46 f. and Tran Tam Tinh, op. cit. 36 f. Perdrizet's discussion (*Terr.* 75-7) of 'Sarapis Hydreios' is not among his best. It includes the astonishing statement (p. 76), 'or Isis n'est pas à proprement parler une divinité funéraire'. What is clear is that the long-spouted type of vessel is for pouring water. The Osiris or Sarapis Hydreios is really a cult image and cannot, in a strict sense, be linked with the function of the sprinkler. Tran Tam Tinh, op. cit. 37, may be right in stressing the idea that Apuleius is thinking especially of the contents of the vase — the fructifying water of the Nile with which Osiris is identified. He is also thinking of the importance of the uraeus, and this he is probably associating with Isis.

The Osiris Hydreios, in view of its origin and ritual decoration, must be basically explained in another way. This type of jar was originally a receptacle for visceral remains carefully preserved; it was a symbol therefore of continued life. The themes of the reliefs on the Graeco-Roman type of jar show how this idea is now associated especially with Osiris and his circle; the vessel is a symbol of physical immortality. Since the vessel described by Apuleius combines two quite different types, the explanation may lie in a mental telescoping of two objects. On the other hand, the two types may of course have been amalgamated in a form which the archaeological record does not happen to attest.

In 'Diva Matrix', 200-202 ('The Isis-Emblem in the "Golden Ass"') A. A. Barb wishes to explain the *urnula* as a form of the magical uterus which furthers child-bearing; of this he finds many manifestation in far-flung regions and religions. He says (p. 201) of the present passage : 'This description not only uses the words we find in anatomical descriptions for parts of the uterus, but also fits well with the magical and anatomical pictures with which we had to deal.' An instance of his first point is the word *canalis* : on p. 224 n. 124 he says that this is, according to Celsus, *De medicina*, 4.1 'the correct medical name for what he also calls "Cervix" ... of the "Vulva" '. The word is also used in medicine for several other parts of the body, as in the ear and throat : v. *Thes. L.L.* 3, 225, 23 ff. Elsewhere Apuleius uses it to mean the valley of a stream, as in *Metam.* 6.14 (138, 22) or a path or track as in 6.18 (141, 21); 9.11 (211, 7). A specialized medical application seems unlikely here. On p. 224 n. 125 Barb admits to finding the last sentence (beginning *eius orificium* ...) 'the obscurest part of the description'; he objects to taking *orificium* as 'spout' and himself translates (p. 201) : 'its mouth, slightly raised (rimmed?), jutted out in an extended channel with long neck (? "rivulo").' The figure of the uterus on his pls. 25 and 26 hardly show a 'long neck' with the exception of

26 b, which is from an anatomical work; pl. 33 g (a gem in Athens) is more convincing. Barb is forced to concede (p. 224 n. 125) that 'it might be that Apuleius himself relied here less on autopsy than on a written description which he did not fully understand.' There are few signs elsewhere of a written *Vorlage* to Book XI. Of inaccuracy there may be signs. Thus it does seem that the features of two types of vessels are being combined in the description, but this, after all, can easily happen to a quite observant commentator. Again, the Latin word *ansa* definitely means 'handle', and when Barb (p. 225 n. 126) claims that 'the description of the "handle" could well apply to the two snake-like appendices extending (horizontally) from the "*fundus*" of the uterus, he snaps the cord of credibility; 'snake-like' can well be conceded, but *ansa* is singular. The initial *urnula* is equally unequivocal, and there is no suggestion of a metaphorical use.

These details apart, one is tempted to ask what possible place there was for a symbolic uterus in a festival of Isis. On this point Barb (p. 201) refers to a haematite intaglio in Paris as evidence 'that an image of the uterus was really carried about or at least shown held in the hand of a divine figure.' The gem is reproduced in his pl. 33 d; see also Delatte and Derchain, *Intailles Magiques*, 255, no. 359 and cf. Bonner, *Stud. Mag. Am.* D 143. Here the main figure is the ram-headed Khnum, and it is he who holds the uterus in his right hand; he is presenting it to an infant who is emerging from the head of the god Bes, or at least is seated on his head; behind Khnum stands Isis with a sistrum in one hand and a vase in the other. No procession or rite in involved here. Khnum is a major creator-god in the Egyptian tradition; Bes has affinities too with procreation and birth. Isis here plays a subsidiary role, and the general purpose of the amulet is clearly to confer success in child-bearing. Barb thinks that the child is Harpocrates, but although Bonner, *op. cit.* 276 finds a 'tiny Harpocrates' seated on the uterine symbol in the rather similar gem published by him, this is not beyond question. Indeed the Isiac significance is belied rather by the reverse of Barb's gem, which shows Seth on an uterus; v. Delatte and Derchain, *loc. cit.* and Barb. pl, 33 e; surely Seth here is benign and not hostile, akthough he may be used as a threat 'in case the womb becomes troublesome' (Barb, *JWCI* 22 [1959], 370). If Barb is right, the reference of *summi numinis ... effigies* will be to Isis and not Osiris, since to him the *urnula* is the 'uterus-image of the great mother-goddess Isis'. In ch. 30 (291, 6) Osiris is called *maiorum summus et summorum maximus*, but in ch. 5 (269, 10-11) Isis too is *summa numinum*, so that the choice here lies open. It is of interest that some of the representations discussed by Barb (pl. 25 a) were explained by Max Pieper in *MDAIK* 5 (1934), 141, as figures of the reliquary containing the head of Osiris; cf. his pl. 22, no. 11915 (Berlin). Delatte and Derchain, Bonner and Barb are undoubtedly right in seeing an uterus in them, but in his *Addenda* on p. 238 Barb says that 'the vessel carried by the priest on the relief in Rome (= Leipoldt, *Bilderatlas* 56 [292], discussed above) clearly shows the uterus-shape and serpent-handle'; he also compares a pot from

Hadra, published by Adriani, *Annuaire* 3 (1952), pl. 12, 1-3 and p. 21. Here, then, Barb seems to change his ground; the *urnula* is now a real *urnula*, but with suggestions of an uterus.

Gressmann, *Orient. Rel.* 39 f. seems to regard the *urnula* as part of the *cista*, and it is true that Plutarch, *De Is. et Os.* 39 describes a casket (κιβώτιον) as being inside the sacred box, and Chassinat regards the κιβώτιον as being a vase; cf. my *Plut. De Is. et Os.* 452 with a brief reference to Barb's view. In fact Barb does not connect the *urnula* and the *cista*, although it could be urged, on the analogy of the Eleusinian *cista mystica*, that if a divine uterus appeared anywhere in the Graeco-Roman rites of Isis, it would have been in the *cista*. A good point in Barb's theory is that it would explain the strangeness or novelty (*ipsa novitate reverendam*) assigned by Apuleius to the object. But that might be the subjective emphasis of an author not himself familiar, previously, with all the sacred objects of the cult.

p. 275, 6 **quam rutundo** : The use of *quam* by itself to intensify the meaning of the following adjective probably derives from its common introduction of an exclamation as in *quam multa, quam paucis!* (Cic. *Fam.* 11.24.1). Médan compares the use of ὡς in ὡς ἀληθῶς. Plautus and Terence use *quam* similarly; v. *Amph.* 1.3.43; *Andr.* 1.1.109 (with an abverb).

p. 275, 7 **simulacris Aegyptiorum** : These were mainly of gods in the Osirian circle : see n. *ad urnula* above. The prototype of the Osiris Hydreios was the Canopic jar in which the entrails were kept; this had a lid representing the head of one of the four Sons of Horus, while on the body of the jar there were hieroglyphs which included the name of the deceased; see e.g. H. W. Müller, *Sammlung München*, 55, 89 (nos. 27 and 28) with pp. 93 and 97. On the Osiris Hydreios the hieroglyphs were replaced by figures in relief, usually of gods or of divine symbols; see e.g. Anne Roullet, *Rome*, figs. 66 and 163.

effigiata : Apuleius is the first author to use this word; v. *Thes. L.L.* 5, 2, 184, 26 ff.

orificium : Used three times by Apuleius, the word is found elsewhere only in Macrobius. See also above *ad* line 6, *urnula*.

p. 275, 8 **altiuscule** : Although Apuleius is the only author to use this adverbial diminutive, the adjective *altiusculus* is found in Suetonius, *Aug.* 73; v. *Thes. L.L.* 1, 1770, 1 ff. See further Bernhard, *Stil*, 136 f.

canalem : See n. above *ad* line 6, *urnula*.

p. 275, 10 **aspis** : Cf. n. *ad* ch. 4 (269, 5), *aspis* and *ad* p. 274 20 above, *cista*; also ad line 6, *urnula*. The relief in the Vatican (Leipoldt, *Bilderatlas*, 56 [292]) shows a uraeus immediately above the handle of the pitcher. In this procession the first figure, too, a priestess, holds forward her left hand round which a uraeus is coiled, raising its head. Unlike the case with the *cista*, Greek parallels are not forthcoming here, and the uraeus is a divine serpent (the hooded cobra) with a distinctive role in Egyptian religion. Originally Wedjoyet, the cobra-goddess of Buto, she was the traditional protectress of the Pharaoh, appearing on his head-dress. One must assume that as an attribute of Isis or her priests, the uraeus still derives from this source, but that in Graeco-Roman times its appearance is proliferated. The description by Apuleius suits the uraeus very well, especially the 'streaked swelling' of the neck; cf. Margaret A. Murray on the *Naja nigricollis*. *JEA* 34 (1948), 117 f. with a reference to the black lines on the hooded cobra's neck as shown in early hieroglyphs.

CHAPTER 12

p. 275, 12 **accedunt** : L. Callebat, *Sermo Cotid.* 394 ff. notes the fondness shown by Apuleius for verbs compounded with prefixes; on p. 397 he examines the verbal forms of this chapter. He concludes that here, as elsewhere, the frequency of such forms derives from a striving for the picturesque and the dramatic, and rightly recognizes the literary and archaizing impetus.

p. 275, 13 **salutemque** : Cf. n. ad ch. 5 (270, 4), *dies salutaris*; also *ad* ch. 21 (283, 5-6), *precariae salutis*; and the use of *salus* in ch. 21 (283, 5, 6, 9). Whereas the phrase *spem salutis* in ch. 1 (266, 19) implies hope of deliverance in the physical sense only, the idea of spiritual salvation is probably present here in addition, since the transformation back into human form is to be accompanied by conversion to the faith of Isis.

p. 275, 13-14 **ad ipsum praescriptum ... ornatum** : See ch. 6, *init.* : 'a priest ... will carry a crown of roses attached to the sistrum in his right hand.' Hildebrand and Médan construe *ornatum* as a participle with *sistrum*, the former denying that ch. 6 says anything about the *ornatus* of the priest. Clearly he takes the word in the sense of 'dress'; in the sense of 'equipment' the reference is plain.

275, 15 **coronam consequenter** : For the adverb cf. *Metam.* 9.21 (218, 29); 10.2 (237, 4); 11.1 (266, 18), where 'as a result' or the like is the sense. See *Thes. L.L.* 4, 412, 71 ff. Here a meaning 'suitably', 'fittingly', i.e. 'as a fitting result', emerges from the *quod*-clause, for the crown is one of victory given to one who is overcoming Fortune; cf. n. ad ch. 6 (270, 10-11), *roseam ... coronam*.

p. 275, 16 **exanclatis** : Cf. ch. 6 (267, 17) and n.

p. 275, 17 **providentia** : This religious concept is likewise assigned to Isis in chs. 5 (270, 4); 10 (274, 6); and 15 (277, 20); v. n. *ad loc. ult.*

adluctantem : An Apuleian neologism; cf. *Metam.* 10.17 (250, 1) and *Thes. L.L.* 1, 1697, 59.

Fortunam : See n. *ad* ch. 15 (277, 4).

superarem : The subjunctive may be due to *oratio obliqua* implied by the previous mention of 'divine promise'. Its imperfect tense is apt : the victory is not yet complete.

p. 275, 18 **inclementi** : The meaning of this adjective elsewhere is 'harsh, rigorous', of persons or things; v. *Thes. L.L.* 7, 1. 937, 41 ff. Here it is plainly opposed to *placido ac prorsus humano gradu*.

p. 275, 21 **divinitus decedente** : Cf. the promise of Isis in ch. 6 (270, 17-18) : *meo iussu tibi constricti comitatus decedent populi.*

inrepo : The chapter begins with vivid present tenses, and now, after the intervening perfect *proripui*, a present tense recurs. Cf. ch. 26 (287, 19), *pervolavi*, and n. A desire for variety is perhaps the main factor. There are precedents in comedy, and Petronius combines the tenses; v. Hofmann and Szantyr, *Lat. Synt.* 307 and Callebat, *Sermo Cotid.* 429 f., who also cites J. M. H. Fernhout's Comm. on Book V, p. 24 (on a perfect tense surrounded by present tenses).

CHAPTER 13

p. 275, 22 **reabse** : For the form cf. *Metam.* 1.13 (12, 9) and *Apol.* 67 (76, 11) with Butler and Owen's n. ad loc. Forcellini cites Seneca, *Ep.* 108.32 for the view that *reapse*, used by Cicero, is an old form for *reipsa*. Lewis and Short, s.v., say that it is 'an old word which does not occur after Cicero', oddly ignoring the instances in Apuleius. Its use by him must, at the same time, be a conscious archaism.

p. 275, 22-23 **nocturni commonefactus oraculi** : Butler, who rarely misleads, here renders, 'But the priest ... had been warned of the oracle delivered to me during the night.' In ch. 6 (270, 15-17), however, Isis tells Lucius that she is also with the priest, 'instructing him in his sleep'. Now the priest is being reminded of his own experience. See n. *ad* ch. 6 (270, 16-17), *per quietem.*

p. 276, 1 **micanti corde** : The Ablative singular ending of the present participle in -*i* rather than -*e* is unclassical, as Médan notes; the ending in -*e* is particularly preferred in classical prose when the participle is not merely adjectival but acts as the predicate of the Ablative Absolute, as here. Hildebrand's *Index Rerum Gramm.* 671 s.v. Ablativus, suggests that Apuleius was somewhat perverse in this matter, preferring occasionally even forms like *decori* and *oneri* as Ablatives. He may, of course, have suffered at the hands of scribes.

p. 276, 1-3 **coronam devoravi** : The sight of an ass eating a garland of flowers was not unfamiliar to Romans in a ritual context, argues Berreth, p. 98, citing mainly Ovid, *Fasti*, 6.311, where reference is made to the festival of Vesta in which 'loaves are hung on asses decked with wreaths' (*coronatis ... asellis*); but in fact these wreaths seem to have been made of miniature loaves : see G. Wissowa in Roscher, *Lex. Myth.* VI, 256 f. s.v. Vesta on the Pompeian wall-painting of which he reproduces a drawing (fig. 2); cf. J. G. Frazer *ad* Ovid, *Fasti*, 6.311 (p. 230) and Franz Bömer (Heidelberg, 1938), p. 361; also Propertius, 4.1.21; Tib. 2.1.8; J. Lydus, *De mens.* 4.94. On the other hand Ovid, *Fasti*, 6.469, tells us that the asses were also decked with violets, so that Berreth's point may well be valid.

In *Lucius or Ass*, 54, the eating of roses is similarly the instrument of metamorphosis. The setting, however, is different, for there Lucius as an ass is compelled to take part in a theatrical show in Thessalonica which is to highlight the sexual union of an ass and a woman; and when a basket of flowers, including roses, is brought around, he immediately eats the roses and so achieves his transformation into a man, standing up naked before everyone. A similar show is arranged at the end of Book X in Apuleius, but Lucius the ass flees from it; and the deliverance through eating roses is artistically and effectively transferred to a religious procession.

p. 276, 2 **cupidus promissi cupidissime** : Max Bernhard, *Gnomon* 7 (1931), 666, approves of this proposal by Giarratano which conflates two groups of readings and combines, as Bernhard aptly notes, an Apuleian pleonasm with paronomasia. Zeugma might be a better term, since *cupidus* and *cupidissime* are used of mental and physical greed. For the pleonasm cf. ch. 16 (278, 16), *quam purissime purificatam.*

p. 276, 3-4 **protinus mihi delabitur etc.** : In *Metam.* 3.24 Apuleius goes into similar detail in describing the metamorphosis of Lucius into an ass. In *Lucius or Ass*, on the other hand, although the initial transformation is minutely portrayed (ch. 13), the change back into human form lacks any detail except for the stress on nakedness which Apuleius touches on more delicately in ch. 14. Literature dealing with miracles of healing naturally elaborates each event, as the Sarapis-Aretalogy from Delos does (v. H. Engelmann, *Die delische Sarapisaretalogie*, Meisenheim, 1964, 34 ff.) or the Praise of Imouthes—Asclepius (P. Oxy. 1381). Ovid, of course, often portrays metamorphosis, but with a very different atmosphere of far-removed mythology. *Mihi*, a 'Dativus sympatheticus', has poetic and popular associations, and probably derives from living speech; cf. Hofmann and Szantyr, *Lat. Syntax*, 94 f.; Callebat, *Sermo Cotid.* 261 f.

p. 276, 4 **deformis et ferina facies** : The thrice repeated *f*-sound admirably supports the idea expressed; cf. *ad* lines 5, 8 and 15-16.

p. 276, 5 **residet** : Van der Vliet proposes to emend to *residit*, and Latin usage in general would certainly support this. The codices, however, including the twelve consulted by me, are unanimous in reading *residet*, and Helm compares *Metam.* 1.14 (13, 4), *cardines ad foramina resident*, where most of the codices give this reading; F has a correction superscript in the same hand to *residunt*, and Robertson gives it in his text. Here, however, Robertson reads *residet*, bowing presumably to the unanimity of the manuscripts. The second vowel in *residet* is short, while that in *residit* is long, and Ryle, who supports van der Vliet's emendation, makes the point that *obesus residit* would 'give Apuleius' most frequent clausula, while *residet* would give a much less common one.' He cites Bernhard's discussion of the clausulae (*Stil*, 250 f.). The double trochee is indeed the most favoured clausula according to Bernhard's analysis, but the fact that he confined his attention to sentence-endings rather invalidates this interesting point.

pedum plantae per : A triple alliteration is not common, but in a sense it occurs, as we have seen, in *deformis et ferina facies* (line 4) and in *repetunt pristinam parvitatem* below (line 8); cf. n. *ad* lines 15-16.

p. 276, 9 **minutiem** : Cf. *Metam.* 9.27 (223, 15). Apuleius is the first to use this post-classical collateral form of *minutia*; v. *Thes. L.L.* 8, 1046, 10 ff.

p. 276, 10 **nusquam comparuit** : The record of readings given in previous editions is at fault here, the idea indicated being that only a much later hand in F gives the reading *comparuit*. This reading actually occurs also in B2, B3, D and O; further, it appears too in the *Editio Princeps*, which Robertson once described (CQ 18 [1924], 30) as 'an important witness', adding that it 'seems to be based on a lost MS. or MSS.' The adjacent tenses are, admittedly, present; hence van der Vliet's proposal *comparet*, for which cf. *Metam.* 8.21 (193, 15); 10.15 (248, 4); in these cases, however, the infinitive is used. Schober, *Comp. num.* 10, accepts van der Vliet's reading and notes with pleasure that *comparet. populi mirantur religiosis* yields a hexameter — a doubtful procedure in view of the stop after *comparet*. More plausible, metrically, is L. Chodaczek's argument in *Eos* 33 (1930-31), 534. He rejects *comparet*, urging that *cauda nusquam*, a double trochee, constitutes a favourite clausula (cf. n. *ad* line 5, *residet*). He also finds the ellipse of a verb an elegant process here, supplemented perhaps by an effective gesture. Cf. Callebat, *Sermo Cotid.* 447.

populi ... religiosi : In ch. 16 (279, 3) occurs the phrase *cuncti populi tam religiosi quam profani*, indicating that *populi* is the wider term which includes the faithful and the unattached bystanders. This belies Médan's attempt to take *religiosi* here as virtually adverbial.

p. 276, 12 **facilitatem reformationis** : The miracle wrought by Isis is here the power of metamorphosis. In the Egyptian tradition her miraculous deeds are often concerned with healing. It is she who heals and revives Osiris after finding him dead : see the *Songs of Isis and Nephthys*, 14, 25 ff. : 'She dispels the evil which appertains to thy flesh, / And the stroke as though it had never been' (Faulkner's translation, *JEA* 22 [1936], 130; further details follow). Cf. my *Plut. De Is. et Os.* 434. Medical and magical papyri refer to her role as the healer of Horus and invoke this situation as the paradigm for other sufferers. Cf. R. E. Witt, *Isis Gr.-R.* 185 ff. ('Healing the Sick'). Thus P. Ebers, 1, 12 ff., states that 'Horus was released by Isis from the evil done against him by his brother Seth, when he slew his father Osiris;' then comes the prayer, 'O Isis, great in magic, release me!' Cf. Diod. Sic. 1.25.6, where there is a confusion, however, between Horus and Osiris; v. my *Plut. De Is. et Os.* 355. Isis functions similarly in the episodes of the Metternich Stela and parallel texts; cf. C. E. Sander-Hansen, *Die Texte der Metternichstele* (Copenhagen, 1956); A. Klasens, *A Magical Statue Base*, 52 ff. In the Delian Sarapis-Aretalogy, for which see H. Engelmann, *Die delische Sarapisaretalogie*, 18 and 36 ff., Isis and Sarapis are called the 'saviours' of good men who have the correct religious beliefs; cf. P. Cair. Zen. 59,034 (= Grant, *Hellenistic Rel.* 144 f.) and P. M Fraser, 'Two Studies', 41 and 54; Artemidorus, *Oneir.* 2.39 (= Hopfner, *Fontes*, 357; Anubis and Harpocrates are named too). In the Sarapis-Hymn of Aelius Aristides, Sarapis is both healer and miracle-performer in other ways; cf. Anton Höfler, *Der Sarapishymnus des Ailios Aristeides* (Stuttgart, 1935), 46 ff.

and 71 ff. Tibullus, 1.3.27 f., tells us that votive tablets in the temples of Isis
attested her power to heal; she could cause or cure blindness according to
Ovid, *Ex Ponto*, 1.1.50-54; cf. Juv. 13.92-4; in the Delian Aretalogy Sarapis
makes the enemies of the faith speechless. The many silver and gold votive
eyes found in Delos seem to attribute a special power over eyesight to both
Isis and Sarapis; v. Roussel, *CED* 290 f. and for Egyptian antecedents H. de
Meulenaere, *CdÉ* 28 (1953), 255 f. The depiction of eyes and ears on Egyptian
stelae probably implied a divinity who beheld and heard his worshipper;
cf. P. F. Tschudin, *Isis in Rom*, 33 and 56 n. 179. Vespasian was said to have
healed two people at Alexandria through the power of Sarapis; v. Hopfner,
Fontes, 286; 293; 375 f. On the temper of credulity see R. M. Grant, *Miracle
and Natural Law* (Amsterdam, 1952), 64 f. As for miraculous metamorphosis,
Egyptian mythology is replete with this. In the *Contendings of Horus and Seth*,
for instance, Isis herself changes her form four times — into an old woman, a
beautiful maid, a bird (a kite), and a headless statue. Seth and his followers,
according to the myth, changed themselves into various animals; v. my *Conflict*,
102; 116 and my *Plut. De Is. et Os.* 545 f. There is also the belief, often expressed
in the *Book of the Dead*, that a deceased person's *ba* could achieve many kinds
of transformations. Further, Isis was regarded as especially potent in magic;
cf. Maria Münster, *Isis*, 192-6. According to Ovid, *Metam.* 9.771 ff. Isis changed
Iphis, the daughter of Telethusa, into a boy; see F. Arnaldi, 'L'episodio di
Ifi nelle "Metamorfosi" di Ovidio (IX, 666 sgg.) e l'IX Libro di Apuleio',
Atti del Convegno Internazionale Ovidiano, II (Rome, 1959), 371-5. Wittman
rightly stresses that the whole atmosphere of the book by Apuleius is fraught
with an aura of supernatural intervention; it begins with the epiphany of the
goddess and continues with a portrayal of a colourful procession which is
accompanied by music and sacred singing as well as by the display of the holiest
symbols of the faith. The metamorphosis of Lucius is the climax, and it supplies
the glorifying miracle which the age demanded as the confirmation of a religious
faith; cf. Reitzenstein, *Hellenistische Wundererzählungen*, 36; Merkelbach,
Isisfeste, 35 n. 28; E. R. Dodds *ad* Euripides, *Bacchae*, 704 ff. (on Dionysus
changing water into wine) and Merkelbach, *Roman und Mysterium*, 221. For an
Isis-procession in the reign of Ramesses II which prophesied the promotion
of a police-officer to the post of royal ambassador, see Erman, *Rel.* (tr. Wild,
1952), 187, citing Petrie, *Koptos*, pl. 19 (cf. p. 16). There the sacred barque of
Isis is borne on priests' shoulders; in line 9 we are told that he is chief of the
medjay (Nubian police). Isis is said to have stopped and beckoned to him,
indicating the promotion both to the status of *wpwty nsw* (royal ambassador)
and to the office of overseer of works.

p. 276, 12 **consona voce** : A doxology in regular use is suggested although
its timing is a spontaneous reaction to the miracle. In ch. 16 (278, 6-10) the
people address to Lucius an acclamation which begins *hunc omnipotentis hodie
numen augustum reformavit ad homines*; there the reference is too detailed and
deae numen specific to apply to a brief song of praise. Wittmann aptly compares

the scene in Xenophon's *Ephesiaca*, 5.13, when Habrocomes and Anthia find each other again through the help of Isis: the people of Rhodes salute Isis as the Great Goddess (μεγάλην θεὸν ἀνακαλοῦντες τὴν *Ἶσιν). The lovers, it may be added, proceed to proffer a more elaborate expression of thanks in the temple of Isis : 'O greatest goddess, we thank thee for our deliverance ...'; cf. Merkelbach, *Roman und Mysterium*, 111 ff. who compares *PGM* 24,1 : 'Great is Isis the Sovereign' (Μεγάλη *Ἶσις ἡ κυρία) and the reference to the reaction of the people in the Sarapis-Aretalogy of Maiistas (Powell, *Collectanea Alex.* 71,61 f.; Engelmann, *Die delische Sarapisaretalogie*, lines 30 ff. with Commentary, pp. 34 ff.) Cf. R. E. Witt, *Isis. Gr.-R.* ch. 18 and p. 254. The epithet μέγας was naturally used of other gods, and the precise reference of μέγα τὸ ὄνομα τοῦ θεοῦ in Vidman, *SIRIS* nos. 245, 304, 357 *not.* remains doubtful. In the first Hymn of Isidorus, 26 (*SEG* 8, 548) Isis is addressed as 'immortal Saviour' (σώτειρ' ἀθανάτη); see Vanderlip, *Hymns of Isidorus*, 31-2.

p. 276, 13 **beneficium** : Cf. ch. 12 (275, 12), *praesentissimi numinis promissa nobis accedunt beneficia*; 18 (280, 8), *deae providentis adorabile beneficium*; 21 (282, 10), *spe futura beneficiis praesentibus pignerata*; 24 (286, 10-11), *inremunerabili quippe beneficio pigneratus*. Jack Lindsay translates as 'lovingkindness' here— an attractive idea. But although *Thes. L.L.* 2, 1889, 1 ff. lists among the synonyms of *beneficium* words like *amicitia, liberalitas, munificentia*, and *gratia*, the word itself denotes a particular expression of loving-kindness (*benevolentia* or *beneficentia*) which is especially clear when a plural is used.

CHAPTER 14

p. 276, 14 **nimio** : For this meaning of *nimius* cf. ch. 1 (266, 12, *candore nimio*). Médan points out that *nimius* with the sense of *magnus* is frequent in Plautus. It seems that Martial, however, (5.64.3), was the first to revive the Plautine usage.

p. 276, 15-16 **potissimum praefarer primarium** : Triple alliteration; cf. ch. 13 (276, 4; 5; 8). In ch. 8 (272, 3) it is combined with rhyme.

p. 276, 15 **praefarer** : Later in the book Apuleius uses the word of religious speech : ch. 16 (278, 16), *preces de casto praefatus ore*; ch. 17 (279, 17), *fausta vota praefatus*; ch. 23 (284, 21), *praefatus deum veniam*. At other times there is no religious context, as in *Metam.* 1.1 (1, 13), *praefamur veniam* and *Flor.* 1 (1, 5), *praefanda venia*; nor is there any necessary reference here to a prayer. A similar variety of usage is found in other authors.

p. 276, 17 **renatam linguam** : Hildebrand notes that Apuleius always uses an Accusative with *auspicari*, as in *Metam.* 8.8 (183, 17 f.), *noli parricidio nuptias auspicari* and *Apol.* 73 (82, 13 f.), *frater eius virilis togae usum auspicaretur*. While several of the codices read *sermonem*, what is being inaugurated is the 'new-born tongue'. Van der Vliet's emendation is therefore convincing; cf. Robertson, 'fort. recte'. An Accusative *renatam linguam* could easily have been copied as a Nominative or Ablative because the *m* is often denoted by a minute supralineal sign and can thus be easily missed; an intelligent scribe then changed *sermone* into *sermonem*, but chose the wrong object.

p. 276, 17 **auspicarer** : Here, as in the two instances quoted in the previous note, Apuleius is using the word in the general sense of 'begin', but doubtless with a colouring derived from the basically religious meaning of the word; cf. Neuenschwander, *Der bildliche Ausdruck*, 55.

quibus quantisque : The alliteration is clearly purposive since *quibus verbis quantisque* might seem the natural sequence.

p. 276, 18 **utcumque** : Perhaps 'as ever'; cf. Hofmann and Szantyr, *Lat. Synt*. 635, § 344, although an indefinite sense, 'somehow', 'in whatever way', seems also possible. Cf. n. *ad* ch. 15 (277, 9).

divino monitu : Cf. ch. 6 (270, 9), *meo monitu* and n. Cf. too Vidman, *SIRIS* 271, no. 597, an inscription on an altar in Verona (perhaps A.D. i) : *Isidi | sacrum | Ex monit(u) eius d(ono) d(edit) || L. Valerius*.

p. 276, 20 **nutu significato** : The participle is an Ablative Absolute with unexpressed subject, like *composito* and *auspicato*; cf. Hofmann and Szantyr, *Lat. Syntax*, 141 f. The relation of *nutu* to the verb is the same as in *Metam*. 10.30 (261, 17 f.), *nutu significans*.

prius praecepit : Alliteration.

linteam dari laciniam : The form *licinia* is found in the best codices, and one is tempted at first to see an Apuleian coinage here, meaning 'a thin dress', from *liciniare*, 'show through, disclose', as in *Metam*. 10.31 (262,4), *membrorum voluptatem ... liciniaret*. In the latter context, however, *lacinia* is used of a tunic or cloak (262, 1); cf. too 3.21 (68, 4) and 6.3 (131, 1). Further, the adjective *lintea* suffices here to differentiate this linen cloak of the Isiac type from the sort of *lacinia* worn by others. In ch. 15 (277, 17) it is described as white. Cf. n. *ad* ch. 10 (273, 15), *linteae vestis*. Clearly the bestowal of the linen cloak is a token of the spiritual future which awaits Lucius.

p. 276, 21 **me** : Van der Vliet wishes to delete this word, and it appears that *mecum* stood originally in F. The Accusative and Ablative are, however, attested with *despoliare*, as in Caesar, *B.G.* 2.31.4, *ne se armis despoliaret*; cf. Petronius, 79, *gaudio despoliatum torum*; *Thes. L.L.* 5, 749, 27 ff.

nefando : Cf. *Metam*. 8.8 (183, 2), *vocem nefandam*; *Apol*. 25 (29, 12), *artis nefandas*; *Apol*. 85 (95, 2 f.), *sceleri ... nefando*. This is the reading of U and S as well as of the *Editio Princeps*, and since it is usually rather wider in meaning than *nefastus*, it agrees better with the recent allusion in ch. 13 (276, 4) to the asinine *deformis et ferina facies*. On the other hand, *nefastus* suits well enough the reference made by Isis in ch. 6 (270, 14-15) to the ass as an animal hateful to her. *Nefarius* is more frequent in Apuleius; v. *Index Apul*.

p. 276, 22 **in artum** : The emendation by Beroaldus cannot well be rejected. *In altum*, the reading of the codices, would make sense if Lucius were in a sitting posture, since he might then hide his *pudenda* by raising his thighs. But we are told above that he was standing (276, 6-7, *in erecta porriguntur* *officia*, of his hands). For the neuter Accusative of the adjective after *in* cf. ch. 20 (281, 20), *in diversum*; Hofmann and Szantyr, *Lat. Syntax*, 276; Callebat, *Sermo Cotid.* 228.

p. 276, 22 **nudo** : Nakedness in a religious procession was a shocking phenomenon unless the rite itself demanded it; such rites (e.g. the *Lupercalia* and some Dionysiac ceremonies) were normally connected with fertility; cf. G. van der Leeuw, *Rel. in Essence and Manifestation* (tr. J. E. Turner, London, 1964), 240; 340 f.; 377; 411.

p. 276, 23 f. **e cohorte religionis** : Cf. ch. 23 (284, 20), *religiosa cohorte*. Whereas the military sense of *cohors* is not its first meaning (an enclosure for cattle or fowl seems to be the original idea), it is the widespread military association that apparently gave rise to the extended sense of 'band, multitude, retinue' in poetry and post-Augustan prose, as in Hor. *Epod.* 16.60 (of the followers of Ulysses) and Ovid, *Metam.* 11.89 (of the band of Bacchanals with Bacchus). In this case the military association is probably deliberate since the Isis-religion is presented in ch. 15 as a spiritual struggle with quasi-military significance (277, 21, *da nomen sanctae huic militiae*).

p. 277, 2 **vultu geniali** : Cf. n. *ad* ch. 9 (273, 4).

perhumanum : The word *inhumanum* means usually 'barbarous' or 'boorish'. Apuleius alone gives it a favourable sense, as in *De deo Socr.* 5 (12, 5), *post istam caelestem quidem sed paene inhumanam* ('superhuman') *tuam sententiam*; *Metam.* 5.8 (109, 5), *inhumanae mensae lautitiis* ('tables divinely loaded with delicacies'). At the same time an elaboration of the description of the priest's countenance seems needless. On the other hand, the reason for his astonishment is omitted. Clearly he is astonished because Lucius now has a human form, and the word *perhumanus*, which occurs in seven of the manuscripts (including F at one stage) provides the clue although it occurs everywhere in the Ablative, agreeing with *vultu*. Oudendorp's emendation, *humanum in aspectum meum* meets the case almost exactly; *perhumanum* in the sense of 'thoroughly human' is better, and the occurrence of the prefix in the textual tradition demands its retention. Elsewhere *perhumanus* means 'kind', but a more literal meaning is necessary here, and it would be quite like the Apuleian approach to provide the only occurrence of such a meaning.

p. 277, 3 **effatur** : *Affatur* is found in several codices; cf. *Metam.* 5.24 (121, 25), where the god of love addresses Psyche, and 4.33 (101, 5), *affatu sanctae vaticinationis accepto*. But *effari* is often used of sacred pronouncements; *effatur* occurs here in F and Φ and probably, as Hildebrand suggests, it was changed to *affatur* by a scribe who thought that the latter was more suitable to an address by one person to another.

CHAPTER 15

p. 277, 4 **exanclatis** : See n. *ad* ch. 2 (267, 17). The phrase *exanclatis laboribus* occurs too in ch. 12 (275, 16).

p. 277, 4 **Fortunae** : A foretaste of the sentiment expressed here is found in the narrative in ch. 12, where Lucius, on seeing the priest with the sistrum and crown of roses, looks forward to his imminent salvation and to the victory over Fortune which the providence of Isis has arranged. There is a similar emphasis in the speech of self-revelation made by Isis to Lucius in chs. 5-6, especially at the end of ch. 6, where she promises that he shall live beyond the limit set by fate. In the prayer offered to Isis in ch. 25 both Fortune and Fate are mentioned. The present speech, which forms the impressive centrepiece of the book, is not only an address to Lucius; it is intended to be heard by all the bystanders, including those who are not of the faith, since a pointed allusion is made to them at the end in the form of a proselytising challenge. The priest is tired at the end (ch. 16), and there is then a joyous reaction on the part of the people. Wittmann is therefore justified in calling the speech a sermon with a missionary purpose.

The doctrine about Fortune is the main theme of this sermon; it is applied in a personal and confessional manner. Lucius has suffered immensely at the hands of Fortune, but in spite of her blindness and malice the whole process has led to a state of religious blessedness. A moral law has operated in the suffering, for Lucius has gained a grim reward for his ill-starred curiosity, which has led him to low pleasures. In *Metam.* 9.1 (203, 12 ff.) Apuleius has expressed a fatalistic view : no wisdom profits a man if Fortune is against him. Now Fortune is exhorted to choose another target for her frenzy, since in respect to Lucius Isis has replaced Fortune; and she is *videns* and *sospitatrix.* as opposed to Fortune which is *caeca* and *nefaria*. A striking equation is implied : Isis is herself Fortune, but a Fortune that is in no way blind. Clearly there is a correspondence here to the composite Isis-Fortuna or -Tychê, a well-known artistic form in which Isis in her Hellenistic guise is accompanied by two symbols of Fortune, the cornucopia and rudder (the latter sometimes resting on a globe). See Leipoldt, *Bilderatlas*, 31 and *Umwelt.* III, 265; Drexler in Roscher, *Lex. Myth.* s.v. Fortuna (Nachtr. Isis-Fortuna); also R. Peter, ibid. s.v. Fortuna (pp. 1530 ff.). It was a favourite theme at Pompeii for statues, statuettes and amulets; v. Tran Tam Tinh, *Isis à Pompéi*, pl. 22,1 (cf. 20, 2) and index refs. on p. 193; also the refs. in Schefold, *Vergessenes Pompeji*, 200 ff.; Boyce, *Lararia of Pompeii*, pl. 26,1 cf. no. 372 on p. 78. For a statuette in Delos see Roussel, *CED* 67, and his p. 91 for Isis and Agathê Tychê; in two inscriptions from Delos the goddess is called Isis Tychê Protogeneia : v. Roussel, *CED* 148 ff.; Vidman, *SIRIS* nos. 358 and 614, where the representations concern Isis-Fortuna but the inscriptions mention, respectively, Isis Pharia and Fortis Fortuna. Statuettes are reproduced by Wessetzky, *Ägypt. Kulte in Ungarn*, pls. 14 and 16,20; see also Grimm, *Ägypt. Rel. im röm. Deutschland*, pls. 24-5 and 28-9 with several discussions by him (v. his Index s.v. Isis-Fortuna, Fortuna). Vidman, *SIRIS* 205, no. 412, records the rare composite form Isitychê; cf. R. Peter in Roscher, *Lex. Myth.* s.v. and A.W. Van Buren, *AJPh* 47 (1926), 179 (on *CIL* IV, 4138).

It seems that the origin of the appellation Isis-Tychê is to be sought in Alexandria, and that it begins with the equation of Isis-Thermuthis with the snake-goddess of fertility, Agathê Tychê, who was distinctively the goddess of Alexandria; cf. Vandebeek, *Isisfiguur*, 58 f. Thus the first Hymn of Isidorus, which belongs to the first century B.C., addresses Isis in line 2 as παντοκράτειρα, Τύχη 'Αγαθή, μεγαλώνυμε 'Ισι (*SEG* 8, 548), after calling her Hermuthis in the first line. Cf. Hymn 2, 1 (*SEG* 8, 549) and 3,19 (*SEG* 8, 550) and J. Broekhuis, *De godin Renenwetet* (Assen, 1971), 127-9; also Vanderlip, *Hymns of Isidorus*, 19-21. The aspect of Bona Fortuna which derives from this serpent-goddess is that of material prosperity; she was the guardian of the crops. According to Étienne Bernand, *Inscriptions Métriques de l'Égypte Gréco-Romaine* (Paris, 1969), 641, this is the first appearance of the adjective παντο-κράτειρα 'ruler of all', but it agrees with the general position of the goddess here; she is also addressed as 'queen of the gods' (Hymn 1, 1). Pliny tells us that in his time the worship of Fortune was overwhelmingly dominant (*HN* 2.4.22, *toto quippe mundo ... Fortuna sola invocatur ac nominatur*). According to the priest in Apuleius Fortune is both blind and malicious, but Isis-Fortuna is both prescient and beneficent. It is through her that Lucius gains his victory over Fortune : 'rejoicing in the providence of mighty Isis, he is victorious over his Fortune.' Yet in the next sentence he is exhorted to enrol his name in this 'holy military service'. His victory over Fortune, then, is in one sense a gift of Isis; but in another sense it depends on his personal commitment to her service. Other systems offered an escape from the personal fate (stressed in *de sua Fortuna*) which astrology, according to current beliefs, had revealed — the εἱμαρμένη or ἀνάγκη with which Stoic thought was much engrossed.

The Stoic answer was certainly the most distinctive. Whereas it proclaimed a faith in the law of the universe and in providence (πρόνοια), it courageously accepted what was fated as being necessary and good; thus Cleanthes addresses Zeus and Destiny (*Peprêmenê*) in his prayer : 'Lead me, O Zeus, and lead me, Destiny, Whither I go is fixed by your decree.' (Von Arnim, *Stoic. Vet. Fr.* I, no. 527; cf. M. Pohlenz, *Die Stoa*, 106). The modern Stoic, W. E. Henley, has therefore deviated from the ancient creed in his arrogant challenge to fate in the lines 'I am the master of my fate, / I am the captain of my soul.' The fatalism engendered by astrology is often exposed in the magical papyri; here the way out is sometimes, naturally, magical, but religion is deployed too, as when, in *PGM* 13, 708 ff., an all-powerful god is offered as an instrument to cancel or change what is fated; cf. H. G. Gundel, *Weltbild und Astrologie in den griechischen Zauberpapyri*, 16 and 68 and my remarks in *C.R.* 19 (1969), 358. Sometimes a kind of *captatio benevolentiae* leads the magician to enlist the help of Anankê and the Moirae themselves; see Gundel, 72 f. Vettius Valens, an astrologer of the second century A.D. claimed that the versed astrologer could accept his destiny with discipline like a 'soldier of fate'; cf. K. Latte, *Die Rel der Römer*, 32, no. 26 (where 'v. Chr.' appears for 'n. Chr.'); a version of the text appears in G. Kroll, *Vetti Valentis Anthol. Libri*

(Berlin, 1908), 5.9 (pp. 219 ff.). However, it is in religion that the firmest answers appear. In Mithraism the concept of time as Zervan or Aion is that most akin to the idea of Fortune or Heimarmenê; cf. Vermaseren, *Mithras, the Secret God*, 106 ff.; and Mithras himself becomes the master of time, bearing the title *saecularis*, 'eternal' (ibid. 125), although the essence of his final victory is the triumph of *Sol Invictus* over the evil spirit of darkness; cf. Vermaseren and van Essen, *The Excavations in the Mithraeum of the Church of Santa Prisca in Rome* (Leiden, 1965), 231. In Christian thought victory is gained over all the tribulations brought by fate through Christ and his love; cf. Rom. 8.31-9, esp. 38 : 'In all these things we are more than conquerors ($\dot{\upsilon}\pi\epsilon\rho\kappa\rho\iota\nu\hat{\omega}\mu\epsilon\nu$) through him that loved us.' In one respect Christianity and the religion of Isis were similar : the victory over Fortune is not achieved by the believer unaided, but neither is it entirely the result of a battle fought outside him. Personal responsibility is combined with commitment to divine guidance. In the Aretalogies, admittedly, the victory is that of Isis alone : 'I conquer Heimarmenê, Heimarmenê is subservient to me' (M 55, D. Müller, pp. 74 ff.; Peek, *Isishymnus*, 124, 55 f. from Cyme). Apuleius allows one to see how the claim is shared with the believer. J. Bergman, 'I Overcome Fate etc.' in H. Ringgren (ed.), *Fatalistic Beliefs* (Stockholm, 1967), 35-51, compares, with regard to the concrete and personal emphasis, the claim of Valentinian Gnosticism 'to transfer those who believe in Christ from heimarmenē to His providence' (Clem. Alex. *Excerpta ex Theodoto*, 74).

In Egyptian religion the tradition is very clear that the gods are rulers over destiny; see the detailed study by S. Morenz and D. Müller, *Untersuchungen zur Rolle des Schicksals in der ägyptischen Religion* (*Abh. Leipzig*, 1960), especially the conclusions on pp. 29 ff. The power attributed in Apuleius to Isis can be traced back to Egyptian sources, in particular the promise made in ch. 6 to lengthen the span of life. See n. *ad loc.* Isis is called 'the mistress of fate, she who brings Prosperity (Renenet) into being' (BM 70, quoted by D. Müller, *Isis-Aret.* 84). Several other deities are named in similar expressions, where the Egn. word for 'fate' is *š3ì*. D. Müller's discussion is mainly concerned with the concept of *Shai* as a possible equivalent to Heimarmenê in the Aretalogy from Cyme, and he shows how the Egyptian attitude, in contrast to the Greek, always makes the idea of fate subordinate to the power of the gods. To Apuleius the sovereignty of Isis over Fortuna meant other things too. apart from her ability to extend one's life-span. In the present context it is her magical power that has wrought the miraculous metamorphosis from ass to man. In doing so she obviously interfered crucially in the course of Lucius's Fortune through her sway over life's processes. Eschatology may also be included in the victory over Fortune, since Isis emphasizes this to Lucius in ch. 6, where blessed immortality is promised; in the full Isiac doctrine this is accompanied by justification in the tribunal after death. Berreth, p. 103, compares the phrase *sua Fortuna* with the Egn. *ka*, citing the connection in Iamblichus *De myst.* 9.3 between fate and the personal *daemon*. But Egyptian thought

244 COMMENTARY CH. 15

would scarcely envisage a victory over one's *ka*, although there is a dispute with the *ba* in the early text called the *Lebensmüde*. What is more relevant here is that in Hermetic and Gnostic thought a victory over Heimarmenê is assigned to Nous, a quality which the pious man shares with God; cf. *Corp. Herm.* 12.9 (vol. I, 177), 'Mind (Nous), the spirit of God, rules everything, both Heimarmenê and law and everything else', on which see Reitzenstein, *Poimandres*, 78 f. Cf. Lactantius, *Div. Inst.* 2.15.6 : 'Finally Hermes maintains that those who know God are not only safe from the attacks of daemons, but are also immune from the grasp of fate; the one defence, he says, is piety, for the pious man is ruled neither by an evil daemon nor by fate;' Iamblichus, *De myst* 8.7 : 'Nor have we attached Heimarmenê to the gods, whom we worship in temples and statues as liberators from Heimarmenê.' Similarly in a magical papyrus in Leiden Sarapis is called on to delete the wretched fate that threatens a man (*PGM* 13, 634 f.), and D. Müller, *Isis-Aret.* 79, rightly invokes a truly Egyptian approach. This may well be ultimately true also of the Gnostic view of the supremacy of the pious Nous over fate, a classic theme in Gnosis as Festugière, *Corp. Herm.* I, 186 n. 25 remarks; cf. H. Jonas, *Gnosis und spätantiker Geist* (Ed. 3, Göttingen, 1964), 156-80, esp. 180. Nous and Gnosis are, of course, both Greek terms, but in an Alexandrian context they may have taken on an Egyptian colouring; certainly correct knowledge (*rḫ*) is often stressed in Egyptian texts as Bleeker points out in an essay on 'The Egyptian Background of Gnosticism' in *The Origins of Gnosticism* ed. U. Bianchi, Leiden, 1967, p. 232; cf. L. Kákosy on p. 247; and the similar attitude to fate is touched on by L. Kákosy, ibid. 239 f. If there is a like element in Iranian thought, as we have seen above, (cf. too G. Gnoli in *The Origins of Gnosticism*, 287, and U. Bianchi, ibid. 719), it can safely be discarded in the interpretation of Fortuna in Apuleius. He is dealing with a concept of fate worshipped and feared in Hellenistic and Roman times, and bolstered up by astrology. Isis, who is herself Fortuna and Tychê, is acclaimed as superior to this concept and she imparts her victory to Lucius, a victory that derives from the Egyptian tradition.

p. 277, 4-5 **tempestatibus et maximis actus procellis** : For the oratorical stylistic *abundantia* cf. ch. 5 (270, 6 f.) alluding to the *dies salutaris* which is to come : *quo sedatis hibernis tempestatibus et lenitis maris procellosis fluctibus* ...; the phrase *Fortunae tempestates* occurs too in ch. 25 (286, 22). *Maximis* repeats the *m* of *multis* and *magnisque*. Wittmann, pp. 78 f., finds a triadic arrangement in this sentence as well as rhyme and alliteration :

> *M*ultis et variis exanclatis labor*ibus*
> *m*agnisque Fortunae tempesta*tibus*
> et *m*aximis actus procellis
> ad portum Quietis
> et aram Misericordiae
> tandem, Luci, venisti.

The arrangement varies in the rest of the speech, but rhyme and alliteration are again freely used, as well as anaphora (*quid latrones, quid ferae* ...; *videant inreligiosi, videant* ...)

p. 277, 5 **ad portum Quietis** : The metaphor suits a rite in the harbour of Cenchreae, especially the rite of the *Isidis Navigium*, although it concerns the launching rather than the arrival of a ship. It is not uncommon, however, in earlier writers in both Greek and Latin. Cf. Sophocles, *Ajax*, 683, a 'haven of friendship' and J. C. Kamerbeek *ad loc.*; Euripides, *Medea*, 769, 'haven of resolutions'; with a different kind of Genitive in Aeschylus, *Supp.* 471, 'haven from ills'; Cic. *Ad fam.* 7.30, *in philosophiae portum*: id. *Tusc.* 5.2.5; *Corp. Herm.* 7.2 (vol. I, 81), 'haven of salvation' (τοῦ τῆς σωτηρίας λιμένος). An Attic epitaph (perhaps A.D. iii) includes the line σωθεὶς ἐκ πελάγους τοῦτον ἔχω λιμέναν : v. *IG* III, 1379 = Kaibel, *Epigr.* 168 and cf. J. Carcopino, *Aspects mystiques de la Rome païenne* (Paris, 1942), 226 f., who sees an Epicurean influence here; S. Lancel, *Rev. Hist. Rel.* 160 (1961), 32, who also cites Buecheler, *Carmina lat. epigr.* 434. For the 'haven of salvation' in Christian symbolism see Hugo Rahner, *Greek Myths and Christian Mystery* (London, 1963), 346 ff. Here again it is possible that the Apuleian source is Egyptian, for the idea of the ship of the soul was common in Egypt, and Campbell Bonner in his study 'The Ship of the Soul on a Group of Grave-Stelae from Terenuthis', *Amer. Phil. Soc.* 85.1 (1941), 84-91, interprets a number of stelae from Lower Egypt which represent the deceased person in a boat, in one case accompanied by a kindly ferryman. These stelae belong to the fourth or fifth century A.D., and Bonner also reproduces Crum, *Coptic Monuments* (*CCG*, 1902), no. 8574, pl. 30, where a monk's grave-stone bears a ship surmounted by a Chi-Rho. Bonner cogently argues that the ancient Egyptian idea of the journey to the celestial and blessed afterworld has here been revived. In 'Desired Haven', *Harv. Theol. Rev.* 34 (1941), 49-67, Bonner collected a large number of literary allusions involving a similar metaphorical use of 'harbour' or 'haven'. In Hymns of Isidorus, 4,6 (*SEG* 8, 551) the temple built for Isis and related gods by a divine king is described as 'a most just haven' (ὅρμον εὗρε δικαιότατον). Vanderlip *ad loc.*, p. 66, compares P. Oxy. 1380, 15 f. and 74, where Isis is entitled ὁρμίστρια ('bringer to harbour'). In Egn. texts the frequent use of *mni*, 'to land, come ashore', of death confirms Bonner's argument : see *Wb.* II, 73 f. Yet it is not death, but a desired goal within life that is indicated by the phrase in Apuleius. Cf. Spenser, *Faerie Queene*, 9,40 :

Sleep after toil, port after stormy seas
Ease after war, death after life does greatly please.

p. 277, 5-6 **et aram Misericordiae** : Wittmann, p. 80, remarks that the collocation 'haven of Peace and altar of Mercy' occurs nowhere else in Greek or Latin literature. This may be true of the detailed expression, but *portus* and *ara* are combined in Ovid, *Ex Ponto*, 2.8.68 : *vos eritis nostrae portus et ara fugae* (of small figures of the imperial family sent to him — 'you shall be the haven and altar of my exile'); cf. *Her.* 1.110 (Penelope to Ulysses) : *tu citius venias, portus et ara tuis.* Evidently the phrase was almost proverbial, the idea being that a harbour offered safe physical landing and an altar the divine protection connected with that. *Ara Misericordiae* does not apparently occur elsewhere but Elmenhorst cites Paus. 1.17.1 on the Altar of Mercy (*'Ελέον βωμός*) in the Athenian agora; Pausanias says here that the Athenians alone among the Greeks honoured Mercy, although the deity is very helpful in human life and in the changes of their affairs; cf. Diod. Sic. 13.22.7. There was a similar altar at Epidaurus in the Roman era; v. Dittenberger, *Syll.*³ 1149.

The concept of mercy accords well with the main characteristics of Isis as a loving wife and mother. In the Aretalogies (M 36) she claims, 'I decreed mercy to suppliants', and D. Müller, *Isis-Aret.* 60, sees here a function derived from Zeus Hikesios. In a more general context, however, the attribute of mercy belongs to Isis. The prayers to Isis as a healer show this, where her benefactions to Horus are the prototype. Although it is Osiris rather than Isis who is prominent in the judgement after death, an approach to the idea of mercy and even forgiveness is present in some form as early as the Coffin Texts, since the deceased is promised that his evil deeds shall not weigh against him; cf. R. Grieshammer, *Das Jenseitsgericht in den Sargtexten* (Wiesbaden, 1970), 46 f.; J. Gwyn Griffiths, *Conflict*, 75. In the 25th Dynasty Osiris is described as 'he who responds to the unfortunate (*p3-wšb-i3d*);v. J. Leclant, *Mons. Thébains*, 272. In a Turin Stela of the 19th Dynasty (no. 296) Isis is identified with the Peak of the West (in the Valley of the Tombs) and it is said of her, 'Great Isis, Mother of the God ... the Great Peak of the West, who gives her hand to him that she loves, and gives protection to him that sets her in his heart'; v. Maspero, *Rec. trav.* 2 (1886), 112; B. Gunn, *JEA* 3 (1916), 87 f.; cf. what is said of the associated Meretseger as 'the mistress who turns herself towards mercy' (*r ḥtp*), B. M. Stela, no. 374, ed. H. R. Hall, and Gunn, ibid. An inscription in the temple of Philae calls Isis 'the strong Saviour (*nḏt*) ... who rescues (*nḥm*) everyone whom she wishes', Lepsius, *Dkm.* IV, 74 c and cf. E. Otto, *Gott und Mensch*, 17; the accompanying relief shows Tiberius smiting bound enemies. Apuleius has already referred to Isis in ch. 5 (270, 2-3) as *favens et propitia*; cf. her *altaria, id est auxilia* in ch. 10 (274, 5.). Her consort Sarapis is described in Aristides, *In Sarap.* 26 ed. Keil p. 360 (= Hopfner, *Fontes*, 305) as one who, although much feared, 'prefers to turn to mercy'; and the prayer '*Ελέησον* 'Have mercy!' is addressed to the One Zeus Serapis in *IG* XIV, 2413, 3. In *Corp. Herm.* 1.22 (vol. I, 14) God says, 'I am come as Nous to the holy, the good, the pure, the merciful;' cf. 13. 8 (vol. II, 203) on God's constant mercy.

p. 277, 6 ff. **nec tibi natales atc.** : Médan finds a touch of autobiography here. The Lucius of the story tells us in *Metam.* 1.1 that his ancestors lived in

Hymettus in Attica, in the Isthmus near Ephyra, and in Taenarus in Sparta; he himself, he goes on, learnt Attic Greek, and later mastered Latin in Rome. In the following chapter he says that his mother was descended from the famous Plutarch and his nephew Sextus the philosopher. In 3.15 Photis tells him that she has confidence in him because of his learning (*doctrina*), his nobility of birth (*generosa natalium dignitas*) and his highly gifted talent (*sublime ingenium*); she adds an allusion to his initiation into many sacred rites. Perhaps Apuleius himself also prided himself on all these things. According to the Stoics, who advocated the simple life, noble birth, reputation and cleverness are among the 'indifferent' things, although they are in the 'preferred' class : v. Diog. Laert. 7.106, and cf. E. Bevan, *Stoics and Sceptics*, 63. To maintain, however, as Wittmann, p. 80, does, that the Isis-cult was opposed to *doctrina*, is somewhat misleading. In Plut. *De Is. et Os.* 2, 351 E, Clea is said to worship Isis 'as one who is exceptionally wise and devoted to wisdom', and Plutarch's discussion implies that the cult inculcated a pursuit both of the intellectual aspect of truth and of the intuitive *gnôsis* by which God was known after initiation; cf. my remarks *ad loc*. p. 256. Apuleius himself (*Apol.* 55) describes his acquaintance with many religious rites as arising from his 'enthusiasm for the truth and sense of duty towards the gods'. *Studium veri* there certainly was, although the present context suggests that secular, as opposed to divine, wisdom is of no avail, as the experience of Lucius proved. On the question of social rank (*dignitas*) the teaching of the cult was unequivocal : men and women of any origin or age were welcome; cf. ch. 10 (273, 15) on the initiates, *viri feminaeque omnis dignitatis et omnis aetatis* and n. *ad loc*.

p. 277, 7 **lubrico virentis aetatulae** : Fond as he is of using the neuter adjective substantivally with a following Genitive (cf. Médan, *Lat.* 250), Apuleius rarely uses it in the Ablative as here; the Ablative is modal or may be one of cause; cf. *Apol.* 27 (32, 18), *lubrico soli prolapsus*, and Butler and Owen *ad loc*. The adjective is often used of the passions of youth, as in Cic. *Pro Cael.* 41, *multas vias adulescentiae lubricas* and Austin *ad loc*. p. 170; Tac. *Ann.* 6.49, *lubricum iuventae*: 14.56, *lubricum adulescentiae*; Plin. *Ep.* 3.3.4, *in hoc lubrico aetatis*; Seneca, *Controv.* 2.6.4, *lubricum tempus*; St Jerome, *Ep.* 7.4.1, *lubricum adulescentiae iter*. Similarly the diminutive *aetatula* is often used of the bloom of adolescence; v. *Thes. L.L.* 1, 1138, 45 ff., and Apuleius twice uses it of the state of virginity : *Metam.* 1.12 (11, 12 f.); 7.9 (162, 12); cf. 10.31 (262, 3).

p. 277. 8 **serviles ... voluptates** : The reference must be to the erotic pleasures, especially with Photis, before Lucius becomes an ass. S. Lancel, *Rev. Hist. Rel.* 160 (1961), 32 f., argues that eroticism in liaison with magic is what is being condemned. He cites Theocritus and Petronius as authors who supply instances of the combination, and he finds the two practices sharing the same spirit — that of appropriation, of exerting one's will over another, and of enjoyment for its own sake. But it is in the next phrase that Apuleius refers to magic. Price advanced three possible reasons for the adjective : Photis was a slave; his passion held Lucius as a slave; or it was unworthy of him as a free man.

Perhaps more than one sense is present. Hildebrand rightly contrasts the idea of *servitium* to Isis that follows.

curiositatis : A review of the whole story is implied here, and it is clear from this important sentence that Book XI is not an appendix added inconsequently; it is regarded by Apuleius as providing the basic interpretation which gives unity to the whole. Serge Lancel in *Rev. Hist. Rel.* 160 (1961), 26, (reprinted in tr, in Merkelbach and Binding, *Amor und Psyche* [Darmstadt, 1968], 408-432) points out how fond Apuleius is of this noun and of the related adjective and adverb; he has counted twelve instances of the noun in his works, twelve of the adjective, and eighteen of the adverb. (He has curiously used only the *Thes. L.L.* in his count; the *Index Apul.* is a more convenient instrument for this purpose, and it gives two fewer instances of the adverb.) In recent times the significance of the motif in Apuleius was first recognized by H. J. Mette in his article 'Curiositas' in *FS. Bruno Snell* (Munich, 1956), 227-235. Mette begins with an engaging modern comparison of the quality shown by Felix Krull in the amusing picaresque novel by Thomas Mann. In the main, however, he is concerned with the role of *curiositas* or περιεργία in the prototype of the *Metamorphoses*, namely *Lucius or Ass*. 'Alas for this inopportune curiosity of mine!' exclaims the hero in that work (15), after being changed into an ass. When he is changed back again after eating roses, he remarks that he has been brought safe home 'from the curiosity of an ass' (ἐξ ὄνου περιεργίας, 56). Mette shows that Apuleius has similar allusions. When Lucius gets a chance of learning about magic, his curiosity impels him onwards (2.6 *init At ego curiosus alioquin, ut primum artis magicae semper optatum nomen audivi* ...); and this quality causes his transformation into an ass (cf. 3.14 *init. Tunc ego familiaris curiositatis admonitus* ...) Even as an ass he is still marked by the same quality : *curiosus alioquin et inquieti procacitate praeditus asinus*, 9.42 (235, 22 f.). The great divergence from the Greek prototype comes, as Mette shows, in the deeper and more elaborate exposition of *curiositas* in the Isis-book; it is recognized as the flaw which led Lucius astray, and when he has accepted the Isis-religion, he resolves not to yield to the *temeraria curiositas* which could injure those who got to know the *arcana* of the cult illicitly.

Apuleius has led up to this climax with many previous emphases that are not found in his prototype. Mette cites the detail in 1.2 *ad fin.*, where Lucius is *sititor alioquin novitatis*; then he refers to himself as *non quidem curiosum, sed qui velim scire vel cuncta vel certe plurima*; cf. 1.12 *fin. ut ... instantis curiositatis paeniteat*; 2.1 *ad. init. nimis cupidus cognoscendi quae rara miraque sunt*; the allusion to Actaeon at the end of 2.4 (*curioso optutu*); and the repeated reference in 3.19 (66, 14) to the curiosity about magic (*coram magiae noscendae ardentissimus cupitor*). Many have noted how prominent the theme is in the story of Amor and Psyche. Mette (p. 231) sees Psyche as none other than the *anima curiosa* of the narrator himself; certainly the quality is often stressed in the narrative. There are further allusions, however, to the quality in Lucius himself as an ass : 9.12 (211, 29), *familiari curiositate attonitus* and 9.13 (212, 24), *nisi quod ingenita mihi curiositate recreabar* — it was a source of comfort to him; 9.15 (214, 4, the baker's wife magnified his *genuinam curiositatem*). Mette ends with quotations from the Hermetic literature in which *curiositas* or περιεργία is belittled : see *Corp. Herm.* : *Asclepius*, 14 (vol. II, 312 f.), qualifying the exaltation of man (cf. 6, *magnum miraculum est homo*); *Korê Kosmou*, 44 ff. (vol. IV, 14 ff.). The attitude is like that of the Stoic diatribes on the audacity of man; cf. Scott and Ferguson, *Hermetica*, IV, 456 f. Wittmann, pp. 81 f., argues that the view is oriental rather than Greek, and notes the condemnation of *curiositas* in two other African writers, Tertullian and Augustine. Mette follows the view into early Christian literature, and cites Augustine on Psalm 8.13 : three kinds of vice are *voluptas carnis et superbia et curiositas*.

Further detail on the history of the idea and terminology is given by André Labhardt, 'Curiositas, notes sur l'histoire d'un mot et d'une notion', *Mus. Helv.* 17 (1960), 206-24. He points out (p. 206) that Augustine contrasts *studiosus* and *curiosus*, the pejorative sense of the latter deriving from a desire to know what one has no business to know (*ea requirit quae nihil ad se adtinent*). Labhardt discusses the occurrences of the adjective in Plautus and Cicero, and finds a good instance of the derogatory meaning in Catull. 7.11 (on the *curiosi* who want to count the kisses). *Curiositas*, on the other hand, occurs only once before Apuleius, in Cic. *Ad Att.* 2.12.2. Labhardt (p. 216) makes a good point in citing *Apol.* 27, where Apuleius defends his research into certain kinds of fishes; a philosopher, he suggests, has the right to do a thing like this for the sake of knowledge (*quasi id cognitionis gratia philosopho facere non liceat*); and before this he has mentioned the popular charge against Anaxagoras, Leucippus and others, *qui providentiam mundi curiosius vestigant*. It seems, then, that Apuleius supports scientific enquiry in which intellectual curiosity, according to our terminology, is so vital a factor; but he does not apply the term *curiositas* to it, in spite of the adverb in the last sentence quoted. This is where it is hard to follow the initial argument in Serge Lancel's study cited above. He would see two types of *curiositas*, the good and the bad. The first type he terms 'la *curiositas* des *mirabilia*', the second he qualifies as 'ubristique'. It is true, as he says, that the adjectives *familiaris*, *ingenita* and *genuina* are sometimes applied to the noun, suggesting that it is a natural quality (elsewhere it is *sacrilega, inprospera, temeraria*), and that the description at the and of 1.2 (cf. above) might seems to agree with the attitude defended in *Apol.* 27. But nowhere in the romance does he suggest an approval of the idea, and one is driven to the conclusion that other expressions are used for the spirit of healthy scientific enquiry, e.g. *studium veri* in *Apol.* 55. Such a spirit is lauded, as Lancel points out, in the prelude to the *De mundo* (p. 136), but it is noteworthy that *curiosus* and related words are missing; and the avid readers are referred to in *plerique studiose legunt*. The truth is that *curiositas* often relates to magic and religion, and Lancel well cites the myth of Eden, where the tree of knowledge is forbidden; a similar taboo is present, as he shows, in the story of Amor and Psyche. One of the principles of magic is that its secrets should not be divulged; a spell may be broken if this occurs. The same principle applies pre-eminently to the Mysteries, and it was a sanction observed by the priests of ancient Egypt in relation to *sštꝫ*, 'what is secret'. Cf. one of the Declarations of Innocence, *BD* 125 ed. Naville : 'I have not spied' (that is, on what is not my business; T. G. Allen, *BD* p. 197, 'I have not eavesdropped'). Whether Merkelbach is right or not in his elaborately Isiac interpretation of the story of Amor and Psyche — there are certainly striking resemblances between Psyche and Io-Isis — his emphasis on the sin of *curiositas* in relation to the Mysteries is well placed; cf. his *Roman und Mysterium*, 48 (on the prohibition against opening the *cista mystica*).

p. 277, 8-9 **sinistrum praemium** : Oxymoron. Cf. Bernhard, *Stil*, 237 f.

p. 277, 9 **utcumque** : The sense here is 'nevertheless', rather like that of *utique*. Cf. n. *ad* ch. 14 (276, 18).

Fortunae caecitas : An abstraction is preferred to *Fortuna caeca*. For *Fortuna* as blind cf. *Metam.* 7.2 (155, 21); 8.24 (195, 21 ff.); and frequent literary allusions in *Thes. L.L.* 6, 1, 1186, 22 ff.; A. Otto, *Die Sprichwörter und Sprichwörtlichen Redensarten der Römer*, 142 (the same epithet is cited for Tychê in Greek). In representations connected with the cult of Fortuna, the goddess is shown with a cornucopia and rudder : see R. Peter in Roscher, *Lex. Myth.* s.v. Fortuna (1884), 1503 ff. Her blindness is not represented or mentioned, it seems, in such a context, but is a purely literary creation. In cult, on the contrary, a *Fortuna respiciens* was known; cf. Latte, *Röm. Rel.* 182.

p. 277, 9-10 **pessimis periculis** : Alliteration has doubtless dictated the choice of adjective, as Médan observes.

p. 277, 10 **istam** : The pronoun implies a reference to the second person; cf. line 17, *isto habitu tuo*; Hofmann and Szantyr, *Lat. Syntax*, 183.

beatitudinem : Cf. ch. 16 (278, 7), *ter beatus*, where the expression belongs to a liturgical utterance, as is noted by Fugier, *L'Expression du Sacré*, 304.

p. 277, 11 **malitia** : Cf. Petronius, *Sat.* fr. 49, 7 f. (ed. A. Ernout, Budé, 1950), *Pervixi* : *neque enim fortuna malignior umquam | eripiet nobis quod prior hora dedit*, and the remarks by Vincenzo Ciaffi, *Petronio in Apuleio* (Turin, 1960), 149.

eat nunc : Berreth, p. 102, rightly sees primitive elements in this sentence. In the magical impetus against evil, the opposing power is commanded to leave. Weinreich in an essay entitled 'Primitiver Gebetsegoismus' (*Genethliakon Wilhelm Schmid, Tübinger Beitr. zum Altertumswiss.* 5, Stuttgart, 1929, pp. 175 ff.) distinguishes ἀποπομπή and ἐπιπομπή, the first implying a mere expulsion, the second adding the detail as to whither. He compares, for the second type, ἐς κόρακας; one might add 'Go to hell!' and the instance of the swine of Gadara. Cf. J. P. Sullivan, *The Satyricon of Petronius* (Londen, 1968), 204, on a similar usage in Seneca and Petronius. Weinreich cites (p. 180) Hor. *Carm.* 1.21.13 ff. as an example in poetry : Apollo is asked to send war and other evils from the Roman people to the Persians and Britons. Since Fortune was worshipped as a goddess, there is scarcely an original personification here; and it may be doubted whether Apuleius is thinking of her, as Berreth suggests, as a raging animal.

p. 277, 11 **crudelitati** : Cf. Petronius, *Sat.* 114.8, *sed non crudelis Fortuna concedit* and V. Ciaffi, op. cit. 14.

p. 277, 12 **vitas** : The codices read *servitium* after this word, but Oudendorp convincingly secluded it as an intrusion wrongly inserted from the next sentence. Adding *in* before *servitium* is not much use. Ryle points out that *vindicare in* is used by Apuleius to mean 'to avenge oneself on'; cf. *Metam.* 2.27 (47, 15 f.); 4.31 (99, 5 f.); 8.13 (187, 16). In 9.37 (231, 11) *de* follows the verb with this sense. Without a preposition the meaning is 'claim' : cf. *Metam.* 9.28 (224, 4 f.); 9.35 (229, 23); though in one case the passive infinitive means 'avenge', 10.6 (241, 14); and in another *de* is used in a context unconnected with vengeance, 10.14 (247, 13 f.), *de reliquis aequam vindicare divisionem.*

deae nostrae maiestas : The abstraction is preferred.

p. 277, 13 **quid latrones etc.** : Price compares the words of Juno in Vergil, *Aen.* 7.302 f., *Quid Syrtes aut Scylla mihi, quid vasta Charybdis / profuit*? Wittmann invokes Cic. *Tusc.* 5.2.6, but misfortunes are not listed there. The series is more reminiscent of Rom. 8.35-9.

p. 277, 15 **cotidianae nefariae** : The arrangement is chiastic, and ambiguity is avoided through the differential choice of adjectives. In *cotidianae nefariae Fortunae* rhyme is followed by the repetition of the two consonants *f* and *r*. Cf. n. *ad* p. 266, 16 and p. 278, 5-6.

in tutelam : Cf. the use of the terms *vadata* and *ei totum debere* by Isis in her address to Lucius in ch. 6; also *vitas ... vindicavit* above, lines 12-13. Wittmann, p. 84, aptly cites *CIL* VI, 573, *Sarapi conservatori deo in cuius tutela domus est*, but the legal metaphors involved are more varied than he suggests. *Servire* at the end of the chapter (278, 2) implies the relationship of *dominus* and *servus*, but *tutela* that of guardian and ward. Roman law knew two types of *tutela*, that over minors and that over women; v. F. Schulz, *Classical Roman Law* (Oxford, 1951), 164 ff. and 180 ff.

p. 277, 16 **Fortunae, sed videntis** : Cf. notes *ad* line 4., *Fortunae*, and line 9, *Fortunae caecitas.*

p. 277, 16-17 **ceteros etiam deos illuminat** : The sovereignty of Isis over other gods is suggested. Cf. 'She who leads all the gods' (of Isis), Kalabsha, 16; 'she who gives orders to the Ennead and leads with her utterance', ibid. 118 (also of Isis); both quoted by E. Otto, *Gott und Mensch*, 152.

p. 277, 17 **isto habitu tuo** : For *iste* in reference to the second person cf. n. *ad* line 10, *istam*. The case is Dative. For *isto* cf. 5.31 (127, 29); 6.17 (141, 14); 7.26 (174, 21). On the use of white Isiac garments see *ad* ch. 10 (273, 15), *linteae vestis*. The original significane of the use of white in an Egyptian priestly context — and white linen was the normal dress of most priests — is not joy but purity; cf. *wʿb*, 'pure one' the generic term for 'priest'.

p. 277, 18 **sospitatricis** : See n. *ad* ch. 8 (272, 18).

p. 277, 8 **inovanti** : Accepting the reading of A, which is also given by Beroaldus (in his text), one is tempted to follow the suggestion of Oudendorp, followed by Médan, after noting other compounds with -*in* which Apuleius uses (Médan cites *intollo, intraho, inunco, inolbo, incapistro*), that an Africanism is involved, since Tertullian shows a similar fondness. The suggestion can be made more specific, however; Hebrew can regularly introduce different verbal meanings by the use of prefixes, as in the Niph'al and Hithpa'ēl forms; cf. A. B. Davidson, rev. McFadyen, *Hebrew Gr.* (1932), 89 f. and 93. Neither of these is, admittedly, a precise parallel since the prefix is not a preposition, but -*in* of *inovanti* does not have a prepositional force; it may have the intensive sense of the Hithpa'ēl, 'a step that shows itself as triumphant'. The reading *innovanti* could refer to the new gait now used by Lucius (the human, as opposed to the asinine walk), but the notion of triumph, as Hildebrand shows, is underlined in the sequel.

p. 277, 18 **videant inreligiosi etc.** : The call to repentance in a missionary address is paralleled in *Poimandres*, which belongs to the second or third century A.D.; v. *Corp. Herm.* I, 27-8 (vol. I, 16 f.) and cf. A. D. Nock, *Conversion*, 4. Other instructive parallels are set out by Ed. Norden, *Agnostos Theos*, 6 f. (though he does not cite our locus); with the Hermetic passage he prints Acts 17.23 ff.; the 23rd Ode of Solomon, an early second century writing which is a Syrian version of an originally Greek work, though Semitic in inspiration; and parts of the Kerygma of Peter (A.D. iii) and of the so-called Sermon of Barnabas, which is probably later than the others. In P. Oxy. 1381, after the miracle of healing by Imouthes Asclepius has been related, an obligation to propagate the faith in him is accepted; but while the pious are welcomed, the impious are rebutted : 'Go hence, O envious and impious ...'; cf. Nock, *Conversion*, 88. Norden, *Agnostos Theos*, 134 ff., was able to show that the idea of μετάνοια, involving as it did both a turning to God and regret for sins committed, derives from Jewish sources; and it is strange that Nock, *Conversion*, 179 f., while noting the use of the idea of the 'turning around of the soul' in Plato, *Resp.* 518 D ff. and of *conversio* in Cic. *De nat. deor.* 1.77, appears to ignore the discussion by Norden. The clause *errorem suum recognoscant* expresses the traditional Egyptian attitude very well, for the sense of personal remorse is not often evident in Egyptian texts. Failure to recognize the truth is what is wrong, and in our context the truth is that Isis is a mighty goddess, capable of miracles of metamorphosis. Cf. the inscription of Nefer-abu : 'I was an ignorant man, and knew not what good and evil is.' Cf. Morenz, *Rel.* 138 ff. and the texts studied by G. Fecht in *Literarische Zeugnisse zur "Persönlichen Frömmigkeit" in Ägypten* (Abh. Heidelberg, 1965). Frankfort, *Rel.* 73, states that 'the Egyptian viewed his misdeeds not as sins, but as aberrations'. Yet the word 'sin' is applicable if we remember that the basic stress is on wrong thinking.

p. 277, 19 **en ecce** : The pleonasm occurs in Seneca, *Oed.* 1004 and three other times in Apuleius; see Bernhard, *Stil*, 129, who thinks that it may derive from popular speech.

aerumnis : Cf. ch. 2 (267, 16) and n.

p. 277, 20 **Isidis magnae providentia** : This is in line with the previous allusion in this chapter to Isis Fortuna as a deity who is not blind, but sees. Cf. also ch. 5 (270, 4), *iam tibi providentia mea inlucescit dies salutaris*; ch. 10 (274, 6), *deae summatis auxiliaris providentia*; ch. 18 (280, 8), *deae providentis adorabile beneficium*. Providence was an important concept in Stoic teaching; cf. von Arnim, *St. Vet. Fr.* 322 ff.; on Chrysippus see Weinreich, *Antike Heilungswunder* (Giessen, 1909), 128 ff.; Cic. *De nat. deor.* 3.92; Plut. *De Is. et Os.* 45, 369 A and my remarks *ad loc.* p. 469; in this passage Plutarch is rejecting the Stoic view, but later in the same work he appears to accept it : v. 67, 377 F. Apuleius, however, firmly links the idea of providence with Isis in a personal way. Plutarch has only an indirect suggestion of this (4, 352 A, Isis as the daughter of Prometheus). In P. Oxy. 1380, 43 f. Isis Pronoia probably reflects Stoic influence; Grenfell and Hunt *ad loc.* state that 'Isis appears as Pronoia on Alexandrian coins', citing Poole, *Cat. of the Coins of Alexandria*, 176; Pronoia appears there on coins numbered 1416 and 1417, but there is no indication that Isis is also being represented. The previous references in Apuleius as well as the present exposition make it doubtful whether the Stoic concept is operative. Isis herself is envisaged as exercising providential care in relation to Lucius, and this very personal interpretation is fully in accord with the Egyptian idea of the gods as kindly arbiters of providence. A part of the idea is that a god has elected a person for favoured care and protection. This was an attitude often expressed in relation to the King, especially in the New Kingdom, and a reciprocal facet was that the King too had chosen a particular god for special veneration; see Morenz, 'Die Erwählung zwischen Gott und König in Ägypten', *Sino-Japonica* (FS. A. Wedemeyer, Leipzig, 1956), 118-137. A related idea is that of predetermination or predestination, which is sometimes applied to both character and occupation : see H. Brunner, *Die Lehre des Cheti* (Glückstadt, 1944), 68 f. (on the occupation of scribe); also the detailed exposition by Morenz and D. Müller, *Unters. zur Rolle des Schicksals in der ägypt. Rel.* 8 ff. Here the idea of foretelling is also prominent, as when Ramesses III says of his successor, 'You (Amûn) have destined him beforehand as King, when he was only a child' (P. Harris, I, 22, 5); cf. Morenz and Müller, op. cit. 13.

de sua Fortuna triumphat : V. Ciaffi, *Petronio in Apuleio*, 147 ff., compares the treatment of Fortuna in Petronius, Apuleius and Heliodorus. He shows that Petronius and Apuleius use bellicose expressions about Fortuna. Thus in *Metam.* 7.3 (156, 1 f.) Apuleius speaks of Fortuna's 'very fierce attack' on Lucius (*saevissimus eius impetus*) and in 7.25 (173,4 ff.) of the ambushes prepared by her (*novas instruxit insidias*); cf. Petronius, *Sat.* 101.1, *totum me, Fortuna, vicisti*, and the phrase *mutare in proelia vultum*, used of Fortuna in 120.94. But here and in ch. 12 (275, 17), *Fortunam superarem*, Apuleius can be credited with a significant conceptual difference which arises from his religious theme : now it is Fortune that is being conquered. Cf. H. Gressmann,

Die hellenistische Gestirnreligion (Leipzig, 1925), 30 f., where, however, the role of astrology is unduly magnified.

p. 277, 21 **da nomen** : In pronouncing the military oath (*sacramentum*) the soldier supplied his name and thus enrolled himself for military service. Cf. Valerius Maximus, 5.2.2. (ed. Kempf p. 228), (*iuventus*) *ultro nomina sua militari sacramento obtulit.*

sanctae huic militiae : The idea of conflict is deeply embedded in the Osirian religion since the myth of Osiris in its earliest known form, as expressed in the Pyramid Texts, has already subsumed the legend of Horus and Seth : see J. Gwyn Griffiths *The Conflict of Horus and Seth* (Liverpool, 1960). Seth becomes the enemy of Osiris and Isis, and the campaign of Horus against Seth and his confederates takes on the colour of a vendetta, since Seth is regarded as the slayer of Osiris. The Stela of Ikhernnofret in the Twelfth Dynasty describes a fight on a lake as a part of Osirian ceremonies, where Osiris is in his *neshmet-* barque; cf. Introd. V, pp. 48 ff., In the Late and Ptolemaic Eras, with the degeneration in the status of Seth, the call to resist and overcome him becomes still more fierce in tone; this is particularly clear in the *Urkunden Mythologischen Inhalts* (*Urk.* VI) edited by Schott, the first part of which (*Das Buch vom Sieg über Seth*) comprises a ritual for use in the temple of Osiris in Abydos and in other temples. Other late texts do not show the same concentration of theme in this respect, but they show a similar militant attitude against Seth and the evil associated with him; cf. the *Songs of Isis and Nephthys* = P. Bremner-Rhind, 2, 14 ff. for which see Faulkner, *JEA* 22 (1936), 123 f.; Junker, *Die Stundenwachen in den Osirismysterien*, 39, 16 (and often in allusions to 'enemies'); the texts from the temple of Edfu, in which the fight of Horus against Seth is elaborated in several phases (cf. the analysis by Fairman in *JEA* 21 [1935], 26 f. and my interpretation in *JEA* 44 [1958], 75-85). Wittmann, though he largely ignores this material, aptly cites the Paris Great Magical Papyrus (*PGM* 4, 193) where a prayer addressed to Typhon contains the words, 'I, your soldier (ὁ σὸς στρατιώτης), have been conquered by the gods.' Nor does Plutarch neglect this aspect. Osiris, we are told, came from the underworld to equip and train Horus for battle (*De Is. et Os.* 19, 358 B); Horus here chooses the horse as the animal most useful in battle, and in iconography this fighting Horus seems to have influenced the cavalier saints of Coptic art; v. my *Plut. De Is. et Os.* 346; cf. Bonner, *Stud. Mag. Am.* 40. When Plutarch describes Isis as a 'pattern of piety' (27, 361 D-E), he refers to 'the contests and struggles which she had undertaken, her wanderings and her many deeds of wisdom and bravery'. Cf. P. Oxy. 1380, 43 : in Rome Isis is στρατία, 'she who goes into battle'.

Apuleius has used military symbolism before this in connection with the triumph over Fortuna; cf. too ch. 7 (271, 7), *numen invictum* and ch. 14 (276,23 f.), *e cohorte religionis*. Vettius Valens, a contemporary, speaks of 'a soldier of fate'; cf. n. *ad* line 4, *Fortunae*. Both Mithraism and Christianity used a similar symbolism, and in the former case the term *miles* was applied to the third grade of initiate : see Vermaseren and van Essen, *Santa Prisca*, 157; Vermaseren, *Mithras, the Secret God*, 177 ff.; Cumont, *Or. Rel.* (German tr., 1959), xii; Reitzenstein, *Hellenist. Myst.* 194. Paul urges Timothy to be 'a good soldier of Jesus Christ' (2 Tim. 2.3). We are dealing, however, with an Egyptian cult, and in this case an ancient and prominent precedent comes from the Egyptian tradition.

p. 277, 22 **sacramento** : The term is again probably taken from a military association, but the oath of loyalty is that of a voluntary soldier, not a conscript; cf. Reitzenstein, *Hellenist. Myst.* 20 and 192; Cumont, *Or Rel.* (German tr.), 207 n. 5; A. D. Nock, *C.R.* 38 (1924), 58 f. Isis in her address to Lucius in ch. 6, although she mentions no *sacramentum*, certainly implies that she will be expecting a sacred oath of loyalty to her (*semper tenebis mihi reliqua vitae tuae curricula ...*) While no such oath is extant, Verne B. Schuman, 'A Second-Century [A.D.] Treatise on Egyptian Priests and Temples', *Harv. Theol. Rev.* 53 (1960), 159-70, publishes a papyrus in which a priestly oath is incorporated, and R. Merkelbach, 'Ein Griechisch-Ägyptischer Priestereid und das Totenbuch' (Derchain, ed. *Rel. en Égypte*, 69-73) was able to show that some of the abstentions promised revert to Spell 125 of the *Book of the Dead*; see too his article in *ZPE* 1 (1967), 55-73, 'Der Eid der Isismysten', where he interprets *PGM* 5, 98-159 and 459-86 as Osirian texts and compares P. Soc. It. 1290 and 1162; the last two texts he views as forming the vow of an Isiac or Osirian initiate. Since the papyrus edited by Schuman emanated from the same era as the work of Apuleius, a salutary reminder emerges : an Egyptian cult at this time may preserve very ancient elements in spite of certain transmutations of language and scene. Ryle argues that the transformation of Lucius 'could be considered a "sacrament" in a quasi-Christian sense, as a sign of his rebirth, analogous to baptism', and he cites a similar opinion of Vallette's. The previous mention of *militia* prompts one rather to see in *sacramentum* the sacred bond undertaken by the initiate; the sequel too confirms this.

p. 278, 1 **ministerii iugum** ; Cf. ch. 30 (290,27), *castimoniae iugum subeo*. The words used by the goddess at the end of ch. 6 are rather similar (*sedulis obsequiis et religiosis ministeriis*). Like ζυγόν, *iugum* in commonly used of the yoke of slavery. The military metaphor has now given way to the symbolism of slave and master. Its application to religion had already occurred in Christian writings; cf. Mt. 11.29, ἄρατε τὸν ζυγόν μου ἐφ᾽ ὑμᾶς. Fugier, *L'Expression du Sacré*, 305 n. 35, argues that *obsequium*, in the statement of the priest, denotes the total consecration of life to the service of the goddess, whereas *iugum* implies the priesthood; but every believer, she rightly adds, accepted a kind of *obsequium* and *iugum*.

p. 278, 2 **deae servire ... fructum tuae libertatis** : This kind of paradox is first found in Stoic literature. Thus Seneca, Ep. 47.17, states that a man may be technically free, but may be nonetheless a slave of his passions. In earlier Stoic writings the acceptance of fate is made a source of comfort, as in the prayer of Cleanthes in von Arnim, *St. Vet. Fr.* I, 527 = Bevan, *Later Greek Religion*,

15. The Pauline epistles contain a similar idea : Paul is a slave of Christ (Rom. 1.1), but in this condition finds true freedom (Gal. 5.1). Cf. ch. 27 (288, 11), *deo famulum*.

CHAPTER 16

p. 278, 3 **Ad istum modum** : See n. *ad* ch. 3 (267, 22).

p. 278, 3-4 **fatigatos anhelitus trahens** : Cf. Vergil, *Aen.* 6.48 f. of the Sibyl, *sed pectus anhelum | Et rabie fera corda tument*; Seneca, *Ag.* 713, *anhela corda murmure incluso fremunt*. The phrase is consciously poetical; cf. Médan, *Lat.* 251. In *Metam.* 8.27 (199, 5) a similar state of priestly frenzy is described with the words *anhelitos crebros referens*; there the priest belongs to the Dea Syria. In 10.2 (237, 26 f.) *fatigatus anhelitus* is one of the symptoms of love, here compared with disease, as in the song where Peter Sellars impersonates an Indian doctor.

p. 278, 5 **sacrarium** : The reference is probably to the *cista* mentioned in ch. 11; in its most elaborate form it certainly amounted to a small shrine.

totae : An old form. Leumann, *Lat. Gr.* (1963), 291, shows that a feminine Dative in -ae is quite common in early times; he cites *illae, istae, aliae, alterae, solae*, and *totae* as occurring in Plautus.

p. 278, 5-6 **nutibusque notabilis** : Here the alliteration involves a sequence of three consonants — *n, t, b*. Such alliterative sequences are a common feature of the Welsh strict metres (*Cynghanedd*).

p. 278, 6 **fabulabantur** : The word is frequent in Plautus, but does not occur in Cicero. See *Thes. L.L.* 6, 1, 34, 79 ff. In *De deo Socr.* 108 (prol.) Apuleius twice uses the word of relating a fable, but there is clearly no similar sense here. There is apparently no other example of the verb being followed by *in*; but Médan compares Cic. *De orat.* 2.61.248, *quod idem in bono servo dici solet*.

omnipotentis : Cf. *Metam.* 8.25 (196, 24 f.), *Omnipotens et omniparens dea Syria*. Elsewhere the word occurs mainly in poetry. The blessing or *makarismos* pronounced by the people was a regular sequel to a miraculous occurrence assigned to a deity. Here it is conjoined to the act of welcoming a new initiate; cf. the felicitation extended to Lucius by the priest in ch. 22 (284, 5 f.), '*O*', *inquit*, '*Luci, te felicem, te beatum, quem propitia voluntate numen augustum tantopere dignatur*', where three terms are repeated from the present passage (*felix, beatus, numen augustum*). Wittmann, p. 87, rightly invokes a known liturgy, pointing to the solemn rhythms of the piece.

p. 278, 7 **ter beatus** : The intensive force of *ter* is well known; cf. Hor. *Carm.* 1.13.17, *felices ter et amplius*; Ovid, *Metam.* 8.51, *O ego ter felix*; and the use of τρίς in Greek as in τρίσμακαρ, Aristoph. *Pax*, 1333. In Egyptian 'three' was a term of plurality, and in the name Hermes Trismegistus the intensive *tris* undoubtedly derives from Egyptian usage; cf. my *Plut. De Is. et Os.*

439. G. L. Dirichlet, *De veterum macarismis* (Giessen, 1914), 5, points out that Homer uses two adjectives for beatitude, μάκαρ and ὄλβιος, while Aeschylus uses εὐδαίμων (p. 13); a love context often shows *felix* and *beatus* used by the Latin poets (p. 43; cf. the example from Horace above). But in the material surveyed by Dirichlet it is that pertaining to the Eleusinian Mysteries that is most apposite to our purpose; he shows (p. 62) that the idea of eternal bliss first appears in Greek with this background, in the Homeric Hymn to Demeter, 480 : 'Happy is he among men on earth who has seen these things' (ὄλβιος ὃς τάδ'ὄπωπεν ἐπιχθονίων ἀνθρώπων); the uninitiate, it is then said, have no such happiness. Sophocles, fr. 753 (ed. Nauck), uses τρισόλβιοι of the Eleusinian beatitude (Dirichlet, p. 63). Orphic usage is compared; also Eur. *Bacch.* 72 ff. on Dionysiac bliss; Demosthenes, *De cor.* 260 on that of the devotees of Sabazius. The Egyptian adjective was *nfr*, but in an Isiac or Osirian context m3ꜥ ḫrw was the constant phrase used of the blessed believer who secures eternal happiness. Paul Foucart's attempt in *Les Mystères d'Éleusis* (Paris, 1914) to derive the Eleusinian concepts from Egypt did not succeed because there is really a lack of detailed correspondence, and A. A. Barb 'Mystery, Myth, and Magic' in *The Legacy of Egypt*[2] ed. J. R. Harris (Oxford, 1971), scarcely faces up to this in his attempt to revive it. (see his pp. 151 ff.).

p. 278, 8 **innocentia fideque** : In view of the priest's words in ch. 15, condemning Lucius for falling into low pleasures and serving an ill-starred curiosity and in view of what the reader has been told about his previous life, this attribution of merit to him is very strange. Berreth, p. 102, suggests that the strangeness is mitigated by *praecedentis*, taking this apparently as referring to the life of Lucius *before* the adventures related in the novel begin. Certainly he is given an eminently respectable character in the opening chapters. A more satisfactory explanation, also suggested by Berreth, is that the words of the *macarismos* are a set formula; cf. Wittmann, p. 87; Festugière, 'Lucius and Isis', 78 and 164 f. *Innocentia* was certainly demanded of the Isiac initiate; and personal guilt was believed to be deleted only through identification with Osiris. Pardon or forgiveness is extended to Lucius according to ch. 23 (284,21), *praefatus deum veniam*. What is connoted by *fides* is best appreciated from the words of Isis in ch. 6. Lucius has to trust her (*mea volentia fretus*) and carry out her instructions; he must believe in the truth of her promises. Doubtless there is an approach here to the Christian doctrine of πίστις, except that the formula which Apuleius is reproducing portrays a spiritual achievement based on merit. It is clearly a subjective quality corresponding to the meaning 'true piety' in Bauer's *Wb. N.T.*[5] (Berlin, 1958) s.v. πίστις 2 d, p. 1314, where other pagan instances are cited. See further p. 354.

p. 278, 9 **de caelo** : While this use of *de* is found in Plautus and Cicero, the extensive employment of the preposition in Apuleius probably reflects its contemporary use in the province of Africa : v. Callebat, *Sermo Cotid.* 201 and 199 n. 297; cf. Fernhout, *Metam. V*, 81 f.; van der Paardt, *Metam. III*, 73.

p. 278, 9 **patrocinium** : The heavenly *patrocinium* is not accorded, for all its beneficence, without human desert; a *vadimonium* pledged by Lucius is also implicated, as ch. 6 makes clear. Cf. Fugièr, *L'Expression du Sacré*, 305.

renatus ; A double meaning is present : Lucius has been born again in the sense that he has been restored to human shape; he has also been born again spiritually in his acceptance of the protection and favour of Isis. Plutarch, *De Is. et Os.* 35, 364 E, refers to the 'episodes of dismemberment, return to life, and rebirth, related of Osiris', and he compares these with the saga of the Titans, doubtless that in which Zagreus figured. The Osirian believer was favoured with a guarantee that rebirth after death (*wḥm 'nḫ*, 'repeating life', is the Egyptian phrase, see *Wb.* I, 341) would be his experience also, and funerary iconography constantly stresses the idea by equating the dead with Osiris and representing the latter's triumph over death. Osirian ritual texts were freely used in the service of the dead, and even the kingship of Osiris was assigned to the believer, as in the celebrated case of Antinous; cf. Morenz, "Problem des Werdens zu Osiris', 79. Spiritual rebirth in this life, however, might seem a rather different concept, and in Apuleius it is clearly related to the idea, expounded in ch. 21, that initiation means a voluntary death on the part of the initiate; indeed the expression *quodam modo renatos* occurs also in ch. 21 (283, 9). In the present context, at the same time, the first reference is to the re-shaping in human form; *renatus* echoes *reformavit* in line 7; cf. Reitzenstein, *Hellenist. Myst.* 39; on p. 262 he compares the use of παλιγγεν-εσία in Plut. *De Is. et Os.* 72, 379 E. although the theme there is metempsychosis into animal forms. H. Wagenvoort in his *Studies in Roman Literature, Culture and Religion* (Leiden, 1956), 132-49, admirably discusses ' "Rebirth" in Antique Profane Literature', showing that the concept is present in many primitive religions; he points out (p. 139) that Plato uses πάλιν γίγνεσθαι of reincarnation. It is a striking fact that the reflex image of death and new life in the spiritual experience of the believer is parallel to the interpretation given by Paul in Rom. 6.4, where the death and resurrection of Christ are said to be mirrored in Christian baptism : 'Therefore we are all buried with him by baptism into death; that like as Christ was raised up from the dead by the glory of the Father, even so we also should walk in newness of life.' Cf. M. Dibelius, 'Isisweihe', 46 ff., where it is argued that Paul has transferred the idea of the Mystery Cult to the mystery of life in Christ. The Johannine idea of 'being born from above (or again)' (John 3.3) is not so precisely related; cf. D. R. Griffiths in *Christian Baptism* ed. A. Gilmore (London, 1959), 157 and M. de Jonge in *Bull. J. Ryl.* 53 (1971), 348 f. Wagner, 'Problem', 121, argues that *renatus* implies the death of the old frivolous life and new birth to the life of the initiate; he admits a metaphorical usage, yet denies that it is tantamount to a 'mystische Wiedergeburt'. Whereas the functions of Osiris and Isis were inclined, in the Late and Ptolemaic Eras, to be extended to the world of the living, it is doubtful whether the Egyptians had taken the step of transferring the concept of rebirth after death to the spiritual regeneration of the believer in the present life. Such a step is more likely to have derived from the application of Greek thought to the Egyptian rites. The idea of rebirth is of course found elsewhere; cf. treatises 4 and 13 of the *Corpus Hermeticum*; the rites of Eleusis and Cybele; on the latter see Sallustius, *De diis et mundo*, 4, ed. Nock pp. 8 f., '... we are fed on milk as though being reborn', and *in aeternum renatus*, Hepding, *Attis*, 173; Nock, *Early Gentile Christianity* (1928, repr. 1964), 65 f. The word *renatus* is again attested in the rites of Mithras : see Vermaseren and van Essen, *Santa Prisca*, 207, line 11, *pi(e) r(e) b(u) s renatum dulcibus atque creatum*, with the following discussion, where it is shown that this is the first instance of the word's occurrence in the Mithraic cult. Festugière, 'Lucius and Isis', 164 n. 45, interprets the Apuleian context thus : 'Man is *renatus* for a new term of temporal life, not for a divine life given by supernatural grace.' This ignores the emphasis on the pledge given by Lucius to serve the goddess and also misses the significance of the ritual death in ch. 21. Cf. P. Veyne, *Rev. Phil.* 39 (1965), 247 n. 4, who suggests 'spiritual rebirth'as the sense implied. Reitzenstein, *Arch. Rel.* 7 (1094), 406 ff., discusses the idea in relation to the baptism described in ch. 23. He well quotes (p. 406 n. 2) from the statement addressed by Firmicus Maternus, *Err. prof. rel.* 2.5, to the Isiacs : *alia est aqua, qua renovati homines renascantur*. The claim made by the Egyptian cult concerning regeneration is thus made incisively clear.

p. 278, 10 **desponderetur** : Cf. ch. 28 (289, 8-9), *ad istum modum desponsus sacris*.

p. 278, 12-13 **meus ... asinus** : The former mode of being is similarly mentioned in ch. 2 (267, 19-20), *redde me meo Lucio*.

p. 278, 13 **simulacris rite dispositis** : A *corpus pausariorum* is mentioned in an inscription from Rome (A.D. i-ii) relating to Isis and Osiris; v. *CIL* VI, 348 = Vidman, *SIRIS* 201, no. 400; cf. *SHA V. Caracall.* 9.11, *et Anubin portaret et pausas ederet*; also *V. Pesc. Niger*, 6.9. *Pausarii* may occur too in *CIL* XII, 734 = *SIRIS* 311, no. 727. They have been explained as ministrants who arranged the pauses or stops in the processions of Isis, and H. J. Boeken, *Adnot.* 93 f., believes that these officials are implied here. Vidman, *Isis und Sarapis*, 88, seems to be a little doubtful about the occurrence in *SIRIS* no. 400; *ex corpore pausariorum et argentariorum* has been emended to read ... *aurariorum*. The other references, however, combine to establish the office.

p. 278, 13-14 **navem faberrime factam** : Cf. *Flor.* 23 (p. 43), *navem bonam, fabre factam ... eleganter depictam, ... insigni carchesio, splendentibus velis*, and Introd. p. 77. The climax of the public festival is the launching of a new ship consecrated to Isis. Representations of Isis Pelagia or Isis Pharia do not, naturally, provide detail about the festive ship which was the centre of the rite of the *Isidis Navigium* on March 5th; they concern rather the form of the goddess; cf. Ph. Bruneau, *BCH* 85 (1961), 435-446 and 87 (1963), 301-8 and Introd. pp. 46 ff. Tran Tam Tinh, *Isis à Pompéi*, 99, states that the festival is probably represented on the walls of the *peribolê* of the Pompeian Iseum; cf. Introd. pp. 69 ff.; he refers also to eight tableaux of a naval parade preserved in the Naples Museum; the ships, he says, are well equipped, have two tiers of rowers, and have a trophy erected on the stern or prow. His own pl. 10,1, which he entitles 'Découverte d'Osiris', is perhaps connected, as our discussion on p. 41 has made clear. Olga Elia, *Pitture murali e mosaici nel museo nazionale di Napoli* (Rome, 1932), 120, no. 357, entitles her note on it *Navigium Isidis* (?); she gives a good reproduction in her *Pitture del Tempio di Iside* (Rome, 1942 = E.F. XX), 22, fig. 26, but here she entitles it *Inventio Osiridis* and rejects a connection with the *Navigium*. She interprets a female figure standing in one of the barques as Isis seeking and finding Osiris. The falcon in a chest, as we have seen above, may well represent Sokar or Osiris-Sokar. While Elia's general interpretation may be correct, there may still be a connection with the *Navigium*; the myth and rite may thus be linked. Cf. Schefold, *Die Wände Pompejis* (Berlin, 1957), 233, 'Auffindung des Osiris'. The representations on coins are reproduced by Alföldi, *Festival of Isis*, 46 ff. and pls. 1, 1-6; 12, 3-4 and his later study, 'Die alexandrinischen Götter'; also the studies by J.-G. Szilágyi and L. Castiglione discussed in our Introd. pp. 46 ff. These representations sometimes show Isis herself in the ship. See further Lafaye, *Hist. du culte*, 120 ff.; Drexler, 'Isis', 474 ff.; Vandebeek, *Isisfiguur*, 48 ff.; Merkelbach, *Isisfeste*, 39 ff.; Bergman, *Ich bin Isis*, 202; Vidman, *Isis und Sarapis*, 77 ff. On the temple of Isis at Cenchreae see Introd. II. See further p. 355.

p. 278, 14 **picturis miris Aegyptiorum** : Cf. ch. 11 (275, 7) of the *urnula* : *miris extrinsecus simulacris Aegyptiorum effigiata*. Paintings are probably meant. At the end of ch. 22 hieroglyphs are described, but the expressions used are different. On Egyptian ships see Petrie, *Ancient Egypt* 1933, 1-14; 65-75; R. O. Faulkner, *JEA* 26 (1940), 3-9; T. Säve-Söderbergh, *The Navy of the Eighteenth Egyptian Dynasty* (Uppsala, 1946); B. Landström, *Ships of the Pharaohs* (London, 1970). Nina M. Davies, *Ancient Egyptian Paintings*, I (Chicago, 1936), pl. 2, reproduces a ship depicted in the Sixth Dynasty; the colours are bright and decorations are simple and geometric. By the 18th Dynasty the decorations of the hull and steering-oars are lusciously extravagant. Nina M. Davies, op. cit., pls. 28, 56, 82, gives good examples. There is a raised structure at the stern showing painted figures of the falcon-headed god Mont; on the hull the Pharaoh is shown as a lion slaying his enemies. Pl. 56 shows a big oar adorned with lotus-flowers and eyes; stern and prow also have lotus decorations. The god Mont is depicted on pl. 82 on cabins fore and aft; the hull has several paintings too; and a figure of Rē'-Ḥarakhty tops the cabin on the stern.

circumsecus : Cf. *Metam.* 2.14 (36,24 f.); 5.17 (116, 21). The word is not apparently found in any other author; cf. *Thes. L.L.* 3, 1165, 3 ff.

p. 278, 15 **summus sacerdos** : Cf. ch. 20 *init.* and n. *ad* ch. 21 (282, 12), *primarium sacerdotem*. This official is perhaps mentioned in an inscription from Byzantium discussed by L. Deubner, *Ath. Mitt.* 37 (1912), 180-182, where the participle ναυαρχήσας may well refer to him. See also Vidman, *SIRIS* 58 f., no. 130 and *Isis und Sarapis*, 79. The nautical title of nauarch was used in the cult, it seems, because of the prominence of Isis Pelagia and of the rite of the *Isidis Navigium*; cf. Alföldi, 'Die alexandrinischen Götter', 77 f. and Vidman's valuable exposition, *Isis und Sarapis*, 76-87. On pp. 86 f. Vidman doubts whether the nauarchy held in Byzantium could be equated with the office of *summus sacerdos*; he shows that it is very likely that the nauarchs formed a *Kultverein*, but there is no reason why priests should have been excluded. If the equation here must remain a little doubtful, it is hard to follow Vidman's suggestion (p. 51) that *summus sacerdos* (here and ch. 20), *sacerdos maximus* (ch. 17 init.), and *primarius sacerdos* (ch. 21, p. 282, 12) denote different grades at the top of the hierarchy. They are surely synonymous expressions referring to the same person.

p. 278, 15 **taeda lucida et ovo et sulpure** : Torches and sulphur are often attested as elements in purification ceremonies; fire has a widespread use in such connections. Cf. *Od.* 22.481 f. (after killing the suitors Odysseus requests sulphur and fire); Servius *ad Aen.* 6.226, *lustratio a circumlatione dicta vel taedae vel sulphuris*; Juv. 2.157 f.; Budge, *Amulets and Superstitions* (London, 1930), 324 f. (on sulphur); Blümner, *PW* s.v. Schwefel (1923), 796-801, who suggests that sulphur was assigned purificatory potency because it was easily inflammable and was observed to have disinfectant qualities. Eggs are mentioned with sulphur in Ovid, *Ars Amat.* 2.329 f.; cf. Juv. 6.518; Lucian, *Dial, Mort.* 1.1 (ᾠὸν ἐκ καθαρσίου). Ryle suggests that the purificatory use of eggs derives from the fact that eggs contain sulphur and that bad eggs emit sulphuretted hydrogen. He also cites Jane Harrison, *Prolegomena*, 628 f., who is discussing the 'world-egg' of the Orphics and its relations to ritual; cf. Lobeck, *Aglaophamus*, 477. Now Morenz has shown that this concept derives from Egypt, and an Egyptian magical papyrus gives a good example of a ritual use of an egg designed to protect a ship. In P. Mag. Harris 6, 10 ff. a cosmic egg is addressed as one that is 'great in heaven and great in the underworld'. A spell is to be recited then over an egg of clay and placed in the hand of a person on the front of a ship; then it is said, 'If he who is on the water (a crocodile) comes out, throw it into the water (or, he is thrown into the water);' that is, the egg and the spell are a defence against the crocodile. See H. O. Lange, *Der magische Papyrus Harris* (Copenhagen, 1927), 54; cf. Erman and Ranke, *Aegypten*, 407.

sollemnissimas : The form seems to occur first in Fronto; cf. Callebat, *Sermo Cotid.* 401.

p. 278, 16 **purissime purificatam** ; The alliteration derives from the remarkable pleonasm. The phrase recalls the even more tautological Mithraic formula, 'purified pure by pure purifications' (ἁγίοις ἁγιασθεὶς ἁγιάσμασι ἅγιος), Dieterich, *Mithrasliturgie³* 4, 22 f. = Preisendanz, *PGM* 4, 523. In the Egyptian tradition purity, both ritual and moral, is much emphasized. A text from the temple of Edfu says, 'Beware of entering in impurity, for God loves purity more than millions of offerings' (*Edfou*, VI, 349, 5); cf. Fairman,

MDAIK 16 (FS. Junker, 1958), 89 and Sauneron, *Priests*, 25 (on Apuleius, p. 50).

p. 278, 16-17 **deae nuncupavit** : The verb (< *nomen capio*) will imply that the ship is called the ISIS. A ship is so called in Lucian, *Navigium*, 5, and the goddess is said to be figured on each side of the prow; cf. Geneviève Husson, *Lucien, Le Navire ou Les Souhaits* (Paris, 1970), II, 15 f. Other examples of ships with the name of the goddess are provided by *CIL* VI, 3123; X, 3615; 3618; 3640; also a papyrus of the third century A.D., *PSI* 1048, 9, on which see Maria Merzagora, *Aegyptus* 10 (1929), 148, in an article on 'La navigazione in Egitto nell'età greco-romana'. An inscription from Ostia, *CIL* XIV, 2028, refers to a ship with the name ISIS GIMINIANA; and *CIL* III, 3, from Crete, to a ship called ISOPHARIA. See also Drexler, 'Isis', 477, and J. Rougé, *Recherches sur l'organisation du commerce maritime en Méditerranée sous l'Empire romain* (Paris, 1966), 327 f.; he refers to other theophorous names attested for ships, as does M. Merzagora, loc. cit.

p. 278, 17 **aureas** : Giarratano's emendation introduces an adjective which is a favourite with Apuleius. The codices have clearly inserted *votum* by a dittography from the following line.

p. 278, 18 **votum instaurabant** : Although there are plainly some Egyptian ritual elements in the description of this ship, it need not be assumed to be an Egyptian vessel. Probably it would be wise to equate it roughly with the ISIS of Lucian's *Navigium*; on this see Lionel Casson, *TAPA* 81 (1950), 43-56 ('The Isis and her Voyage'), especially the relief from Ostia which he reproduces on p. 50. The inscribed *votum* may have been in Latin; Médan cites *Salus Aug.* from a coin of Hadrian; *votis felicibus* (Commodus); *vota publica* (Julian, with Isis figured on the ship). Greek parallels occur on lamps in the form of ships; see n. *ad* ch. 10 (274, 3). A prayer for good luck is the essence of the inscription. Here is a new ship and its auspicious future is prayed for. The whole idea has doubtless a symbolical sense too : here is a new man, Lucius, and his future is thought of; cf. Junghanns, *Erzählungstechnik*, 180 n. 106.

p. 278, 19 **pinus rutunda** : The body of a ship would also be doubtless made of pine normally. Cf. Mme. Nicole Fick, *Latomus* 30 (1971), 334, who wisely rejects the idea that the importance of the pine-tree in the religion of Attis might be reflected here. She goes on to suggest that to Apuleius the pine will recall either the sacred pine of Poseidon, a great god of Corinth. or a traditional symbol of fertility. At the same time one demurs to the idea that every single detail must have symbolic significance.

p. 279, 1 **insigni carchesio** : Cf. *Flor.* 23 (43 (15) where the very same phrase should have deterred editors from transposing the order of words in this line. For other instances of the meaning 'mast-head' see *Thes. L.L.* 3, 439, 61 ff.; the word is Greek in origin, and its first meaning is 'drinking-cup'. According to Cecil Torr, *Ancient Ships* (Chicago, 1964), 92, the *carchesium* functioned as a 'military-top'; a few men could be lodged in it to shoot at enemy ships, and this was the case sometimes even in merchant-ships.

p. 279, 1 **chenisco** : The word occurs only here in Latin; see *Thes. L.L.* 3, 1006, 71 ff. Lucian, *Navigium*, 5, speaks of a 'gilded *cheniscus*'. Torr, *Ancient Ships*, pl. 6, fig. 29, figures a Roman ship of about A.D. 200; here 'the stern… is prolonged into a kind of gallery, while its true contour is marked by the swan's neck that rises in a curve within'; earlier the swan or goose was a recognized feature (p. 67). Cf. J. S. Morrison and R. T. Williams, *Greek Oared Ships* (Cambridge, 1968), pl. 12 *f* and p. 90. The Greek means 'little goose', but the nautical sense is common. Sterns ending in this shape are not attested in Egypt, as Dr R. O. Faulkner points out to me (22.4.71); some of the ships in the naval scenes in the temple of Medinet Habu, where foreign vessels are also figured, have animal figure-heads, but the goose is not among them; the lashed papyrus-bundle or the lotus are the shapes used in Egyptian ships. Suggestions, therefore, that Apuleius is invoking here a goose sacred to Isis or Harpocrates riding a goose (Médan) are out of place, unless one cares to stress the bird's head in which the prow of the ship of Isis ends on a mural painting in the Iseum of Pompeii (Tran Tam Tinh, *Isis à Pompéi*, pl. 10, 1).

p. 279, 2 **bracteis aureis** : This type of decoration was much liked in Egypt, as the treasure of Tut'ankhamûn shows. Wittman, p. 91, compares the inscriptions of lamps in the form of ships and also the votive-tablets set up in temples of Isis in gratitude for rescue from dangers at sea, for which he cites Juv. 12.22 ff. with the Scholiast. But the gold-leaf plates were probably purely decorative; cf. the 'eighty gold leaves' mentioned in an inscription from Pergamon : *SIG*² 754 = Vidman, *SIRIS* 161, no. 313: the dedicants are *hieraphoroi* of Isis and the inscription perhaps dates from the first century A.D.

citro : Cf. *Metam.* 5.1 (103, 16), where the palace assigned to Psyche has its *laquearia* made of citrus and ivory. It was a prized African tree of great fragrance and elegance; see Olck, *PW* s.v. Citrus (1899), 2621 ff.

p. 279, 3 **tam … quam** : The use of these correlatives as equivalent to *cum … tum* is common in Late Latin, but not earlier; see Hofmann and Szantyr, *Lat. Syntax*, 590 f.

vannos : Cf. ch. 10 (274, 12), *auream vannum* with n.

p. 279, 4 **aromatis** : The form is an Ablative, for the more usual *aromatibus*: cf. *Metam.* 3.17 (65,4 f.) and *Flor.* 19 (40,2 f.). Van der Paardt, *Metam. III*, 132, points out that Apuleius sometimes ends the Ablative plural of Greek words in *-is*, at other times in *-ibus*. The ritual procedure recalls the statement of Isis in ch. 5 (270, 8), *primitias commeatus libant*.

insuper : For the preposition cf. *Metam.* 1.25 (23,14); 7.18 (168, 2); 8.5 (180,3 f.); it is a somewhat archaistic use and much more limited than the use as an adverb; v. *Thes. L.L.* 7, 1, 2059, 27 ff. Callebat, *Sermo Cotid.* 238 f., does not here convince in his attempt to invoke everyday speech.

p. 279, 5 **intritum lacte confectum** : A feminine form *intrita* is found in Pliny, *HN* 36.23.55 and Colum. 12.55: see further Forcellini, *Lex.* 597. Milk is prominent among Egyptian offerings in a general sense, but a libation of milk poured on to the sea may have here an apotropaic meaning. Berreth indeed tends to interpret the whole rite as apotropaic. The other offerings, however, are intended for Isis as mistress of the sea.

p. 279, 7 **redderetur** : After the vivid narrative present *libant* (line 5) the sequence has every sanction, but Apuleius shows a preference for it; cf. ch. 22 (284, 17), *forent* with n.; and Callebat, *Sermo Cotid.* 360 f.

p. 279, 8 **incertat** : Cf. *Metam.* 5.13 (113, 15), *Psyche singultu lacrimoso sermonem incertans.*

sacrorum geruli : These are clearly the same as the ministrants mentioned in ch. 17 *init.* : *quique divinas effigies progerebant.* They seem to correspond to the *hieraphoroi* of Plut. *De Is. et Os.* 3, 352 B; cf. my comment *ad loc.* p. 265; they may well have been servants of the *pastophori* of chs. 17. 27 and 30.

CHAPTER 17

p. 279, 11 **sacerdos maximus** : See n. ad ch. 21 (282, 12), *primarium sacerdotem.*

p. 279, 12 **progerebant** : Cf. the opening of ch. 11, and ch. 16 (279, 8), *sacrorum geruli*, with n.

p. 279, 13 **cubiculum deae** : Egyptian tradition was in agreement with that of the Greeks and Romans in one aspect of temple architecture : within the temple the most sacred room was that in which the statue of the god was kept. Whereas the Graeco-Roman custom was to allow the statue to be seen by all worshippers, in Egypt it was only the higher priesthood that had access to this room; cf. Dieter Arnold, *Wandrelief und Raumfunktion in ägyptischen Tempeln des Neuen Reiches* (Berlin, 1962), 7 f. and J. Gwyn Griffiths, *JEA* 51 (1965), 220. The Graeco-Roman phase of the Isis cult has extended the range of esoteric privilege in that initiates are allowed entrance, although the phrasing used by Apuleius suggests that only a certain grade of initiates has access to the *cubiculum.* Ryle argues that the temple involved was in Corinth; he cites the statement of Pausanias, 2.4.6 that there were two precincts of Isis in Corinth, one of Isis Pelagia and the other of Egyptian Isis, both on the way up to Acrocorinth. Pausanias, however, also states (2.2.3) that there were sanctuaries of Asclepius and Isis in Cenchreae, and now there is the probability that an American expedition has revealed a part of the sanctuary of Isis in Cenchreae; see R. L. Scranton, *Archaeology* 20 (1967), 171 and Introd. III.

p. 279, 14 **simulacra spirantia** : Cf. Vergil, *Georg.* 3.34, *spirantia signa* and *Aen.* 6.847, *excudent alii spirantia mollius aera*: Arnobius, *Adv. nat.* 6.16, *spirantia haec signa.* If Apuleius, in relation to Vergil, is following a traditional manner of expression, yet his meaning is not simply that these images had been made with such artistic skill as to appear life-like. Egyptian belief held strongly that the gods were present in their images. The *Memphite Theology,* 59 f., speaks of the gods 'entering into their body' of various material, and the later tradition establishes a rite of 'Opening the Mouth' of statues after they had been finished by the sculptor, thus enabling the immanence of the respective deities to be secured; see Morenz, *Rel.* 161 ff. (an admirable discussion); Schott, *Altägyptische Festdaten*, 64; Bonnet, *Reallexikon*, 118 ff.; E. Otto, *Das altägyptische Mundöffnungsritual*, II, 2 ff. It follows that *spirantia* here is most apposite.

p. 279, 14 **grammatea** : This is the only occurrence in Apuleius of the Greek term; he uses *grammaticus* elsewhere, doubtless with a different meaning. Elsewhere the word occurs in Latin only in inscriptions; v. *Thes. L.L.* 6, 2, 2170, 9 ff. The temple scribes, usually called ἱερογραμματεῖς in Greek, were priests of some importance in the second class; see Canopus Decree, 14 (*Urk.* II, 126, 10); Rosetta Stone, 27 (*Urk.* II, 172, 5); Diod. Sic. 1.87.8; Chaeremon in Hopfner, *Fontes*, 182; Clem. Alex. *Strom.* 6.4.36.1 ed. Stählin p. 449 (according to him the *hierogrammateus* carries a book and a basket with writing materials); Aelian, *NA* 11.10; Iamblichus, *De myst.* 1.3, ed. Des Places p. 39; and cf. the mention by Herodotus 2.28 of the scribe of the treasury of Athena in Saïs. The discussion by W. Otto, *Priester und Tempel*, I, 87, is still of basic importance; see also Wilcken, *UPZ* II, 218; Preisigke, *WB.* III, 377; Cumont, *L'Égypte des astrologues*, 121; Tran Tam Tinh, *Isis à Pompéi*, 92 with his pl. 5,2 from the *peribolê* of the Pompeian temple (see too p. 136, no. 30), where a sacred scribe is shown reading from a papyrus roll; a similar figure appears in the Isiac procession on a relief in the Vatican Museum : see Amelung, *Sculpturen des Vaticanischen Museums*, II, pl. 7,55 = Leipoldt, *Bilderatlas* 56 [292]. It is remarkable, as Vidman, *Isis und Sarapis*, 63, points out, that inscriptions from outside Egypt do not mention the sacred scribes at all. Most Egyptian priests were scribes in a general sense, and their office varied according to the special tasks assigned, one of which was land mensuration of temple property; cf. my remarks in *C.R.* 2 (1952), 10 f. The scribe mentioned in Apuleius is obviously a lector-priest, Egn, ẖry-ḥbt; cf. Morenz, *Rel.* 68 and 236; Sauneron, *Priests*, 123 ff.

p. 279, 15 **pastophorum** : Cf. ch. 27. (288, 19) and 30 (291, 12). Although Apuleius speaks with great respect of the *pastophori* both here and in ch. 30 (where he prides himself on being elected a *decurio quinquennalis* of the college), they belonged to a lower priestly grade, on the border-line between priests and temple servants. Lucius, of course, as a recent novitiate, could not have aspired to a grade of importance, and the pride he shows, in spite of this, is natural in the context of veneration for the whole exalted hierarchy of the cult. Apuleius has already mentioned, in chs. 11 and 16 (*ad. fin.*, *sacrorum geruli*) as well as at the opening of the present chapter, ministrants who carried the sacred objects or images; but he has not used the term *pastophori* of these. Clearly he regards the *pastophori* as more important than the *sacrorum geruli*; perhaps he regards the latter as servants of the former. The *pastophori*, to him, formed a 'most sacred college' and also a 'most ancient college' (ch. 30), reverting in Rome to the days of Sulla. As for the considerable evidence outside Apuleius, the lowest level is reached, from the pastophoric viewpoint, by the

Gnonom of the Idios Logos (A.D. ii) which states (line 94) that *pastophori* are not allowed to take part in processions nor to claim the places of priests; see the text by Schubart (Berlin, 1919), p. 35 and his comments in *ZÄS* 56 (1920), 92 f.; also the commentary by Graf Uxkull-Gyllenband (Berlin, 1934), 89 ff.; cf. Nock, *Harv. Theol. Rev.* 29 (1936), 83 f. Obviously this can only be a qualified ban, and Uxkull-Gyllenband, p. 91, interprets it as meaning that the *pastophori* must not take part in a procession reserved for priests only; on the other hand it would not exclude priestly participation in a procession of *pastophori*. The whole material is surveyed scrupulously by W. Otto in his *Priester und Tempel*, I, 94 ff. and in his *Beiträge zur Hierodulie* (Munich, 1950), 22 ff.; on p. 56 n. 89 of the latter work he faces the puzzle of παστός : if it means 'shrine', as is often claimed, where is that meaning attested? The *Idios Logos*, 93, uses the term ναὸν κωμάζειν. Many varied terms are attested from inscriptions and in literature; cf. my *Plut. De Is. et Os.* 265 f. A *pastophorus* is probably represented in a relief in the Alexandria Museum; see n. *ad* ch. 10 (274, 5), *altaria*, where it was concluded that a *pastophorus* was carrying this object in the procession there described. See also Breccia. *Monuments*, I (1926), pl. 25, fig. 3 and p. 58 n. 6. It is in black granite and shows a priest holding in front of him a conventional shrine in which a figure of the warrior Horus, wearing the Double Crown, is represented in marching posture; his left arm is stretched to hold a defeated enemy, while his right arm is raised aloft to strike with a spear or club. In addition to the parallels cited s.v. *altaria* in ch. 10 see P. Graindor, *Terres cuites de l'Égypte Gréco-Romaine* (Antwerp, 1939), pl. 10, 24 with p. 95. Fragments of a papyrus in Strassburg (A.D. i-ii) concern a complaint made by *pastophori*, probably to the Prefect of Egypt, about the conduct of priests in relation to revenues and about priestly irregularities in other ways (perhaps their dealings with the temple bakers); the papyrus mentions 'festivals and processions of the supreme gods Isis and Sarapis'; see F. Dunand. 'Une plainte de pastophores', *CdÉ* 44 (1969), 301-12, where it is argued (p. 305) that the *pastophori* played a more important role than has been generally thought.

p. 279, 16 **indidem de sublime suggestu** : For the adverb of place followed by a prepositional phrase cf. ch. 6 (271, 1-2), *ibi quoque etc.* with n.

suggestu : Wittmann, p. 92, compares the podium on which priests appear to be standing in the pillar-reliefs from the Iseum in the Campus Martius; v. Leipoldt, *Bilderatlas*, 60-61 [288-90] = Anne Roullet, *Rome*, pls. 27-30. The priests are carrying sacred objects and the stands look like benches. The mounts for the Anubis-figures in a grave at Kom esh-Shukafa, also cited by Wittmann (Sieglin Exp. I, pl. 25) are in a very different context. In the two ritual scenes from Herculaneum the top of the temple-steps serves as a raised platform for the important figures.

p. 279, 17 **de litteris** : The addition of these words after *de libro* suggests that the ordained and traditional formulae are being strictly followed.

fausta vota : A festival referred to as *vota, vota publica,* or *votorum nuncupatio* was in origin a New Year ceremony on January 1st and 3rd; cf. Lucian, *Pseudol.* 8; Dio Cassius, 59. 3.4. It involved prayers for the prosperity of rulers, state and people; see Latte, *Röm. Rel.* 361 f. Various accretions, such as circus-processions and impersonations of a carnival nature, later became part of the rites. What is striking here is that the prayers are incorporated into an oriental cult. Plainly it was the desire of these religious leaders to court the favour of the authorities. The same was conspicuously true of the cult of Mithras; cf. Gressmann, *Orient. Rel.* 145; and eventually the imperial rulers themselves supported the cult; v. Vermaseren, *Mithras, the Secret God,* 34 f.

p. 279, 17 **principi magno** : In the Roman state rites the members of the imperial family were named in the prayers with the prophylactic words *si vivent et incolumes erunt*; v. Mommsen, *Röm. Staatsrecht,* II, 810 ff. A prayer for the ruling emperors came easily to adherents of the Isis-cult in Egypt itself, since in Pharaonic times the King was a god in his own right, and in the Ptolemaic era the ruler-cult was continued with apparently little embarrassment to its Greek participants; v. C. E. Visser, *Götter und Kulte im Ptolemäischen Alexandrien,* 13 ff.; P. M. Fraser, *Ptolemaic Alexandria,* I, 115 ff. and 213 ff. The Roman ruler-cult probably owed something to Egyptian influence, and prayers for the emperor began with Augustus; cf. L. R. Taylor, *The Divinity of the Roman Emperor,* 181 ff. Wittmann, p. 92, following Weber, *Aegyptisch-Griechische Götter im Hellenismus* (Groningen, 1912), 31, suggests that the Egyptian cults began to introduce aspects of the Roman ruler-cult into their rites from the time of Trajan. Yet in another way the ruler-cult, as we have noted, was fully established in Egypt itself as the full heir of the Pharaonic ruler-cult, as countless hieroglyphic inscriptions and reliefs in the temples show. The Christians, on the other hand, who rejected the ruler-cult, were at the same time prepared to offer prayers for the Roman emperors; cf. 1 Tim. 2.1-2; 1 Clem. 60.4; 61.1. Cumont, *Rel. Or.*[4] 72, followed by Alföldi, *Festival of Isis,* 42 ff., denies that the solemn vows of the Isiac cult are Roman in origin at all. Certainly *vota publica* are connected on coins of the fourth century, as Alföldi shows, with motifs reflecting the worship of Isis and Sarapis, though one cannot accept his claim that the *Navigium* was involved; he argues justly that there was a long tradition behind the association of the Isiac cult and the *vota*; see his 'Die alexandrinischen Götter', 74 f.

In the phrase *principi magno* the adjective is unusual, and Alföldi, *Festival of Isis,* 47 f., proposes to derive it from the term Μέγας Βασιλεύς, which he locates, without further detail, in the Egyptian liturgy. It was of course used of the Persian king in the fifth century B.C (cf. Hdt. 1.188) and afterwards applied to other rulers, as in Lucian, *Toxaris,* 17 (of the Roman emperor). A more likely derivation is the well-known Egyptian title *Pr-ʻ3*, lit. 'Great House', used of the King of Egypt from the 18th Dynasty onwards; cf. Assyrian Pirʼu and Hebrew פַּרְעֹה whence Pharaoh; the Septuagint transcribes Φαραώ. See *Wb.* I, 516 (esp. 10, of its use in Ptolemaic inscriptions instead of the King's name) and Gardiner, *Egn. Gr.* 75. The same Egyptian adjective occurs in the phrase *nṯr ʿ3*, 'Great God', used of both gods and kings, but not so much of kings in later times; see *Wb*. II, 361, 4-6.

p. 279, 18 **totoque ... populo** : For the Dative form *toto* cf. n. *ad* ch. 16 (278, 5), *totae civitati*; Leumann and Hofmann, *Lat. Gr.* 291, cite *toto orbi* (Propertius).

nauticis navibus ; Since *nauta* derives from *navis*, here is an alliteration of cognates. Cf. ch. 22 (284, 2), *luce lucida*.

p. 279, 19 f. πλοιαφέσια : The term is a neuter plural, and occurs in an inscription from Byzantium, as convincingly read by Deubner, *Ath. Mitt.* 37 (1912), 180, which may derive from the first century A.D.; cf. n. *ad* ch. 16 (278.15), *summus sacerdos*. See also Joannes Lydus (A.D. vi). *De mens.* 4.45 = Hopfner, *Fontes*, 698, τῇ πρὸ τριῶν Νωνῶν Μαρτίων ὁ πλοῦς τῆς ῎Ισιδος ἐπετελεῖτο, ὃν ἔτι καὶ νῦν τελοῦντες καλοῦσι πλοιαφέσια. For the same date (March 5th) the Calendar of Philocalus (A.D. 354) has *Isidis navigium* (ibid. 523); the *Menologium rusticum Colotianum* also puts it in March (ibid. 527). *navigium*; v. Hopfner, *Fontes*, 532; Whereas Mommsen's emendation of the meaningless manuscript readings carries full conviction in relation to πλοιαφέσια, the *ita* which he proposed (and which is present in φ as *Ita*) was plausibly corrected by van der Vliet to τά. The reading of φ was defended by Dietrich, *Mithrasliturgie* (Leipzig, 1903), 36 ff., who pointed out that in Mithraic rites there was veneration for unintelligible foreign words such as *Nabarze* and *Nama*; perhaps for *ita*, he remarked, we should read *i e a*; the ἐφέσια which ends the group is explanatory; cf. the ᾿Εφέσια γράμματα, the six magical words, on which see Kuhnert, *PW* s.v. (1905), 2771-3. Thus too F. Dornseiff, *Das Alphabet in Mystik und Magie* (Berlin, 1922), 49 : 'das ephesische itaaoia'. Cf. Festugière's view, discussed by Vidman, *Isis und Sarapis*, 77, citing *Mons. Piot.* 53 (1963), 142-4, that the mystical formulae mentioned on a sarcophagus from Ravenna are involved (Vidman, *SIRIS* 266 ff., no. 586); in this inscription a woman who is an Isiac thanks her husband (?) for teaching her the ἀοίδιμα γράμματα ('the glorious words'). Vidman, *Isis und Sarapis*, 77, replies well to this approach by remarking that a secret mystic formula would hardly have been publicly pronounced to an assembly of worshippers.

p. 280, 1 **signavit** : *Significavit* would normally express the meaning here ('indicated').

p. 280, 2 **gaudio delibuti** : Cf. *Metam.* 7.13 (163, 23); 10.17 (249, 23). Lit. 'besmeared or anointed with joy'. Cf. *Metam.* 3.10 (59, 14), *laetitia delibuti*, and van der Paardt, p. 83; Ter. *Phorm.* 856; and further *Thes. L.L.* 5, 1, 442, 75 ff.

thallos : The Greek θάλλος; and in the Greek tradition suppliants carried boughs of olive; cf. Eur. *Suppl.* 10. In the procession of the Panathenaea old men carried young olive-shoots and were called θαλλοφόροι; v. Aristoph. *Vesp.* 544; Xen. *Symp.* 4.17.

p. 280, 3 **exosculatis vestigiis deae** : In Egypt the constant form of *proskynesis* was kissing the earth (*sn t3*) before a god or king; see *Wb.* IV, 154,

But there are allusions also to kissing the foot of the King; see *Urk*. I, 53, 2 and P. Mag. Leid. 347, 6, 2. *Vestigia* with the sense of *pedes* occurs in Catull. 64.162 (see Fordyce ad loc.) and Vergil, *Aen*. 5.566; cf. *Metam*. 2.32 (51, 23), *ante ipsa vestigia mea*. In ch. 24 *ad fin*. Lucius himself kisses the feet of the goddess when he bids farewell to the temple of Cenchreae. Seymour de Ricci, *Rev. Arch*. 16 (2, 1910), 98, refers to the colossal statue of Sarapis in the Alexandria Museum; the foot, he argues, was the only part which a pilgrim could touch and kiss; cf. Otto Weinreich, *Ausgewählte Schriften*, I (Amsterdam, 1969), 418 ('Neue Urkunden zur Sarapis-Rel.'). There are parallels to the custom in the traditional usage of the Catholic and Orthodox Churches. Drexler, 'Isis', 526 f., wisely rejects suggestions that there may be a connection with the '*wnpt* of Nephthys' mentioned in *BD* 125, 60 ed. Lepsius as a name of the left foot of the deceased; cf. G. Ebers, *ZÄS* 9 (1871), 48-50 and T. G. Allen, *The Egyptian Book of the Dead* (Chicago, 1960), 201. Nor is there any connection with the *vestigia* represented on the stones of Egyptian temples; L. Castiglione has shown in his study 'Vestigia', *Acta Arch. Hung.* 22 (1970), 95-130 that these footprints are a 'picture-like "formula" of the proscynemata of the Egyptian Temples' (p. 128). Vidman, *Isis und Sarapis*, 121, wrongly interprets such *vestigia* as implying pilgrims' vows.

p. 280, 3 **gradibus** : Neither Egyptian nor Greek temples had steps in front; this was a normal feature of Roman temples, and the temple of Isis in Pompeii exemplifies such an approach; cf. Moret, *Rois et Dieux d'Égypte*, pl. 13 (p. 168); Tran Tam Tinh, *Isis à Pompéi*, pl. 1, 3; Leipoldt, *Bilderatlas*, 45 [276]. One should not assume that a statue of the goddess was permanently placed on the temple steps, but the frescoes from Herculaneum which depict Isiac services in front of temples suggest that a statue might well have been placed on the top step in front of the entrance. Von Bissing, 'Paintings from Pompeii', 227, suggested, it is true, that these paintings reflect an Alexandrian sanctuary rather than one at Pompeii, since palm-groves and large gardens seem to be near. The frontal steps in the frescoes are much wider in appearance than those in the Pompeian temple, but the presence of such steps constitutes a similarity. T. Szentléleky, 'Architektonische Herausbildung und Entwicklung der Iseen in Ägypten, ihre Auswirkungen in Pannonien' in *Acta Ant. Hung.* 15 (1967), 457-66, compares the type of Iseum and Serapeum developed in Lower Egypt with the sanctuaries of the cult outside Egypt, and shows that a number of features were borrowed, including the large encircling court and a series of crypts. The podium or platform, however, is a feature that results from Roman influence; it is seen, naturally, in the Isis-temple of the Campus Martius, as shown on a coin of Vespasian : see Leipoldt, *Bilderatlas* 46 [274] = Anne Roullet, *Rome*, pl. 15 with pp. 23 ff.

p. 280, 4 **ungue latius** : Cf. *Metam*. 2.18 (39,19 f.); 10.26 (257, 25). Médan compares Plaut. *Aul.* 57 and Cic. *Ad Att.* 13.20. See also A. Otto, *Sprichwörter der Römer*, 356; Koziol, *Stil*, 248.

CHAPTER 18

p. 280, 7 **volucris pigra** : Antithetic juxtaposition is achieved here. Cf. J. P. Postgate, *Sermo Latinus*, 40. For the picture of Fame cf. Vergil, *Aen.* 4.173 ff. and R. G. Austin *ad. loc.*

pigra pinnatum : Alliteration.

p. 280, 8 **patria** : According to *Metam.* 1.1 Lucius has Attic, Isthmian and Spartan connexions. Greece, then, is his country.

deae providentis : Cf. ch. 15 (277, 20), *Isidis magnae providentia* and n.

adorabile : A neologism; see *Thes. L.L.* I, 812, 31 ff.

beneficium : Cf. ch. 13 (276, 13) and n.

p. 280, 12 **munerabundi** : Another neologism; in this case the only occurrence of the word, formed from *munerare* or *munerari*; see *Thes. L.L.* 8, 1640, 39 ff.

p. 280, 12-13 **ad meum ... conspectum** : Apuleius, as Médan points out, has boldly and loosely used the pronominal adjective for the pronoun. One would expect *ad conspectum mei diurni reducisque.*

p. 280, 13 **reducemque ab inferis** : Cf. ch. 16 (278, 9), *renatus.* Vallette rightly recognizes the double allusion to physical metamorphosis and spiritual regeneration.

p. 280, 14 **oblationes** : The meaning is *dona*; cf. Koziol, *Stil*, 254 (*Abstracta für Concreta*); Bernhard, *Stil*, 97 f.

aequi bonique facio : Cf. *Metam.* 1.5 (4, 17 f.), *istud quidem, quod polliceris, aequi bonique facio*; Plautus, *Mil.* 784; Ter. *Haut.* 788; and see further Hofmann and Szantyr, *Lat. Synt.* 71 on the adverbial use of the genitive. P. McGlynn, *Lex. Terentianum* (London, 1963), 25, explains the phrase in Terence as meaning *placent mihi quae facis.*

p. 280, 15 **ad cultum sumptumque** : In ch. 27 Lucius is ordered to give a banquet in honour of the faith, but at the end of the chapter, one of the *pastophori* describes him as 'quite a poor man' (*admodum pauperum*), a fact stressed again at the beginning of ch. 28; his poverty impels him to sell his wardrobe. In ch. 30, on the other hand, he says that he spared nothing in securing everything necessary for his initiation, a point made also at the beginning of ch. 23.

largiter : Cf. n. *ad* ch. 30 (291, 2), *largitus.* Callebat, *Sermo Cotid.* 175 regards *largiter*, of which he cites five examples in *Metam.*, as an example of *sermo familiaris* inserted into the literary language. This he defines, following Hofmann, as the less purist mode of expression, sometimes used by cultivated persons, but not a part of the *sermo vulgaris.*

p. 280, 16 **prospicue** : Cf. *Metam.* 1.21 (20, 1). The adverb occurs in no other author, although *prospicuus* is an adjective used by Statius, *Theb.* 12.15 (but emended from *perspicuus*).

CHAPTER 19

p. 280, 17 **adfatis** : For the passive use of this deponent verb cf. Seneca, *Quaest. nat.* 2.38. 2, ed. Oltramare p. 38; Statius, *Theb.* 6.51; and see further *Thes. L.L.* 1, 1245, 41 ff.

p. 280, 17-18 **narratisque meis ... aerumnis et ... gaudiis** : Lucius tells his life-story to his relatives and reveals too his present state of mind. It is tantamount to a confessional statement. Ovid, *Ep. ex Ponto*, 1.1.50 ff. describes a person making a confession (*fatentem*) before Isiac altars that he has offended the goddess, while another, who was blinded by her, cries that he deserved it. Personal confessions of sin are not common in Egyptian texts, but the fear of being convicted of sin is present in many protestations of innocence, as in *BD* 125. Fairman, *MDAIK* 16 (FS. Junker, 1958), 91, quotes a passage where the priest-king denies a series of evil deeds, beginning, 'I have not shown partiality in judgement' (*Edfou*, III, 78, 10 ff.). See also C. H. Roberts, *JEA* 20 (1934), 25; R. Pettazzoni (tr. H. J. Rose), *Essays on the History of Religions* (Leiden, 1954), 55 ff.; Reitzenstein, *Hellenist. Myst.* 137 ff.; Merkelbach, *Roman und Mysterium*, 170 n. 1, who cites *inter alia* P. Dem. Dodgson 2, 30, where a man convicted of sacrilegious behaviour is urged to seek forgiveness and perhaps to make confession; cf. Roeder, *Rel.* I, 340 (there is some restoration, however). Morenz, *Rel.* 129, cites a prayer in which a man pleads for forgiveness, saying, 'Do not bring up against me my many crimes; I am one who knows not his own self. I am a senseless man and spend the whole time following after my (own) dictate like an ox after grass' (Caminos, *Late-Egyptian Miscellanies*, 62, translating the text in Gardiner, 18 f.). The attitude of plaintive humility appears too in the texts discussed by G. Fecht, *Literarische Zeugnisse zur 'Persönlichen Frömmigkeit' in Ägypten* (Abh. Heidelberg, 1965).

p. 280, 19 f. **intra conseptum templi** : Isiac temples in the Greek and Roman world were not usually large as far as the main building was concerned, but the temple precincts were extensive by comparison and contained several subsidiary buildings. At Pergamon the main building was larger than elsewhere, but the huge court in front of it was about 200 metres long; see Regina Salditt-Trappmann, *Tempel der ägyptischen Götter in Griechenland und an der Westküste Kleinasiens* (Leiden, 1970), 1 and pls. 1 ff. Any one who has visited the Isea at Pompeii and Savaria will have received a similar impression. At Pompeii several of the subsidiary buildings are larger than the *naos* of the second Iseum; v. Tran Tam Tinh, *Isis à Pompéi*, 33 ff. Naturally their exact purpose is not easy to discern. On the size of the Iseum at Savaria see Wessetzky, *Ägypt. Kulte in Ungarn*, 28; T. Szentléleky, *Das Isis-Heiligtum von Szombathely* (Savaria Museum, 1955), 39 ff. The general plan of temples of Isis and Sarapis is discussed by P. F. Tschudin, *Isis in Rom*, 21 ff. and Anne Roullet, *Rome*, 30 ff. In his description of the Alexandrian Serapeum Rufinus, *Hist. eccles.* (A.D. iv) 11.23 (= Hopfner, *Fontes*, 627), tells us that above the ground (he has been discussing the crypts) there were halls and rooms for the *pastophori* and lofty houses in which the temple guardians lived and also those undergoing initiation (*in quibus vel aeditui vel hi, quos appellabant ἁγνεύοντας, id est, qui se castificant, commanere soliti erant*). Lucius was, of course, precisely in the latter group. See further p. 355.

p. 281, 1 **ministeriis adhuc privatis** : As a candidate for initiation he was not yet permitted to take part in public and official rites.

p. 281, 2 **individuus** : Cf. *Apol.* 53 (60, 19), where it is said of Pontianus *individuo contubernio mecum vixit*, i.e. in a shared lodging. Here close proximity is suggested.

p. 281, 3-4 **visu deae monituque ieiuna** : Cf. the epiphany of the goddess to Lucius in ch. 5 and the reference to her guidance of the priest in ch. 6 *init.* (*meo monitu sacerdos* ...) on which see n.; also ch. 6 (270, 16-17), *sacerdoti meo per quietem facienda praecipio*; ch. 14 (276, 18), *divino monitu*; ch. 24 (286, 11), *deae monitu.* The previous visions and injunctions were, however, unsought by Lucius. Now he is following the planned and meditated course of incubation which candidates for initiation were evidently expected to follow. Cf. Festugière, 'Lucius and Isis', 79.

p. 281, 5 **censebat initiari** : The infinitive bears the sense of *initiandum.* There are several parallels, and Hofmann and Szantyr, *Lat. Syntax,* 347, explain the usage as deriving from the treatment of *censeo* and other verbs as *verba voluntatis* and not simply as *verba sentiendi.* It is the goddess, then, who summons Lucius to be initiated, although her vocation is at first conducive to uncertainty in him. Before this she has elected or predestined him for his religious career : *iam dudum destinatum* (line 4). The idea of election is prominent in Egypt in the relation between God and King; the god Amûn, in particular, expresses his special favour for the King, including, sometimes, his decision to lengthen his life-span. Cf. notes ad ch. 6 (271, 5-6), *ultra statuta fato tuo spatia* and ad ch. 15 (277, 20), *Isidis magnae providentia.* The idea that Isis elects and decides is found in the Aretalogies, as in M 40, 'No one is exalted without my agreement' and M 46, 'What I decide is also implemented' (D. Müller, *Isis-Aret.* 69-71). Nock, *Conversion,* 153, quotes Pausanias, 10.32.13 (actually 10.32.9) on the temple of Isis at Tithorea in Phocis : only those were admitted who were summoned beforehand by the goddess in dream-visions; cf. Festugière, 'Lucius and Isis', 77 ff. Divine commands are, of course, attested in the Greek tradition, but they are more conspicuous in Hebrew and Egyptian religion; cf. Nock, op. cit. 154.

p. 281, 6 **religiosa formidine retardabar** : Cf. line 10, *differebam.* Festugière, 'Lucius and Isis', 79, argues that it may be that 'Lucius' hesitation to obey the goddess after he has been called is but a literary convention.' He compares P. Oxy. 1381, where Asclepius orders a man to translate an account of his miracles from Egyptian into Greek; the man is uncertain and hesitant and becomes ill; then Asclepius reappears to him and he finally agrees. A similar situation occurs in Aelius Aristides, 48.71 ff. Yet there is a difference in that in these two cases it is the god's punishment that produces the final result. Festugière points out that Lucius holds back on two subsequent occasions after receiving calls to initiation; he is made hesitant the second time by his poverty (ch. 28, *init.*); and the third time by the thought that two initiations are enough (ch. 29 *init.*). A distinctive point conceded by Festugière is that

Lucius is called not merely to initiation, but to consecrate his whole life to the service of the goddess (ch. 6). Moreover, the reasons advanced by Lucius here are psychologically convincing; and the whole impression is that, far from following slavishly a literary convention, he is presenting cogently an impressive piece of self-analysis. Cf. p. 53 above.

p. 281, 6 **quod enim** : For the pleonasm see Bernhard, *Stil*, 172 f.

p. 281, 6-7 **percontaveram** : Elsewhere Apuleius uses the normal deponent form of this verb; v. Oldfather et al. *Index Apul.* The active form occurs in Naevius; see Wladyslaw Strzelecki, *Naevii Bell. Pun. Carm. Quae Supersunt* (Teubner, 1964), 23; II, 23, p. 10; cf. Enzo V. Marmorale, *Naevius Poeta* (Florence, 1950), 245; Marino Barchiesi, *Nevio Epico* (Padua, 1962), 481.

p. 281, 7 **castimoniorum abstinentiam** : Cf. ch. 6 (271, 5), *tenacibus castimoniis* with n. The Genitive with *abstinentia* usually denotes what is abstained from, as in *abstinentia vini*, Pliny, *HN* 25.24.59; cf. 26.7.13; see further *Thes. L.L.* 1, 192, 2 ff. Here, however, the Genitive is generic or defining : 'abstinence consisting of rules of chastity'. For the details involved in the cult see ch. 23 (284, 24 ff.). Bernhard, *Stil*, 174, classifies it as a *Genitivus Inhaerentiae*; cf. Hofmann and Szantyr, *Lat. Syntax*, 794 f. Semitic influence cannot be ruled out in view of the frequency of Genitives of this kind in Hebrew. *Casta abstinentia*, 'a chaste abstinence', might have expressed the idea more normally, and Hebrew often prefers a Genitive to an adjective, as in expressions like 'a possession of everlasting' and 'garments of holiness'; see Gesenius and Kautzsch, rev. Cowley, *Hebrew Gr.* (Oxford, 1910), 417.

p. 281, 10 **differebam** : See n. ad. line 6, *retardabar*.

CHAPTER 20

p. 281, 11-12 **summus sacerdos** : See n. *ad* ch. 17 (279, 11), *sacerdos maximus* and ch. 21 (282, 12), *primarium sacerdotem*.

p. 281, 12 **quid utique istud** : In Late Latin, from the time of Tertullian, *utique* is often used with interrogative pronouns with the sense of *ergo, igitur*; thus Hofmann and Szantyr, *Lat. Syntax*, 493. Apuleius normally uses it with verbs to give the meaning 'at least', 'at any rate'; but in *Metam.* 10.26 (257, 11) he uses it with a relative pronoun (*quae res utique*) and in 9.23 (220, 18) with the interrogative *cur*, which comes near to the present usage. The omission of the verb doubtless reflects the direct colloquial form of the question; cf. Callebat, *Sermo Cotid.* 447; Fernhout, *Metam. V*, 171.

partes : Cf. Suetonius, *Calig.* 18, of a portion or share of food, here applied more generally perhaps, but referring still to gifts of food.

p. 281, 14 **hanc ... imaginem etc.** : The Accusative would more normally be the Nominative of the following clause, *quid rei haec imago portenderet*. Such a prolepsis may reflect Greek influence; cf. Hofmann and Szantyr, *Lat. Syntax*, 413 f.; but for similar instances in Cicero and Varro see K. F. von Nägelsbach, *Lateinische Stilistik*, 628 f.

p. 281, 14 **diu diuque** : Such a doubling is commonly found in the phrases *iam iam, magis magis* or *magis magisque, modo modo* and *longe longeque*; see Hofmann and Szantyr, *Lat. Syntax*, 809, who do not find the present instance before Apuleius. In ch. 26 (287, 14) we find *diu denique*.

p. 281, 14-15 **apud cogitationes meas revolvebam** : Cf. ch. 27 (288, 5), *apud meum sensum disputo*; ch, 29 (290, 7-8), *mecum ipse cogitationes exercitius agitabam*; Callebat, *Sermo Cotid.* 216. An intensity of introspection is implied.

p. 281, 17 **utut** : According to Hofmann and Szantyr, *Lat. Syntax*, 635, this word is almost confined to Old Latin, where it is mostly followed by forms of *esse*, as in Plaut. *Merc.* 558, *utut est*. The Subjunctive that follows here derives from the general or indefinite sense of the clause.

p. 281, 18-19 **in proventum ... attonitus** : Cf. ch. 14 (277, 2-3), *in aspectum meum attonitus* with n.

p. 281, 19 **templi matutinas apertiones** : Cf. ch. 22 (284, 11-12), *rituque sollemni apertionis celebrato ministerio ac matutino peracto sacrificio* and ch. 27 (288, 17-18), *deae matutinis perfectis salutationibus*. There are some resemblances to this account by Apuleius in the description given by Porphyry, *De abst.* 4.9, ed. Nauck p. 242, of the opening of a temple of Sarapis, where Porphyry emphasizes the function of fire and water in the rites. Perhaps there is some doubt as to whether Porphyry's account concerns the morning opening of a temple as opposed to its initial opening and consecration; at the end he says that the choral leader makes a libation of water and kindles fire when he stands on the threshold and awakens the god (ἐγείρει τὸν θεόν) with the traditional Egyptian words. The description could apply to either ceremony, and indeed it is apparent that this was true of the ancient rites known to us. In his *Le rituel du culte divin journalier en Égypte* (Paris, 1902), 35 ff. Moret collated two texts (inscriptions from the temple of Abydos and P. Berl. 3055) dealing with the normal daily rites of a temple. In *JEA* 32 (1946), 75-91 Blackman and Fairman published the much later texts from the temple of Edfu (Ptolemy VIII, Soter II is named in them) which they entitled 'The Consecration of an Egyptian Temple according to the Use of Edfu'. They point out (p. 86) that the rite of Opening the Mouth is a basic common element in the two records; this rite was applied to statues and mummies, and in a temple context was applied to the cult-statues and also to the temple itself, the idea being that all reliefs and inscriptions became animated, as a result, by the presence of the gods. Other features, which constantly occur in Egyptian rites, were libations and purificatory sprinklings of water; fumigation or censing; and the sacrifice of animal victims; see Blackman and Fairman, op. cit. 76 f.; Blackman, 'The Sequence of the Episodes in the Egyptian Daily Temple Liturgy', *JMEOS* 1918, 27-53. The first two features are prominent in the account by Porphyry and also in that by Apuleius; Porphyry's fire could be involved in the censing as well as in burnt offerings, and here the allusion to altars implies it too. 'Lighting the fire' was important in the daily rites of the temple, and the first kind of fire was the means of illuminating the temple; it was interpreted mythologically as symbolizing the eye of Horus; see my study of 'The Horus-Seth Myth in the Temple Liturgy', *Aegyptus* 38 (1958), 1-10. One of the ritual frescoes from Herculaneum has been interpreted as depicting an *apertio templi* : v. Leipoldt, *Bilderatlas*, 53 [294] and Tran Tam Tinh, *Herculanum*, pl. 27 with pp. 42 ff. Certainly there are elements that correspond to the account in Apuleius : the central priestly figure on the threshold holds a water-vessel; another priest attends with a fan to an altar from which smoke arises; two groups of worshippers appear to be singing, and there is a flute-player on the right. But this fresco seems to attach much greater significance to the vessel in the High Priest's hands than does the Apuleian account; probably the scene is related to a ceremony more basically related to the cult of Isis and Osiris, the water being a symbol of the recovered Osiris. Such a rite could doubtless precede or end an Isiac procession, whatever other special ceremonies might be included afterwards or previously; cf. the view of Tran Tam Tinh, op. cit. 48, who interprets the fresco as depicting the solemn beginning of the festivities of the *Isidis Navigium*.

p. 281, 20 **velis candentibus reductis** : The curtains clearly enveloped the *cella* in which the statue of the goddess was kept. A rite which will have preceded this was the 'drawing of the bolt'; cf. my remarks in *Aegyptus* 38 (1958), 1-10. Apuleius is accurately reflecting the Egyptian tradition in that the whole rite is directed to the statue of the goddess. Where he differs from it is in the suggestion that the worshippers have now entered the temple to the *cella*; in the ancient tradition only important priests were permitted to do this, but there was doubtless a relaxation of this rule in Graeco-Roman times in a manner parallel to the whole democratization of the cult. In essence the daily temple service meant attention to the deity in a sense transferred from the human plane; just as a man is awakened in the morning and is washed, dressed and fed, so are the rites directed to the divine statue with similar apparent aims; cf. Blackman and Fairman, *JEA* 32 (1946), 86 and Bonnet, *Reallexikon*, 640. In the texts concerned with the Osirian 'Hour-Watches' the first hour of the day is involved with the Opening of the Mouth and with the protection of the god generally; see Junker, *Stundenwachen*, 33-37. Wittmann, p. 100, oddly quotes Roeder, *Urk. Rel.* 38, from the text for the tenth hour of the day, which includes the exhortation 'Awake in peace!' Here the meaning is 'Awake from the sleep of death!' ; cf. *Wb.* II, 450, 2. In the 'Morgenlieder', on the other hand, of Erman's *Hymnen an das Diadem der Pharaonen* (Abh. Berlin, 1911), 24 ff. the expression has its first and more literal meaning.

in diversum : Cf. n. *ad* ch. 14 (276, 22), *in artum*.

p. 281, 21 **per dispositas aras** : The fresco from Herculaneum which we have discussed in the note on the previous line shows an altar in the foreground. The precincts of the Pompeian Iseum contained altars; see Leipoldt, *Bilderatlas*, 45 [276]; Moret, *Rois et Dieux d'Égypte*, pl. 13.

p. 281, 22 **supplicamentis** : Cf. ch. 22 (283, 21), *procurare supplicamentis*. The word seems to occur only in Apuleius and Arnobius, two African writers;

it has apparently the same meaning as *supplicatio*, but the advantage of being freed from the Roman associations of that term, for which see Latte, *Röm. Rel.* 245.

p. 281, 22 **de penetrali fontem** : Cf. ch. 23 (285, 5 f.) where Lucius is led by the priest to the innermost parts or the sanctuary (*ad ipsius sacrarii penetralia*). Water in Egyptian temples was usually obtained from sacred pools within the precincts. In the Isiac temples outside Egypt crypts were connected with water which simulated that of the Nile. There was an elaborate system at Delos, for which see Roussel, *CED* 286 f.; also at Pompeii where the River Sarno provided. the water; see Tran Tam Tinh, *Isis à Pompéi*, 85 and my *Plut. De Is. et Os.* 361.

p. 282, 1 **spondeo** : Apuleius alone uses this term in Latin; it is the Greek σπονδεῖον, a cup from which libations were poured; cf. Clem. Alex. *Strom.* 6.4.36.2 (= Hopfner, *Fontes*, 373). It is the same vessel, probably, as that mentioned in ch. 10 (274, 11), *aureum vasculum*; see n. *ad loc.*; or it might correspond to a sprinkler with a rather different shape such as those depicted in Leipoldt, *Bilderatlas*, 55 [286]. Sprinkling in a temple ceremony is mentioned in a text of the Ptolemaic era translated by Blackman and Fairman, *JEA* 32 (1946), 76 : 'Asperging with the *nmst*-ewers and red pitchers'; cf. their note on p. 79. The early Egyptian rite included a washing or sprinkling of the deity's statue; cf. Blackman, *Rec. trav.* 39 (1921), 44 f. Purification was the first meaning implied; but the water was also regarded as life-renewing; see Blackman in Hastings, *ERE* 10, 79; Junker, *Stundenwachen*, 79 f.

p. 282, 2 **primam nuntiantes horam** : The whole congregation are regarded as having done this ritually. Wittmann states that the announcer of hours in the temple was the ὡροσκόπος or ὡρολόγος, but W. Otto, *Priester und Tempel*, I, 89, shows that the priest so named was concerned with astronomy and astrology in a more elaborate sense. Cf. n. *ad* ch. 22 (283, 22), *stellarum consortio.*

p. 282, 3 **Hypata** : In *Metam.* 1.5 (5,5 f.) Hypata is said to be the outstanding town of Thessaly; cf. *Lucius or Ass*, 1. Purser, *Cupid and Psyche*, xix n. 1, shares the disbelief of Mahaffy and Rohde about the prosperity of the city at this time. But Bowersock, *Rhein Mus.* 108 (1965), 279, is prepared to accept the evidence of the novel.

p. 282, 4 **incapistrasset** : A neologism which occurs only here, formed from *in* and *capistrare*, 'tie with halter'. See *Thes. L.L.* 7, 1, 848, 29 ff. which notes the interesting survival in the modern Italian *incapestrare*.

p. 282, 5 **diverse distractum** : Ryle suggests 'sold repeatedly' as the meaning; cf. Vallette and Brandt. He argues that 'the term was used of the sale of individual items from a large stock.' The verb certainly seems to have that meaning, as Ryle goes on to say, in ch. 28 (289, 15-16), *veste ipsa mea ... distracta* and in 1.5 (5, 7), *commodo pretio distrahi*; cf. M. Molt, *Metam. I*, 51. *Diverse*, however, will mean 'to different people'.

p. 282, 5-6 **notae dorsualis agnitione** : A natural mark is probably meant. Owners branded signs of ownership on the backs of animals; cf. Vergil, *Georg.*

3.158, *continuoque notas et nomina gentis inurunt*; so that the repeated change
of ownership would have removed any mark imposed by Lucius. See also p. 355.

p. 282, 7 **congruentiam lucrosae pollicitationis** : Cf. ch. 13 (275, 23), *miratusque congruentiam mandati muneris.* The fondness for abstractions is accompanied here by a degree of compression.

p. 282, 8 **candidum** : On the interpretation of dreams see n. *ad* ch. 5 (269, 9),
tuis commota ... precibus. The slave called Candidus turns out, then, to be
a white horse; here is an instance of the riddling and round-about method followed in symbolic dreams, which constituted the first category according to
Artemidorus and Macrobius; cf. E. R. Dodds, *The Greeks and the Irrational,*
107; D. Del Corno, *Graecorum De Re Onirocritica Scriptorum Reliquiae* (Milan,
1969), 41 and 126. Mme. N. Fick, *Rev. Ét. Lat.* 47 (1969), 378, suggests that
candidus here prefigures the robes of white linen used in the Isiac ritual. The
adjective is indeed employed several times in ch. 9 of the Isiacs, and according
to ch. 14 Lucius has been given a linen garment already, at the very moment
which followed his transformation. A conscious association seems therefore
unlikely. See further p. 355.

CHAPTER 21

p. 282, 9 **idem** : There is a slight awkwardness about the unnecessary
emphasis of *idem*, whether it is construed with the subject or with *ministerium.*
Hence Kroll's *pridem*, which, however, is hardly suitable after *quo facto.*

colendi : The Genitive probably depends on *ministerium* rather than on
sedulum; cf. ch. 22 (283, 16-17), *sedulum ... obibam culturae sacrorum ministerium.*

p. 282, 11 **magis magisque** : Cf. ch. 20 (281, 14), *diu diuque* with n.

accipiendorum sacrorum : Cf. ch. 26 (287, 14), *gratiarum gerendarum,*
also 16 (278, 11). The double Genitive plural ending is not avoided, but
Cicero and Caesar sometimes do likewise; v. Hofmann and Szantyr, *Lat.
Syntax,* 373. For the expression cf. Arnobius, *Adv. nat.* 5.19, *sumentes ea
(initia).* Paul uses παραλαμβάνειν of receiving instruction; cf. Clemen, *Einfluss
der Mysterienrel.* 17 f. and 25; Nock, *Early Gentile Christianity,* 69.

p. 282, 12 **primarium sacerdotem** : A synonym for *summus*, used of the
sacerdos in question in ch. 16 (278, 15) and 20 (281, 11); in ch. 17 (279, 11)
sacerdos maximus is the phrase, and this title is found in inscriptions probably
relating to Sarapis; v. Vidman, *SIRIS* 328 f., nos. 780 f.; in *Isis und Sarapis,*
51, Vidman interprets the varying titles in Apuleius as referring to different
priests, but *ipsumque Mithram illum sacerdotem praecipuum* in ch. 22 (283,
21-22) clearly implies that he is the same priest as in ch. 21, and the *summus
sacerdos* in ch. 20 is probably also the same one, as he appears to Lucius in
a dream. In ch. 22 (283, 21-22), as we have just seen, *sacerdos praecipuus* is
the phrase. His name is there given as Mithras. Presumably this priest must

be taken to be the author of the important speech in ch. 15, although the term *sacerdos* alone is used of him in chs. 14 and 16 (with *egregius* in the latter place, p. 278, 3). Cf. Tertull. *Apol.* 8 : *Atqui volentibus initiari moris est, opinor, prius patrem illum sacrorum adire, quae praeparanda sint describere*; in *Ad nat.* 1.7.23 he calls the officiating priest *magister sacrorum* as well as *pater*; cf. Vermaseren, *Mithras, the Secret God*, 129.

p. 282, 13 **noctis sacratae** : Why is the initiation to be in the night? Cf. ch. 23 (285, 2), *et sol curvatus intrahebat vesperam*. Magical potency was strongest at night. Medea in Ovid, *Metam.* 7.192, appeals to the night as *Nox ... arcanis fidissima*; so does Canidia in Hor. *Epod.* 5.51 (to night and Diana as moon-goddess) : *Nox et Diana, quae silentium regis, / Arcana cum fiunt sacra*. See further Hopfner, *PW* s.v. Mageia (1928), 354 and J. Gwyn Griffiths, *Anthropos* 60 (1965), 109. The Horatian allusion underlines an aspect relevant to the Mystery Religions : secrecy was expected, and night was conducive to this. But a more specific reason lies in the nocturnal rites of the initiation ceremonies. In the Abydene festival called Haker, Osiris was said to have called for help on the 'night of the Great Sleep'; see the Belegstellen for *Wb.* II, 482, 2-5 and Bonnet, *Reallexikon*, 574; Rundle Clark, *Myth and Symbol in Ancient Egypt*, 130. The Osirian and Isiac lamp-festivals were naturally intended for the night, and in the Khoiak festival recorded in the Denderah texts it was on the night of the 24th day of the month that the effigy of Sokar was put in a wooden box and placed in a special chamber, after which the effigy of the previous year was removed; v. Chassinat, *Le Mystère d'Osiris*, 71 f. and Blackman in *Myth and Ritual*, ed. Hooke, 20. According to Plut. *De Is. et Os.* 39, 366 f. it is a nocturnal procession to the sea that culminates in the rite of the 'Finding of Osiris'. Doubtless there were parallels in the other Mystery cults. Thus Plutarch, ibid. 35, 364 F, refers to the Dionysiac 'Night-Festivals'. In Mithraism the temple ceiling was often decorated with stars, and the emergence of light in darkness was an essential part of the ceremonies; cf. Vermaseren, *Mithras, the Secret God*, 37 f. Indeed the birth of Mithras was regarded as that of light from darkness; cf. Fritz Saxl, *Mithras*, 73 f.; and Luke 1.79 ('to give light to them that sit in darkness', of the birth of John the Baptist).

alioquin : This is a favourite particle of Apuleius, at least in the *Metam.* According to *Thes. L.L.* 1, 1591, 9 ff. it does not occur in Cicero. Apuleius uses it often to join two adjectives, as here; see Bernhard, *Stil*, 127; Hofmann and Szantyr, *Lat. Syntax*, 677; van der Paardt, *Metam. III*, 52.

p. 282, 14 **famosus** : Unlike writers of the classical era, Apuleius always gives this word a favourable sense, as in *Metam.* 9.18 (216, 9), *famosa castitate*.

p. 282, 15 **parentes** : Cf. ch. 25 (287, 11-12), where Lucius embraces and kisses Mithras, described as 'the priest and now my father' (*sacerdotem et meum iam parentem*). As we have remarked in the note to line 12 (*primarium sacerdotem*) Tertullian uses the term *pater sacrorum* and *pater* of the priest who presides at initiation ceremonies, though he is not referring specifically to Isiac rites. *Pater sacrorum* is used of a grade in the Mithraic cult; cf. n. *ad*

ch. 22 (283, 23), *sacrorum ministrum*. The concept of a priest as a spiritual
father is based on the idea of rebirth : the initiate is one who is reborn. Cf.
H. Wagenvoort, *Studies in Roman Literature, Culture and Religion*, 141 ff.,
where it is shown that the idea is ancient; on p. 144 he quotes the Dionysiac
formula, 'As a kid I fell to the milk', and compares 1 Cor. 3.2 ('I have fed you
with milk and not with meat'). He also aptly quotes Gal. 4.19 for the idea
of the spiritual father : 'My little children, of whom I travail in birth again ...'.

p. 282, 15 **modificari** : The use of this verb with a Dative is confined to
Fronto and Apuleius; v. *Thes. L.L.* 8, 1238, 44 ff.

p. 282, 16 **instantiam** : The sense of 'importunity' or 'insistence' is post-
Augustan. Cf. ch. 28 (289, 14), *numinis premebar instantia*.

solaciis : Poetical plural for singular; cf. J. von Geisau, *De Apul. Synt.* 22.

p. 282, 17 **deae nutu** : The expression recalls the method of oracular response
in Egypt from the New Kingdom onwards. The statue of the god indicated
what was best, and consultation with the god was possible in public processions.
The god was carried in a shrine mounted on a barque, and when a question
was put, the statue walked backwards to say 'No' and forwards to say 'Yes'.
When a written query was presented, two versions were submitted, one positive,
one negative, and the answer drawn from a vessel. A stela from the time of
Ramesses II (v. Petrie, *Koptos*, pl. 19, top) shows a shrine and barque of Isis
when she issued an oracular decision concerning the promotion of one who
had been a police-officer; ch. n. *ad* ch. 13 (276. 12), *facilitatem reformationis*.
See further J. Černý, 'Egyptian Oracles' in R. A. Parker, *A Saïte Oracle Papyrus
from Thebes* (Brown U.P., 1962), 35-48. But it was in dreams and visions
that the goddess made her purpose known to most of her worshippers in the
Graeco-Roman world; cf. ch. 6 (270, 9), *meo monitu* and n.; ch. 5 (269, 9),
tuis commota precibus and n.; ch. 6 (270, 16-17), *per quietem* and n. The goddess
has divulged in this way her initial election of Lucius; the choice of priest
and the indication of the expenses are similarly to be revealed.

p. 282, 20 **nos** : Apparently with singular meaning, as *quippe cum ... deberem*
shows.

observabili : Such adjectives are mostly passive in meaning; cf. Kühner
and Holzweissig, *Gr. Lat.*² 992, where *terribilis* is cited as active; Hofmann
and Szantyr, *Lat. Syntax*, 371 (on their interchange with the Gerundive).
Observabilis is rare, and Apuleius seems to be using it in the active Ciceronian
sense of *observans*, 'respectful', 'reverent'. Cf. n. *ad* ch. 23 (285, 1), *venerabili*.

p. 282, 21 **aviditate contumaciaque** : Elsewhere Apuleius uses *cavere* with
a and the Ablative, as in *Metam.* 2.5 (28, 16 f.), *sed cave fortiter a malis artibus*,
or with the Ablative alone as in 8.17 (190, 27), *qua potissimum caveremus clade*.
He has a Genitive in *De deo Socr.* 21 (31, 8) unless the adjective *par* there
governs it. The text should therefore be emended to conform with one of these
modes, preferably the Ablative; cf. Oudendorp's proposals. The Dative does
not occur elsewhere in Apuleius.

p. 283, 2 **immo** : A favourite climactic particle in Apuleius; v. Bernhard, *Stil*, 127 f.

sibi ... iubente : The Dative after *iubeo* is found occasionally in earlier authors; v. Hofmann and Szantyr, *Lat. Syntax*, 31

p. 283, 3 **domina** : Cf. ch. 5 (269, 10), *elementorum omnium domina* and n.; ch. 7 (271, 18-19), *orbisque totius dominam* and n.

p. 283, 3-4 **noxamque letalem contrahere** : A juridical metaphor; cf. ch. 23 (285, 9), *parem noxam contraherent*.

p. 283, 5 **traditionem** : Cf. ch. 29 (290, 9-10), *iteratae iam, traditioni remansisset*; ch. 29 (290, 18), *ceterum futura tibi sacrorum traditio pernecessaria est.* The vow made during initiation is meant. Dibelius, 'Isisweihe', 32 n. 3, compares the use, in similar contexts, of *tradere* and of παράδοσις and παραδιδόναι. Athenaeus, 2.40 D, refers to τελεταί as festivals 'with a certain mystic tradition' (μετά τινος μυστικῆς παραδόσεως); cf. Diod. Sic. 5.49.5; Theon of Smyrna *ap.* Turchi, *Fontes Hist. Myst.* 49; Reitzenstein, *Hellenist. Myst.* 196 (an example from Hippolytus), G. Anrich, *Das antike Mysterienwesen* (Göttingen, 1894), 54 n. 4, also cites Diod. Sic. 5.48.4, μυστηρίων τελετὴν, ... παραδοθεῖσαν; and Strabo, 10.3.7, οἱ παραδόντες τὰ Κρητικὰ καὶ τὰ Φρύγια.

ad instar : Cf. ch. 24 (286, 4), where the phrase is synonymous with the preceding *in speciem* and *in modum*; ch. 29 (290, 12), *ad instar insaniae*.

voluntariae mortis : Médan notes a sequence of four cretics in *(traditi)onem ad instar voluntariae mortis et*, but it can hardly be an effect deliberately encompassed. Conceptually the phrase is of basic importance, linking as it does with the description of the first rite of initiation in ch. 23 (285, 11 ff.), *accessi confinium mortis et calcato Proserpinae limine etc.* See n. *ad illum loc.*

p. 283, 5-6 **precariae salutis** : Here and in the other two occurrences of *salus* in this chapter — *salutis tutelam in deae manu* and *salutis curricula* — life in the spiritual as well as the physical sense is connoted, so that the idea of salvation is present. The present phrase implies that *salus* comes only as the result of prayer and the deity's responding grace. Now that the metamorphosis into man is achieved, *salus* in that sense is no longer the question. There is still the question, it is true, of the promised extension of life, and this involves a kind of rebirth at the beginning of a new life (*quodam modo renatos etc.* line 9). While a physical factor appears here, why should it be described as a new life unless a spiritual regeneration is also implied? Cf. n. *ad* ch. 5 (270, 4), *dies salutaris* and *ad* ch. 12 (275, 13), *salutemque.*

p. 283, 7 **lucis** : Like φῶς in Greek, *lux* sometimes signifies 'life'. The alliteration in *lucis limine* and *tamen tuto* reminds one of the elevated poetical style in which the priest's whole statement is couched.

p. 283, 8 **eligere** : Whereas *elicere* is used of evoking the souls of the dead (cf. Tib. 1.2.45 f. *manesque sepulcris / elicit*; Apul. *Apol.* 34 (40, 14), *eliciendis mortuis*), the association is not exactly apposite here in spite of the *voluntaria mors* mentioned above. The choice and election of the goddess is several times stressed; cf. ch. 5 (270, 4.), *providentia mea*; the whole tenor of ch. 6; ch. 12 (275, 13-14), *ad ipsum praescriptum divinae promissionis*; ch. 15 (277, 20), *Isidis magnae providentia gaudens*; ch. 21 (282, 17 ff.), where the day is chosen *deae nutu* and the priest is selected by her providence (*eiusdem providentia deligi*). The emendation by Beroaldus is therefore almost certain to be right.

p. 283, 9 **renatos** : Cf. ch. 16 (278, 9), *renatus quodam modo* and n.

curricula : Cf. ch. 5 (270, 21-22), *reliqua vitae tuae curricula*.

p. 283, 10 **ergo igitur** : Cf. ch. 5 (270, 4) and n.; ch. 28 (289, 20).

p. 283, 11 : **praecipua** : Whereas *perspicua* cannot be objected to because its meaning is repeated in the following adjective, Hildebrand rightly upholds the admirable sense provided by *praecipua*, and this is the first version of F, as well as the reading of several other codices.

dignatione : Cf. ch. 29 (290, 15), *ista numinum dignatione laetus*; ch. 4 *fin.*, *divina me voce dignata est*; ch. 22 (284, 6-7), *quem ... numen augustum tantopere dignatur*. The special favour shown to Lucius by the goddess is linked with the idea of personal election and predestination; cf. Reitzenstein, *Hellenist. Myst.* 253 f.

p. 283, 12 **cultores ceteri cibis** : Triple alliteration.

cibis : Cf. ch. 6 (271, 5), *castimoniis*; ch. 19 (281, 7), *castimoniorum abstinentiam* with n.; ch. 23 (284, 25), *cibariam voluntatem cohercerem* with n.

p. 283, 13-14 **arcana ... secreta** : For the pleonasm cf. *Metam.* 3.15 (63, 5 f.), *arcana dominae meae revelare secreta*; Bernhard, *Stil*, 175.

CHAPTER 22

p. 283, 16 **aliquot** : Van der Viet's correction of *quot* is desirable for several reasons. An interrogative or relative abverb is syntactically out of place here; nor is *quot* usual with an Accusative. In similar contexts Apuleius gives the number of the days; cf. ch. 23 (284, 24), *decem ... diebus*; ch. 28 (289, 20), *decem rursus diebus*; so that Eyssenhart's *quinque* has some attraction.

p. 283, 18 **salutaris** : Cf. ch. 5 (270, 4), *dies salutaris and* n.

p. 283, 18-19 **obscurae non obscuris** : The night is dark, the commands are clear; a rhetorical juxtaposition of literal and metaphorical meanings.

p. 283, 19 **monuit** : Cf. ch. 6 (270, 9) *meo monitu* and n.

advenisse diem mihi : Schober, *Comp. num.*, 12, and Médan, *Lat.* 254, point to the dactylic sequence in the middle of the period.

p. 283, 21 **procurare supplicamentis** : Cf. ch. 20 (281, 22) and n.; in that phrase (*rem divinam procurans supplicamentis*) Apuleius use an Accusative with the verb as opposed to the Dative here.

Mithram : Wittmann, p. 218 n. 545 argues that no significance need be attached to the name here. He cites *CIL VI*, 571, where a freedman of the emperor, called Mithras, dedicates an altar to Sarapis; he also notes that several priests are known who held priestly offices similtaneously in differing cults. In this sense, however, it could be urged that an atmosphere of friendly syncretism contributed some aura of dignity to the name; the relationship is seen in the fact that Clea, the friend of Plutarch, was a priestess of Dionysus as well as of Isis : see Plutarch, *De Is. et Os.* 35,364 D ff. and my remarks *ad loc.* pp. 430 f. and also p. 95. J. Leipoldt, *Von den Mysterien zur Kirche* (1962), 47 f., cites the case of Vettius Agorius Praetextatus (A.D. iv) who had been initiated into the Dionysiac and Eleusinian Mysteries; he was also *tauroboliatus*, thus an adherent of Attis or of Mithras, while his title *pater patrum* proves that he had an honoured place in the Mithraic cult (cf. Vermaseren, *Mithras, the Secret God*, 153 and for the inscription see id. *CIM Rel. Mithr.* I, no. 420); his wife Fabia was likewise attached to several cults, including that of Isis.

Theophoric names do, of course, become atrophied in certain situations and this may apply also to a simple divine name; Wittmann, loc. cit., states that Mithras occurs as a personal name with Epicureans and Christians, and the latter category, at any rate, could not have used it meaningfully. In our context it is hard to believe that such an atrophy has occurred. Reitzenstein, *Hellenist. Myst.* 228, interprets the name here as indicating the syncretistic nature of the cult and he refers to the representation of Mithras as leader of souls on the monument of King Antiochus IV of Commagene; it is Antiochus I that is really involved, and whether Mithras is figured here as a leader of souls is a moot point : see Fritz Saxl, *Mithras*, fig. 5, and Vermaseren, *CIM Rel. Mithr.* I, fig. 5. The inscription, however, names the god as Apollo-Mithras-Helius-Hermes : v. Fritz Saxl, *Mithras*, 3 and Vermaseren *CIM Rel. Mithr.* no. 32, 55; also Tarn and Griffith, *Hellenistic Civilisation*[3] 170; cf. the remarks of Vermaseren, *Mithras, the Secret God*, 113, on inscriptions in Germany and Gaul in which Mithras is equated with Mercury, the two gods being envisaged as 'patrons of the traveller and guides on the final voyage to eternity'; for an example see id. *CIM Rel, Mithr.* II, no. 1211; see also Cumont, *Mystères de Mithra*[3], 146, citing Julian, *Caes.* 338 C. As for Hermes or Hermes-Thoth, he has a relation also to Isis : he is her father according to Plut. *De Is. et Os.* 3 and 12; cf. *PGM* 4, 95 ff. and 2289 ff.; Adam Abt, *Apologie des Apuleius* (Giessen, 1908), 109; the association probably arose through the attribution of wisdom to Isis; see my *Plut. De Is. et Os.* 363. In our present context it is the explanation suggested by Reitzenstein that is probably operative; we have here a syncretistic borrowing in that the High Priest is equated with Mithras as the guide of souls. Reitzenstein compares, for the transference of a divine name to a priest, instances in the Phrygian cult of Attis. Berreth, p. 109, interprets the name differently, although accepting the idea of syncretism : the first initiation, he points out, has a strongly solar element and he connects this with the priest's name and with the god Mithras as ὁ μέγας θεὸς "Ηλιος Μίθρας (*PGM* 4, 475 ff.). The solar aspect of the first initiation can, however, be derived more convincingly from Egyptian religion.

p. 283, 21-22 **sacerdotem praecipuum** : See n. *ad* ch. 21 (282, 12), *primarium sacerdotem.*

p. 283, 22 **stellarum consortio** : Cf. ch. 22 (286, 23) : Isis checks the *stellarum noxios meatus*. Isis is here using an astrological datum to justify her choice of priest. The oriental cults had all been heavily influenced by astrology; v. Cumont, *Astrology and Rel. among the Greeks and Romans*, 51 ff.; id. *L'Égypte des Astrologues*, 113 ff.; Vermaseren, *Mithras, the Secret God*, 73 f. Many astral connections of the Osirian gods are apparent in the Greek magical papyri; v. H. G. Gundel, *Weltbild und Astrologie in den griechischen Zauberpapyri*; and the Egyptian priest Chaeremon, who became one of Nero's teachers, is credited with the process of furnishing the myths, including that of Osiris and Isis, with astral interpretations; v. Eusebius, *Praep. Evang.* 3.4 and Iamblichus, *De myst.* 8.4, both loci in Hopfner, *Fontes*, 182 f.; cf. W. Gundel, *Dekane und Dekansternbilder*[2] (1969), 28 and 342. Chaeremon *ap.* Porphyr, *De abst.* 4.8 (= Hopfner, *Fontes*, 182) places astrologers (ὡρολόγοι) among the important priests, and Clem. Alex. *Strom.* 6.4.35.3 (= Hopfner, *Fontes*, 372) assigns to the astrologer (ὡροσκόπος) the second place in a religious procession; cf. W. Otto, *Priester und Tempel*, I, 89; Cumont, *L'Égypte des Astrologues*, 124; and n. above *ad* ch. 20 (282,2 f.), *primam nuntiantes horam*. It is likely that *stella* in our phrase has the meaning of *sidus*, 'constellation', a usage that occurs in poetry; the 'association of constellations' will perhaps refer to the birth of Lucius and Mithras as having happened in the same month, that is, under the same constellation in the zodiac. According to Cicero, *De div.* 2.42.87, Eudoxus of Cnidos said of the Chaldaeans that they 'predict and mark out the life of every man on the basis of his birthday'; Eudoxus himself may have opposed the idea, but he was intensely interested in the subject; cf. Jack Lindsay, *Origins of Astrology* (London, 1971,) 83 f.; O. Neugebauer, *The Exact Sciences in Antiquity*[2] (New York, 1969), 188. Elaborate instances of the horoscopic method are found in Albumasaris, *De revolutionibus nativitatum*, the Arabic original of which derives from the ninth century A.D., but which doubtless incorporates much earlier speculations; see the Teubner edition (1968) by David Pingree and my remarks in *C.R.* 20 (1970), 403.

p. 283, 23 **sacrorum ministrum** : Cf. ch. 21 (282, 18), *sacerdotem, qui sacra debeat ministrare*, where the allusion is to the 'holy night' when Lucius is to be initated; also line 17, (p. 283), *sacrorum ministerium*, of a lowlier service. The term *pater sacrorum* occurs in Vidman, *SIRIS* nos. 438 and 439, inscriptions from the outskirts of Rome; Vidman recognizes that this title is used, however, in the cult of Mithras, as in Vermaseren, *CIM Rel. Mithr.* I, 513 and 522, see further p. 352; indeed Vermaseren includes the two Roman inscriptions cited above in his own *Corpus*, I, 623 f. Plutarch, *V. Alc.* 34 uses the term μυσταγωγός; cf. id. *De Is. et Os.* 68, 378 A (philosophy as a guide to the Mysteries) and my remarks *ad loc.* p. 533. In some Latin inscriptions *sacrorum Isidis* occurs after a name; v. Vidman, *Isis und Sarapis*, 53; here it is likely that only subordinate ministrants are involved, whereas Apuleius is referring to the priest in charge. A word like *minister* way well be understood with the inscriptions, since it is hard to construe *sacrorum* as a masculine form, though Vidman appears to do so.

p. 284, 1 **summatis** : Cf. ch. 1 (266, 14) and n.; ch. 10 (274, 6) and n.

p. 284, 2 **luce lucida** : The alliteration here involves cognate words in a playful sort of pleonasm. Cf. ch. 17 (279, 18), *nauticis navibus*.

discussa quiete : Ch. ch. 1 (266, 21), *discussa pigra quiete*.

p. 284, 2-3 **receptaculum sacerdotis** : The temple area had room for the accommodation of priests and initiates; see n. *ad* ch. 19 (280, 19 f.), *intra conseptum templi*. In *Metam.* 1.23 (21, 12 f.) *receptaculum* is apparently equated with *cubiculum*; cf. M. Molt, *Metam. I*, 104.

p. 284, 4 **continatus** : Cf. n. *ad* ch. 6 (270, 11-12), *continuare*.

p. 284, 6 **te felicem, te beatum** : This recalls *felix hercules et ter beatus* in the *macarismos* of the people in ch. 16 (278, 7); cf. n. *ad loc.*

p. 284, 7 **dignatur** : Cf. n. ad ch. 15 (283, 11), *dignatione*.

p. 284, 9 **multinominis** : Cf. ch. 5 (269, 14), *nomine multiiugo*, also of Isis, with n. *Multinominis* occurs only here, and *Thes. L.L.* 8, 1590, 24 ff. compares *binominis* and the Greek πολυώνυμος, which is used of several deities.

istas meas manus : See n. *ad* ch. 5 (270, 5), *istis meis*.

piissimis : This superlative form is frequent in the post-Augustan era and is often found in Seneca. Cicero, *Phil.* 13.43, denied its existence as a Latin word — foolishly, because his outburst reveals that it was used by Mark Antony.

p. 284, 10 **iniecta dextera** : Cf. ch. 25 (286, 21) of Isis, *salutarem porrigas dexteram*. Although different verbs are used, the basic gesture involved seems to be *dexteram dare*, with the sense of a profession of trust and friendship; see *Thes. L.L.* 5, 1, 927, 64 ff. quoting, *inter alios*, Nep. *Them.* 8.4, *data dextra in fidem reciperet* and Vergil, *Aen.* 3.610 f. Apuleius uses *porrigere* with *dextera* in *Metam.* 1.12 (11, 16 f.) and 2.21 (42, 11); in 1.25 (23, 3) he has *adrepta dextera*, a phrase used, however, in 9.38 (232, 10) of a hostile attack. The present phrase occurs in 1.17 (16, 3), *et iniecta dextera*: *"quin imus"*, inquam, which Vallette renders 'lui metant la main sur l'épaule'; here he says, 'posant ... sa main droite sur moi'. It is more likely that it is a variant of *dexteram dare* or *porrigere*.

p. 284, 11 **apertionis** : Cf. the description of this rite in ch. 20.

p. 284, 12 **de opertis adyti** : *Adytum* is used of the holiest part or innermost recess of the temple, while de *opertis* suggests crypts; cf. *de penetrali* ch. 20 (281, 22) and n. In the Pompeian temple there were small crypts immediately behind and below the *cella* itself. For crypts in the Iseum at Gortyn see R. Salditt-Trappmann, *Tempel der ägyptischen Gotter usw.* pl. 50 and p. 62 f. In the great Egyptian temples, on the other hand, books were kept in the 'House of Life' (*pr 'nḫ*), a room in which copies were made of existing manuscripts and new texts also composed : see Derchain, *Le Papyrus Salt* 825, 55 f. and J. Gwyn Griffiths, *JEA* 53 (1967), 187. In effect this was the temple library. A smaller room is probably referred to by Apuleius, corresponding to the Egyptian *pr mḏ3t*, where a selection of papyrus rolls were kept in readiness for particular rites; cf. Fairman, *Worship and Festivals in an Egyptian Temple*, 69.

p. 284, 13 **litteris ignorabilibus** : The meaning of *ignorabilis* here is not simply *ignotus*, as *Thes. L.L.* 7, 1, 306, 72 ff. suggests, but 'unknowable', that is 'undecipherable', to the illiterate stranger.

Pierre Marestaing, *Les écritures égyptiennes et l'antiquité classique* (Paris, 1913), 59 ff. concludes, after some hesitation, that Apuleius is referring here to the hieroglyphic script; if he were dealing with the hieratic script, it is argued, he would not have been able to recognize the figures of animals which become heavily disguised in hieratic. It is possible, however, that the animal figures were in the form of small vignettes such as those which accompany texts of the *Book of the Dead*. The other peculiarities are certainly preserved in hieratic; see G. Möller, *Hieratische Paläographie*, III (which covers hieratic from the 22nd Dynasty to the third century A.D.), 520, 523 and 525 for knotted extremities (not so clear, admittedly, in 525); circular forms are roughly retained the same, as in 303; there are plenty of close intertwinings, as in 215, 297, 368, 523, 526. A papyrus in the Hellenistic or Roman era might use demotic, but the forms of this script are much more abbreviated and could hardly apply to the present description; cf. W. Erichsen, *Demotische Lesestücke*, I & II (Leipzig, 1937 and 1939). Late Hieratic seems more likely to be involved, althoug Marestaing's suggestion that cursive hieroglyphs are meant is also possible, as in the Turin papyrus of the *Book of the Dead* published by Lepsius (*Das Todtenbuch*). Apuleius may well be referring to hieroglyphs in his allusion to animal figures, and he is clearly interpreting them as ideograms rather than as phonograms. There is more to his account than the ' "naiveté" and unpretentious simplicity' seen in it by Erik Iversen, *The Myth of Egypt and its Hieroglyphs* (Copenhagen, 1961), 41 f., who quotes Adlington's misleading translation (misleading at least in one important clause). Apuleius begins the *Metam.* with a description of an Egyptian papyrus roll, and there is every reason to believe that he was acquainted with papyri on which various Egyptian scripts were used,

praenotatos : The force of the prefix has been atrophied, for the reference must be to all the writing and not merely to the titles, although Butler takes the latter view. *Metam.* 6.25 (147, 6) exemplifies the wider sense.

p. 284, 14 **concepti** : For this meaning of the participle ('traditional', 'liturgical', 'formulaic') compare Varro, *De ling. Lat.* 7.8, *locus ... quibusdam conceptis verbis finitus*, 'a place ... set aside and limited by certain formulaic words' (tr. R. G. Kent, Loeb ed., p. 275).

p. 284, 15 **capreolatimque** : The word occurs only here and derives from *capreolus*, 'vine-tendril'; v. *Thes. L.L.* 3, 356, 57 ff.

p. 284, 16 **munita** : As a parallel expression to *suggerentes* the Ablative Absolute *lectione munita* is syntactically irregular. The use of an Egyptian script even in a Greek cult-centre is a mark of religious conservatism; its inaccessibilty agrees with the spirit of the *mysteria* as matters not to be generally divulged.

p. 284, 17 **forent** : The imperfect naturally follows a present which is historic; cf. ch. 16 (279, 7), *redderetur* and n.

teletae : See n. ad ch. 24 (286, 8).

CHAPTER 23

p. 284, 18 **partim ... partim** : Cf. *Metam.* 8.7 (182, 2 f.), *partim per semet ipsum, partim per ceteros familiares ac necessarios*. Stewechius argued that *partim ipse* was added by a scribe who wrongly thought that *partim* could not stand by itself; he also urged that it was unlikely that Lucius himself had now to rush around to buy the necessary objects. The omission of *partim ipse* would not, however, alter the sense. What Lucius was able to procure personally is envisaged as available within the precincts of the temple; the friends would buy objects which could only be got outside. Médan compares the buying and selling in the temple at Jerusalem; bankers deposited their money there : v. J. Jeremias, *Jerusalem in the Time of Jesus* (London, 1969), 56. Corinth and Cenchreae doubtless offered many such facilities.

p. 284, 20 **religiosa cohorte** : Cf. ch. 14 (276, 23 f.), *e cohorte religionis unus* and n.

ad proximas balneas : Remains of Graeco-Roman Isiac temples attest the presence of baths used for baptism. See n. *ad* ch. 20 (281, 22), *de penetrali fontem*. The phrase *ad proximas balneas* might admittedly refer to the town baths outside the temple; cf. *Metam.* 1.5 (5, 12), *ad balneas*, of baths in the Thessalian Hypata; 1.7 (6,16), *lavacro trado*; 1.23 (21,21 f.), *ad proximas balneas*, also of Hypata; 3.12 (61,9), *ad lavacrum proximum*, where the public baths of Hypata are once again meant. But the ritual nature of the present ablutions prevent such an interpretation.

sueto lavacro : Cf. Tib. 1.3.25, *pureque lavari*. Two purificatory ablutions are described by Apuleius. The first is the preliminary washing which was a prelude, probably, to most acts of worship. In the ancient Egyptian rite the Pharaoh had to be purified before he could enter a temple to take part in any ceremony, and the water was provided from the sacred pool with which every temple was equipped; v. Blackman, Hastings, *ERE* 10 (1918), 478 and Schott, *Die Reinigung Pharaos in einem memphitischen Tempel* (Nachr. Göttingen, 1957), where a text from the reign of Augustus is dealt with. Priests had naturally to undertake this ceremony. That the concept was applied to the laity is shown by parallel scenes in the *Book of the Dead* and in paintings and reliefs from tombs (e.g. Leipoldt, *Bilderatlas*, 1 and 2 [233 and 234]) where the deceased person is thus purified. Cf. Schott, op. cit. pls. 2 a ff. Some of these scenes concern the statue of the deceased during the ceremony of Opening the Mouth. According to *BD* 64,46 ed. Naville a worshipper's hands are pure

when he praises the god. Hero of Alexandria (fl. A.D. 20), *Pneumatica*, 1.32
(= Hopfner, *Fontes*, 177), states that 'stoups (περιρραντήρια) for the sprinkling of those who enter' were found at the entrance of Egyptian temples, and
the statement has been connected with stone vessels deriving from temples
of the Ptolemaic era; v. W. Otto, *Priester und Tempel*, I, 396 f.; Blackman,
ERE 10, 481. Herodotus, 2.37, mentions the regular ablutions of the priesthood
with cold water; cf. Chaeremon *ap.* Porphyr. *De abst.* 4.7 (= Hopfner, *Fontes*,
181).

The first ablution in the present context is probably not a sprinkling, for the
phrase *ad proximas balneas* suggests a washing of the whole body. An Egyptian
rite of purification corresponded to this form, in which priests bathed themselves
in the sacred lake; v. Schott, *Die Reinigung Pharaos usw.* 81 with fig. 8 and
pl. 8 a. Water flowing from a vase is shown above them, but this is merely
symbolic of the act of self-ablution, as Schott shows from various texts, e.g.
Urk. III, 37 f. (of Piankhi), 'He washes his face in the stream of Nun, in which
Rē' has washed his face.' Apuleius, however, describes the second ablution
as a sprinkling. Joseph Dey, Παλιγγενεσία (Münster, 1937), 87 n. 5, doubts
whether two separate rites are meant. It is true, as he says, that the adjective
suetus here does not necessarily imply this, since it could refer to a rite customary in initiation, and not one which was customary in a more general sense;
cf. G. Wagner, *Problem*, 110. Yet the terminology suggests two rites distinct
in form and meaning; cf. Reitzenstein, *Hellenist. Myst.* 41 and 221; Wittmann,
pp. 109 f.

p. 284, 21 **praefatus deum veniam** : This prayer is a prelude to the main
baptism of initiation, and its stress on forgiveness is in accord with the central
spiritual experience of the work : Lucius is saved through the grace and mercy
of Isis. Festugière, 'Lucius and Isis', 79, draws a contrast between this account
and initiation in the Eleusinian Mysteries, where ritual purity was the essential
prerequisite, whereas here it is the vocation and grace of the goddess that is
needed.

In ch. 25 *ad fin.* Lucius embraces Mithras and asks for forgiveness (*veniam
postulabam*). The attitude was doubtless traditional in the Isis-cult although
few documents are extant recording a purely personal experience. Its persistence is well illustrated by the words of a consul who had been converted to
the cult : *Dea, erravi, ignosce, redivi*! (Cyprian, 4.25 ff. ed. D. Hartel p. 303)
Cf. the notes *ad* ch. 15 (277, 5-6), *aram Misericordiae* and ch. 21 (283, 11),
dignatione. Huguette Fugier, *L'Expression du sacré*, 297 f., argues that the
phrase *deum veniam* really refers to Isis; it is her belief that it is Isis that appears
to Lucius in ch. 29 after he has been disturbed by 'wonderful commands from
the gods' (*mirificis imperiis deum*). This is doubtful. Fugier notes further that
Apuleius does not use the term *pax deorum*; the term *venia* denotes the charm
and grace emanating from a personal relationship.

purissime circumrorans abluit : The ancient Egyptian rite, as applied to the
Pharaoh or to a private persons, involved pouring water from a vessel over

the head of the person who was being purified; v. Schott, *Die Reinigung Pharaos usw.* pls. 3 b, 4 b, 5 a, 5 b, where private persons are involved. Apuleius uses the term *circumrorans*, which occurs only here; v. *Thes. L.L.* 3, 1159, 45 f.; and this suggests sprinkling, so that of the several vessels mentioned by him previously, the small golden breast-shaped vessel described at the end of ch. 10 seems to be implied; on the other hand some of the qualities of the *urnula* portrayed at the end of ch. 11 would suit. In the representations various vessels are shown, but the situla and long-spouted sprinkler are specially apt for the purpose. The Rhind papyrus of *BD*, which belongs to the first century B.C., illustrates a washing, that is, the first rite; v. G. Möller, *Die beiden Totenpapyrus Rhind* (Leipzig, 1913), pls. 1 and 6 = Leipoldt, *Bilderatlas*, 1 and 2 [233 and 234]. A sprinkling seems to be indicated by Gabra and Drioton, *Touna el-Gebel*, pl. 25, where a deceased woman, in Greek costume, is depicted being thus baptised by Thoth and Horus. These depictions may, however, involve the same rite. The gods are identical, and the demotic text in the first Rhind papyrus (pl. 6) includes the following (Möller's tr., p. 31) : 'Spell for purification by Horus and Thoth. To be recited. Horus purifies you as you enter the glorious underworld (*Dw3t*), to worship the great god who is in Amenthes.' That baptism was a part of initiation in the Isiac cult of the Graeco-Roman era is borne out by Tertullian, *De baptismo*, 5 (= Hopfner, *Fontes*, 381), and he was writing barely a generation after Apuleius : 'In certain sacred rites the people are initiated by baptism, of an Isis or of a Mithras' (*sacris quibusdam per lavacrum initiantur, Isidis alicuius aut Mithrae*; here *alicuius* is awkward, since Isis and Mithras were well known, but Bruno Luiselli [Turin, 1969], p. 10 does not record a variant reading, any more than prevous editors do). Tertullian goes on to say that 'they carry out their very gods for baptisms' (*ipsos etiam deos suos lavationibus efferunt*), where *efferunt*, as Nock has shown, *JTS* 28 (1927), 290, probably has a literal meaning, rather than that of 'exalt', extol'. Cf. Zimmermann, *Rel.* 40; Wagner, *Problem*, 110 n. 69. In the Egyptian tradition it was a constant necessity to administer ablutions to statues of the gods, and an interesting allusion from the second or third century A.D. in a funerary inscription from Megalopolis in Arcadia tells how a priestess of Isis called Dionysia administered ablutions to the statue of the goddess; v. F. Dunand, *ZPE* 1 (1967), 221. W. Peek, *Griechische Grabgedichte*, 186, no. 317, takes it as referring to the bath of the priestess herself; but A. Henrichs, *ZPE* 3 (1968), 109-10, agrees with F. Dunand, while proposing two different readings; he cites Porphyr. *De abst.* 2.16 (ed. Nauck p. 146) on the washing (φαιδρύνειν) of statues.

Baptism with water had a place too in the rites of Mithras; according to Vermaseren and van Essen, *Santa Prisca*, 229, 'before the *mystes* became a Lion he received two purifying baptisms, one by water and one by fire', and two chapels in the Mithraeum of Santa Prisca may have been used for these ceremonies; see op. cit. 141. Mithraism, indeed, may have included a similar baptismal idea to that of the Isiac baptism — that of rebirth — for in the text edited by Dieterich, *Mithrasliturgie*² (cf. Preisendanz, *PGM* 4,

475 ff.) 4, 22 f. (= *PGM* 4, 523), the initiate is said to be 'purified pure by pure purifications'. This, at any rate, may be one of the Iranian or Mithraic elements in a text which Nock has described as neither liturgical nor Mithraic, but mainly a Graeco-Egyptian revelation text; at the same time he lists some Persian and Mithraic elements; see his *Essays*, I, 192; cf. Reitzenstein, *Hellenist. Myst.* 46, who stresses Manichaean and Mandaean affinities; Nilsson, *Rel. in den griechischen Zauberpapyri*, 4. n. 1, emphasizes the astrological element. It seems natural to connect this with the term *renatus* used in Vermaseren, *CIM Rel. Mithr.* I, 520, as well as in Vermaseren and van Essen, *Santa Prisca*, 207, line 11; in his discussion on p. 209 Vermaseren links the term not with baptism, but with feeding the *mystes* with milk and honey, and he suggests that such a rite was introduced into the Mithraic cult from the rites of Attis and Dionysus and the Orphic Mysteries. There was a purification in the sea before Eleusinian initiation, and also a further rite of baptism : see Deubner, *Attische Feste*, 72 and 75 f. with pl. 6, 3. Deubner takes the statement in Philostratus, *V. Apoll.* 4.18 (Eleusis was not open to a man μὴ καθαρῷ τὰ δαιμόνια) as referring to purity from unclean daemons. We have seen that Apuleius uses the term *renatus* twice : ch. 16 (278,9) and 21 (283, 9). The second occurrence is in a preview of the rites of initiation, so that Reitzenstein, *Hellenist. Myst.* 220 f., seems thoroughly justified in connecting the idea with the baptism here described. Life, strength, and rebirth were constant spiritual concomitants in the fully sacramental purifications of the Egyptian tradition; cf. 'the water of life and good fortune' and '(the water) which renews life' in the inscriptions above a scene of water ablution in Mariette, *Dendérah*, I, pl. 10 and see Bonnet, *Reallexikon*, 633 ff. s.v. Reinigung.

Bonnet stresses this idea in the cult of the dead, and he is undoubtedly right (p. 636) in his attempt to link the present locus with the Egyptian funerary cult. It is true that Apuleius at this point adds no elucidatory comments, and Dibelius, 'Isisweihe', 32 n. 4, questions whether the baptism should be conceptually connected with the visit to the realm of the dead portrayed in the second half of the chapter. G. Wagner, *Problem*, 110, carries the scepticism to a point of vigorous denial : 'Das Bad steht nicht in direkter Verbindung zum Mysterium.' He stresses, in a brief discussion of Egyptian purifications, that the rite was never understood as death. This is true; but it can be interpreted prospectively as anticipating the triumph over death. Such a baptism is admittedly not attested in documents relating to the cult of Isis specifically, as applied to living persons. Both Isis and Osiris, however, were essentially funerary deities, and the presence of such a rite in their Mysteries is wholly natural and credible. J. Dey, Παλιγγενεσία, 89 n. 9 raises the objection, as against Reitzenstein's view, that the purification of the Pharaoh's successor is not apposite to the Isis-cult; but he overlooks the fact that such a purification was widely extended to the individual dead person, a point well appreciated by Reitzenstein, 220 f. The purification of the Pharaoh is expounded by Gardiner, 'The Baptism of Pharaoh', *JEA* 36 (1950), 3-12, though he misleads by applying to it the term 'religious life' in a personal sense; see my *Conflict*, 123. Indeed the whole comparison of the ancient Egyptian rites with the Apuleian baptism needs to be tempered by the consideration that it was not until the Hellenistic era that a deeply personal approach to religion found frequent expression.

p. 284, 21-22 **ad templum** : This need not, of course, imply that the previous rites occurred outside the temple precincts.

p. 284, 22-3 **deae vestigia** : The reference is probably to the temple's principal statue of Isis, in the *cella*. Cf. n. *ad* ch. 17 (280, 3), *exosculatis vestigiis deae*.

p. 284, 23 **voce meliora** : An imitation, it seems, of a Greek idiom; cf. Eur. *Suppl.* 844 f. κρεῖσσον᾽ἢ λέξαι λόγῳ | τολμήματα; id. *Iph. T.* 837 f.; Xen. *Mem.* 3.11.1, κρεῖττον εἴη λόγου τὸ κάλλος τῆς γυναικός. Apuleius includes a further idea : these matters are not permitted to be uttered.

p. 284, 24 **cunctis arbitris** : A Dative is natural with *praecipit*, but since it is Lucius that is receiving the instructions, this phrase must be an Ablative Absolute.

decem ... diebus : A regimen of ten days is also laid down before the second and third initiations; see ch. 28 *ad fin.* and 30 (291, 1). The period may well derive from the Egyptian ten-day week, a unit of time presided over by a decan-god; cf. Bonnet, *Reallexikon*, 154; Caminos, *Late-Egyptian Miscellanies*, 309; B. R. Rees, *C.R.* 5 (1955), 143 (on the adoption of the unit by the Greeks); my *Plut. De Is. et Os.* 418. According to Livy, 39.9 an abstinence of ten days was demanded as a prelude to initiation into the Bacchanalian Mysteries at Rome in 186 B.C. (*decem dierum castimonia opus esse*; *decimo die cenatum, deinde pure lautum in sacrarium deducturam*); cf. Nilsson, *Dionysiac Mysteries*, 16, where *castimonia*, however, is too narrowly interpreted as 'abstinence from sexual intercourse'; of course it includes this, but is a wider term, and *decimo die cenatum* clearly alludes to a measure of fasting. The asceticism imposed on Isiac initiates doubtless included sexual abstention. Propertius, 2.33 A. 1-2, complains of Cynthia's adherence to the rule, and mentions like-wise a ten-day period : *Cynthia iam noctes est operata decem.* Cf. id. 2.28.62, *votivas noctes et mihi solve decem.* At the same time, in the case of Cynthia it is not the first initiation that is referred to, but a recurring rite, as 2.33 A. 1 shows : *Tristia iam redeunt iterum sollemnia nobis*; cf. W. A. Camps (Cambridge, 1967) *ad loc.* Tibullus makes a like complaint in 1.3.23 ff. See further pp. 355 f.

p. 284, 25 : **cohercevem** : Cf. ch. 6 *ad fin.* (271, 5), *tenacibus castimoniis*; 19 (281, 7-8), *castimoniorum abstinentiam satis arduam*; 21 (283, 12-13), *cibis profanis ac nefariis iam nunc temperarem.* General restraint with food is denoted in ch. 30 (290, 26-7), *inanimae ... castimoniae.* Vegetarianism and total absti-nence from wine are to some extent confirmed in Plutarch's allusions to such rules; in his *De Is. et Os.* 4, 352 C he says that priests must abstain from mutton; cf. a papyrus of the second century A.D. edited by Verne B. Schuman in *Harv. Theol. Rev.* 53 (1960), 157-70, esp. pp. 168 f. This document (Recto col. 2, 6 ff.) contains the statement 'I will not eat and I will not drink the things that are not lawful, nor all those things which have been written in the books, nor will I attach my fingers to them' (Schuman's tr., p. 170). Merkelbach, *ZPE* 2 (1968), 7-30, has well drawn attention to the parallels between this text and *BD* 125 (cf. our n. *ad* ch. 15, p. 277, 22, *sacramento*), and on p. 16 he compares the abstinences of Lucius here to those of the ἁγνεύοντες perhaps mentioned in the papyrus. Total vegetarianism is not attested, however, as a doctrine in Egypt. Plutarch, *De Is. et Os.* 7, 353 C, mentions priestly abstinence from fish or from certain sea fish; and Chaeremon *ap*. Porphyr. *De abst.* 4.7, while he claims that many Egyptian priests abstained from living creatures in general, yet admits considerable variety in their practices. In many cases they probably ate freely of the flesh of oxen and geese; cf. Hdt. 2.37. As for abstaining from wine, Plutarch, *De Is. et Os.* 6, 353 B, says that priests 'have many periods of purification when they do not touch it'; for possible Pythagorean influences see my n. *ad loc.* p. 376. The other side of the picture is recorded by Apuleius in ch. 24 (286, 7), *suaves epulae et faceta convivia*. Gilds of worshippers had regular sessions of drinking wine and beer. Abstinences were a feature, on the other hand, of the Eleusinian rites; wine was forbidden and many kinds of meat; also there were periods of complete fasting; v. P. R. Arbesmann, *Das Fasten bei den Griechen und Römern* (Giessen, 1929), 76 f.; G. E. Mylonas, *Eleusis and the Eleusinian Mysteries* (Princeton, 1962), 258 f. That the Isiac rule included abstention from bread is maintained by Arbesmann, op. cit. 86, citing Tertull. *De ieiun.* 16 (= Hopfner, *Fontes*, 381; cf. also ch. 2, quoted there; the relevant word is *xerophagia*, which doubtless includes bread); also Jerome, *Ep.* 107.10 *ad Laetam*, quoted by Arbesmann, p. 84 : *Faciant hoc cultores Isidis et Cybelae ... ne scilicet Cerealia dona contaminent*. There was a period of abstinence from food and sexual intercourse in the rites of Attis too; v. Vermaseren, *The Legend of Attis in Greek and Roman Art*, 44; cf. H. Graillot, *Le Culte de Cybèle*, 119, on the nine days called the *Castus Matris Deum*. According to Peter Gerlitz, 'Fasten als Reinigungsritus', *Z. f. Religions- und Geistesgeschichte* 20 (1968), 212-222, rites of fasting derive from apotropaic and cathartic motives and are based on magic; fasting repels the daemons that pollute men's bodies, for the daemons leave an inhospitable body which gives them nothing to eat. A later stage brings ethical considerations to bear, and the Mystery Religions certainly reflect a desire for ritual and moral purity.

p. 284, 25 **essem et essem** : In spite of his serious subject Apuleius cannot forego a playful repetition of the identical form which happens to be produced by the two different verbs *edo* and *esse*. It is just possible, though, that the second form is also from *edo* — 'that I should eat wineless'. Médan's transposition of *invinius essem* results in a chiasmic pattern which Apuleius, one feels, would not have overlooked, although he does not regularly take every opportunity of using chiasmus. Cf. the symmetrical phrases of ch. 2.

p. 285, 1 **invinius** : A neologism which occurs only here; perhaps modelled on ἄοινος, found in a favourite author of Apuleius, Plato (*Phileb.* 61 C); cf. *Thes. L.L.* 7, 2, 214, 31 f.

p. 285, 1 **venerabili** : In ch. 7 (271, 7), *oraculi venerabilis*, the adjective has a passive sense; so too in 20 (281, 20-21), *deae venerabilem conspectum*. Here, however, the sense is clearly active, a post-classical usage; cf. Valerius Max. 1.1.15 ed. Kempf p. 8, *quanto nostrae civitatis senatus venerabilior in deos*! For the active-passive ambivalence of adjectives in *-bilis* see n. *ad* ch. 21 (282, 20), *observabili*.

p. 285, 2 **vadimonio** : Cf. ch. 6 (270, 22), *vadata* and n.

sol curvatus intrahebat vesperam : This was the night of the tenth day; cf. ch. 21 (282, 13), *noctis sacratae* and n. For the expression cf. *Metam.* 5.21 (119, 16), *vespera tamen iam noctem trahente*.

p. 285, 3 **sacratorum** : Ch. 27 (288, 6), *sacratorum consiliis*, justifies Brant's emendation; cf. ch. 24 (285, 18), *sacratus*. So does the absence of suitable parallels to such a meaning of *sacri*, used favourably of persons; cf. W. W. Fowler, *Roman Essays and Interpretations* (Oxford, 1920), 15 ff.; H. Bennett, *TAPA* 61 (1930), 5 ff.; H. Fugier, *L'Expression du Sacré*, 238; Latte, *Röm. Rel.* 38 f. In the post-classical era an extension of the beneficent sense in phrases like *sacri lateris custos*, Martial, 6.71.1 (of guarding the emperor) does not achieve an exact parallel. It is true that the term *pater sacrorum* or simply *sacrorum* occurs in a number of funerary inscriptions from Rome relating probably, in the case of *sacrorum*, to Isiacs; see *CIL* VI, 2277-2282 = Vidman, SIRIS nos. 438-443; but *sacrorum* here is clearly a neuter plural. Cf. *pater sacrorum* in the Mithras cult, 'Father of the mysteries', as Vermaseren, *Mithras, the Secret God*, 153, renders it; indeed the examples with this phrase may all belong to the Mithras cult, as Vermaseren, *CIM Rel. Mithr.* nos. 623 and 624, maintains. *Sacra* is interpreted as a neuter plural, apparently, by W. Henzen, *CIL* VI, p. 622; cf. Dessau, *ILS* 4410ᵃ n. 1 ('sacra Isidis') and Lafaye, *Hist. du culte*, 145, 'ils se disent simplement *de la Religion*.' Yet Vidman, *Isis und* Sarapis, 88 f., wishes to see a masculine plural in *sacrorum* in these and other inscriptions and thereby to defend the reading *sacrorum* in our locus. The epigraphic evidence in no way justifies this. The only way to retain *sacrorum* here is to follow Oudendorp and construe it with *ritu vetusto* which follows. See further ch. 22 (283, 23), *sacrorum ministrum* and n.

p. 285, 3-4 **muneribus honorantes** : Médan compares the gifts presented to children in the lesser Mysteries of Eleusis. This certainly happened in the Athenian Anthesteria; v. Deubner, *Attische Feste*, 115 with pl. 13,4. In the Egyptian cult the gifts would probably be of amuletic or ritual significance, such as the saving *wedjat*-eye of Horus (cf. Lepsius, *Tb.* pl. 57, where a kneeling, human figure bears one on his head) or a knot of Isis (cf. Gabra and Drioton, *Touna el-Gebel*, pl. 18). Eitrem, *Symb. Oslo.* 4 (1926), 52, regards the *munera* as 'Todesgaben' and the symbolism of the whole context certainly agrees with this. He rejects the idea that they are birthday-gifts, since the birthday is celebrated on the following day.

p. 285, 4 **semotis procul profanis** : The implication is that non-members of the cult, although admitted to the temple precincts, are not allowed to enter the temple itself where the rite of initiation, in the proper sense, is to occur.

p. 285, 4 **linteo** : Cf. ch. 3 (268, 11), *bysso tenuit*; 10 (273, 15-16), *linteae vestis candore*; 14 (276, 20), *linteam dari laciniam*, with notes.

p. 285, 5 **amicimine** : Cf. ch. 9 (272, 19) and n. Eitrem, *Symb. Oslo.* 4 (1926), 52, explains it as a 'Todeskleid', and the suggestion of *rudis*, as denoting a dress hitherto unworn, agrees with this.

p. 285, 6 **penetralia** : Cf. ch. 20 (281, 22), *deae de penetrali* and n.

p. 285, 8 **si dicere liceret** ; The penalty for divulging the secrets of the Eleusinian Mysteries was death; see Andocides, *De myst.* 20 and D. Macdowell (Oxford, 1962) *ad loc.* as well as pp. 6 ff. Aeschylus was thus charged, but acquitted; v. Aristot. *Eth. Nic.* 3.1.1111 a 10; Clem. Alex. *Strom.* 2.14.60.3 ed. Stählin p. 145. The notion of secrecy was strongly present in the Egyptian cult, and in its early phase only the priesthood witnessed the whole rites. Cf. *BD* 125 (Nu) Introd. 8, ed. Budge, p. 250, 'I have not got to know that which is not (to be known);' Barguet, *Livre des Morts*, 158, 'Je n'ai pas (cherché à) connaître ce qui n'est pas (à connaître).' In an address to priests in the temple of Edfu, they are adjured, 'Do not reveal what you have seen in all the mysteries of the temples', and the text refers to them, in the beginning, as 'guardians of the mysteries'; see Alliot, *Le culte d'Horus à Edfou*, I (Cairo, 1949), 184 f.; Fairman, *MDAIK* 16 (FS. Junker, 1958), 90; Sauneron, *Priests*, 25. According to P. Wash. U. Inv. 138, recto 20, an Egyptian priest denies association with others during the period of purification; v. V. B. Schuman, *Harv. Theol. Rev.* 53 (1960), 166, where Porphyr. *De abst.* 4.6 is compared (only in festivals did the priests mingle with others, a statement cited from Chaeremon. *temp. Neronis*). Cf. Hdt. 2.171; Diod. Sic. 1.27.6; Merkelbach in *Rel. en Égypte*, ed. Derchain, 72 f.; R. E. Witt, *Isis Gr.-R.* 153. In the age of Apuleius the secrecy pertaining to the rites had been reinforced by the similar tradition in the Eleusinian Mysteries. The Dionysiac Mysteries, on the other hand, seem by now to have lost the prohibition originally present : see Nilsson, *Dionysiac Mysteries*, 4, who cogently argues that the numerous representations of these ceremonies negate any idea of secrecy; cf. my *Plut. De Is. et Os.* 392.

p. 285, 9 **parem noxam contraherent** : Cf. ch. 22 (283, 3-4), *noxamque letalem contrahere* and n. In *Apol.* 55 Apuleius states, after claiming that he has taken part in several initiation ceremonies in Greece, that he carefully preserves certain tokens and memorials consigned to him by the priests. He then says that those who are initiates of *unus Liber pater* know that they keep something concealed at home and silently revere it 'away from all the unholy' (*absque omnibus profanis*). The Lesser Eleusinian Rites seem to be implied. Butler and Owen *ad loc.* (p. 118) suggest that the reference is to the *cista mystica*, but it is highly unlikely that initiates were entrusted with this; still more unlikely is their statement that in the Mysteries of Isis the *cista mystica* 'held the phallus and salt'.

p. 285, 9-10 **linguae illae temerariae curiositatis** : The emendation by van der Vliet (*lingua ista ⟨impiae loquacitatis⟩*) introduces greater precision since the hypothetical divulger of secrets has only one tongue — unless the hearer too be imagined as repeating the information. But is it the hearer only who is the prey of curiosity? If so, van der Vliet's restoration is plausible. In a sense, however, the teller also is involved in the guilt of curiosity since he is attempting to satisfy it in another. For *illae* as a Genitive F. Neue, rev. C. Wagener, *Formenlehre der Lateinischen Sprache*, II (Berlin, 1892), 427, quotes Gellius, 1.12.12, *gratia Papiae illae legis per senatum fit*; but *illae* is a restoration by Hertz, v. P. K. Marshall's text (Oxford, 1968), I, p. 62 (several MSS. read *Popiliae*). Nor is the reading *illae* beyond doubt in Charisius, *Ars Gr.* 2.7 (158, p. 201 ed. Barwick and Kuhnert, 1964) although it occurs in MSS; however, *istae* and *ipsae* are given as Genitives on p. 206, so that *illae* may well be intended. Stolz and Schmalz (rev. Leumann and Hofmann), *Lat. Gr.* 291, find *illae* as a frequent substitute of the Dative, but not of the Genitive. The grammarian Virgil (A.D. vii) attests *illae* as a Genitive : v. Huemer's ed. 6, p. 45; and see further *Thes. L.L.* 7, 340, 80 ff. Since Apuleius occasionally uses *illae* for the Dative, here he is probably using the same form for the Genitive. Hildebrand suggests that *linguae* may be a plural attracted to the number of *aures*, but this seems unlikely.

For *curiositas* see n. *ad* ch. 15 (277, 8). Here a healthy kind of spiritual curiosity, *desiderium religiosum*, is contrasted. It concerns what was said and done (*quid deinde dictum, quid factum*).

p. 285, 11 **crede, quae vera sunt** ; The propagandist fervour is comparable to the emphasis in the N.T., especially in the Johannine literature, that the testimony is true; e.g. Joh. 5.31 f. and see further Bauer, *Wb.*; also πιστὸς ὁ λόγος in 1 Tim. 1.15. That Apuleius proceeds to give some indication of the ritual significance of what was experienced may appear to contradict the resolve not to satisfy *temeraria curiositas*; it is justified as being a proper gesture to *desiderium religiosum*, the healthy curiosity which a missionary urge may naturally bow to. But even this curiosity is not fully satisfied, for the brief *exposé* does not reveal what was said or what was done, neither the ἱερὸς λόγος nor the δρώμενον. R. T. van der Paardt, *Metam. III*, 209, urges that the religious meaning of *curiositas* should not be overestimated. In this book, particularly in ch. 15 and here, it is a very significant motif.

Dibelius, 'Isisweihe', 35, rightly points to the 'hieratic simplicity' of the statement that follows. He compares the συνθήματα of other Mysteries which are extant : first, that by Clem. Alex. *Protr.* 2.21.2 ed. Stählin p. 16, on the Eleusinian Mysteries : 'This is the *synthema* of the Eleusinian Mysteries : "I fasted, I drank the *kykeon*, I took from the box. After handling (them) I removed (the objects) to the basket and from the basket to the box." ' Deubner, *Attische Feste*, 79 ff., shows that these words point to a ceremony which preceded the beholding of the δρώμενα and δεικνύμενα and was a prerequisite to this; cf. Mylonas, *Eleusis*, 294 f. Further, they are words spoken by the initiate. A second *synthema* probably concerns the mysteries of Attis, and it is given thus by Firmicus Maternus, *De err. prof. rel.* 18.1 ed. G. Heuten p. 85 : 'I have eaten from the tambourine, I have drunk from the cymbal, I have become an initiate of Attis;' cf. Clem. Alex. *Protr.* 2.15.3 ed. Stählin p. 13, where the words are introduced as the *symbola* of the initiation to Attis, Cybele and the Corybantes. Firmicus Maternus speaks in this context of *signa* and *symbola*, of *propria signa, propria responsa*. In both reports we are dealing with words spoken by initiates during, or at the end of, the rites; the words operate as 'passwords', *synthemata*. Dibelius, op. cit. 41, applies the meaning to the initiate's position after taking the vows : they are probably sayings, he urges, through which the initiate of the Eleusinian or Phrygian or Isiac rites enabled himself to be recognized, in the world outside, as a member of his sacral community. Now this can hardly be true of the statement in Apuleius, nor do the other interpretations apply; and the arguments by which Dibelius seeks to make a *synthema* of this account are not convincing. He points out (p. 40) that the Apuleian passage, like the other loci, consists of short sentences in the aorist or perfect, juxtaposed without syntactical conjunction, and enriched by participial constructions. Again, he urges, in all the instances the initiate speaks in the first person and intimates briefly, without describing, the sacred proceedings. So far we can agree : there is a stylistic resemblance. On the question of content, however, a clear difference emerges : the Eleusinian and Phrygian statements do describe, even if very briefly, ritual actions that have been performed, whereas the Apuleian initiate describes his movements and what he has seen, and all this in a heightened symbolical sense. Perhaps Dibelius is right to compare the end of the Phrygian formula with ours : 'I have become an initiate of Attis' and 'I worshipped them (the gods) face to face'; even here the correspondence relates to a climax, while a detailed parallel is missing. Dibelius goes too far when he claims that the final sentence in Apuleius means 'I have become a god', and that in the next chapter the initiate is revealed to the people as a god; certainly an assimilation to a god has happened, but it is not a simple apotheosis; cf. Wagner, *Problem*, 122.

There are other comparable sayings, as at the end of the so-called Mithras-Liturgy : 'Lord, as one reborn do I depart, as one who is being exalted and is already exalted do I die' (Dieterich, *Mithrasliturgie*[2], 14,31 f. = *PGM* 4, 719 f.). Berreth, p. 109, points to the conceptual resemblance to our passage, in that the initiate is united with the sun. But a functional and formal resemblance is missing. The same applies to the saying from a rite of Sabazius quoted by Demosthenes, *De cor.* 259 : 'I escaped the evil. I found the better lot;' and to the saying recorded in Irenaeus (A.D. ii) 1.21.3, ed. W. W. Harvey (1857), I, p. 185 : 'I have been confirmed and redeemed, and I shall redeem my soul from this age and everything from it in the name of Iao, who redeemed his soul unto deliverance in the living Christ', a passage rightly dubbed by Dibelius, p. 40, as a 'liturgical response'. So too an inscription from Thurii (*IG* XIV, 641) ends with a *macarismos* addressed to the initiate : 'Happy and blessed, you shall be divine instead of mortal'; after which comes the line 'A kid, I fell into the milk' (ἔριφος ἐς γάλ' ἔπετον) — clearly the initiate's response, in which 'kid' refers perhaps to his grade, and the ritual action to a bath in milk in a Dionysiac rite; cf. Dieterich, *Mithrasliturgie*², 171, where Reinach is cited for the view that a drink of milk is implied. According to de Jong, *Myst.* 77, the expression symbolizes the initiate's return to his god. In his Appendix Dieterich assembled a number of other liturgical fragments. Our passage has stylistic affinities with them, but its content is sharply distinguished from them. The rite at Cenchreae must have been conducted in the main in Greek, so that in any case the words of Apuleius cannot have preserved their original form; cf. Dibelius, p. 41 n. 20. The simplicity echoes the *synthemata*, but it is a highly sophisticated simplicity. *Limine* rhymes with *lumine*, and the poetical aim is clear in other ways — the repetition of *accessi*; the alliteration in *candido coruscantem* and the hard gutterals elsewhere; and in the choice of words : *confinium, calcare, coruscare, proxumus*, Wittmann points out that these words had been previously used in prose, but this does not mean that their poetic glow has been fully chilled. The brief record refrains from naming gods, apart from Proserpina; nor does it specify ritual actions carried out. This may stem from religious reticence, and the early Christian community exersised a similar *disciplina arcani*, particularly with regard to the sacraments of baptism and the eucharist; cf. Gustav Mensching, *Das heilige Schweigen* (Giessen, 1926), 125 f. In Egypt itself in the post-Persian era the defensive psychological mechanism of a subject people may have operated, just as the pre-Greek population intensified the secrecy of Eleusis in the face of newcomers; cf. Deubner, *Attische Feste*, 71. Yet outside Egypt the faith was now a missionary movement, and secrecy in this context was a mark of pride attaching to a tradition of high antiquity.

　　　p. 285, 11-12 **accessi confinium mortis** : Cf. *Metam.* 2.28 (48, 6 f.), *corpusque istud postliminio mortis animare* (of the promise made by an Egyptian priest). While the Egyptian affinities of this domain of death are unmistakable, the rites of other Mystery cults show concern with the same theme. Thus the candidate for admission into the following of Attis is described in Firmicus Maternus, *De err. prof. rel.* 18.1 as *homo moriturus*; de Jong, *De Apul.* 99, compares Plut. *Fr. de an.* 2 = Fr. 178 in F. H. Sandbach, *Plutarch's Moralia*, vol. 15 (Loeb, 1969), p. 316; Plutarch is quoting from Themistius, *On the Soul* : 'but when that time (of death) comes, it has an experience like that of men who are undergoing initiation into great mysteries; and so the verbs *teleutân* (die) and *teleisthai* (be initiated), and the actions they denote, have a similarity.' The translation is Sandbach's, and he cites Mylonas, *Eleusis*, 264 ff. for the view that the statement does not relate to the Eleusinian Mysteries. The statement goes on to describe the wonderful light and divine bliss which follow an experience of terrible darkness and wandering; this, according to Mylonas, is the impress of Orphism. It is clear that a false etymology has motivated the contrast in Themistius—Plutarch; but Deubner, *Attische Feste*, 78 f., believes that a blessed life after death was a certainly promised to initiates at Eleusis. He points to the Homeric Hymn to Demeter, 481 f., and goes on to admit that the contrasted Heaven and Hell was an accretion elaborated by the Orphics.

On the importance of the 'Totenreich' in Eleusis see also Nilsson, *Gesch. Gr. Rel.* I, 475. At the same time the theme of death and resurrection was strongly expressed in the rites of Attis : v. Hepding, *Attis*, 195 ff.; Vermaseren, *The Legend of Attis in Greek and Roman Art*, 44 ff.

The experience thus introduced by Apuleius is tentatively explained by de Jong, *Myst.* 203 ff. as one belonging to a state of ecstasy or trance. Dreams and incubation, he urges, permeate the whole Isiac approach. Dibelius, 'Isisweihe', p. 46, well points out that these elements characterise the period of promise and waiting, as in the epiphany of the goddess (chs. 3-6), the nocturnal instructions from her (ch. 19), the oracular dream (ch. 20), and her nocturnal intimation of the call to initiation (ch. 22). But now the longed-for culmination has come; now it is not a case of trance or dream, it is the reality of revelation.

That the expression *accessi confinium mortis* means 'I was in danger of death' is not likely, although de Jong, *Myst.* 230, quotes the words of a medium in illustration ('The soul clings to the body with only a very thin thread'). It is true that the words *ad instar voluntariae mortis et precariae salutis* in ch. 12 can be pressed to imply that the initiate is submitting to death and achieves redemption from it through prayer. H. Wagenvoort, *Studies in Roman Literature, Culture and Rel.* 135, cites the symbolic facing of death in rites of puberty; also the fact that the candidate for Benedictine ordination lies on the ground and is covered with a shroud to the sounds of the *Miserere* before rising to receive his new life and status. Yet the whole description in Apuleius makes it clear that he is being introduced to the realm of the dead, which the Egyptians located in Dat or Dewat, the underworld, a region which the sun was believed to visit in the night. Texts and pictures deriving mainly from the royal tombs of the New Kingdom set forth the doctrine of *'Imy Dw3t* ('He who is in the Underworld'); v. Erik Hornung, *Das Amduat* (3 vols., Wiesbaden, 1963 and 1967). That the text was not specifically royal in origin was shown by Grapow, *ZÄS* 72 (1936),38 f. It is a funerary concept that unites the belief in Osiris with solar worship. The deceased is identified with Osiris, and his glorified body remains in the underworld, the realm of Osiris; but his soul accompanies Rē', the sun-god, in his daily encircling of the world through heaven, earth and underworld. In the following of Rē' the soul returns every night to the underworld and reunites with his body. At dawn comes the experience of rejuvenation and rebirth, recalling the line of Catullus, *Soles occidere et redire possunt*, but here the fate of man is happily linked to the solar return in the dawn. Representations show the Osiris-King in the full flush of ithyphallic power greeting the dawn. The text of the Twelfth Hour includes the words : 'May the living breath of Rē' be in your nose, may the breath of Khepri be with you, so that you live and remain in life. Hail, Osiris, Lord of Life!' (Hornung, vol. I, 204; vol. II, 192-4). The tradition flourished after the New Kingdom, though in different forms; for the papyri see Bonnet, *Reallexikon*, 78; Lanzone, *Diz. Mit.* 1293 ff. and pl. 267 (lower reg.); id. *Le domicile des esprits* (Paris, 1879); Jequier, *Livre de ce qu'il y a dans l'Hadès* (Paris, 1894); Hornung,

Das Amduat, III (Wiesbaden, 1967), vii and pls. 5-10. The theme was displayed on sarcophagi, as on that of Ramesses III; v. C. Boreux, *Louvre Cat.* (1932), pl. 10 and pp. 109 f.; that of Pediêse in the Saïte era shows the revivified dead adoring the sun barque : v. A. Moret, *Sarcophages de l'époque Bubastite à l'époque Saïte* (Cairo, 1913), 271 (no. 41029); cf. ibid. pls. 19, 23, 30, 32, 34, 35 (côtè 3, top) and 39, where phases of the solar journey are shown. Adoration of the solar barque is often represented on stelae, as on no. 22047 in the Cairo Museum, see A. Kamal, *Stèles ptolémaiques et romaines* (Cairo, 1905), II, pl. 14 and I, pp. 42 ff.; cf. U. Bouriant, *Rec. trav.* 10 (1888), 195, where this and other instances are noted; see also Kamal, op. cit. II, pl. 15, no 22049 and I, pp. 44 ff.; II, pl. 16, no 22052 and I, pl. 48 ff.; II, pl. 18, no. 22057 and I, p. 55. The barque of Rē' is conspicuous too in the late funerary literature; v. J.-C. Goyon *Rituels funéraires de l'ancienne Égypte* (Paris, 1972), 160, 255, 259, 261; on p. 255 the privilege of joining Rē' here is linked to the power of making transformations in the afterlife : 'Quand Atoum m'a placé à bord de la barque de Rê, il m'accorde d'accomplir toutes les tranformations que je souhaite' (from the *Second Book of Breathings*; tr. by Goyon). Isis, it may be noted, is a prominent figure in the solar barque as figured on the stelae.

The relevance of this vital theme to Apuleius has been questioned because it is not pure Osirianism. Such scepticism is ill-founded, for the fusion of solar and Osirian beliefs had occurred very long since. Dibelius, 'Isisweihe', 49, objects that Apuleius never states that the initiate is experiencing the same fate as Osiris; the concept is so basic, however, in the Egyptian tradition that it can scarcely be avoided. Wagner, *Problem*, 114, objects that an association of Osiris and the sun is a late and quite artificial phenomenon. He is thinking of Osiris as a sun-god, and in this sense he is right. But the concept set out in *Amduat* is not an equation of Osiris and the sun; it involves a fusion of two theologies enabling the Osirian dead to be endowed with solar immortality. Plutarch, *De Is. et Os.* 52 *init.*, says that 'in the sacred hymns of Osiris they call on him who is hidden in the arms of the sun'; in my commentary *ad loc.* (p. 498) I have recorded Zandee's very probable suggestion that what is meant is the revivification of Osiris by Rē' when the latter visits the underworld — the very situation depicted by Apuleius if we concede that the initiate is identified with Osiris. Wittmann's interpretation is on the right lines; so too is that of Reitzenstein, *Hellenist. Myst.* 220 ff., although he concentrates too much on the evidence of the Rhind Funerary Papyrus I; his invocation of 'Apotheosis by Drowning' involves a valid Osirian concept, but one not likely to be induced in ritual. The essential relation to Egyptian funerary ideas was pointed out by Erman, *Rel.* (tr. Wild), 492 f.; cf. Lüddeckens, *MDAIK* 11 (1943), 59.

Several details remain, nevertheless, problematic since the presentation of the central concept does not appear in any text or figure relating directly to the rites of Isis and Osiris. The ceremonies probably took place in an underground chamber. Crypts were a regular feature of temples of Isis and Serapis, and they were found both in the main sanctuary and in subsidiary buildings;

see Tran Tam Tinh, *Isis à Pompéi*, 34; my *Plut. De Is. et Os.* 385 ff. Crypts were used too in other Mystery cults; the Mithraeum is the example *par excellence*. E. Maass, *Orpheus*, 176 n. 3 (cf. 132 n. 10) cites Pausanias 2.2.1 on the Corinthian temple of Palaemon for the idea in a Greek context, as well as the tradition that Diocletian built an underground temple for the goddess Hecate in Antiochia (according to Joh. Malalas, A.D. vi). Mylonas, however, *Eleusis*, 268, says of Eleusis that 'no underground rooms and passages exist into which the mystai might have descended to get a glimpse of Hades.' The *voluntaria mors* was a ritual submission through identification with Osiris, and the walls of the chamber probably bore depictions of the realm of the dead, such as the *Book of Amduat* shows. The most splendidly impressive of such extant representations are those preserved in the tomb of Sethos I.

What exactly was done to the initiate? Hopfner, *PW* s.v. Mysterien (oriental-hellenist.) [1933], 1332, believes that, just as Osiris was slain and enclosed in a coffin, so the initiate was anaesthetized and boxed up, after which came the reawakening and resurrection through the suggestive commands of priestesses or priests. The anaesthetization, he opines, was achieved through a purely physical narcosis or through a hypnotic catalepsy. The latter mode is championed by O. E. Briem, *Les sociétés secrètes de Mystères* (Paris, 1941), 371, who invokes Aelius Aristides on hypnotic sleep. That a sarcophagus was used does not seem likely, but many funerary reliefs show Osiris being awakened and revived from death by Isis while he lies on a couch or catafalque; see those in the temple of Denderah and one in the Cairo Museum, both reproduced by E. Otto, *Cults of Osiris and Amon*, pls. 18-20 cf. pls. 16-17; also Lanzone, *Diz. Mit.* pls. 269 ff. The *Songs* and *Lamentations of Isis and Nephthys* show that the call to the moribund Osiris was carried out in festival rites in poetic language full of sexual appeal and with an accompaniment of music; detailed instructions are also given concerning the toilet of the priestesses who were to impersonate the two goddesses; for instance, they were to remove body hair. Hopfner's suggestion is, therefore, in this respect well founded. How the initiate was 'put to sleep' is more questionable; Hopfner refers to his article in *Griffith Studies* (1932), 218-232, which deals with magical practices from mediaeval and modern Greek sources, but their relevance may be doubted. Plutarch, however, writing some fifty years before Apuleius, tells of a preparation called *cyphi*, through the aromatic charms of which the body 'acquires a temper that seductively brings on sleep' (*De Is. et Os.* 80, 383 F). Furthermore, Apuleius *Apol.* 43, states his belief that sleep and oblivion can be induced by singing or by incense (*seu carminum avocamento sive odorum delenimento*); cf. de Jong, *Myst.* 228. Carl du Prel, *Die Mystik der alten Griechen* (Leipzig, 1888), 83, believes that the state there described is that of the somnambulist. A similarity in a monastic rite has been referred to above, and Berreth, p. 112, also invokes it : the Christian monk makes a vow, taking on a funerary garment and undergoing an emblematic death, the sense of which is that he becomes dead to this world (Col. 3.3, 'For ye are dead and your life is hid with Christ in God').

After a fast an *aperitio oris* takes place, recalling the Ancient Egyptian rite, and the monk dons a white dress. Monasticism, as Berreth rightly stresses, began in Egypt. In the modern world some American evangelists have been known to place converts in coffins, after which they are called out to a new life; Dr Pennar Davies supplies this information verbally, and he has embodied the idea into his Welsh novel, *Anadl o'r Uchelder* (*Breath from on High*). But in the Isiac cult, as we have already suggested, the funerary couch was probably used. It is the couch of Osiris himself, represented in the scenes of awakening in the temples of Abydos and Denderah. Eberhard Otto has found the earliest instance of this cult-form, which he justly regards as the prototype of the Osiris-Mysteries in the Late Era, in a representation in Room 19 of the funerary temple of Sethos I in Qurna : see his 'Eine Darstellung der "Osiris-Mysterien" in Theben', *FS. Siegfried Schott*, ed. W. Helck (Wiesbaden, 1968), 99-105.

That a mosaic from a house in Antioch of the imperial era depicts our scene has been claimed by Doro Levi in *Berytus* 7 (1942), 19-55 ('Mors Voluntaria : Mystery Cults on Mosaics from Antioch'); also in *Antioch Mosaic Pavements* (Princeton, 1947), I, 163 ff. and II, pl. 33 a. Cf. R. E. Witt, *Isis Gr.-R.* 34 and p. 161. There are three figures in the scene, one of which is Hermes with his *caduceus*; in the middle is a scantily clothed human figure; on the left is a goddess with a veil and wreath of green leaves on her head, while rising above her head-dress is the top of a trumpet-shaped torch which the missing left hand of the goddess is apparently holding. The torch, according to Doro Levi, is of floral origin, 'imitating a double papyrus stem', but its design is seen to occur in two instances of Demeter's long torch in frescoes from Pompeii. It seems likely that the figure is indeed Demeter, and that the scene is Eleusinian, relating to Hades. It is true that Doro Levi can point to several contexts where Hermes and Isis are connected; and a Pompeian fresco (= Schefold, *Verges-senes Pompeji*, pl. 169, 2) is interpreted by him as depicting Hermes and Isis-Fortuna; Schefold and others see Demeter here, and the torch is similar. In the absence of anything distinctively and indubitably Isiac, the mosaic from Antioch cannot confidently be assigned to the Apuleian context. In one panel admittedly there is a figure who is probably Isis or an Isiac priestess since she has a sash with moon and stars depicted on it; cf. n. *ad* ch. 4 (268, 17-18), *stellae ... semenstris luna*. But it may be questioned whether this figure confers an Isiac meaning on the whole of the rest.

In ch. 3 of *Chaldaean Oracles and Theurgy* (Cairo, 1956), 177 ff. Hans Lewy states that 'theurgical elevation, known as ἀναγωγή is the chief mystery of the Chaldaean sacramental community, its goal being the immortalization of the soul' (p. 177). After an attempted reconstruction of the rites furthering 'the ascent of the soul', Lewy, pp. 204-7, maintains that it was preceded by 'another act which signified the death of the mortal body' (p. 205). He is inter-preting Proclus, *Theol. Plat.* 4.9, here; when he claims that 'mystic voluntary suicide' was a part of the rite, he is explaining Psellus, *Comm.* 1141 B (Kroll,

61, 3) thus, in a sentence which he translates, 'The souls of those who have left their body violently are the purest.' It is very doubtful whether this implies 'mystic voluntary suicide'; cf. Dodds, *Harv. Theol. Rev.* 54 (1961), 268 f.

p. 285, 12 **Proserpinae limine** : In ch. 5 (269, 11) Isis calls herself *regina manium* and says that the Siculi refer to her as *Ortygiam Proserpinam* (269, 17-18); in ch. 6 *ad fin.* she claims to rule over the Stygian depths; cf. ch. 21 (283, 4-5), *inferum claustra … in deae manu posita*; ch. 25 (286, 23-4), *te … observant inferi … calcas Tartarum.* Yet the identification of Isis and Proserpina is not vital to the theme; what is meant is the realm of the dead. That the Eleusinian rites also included a view of Hades is suggested by Lucian, *Catapl.* 22; cf. de Jong, *Myst.* 255; such an episode, perhaps dramatic, would naturally relate to the rape of Korê; cf. Paul Foucart, *Les Mystères d'Éleusis* (Paris, 1914), 460 ff.; Deubner, *Attische Feste*, 84; Mylonas, *Eleusis*, 261 ff., believes that the 'sacred pageant' included the abduction of Korê, but denies the idea that Hades and its horrors were represented.

per omnia vectus elementa : In ch. 5 (269, 10) Isis claims to be *elementorum omnium domina*; see n. Cf. the text from a Theban tomb, quoted by Lüddeckens, *MDAIK* 11 (1943), 57 : 'Going in peace to the heaven, to the horizon, to the fields of rushes, to the underworld (Dat), to the *sšmt*-hall, to the place where this god tarries.' Stages are thus portrayed in the journey of the dead to Osiris in the afterworld. The three regions stressed in the *Book of Amduat* are heaven, earth and the underworld; the sun's nocturnal journey in the evening barque (*mesketet*) ends at dawn at a point where the three regions converge; cf. Hornung, *Das Amduat*, II, 194 f. We must assume that the initiate's movement through the cosmic regions is symbolic only; they are depicted before him on the surrounding walls of the crypt, and his involvement is ensured by spells. It is true that Merkelbach, *Roman und Mysterium*, 13, invokes cult realities in connection with our passage and with the *mitis aura* which bears Psyche away in *Metam.* 4.35; he quotes *PGM* 4, 539 ('You shall see yourself being lifted up and ascending aloft') and on p. 151 he refers to the flight of the winged Clitophon to the shrine of Artemis in the romance by Achilles Tatius. The vital evidence from cult, however, is cited by him from Livy, 39.13.13, where initiates into the Bacchic Mysteries in Italy are said to be snatched away by the gods; in the process they are said to be tied to machines which take them out of sight into hidden caves; cf. Reitzenstein in *Amor und Psyche*, ed. Binder and Merkelbach, 106 f. The custom may have derived from the use of the *méchanê* in the production of Greek tragedies, although its application was to the lower world rather than to the heaven in which actors moved upwards and downwards. Egyptian temples often had crypts, but there is no clear testimony to their use in this way.

If our central interpretation is correct, it is vain to adduce the four Empedoclean elements of air, earth, fire and water, which are invoked by Plutarch, *De Is. et Os.* 63, 376 D, in a remark on the symbolism of the sistrum. Certainly Apuleius is familar with these; v. *De Plat.* 1.7 (88, 21 ff.). But he uses *elementa* in a wider sense, as in *Metam.* 3.15 (63, 17), *serviunt elementa*, of the magic powers of Pamphile, a sentence used later of Isis in ch. 25 (286, 25 f.); cf. too of Isis the phrase quoted above, *elementorum omnium domina* (269, 10). De Jong, *De Apul.* 111 ff. and *Myst.* 270 ff., sympathetically presents the ideas of du Prel, who adduces Iamblichus, *De myst.* 3.4 (des Places, p. 104) for the claim that men who are ecstatically and religiously inspired are not harmed by fire. The present sentence would accordingly mean that the initiate is assailed by trials of water, fire, and air, but successfully survives them (*remeavi*); he does not sink in water, he is not burnt by fire, and when thrown into air he enjoys levitation. Although some parallels are adduced from religious rites — the flaming hair of the Maenads (Eur. *Bacch.* 757 ff.) and the torches of the Bacchantes which are unquenched after being dipped in the river (Livy, 39. 13) — Apuleius would surely have suggested the miracles more clearly had he intended this sense. Mithraic ritual included some kind of 'baptism by fire' and purification with water, but not of the ordeal type which du Prel had in mind; v. de Jong, *Myst.* 295 and Vermaseren, *Mithras, the Secret God*, 129 ff., esp. 134. Graillot, *Le culte de Cybèle*, 179 f., adduces usages in the cult of Cybele to suggest that Apuleius is referring to baptisms with water, mud and fire. More pertinent might well be the Mithraic concept of the 'souls's journey through the separate spheres of the planets' (Vermaseren, op. cit. 162); for a possible impress on Egyptian ideas see Kákosy in *Rel. en Égypte*, ed. Derchain, 64 f.; W. R. Halliday, *The Pagan Background of Early Christianity* (London, 1925), 260 f., takes the view that this is implied here. The four elements were also important in the Mithraic cult; v. Vermaseren, *op. cit.* 159. Cf. p. 356 below. There is no need, however, to seek a syncretistic explanation.

Reitzenstein, *Hellenist. Myst.* 223, following Cumont, quotes a passage in *Asclepius*, 28, where the guilty soul after death is said to be delivered to storms in which air, fire and water are in conflict: there it must pay the penalty between sky and earth. Another possible parallel from the Hermetic literature is 11.20 (vol. I, p. 155), where man is exhorted to think of himself as immortal and to assemble in himself the sensations of all created things, of heat and cold, dryness and fluidity. Dibelius, 'Isisweihe', 50 n. 44, rightly remarks that the Apuleian passage does not share this combination of contemplation and ecstasy. It does contain ecstasy, but is a product of revelation in a ritual procedure. A union with cosmic powers is part of the process of regeneration in several Mystery religions according to Eitrem, *Symb. Oslo.* 4 (1926), 39-59 and 5 (1927), 39-59; in the first part (pp. 52-4) he maintains, with Dibelius, that the initiate is always in movement, from room to room; in these rooms, he suggests, he is subjected to cold, heat and water. On p. 53 it is surprising to find him quoting Freimaurer's libretto of Mozart's *Zauberflöte* (act 4, Scene 9) as a serious illustration : Tamino and Pamino go through two rocky holes, equipped with fire and water, in order 'durch Feuer, Wasser, Erde und Luft gereinigt zu werden'. Doubtless some of the rites of modern Freemasonry are connected with this; cf. Colin Cross, *The Observer*, 18 June 1967, of the person who is raised to the grade of master mason, 'the third degree' : 'it involves the candidate being "murdered" and then "raised from the dead"; ... on occasion — though this is becoming extinct — the candidate may be placed in a coffin.' But it is all too removed in time and place to have any validity in our quest.

The Pauline allusions to the elements (in Gal. 4.3 and 4.9; Col. 2.8 and 2.20) are eagerly compared with our locus by Dibelius, 'Isisweihe', 55 ff. Col. 2.20 indeed seems to offer a double parallel ('Did you not die with Christ and pass beyond reach of the elemental spirits of the universe?'; thus *NEB*). Dibelius believed that in Colossae there was a Mystery-cult of the Elements, and that the prohibitions referred to in Col. 2.18 ('Do not handle this, do not taste that!') are comparable also to those mentioned by Apuleius. R. E. Witt, *Isis Gr.-R.* 263 is likewise ready to identify the 'weak and beggarly spirits of the elements' (Gal. 4.9) with our *elementa*. Both indeed have a cosmic reference, but Apuleius is alluding to vast cosmic regions, whereas Paul in Gal. 4.9 is contrasting the spirits of the elements ironically with God himself; cf. G. Bornkamm, *Paul* (tr. Stalker, 1971), 83 (he regards Col. as post-Pauline, p. 242). Wagner, *Problem* 117 f., argues that Apuleius too regards the *elementa* as divinities; he cites ch. 25 (286, 25f.), *gaudent numina, serviunt elementa*; yet the series begins with *respondent sidera*, suggesting personification of inanimate objects. Still, Wagner may be right about ch. 25, since stars can well be gods. Here, however, *per vectus elementa* is clearly spatial in reference, as *remeavi* shows.

p. 285, 12 **remeavi** : Dibelius, 'Isisweihe', 46, argues that this marks the end of the experience in the realm of the dead, since it indicates return. The subsequent mention of the sun suggests a return to the upper air. In fact, however, this detail does not contradict a continuation of the description, in what follows, of the underworld.

p. 285, 13 **nocte media vidi solem** : This remarkable phenomenon is presented, on the first level, as something bizarre. Yet it admirably suits the situation in the *Book of Amduat*, where the sun-god is depicted as voyaging through the twelve hours of night in the Osirian underworld. This, in fact, is the crucial point in determining the exact Egyptian context. If the experience of the realm of the dead was imparted through representations on the walls of the rooms through which the initiate passed (here the precedent of the New Kingdom tombs would provide a sequence of scenes divided between several rooms and passages), then the depiction of the sun-god would occur frequently. He is normally shown in the centre of the solar barque in the form of a ram-headed figure with the sun-disk on his head; at other times he appears as Khepri, in the shape of the scarab beetle. The glorified dead are in the following of the sun-god, and at the end of the twelfth hour (Hornung, *Das Amduat*, fig. 908), at the moment of dawn, is shown the figure of the mummy, here called *sšmw-ỉwf* ('Image of the flesh') and previously *sšmw-Wsỉr* ('Image of Osiris'). Rē' and Osiris are united in him; cf. Hornung, op. cit. II, 193 and 124; on p. 124 he shows that the fusion of Rē' and Osiris in this context goes back to the beginning of the New Kingdom and so ante-dates the Amarna origin for it which was posited by Drioton, *ASAE* 43 (1943), 15-43, esp. 42. (A very clear and conscious assimilation of Osiris and Rē‘ occurs in the hymn from the lintel of Ḥatiay on p. 37 : 'You (Osiris) have risen like Rē‘ in the horizon. His disk is your disk, his image is your image.') The basic thought is that the sun-god too, in entering the realm of the dead, becomes Osiris like other dead persons. It seems that the precise midnight hour was not emphasized in the Amduat tradition; a female divine figure in the First Hour (Hornung, fig. 38; see II, p. 16) is called *wš3ỉt*, 'the midnight one'; Hornung compares the term *nbt wš3w*, 'Mistress of Midnight', applied to the Eighth Hour in the shortened version (see his vol. III, 19, line 1 and p. 33, 'Herrin der tiefen Nacht'). In the Sixth Hour one reaches 'the depth (called) Mistress of those in the Underworld'; thus at midnight one encounters Khepri-Osiris or 'the body of Osiris'; in the Seventh Hour appears the 'Cavern of Osiris', where 'the flesh of Osiris' reigns as King; v. Hornung, II, 109; 114 f.: 116; 124; cf. Budge, *The Egyptian Heaven and Hell* (London, 1906), 117; 139; Bonnet, *Reallexikon*, 19. There are other Egyptian texts and representations which are concerned with the sun-god's nocturnal journey, especially the *Book of Night*, the *Book of Gates*, the *Book of Traversing Eternity*, and parts of the *Book of the Dead*. The *Book of Amduat*, however, propounds the doctrine of immortality on the pattern of Rē‘ and Osiris in a way which is especially apposite to the account in Apuleius.

Cumont in *CRAIBL* 1920, 280, claims that the idea was ancient in Greece that the sun by night illumined the abode of the dead. He cites Pindar, Fr. 129 : 'For them in the world below the sun gleameth brightly in his strength, while 'tis night with us' (Farnell's tr.). The underlying concept, however, may be different. Farnell, *Comm.* 433, says : 'the obvious meaning is that in Paradise the sun shines for ever, even while it is night with us'; he compares Vergil, *Aen.* 6.641, *solemque suum sua sidera norunt.* Rohde, *Psyche*[19] (1925), 210 n. 1, was able to cite vague parallels from both Homeric and Orphic sources.

It is noteworthy that the idea of 'Mysteries' is associated with the underworld in the *Book of the Dead*, 15, where the hymns to the sun-god have been elaborately studied by Jan Assmann in his *Liturgische Leider an den Sonnengott* (MÄS 19, Berlin, 1969). On p. 28 he thus translates the opening lines of one text : 'The secrets of the underworld, an initiation into the mysteries of the realm of the dead, seeing the sun when it sets in life, in the West, when it is venerated by the gods and glorified ones in the underworld.' The recitation of the spell, urges Assmann (p. 31), had the magical effect of enabling the sun to be seen in the underworld. He aptly quotes from the Setna-Romance (Griffith, *Stories of the High Priests of Memphis*, 92 f.) : 'Reading the second formula : if it be that thou art in Amenti, thou art again on earth in thy (usual) form; thou wilst see the sun rising in heaven with his cycle of deities, and the moon in his form of shining.' The situation, of course, is the reverse of that in Apuleius; here it is the living on earth who is transported, for the nonce, to the underworld.

At the same time the Apuleian ceremonies probably included also those Osirian rites of reawakening which gave special attention to the individual. Moreover, the dramatic or pictorial representation of the Amduat theme may well have included techniques which went beyond the funerary records of it which we possess. Dibelius, 'Isisweihe', 52, points to the popularity in Mystery-cults of the contrast between light and darkness. He cites Dio Chrys. *Or.* 12.33 (ed. J. W. Cohoon, Loeb, 1950, pp. 34 ff.), where rites of initiation are described in which the participant would find that 'light and darkness would appear to him alternately'; the allusion is probably to the Eleusinian Mysteries; v. Deubner, *Attische Feste*, 87 n. 5; Mylonas, *Eleusis*, 263. Cf. the 'wonderful light' (φῶς τι θαυμάσιον) in Plut. *Fr. de an.* 178 (ed. Sandbach, Loeb, 1969, p. 316), perhaps also of Eleusis; Firmicus Maternus, *De err. prof. rel.* 2.4, p. 43 ed. Heuten ('you are not disillusioned by the brilliance of the light shown to you'; Heuten, p. 135, thinks it is the light of Christianity, while Dibelius, p. 52 n. 50, rather boldly assigns it to the rites of Isis); Firmicus Maternus, ibid. 22.1, p. 99 ed. Heuten (*lumen infertur* in the rites of Attis); Aelius Aristides, *Sacr. serm.* 3.46, p. 424 ed. Keil : 'Light also came from Isis and other untold blessings contributing to salvation', but here the context is about miraculous happenings. Certainly the interplay of light and darkness must have strongly marked the rites of Mithras; Tertullian, *De cor.* 15, describes the cult as taking place 'in a cave, in truth a camp of darkness' (*in spelaeo, in castris vere tenebrarum*); cf. J. Fontaine (Paris, 1966) ad loc. p. 180 and Vermaseren, *Mithras, the Secret God*, 38. Doubtless there was an array of numerous lamps skilfully used; v. Cumont, *Mysteries of Mithra*, 162.

Priestly representatives of Cautes and Cautopates acted as torchbearers; v. Vermaseren, op. cit. 72 f.; cf. Reitzenstein, *Hellenist. Myst.* 264, on the Iranian concept of light. Indeed Vermaseren and van Essen, *Santa Prisca*, 145, argue that in spite of some differing detail the Isiac and Mithraic Mysteries were essentially similar : the Mithraist also passed through the four elements, and after his symbolic death was reborn, to find, later, 'the Sun shining with a bright light during the night'. They then refer to the leaden image of Sol with pierced rays, which was found in the Mithraeum of Santa Prisca; it could be illuminated from behind. The resemblance is striking, but the Egyptian experience is very different in origin. Christian liturgy and ceremonial also used the concept and practice of illumination, perhaps under Iranian influence, as Cumont suggests in *Lux Perpetua*, 460, referring, *inter alia*, to the use of the phrase adopted as his title. There are Jewish antecedents too; cf. 'the sun of righteousness' (Mal. 4.2). Dibelius, 'Isisweihe', 53, compares the concurrence of light and theophany in Paul's experience; v. 2 Cor. 4.6 ('God, who commanded the light to shine out of darkness ...') It is not unlikely that the Isiac rites were formally influenced by these parallel usages, although the Egyptian tradition was itself well acquainted with similar practices. It is less likely that the Isiac initiate was at one stage naked and blindfolded as was his Mithraic counterpart (Vermaseren, *Mithras, the Secret God*, 131). De Jong, *Myst.* 314, recalls that in one room of the Pompeian Iseum no fewer than fifty-eight pottery lamps were found; v. Mau (tr. Kelsey), *Pompeii* (N. York, 1902), 181, where they are said to be 'in part provided with iron rings, so that they could be suspended'. Twenty lamps were found near the Isiac *sacellum* in the house of Loreius Tiburtinus : v. Tran Tam Tinh, *Isis à Pompéi*, 44. Yet de Jong goes on to cite approvingly the view of du Prel that Apuleius is describing 'mystic light phenomena'. Du Prel, *Die Mystik der alten Griechen*, 105, ascribes the first move (*accessi confinium mortis*) to 'somnambulist ecstasy', and he consistently follows the line of psychic interpretation. De Jong is more circumspect; he often leaves the matter undecided, but in this case (p. 322) he maintains it to be a very reasonable assumption that in rites such as the Isiac mysteries, gifted persons who had been induced to a nervous state of suggestibility often experienced light-phenomena of a hallucinatory nature. The evidence, however, shows that such phenomena were systematically planned.

p. 285, 13-14 **deos inferos et deos superos** : The grouping of the categories is further proof that the whole description refers to the underworld; so rightly Hopfner and Wittmann. Wagner, *Problem*, 118 f., follows Dibelius in denying this. He justly avers that the Egyptians did not believe that the sun in Dat shone as brightly as the day-time sun. But that it shone at all at night was sufficient wonder to Apuleius, whose poetic verve adds to the phenomenon. Chief of the *dei inferi*, whom Apuleius pointedly puts first, was Osiris. This reflects his primary function as king and leader of the dead; cf. his epithet 'head of the primal darkness' in the Twelfth Hour of Amduat (Hornung, II, 192 f.). The other *inferi* will include Anubis, Khentamenthes, and a host of gate-keeping daemons. Chief of the *superi* is the sun-god Rē', found and depicted also as Khepri and Atum; although the lord of the *superi*, he is here present in the underworld. To Apuleius the role of Isis is above all these; she is the presiding genius of the whole cosmos, although she has special relations with the underworld. At the same time she illumines the very sun : ch. 25 (286, 23-4), *te superi colunt, observant inferi, tu rotas orbem, luminas solem, regis mundum, calcas Tartarum*. The culmination of the rite is therefore the *epopteia*, the beholding of these gods. Hopfner, *PW* s.v. Mysterien (1933), 1339, interprets *deos inferos et deos superos* as all gods of the underworld. While the classification is Graeco-Roman, its application to the Egyptian context would clearly allow the sun-god to lead the *dei superi*. Reitzenstein, *Hellenist. Wundererzählungen*, 116, compares the journey of the prophet in the Book of Ostanes to the seven portals of heaven; after entering the seventh he finds an inscription offering the sum of all wisdom. But the underworld is missing in this parallel. A second parallel adduced by Reitzenstein is more apposite : in Spell 148 of the Coffin Texts the Horus-falcon claims to span both heaven and the underworld; see my *Conflict*, 52.; Faulkner, *JEA* 54 (1968), 40-4; M. Gilula, *JEA* 57 (1971), 14-19; Fairman, *The Triumph of Horus* (London, 1974), 10 ff.

p. 285, 14 **adoravi de proxumo** : For the adverblal phrase cf. 1 Cor. 13.12, τότε δὲ πρόσωπον πρὸς πρόσωπον. Isis, Osiris, and Rē' are clearly the chief objects of this adoration, and the description as it stands refers to no *unio mystica* on the part of the initiate with any of these deities. Yet implied in the whole Egyptian tradition is the union with Osiris; it is on the pattern of his death and immortality that the believer is blessed. Morenz has shown how the personal sense of identification with Osiris became more pronounced in Egypt in the Graeco-Roman era; see his study in *Rel. en Égypte*, ed. Derchain 75-91. Here Morenz deals especially with the increased consciousness of this as expressed in funerary pictorial representations, but he points also (pp. 78-80) to the clear tendency in this era to attach Osirian ritual texts to the private cult of individuals, as in the case of the Abydene temple texts which were used as an appendix to the *Book of the Dead* or otherwise attached to the private cult (P. Louvre 3129 and P.B.W 10252). A similar use was made of the *Songs of Isis and Nephthys*, while a recently published papyrus of Spell 175 of the *Book of the Dead* in Cracow includes also, remarkably enough, parts of the ritual of the *Stundenwachen* of Osiris. To this should be added the fact that several of these texts of the Graeco-Roman era exhibit a warmth of feeling that is absent in the earlier hymns; the *Songs* and the *Stundenwachen* are notable instances. The Hellenistic world is known to have experienced, in general, a new growth of individual consciousness, and its influence is perhaps perceptible in these developments. A parallel tendency is noted by L. Kákosy in *Rel. en Égypte*, ed. Derchain, 66 f. : the fours sons of Horus, the traditional guardians of the so-called Canopic vases, now tend to be identified with aspects of the deceased's personality. These are considerations that confirm an interpretation of Apuleius on the lines of a 'werden zu Osiris'. One may agree with Dibelius (p. 54) that this experience does not suggest a mystic union with Isis except in the sense that the initiate shares adoringly in her cosmic sovereignty.

Of the promises she has made to Lucius in ch. 6, it is that of eternal happiness which stands out here : when he goes down to the netherworld he shall see her shining through the darkness of Acheron; he shall dwell in the Elysian fields and constantly worship her. In view of this it is hard to understand how Wagner, *Problem*, 120 f., following Nilsson, *Gesch. Gr. Rel.* II² 636 denies that Isis promises immortality; his summary omits *campos Elysios incolens*. The concept is rightly admitted by Dibelius, 'Isisweihe', 54. Nilsson, loc. cit. includes these important words in his translation of the passage, so that his denial is still more strange. A promise of immortality is the core and kernel of the Osirian religion. It is true that in ch. 6 Isis also promises a prolonged life in this world; but to seize on this as the only important pledge is misleading, nor are the attempts to adduce the Egyptian *sed*-festival in illustration of this idea in a ritual sense at all successful, since this festival was a royal rite and remained so exclusively, as Nilsson, *Gesch. Gr. Rel.* II², 634, properly points out. Loisy, *Les mystères païens et le mystère chrétien* (Paris, 1919), 139, invokes Moret's interpretion of the *sed*-festival, according to which the Pharaoh was enthroned as a revived Osiris; for a rebuttal of this view see my remarks in *JEA* 28 (1942), 71; cf. Wagner, *Problem*, 130 f. He is also misleading about 'eating the flesh' of Osiris (p. 141). If these errors are no longer accepted, there remains the objection that in the Graeco-Roman Mysteries Osirian rites are applied, according to the view here presented, to a living person. Efraim Briem, *Zur Frage nach dem Ursprung der hellenistischen Mysterien* (Lund, 1928), 43, says that no evidence exists for this, as far as he knows; cf. Nilsson, loc. cit.; Wagner, *Problem*, 131 ff. We know, nonetheless, that Osirian rites in a special sense, such as those for the month of Khoiak recorded in the Denderah texts, as well as the thoroughly Osirian funerary rites, were based on the concept of the death and rebirth of Osiris, often in link with vegetation. The Hellenistic Mysteries, in all probability, applied the concept to the individual living person. When Apuleius, therefore, talks of *voluntaria mors* and *confinium mortis*, he means, in the first place, a spiritual preview of death and rebirth; secondly, though less obviously in the present chapter, he means the death of the initiate to the old life of immorality; this sense is clear in chs. 15 and 21 especially, as Wagner, *Problem*, 121, admits, although he strangely denies the first meaning; cf. Nilsson, op. cit. 637.

Renatus bears several senses, as we have seen, A problem is raised by Dey, Παλιγγενεσία, 91 f. He wishes to deny any Osirian meaning to the rite recorded in this chapter and stresses, for instance, that Osiris is not named; this objection has been discussed above. He goes on, however, to note that in ch. 27 a second initiation is designated as that of Osiris, and the previous rites, it is suggested, are those of Isis only. The distinction implied is itself problematic, since the two deities are so closely linked. But certainly it is possible that a specifically Osirian ceremony like the judgement was reserved for the second initiation.

p. 285, 15 **ignores tamen** : A suggestion that even the brief indication given has gone too far, although its bald outline will not inform much. The phrase *sine piaculo* in the next sentence confirms this; the author returns to record in detail what can be described with impunity.

CHAPTER 24

p. 285, 17 **mane** : Since the substantival use of this word is rare, it seems advisable to retain the normal adverbial sense and interpret *factum est* in relation to all the events of the night, even though the idea is then partly repeated in *perfectis sollemnibus*.

p. 285, 18 **duodecim sacratus stolis** : For *sacratus* cf. n. *ad* ch. 23 (285, 3), *sacratorum*; here lit. 'I went forth as an initiate with twelve robes,' although the Ablative could also possibly be taken closely with *sacratus* : 'made sacred with twelve robes'; cf. Reitzenstein, *Hellenist. Myst.* 226, who compares the Greek ἁγιασθείς. New clothing indicates a new man in this context; Lucius is *renatus*. Reitzenstein, loc. cit., after citing Manichaean and Indian parallels (the latter involving the twelve months of the year), mentions what is without doubt the true explanation : the Twelve Robes represent the twelve hours of the night through which the sun-god has travelled. In the *Book of Amduat* each of those hours is assigned a distinctive name which occurs at the end of the text devoted to it : see, e.g., Hornung, *Das Amduat* III (*Die Kurzfassung*), 27-35 (translation). Cf. Wittmann, p. 114, and Dibelius, 'Isisweihe', 51 on the relation to the twelve traversed zones. Cumont in *CRAIBL* 1920, 272-85 propounded the interesting theory that the astrological speculations of Peto-siris influenced the Alexandrian Mysteries; cf. his *Égypte des Astrologues*, 202. He is dealing with the Pseudo-Platonic *Axiochus* (v. Stobaeus, *Florilegium* ed. Meineke, III, 236-39; IV, 113; 122) and one must agree with Reitzenstein (p. 227 n. 2) that the description of Hades presented in these writings hardly agrees in general with the account in Apuleius; certainly Serapis, as he says, became the sun, but this can be explained as the development of Egyptian tradition. Astrology was a pervasive influence in the second century, and Nils-son's statement is therefore not implausible (*Gesch. Gr. Rel.* II², 635) when he maintains, as opposed to Wittmann, that the Twelve Robes relate to the twelve zodiacal signs through which the sun moves. Dey, Παλιγγενεσία, 88 n. 6, argues soundly that these Twelve Robes must have some cosmic meaning and be related to the way through the elements described in ch. 23. Nilsson's case would have been stronger if he had explained this journey as a Mithraic astral course; he is content, however, to take the *elementa* in the traditional Greek sense, adding an Aristotelian fifth; he also maintains (cf. Cumont's remarks, quoted above) that the idea of the sun shining in the underworld for the initiates is old among the Greeks. (He cites Pindar, Fr. 129, but this does not, it seems, refer to initiates; Aristoph. *Ran.* 154 f. does concern initiates of Eleusis, but does not allude, more than the Pindar fragment, to the sun shining at night.)

We are not told how the Twelve Robes were differentiated. J. Pascher, ῾Η βασιλικὴ ὁδός (Paderborn, 1961), 55, suggests that they were worn together. If so, this would be preceded in each case by a ceremonial conferment, perhaps with an accompanying ritual utterance. It is more likely that they were worn separately, in the first place, and then kept for funerary purposes — to serve the occasion of real death when the twelve regions of the realm of the dead would be encountered.

The putting on of sacral robes implies, in a previous stage, the discarding of garments worn before, so that the initiate would have been naked in the interim. Merkelbach, *Roman und Mysterium*, 318, refers to the tradition that the initiate into the Mysteries took off his clothes; he quotes Plotinus, 1.6.7 ('... so, to those that approach the Holy Celebrations of the Mysteries, there were appointed purifications and the laying aside of the garments worn before, and the entry in nakedness' : tr. by Stephen MacKenna, London, 1969, p. 62), where the reference may well be to the rites of Isis; cf. J. M. Rist, *Plotinus : The Road to Reality* (Cambridge, 1967), 17 and 191. Cf. also Porphyr. *De abst.* 1.31 and Chaldaean Or. fr. 116, 2 (ed. E. des Places, p. 95 : 'the divine is not accessible to mortals who think of the body, but to those who, naked, hasten to the height'); but in these cases the involvement of ritual is not indubitable. R. E. Witt, *Isis Gr.-R.* 161, claims to adduce archaeological evidence in favour of 'nudity in the Isiac cult'. His search for nudes can hardly be said to be successful. Priests of Isis 'with at least a half-naked torso' are not a convincing argument, nor is the depiction of Isis and Luna as topless in Tran Tam Tinh, *Isis à Pompéi*, pl. 14,1. (The motive there is very different.) The almost naked initiate from Antioch (Witt's pl. 34) is very doubtfully Isiac. Before this Witt properly emphasizes that in our book the stress is on the necessity of clothing the naked body. In ch. 14 *fin.*, when Lucius recovers human form, he is very nervous about being nude. A priest quickly clothes him (*supertexit me celerrume*). Yet there was obviously a brief moment in the mystic rites when the initiate was naked; he had discarded his old clothes with his old life, and was facing a series of new and richly-symbolic garments. Plotinus was doubtless referring to the moment between the old and the new. See also pp. 356 f.

p. 285, 19 **effari ... prohibeor**: The construction is old, with either passive or active infinitives : v. Hofmann and Szantyr, *Lat. Syntax*, 356.

tunc temporis : An archaism : v. Hofmann and Szantyr, *Lat. Syntax*, 47. Callebat, *Sermo Cotid.* 191 thinks that such expressions were nonetheless stereotyped formulae in familiar speech.

p. 285, 20 **namque** : In *Metam.* 6.19 (942, 22) a sentence begins *Canis namque*, and Hildebrand shows *ad loc.* that Apuleius varies his practice, putting the word first or second. In classical prose it comes first; v. Bernhard, *Stil*, 28.

meditullio : Cf. *Metam.* 3.27 (72, 3f.), *in ipso fere meditullio Eponae deae simulacrum residens aediculae*; and a metaphorical use in *De Plat.* 2.5 (108, 12 f.), *in meditullio quodam vitiorum*. The word seems to mean 'inner land', from *medius* and *tollium* (cf. *tellus*); cf. A. Walde, rev. Hofmann, *Lat. Etym. Wb³.* (1954), 57; *Thes. L.L.* 8, 581, 21 ff.

p. 285, 21 **tribunal ligneum** : Wittmann, p. 114, aptly compares the pedestals on which priests are standing as shown by the pillar-reliefs in the Capitoline Museum, Rome, which have come from the Iseum in the Campus Martius; v. H. Stuart Jones, *Cat.* pl. 92; on p. 360 of his text he calls them 'stools'. They are clearly moveable. See too Leipoldt, *Bilderatlas*, 60-61 [288-90]. A similar type of pedestal, as Wittmann also notes, is seen beneath the figures who guard the chief grave in Kôm-esh-Shukâfa : v. Th. Schreiber, *Die Nekropole von Kôm-esch-Schukâfa* (Sieglin Exp. I, 1908), pl. 25; and add pls. 21-2, with a serpent on a pedestal; cf. Breccia, *Alex.* 107, fig. 28.

p. 285, 21-2 **byssina ... veste** : Cf. ch. 3 (268, 11), *bysso tenui pertexta*, of Isis; see n.

p. 285, 22 **floride** : Apuleius is the first to use the adverb; v. *Thes. L.L.* 6, 1, 926, 23 ff. One is tempted to follow Hildebrand, Médan and Wittmann in giving it a literal sense here, 'decorated with flowers'. Cf. *Metam.* 10.29 (260, 8 f.), *ver ... gemmulis floridis cuncta depingeret.* Flowers do not seem to occur on Isiac dresses; but neither do the elaborate designs later mentioned. Nilsson, *Gesch. Gr. Rel* II²., 635, castigates Wittmann for referring to a 'Blumen-gewand'; the text, he says, speaks not of flowers, but of animals. Wittmann, however (p. 114), when referring to 'ein feines blumenbemaltes Byssosgewand', is clearly translating *floride depicta veste*. He refers to the animals later.

p. 285, 23 **chlamyda** : Normally the chlamys did not reach far below the knee, but instances of more generous proportions occur; v. M. M. Evans, *Chapters on Greek Dress* (London, 1893), 54, fig. 59; L. Heuzey, *Hist. du costume antique* (Paris, 1922), 117, fig. 59; 124, fig. 63; 128, fig. 65 (they are still longer on Heuzey's studies with a *modèle vivant*, but naturally not as authentic). According to Saglio in Dar.-Sag. I (1887), 1116, the garment became more elaborate in the imperial era.

p. 285, 24 **dracones Indici** : The use of a linen tunic beneath the *chlamys* points to Egyptian hieratic custom, and *Indici* here does not necessarily point elsewhere; it may be a purely subjective adjective, although Apuleius includes the *immensi dracones* in an admiring survey of the Indian scene in *Flor.* 5. Indeed, Reitzenstein, *Hellenist. Myst.* 229, adduces the serpents and other animals in the body of the Indian cosmic god of the world : v. Reitzenstein and Schaeder, *Studien zum antiken Synkretismus aus Iran und Griechenland* (Leipzig, 1926), 83 (the Song of Mārkaṇḍeya). He adds that Philostratus, *V. Apoll.* 2.20 (ed. Kayser, p. 33) attests contact between Egypt and India ('Cotton from India comes to many temples in Egypt'); religious contact is another matter. Whereas the relative clause in this sentence probably applies to the griffons only, winged serpents are not lacking in Egyptian religious art. Indeed they are exemplified in the *Book of Amduat*, whose relevance was found crucial to the understanding of ch. 23. See Hornung, *Amduat*, 4th Hour, fig. 285, and remarks in II, 84 ('a great god'); 5th Hour, fig. 394 with the remarks in II, 106 (the winged serpent here is described as a 'great god' whose function is to guard the image of Sokar); the 11th Hour, fig. 756 — discussed in II, 175 (associated with the sun-god Atum). Cf. Piankoff and Rambova, *Mythological Papyri* (N.Y., 1967), no. 20, Scene 3 below (text vol. 165 f.) and no. 29, lower reg., Scene 3 (text vol. 208). These, it should be noted, are beneficent winged serpents, such as the context clearly demands. Other serpents, notably Apopis, are maleficent. On the other hand, the serpent-figures of Amduat, although sometimes called '*great god*', are very minor beings really, and the dress of an Isiac initiate might be expected to show symbols more obviously related to Isis or Osiris. The emblematic affiliations here must probably he sought in the religious art of Alexandria, as Wittmann has effectively done. Both Isis and Osiris assume serpent forms in this tradition. See n. above *ad* ch. 3 (268, 9-10), *viperarum* and ch. 11 (275, 10), *aspis*. Wittmann, at the same time, should be corrected on one point : it is not from Nemesis and Demeter that Isis derives her form as serpent but mainly from Renenutet (Thermuthis). Cf. ch. 4 (269, 5) *aspis* and n. Nilsson, *Gesch. Gr. Rel.* II² 635 compares the representations of Iuppiter Heliopolitanus shown in A. B. Cook, *Zeus*, I, 567 ff. Some Egyptian motifs appear in these figures, but there are no detailed resemblances to our passage. Berreth, p. 112, finds the signs of the zodiac suggested by the animals of the 'heavenly dress'. (He is apparently following the earlier view propounded by Reitzenstein). This implies that the *Olympiaca stola* is the last of the twelve robes mentioned in the beginning of the chapter, an interpretation shared also by Gressmann, *Orient. Rel.* 42 and J. Pascher, ʽΗ βασιλικὴ ὁδός, 55. Gressmann advances too the connexion with zodiacal signs. The intervening piece of narrative rather suggests that the twelve robes have by now been laid aside. Further, the animals mentioned here do not occur in the signs of the zodiac. Berreth is able to cite in *PGM* 4, 1596 ff., an instructive magical prayer to Helius in which twelve different animal forms, beginning with a cat, dog, and serpent are assigned to the sun-god for twelve hours. The prayer ends with the advice, 'When you vow say "There is only one Zeus Serapis".' The piece is clearly Egyptian in origin.

285, 24 f. **grypes Hyperborei** : Pliny, *NH* 10.70.136, refers to the long ears and crooked beak of the griffon. Its oriental origin is clear, the components of its fabulous nature being often derived from the lion and the eagle : v. A. Furt-wängler in Roscher, *Lex. Myth.* s.v. Gryps (1890), 1742-77 and K. Ziegler, *PW* s.v. (1912), 1902-29. J. Leibovitch in *BIFAO* 25 (1943), 183-203, shows that plentiful Egyptian examples derive from the Middle Kingdom. The body in these looks like that of a cheetah while the head is that of a falcon, the latter doubtless referring to Horus. In the New Kingdom it was often shown in aggressive postures and the body is frequently that of a lion. In Leibovitch's fig. 7, p. 189 (= Lanzone, *Diz. Mit.* III, pl. 13) the griffon is destroying enemies; on its head it carries the double plume and sun-disk of Amûn. The warlike god Mont is also associated with a griffon form sometimes, and in the 21st and 22nd Dynasties stelae show chariots being drawn by griffons (Leibovitch, pp. 196 f.). In the Demotic P. Leiden I, 384, col. 15, 2, the beak is said to be that of a falcon : v. Spiegelberg, *Mythus vom Sonnenauge*, 39; in a text quoted by Griffith and Thompson *ad.* P. Mag. Lond. Leid I, 16, p. 23 ff. a lion's limbs are assigned to it. Crete, Syria and Samaria produced griffons too. A form borrowed by Syria from Egypt was in turn borrowed by Crete, and this Cretan form was again borrowed unchanged by Egypt; thus Helck and Otto, *Kl. Wb.* 132 f. The griffon had several divine connections. P. Dem. Mag. Lond. Leid. 19,27 shows it linked with Osiris : 'Gryphon is my real name, for Osiris is he who is my hand' (Griffith and Thompson, p. 127); cf. 12,16 and 21, 'this (that) gryphon which is in Abydos'. In Graeco-Egyptian art the female griffon is sometimes identified with Nemesis, a not unexpected development from the Egyptian antecedents : v. F. H. Marshall, *JHS* 33 (1913), 83-6 with pl. 7 and fig. 1 (the limestone mould is of unknown provenance, but Marshall rightly assigned it to Alexandria; the griffon has a uraeus tail, which is paralleled, as is shown, on a coin of Alexandria); P. Perdrizet, *BCH* 36 (1912), 256-62, who notes also the emergence of Isis-Nemesis; id. *BCH* 38 (1914), 94-6; id. *Terr.* pl. 57 (top left) and pp. 105 f., no. 274 (from Memphis, a Nemesis-griffon with the wheel of fortune); on the same plate (top right) is a Memphite relief of a Cretan griffon; id. *Bronzes Fouquet*, pl. 18 (left) and p. 38, no. 62;

Breccia, *Terr.* 2, pl. 110, no 634 and p. 57; Edgar, *Greek Vases*, no. 26238 on pl. 16 ad p. 42; Edgar, *Greek Sculpture*, pl. 16, no 27512 and pp. 30 f.; another instance in Edgar, *op. cit.* pl. 24, no 275 28 is instructive because this limestone stela shows a small winged griffon between a uraeus with the head-dress of Isis and a serpent with the crown of Upper Egypt (undoubtedly a mark of Osiris here). This is a contact which suits Isiac initiation. See also p. 357.

The adjective *Hyperborei* points to a belief in its northern origin; cf. Pliny, *NH* 10.70.136 (perhaps Scythia); Herodotus, 4.13 and 32 (griffons guarded gold in the far north and the Hyperboreans lived further north again) cf. J.D.P. Bolton, *Aristeas of Proconnesus* (Oxford, 1962), 100 f. and 195 ff. (he believes that the Hyperboreans are 'a fabled people', 'not a real people but a folk-memory'). The Greek myth is illustrated on a vase from Alexandria : v. Breccia, *Necropoli di Sciatbi* (*CCG*, 1912), II, pl. 47 and I, 49 f.

286, 1 **mundus alter** : A geographical explanation in the strict sense is suggested by Oudendorp : *apud antipodas*. Wittmann, p. 115, suggests that the afterworld is meant. A wondrous world of fable may rather be implied : such creatures do not really exist.

p. 286, 2 **Olympiacam stolam** : Helm rejects Kaibel's emendation *Osiriacam* with a reference to ch. 27 (288, 8) which mentions the Osirian rite which was still to come. The objection is hardly valid since Osiris has certainly been a part of the first rite. While there is no support for *Osiriacam* in the MSS, save in the spelling *olimpiacam*, Ryle points out that in the Beneventan script *s* was curved only at the top; he cites E. A. Lowe, *The Beneventan Script*, 138. This leaves, however, the discrepancy of *mp* as against *r*. Médan argues that the MSS reading is suspect because the Egyptian gods were the enemies of the Olympian gods (cf. Kaibel) and the Egyptian priests were very jealous of their mysteries and their original deities. It may be added that the experience recorded in ch. 23 is definitely concerned with the underworld and is quite un-Olympian. But Apuleius does not seem averse to using the traditional Graeco-Roman terminology, even when, as in ch. 6, Egyptian ideas are really being presented; cf. Proserpina in ch. 23; and, in a strictly Olympian sense, the claim of Isis in ch. 5 that she is *prima caelitum*, Venus, Diana, and Juno. According to Plutarch, *De Is. et Os.* 77, 382 C, the robe of Osiris is 'of one simple colour, the colour of light'; cf. 51, 371 F f.; see my comments *ad loc.* p. 562. According to Damascius (A.D. vi) the Osirian funerary garment was both radiant and elaborate in its decoration (Hopfner, *Fontes* 690). This robe or *chlamys* has many colours (*colore vario*, 285, 23, probably applies to the *chlamys* rather than to the linen tunic below it; but it may apply to both, and we know that linen was produced in several colours : see my *Plut., De Is. et Os.* 271). The *stola Olympiaca* will have had both solar and Osirian associations. Whereas Osiris is the god of the dead and of the underworld, he is connected too with heaven and the sun. In *Metam.* 5.1, where the palace of Eros is described, it is said that the walls were covered with figures of wild beasts and creatures of the field, wrought in chased silver. Mme. N. Fick, *Rev. Ét. Lat.* 47 (1969), 378-96, argues that these animals reappear in a sense in ch. 22, where the hieroglyphic books are described, and also here in the account of the Olympian robe. The allusion to the animals shown in the palace of Eros is, however, so brief that there is no compelling reason to make these connections.

p. 286, 2 **sacrati** : Cf. ch. 24 (285, 18), *sacratus*, and n.; ch. 23 (285, 3: emended) *sacratorum*, and n.

p. 286, 3 **flammis adultam facem** : The verb is similarly used in Verg. *Aen.* 1.704, *flammis adolere penates*; cf. the verb *adolesco* in *Georg.* 4.379, *adolescunt ignibus arae*. No other instance seems to occur of the participle *adultus* so used; cf. *Thes. L.L.* 1, 794, 8 ff.

A torch is a frequent priestly attribute in cult scenes; cf. n. *ad* ch. 16 (278, 15), *taeda lucida*. Thus a priest or initiate in an Isiac scene on a pillar from the Iseum Campestre is shown carrying torches : v. Gressmann, *Orient. Rel.* 43, fig. 17; Leipoldt, *Bilderatlas* 60 (centre) [289]. In a mosaic from Antioch of the imperial era Doro Levi has interpreted as Isis a figure which has a torch rising from her head-dress : v. *Berytus* 7 (1942), pl. 1,1 and pp. 19 ff.; also id. *Antioch Mosaic Pavements* (Princeton, 1947), I, 163 ff and II, pl. 33 a; Hermes also occurs in the group, and the goddess may well be Demeter. Cf. p. 300 above. But Isis with a torch appears on a lamp in Drexler,‘ Isis’, 451, where the head-dress is Isiac. H. Stuart Jones, text vol. 360, explains them as ‘two lotus flowers’. An elaborate terracotta torch-carrier in Alexandria has on it a figure of Sarapis : v. Breccia, *Terr.* 2, pl. 119, 693 and p. 60; cf. *ibid.*, pl. 118, 689 and p. 60; pl. 119, 694 and p. 60. Perhaps the double lotus capsule on pl. 119: 697 and p. 60 was used as a torch; the Isiac head-dress is figured on it. There is therefore no need to adduce the use of the torch in the Eleusinian Mysteries or on the coins of cities in Asia Minor or those of Hadrianopolis in Thrace under Gordian III, as Wittmann, p. 115, does. Doubtless the big torch held by Demeter-Isis in P. Graindor, *Terres cuites de l'Égypte Gréco-Romaine*, pl. 5,5 and pp. 74 f. is originally Demeter's; cf. Breccia, *Terr.* 2, pl. 147, 235 and p. 31. That Hopfner should have pronounced the torch here as ‘un-Egyptian’ is very strange (*PW* s.v. *Mysterien* (1933), 1340).

p. 286, 3 **corona ... palmae** : A crown suggesting the radiate sun is clearly implied. There is a good example on a vase in Alexandria which is a cinerary urn : v. Edgar, *Greek Vases* (*CCG*, 1911), pl. 15, no. 26.232 and pp. 38 f., where Edgar describes the design as the ‘head of Helios with large palmette-spray on each side’; another detail of the Apuleian account is present too in the ‘white paint on face of Helios and alongside the rays’; cf. *candidae foliis*. Cf. a partly similar instance in Edgar, op. cit. 40, no. 26.324. It does not follow, of course, that the Greek Helius or indeed any sun-god other than the Egyptian Rē‘ is intended by Apuleius. See further p. 357.

p. 286, 4 **ad instar Solis** ; The radiate head is common in Mithraic depictions: v. Vermaseren, *Mithras, the Secret God*, facing pp. 112 and 113 and *passim*; and Nilsson, *Gesch. Gr. Rel.* II² 635 has no hesitation in assigning the crown of our context and the allusion to solar decoration to the popular sun cult of the era, though he grudgingly admits that the Egyptian sun-cult provided a good link. While the palm crown is here solar in form, it probably derives from the Osirian 'crown of justification or victory' on which v.n. *ad* ch. 4 (269, 7), *palmae victricis* and *ad* ch. 12 (275, 15), *coronam*. Drexler, 'Isis', 464, cites gems on which the Osiris mummy bears a radiate crown. Such a crown is also borne by Serapis, but he derives it from Helius; cf. R. S. Poole, *Cat. Coins of Alexandria* (London, 1892), lxii; on p. lxix he points to an instance with Hermanubis; cf. Tran Tam Tinh, *Isis à Pompéi*, pl. 14, 3, showing Harpocrates-Helius thus adorned. For Osiris with a radiate crown Derchain, *CdÉ* 30 (1955), 240, compares Pieper, 'Abraxasgemmen' in *MDAIK* 5 (1934), 140 and pl. 22 no. 9782, and a stone published by Delatte, *BCH* 38 (1914), 193, where the head of a mummy is replaced by twigs and leaves. There are clearly signs that in the Graeco-Roman era solar symbolism became popular in Osirian contexts. In Edgar, *Greek Vases*, pl. 21, no. 26.281 and p. 56 an Egyptian winged disk is shown above the crowns of Osiris and Isis, and the winged disk occurs on several of the *Graeco-Egyptian Coffins* published also by Edgar. The sun-disk appears on the head of persons in Adriani, *Rep. d'Arte* Ser. C, vol. I-II, pl. 101, fig. 342, N. 91 a (from Kôm esh-Shukâfa). A token of the same emphasis is the depiction of the *ba*-bird, which symbolizes the soul, with a sun-disk on its head; there are two beautifully elaborate examples from masks of female mummies in Edgar, *Graeco-Roman Coffins*, pl. II, no. 33.130 (p 22) and pl. 15, no. 33, 135 centre (pp. 29 ff.); on pl. 12, no. 33. 131 (middle) and p. 23 the solar theme is present in two ways : above is a Horus falcon with sun-disk and uraei, while in adjacent paintings a male figure arising from a lotus adores Osiris and Sokar; the lotus has of course a solar association. Osiris himself sometimes carries a sun-disk on top of his crown : v. Petrie, *Koptos*, pl. 21, nos. 12 and 13 (26th Dynasty, cf. p. 24), and the quantity of figurines of the god produced by this site resulted in the use of conjoined moulds which gave the effect of 'a sort of radiating ornament' (Petrie, p. 24). The latter impression is, however, purely coincidental to our theme.

The possibility that the solar emphasis here is due to Serapis is suggested by Wagner, *Problem*, 114 n. 90, who cites Roeder, *PW* s.v. Sarapis (1920), 2421 for the prevalence of the syncretism Helius-Sarapis; the association of Zeus with Sarapis points in a similar direction; cf. Milne, *Hist. of Egypt under Roman Rule*[3] (1924), 206, who suggests that Amen-Rē' was subsumed. The objection to seeing Serapis here is that it would be a *non-sequitur*; there is nothing in the account of the ceremony to suggest his presence. For an association of Isis and the sun see ch. 25 (286, 24) *luminas solem* and n. The phrase *ad instar Solis* must be viewed as a simplification. In this cult the initiate can be identified with none other than Osiris, but here, after a ceremony which depicts the visit of the sun-god to the Osirian realm of the dead, the triumph over death is fittingly symbolized by an Osiris-figure with solar attributes. An identification with the god is therefore present. Wagner, *Problem*, 122 denies this, following

Dey, *Παλιγγενεσία*, 97, by divorcing the symbolism from its Egyptian context. See further p. 357.

p. 286, **5 in vicem simulacri**: The identity of the *mystes* and his god could not be more clearly expressed. In Egyptian funerary texts the identity is proclaimed simply by prefixing *Osiris* to the name of the deceased. As we have seen above, the concept was pushed further in Graeco-Roman times. Morenz, 'Problem des Werdens zu Osiris', pl. 3 (facing p. 80), publishes a representation from a sarcophagus in Budapest in which the deceased, who is making offerings to Osiris, is himself equipped with the crown of Osiris and also boasts a royal cartouche. That the initiate is being treated like his god is implied not only by this phrase but also by the following *repente velis reductis*; cf. ch. 20 (281, 20), *velis candentibus reductis*, used of the goddess herself in the *apertio templi*. Although attestation in the ritual applied to living persons is lacking, the identification with Osiris is abundantly confirmed in funerary contexts. In the Graeco-Roman era women are sometimes identified with Hathor: v. Spiegelberg, *ZÄS* 62 (1927), 27 ff; cf. G. Lefebvre, *ASAE* 23 (1923,) 239, on a woman, perhaps a relative of Petosiris, who is called 'Osiris-Hathor Tadipakem' on her sarcophagus. Now the variation according to sex is itself a token of increased awareness of the individual; it reflects a desire to pursue the divine identification in something other than a purely magical sense; cf. Morenz, *Rel. en Ég.* 81. The Osirian motif remains predominant, however, as in the text published by Spiegelberg in *ZÄS* 54 (1918), 86-92 ('Eine Totenliturgie der Ptolemäerzeit'), where a deceased woman is called Hathor-Artemis; in the last part of the text (pp. 89 ff) it is said of her, 'You are happy in heaven with Rē'', and then her body is said to be taken to four places corresponding to the four regions of heaven, but the dramatic ritual mirrors a fight in which Horus smites the foes of his father Osiris; on p. 91 ff., line 6, she is referred to as 'the god' — clearly the identity with Osiris is here meant. This use of *p3 nṯr* of the deceased underlines the idea of deification; for other occurrences see Spiegelberg, *ZÄS* 62 (1927), 27; two cases are cited in Spiegelberg and Preisigke, *Die Prinz-Joachim-Ostraka* (Strassburg, 1914), 14 n. 6 (P. Louvre 2891 and P. Louvre 2431). Morenz in *Rel. en Égypte*, 82 f. points out that in the Ptolemaic and Roman eras the mummy-binding is called *sntrỉ*, a causative, 'that which makes divine'. That the idea of *ἀποθέωσις* or *ἐκθέωσις* was important in Egypt is amply demonstrated by Morenz in his article 'Zur Vergöttlichung in Ägypten', *ZÄS* 84 (1959), 132-43, although E. Otto, *MDAIK* 15 (1957), 195, tends to deny it. Morenz shows, for instance, that the ritual burial of the Apis was called *sntrỉ* while a Greek papyrus text speaks of the procedure as *ὑπὲρ ἀποθεώσεως* ῎*Απιδος* (Wilcken, *Gdz.* I. 2 (1912), n⁰ 85 (pp. 112 f.); and here the idea is that when the Apis bull dies, its equation with Osiris made it divine. This process is naturally prominent with mortal men: 'You (Osiris) make divine the souls of ......' (Berlin 12441, a text of the Roman era, Morenz, p. 133). Offerings are made divine by becoming the 'Eye of Horus'; in P. Mag. Lond. Leid. 15,13 wine is called 'the blood of Osiris', a process of transubstantiation. Apotheosis by drowning is a well-established, though special, category. It is the deification through identity with Osiris in the traditional sense that concerns us. The epithet *mȝꜥ ḫrw*, 'justified' or 'triumphant', which refers to posthumous judgement, is an instance of it; for this is conferred on the dead through the equation with Osiris. The beginnings of the concept go back to the Old Kingdom; v. my *Origins of Osiris*, 119 ff. The consequent gift, of course, is life which endures and rejuvenation; cf. the short text translated by N. J. Reich, 'An abbreviated Demotic Book of the Dead' (P.B.M. 10072) : 'Thy soul liveth, she rejuvenateth (herself), she knoweth in eternity, for ever. She goeth to the place where Osiris is; she goeth (and) cometh upon the earth for ever : Tikos, daughter of Eserashe.' (*JEA* 17 [1931], 88). See also p. 357.

The assimilation of the worshipper to his god includes his identity with the symbol he is bearing; cf. J. Pascher, ʽH βασιλικὴ ὁδός, 60, who finds a similar approach in Philo. Plutarch, *De Is. et Os.* 3,351 B f. says that the garments of the devotees imply possession of the sacred lore; in my comments *ad loc.* (pp. 267 ff) the significance of the clothing of the gods is shown. By wearing them the worshipper becomes the god, as *CT* VI, 62, *i-k*, succinctly expresses it : 'I have clothed myself with the garment of the great one (Hathor); I am the great one.'

p. 286, 5-6 **in aspectum populus errabat** : Wagner, *Problem*, 122, argues that this clause implies not veneration, but the astonished stare of the people. It implies both. The element of veneration is clearly suggested in what precedes, for on any interpretation Lucius has been exalted in a very special way. Wagner, loc. cit. tends to favour Oudendorp's emendation *haerebat*, comparing ch. 14 (276, 13 f.), *at ego stupore nimio defixus tacitus haerebam*; here, however, *in aspectum* could not go well with *haerebat*; *in aspectu*, as Hildebrand points out, would then be expected.

p. 286, 6-7 **natalem sacrorum** : The initiation has meant a new birth after the death which has been dramatized; it is also a new birth morally, as Lucius has now died to the frivolity of his old life. W. L. Knox, *Some Hellenistic Elements in Primitive Christianity* (London, 1944), 81, says that 'it is difficult to see that the description of his initiation as a "birthday" implies that the rite was habitually interpreted as a "new birth"; the account of it implies rather an approach to death in the form of a visit to the lower world and a more or less miraculous return ...'. Knox does not elaborate on the kind of 'new birth' which he thinks is implied; perhaps he views it as something purely physical, the achievement of safety after the hazard of death. There is a clear link with *renatus* in chs. 16 and 21. Vermaseren and Van Essen, *Santa Prisca*, 208 f., compare the practice in the cult of Cybele of calling the day of the *taurobolium* the *natalicium*; cf. Hepding, *Attis*, 198 citing *CIL* II, 5260, an inscription in Madrid which includes the words *sui natalici redditi*. Wagner, *Problem*, 121 f., who denies any sense of mystic rebirth to *renatus*, similarly devalues the notion to imply merely the first day in the service of Isis; he points to Nock's translation 'birthday of the rites', but the rites are those of initiation, and it is unnatural not to apply the whole concept in a personal way to Lucius; cf. H. Wagenvoort, *Studies in Roman Literature, Culture and Religion*, 143; Rohde's emendation, *natalem sacrum*, accepted by Hopfner, *PW* s.v. *Mysterien*, 1340, would make the personal application clearer, but it is unnecessary.

p. 286, 7 **epulae et faceta convivia** : Whereas banquets and gifts on a birthday could imply a religious offering to a person's *daemon* or genius (cf. Hopfner, *Griechisch-Ägyptischer Offenbarungszauber* II, 27 f. and H. J. Rose, *OCD* 138), there is no suggestion here of a charismatic nature. His friends and fellow-worshippers have done this for Lucius; an impersonal verb such as *fiebant* must be understood.

p. 286, 8 **ientaculum religiosum** : Cf. ch. 27 (288, 14): *epulas* and n. A cult meal is well attested for Serapis. Two invitations to dinner in P. Oxy. 110 and 523, both of the second century A.D., concern meals at the table of the Lord Sarapis, the one in the Serapeum and the other in a private house. Cf. Schubart, *Papyruskunde*, 367; Wilcken, *Chrest.* 99 and *Arch. Pap.* 4 (1908), 211; Deissmann, *Licht vom Osten* 4 (1923), 299 n. 1; Youtie, *Harv. Theol. Rev.* 41 (1948), 9 ff.; Bell, *Cults and Creeds*, 21. W. Otto, *Priester und Tempel*, II, 16 refers to the complaints of Tertullian (*Apol.* 19.15) about the banquetings in pagan festivals; he says that the fire-watchmen will be called out to the smoke of the *cena Serapiaca*. That Serapis was not the only Egyptian deity involved in such a practice is shown by Josephus, *Ant.* 18.73 (ed. L. H. Feldman, Loeb, p. 54), telling the story of the noble Paulina (in the reign of Tiberius) who was deceived to sleep with Decius Mundus when the latter, with the bribed collusion of the priests, took on the role of Anubis and invited her to dinner, which is specifically called the *dinner of Anubis*. In full the phrase here is δεῖπνόν τε αὐτῇ καὶ εὐνὴν τοῦ Ἀνούβιδος; the combination is similar to that of a charm in Preisendanz, *PGM* 1,1 ff (A.D. iv or v) which is designed to make a daemon friendly and informative, eating and sleeping with one. According to Aelius Aristides, *In Sarap.* 27, Keil p. 360 = Hopfner, *Fontes*, 305, banquets involving fellowship were prominent in the cult of Sarapis. A δειπνητήριον mentioned in *OGIS* II, 671 (*temp.* Vespasian) may be connected with him although gods are not named there. A charming terra cotta in Vogt, *Terr.* text vol. 1, fig. 1 shows a *Theoxenion* : on the *Klinê* or sofa are Sarapis, Harpo-crates, Isis, Anubis and Hermanubis, while in the niches in the front are *Canopi* and Harpocrates; the deities cannot easily all be recognized from the photographs, but see Vogt's description on p. 14. There is plentiful evidence, too, in Greek and Roman lands for the popularity of the banquets of the *Kultverein* connected with Isis or Sarapis; at least, the associations themselves are well attested; see Vidman, *Isis und Sarapis*, 87 f., referring to inscriptions from Potaïssa (in Dacia) and Spain; García y Bellido in *Hommages à W. Deonna* (Brussels, 1957), 238-44. The Helen-mosaic found in Trier in 1950 may not be overtly Isiac, but the banquets of a guild are clearly suggested by the food-bearing figures around the mosaic; see K. Parlasca, *Die römischen*

Mosaiken in Deutschland (Berlin, 1959), 56 f., qualifying his earlier interpretation in *Trierer Zeitschrift* 19 (1950), 109-25. An inscription from Prusa may bear witness to a 'dining club of initiates' : see Youtie, *Harv. Theol. Rev.* 41 (1948), 15 n. 34, citing Mendel, *BCH* 24 (1900), 366 f. *Sol-Serapis cum sua cline* are words in an inscription from Cologne : see G. Grimm, *Ägypt. Rel. im röm. Deutschland*, pl. 30 with p. 83; cf. the vessel-lid from Westheim near Augsburg figuring Sarapis and Isis on the banqueting-couch, for which see Grimm, op. cit. figs. 39 f. and pl. 44 with p. 81. Cf. my remarks on 'The Isiac Jug from Southwark', *JEA* 59 (1973), 233-6. Sacred meals were well known, of course, in the other mysteries. In the ceremonies of Attis the meal which followed a period of fasting offered magical life-giving sustenance : v. Hepding, *Attis*, 185 ff. In Mithraism it is a meal, initially, between the gods Sol and Mithras, but they are imitated by their followers, and some representations show only initiates partaking; meat, bread and wine were taken, the meat being, if possible, the flesh of a bull; its blood was also drunk, and the significance was more than physical — new life and spiritual salvation were implied; v. Vermaseren, *Mithras the Secret God*, 98 ff.

p. 286, 8-9 **teletae legitima consummatio** : *Teleta* is an Apuleian Latinisation of τελετή, 'initiation'; the word occurs afterwards in Augustine. The Latinized Greek term is comprehensive, including the rites and words, and also the doctrine emanating from them; cf. Reitzenstein, *Hellenist. Myst.* 242 f. *Consummatio* implies 'end', and in *legitima* there is a suggestion of the just physical solace experienced by Lucius after his fast.

p. 286, 10 **voluptate simulacri divini** : The pleasure is adoration of the goddess, for she is deemed to be fully present in her image. Happiness and gratitude follow initiation because one has begun a new existence; cf. Geo Widengren in *Initiation* ed. C. J. Bleeker (Leiden, 1965), 306 f. Whereas identification with Osiris is implied in the symbolism of the First Initiation, Festugière, 'Lucius and Isis', 80-84, justly observes that it is the contemplative adoration of Isis that is the most striking feature of the religious experience portrayed in the book. At the end of ch. 17 Lucius cannot stir from the temple although others have gone home, for he is *intentus in deae specimen*; when he has made his lodging in the precincts he becomes a *cultor inseparabilis* (ch. 19, p. 281, 3); the visit of former servants from Hypata is presented almost as a distraction, and Lucius keenly returns to the service of the goddess (ch. 20 *fin.* - 21 *init.*); then in the quiet period of waiting he experiences serene visitations from her in the dark nights (ch. 22). Festugière feels that parallels to this contemplative attitude of adoration are hard to find in Greek religion, especially as it is absolutely disinterested, with no hint of *do ut des*. Parallels there certainly are in the other sources of the Isis-religion. Cf. Plutarch, *De Is. et Os.* 3,352 A : the end of the sacred rites is 'the knowledge of the First and the Lord, whom only the mind can understand and whom the goddess summons one to seek as a being who is near and with her and united to her'; 78,383 A : 'then is this god their leader and king, for depending on him, they behold insatiably and desire the beauty which is, to men, ineffable and unutterable.' Isis appears in each passage as a kind of mediator; Osiris is the supreme end of the devotion. The Hymns of Isidorus direct this devotion, as does Apuleius, to Isis (equated in this case with Hermuthis). Cf. the sentiment of the Egyptian text : '(My dear) brother, delight your heart with Isis, for she is more splendid than millions of soldiers.' (See prefatory quotation to this book). A sarcophagus from Ravenna (A.D. iii) shows a lady, Tetratia Isias, in an attitude of contemplation related to the cult : v. *MDAI* 4 (1951), pl. 15,2 and Rudolf Egger, pp. 51 ff. : Festugière, 'Lucius and Isis', 84, cites his frontispiece (Louvre bronze 4165), 'Servant of Isis', a figure with upturned face, as an instance.

p. 286, 10 **inremunerabili** : An Apuleian coinage found only in his work; v. *Thes. L.L.* 7, 2, 400, 8 ff.

beneficio : Cf. ch. 13 (276, 13) and n.

p. 286, 11 **deae monitu** : Cf. ch. 19 (281, 3-4) and n.

p. 286, 12 **supplicue** : The adverb occurs only in Apuleius.

domuitionem : A word derived from much earlier usage by Pacuvius, Lucilius and Accius; v. *Thes. L.L.* 5, 1, 1948, 56 ff.

p. 286, 14 **detersis vestigiis** : Cf. ch. 17 (280, 3), *exosculatis vestigiis deae*, and n.

p. 286, 15 **verba devorans** : The expression occurs also in Seneca and Quintilian : v. *Thes. L.L.* 5, 1, 876, 4 ff.

CHAPTER 25

p. 286, 17 **Tu** : Norden, *Agnostos Theos*, 157, in a discussion of the prose praises of Isis, hails this as 'das beste Beispiel einer solchen Prosadoxologie'. In his *Die antike Kunstprosa*[5] (1915-19, repr. 1958), 603, Norden observes that Apuleius uses a different style for each of his writings; to this one might add that *within* each writing there is considerable variety. The liturgical pieces of Book XI form a group by themselves, and they are sharply distinguished from the narrative that surrounds them. Some of these are monologues in the first person; in chs. 5-6 there is the long address by Isis to Lucius which begins in a manner reminiscent of the Aretalogies; in ch. 15 is given the priest's address to Lucius. There are two passages which are, for the most part, in the *Du-Stil* : first, the prayer of Lucius to the moon-goddess in ch. 2; secondly, the present prayer to Isis; cf. the remarks by Bernhard, *Stil*, 277-80, who misleadingly refers, however, to this prayer as addressed 'zur Mondgöttin'. Two other prayers in the whole work are that of Psyche to Ceres (6.2) and that of Psyche to Juno (6.5). The present chapter is discussed in some detail by G. Lafaye, 'Litanie grecque d'Isis', *Rev. Phil.* 40 (1916), 55-108, esp. 100-103, who lists points of contact with P. Oxy. 1380; Berreth, pp. 30-37, who strangely calls it a 'Hymnus', pp. 30 f.; Wittmann, pp. 130-139 ('Das Dankgebet'); Festugière, 'Lucius and Isis', 81 f. and 166, also in *Philol.* 102 (1952), 21-42, esp. 27 ff. What intrigues Festugière is the psychological improbablility of the composition. After the description at the end of ch. 24 of the prostrate and agitated state of Lucius when he pronounces the prayer, one expects something disjointed and incoherent; instead we find a piece of superb technical skill with the artist in complete control. Festugière rightly concludes, after considering other instances too, that ancient writers did not aim at psychological verisimilitude; they sought rather to achieve perfection in the particular form in which they were composing.

In ch. 9 (273, 9) a choir of youths is mentioned, *carmen venustum iterantes*, and this *carmen* is said to be the work of a skilled poet. Berreth, p. 31, suggests that the present piece could be regarded as such a hymn in prose. A prayer can of course be a hymn, and this piece can be so regarded up the words *at ego*; from there on a very personal statement by Lucius replaces the more communal tone of what precedes. The self-conscious art revealed can be explained from the tradition that 'the recording of an experience was regarded as an act of piety' (Nock, *Harv. Theol. Rev.* 27 [1934], 61). Stylistically the main difference between this prayer and that in ch. 2 is the use of tetracola as opposed to the triadic form favoured there. In content our chapter adds little to the portrayal of Isis given elsewhere: its chief stress is on the cosmic sovereignty of the goddess. The opening *Tu* reappears anaphorically in *tuis ... te ... tu ... tibi ... tuo ... tuam.*

p. 286, 17 **sancta** : Lafaye, op. cit. 101, compares the use of ἱερά of Isis in P. Oxy. 1380, 18 and 110; also of ἁγία in 34 f. and 89.

sospitatrix : Cf. ch. 9 (272, 18) and 15 (277, 18) and notes.

p. 286, 18 **dulcem matris adfectionem** : Lafaye, op. cit. 101, compares P. Oxy. 1380, 11 and 86, 'gentle' (ἠπία); also 12, 'affectionate' (φιλόστοργος). The concept of motherly love is very much to the fore in the Egyptian picture of Isis; v. my *Plut. De Is. et Os.* 58 and 73 f. Hathor was also a goddess of love, but more in a sexually unsocial sense; see the admirably formulated distinction by Ph. Derchain, *Bibl. Orient.* 27 (1970), 22. In P. Oxy. 1380, 109-10, ἀγάπη is used of Isis; although Stephanie West, *JTS* 18 (1967), 142 f., makes a good case for reading ἀγαθὴν θεόν (= Bona Dea), the reading of the first editors remains cogent; cf. R. E. Witt, *JTS* 19 (1968), 209-211. In full the phrase is 'the love of the gods', and the idea that Isis is able to convey this to humanity implies both her sovereignty and her claim to save man from suffering and death in the manner which the myth ascribed to her in relation to Osiris.

p. 286, 18-19 **miserorum casibus** : Cf. Leclant, *Mons. Thébains*, 272; Osiris is *p3 wšb i3d*, 'celui qui répond au malheureux.'

p. 286, 19 **nec dies nec quies** : There are several further instances of rhyme in the prayer. *Quies* seems to be mean 'night' here; cf. ch. 19 (281, 3), *nec fuit nox una vel quies* and ch. 27 (289, 4), *quiete proxima.*

p. 286, 20 **beneficiis otiosum** : The adjective is normally followed by the Genitive, not the Ablative; cf. Pliny, *NH* praef. 6, *studiorum otiosis.*

p. 286, 21 **depulsis vitae procellis** : Cf. ch. 15 *init.* and n.

salutarem : Cf. ch. 22 (283, 18) and n ; also, for *dextera*, ch. 22 (284, 10), *iniecta dextera* and n. *Dextera* and *sinistra* are contrasted in ch. 10 (274, 8 ff.).

p. 286, 21-2 **fatorum ... Fortunae** : Cf. ch. 6 (271, 5-6), *ultra statuta fato tuo spatia* and n.; and ch. 15, the several references to Fortuna with notes.

p. 286, 22 **inextricabiliter** : While *inextricabilis* is common, Apuleius is the first to use the adverb, which *Thes. L.L.* 7, 1, 1335, 67 ff. quotes otherwise only from Cassianus (A.D. iv-v).

p. 286, 23 **stellarum noxios meatus** : *Meatus* is used of stellar movements by Lucr. 1.128, *solis lunaeque meatus* and Vergil, *Aen.* 6.849, *caelique meatus*. In ch. 22 (283, 22) a favourable phenomenon is noted, and it would be clearly wrong to interpret the present allusion as implying that stellar movements generally are baleful. What emerges strongly is the claim of Isis to be able to restrain such movements as appeared ominous. The fatalism inherent in astrology was modified in both Babylon and Egypt by the belief that the king or a priest could intervene to prevent ill-boding influences exerting their sway; v. W. Gundel in F. Boll, C. Bezold and W. Gundel, *Sternglaube und Sterndeutung*[5] (Darmstadt, 1966, repr. of 1931), 169 f.; he quotes Firmicus Maternus, *Math.* 4.16.9 (ed. Kroll and Skutsch, p. 236), *unde orare debemus et summis precibus postulare, ne quando Luna se Mercurio ista radiatione coniungat.* D. Müller, *Isis-Aret.* 79, discusses our passage (after misleading slightly with 'bittet Lucius' : he is not imploring, he is praising Isis for doing this) and quotes an instructive allusion in a Sarapis-Aretalogy, where the god claims power over fate : 'Not as Moira wills, but against Moira, for I change the Moirae (lit. change their clothes)' (lines 12 f. in A. Abt's publication of the text, *Arch. Rel.* 18 [1915], 258); cf. O. Weinreich, 'Neue Urkunden', 420 f.

p. 286, 23-4 **te superi colunt, observant inferi** : Cf. ch. 5 (269, 11), *regina manium, prima caelitum* and n.; ch. 23 (285, 13-14), *deos inferos et deos superos* and n.

p. 286, 24 **rotas orbem** : A group of four short clauses begins here, and there is rhyming of nouns (*orbem, solem*; *mundum, Tartarum*) and verbs (*rotas, luminas, calcas*). The ancients imagined the rounded vault of heaven to be turning round the earth. When *orbis* refers to the earth itself, *terrarum* or *terrae* is usually added.

luminas solem : An association of Isis and the sun is attested by P. Oxy. 1380, 157-9 (she is said to control the sun; cf. 112 f. 'name of sun'); in the temple of Kalabsha (now in Aswân) the sun-god Mandulis is often shown with Isis : v. A. D. Nock, *Harv. Theol. Rev.* 27 (1934), 54 and 63 (the end of the hymn to Mandulis Aion). Again, the Aretalogy from Cyme, 44 f. (Peek, p. 124), makes Isis say, 'I am in the rays of the sun, I attend the course of the sun'; cf. D. Müller ad loc. pp. 73 f. and R. E. Witt, *Isis Gr.-R.* 273 (the Panagia in Greek Orthodox tradition is also identified with the ray of the sun). In the Egyptian tradition she is associated with Rē' through her role in the sun-god's barque; see Introd. V. Maria Münster, *Isis*, 89, shows that as the mother of Iehi Isis is sometimes the consort of Rē'. See also p. 358.

mundum : In *Apol.* 27 (31, 21) Apuleius speaks of *providentiam mundi,* where 'the universe' seems implied; in ch. 24 (286, 1), *mundus alter*, 'another world', is more restricted. It is a moot point which meaning applies here. Most translators and commentators favour 'the universe'; Festugière, *Philol.* 102 (1958), 34, gives 'le monde (terre)'; so too Ryle, who argues that in *orbem ... solem ... mundum ... Tartarum* the progression is from the greater to the less and who wants to interpret *orbem* as 'the universe'. The sequence may rather be spatially from the higher to the lower : 'vault of heaven ... sun ... earth ... underworld'. In *Apol.* 13 (16,3) Apuleius speaks of *Cereris mundum*, 'the sphere of Ceres'; cf. Butler and Owen *ad loc.* p. 36. In ch. 8 (272, 6), *mundoque pretioso*, the meaning is quite different.

p. 286, 24 **calcas Tartarum** : In ch. 23 (285, 12), *calcato Proserpinae limine*, the participle seems to have no sense of domination; here it is hard to avoid such a meaning ('trample on') after the verb in *regis mundum*; cf. too *Metam.* 5.29 (126, 16), *dominae praecepta calcares*.

p. 286, 25 **respondent sidera** : Cf. n. ad ch. 5 (269, 11), *prima caelitum*, and ch. 7 (271, 18), *matrem siderum*. Rohde's *resplendent* has the merit of creating a correspondence to *luminas solem* in the previous line. Robertson compares Manilius, 5.720, with Housman's note. Although Isis was identified with Sirius or Sothis in the ancient tradition, and so linked in a crucial way with the inundation of the Nile, which was heralded by the heliacal rising of Sirius (cf. 'the star of Isis' in the Canopus Decree, and the comment by J. Bergman, *Isis-Seele und Osiris-Ei*, 49 n. 2), a more general sovereignty over the stars is envisaged here, as in the Aretalogies : 'I showed the paths of the stars' and 'The stars do not move on their own course unless they receive commands from me' (M 13, D. Müller, p. 39). Cf. *PSI* VII, 844, 5-7 and the discussion by E. Heitsch, *Mus. Helv.* 17 (1960), 185 f.; the sun and the stars are here subservient to Isis. D. Müller quotes several Egyptian precedents in which Isis is mistress of the stars; e.g. Junker, *Der grosse Pylon*, 168, 18-19, where Isis is 'great in heaven, sovereign of the stars, who placed all the stars on their course'. J. Bergman, 'I Overcome Fate etc.', in H. Ringgren, ed., *Fatalistic Beliefs*, 43, compares Stobaeus, 1.82.5, 'The stars serve *heimarmene*', a context where *heimarmenê* itself serves *pronoia* and *anankê*.

redeunt tempora : Cf. n. ad ch. 7 (271, 18), *parentem temporum*.

p. 286, 25 f. **serviunt elementa** : Cf. *Metam.* 15 (63, 17), of Pamphile; cf. ch. 5 (269, 10), *elementorum omnium domina* and n.; ch. 23 (285, 12), *per omnia vectus elementa* and n.

p. 287, 1 **spirant flamina** : Cf. ch. 5 (269, 12-13), *maris salubria flamina ... nutibus meis dispenso* and n. Isis is mistress of the winds in the Aretalogy from Cyme, 39 (Peek, p. 124); cf. p. Oxy. 1380, 237; Lucian, *Dial. deor.* 3, where Isis is exhorted to send the winds. See further D. Müller, *Isis-Aret.* 61 ff. Rhyme is probably deliberate in *flamina ... nubila ... semina ... germina*.

nutriunt nubila : A tradition associating Isis with water appears in Plut. *De Is. et Os.* 12, 355 F, 'Isis was born near very moist places'; v. my remarks *ad loc.* pp. 303 ff. 'Birth of Isis : the heaven rained' (Rhind, Math. P., ed Peet, pl. Y, no. 87 and p. 129) would seem to suggest Isis as rain-maker. It is doubtful whether the tradition belongs to the earliest stratum; indeed Derchain, *Bibl. Orient.* 27 (1970), 22 f., questions its whole validity. He shows that the sending of rain, whether beneficent or otherwise, is associated with various deities. But a later association with Isis is not surprising, for there are many other instances in which the pantheistic Isis absorbs the attributes of other deities. The Cyme Aretalogy, 54, is unequivocal : Isis claims to be 'the mistress of rain'; and in P. Oxy. 1380, 226 ff. she is connected with 'all rain, every spring, all dew and snow'. See further D. Müller, *Isis-Aret.* 67 ff.

p. 287, 1-2 **germinant semina, crescunt germina** : Isis claims to be the discoverer of corn in the Aretalogies, including Diod. Sic. 1.14.1; v. D. Müller, op. cit. 31 ff., who shows that Osiris rather than Isis is credited in the Egyptian texts as the maker of corn. εὑροῦσα, 'she who discovered', being a Greek concept. See also my Plut. *De Is. et Os.* 57 f. and 529. When Plutarch, 32, 363 D, is presenting Osiris as the Nile, then Isis is the land which the Nile fructifies; cf. P. Oxy. 1380, 170, τὴν γῆν σπορίμην. J. Bergman, *Isis-Seele und Osiris-Ei*, 86 f. justly invokes the association of Isis with Renenutet-Thermuthis, a goddess of corn; he also makes the interesting suggestion that Horus was equated with Neper ('corn'), the son of Renenutet, and that the form Carpocrates sometimes given to Horus-Harpocrates reflects this connection, since it implies the idea of καρπός.

p. 287, 3 **labentes** : Hildebrand's emendation of *latentes*, the reading of the codices, is accepted by Médan and approved of to some extent by Robertson. The other animals mentioned are assigned participles describing their movement, and *labentes* fits the series well.

This part of the prayer is very reminiscent in some ways of ancient Egyptian hymns; cf. the Hymn to Isis from Aswân (text and tr, by D. Müller, *Isis-Aret.* 89 ; the Hymn of Amen-mose to Osiris (text in *BIFAO* 30 [1931], 725-50, ed. A. Moret) contains this passage in the translation of Erman and Blackman, *Lit.* 141 f. (cf. Roeder, *Urk. Rel.* 23) :

> Nun hath offered to him his water, and the north wind journeys southward to him; the sky createth air for his nose, for the contentment of his heart. The plants grow according to his desire, and the field createth for him its food. The firmament and the stars hearken into him, and the great portals open to him; to whom men shout for joy in the southern sky, whom men adore in the northern sky. The imperishable stars are under his authority, and the never-wearying ones are his place of abode.

The celebrated long hymn to the Aten provides a detailed parallel to the idea that plants and animals own the sway of the presiding deity. This hymn mentions lions and snakes, birds and lambs, and also the fish : 'The fish in the stream leap before you, and your rays penetrate into the depths of the ocean.' See Maj Sandman, *Texts from the Time of Akhenaten* (Brussels, 1938), 94, 9 f.;

cf. A. Scharff, *Aegyptische Sonnenlieder* (Berlin, 1922), 63; H. M. Stewart, *JEA* 46 (1960), 83-90 for earlier hymns; C. Aldred, *Egypt : The Amarna Period* (*CAH* 1971), 46 f. Assmann, *Liturgische Lieder an den Sonnengott* (1969), deals with hymns in *BD* 15; see e.g. pp. 27 ff.; and 343 ff., where he shows that these hymns, unlike those of Amarna, present the speaker as standing outside the *conditio humana*. The Greek Aretalogies provide several parallels, as we have seen, to the prayer in Apuleius; the correspondences in the much earlier hymns of Egypt bear out Bergman's thesis in *Ich bin Isis* that the Aretalogies themselves have preserved much ancient tradition.

p. 287, 6 **ora mille** : Statius, 'Somnus' (*Silv.* 5.4.11 ff.) speaks of the possibility of having a thousand eyes like Argus; but the present expression does not apparently derive from mythology. 'Not if I had ten tongues and ten mouths ...', says Homer, *Il.* 2.489; Vergil, *Georg.* 2.43 and *Aen.* 6.625, following Ennius, speaks similarly of a hundred tongues and mouths; cf. Norden, *ad loc.* p. 293. Ovid, it seems, was the first to speak of a thousand : *Fasti*, 2.119; v. F. Bömer *ad loc.* Cf. the hymn by Charles Wesley : 'O for a thousand tongues to sing / My dear Redeemer's praise.' Paul, 1 Cor. 1.13 ('the tongues of men and of angels') is probably thinking of a large number too.

p. 287, 8 **alioquin** : Cf. ch. 21 (282, 13) and n.

p. 287, 9-10 **perpetuo custodiens imaginabor** : Cf. the gratitude for blessings received. and the prayer for further beneficence, in the Hymns of Isidorus, 2, 27 ff, (*SEG* 8, 549), where Thermuthis-Isis is addressed : 'In joy do they return home reverently after celebrating your festival, full of the beneficence that comes from you. Grant a share of your gifts also to me, your supplicant, Lady Hermuthis, prosperity and also the blessing of children. Isidorus wrote it. Hearing my prayers and hymns, the gods have recompensed me with the blessing of happiness.' Cf. Vanderlip. *ad loc.* pp. 48 f.

p. 287, 11 **Ad istum modum** : See n. *ad.* ch. 3 (267, 22).

deprecato : An abnormal use of a deponent verb with passive sense; cf. ch. 19 (280, 17), *adfatis*, and n.

p. 287, 12 **meum iam parentem** : Cf. ch. 21 (282, 15), *ut solent parentes* and n.

p. 287, 13 **veniam** : Cf. n. *ad* ch. 23 (284, 21), *praefatus deum veniam.*

p. 287, 14 **nequirem** : Subjunctive in implied Oratio Obliqua.

CHAPTER 26

p. 287, 14 **diu denique** : Cf. ch. 20 (281, 14), *diu diuque*; 2.15 (37, 4 f.), *et tandem denique.*

gratiarum gerendarum : The only instance, it seems, of *gratias gerere* for *gratias agere*; v. *Thes. L.L.* 6, 2, 2225, 56 f. For the non-avoidance of the double Genitive plural ending, cf. ch. 21 (282, 11), *accipiendorum sacrorum.* The Genitive is one of definition.

p. 287, 15 **patrium larem** : In *Metam.* 1.1 Lucius places his ancestors in

Athens, the Isthmus, and the Peloponnese; in 2.12 (35, 1 f.) he talks of a Chaldaean stranger 'even in Corinth now among us' (*et Corinthi nunc apud nos*); and in 1.22 (20, 12), when he goes to Milo's house in Hypata, he says that he has a letter of introduction from Demeas of Corinth. Probably, then, his home must be regarded as in or near Corinth. We are told in ch. 18 that relatives from home come to visit him, but with no further indication; in that chapter (280, 8) *patria* in used of his home, which gives slight support to van der Vliet's emendation here (*patriam, larem* etc.) although it does not seem absolutely necessary. See further P. Veyne, *Rev. phil.* 39 (1965) 243; H. J. Mason, *Phoenix* 25 (1971), 160. Veyne (249 n. 3) believes that one may infer from this that after his initiation at Cenchreae Apuleius went home to Madauros, and then left for Ostia from the port of Hippo. For this there is no firm evidence. The travels of Apuleius in Rome seem rather to have followed his stay in Greece. Merkelbach, *Aegyptus* 49 (1969), 89, takes the native place to be Patrae, apparently assuming that it will correspond to the Patrae named by Lucius in the Greek prototype, 55; cf. H. van Thiel, *Der Eselsroman*, II, 243 and I, 28 ff. A further suggestion by Merkelbach (ibid. 89 n. 1) is that the heavenly home of the human soul may also be implied; during his First Initiation Lucius has already briefly visited this home, but as long as he lives as a man, he cannot remain there; he must move on. Whereas a 'second meaning' is often possible in this work, the context scarcely favours it here, for Lucius is already on the move when he leaves the scene of the First Initiation.

p. 287, 16 **post aliquam multum** : According to Neue and Wagener, *Formenlehre*[3] (1892), II, 578 f. the adverbial use of *aliquam* with *multi* is archaistic since it occurs only once in Cicero in one of his earlier speeches (*Verr.* 4.25.56) and is then resumed by the archaistically inclined Gellius and Apuleius; cf. *Apol.* 4 (6,4) and Butler and Owen *ad loc.* p. 16.

paucisque post diebus : The claims of the goddess make a longer stay impossible. However, his relatives have visited him in Cenchreae (ch. 18) and expressed joy at his transformation.

p. 287, 18 **tutusque** : Although it is December, outside the normal sailing season, Isis Pelagia is doubtless thought to ensure his safety. Cf. P. Veyne *Rev. Phil.* 39 (1965), 249 n. 3. The emendations of Wasse and Price provide a stronger connection with the following Ablative.

prosperitate ventorum ferentium : The abstract expression is preferred to *prosperis ventis*. For the participle cf. Verg. *Aen.* 4, 430, *ventosque ferentis* and R. G. Austin (1953) *ad loc.* p. 130 f. Isis is mistress of the winds : cf. n. *ad* ch. 5 (169, 12), *caeli ... maris ... inferum* and ch. 25 (287, 1).

p. 287, 19 **Augusti portum** : The first harbour of Ostia was built by Claudius; a second inner harbour was built by Trajan; v. R. Meiggs, *Roman Ostia* [2] (Oxford, 1973), 162 ff.

carpento : A carriage with two wheels drawn by two mules. Presumably there were a number available for the sixteen miles journey from Ostia to Rome; cf. Saglio in Dar.-Sag. *Dict.* s.v. (1887), 926 f. with figs. The word is probably of Celtic origin; v. Walde and Hofmann, *Lat. Etym. Wb.*³ (1938), 171; cf. mod. Welsh *cerbyd.*

p. 287, 19 **pervolavi** : For the perfect surrounded by present tenses compare n. *ad* ch. 12 (275, 21), *inrepo.*

p. 287, 20 **quam dies insequebatur Iduum** : Médan observes a sequence of three cretics.

sacrosanctam : Rome housed the temples of many deities (cf. Ammian. Marc. 17.4.13 where Rome is described as *templum mundi totius*), but to Lucius its holiness clearly derives from the prominence now given there to the cult of Isis. It does not follow, of course, that Rome was the central administrative point of the cult, although the higher degrees of initiation are completed there.

p. 287, 23 **Campensis** : The episode of Paulina and Decius Mundus, related by Josephus, *Ant.* 18, 65 ff. (cf. Tac. *Ann.* 2.85; Suet. *Tib.* 36), shows that there was a temple of Isis in Rome in the reign of Tiberius, for the affair took place in the temple, and the net result was the crucifixion of the priests, the throwing of the Isis-statue into the Tiber, and the destruction of the temple. Cf. Ilse Becher, 'Der Isiskult in Rom — ein Kult der Halbwelt?' *ZÄS* 96 (1970), 81-90, esp. 82. It was Caligula who probably built or rebuilt the temple in the Campus Martius : v. Mommsen, *CIL* I², 334 (he argues that the cult was given state sanction at this time); the emperor himself took part in mysteries (Josephus, *Ant.* 19,30) when he put on women's robes; when his wife Caesonia gave birth to a daughter only a month after her marriage, he explained it as a supernatural birth (Dio. 59.6-7), apparently following the Pharaonic theology of the king's birth : v. H. P. L'Orange, *Symb. Osl.* 21 (1941), 105-116. On the other hand, the *Aula Isiaca* on the Palatine, formerly assigned to the reign of Caligula, is now dated to 20 B.C. : v. K. Schefold, following H. G. Beyen, in *FS. G. M. Robinson* II (St. Louis, 1953), 1096. That the Iseum Campense was probably built between A.D. 36 and 39 is cogently argued by Wissowa, *Rel. u. Kultus der Romer*² (1912), 353 f. The site is described by Platner and Ashby, *Top. Dict. of Ancient Rome* (1929), 283-5 and in detail by G. Gatti, 'Topografia dell' Iseo Campense', *Rend. Pont. Acc.* 20 (1913-4), 117-63; see esp. his fig. 1, p. 118, 'Iseum et Serapeum'; Anne Roullet, *Rome*, 23-36, gives an elaborate account. The facade of the temple is shown on a coin of Vespasian (A.D. 71) : v. J. Leipoldt and K. Regling, *Angelos* 1 (1925), pl. 5, 1 with pp. 129 f.; Leipoldt, *Bilderatlas*, 46 [274] : Anne Roullet, *Rome*, fig. 22 with p. 30. On the adjacent Serapeum see Chr. Hülsen, 'Porticus Divorum und Serapeum im Marsfelde', *MDAIR* (1903), 17-57; Anne Roullet, *Rome*, 26 f. See also Drexler, 'Isis', 544; Gressmann, *Orient. Rel.* 40 ff. (with photographs of reliefs); Moret, *Rois et Dieux d'Égypte*, 167 ff; Bonnet, *Reallexikon*, 331; P. F. Tschudin, *Isis in Rom.*, 17; Nock, *CAH* 10 (1934), 496; Latte, *Röm. Rel.* 283 n. 5. After being destroyed in A.D. 80 by fire, it was rebuilt by Domitian; renovations were later made by Alexander Severus, Diocletian and Maximian : v. Wissowa, *Rel. u. Kultus der Romer*² (1912), 353. Juvenal, 6.529, mentions it as being near the old Ovile or Saepta (*antiquo quae proxima surgit ovili*), the assembly point of the Centuria Centuriata. Lucan, who died in A.D. 65, wrote (8.831) *nos in templa tuam Romana accepimus Isim* (he is addressing the land of Egypt). In the second century Hadrian was a notable adherent of the cult.

p. 287, 24 **cultor** : = θεραπευτής, used of the cult of Serapis; v. Reitzenstein, *Hellenist. Myst.* 193 and 204.

p. 287, 24-5 **fani quidem advena, religionis autem indigena** : The faith transcends the bounds of countries and customs, but the individual temple appears to be a self-governing and independent community. Thus Lucius had to have his *Olympiaca stola* in Cenchreae; cf. ch. 29, *ad fin.* An *advena* is a proselyte or newcomer (προσήλυτος or ἐπηλύτης); cf. Reitzenstein, *Hellenist. Myst.* 193 f., who shows that while the Mystery Religions were international in scope, yet their sacral language preserved ideas of national origin, as the words *advena* and *indigena* do here. He compares ἀλλογενής in Luke, 17.18 : and ἀδελφοὶ εἰσποίητοι, 'adopted brothers', in the Jewish-Iranian cult of Hypsistos. The organisation of the 'churches' of the Diaspora must have differed in this respect from that of the cult-centres in Egypt. George La Piana, *Harv. Theol. Rev.* 20 (1927), 336 f. justly states that while there was within Egypt a hierarchical unity, this was not so in the extra-Egyptian cults where the autonomous character of each Isiac congregation is apparent. See also p. 358.

p. 288, 1 f. **Ecce ... et** : Apuleius is fond of this paratactic sequence.

p. 288, 1 **signifero circulo** : Cf. the astrological allusions in ch. 22 (283, 22 ff.) and 25 (286, 23).

Sol magnus : Médan compares Gellius, 3.2, *post meridiem sole magno*. The epithet is merited because it is the sun that demarks the year. Beroald's proposal *magnum annum* belongs to the same association of ideas; he was able to invoke Verg. *Aen.* 3.284, *interea magnum sol circumvolvitur annum*. The particular year intended could be one of three : (1) the calendar year; (2) a year since the arrival of Lucius in Rome; (3) a year since his metamorphosis and the beginning of his initiations. In favour of (1) is the mention, a little previously, of the Ides of December; in favour of (3) is that the festival of the *Isidis Navigium* was on March 5th, and that the completion of a year since that date would seem reasonable. What follows appears to confirm the relation of time here to religious experience. Wittmann, p. 223 n. 634 favours (1) and rightly rejects the idea that the solstice (Dec. 21st) or Dec. 25th is regarded here as a terminal point. More recently Merkelbach in *Aegyptus* 49 (1969), 89-91 has revived precisely this idea. Noting that December 12th is carefully presented here as a date, he locates the vision of Isis mentioned in this context on the night of the same day; on the night of December 13th occurs, according to him, the vision of the initiate carrying wands, ivy and sacred objects; the morning of December 14th is assigned to the salutations to the goddess. At this point Merkelbach admits an element of uncertainty in the time-reckoning. In ch. 28 we are told that Lucius is exhorted to sell his clothes to meet the expenses; he 'was being repeatedly urged on by the persistence of the deity' and he took action only 'after being incited quite often.' Merkelbach wants to telescope these divine instructions into the space of one night in the sense that a dream or vision may recur several times in one night. This enables him to locate the Second Initiation, after the lapse of ten days of dietetic regimen, on the night of December 24th; he admits the doubtful factor in the reckoning, but argues that even if two or three nights have to be added, one is brought to the time of the Christmas season. The Second Initiation, he urges, may well have happened at the time of the great festival of the solstice, and he adduces Epiphanius, *Haer.* 51.22, for the existence of an important festival of Isis and Osiris on December 25th. Insofar as this context is concerned, there is a flaw in the argument quite apart from the doubtful factor which is admitted. After the mention of December 12th in the present chapter, Lucius says that he fervently offered supplications daily at the Iseum Campense and was a constant worshipper (*cultor ... adsiduus*) there. Then comes the mention of the end of the year. If this is the calendar year, the Second Initiation will occur in the second half of January. Clearly the devotions in the temple are presented as covering some time before the occurrence of the first dream-vision in Rome. For the festivals mentioned by Epiphanius, loc. cit. see Ed. Norden, *Geburt des Kindes*, 24 ff. and Merkelbach, *Isisfeste*, 37 ff.; also my comments in *ZDMG* 15 (1965), 348 f.

288, 2 **et quietem etc.** : Médan recognizes a sequence of three cretics beginning here.

pervigilis : Presumably the adjective qualifies *cura*, in which case it is a unique form (instead of *pervigil*).

p. 288, 3 **teletae** : See n. *ad* ch. 24 (286, 8).

p. 288, 4 **quidni** : Cf. ch. 28 (290, 2); 30 (291, 4). The word is followed by a pronoun in 4, 24 (93, 5); 5.30 (127, 8); 6.17 (141, 7); hence Robertson's proposal *quidni*? [*qui*]. But that is not so in the two instances first cited. The literal meaning is probably 'why not?' and the usage occurs in Plautus and Terence; Cicero and Catullus employ a relative clause after it; v. Hofmann and Szantyr, *Lat. Syntax*, 458.

CHAPTER 27

288, 5 **apud meum sensum** : Cf. ch. 20 (281, 14-15), *apud cogitationes meas revolvebam*; and n.

288, 6-7 **comperior** : Although *comperio* is the usual form, the deponent occurs in both Terence and Sallust, and is used six times altogether by Apuleius himself.

p. 288, 7 **magni dei** : The Egyptian *nṭr '3*, 'great god', was often used of Osiris : v. *Wb.* II, 361, 2. It was also used of Rē' and of the King. Cf. Gardiner and Sethe, *Egyptian Letters to the Dead* (London, 1928), 11 n. 9; Leclant, *Enquêtes sur les sacerdoces etc.* (Cairo, 1944), 109; J. Gwyn Griffiths, *Conflict*,

80 f. The phrase μέγας βασιλεύς in Plutarch, *De Is. et Os.* 12, 355 E is perhaps intended to correspond.

p. 288, 7-8 **deumque summi parentis** : The equivalent term in Egyptian *it nṯrw*, 'father of the gods', is used of Atum, Rēʿ, Nun, Geb and other gods, but not, apparently, of Osiris : v. *Wb.* I, 141, 14 with refs. This accords with early cosmogony. Osiris, however, is called *nsw nṯrw*, 'King of the gods' : v. *Wb.* II, 328, 13; and also *nsw nswyw*, 'King of Kings' (ibid. 7); cf. my remarks in *Class. Phil.* 48 (1953), 151.

p. 288, 8 **invicti** : This probably derives from the epithet *wsr*, 'mighty', frequently used of Osiris, sometimes in conscious paranomasia with the name *Wsir* itself : v. my *Plut. De Is. et Os.* 288 and 442; my *Origins of Osiris*, 60 ff. Hermaeus in Plut. *Is. et Os.* 37, 365 E interpreted the name as ὄβριμος, 'mighty'. The question naturally arises, in spite of this tradition, whether *Sol Invictus*, used of Mithras, has influenced the present epithet. Cf. ch. 7 (271, 7), *numen invictum* and n., used of Isis. Stefan Weinstock, 'Victor and Invictus', *Harv. Theol. Rev.* 50 (1957), 211 - 47, shows that the use of these terms in the Roman world was probably inspired by the example of Alexander, to whom the adjective ἀνίκητος and the phrase ὁ ἀνίκητος θεός were applied; Hercules was called *invictus* and Julius Caesar aspired to the title *Deus Invictus*; although Trajan was assigned the epithet, it was not until the reign of Commodus, in A.D. 191, that emperors began regularly to use it. In this context Weinstock (p. 242) believes that Heracles was the pattern; he rejects the view that an intentional rivalry to Mithraism and its Sol Invictus was involved. In the case of the Graeco-Roman Osiris Mithraic influence was a greater possibility. In the Osirian myth it was the victory over Seth-Typhon, including the juridical victory, which made him *m3ʿ-ḫrw*, that was important.

necdum : There is some early evidence for the use of *necdum* with the sense of *nondum* : v. Hofmann and Szantyr, *Lat. Syntax*, 449.

inlustratum : The verb is used of the light of the sun in ch. 5 (269, 20); a spiritual connotation is added here as well as in ch. 28 (289, 21-2), *nocturnis orgiis inlustratus* and 29 (290, 21), *felici illo amictu illustrari*. The verb corresponds to φωτίζεσθαι cf. Reitzenstein, *Hellenist. Myst.* 264.

p. 288, 9 **esset** : The subjunctive following *quamquam* was already common in Tacitus (cf. E. C. Woodcock *The Annals of Tacitus*, *XIV* (London, 1939), 30) even in concessive clauses of fact. Apuleius often uses a participle after it.

p. 288, 10 **discrimen** : Apuleius is at pains to justify the additional initiations in Rome. Isis, Osiris and Sarapis all had some distinctive rites at this time. The temples were in the name of Isis or Sarapis, but an Osirian element was present in all the ceremonies. Those at Cenchreae include the rite of the *Isidis Navigium* and an Isiac initiation; the latter, however, contained an identification of the initiate with Osiris. Several inscriptions from Thessalonica name Osiris; v. Nilsson, *Gesch. Griech. Rel.*, II (1950), 119 n. 12 (from p. 118), Ὀσείριδι μύσται, cf. ibid. 612; also R. E. Witt, 'Macedonia', 331 (five mentions of Osiris and a pathway to the Serapeum called δρόμος Ὀσείριδι). An inscription from

Didyma of the year 288/7 B.C. involves the dedication of a cup of Osiris by Seleucus I ; v. P. M. Fraser 'Two Studies', 33, and Vidman, *Isis und Serapis*, 14 f; but Mr. Francis Piejko, of Chapel Hill, N. Carolina, queries the reading of the god's name and plans to publish an emended reading.

p. 288, 10 **discrimen interesse maximum** : **prohinc** : Médan, *Lat.* 252, notes the Iambic Senarius here.

prohinc : 'Henceforth' (Butler); 'accordingly' is the meaning indicated in *Metam.* 3.8 (58, 7); 3.12 (61, 7); 5.2 (104, 24).

p. 288, 11 **deo famulum** : The terminology of slavery is used to express religious service; cf. ch. 15 fin., *ministerii iugum* and *deae servire*.

p. 288, 12 **de sacratis** : Cf. lines 19-20, *de pastophoris unum*. This variant for the partitive genitive is not uncommon. Apuleius can also use the latter mode; e.g. ch. 10 (274, 1), *quorum primus*.

linteis : See n. ad ch. 10 (273, 15), *linteae vestis*.

iniectum : Cf. *Metam.* 2.28 (48, 7 f.), *iuvenem quempiam linteis amiculis iniectum*, of an Egyptian priest.

thyrsos et hederas : According to J. von Geisau, *De Apul. Synt.* 17, this is a poetic plural for singular; on p. 25 he compares Propertius, 3.3.55, *haec hederas tegit in thyrsos*, where the context is Bacchic. Plutarch, *De Is. et Os.* 37, 365 E, says that 'ivy is consecrated by the Greeks to Dionysus and is said to be named *khenosiris* by the Egyptians, a word which denoted, so they say, "the plant of Osiris".' See my n. *ad loc.* pp. 440 f. Cf. Diod. Sic. 1.17.4; Tib. 1.7.45. By the Roman era, perhaps in Ptolemaic times even, ivy was used in the cult of Osiris. This resulted from the equation of Osiris and Dionysus. Plutarch, *De Is. et Os.* 35, 364 E, also mentions thyrsus-rods (and fawnskins) as figuring in the 'burial of Apis'. The fact that in these details the cult of Osiris was influenced by that of Dionysus should not permit one to infer that a thorough-going process of Dionysiac syncretism had happened, although a phallic rite may also have been adopted; cf. my remarks, op. cit. 299 f.

p. 288, 13 **tacenda quaedam** ; These are meant to refer, probably, to some of the objects mentioned in ch. 10-11, including the *cista secretorum capax* (274, 20 f.). Médan suggests that they might be phallic objects; so too Wittmann, p. 223 n. 638, referring to Plut. *De Is. et Os.* 33 and 37, where Osiris is associated with the principle of generation. It is unlikely that the *cista* contained a phallus; v. n. ad ch. 11 (274, 20), *cista*. In 12, 355 E Plutarch mentions *phallephoria* in connection with Pamyle, the nurse of Osiris; cf. 36, 365 B f. Since phalluses were commonly carried in Dionysiac processions, it is possible that the Graeco-Roman Osirian rites included this element. It is noteworthy that the theme is developed in Egyptian finds of the Hellenistic era; cf. the phallophorous group in terracotta found at Saqqâra in which Bes-figures and Harpocrates are prominent : see G. T. Martin, *JEA* 59 (1973), 11 ff. Apuleius, however, does not mention such an element is his account of the Isiac procession in chs. 10-11, nor is there any reason to infer its presence here, since *tacenda* refers generally to mystic objects which are ἀπόρρητα.

p. 288, 13 **ad ipsos meos lares** : 'Before my housefold gods' (Butler) and thus most interpreters. Lucius must be regarded as staying in a lodging within the precincts of the temple, as he did at Cenchreae, and a reference to household gods is not very fitting to the place or spiritual context. *Lares* can of course mean 'dwelling' or 'home'; usually the singular occurs in this sense, but for the plural thus used see Ovid, *Rem. Am.* 302, *sub titulum nostros misit avara lares*, and Hor. *Carm. Saec.* 39, *iussa pars mutare lares*. Admittedly Apuleius uses a singular in ch. 26 (287, 15), *patrium larem*; but he uses a plural in 4.12 (83, 34), *in alienos lares*; 5.10 (111, 17 f.), *et lares pauperes nostros*; 11.17 (280, 4), *ad suos discedunt lares*. In *Apol.* 53 (59, 18; 27) the plural is used of a cupboard, the religious sense having probably atrophied to some extent; cf. Abt, *Apol.* 280 f. One must agree, then, with F. Carlesi's translation (Florence, 1954), 309, 'le depose proprio innanzi alla mia casa,' save that the sense of 'into' or 'inside' is preferable.

p. 288, 13-14 **collocaret ... denuntiaret** : Cf. ch. 9 (273, 1-4) and n., where the subjunctives *commonstrarent* and *fingerent* are syntactically parallel to the following *conspargebant*. This may be 'Hyperurbanismus', an overstraining for refinement; v. Hofmann and Szantyr, *Lat. Syntax*, 560 f. The indicative would be expected; cf. Callebat, *Sermo Cotid.* 343.

occupato sedili meo : E. Schober, *Comp. num.* 17, remarks on the three cretics. Lafaye, *Hist. du culte*, 184, is anxious to interpret this as a seat or cubicle suitable for incubation. He compares an inscription from the Port of Ostia mentioning the *megaron* of Isis, and he agrees with Lanciani, *Bull. inst. arch. Roma* 40 (1868), 228 f., in explaining the *megaron* as a place of incubation; for the inscription see also H. Thylander, *Inscriptions du port d'Ostie* (Lund, 1952), B 293, cf. 284; L. R. Taylor, *Cults of Ostia*, 68; R. Meiggs, *Roman Ostia²*, 388. The so-called *megaron* at Pompeii is invoked, and certainly the crypt of this building, or a crypt elsewhere, could well have served the purpose; cf. Mau, tr. Kelsey, *Pompeii*, 172 ff.; Tran Tam Tinh, *Isis à Pompéi*, 34. What tends to confirm the interpretation here is that the priest, later described as one of the *pastophori*, has appeared to Lucius in a vision.

p. 288, 14 **epulas** : Cf. ch. 24 (286, 8), *ientaculum religiosum*, and n. In the Cenchreaean initiation the banquets came at the end; here a banquet is to precede the rites. Ch. 28 shows that in this initiation there are nocturnal ceremonies preceded by a vegetarian regimen for ten days. It is possible that this banquet does not belong to the initiation rites in the proper sense, but rather to the convivial meetings which guilds of worshippers are known to have held in Egypt and elsewhere. See A. F. Shore, 'A Drinking-cup with Demotic Inscription', *British Mus. Quarterly* 36 (1971), 16-19, where he translates the first line 'The cups of the shrine of Isis-the-great (Esoeris) of the island of Paos'; the last line gives the date of the cup's dedication (26 October A.D. 73). Shore points out that 'drinking wine and beer on certain occasions was an important element in the religious observations of the guilds' and cites some of the considerable literature on the subject, including W. Erichsen's *Die*

Satzungen einer ägyptischen Kultgenossenschaft aus der Ptolemäerzeit (Copenhagen, 1959). In view of this it may be confidently suggested that the Isiac jug from Southwark with the inscription LONDINI AD FANUM ISIDIS did not belong to a wineshop or tavern, as Eve and John Harris have concluded in *The Oriental Cults in Roman Britain* (Leiden, 1965), 79 f. but was directly connected with the shrine of Isis in this ancillary sense. The *graffito* will then mean not 'In London near the shrine of Isis' (a designation, virtually, of the tavern) but 'In London for the use of the shrine of Isis'. See my remarks in *JEA* 59 (1973), 233-6.

p. 288, 15 **signo** : Witt, *Isis Gr.-R.* 158, compares the tokens of modern Freemasonry.

p. 288, 17 **deum voluntatem** : A similar situation occurs when Lucius approaches the priest who is carrying a crown of of roses, ch. 13 *init.*; both have been previously warned by the goddess, and marvel at the outcome; thus too in ch. 20 *fin.* the significance of a dream is confirmed.

p. 288, 18 **matutinis ... salutationibus** : Cf. chs. 20 and 22.

p. 288, 19 **vestigium similis** : For the Accusative cf. ch. 10 (274, 4-5), *vestitum quidem similis.*

ut somnium : Such a construction after *similis* has naturally led to a number of proposed emendations. Perhaps it is better to bear in mind the unorthodox urge in the syntax of Apuleius; he may really have written this.

de pastophoris : Cf. line 12, *de sacratis*, for the preposition. On *pastophori* see n. *ad* ch. 17 (279, 15).

p. 288, 20 **indicium pedis** : It seems doubtful whether lame or crippled persons were normally admitted to the priesthood of the Egyptian cults. The basic term for priest, *w'b*, 'a pure one', probably implies exclusion of people with physical imperfections. Still, the evidence of this chapter fits in with an attitude which was otherwise liberally comprehensive; cf. ch. 10 *init.* and n. There is no reason to connect this phenomenon with the dedication of representations of feet to Isis or Serapis, on which see L. Castiglione in *Acta Orient. Hung.* 20 (1967), 239-252.

p. 288, 21 **examussim** : A word revived from Plautus, it comes from *ex + amussis*, 'mason's rule'.

p. 288, 21 f. **Asinium Marcellum** : Asinius was not an uncommon *praenomen* in Rome; cf. C. Asinius Pollio, Vergil's friend. That the name might possibly allude to the role of *pastophorus*, a suggestion of Wittmann's, seems hardly likely. The restoration of *non* before *alienum* (289, 1), first made by Beroaldus, is necessary to the general sense; the name is alien to the restored human condition of Lucius, but this would produce an unfavourable emphasis; the name reminds him rather of the happy change.

p. 289, 1 **non** : See previous n.

p. 289, 4 **quiete proxima** : For meaning 'night' cf. ch. 25 (286, 19), *quies ulla* and n.

p. 289, 5 **magno deo coronas** : Doubtless for the statues of the god. Cf. ch. 3

(268, 6), *corona multiformis*, of Isis. In ch. 6, *init.* a priest is to carry a *corona rosea*, and this is probably intended eventually to adorn the statue of Isis. In ch. 24 (286, 3-4) a *corona* ... *palmae candidae* is said to be on the head of Lucius in his state of assimilation, it seems, to the solar Osiris. This kind of crown might be implied here. Highly ornate crowns are shown on figures of Osiris; their basic element is the Upper Egyptian white crown; see our frontispiece, a figure in the Ashmolean Museum. When the white crown is flanked by two large feathers, the Atef-crown is formed; cf. Wessetzky, *Ägypt. Kulte in Ungarn*, pls. 13 and 16 (21); Grimm, *Ägypt. Rel. im röm. Deutschland*, pl. 4; Morenz in *Rel. en Égypte*, ed. Derchain, pls. 3 and 4; Edgar, *Graeco-Egyptian Coffins*, pl. 14. An Osiris Hydreios figured on a pillar of the Iseum Campense is shown with the Double Crown; v. Leipoldt, *Bilderatlas* 60 [288] = Anne Roullet, *Rome*, pl. 30; (pl. 33 here shows another Osiris Hydreios with the Atef Crown).

p. 289, 5 **exaptat** : Helm's conjecture for the lacuna,*c onspexisse numen divinum*, has the merit of preparing the way for the syntax of the following clause, although a masculine subject, such as *Osiris ipse*, would suit *visus est*.

p. 289, 6 **Madaurensem** : Goldbacher's *mane Doriensem* restores cool consistency to the text, but the unwitting self-revelation of *Madaurensem* coheres with the whole tone of the book. Robertson's proposal, *mandare se ⟨religiosum⟩, sed admodum pauperem*, in *CQ* 4 (1910), 221, is not repeated in his edition. See further Introd. I, 'The Autobiographical Element'.

admodum pauperem : Cf. ch. 18 *fin.* and ch. 28.

p. 289, 7 **studiorum gloriam** : This allusion to Apuleius himself confirms the partly autobiographical colouring. A prophecy of glory connected with literature is made to Lucius by Diophanes, the Chaldaean stranger, in *Metam.* 2.12 *fin.*, where the reading *facturum*, as opposed to *futurum*, seems to be demanded by the present allusion, since something much more is meant than being a subject treated in literature. A literary claim is also made by Lucius in *Lucius or Ass*, 55 : 'I am a writer of *historiae* and other prose works, while he (my brother) is an elegiac poet and a good prophet.' Cf. H. van Thiel, *Der Eselroman*, I, 28. Apuleius, then, is partly following his original and partly expressing his own ambitions. Cf. *Flor.* 20 (41, 8 f.), where he makes a claim to polymathy : 'Your friend Apuleius cultivates all these *genres* of art and science and worships all nine Muses with equal fervour.'

CHAPTER 28

p. 289, 8-9 **ad istum modum** : See n. *ad* ch. 3 (267, 22).

p. 289, 9 **desponsus sacris** : Cf. ch. 16 (278, 9-10), *sacrorum absequio desponderetur*. The metaphor is that of betrothal or promise in marriage. This 'Brautmystik' is prominent in the N.T. concept of the relation of Christ and the Church; v. 2 Cor. 11.2; Eph. 5.25-7; Rev. 19.7 ff.

sumptuum : For the sense of 'resources' cf. Spartianus, *Hadr.* 7, p. 24 D. Magie (Loeb), *feminas ... sumptibus iuvit*.

p. 289, 10 **viriculas** ; Cf. *Metam*. 4.13 (85, 4), *patrimonii viribus*. Apuleius is the first to use the diminutive. Both this and *summula* in line 16 are aptly used to describe small means.

p. 289, 12-13 **inter sacrum ego et saxum** : 'Between the altar and the flint knife'; cf. Plaut. *Capt*. 617 and W. M Lindsay *ad loc*.; Neuenschwander, *Der bildliche Ausdruck*, 56; A. Otto, *Sprichwörter ... der Römer*, 305, citing Livy, 1.24 ff. Callebat, *Sermo Cotid*. 69 ff., justly urges that in general the proverbial expressions in Apuleius reflect the influence of popular speech, but in citing this (p. 72) he is careful to note the Plautine parallel. Hildebrand suggests an allegorical explanation here : by *sacrum* is meant the *sacerdotium* into which Lucius is to be initiated, by *saxum* the hard poverty which was an obstacle. To seek a detailed correspondence is perhaps unnecessary. Lucius is saying that he was in a quandary. Médan observes a dactylic series in *(in)ter sacrum et saxum positus cruciabar*.

p. 289, 14 **instantia** : Cf. ch. 21 (282, 15-16), *meam differens instantiam*, but there the quality is ascribed to Lucius.

saepicule : There are seven instances of this diminutive in the *Metam*.; v. Bernhard, *Stil*, 137. M. Molt, *Metam. I*, 73 *ad* 1.12 (11, 4) comments on its previous use in Plautus, as in *Cas*. 704.

p. 289, 15 **veste** : For the collective sense cf. Livy, 21.15.2.

p. 289, 15-16 **distracta** : See n. ad ch. 20 (282, 5), *diverse distractum*.

p. 289, 16 **conrasi** : Cf. Ter. *Ad*. 242; *Phor*. 40.

summulam : Cf. Seneca, *Ep*. 77.8 and n. *ad* line 10, *viriculas*.

p. 289, 16 f. **ipsum praeceptum fuerat specialiter** : 'an tu' : E. Schober, *Comp. num*. 10, observes the hexameter. Cf. n. *ad* ch. 13 (276, 10), *nusquam comparuit*.

p. 289, 18 **parceres** : The imperfect subjunctive answers a present indicative in the protasis (*moliris*), doubtless mirroring the freedom of conversation; cf. Callebat, *Sermo Cotid*. 352.

p. 289, 19 **impaenitendae** : An Apuleian coinage; v. *Thes. L.L*. 7, 1, 515, 74 ff.

p. 289, 20 **Érgo igitur** : Cf. ch. 5 (270, 4) and n.; 21 (283, 10).

decem : Cf. ch. 23 (284, 24) and n.

p. 289, 21 **deraso capite** : Although several of the codices read *de Serapis*, the reading *deras cap* in F and Φ points clearly to *deraso capite*, as Luietjohann saw, comparing *Metam*. 2.28 (48, 9), *deraso capite*, of an Egyptian priest; cf. ch. 10 (273, 17), *capillum derasi*, of initiates; ch. 30 (291, 13-14), *raso capillo*, of the *pastophori*. Further, it has been made clear that the Second Initiation concerns Osiris : v. ch. 27 (288, 7 ff.). There has been no mention of Serapis in this connection. On the other hand, the Iseum in the Campus Martius was adjacent to a Serapeum; cf. Tschudin, *Isis in Rom*, 25 f. and Anne Roullet, *Rome*, 26 ff., for a description of the two temples. It could be argued also that Serapis and Osiris fulfil a similar function, as Hildebrand properly notes. Even so the case for *deraso capite* is very strong.

p. 289, 21-2 **nocturnis orgiis** : Cf. cf. 21 (282, 13), *noctis sacratae* and n.;

23 (285, 2), *sol curvatus intrahebat vesperam* and n.; 23 (285, 13), *nocte media* and n. Orgia (ὄργια) is a word used most frequently of Dionysiac rites; cf. E. R. Dodds *ad* Eur. *Bacch.* 34, p. 65 : 'ὄργια, from the same root as ἔργον, are properly "things done" in a religious sense ...' They too were at night. Dodds adds : 'The modern sense of "orgies" derives from the Hellenistic and Roman conception of the nature of Dionysiac religion : it must not be imported into the *Bacchae*.' Nor should it be imported into the present context.

p. 289, 22 **inlustratus** : Cf. ch. 27 (288, 8) and n.

germanae religionis : It is perfectly possible to construe this, a Médan does, with *fiducia*, but this would imply a previous uncertainty about the associated religion of Osiris; cf. the remarks in ch. 27 (288, 8 ff.) about the unity and distinction of the two cults. It seems better to make the Genitive depend on *obsequium divinum*. The cult of Osiris is understandably described as a 'kindred faith'; the same term could be applied to the cult of Serapis.

p. 290, 2 **quidni** : Cf. ch. 26 (288, 4) and n.

p. 290, 3 **nutrito** : Sc. *mihi* from *peregrinationi meae*.

p. 290, 3-4 **patrocinia sermonis Romani** : An extension apparently, of the *Genitivus Inhaerentiae*; cf. n. ad ch. 19 (281, 7), *castimoniorum abstinentiam*; or perhaps it can be regarded as a Genitive of Description. Whereas the emphasis on the use of Latin as an acquired language suits the situation of Lucius, a Greek, it also suits Apuleius the Madaurian. He refers to his Roman sojourn in *Flor.* 17 (31, 10 f.); probably it was after his stay at Athens; cf. Butler and Owen, *Apol.* x; Bernhard, *Stil*, 359 f.; Walsh, *The Roman Novel*, 249. On the other hand, it was not at Rome that Apuleius acquired a knowledge of Latin, but in his native province of Africa, for when he was about thirty his accusers in the case *De Magia* dubbed him an expert speaker of both Greek and Latin (*Apol.* 4 init., *tam Graece quam Latine ... disertissimum*).

It comes as a surprise, after the rigorous demands of the religious rites, to learn that Lucius is able to practise as an advocate concomitantly with his ritual commitments. Nock, *Conversion*, 155, compares the position of a member of the Third Order of St. Francis 'living in the world but not as of the world'. Helm. *Flor.* praef. xi ff., argues that *patrocinia sermonis Romani* may perhaps refer to work as a rhetorician or grammarian rather than that of an advocate; rhetoricians are known to have had schools in the forum. His final suggestion, that rhetoricians sometimes defended clients in the courts even when they lacked a special training in the law, as in the case of Lucian at Antioch, seems more appostite. This possibility is overlooked by Butler and Owen, *Apol.* xi n. 6. Bernhard, *Stil*, 359 n. 9, cites F. Norden, *Apuleius von Madaura und das römische Privatrecht* (Leipzig, 1912), in support of the view that Apuleius shows considerable knowledge of legal matters. F. Norden, p. 14, urges that not much store should be laid on the fact that Apuleius does not boast of his ability as an advocate; he prided himself rather on being a scholar, writer and philosopher; he also maintains that the *Apology* proves his sharp-wittedness and incisiveness in advocacy. He compares the advocacy of Lucian and

Goethe. F. Norden cites juristic expressions used by Apuleius; on p. 161 n. 3 he cites ch. 20 (282, 5-6), *notae dorsualis agnitione*; on p. 180 n. 2 he refers to ch. 24 (286, 11), *pigneratus*, used in a transferred sense as in three other loci in *Metam*; on p. 166 he notes the term *distrahere* for 'to sell' in ch. 20 (282, 5). Cf. the approval of Richard G. Summers in *Historia* 21 (1972), 121 n. 2 and the remarks of H. Riefstahl, *Der Roman des Apuleius*, 21.

CHAPTER 29

p. 290. 5 **post pauculum tempus** : This diminutive is favoured by Apuleius (there are six instances); cf. ch. 30 (291, 5), *post dies admodum pauculos*.

p. 290, 6 **imperiis deum** : Cf. ch. 23 (284, 21), *praefatus deum veniam*. The divine visitations before the First Initiation are more specifically connected with Isis; cf. ch. 21 (282, 17), *deae nutu*; 22 (283, 18), *deae potentis benignitas* and ff. Perhaps *deum* here is intended to include Isis and Osiris; cf. the plural in *caelestium ... intentio* (lines 8-9), *numinum dignatione* (line 15), *deis magnis auctoribus* (line 23) and *deum providentia* (291, 4)

interpellor : Cf. ch. 26 (288, 2), *quietem meam rursus interpellat numinis beneficii cura*. Perhaps the verb is a *terminus technicus* for disturbance by a divine visitation.

tertiam quoque teletam : For *teletam* see n. *ad* ch. 24 (286, 8). The Second Initiation is designated in ch. 27 as that of Osiris, in contradistinction to the Isíac nature of the First. Probably the Third is envisaged as that of Isis and Osiris; cf. the allusions to deities in the plural. The divine instruction in the second half of this chapter indicates that the *Olympiaca stola* will be bestowed on the initiate as in the first ceremony, the original garment having been deposited in the provincial temple. It does not follow that the Third Initiation is merely a repetition of the First. Indeed, the robe in question is the Osirian solar robe, and its relation to the concept of immortality may have been expressed here other than by a glimpse of the Underworld. On the other hand, the practical need is stressed of a local rite which will enable local participation in the Roman festivals. A mercenary incentive can, of course, be assigned to the Second and Third Initiations; they' have been regarded as invented by the Roman priesthood for their personal gain' (Nock, *Conversion*, 150, who reminds us that according to Josephus the priests of Isis were bribed to further the seduction of Paulina in A.D. 19); but Nock goes on to stress the concept of divine command and vocation which is here reiterated. He thinks that 'it is possible that these additional ceremonies were genuine and due to a tendency ... to multiply rites.' Certainly the number three should not be regarded as definitive; further rites could presumably be enjoined by the divine will, At the same time three is a felicitously sacred figure; cp. ch. 16 (278, 7), *ter beatus* and n. and 29 (290, 16), *ter futurus etc.* (of this initiation).

p. 290, 6-7 **sustinere** : *Suscitare*, the unanimous reading of the MSS, was defended by Floridus and by the modern scholars G. Heraeus and H. Armini. Helm's proposal, *sustinere*, is well supported by ch. 21 (283, 10), *caeleste sustinere praeceptum*. Wower's *susceptare* also suits the meaning, but does not occur elswhere. It is a nice point, whether an emendation involving a *hapax leg.* can be justly applied to an author fond of neologisms.

p. 290, 7 **oppido** : Cf. *Apol.* 3 (4, 22) with the comment of Butler and Owen *ad loc.*, pp. 12 f. Quintilian, *Inst. Or.* 8.3.25 refers to it as obsolescent; cf. Plaut. *Rud.* 207 and 550. The basic meaning is perhaps 'in the (very) place'; cf. Hofmann and Szantyr, *Lat. Syntax*, 217.

p. 290, 8 **cogitationes ... agitabam** : Cf. ch. 20 (281, 14-15), *apud cogitationes meas revolvebam*. The reading *agitabam*, adopted by Oudendorp, is ascribed by Hildebrand to one MS. (his f = Fuxensis). The other MSS. read *cogitabam*, which Hildebrand retains, arguing that the expression in *cogitationes cogitabam* is mitigated by the intervening adverb *exercitius*; also that *agitabam* is the more likely of the two verbs to be the result of scribal interference. Médan also prefers *cogitabam*, claiming that *cogitationes cogitabam* constitutes a 'jeu de mots' which accords with the Apuleian manner. It is not a pun, however; nor does the context favour a playful turn of phrase. Admittedly Apuleius does indulge occasionally in word-play when the context is highly serious; cf. *luce lucida.* ch. 22 (284, 2) and *neque ullum animal essem et essem invinius*, ch. 23 (284, 25 f.) with the remarks of Bernhard, *Stil*, 228 ff. But cognate accusatives do not seem to occur. Although the *figura etymologica* was revived by archaistic writers such as Gellius (v. Hofmann and Szantyr, *Lat. Syntax*, 39), Bernhard, *Stil*, 178 f. can cite only the present example from Apuleius in which the synonymous Accusative uses the same stem; ch. 4 (269, 3), *crispante brachio trigeminos iactus*, shows a verb and object of different stems.

exercitius : Apuleius is the first to use this comparative form, based on a non-existent *exercite* : v. *Thes. L.L.* 5, 2, 1379, 32 ff; *exercitatius*, from *exercitate*, is found earlier : v. ibid. 1389, 61 ff. The meaning is probably intensive. *Exertius*, the proposal by Brantz, from *ex(s)erte*, 'clearly', 'loudly', does not suit the idea of secret thoughts.

p. 290, 8-9 **caelestium ... intentio** : Cf. n. *ad* line 6, *imperiis deum*.

p. 290, 9 **traditioni** : Cf. ch. 21 (283, 5) and n.; below, line 18, *sacrorum traditio*.

p. 290, 10-11 **consuluerunt ... sacerdos uterque** : The synesis is frequent and classical; v. Hofmann and Szantyr, *Lat. Syntax*, 437.

p. 290, 10 **in me** : After *consulere* this construction usually implies action against some one, as in Tac. *Agr.* 16.2, *in deditos ... durius consuleret*. But there are analogies in Plautus and Terence : v. Callebat, *Sermo Cotid.* 233.

p. 290, 12 **sequius** : Cf. ch. 6 (270, 20) and n.

fluctuantem : Apuleius is fond of this metaphor; cf. *Metam.* 4.2 init., *cum in isto cogitationis salo fluctuarem*; 5.21 (119, 10), of Psyche's grief, *aestu pelagi simile maerendo fluctuat*; 7.4 (156, 19); 9.19 (217, 3 f.); *De deo Socr.* 146 (20, 6 ff.).

p. 290, 12 **ad instar insaniae** : Cf. ch. 21 (283, 5), *ad instar voluntariae mortis* and n.; 24 (286, 4), *ad instar Solis.*

p. 290, 12-13 **instar insaniae percitum** : E. Schober, *Comp. num.* 17, notes the three cretic feet.

p. 290, 13 **clemens imago** : Cf. ch. 7 (271, 9-10), *tam claram praesentiam,* of Isis; but in 20 (281, 14) *imago* is used of the figure of the *summus sacerdos* who has appeared to Lucius in a vision, and perhaps a benign priestly figure is intended here. In the speech that follows, the goddess (line 19) and the great gods (line 23) are referred to in the third person, implying that neither Isis nor Osiris is to be seen in the *clemens imago.*

p. 290, 14 **numerosa serie religionis, quasi quicquam** : A sequence of choriambics begins with the last syllable of *numerosa*; v. Médan, *Lat.* 255.

p. 290, 15 **numinum dignatione** : Cf. ch. 21 (283, 11), *magni numinis dignatione* and n.

laetus : *Laetum* (or *letum*) is the reading of the earlier MSS and indeed of all those examined by me. Helm's proposal *laetus* is assigned by Robertson and Giarratano to a MS or MSS, but their abbreviated procedure does not permit them to name it or them. One would doubtless regard *laetus* as more elegant here; Médan argues with justice that *laetum ... gaudium* accords with Apuleian redundance.

p. 290, 16 **ter** : Cf. ch. 16 (278, 7), *ter beatus* and n.; also n. *ad* line 6, *tertiam ... teletam.* A third initiation was not, it seems, a normal procedure.

quod : For the personal reference of the neuter pronoun ch. *Metam.* 3.22 (68, 18 f.), *quidvis aliud magis videbar esse quam Lucius.*

p. 290, 18 **sacrorum traditio** : See n. *ad* ch. 21 (283, 5).

p. 290, 19 **saltem reputaveris exuvias** : Médan, *Lat.* 254 notes the series of three dactyls in the middle of a period; cf. E. Schober, *Comp. num.* 12.

exuvias deae : The reference must be to the various garments with which Lucius is invested in ch. 24, especially the *Olympiaca stola.* It is not stated there that they are the garments of the goddess, but Lucius is invested *ante deae similacrum* (285, 20-21) and *in vicem simulacri* (286, 5). Here there is an instructive allusion to the initiate's act of taking upon himself the raiment of the goddess; cf. end of n. *ad* 286, 5, *in vicem simulacri* : the worshipper thus achieves identity with the deity. In Roman usage the *exuviae* of a god could include his various attributes; cf. K. Latte, *Röm. Rel.* 249 n. 2. One would expect the objects mentioned in chs. 10-11 to be considered among the *exuviae* of Isis since they are carried in procession, and Lucius, as a prospective *pastophorus*, is destined to be concerned with some of them. But in retrospect it is only the sacred garments with their embellishments that are meant. Plutarch, *De Is. et Os.* 77, 382 C, says of the robe of Osiris that 'they put on this dress only once and then take it off, preserving it unseen and untouched, whereas they make use of Isiac robes many times.' It is hard to apply this statement to the facts in Apuleius, save in relation to Isiac robes; when Lucius is given the *exuviae deae* in Rome, he will be free to use them constantly; it is only the regulation of the local temple that forbids their being taken elsewhere.

p. 290, 19-20 **in eodem fano** : The vestments would have been kept in one of the crypts used as *stolisteria*; cf. ch. 22 (284, 12), *de opertis adyti* and n. Hildebrand argues that the variety of reading (*fano* and *funo*) conceals a more specific allusion which has been corrupted; cf. too *solo*. The pronoun *eodem*, however, which is required by the sense, precludes a too detailed sequel, such as *pastophorio*, for which see Rufinus, *Hist. eccles.* 11.23 (= Hopfner, *Fontes*, 627).

p. 290, 21 **iis** : I. e. *exuviis*.

felici illo amictu : The *stola* of ch. 24 (286, 2) is probably meant.

illustrari : Cf. ch. 27 (288, 8), *sacris inlustratum* and n.

p. 290, 22 **felix itaque ac faustum** : Here the alliteration is that which characrizes a stereotyped formula; cf. Bernhard, *Stil*, 220.

gaudiali : The adjective is found only in Apuleius, v. *Thes. L.L.* 6, 1711, 43 ff.

p. 290, 23 **deis magnis auctoribus** : Cf. n. *ad* line 6, *imperiis deum*.

CHAPTER 30

p. 290, 24 **Hactenus** : 'to this extent'.

p. 290, 24-5 **maiestas ... pronuntiavit** : An abstract subject is preferred.

p. 290, 25 **supinam** : For the metaphorical use cf. Quintilian, *Inst. Or.* 10.2.17, *otiosi et supini* (*oratores*).

procrastinationem : A rare word, but found in Cic. *Phil.* 6.3.7.

p. 290, 26 **meo** : This is presumably Asinius Marcellus, the *pastophorus* who admits Lucius to the Second Initiation (ch. 27).

p. 290, 26-7 **inanimae ... castimoniae** : Cf. ch. 6 (271, 5); 19 (281, 7), *castimoniorum abstinentiam* and n. : 23 (284, 25), *neque ullum animal essem* and n. *ad* 284, 25, *cohercerem*.

p. 290, 27 **iugum subeo** : Cf. ch. 15 (278, 1), *iugum ... voluntarium* and n.

p. 291, 1 **decem** : Cf. ch. 23 (284, 24) and n.; 28 (289, 20).

spontali : The adjective occurs only in Apuleius; cf. 4.11 (83, 1).

p. 291, 2 **largitus** : The common adverbial forms are *large* and *largiter*. The latter occurs in ch. 18 (280, 15) on which see n.

Afranius, ap. Non. 514, 13 (ed. Lindsay, p. 30), provides, it seems, the only other occurrence of *largitus*, so that an archaistic choice has been made. Beroaldus recognized this; cf. Piechotta, *Curae Apuleianae*, 51. Elmenhorst proposed *largius*, and was followed by Eyssenhardt; this comparative form occurs in Ter. *Eun.* 1078, but also in writers of the classical age.

p. 291, 2-3 **mensura rerum collatis sumptibus** : In this corrupt locus the reading *mensurarum* in F. seems very likely to have evolved from *mensura rerum*, as Eyssenhardt saw. Brakman's *mensura rerum stipibus* is attractive, but in ch. 21 (282, 19) the word *sumptus* is used for the sum needed; cf. 28 (289, 9), *sumptuum* *tenuitate*, and line 3 here, where the repetition would not be regarded as inelegant.

p. 291, 4 **quidni** : See n. *ad* ch. 26 (288, 4).

deum providentia : For the plural see n. *ad* ch. 29 (290, 6), *imperiis deum*.

p. 291, 5 **bellule** : Cf. *Metam.* 5.31 (128, 12) and 10.16 (249, 3), where however, the reading *vellule* also occurs in each case. The adverb appears to have been revived from Plautus : v. Paul. Fest 36, 4, ed. Lindsay, p. 32; cf. Plaut. *Bacch.* 1068 (Leo). Plautus uses the adjective in *Cas.* 848, *edepol papillam bellulam*.

pauculos : Cf. ch. 29 (290, 5) and n.

p. 291, 5-7 **deus deum magnorum potior** etc. : Cf. *Metam.* 5, 25 (123, 7 f.), *Cupidinem deorum maximum*. The first phrase is clearly an elaboration of the Egyptian and Semitic idiom *god of gods* and *king of kings*; cf. J. Gwyn Griffiths, 'βασιλεὺς βασιλέων : Remarks on the History of a Title,' *Class. Phil.* 48 (1953), 145-54. In Egyptian and Hebrew the idiom does duty for a superlative; cf. L. Friedländer's remarks *ad nummorum nummos* in Petronius, *Sat.* 37 (Ed. 2, 1906, p. 234), comparing the Hebrew for θεὸς θεῶν (see Josh. 22.22, אֵל אֱלֹהִים. where both the Septuagint and the Vulgate have curiously eschewed the plural; in Psalms 49, 1, however, they have θεὸς θεῶν and *deus deorum*). The term אֵל occurs often in Punic inscriptions : v. Friedrich and Röllig, *Phönizisch-Punische Grammatik* (Rome, 1970), 240. That *deus deum* and *magnorum potior* should be taken separately is unlikely in view of the phrases that follow, each demarked by *et*; a periphrasis of *deus deum* is intended. For other occurrences of *deus deum* see *Carmen Saliare*, fr. 1, *divom deo supplicate* (ed. Maurenbrecher, Leipzig, 1894, p. 231); the phrase applies to Ianus; cf. Macrob. *Sat.* 1.9.14 and 1.9.16, ed. Willis, p. 38. The desire for expansion of a stereotyped phrase may be paralleled in the form 'King of Kings of Kings' applied to God in the Hellenistic-Roman period in the Jewish Mishnah; v. J. Gwyn Griffiths, *Class. Phil.* 48 (1953), 151 with n. 62.

It is not surprising that Osiris is described in similar, though not identical phrases in Egyptian texts. He is called 'King of Kings, Chief of Chiefs, Sovereign of Men and Gods'; also 'Lord of Lords, King of Kings, the sovereign, Horus of Horuses '(v. *Wb.* II, 328, 7 Belegstellen); cf. Junker, *Der grosse Pylon*, 5,17 ff., 'Osiris Onnophris, the justified, the Great God on the Abaton, the august power, the lord of Philae, the ruler with the double uraeus diadem'; 6, 18 f., 'King of Eternity, Lord of Everlasting'; 209, 3 f, 'King of the Gods, Lord of Cities, Ruler of Nomes'. See also p. 358.

The expression in Apuleius shows a rare concatenation of climaxes which is achieved by repeating one element in the previous phrase each time and then surpassing it. Cf. Hymns of Isidorus, 4, 23 (*SEG* 8, 551) of Suchos (Sebek), παγκράτορος μεγάλου μεγάλου τε μεγίστου and Vera Vanderlip's note ad loc. (pp. 69 f.) From such magniloquence we infer that if the Third Initiation concerned both Isis and Osiris, yet the latter was the dominant figure.

p. 291, 6 **potior** : The comparative seems here *prima facie* to have superlative sense in line with *summus* and *maximus*. Or it may be viewed as retaining its comparative force and governing a Genitive of Comparison in the Greek manner; cf. Ed. Wölfflin, *Arch. Lat. Lex.* 7 (1892), 118, who quotes the double construction in Plaut. *Capt.* 825, *Non ego nunc parasitus sum, sed regum rex regalior*; also Ennius, *Trag.* 78, *Mater optumarum multo mulier melior mulierum* and Prud. *Peristef* 5.293 f., *O miles invictissime, fortissimorum fortior.* Lindsay *ad Capt.* 825 also quotes the line in Ennius, saying that it 'exhibits the same use of the Comparative for the Superlative.' On the whole, it seems wiser to posit a persisting comparative force; cf. Callebat, *Sermo Cotid.* 189.

p. 291, 7 **reformatus** : For the preposition *in* with this verb cf. *Metam.* 3.23 (69, 23), *in facies hominum tales figuras reformare*; also 6.22 (145, 13 f.); 7.6 (158, 27); in ch. 16 (278, 7) *ad* is used. Apuleius often uses the verb in magical contexts; it occurs in ritual associations of the change wrought in the initiate; cf. Reitzenstein, *Hellenist. Myst.* 39 f. where it is compared with μεταμορφοῦσθαι in the sense of 'be transfigured'. An appearance of Osiris in another form might involve the Apis-bull or the semblance of a serpent or jackal. Traditionally his form was human, and this is here regarded as his true image.

p. 291, 8 **dignatus** : Cf. n. *ad* ch. 21 (283, 11).

adfamine : Cf. n. *ad* ch. 7 (271, 19).

per quietem : Cf. n. *ad* ch. 6 (270, 16-17).

p. 291, 9 **visus est** : Cf. the appearance of Isis to Lucius before the First Initiation (ch. 22). One should not, therefore, it seems, equate this epiphany of Osiris with the Third Initiation itself, as Pascher, ʽΗ βασιλικὴ ὁδός, 122, does. It is striking, at the same time, that the climax of the vision of Osiris, like that of the First Initiation (ch. 23 *fin.* : *accessi coram et adoravi de proxumo*), is a face-tp-face encounter with the divine (here *coram* etc.). See also p. 358.

incunctanter : Cf. ch. 6 (270, 11) and n.

p. 291, 9-10 **patrocinia** : Cf. n. *ad* ch. 28 (290, 3-4), *patrocinia sermonis Romani.* The great god's exhortation seems to be somewhat materialistic in tone.

p. 291, 10 **disseminationes** : A new coinage which Apuleius uses only here, and which is next used by Tertullian; v. *Thes. L.L.* 5, 1, 1452, 33 ff. Jealousy of his learning is given as the cause of the spiteful talk condemning Lucius. Perhaps an exceptional allowance made to him can be regarded as the real reason, unless, as we have suggested above, a class of initiates was regularly permitted to indulge in worldly occupations.

p. 291, 12 **pastophorum** : Cf. n. *ad* ch. 17 (279, 15).

p. 291, 13 **decurionum quinquennales** : Titles indicating a hierarchy among the *pastophori* are found in Egypt in the Roman era; v. W. Otto, *Priester und Tempel*, I, 98 on the ἀρχιπαστοφόροι and πρεσβύτεροι παστοφόρων. The Latin term used by Apuleius is not attested elsewhere in any Isiac context except for the possible application of *decurio* in such a sense to the young N. Popidius Celsinus in an inscription from the temple of Isis in Pompeii.

In the civic sense the term *quinquennalis* refers to officers in the municipalities who were elected every five years to conduct the census : see Io. Neumann, *De quinquennalibus* (Leipzig, 1892) on the *duoviri quinquennales* or *quinquennales* simply; he shows (p. 31) that the *quinquennalis* is mentioned in some inscriptions as having been a priest, a *sacerdos divi Augusti*, but that the post was not in itself religious; he points out too (p. 56) that from the time of Augustus till A.D. 300 the *quinquennales* are often attested in all parts of the empire. See further W. Liebenam, *Städtverwaltung im römischen Kaiserreiche* (Leipzig, 1900), 257 ff.; Hans Rudolph, *Stadt und Staat im römischen Italien* (Leipzig, 1935), 214 f. According to F. F. Abbott in Abbott and Johnson, *Municipal Administration in the Roman Empire* (Princeton, 1926), 65, an important task of the *quinquennales* was to prepare the list of the *ordo decurionum*, so that the phrase *decurionum quinquennales* might possibly refer specially to this, with *decurionum* as a Partitive Genitive — 'the quinquennial officers among the local senators'. However, there is a fatal objection to this political or civic interpretation : Lucius was not in a municipality, he was in Rome. There can be no question that Apuleius is describing a religious office in the Isiac cult, coloured as the terminology may be by Roman municipal administration. Thus rightly Médan, p. 83; Wittmann, p. 824 n. 656; and V. von Gonzenbach, *Knabenweihen*, 117. Whether this proves that the six-year-old N. Popidius Celsinus at Pompeii was a *decurio* in the Isiac sense, as von Gonzenbach argues, is another matter; for arguments against the idea see Tran Tam Tinh, *Isis à Pompéi*, 31 f.; Vidman, *SIRIS*, 227 and *Isis und Sarapis*, 128. Nor can we be sure what the duties of an Isiac *quinquennalis* were; probably, if the civic analogy be followed, the ordering and revision of lists of sacerdotal personnel was involved.

p. 291, 13 **adlegit** : The word is used of the addition of members to various bodies, civic, military and religious : v. *Thes. L.L.* 1, 1663, 83 ff. (religious colleges, 1666, 21 ff.). Médan points to *CIL VI*, 355, an inscription from Rome in which a priest of Isis is called an *adlector collegi ipsius*; see also Dessau, *Inscr. Lat. Sel.* 4360 and Vidman, *SIRIS* no, 413. It is curious that here Osiris himself is co-opting Lucius.

p. 291, 13-14 **raso capillo** : Cf. ch. 28 (289, 21), *deraso capite*, and n.

p. 291, 14 **Syllae temporibus** : The statement accords well with what is otherwise known of the spread of the Egyptian cults in Italy. Already in the second century B.C. they had become popular in maritime centres, and contact with Alexandria and Aegean cities, especially with Delos, had furthered the process; v. P. F. Tschudin *Isis in Rom*, 13 ff. Tschudin, p. 15, argues that the concept of Tychê-Isis, equated with Aphrodite, influenced Sulla's adherence to Fortune; cf. Plut. *Sull.* 35 (on his εὐτυχία) and his adopted name of Epaphroditos, which probably implies 'Darling of Aphrodite-Tychê'; cf. Harry Ericsson, 'Sulla Felix', *Eranos* 41 (1943), 77-89, esp. 84. Tschudin argues further that Lucretius in his invocation and description of Venus is depicting all the qualities of Isis; certainly they are both cosmic and universal goddesses, and although

the symbolic approach of Lucretius is influenced by Stoic ideas, the ascription
of pantheism comes close to the Graeco-Roman concept of Isis. The evidence
from coinage, which Tschudin then adduces, is at its clearest on a coin of the
era 78-55 B.C., showing on its reverse a temple with lotus-capitals; v. E. A
Sydenham, *The Coinage of the Roman Republic* (London, 1952), no. 788,
p. 129 and pl. 22; H. A. Grueber, *Coins of the Roman Republic in the B.M.*,
I (London, 1910, repr. 1970), no. 3276, p. 400, dates it to c. 75 B.C. The figures
explained as those of Iuppiter and Libertas (in the temple) are undoubtedly
Sarapis and Isis; see also A. Alföldi, *Schweiz. Münzblätter* 5 (1954), 25-31, in
an article ('Isiskult und Umsturzbewegung im letzten Jahrhundert der römi-
schen Republik') which demonstrates some of the political influences of the
Isiaci at this time. Alföldi, p. 30, observes that the college of *pastophori* must
have been attached to a specific sanctuary and that tradition placed this on the
Capitol itself; many slaves and freedmen were working on the mint on the
Capitol near the temple of Juno Moneta, and it is cogently urged that their
interest in Isis is reflected in many Nilotic themes that appear on the coinage.
Moreover, the head-dress of Isis occurs : see p. 27, figs 3 and 4 and H. A.
Grueber, *Coins of the Roman Republic in the B.M.*, I, no. 1978, p. 262; also
fig. 5 on p. 27 = Grueber, no. 3807, p. 467. For the altar of Isis on the Capitol,
destroyed in 59 B.C. see Latte, *Röm Rel.* 282. See also pp. 358 ff.

A παστοφόριον is attested in Delos in the second century B.C.; v. Roussel,
CED 152 f., where, however, it is strangely asserted that this need not necessarily imply the existence of a special class of *pastophori* there; cf. Vidman,
Isis und Sarapis, 62 n. 50. In Delos a number of Italians erected dedications
to Egyptian gods, a fact which further confirms the reference in Apuleius;
cf. Latte, *Röm. Rel.* 282; J. Hatzfeld, 'Les Italiens résidant à Délos', *BCH*
36 (1912), 5-218. Tschudin, *Isis in Rom*, 15, also draws attention to the fact
that after Sulla's attack on Praeneste the temple of Fortuna there was decorated
with mosaics presented by Sulla; these are Alexandrian in style and plan, and
show marked Isiac motifs. See pls. 13 and 14 in G. Gullini, *I Mosaici di Palestrina* (Rome, 1956); whereas the former shows a Nilotic landscape with crocodiles and hippopotami, the latter presents a ritual scene before a temple
flanked by two obelisks; there are also ibises and a uraeus; there is a sacred
lake too, and Isis Pelagia rather than Poseidon is suggested; cf. K. Schefold,
Pompejanische Malerei (Basel, 1952), 184 f. (n. to p. 61). R. Pernice, *Pavimente
und figürliche Mosaiken* (Berlin, 1938), 21, gives artistic grounds for assigning
these mosaics to the time of Sulla, so that the scepticism of Balsdon, *JRS* 41
(1951), 8 n. 89 (in an article on 'Sulla Felix') about Sulla's reconstruction
of the temple seems unwarranted, especially in view of Pliny, *NH* 36.62.189
(even if his punctuation be accepted). Vidman, *SIRIS* 243, no. 528, tends to
reject the equation of Fortuna and Isis at Praeneste, but in *Isis und Sarapis*,
98, he gives it a qualified acceptance, suggesting that it was unconscious and
veiled rather than official. The grand plan of the temple of Fortuna in Praeneste
is assigned by Schefold, *Vergessenes Pompeji*, 24, to the middle of the second

century B.C., although he had previously accepted the time of Sulla as the date.

p. 291, 15 **calvitio** : The scorn aroused by the baldness of the initiates is shown in Juvenal, 6. 533, alluding to the priest who represents Anubis, *grege linigero circumdatus et grege calvo*; cf. Martial, 12.28.19, *linigeri fugiunt calvi sistrataque turba*.

gaudens : Joy is one of the dominant notes of the book. At first it is mixed with fear and foreboding, as in ch. 7 (271, 8); it is a joy shared by the glory of the spring day (271, 15); three times there is mention of sudden joy — ch. 12 (275, 18); ch. 14 (276, 14-15); ch. 18 (280, 12, of the relatives of Lucius when they see his transformation). It is a joyful triumph over Fortune in ch. 15 (277, 20); in ch. 19 (280, 18) it is contrasted with former trials (*pristinis aerumnis et praesentibus gaudiis*). It is the mark of the converted and dedicated soul in ch. 29 (290, 15 and 22). Cf. Introd. VII, p. 89. Here the joyful service of the newly appointed *pastophorus* loses a little of the disinterested adoration previously expressed, for it is partly the result of elevation to the lower priesthood, as well as of a promise that success as an advocate will continue.

The whole impact of the ecstatic account of pagan rites presented in this book must have been disturbing to Christian readers. This does not prove, of course, that the book was intended as an attack on Christianity as J.-P. Charpentier argued in his *De Mystica Apuleii Doctrina* (Diss. Paris, 1839), 21. The portrait of the baker's wife in *Metam.* 9.14 seems to include a contemptuous allusion to the Christian or Jewish belief in one God; cf. T. Taylor, *The Metamorphosis ... of Apuleius* (London, 1822), xvi f.; L. Herrmann, 'L'Ane d'or et le christianisme', *Latomus* 12 (1953), 188-91. See further p. 359.

ADDENDA

Four commentaries on books of the *Metamorphoses* have been planned and produced at Groningen University—those of Margaretha Molt on Book I (1938), of B. J. De Jonge on Book II (1941), of R. T. van der Paardt on Book III (1971), and of J. M. H. Fernhout on Book V (1949). From Professor R. E. H. Westendorp Boerma, of Groningen University, comes the welcome information that commentaries on the remaining books have now been planned (with the exception of Book XI) and that a centre of Apuleian Studies is to be established at the Classical Institute of that university.

From the same source came a reference to a Commentary on Book XI (*Kommentar zum Isisbuch des Apuleius*) which was successfully submitted for the degree of *Doctor Philosophiae* at the University of Vienna in July 1973. The author, Dr Christine Harrauer, a pupil of Professor R. Hanslik, has very kindly presented me with a copy. In the nature of things I have here to be content with a brief appraisal of its main features. Her general standpoint on the relation of Book XI to the preceding books involves a firm rejection of the view that Book XI is a mere appendix; there is a deep inner connection, she urges, with the preceding books, in the sense that certain motifs and forms run through the whole. The aim of the work is seen as an attempt to convey, by means of allegory, the striving of mankind, represented by Lucius, after knowledge of the divine; and his transformation into animal form is explained as a figurative delineation of his spiritual decline following his adoption of the wrong means in his quest. An interpretation offered by G. C. Drake in *The Classical Journal* 64 (1968), 102 ff. ('Candidus. A unifying theme in Apuleius' *Metamorphoses*') is accepted as an incidental facet of the general allegory; it is an interesting but unconvincing flight of fancy : see below p. 355.

While this approach has much to commend it, one should not lose sight of the humorous and erotic elements in the first ten books; we have seen that a literary purpose which combined such elements with a moral aim was not at all impossible in some traditions of the early centuries. The relation to the Greek prototype further complicates the question of the unity of the novel. Since a moral purpose is not evident in the prototype, it must be assumed that Apuleius has superimposed it on the material used by him. It can scarcely, therefore, be all-pervading; but the treatment of the themes of magic, *curiositas*, and *voluptates* certainly contributes to a central seriousness, and the story of 'Cupid and Psyche', inserted by Apuleius himself, is related conceptually to Book XI. Dr Harrauer gives some attention to the Platonist element in the attitude of Apuleius to the Isiac Mysteries, and she rightly compares Plutarch's approach; but she seems to have missed the important discussion by R. Thibau (see Bibliography, and p. 53 above).

The prayer beginning *Regina caeli* in ch. 2 is correctly interpreted as referring to a celestial goddess who is not regarded as Isis. A welcome reserve is shown in the treatment of the 'Anteludia' in ch. 8; a thorough-going religious symbolism is rejected, but suggestions relating some of the items to the past experiences of Lucius are sympathetically presented. It is on the linguistic side, however, that this Commentary has most to offer. Dr Harrauer rejects the view that the style of Apuleius attracts merely through its sonorous verbal abundance and emotional intensity; she sees it rather as a medium which is developed with a fine subtlety and elaborated with a delicate feeling for language. She pays special attention to the delight in rhyme which is so often shown. She notes the careful use of prepositions in compound verbs and the occasional imitation of sounds by onomatopeia, as in the representation of the chirping of birds in ch. 7 by the phrase *canorae etiam aviculae* (∪ − −∪∪∪∪∪∪◡̆) and perhaps in the descriptions of the sound of the sistrum in chs. 4 and 10. Frequent analysis of the rhyme-patterns is provided in the Commentary, together with the numbers of syllables occurring in the phrases thus isolated; but there is a welcome avoidance of the 'number mystique' pursued by Wittmann. What emerges is the constant balancing of phrases and clauses in a poetical mode. Attention is also paid in the first five chapters to the metrical pattern of *clausulae*.

Unpublished commentaries which I have not been able to see include those by D. L. Layman on the first book of the *Metamorphoses*, by L. Schutijser on the second book, and by J. Veremans on the third Book. For further details see Carl C. Schlam, *Classical World* 64 (1971), 288.

P. 1 n. 2 :

Brendan Kenny, *Arethusa* 7 (1974), 195, says that 'the flatness of Book XI in comparison with the rest of the story reveals what happens when an author moves from the complexity of enacting a moral problem to direct moral statement.' On the contrary, Book XI has an exciting quality, though it moves on a higher plane; nor is it 'direct moral statement' except occasionally, as in ch. 15, where Kenny rightly sees the importance of the priest's speech in making sense of the whole story. Kenny writes well on the dramatic presentation which serves a 'heuristic purpose'.

P. 2 : The Greek prototype.

Gerardo Bianco, *La fonte greca delle Metamorfosi di Apuleio* (Brescia, 1971), 170 ff., justly maintains that *Lucius or Ass* is a logical and coherent narrative, and that although it has a realistic and popular tone, the treatment is openly ironical.

P. 2 : Sisenna and Aristides.

See also L. Pepe, 'Lucio di Patrae o Aristide—Sisenna?' *Gornale Italiano di Filologia* 16 (1963), 111-142. In a review of a book by the same author Robert Browning emphasizes how little is really known of Sisenna : see *C.R.* n.s. 11 (1961), 50.

P. 7, Section II :

See also Julien Guey, 'Au théâtre de Leptis Magna', *Rev. Ét. Lat.* 29 (1951), 307-317 and 'L'*Apologie* d'Apulée et les inscriptions de Tripolitaine', ibid. 32 (1954), 115-119.

P. 13 : Thessaly in Apuleius.

That the details concerning the application of criminal law in Thessaly have been accurately described by Apuleius in the earlier books of the *Metam.* has been been well shown by Jean Colin, 'Apulée en Thessalie : fiction ou vérité?', *Latomus* 24 (1965), 330-45. He argues that Apuleius could have gained this accuracy only through being there himself, probably as a lawyer and advocate.

P. 13 : Date of Composition.

Ugo Carratello, *Giornale Italiano di Filologia* 16 (1963), 97-110, suggests that Apuleius died in A.D. 163-164, basing his argument mainly on the latest chronological allusions in the *Florida*—a risky form of the *argumentum ex silentio*.

P. 15 n. 4 :

THESSALONICA

R. Merkelbach, 'Zwei Texte aus dem Sarapeum zu Thessalonike', *ZPE* 10 (1973), 45-54, discusses two of the inscriptions published by Charles Edson in his *Inscriptiones Graecae* X (Berlin, 1972), 2, 1. The first of these (Edson's no. 108 with pl. 9) is dated by Edson to a year probably before 100 B.C., although he had previously placed it in the following century : see *Harv. Theol. Rev.* 41 (1948), 182. In the first line Edson restores ᾿Οσε[ῖρι] with conviction since Isis is mentioned later. The second line speaks of 'an elegant chest which carries water', where the word νάμοφόρον is a *hap. leg.* It is explained by Merkelbach as referring to the sacred pitcher which holds the holy water of Osiris; but it is never connected elsewhere with a boat. Very strangly Merkelbach interprets λάρναξ here as 'eine heilige Barke'. It is rather the funerary chest, as mentioned by Plutarch, *De Is. et Os.* 13 and 15, and there is no evidence that it is envisaged as like a boat in shape; although it goes to Byblos it remains a wooden chest. In *Latomus* 24 (1965), 148 Merkelbach wishes to interpret a group from a fresco in Pompeii as 'adoration of the Osiris-barque' (cf. the reproduction on p. 147) since the standing mummy is enveloped by an open sarcophagus which he describes as 'die Sargbarke des Osiris'. This is pure fantasy, for the curved sarcophagus is a very common form and it has nothing to do with a boat. The chest in the inscription is, of course, carried in a boat, just as the sarcophagus is thus depicted in countless Egyptian representations.

In line 3 of the Thessalonican inscription allusion is made to the voyage of Osiris, and Merkelbach rightly connects it with the *periplous* of the god mentioned in the Canopus Decree. He goes on to see a reference to the *Isidis Navigium*, but we have shown above that the calendrical equation is not convincing, although the ship of Osiris can be equated with the ship of Isis and with the ancient *neshmet*-barque. In line 4 Osiris is said to 'make the beloved Isis rejoice', and the following couplet lauds Osiris as the inventor of ship-building and navigation—a distinction hitherto reserved, as Merkelbach points out, for Isis.

Another striking feature is that Osiris voyages, according to line 3, 'under the starry-bright night'. This suggests that a Festival of Lamps is involved, and it recalls the episode described in the Egyptian texts at Denderah. That is in the month of Khoiak, and does not suit the date of the *Navigium*; nor does the Lychnapsia mentioned in the Calendar of Philocalus (August 12th). Other such rites recorded are not necessarily Osirian; cf. Herodotus, 2.62 and Bilabel, *Die gräko-ägyptischen Feste*. See too above pp. 40 ff. Such rites must be distinguished from the ordinary daily lighting of lamps in the temple, for which the term λυχναψία is sometimes used; cf. Elizabeth H. Gilliam, *Yale Class. St.* 10 (1947), 221, misleadingly cited by Merkelbach op. cit. 49 n. 1 as having connection with the Lamp Festivals; so too F. Sokolowski, *Lois sacrées de l'Asie mineure* (Paris, 1955), no. 36, pp. 102 f. We must therefore reject the idea that the Ploiaphesia is involved in this poem by Damaeus, although the traditional barque of Osiris and Isis figures in it. In any case it would be doubtful evidence for the practice of the rite in Thessalonica, since the poem might have a general application.

In *CRAIBL* 1972, 478-87 Georges Daux publishes and discusses a text from the sanctuary of Serapis in Thessalonica; cf. Charles Edson, *IG* X. 2. 1, 259. In line 3 the dedicator is called a *BHCAPTHC*, and Daux suggests a connection with the Egyptian god Bes, adding an explanation by Festugière which sees the term as meaning 'he who raises Bes'; he compares the priest who enacts Anubis in ch. 11 *init* : *attollens canis cervices arduas*.

P. 21 n. 2 : *Roman und Mysterium usw.*

Turcan's study is devoted in the main to Merkelbach's *Roman und Mysterium in der Antike*. Whereas some valid points are made relating to specific interpretations, Turcan is not always a safe guide to the Egyptian tradition; cf. his dictum on p. 153, 'Or Harpocrate apparait souvent chez les Égyptiens et en particulier dans les papyrus magiques comme un dragon.' The first part of the claim is misleading. Merkelbach himself makes the same claim, op. cit. 11 nn. 3 and 4, but the only example he cites from the ancient tradition is the uraeus-serpent on the crown of the Pharaoh which he describes as an incarnation of Horus; this is not so : the uraeus is that of the goddess Wadjet.

P. 25 : The Ass.

See also Jean-G. Préaux, 'Deus Christianorum *Onocoetes*', *Hommages à Léon Herrmann* (Brussels, 1960), 639-654 and B. H. Stricker 'Asinarii', *OMRO* 46 (1955), 52-75. A felicitous account of the role played the ass in Greek and Latin literature is given by Kathleen Freeman, 'Vincent, or the Donkey', *Greece and Rome* 14 (1945), 33-41.

P. 29 : Raising the Dead.

The episode of necromancy in *Metam.* 2. 28-30 has been related to the Egyptian tradition by Siegfried Morenz, 'Totenaussagen im Dienste des Rechts. Ein ägyptisches Element in Hellenismus und Spätantike', *Würzburger Jahrbücher für die Altertumswissenschaft* 3 (1948), 290-300. The Egyptian elements in Apuleus *Metam* have recently been discussed by Pierre Grimal, *REA* 73 (1971), 343-355.

P. 29. Zatchlas.

Another possible derivation might be a by-form of *Ḏḥwty-ir-rḫ-sw*, meaning 'Thoth it is who knows him'; see H. Ranke, *Personennamen*, I, 407, 17 and F. Ll. Griffith, *Rylands Papyri*, III, 463; or again, **Ḏd-ḥr-s*, 'Horus says it'; for Djedḥor cf. H. de Meulenaere, *Le Surnom Égyptien à la basse époque* (Istanbul, 1966), no. 20, p. 8 and no. 20, p. 36; cf. Ranke, op. cit. I, 411, 12 and F. Ll. Griffith, op. cit. III, 465. In none of these suggestions, however, is there a firm correspondence.

P. 53 : Platonic influence.

For Platonic influence see also Carl Schlam, 'Platonica in the *Metamorphoses* of Apuleius', *TAPA* 101 (1970), 477-87; but it is in the books preceding Book XI that 'an abundance of Platonic concepts and motifs' is found.

P. 57 : Variation of Style.

That Apuleius varies his style to a much greater extent than Bernhard allows is maintained by Wolfgang Eicke in his dissertation *Stilunterschiede in den* Metamorphosen *des Apuleius* (Göttingen, 1956). He gives a detailed analysis of seven selections, all of them outside Book XI. He shows that the nature of the theme and situation influences the style in several ways, especially in regard to the use of words with poetical colouring. He does not, however, in my view undermine Bernhard's main position. Dialogue is particularly stereotyped in Apuleius.

P. 62 : Trilingualism.

In the ancient world trilingualism was not a rare phenomenon. It is likely that Jesus, in common with many of his countrymen, had a knowledge, in varying degrees, of three languages—Aramaic, Hebrew (Biblical Hebrew and perhaps Mishnaic Hebrew), and Greek. See James Barr, 'Which Language did Jesus Speak?—Some Remarks of a Semitist', *Bull. John Rylands Library* 53 (1970), 9-29.

P. 114 : Tearful Prayer.

In his article, 'Das Gebetweinen', *Arch. Rel.* 27 (1929), 365-8, Joseph Balogh refers to the idea that the early Christian practice of praying loudly, with much weeping, was changed in the Middle Ages through the more self-controlled Northern temperament. But he quotes (p. 365) from Isidore of Seville, *Sententiae*, 3. 7. 4 : *Numquam est sine gemitu orandum; nam peccatorum recordatio maerorem gignit... Ideoque cum Deo assistimus, gemere et flere debemus.* On p. 368 (n.) he refers to Apuleius, *Apol.* 54 (61, 20 f.) : *Tacitas preces in templo deis allegasti : igitur magus es*—a clear indication that loud and vehement prayer was regarded as the proper manner.

P. 115 : Prayer to the moon-goddess.

Édouard des Places, *Biblica* 38 (1957), 113-29, gives a valuable discussion of the Greek Isis hymns and aretalogies. On p. 128 he rightly adduces the Isis Hymn of Mesomedes and he cites Apuleius, *Metam.* 11.2; the comparison should apply rather to the declaration by Isis in ch. 5.

P. 116 *ad* p. 267, 6 *caelestis Venus.*

The association between the moon and love, and especially Venus, is discussed by Claire Préaux, *La lune dans la pensée grecque* (Acad. Roy. de Belgique, Mém. Lettres, 2ᵉ série, 61, 4, Brussels, 1973), 120, and in n. 2 there she cites Apuleius, *Apol.* 31 (37, 20 : *Venus et Luna noctium conscia et manium potens Trivia*).

P. 165 *ad* p. 271, 1-2 *subterraneo semirutundo etc.*

With the phrase *Acherontis tenebris interlucentem* William R. Nethercut, *Classical Journal* 64 (1968), 111, rightly compares the power ascribed to the witch Meroë in 1.81 (8, 11-12) : she is able to brighten the darkness of Tartarus (*Tartarum ipsum inluminare*). An association of Isis and Meroë is, of course, not unnatural.

P. 177 *ad* p. 272, 12 *ursam mansuem.*

Cf. the show of bears prepared by Demochares of Plataea in *Metam.* 4.13-21, and the remarks by J. M. C. Toynbee, *Animals in Roman Life and Art* (London, 1973), 98 f.

P. 179 *ad* p. 272, 13 *simiam.*

See also H. Sichtermann, 'Ganymed', *Encic. dell'Arte Antica Classica e Orientale*, III (Rome, 1960), 788-90.

P. 180 *ad* p. 272, 15 *Bellerophontem.*

Probing the previous allusions in the *Metam.* to Pegasus and Bellerophon, William R. Nethercut, *Classical Journal* 64 (1968), 117-19, concludes that the 'ass with wings called Pegasus appears to be a specific allusion to Lucius' past.' The argument is hard to follow, mainly because the *anteludia* are regarded as 'metamorphoses', with the characters 'part of a blessed group'. It seems preferable to regard them as simple impersonations.

P. 183 *ad* p. 273, 6 *facticii luminis.*

See also Martin P. Nilsson, 'Lampen und Kerzen im Kult der Antike', *Opusc. Archaeologica* 6 (1950), 96-111. He surveys the use of torches by the Greeks in religious rites, including those carried by the Maenads, Demeter and her initiates, and other goddesses. He suggests that the Mysteries of foreign gods took over the custom from the Greeks; he then cites Cautes and Cautopates and the female who accompanies the Magna Mater. Discussing Egyptian rites (pp. 104 ff.), he recognizes the fact that the cult of both the gods and the dead used such illumination from early times. On this locus (p. 99) he notes that the element had obviously a place in nocturnal ceremonies, but that, as in other cults, it was so closely bound up with the ceremonial that it was practised also in daylight. See also Vermaseren in *Santa Prisca*, 151.

Peremans and Van't Dack, *Prosopographia Ptolemaica* (Louvain, 1956), nos, 7281-5, give cases of men with the title λυχνάπτος With regard to Mithraic rites, Vermaseren notes that a candle-bearer is depicted in the procession in a painting at Santa Prisca : see *Santa Prisca*, 150 f. with pl. 55 and Vermaseren, *Mithras, the Secret God*, 49 (the candle-bearer is leading a procession of members of the Lion grade).

P. 187 : The Initiation of Children.

In *Harv. Theol. Rev.* 52 (1959), 1-7 ('On the Rules regulating the celebration of the Eleusinian Mysteries') F. Sokolowski states (p. 3) that in Roman times children were frequently initiated.

P. 190 *ad* p. 273, 15 *omnis dignitatis et omnis aetatis.*

See now the valuable discussions by Michael Malaise, *Les Conditions de pénétration et de diffusion des cultes égyptiens en Italie* (Leiden, 1972), 25-156 and Françoise Dunand, *Le Culte d'Isis dans le bassin oriental de la Méditerranée*, III (Leiden, 1973), 136-196.

P. 212 : The *Liknon.*

The function of the *liknon* in the Dionysiac ritual is discussed by Friedrich Matz, *Διονυσιακή Τελετή* (Abh. Mainz, 1963, Wiesbaden, 1964), 16 ff. He shows that in some instances it is held above the person who is to be initiated, as in his pl. 22 (Rome, Villa Medici).

P. 217 *ad* p. 274, 20 *attollens.*

Cf. Georges Daux, *CRAIBL* 1972, 487 n. 1, quoting the view of Festugière on the term *Βησάρτης* found on an inscription from the Serapeum at Thessalonica : 'celui qui lève (soulève) Bès' with a reference to this locus.

P. 248 *ad* p. 277, 8 *curiositatis.*

The theme is lucidly discussed by Carl C. Schlam, 'The Curiosity of the Golden Ass', *Classical Journal* 64 (1968), 120-125. He observes on p. 123 that in *Metam.* 9.13 the ass notes the misery of slaves and animals, with the comment *ingenita mihi curiositate recreabar* (cf. above pp. 248-9); and Schlam justly adds that 'this is as close as we come to a favourable view of curiosity.' The whole approach in Book XI contains an element of curiosity, but, as he remarks on p. 125, it is 'a spectacle which combines the satisfaction of curiosity with holy veneration.'

P. 250 *ad* p. 277, 8-9 *sinistrum praemium.*

Brendan Kenny, *Arethusa* 7 (1974), 206, says that 'there is an ambiguity in the Latin *sinistrum* which the English *sinister* does not express, since the Latin can be used to refer to both good and bad luck'. He refers in a note to *LS* and to Fordyce, *Catullus*, 45.8. While the favourable meaning does exist in contexts of divination, it cannot be agreed for one moment that the two meanings ever co-exist, and least of all here. Kenny is fully aware of the narrow application of the good sense, but argues that 'the priest is, in a sense, making a prophetic comment on the outcome of Lucius' behaviour.'

P. 257 *ad* p. 278, 8 *innocentia fideque.*

Worthy of consideration here is the suggestion of William R. Nethercut, *Classical Journal* 64 (1968), 110 n. 4 that the words refer to 'the period just preceding the ass's appeal to Isis'. In support of the view that 'Lucius has lived with greater innocence during Books 9 and 10' he refers to 'his alliance with *caelestis providentia* against the miller's wife in 9.27, his condemnation of the foul woman with whom he is to perform, in 10.29'. But what about his sexual union with the *matrona quaedam pollens et opulens* in 10.19 ff.?

P. 259 *ad* p. 278, 13-14 *navem faberrime factam*.

Twice in this chapter Apuleius uses the term *navis* of the ship of Isis. At the end of ch. 5 he uses the noun *carina* (*rudem dedicantes carinam*); he never employs the phrase *Isidis Navigium* found in the calendar of Philocalus. On the other hand, in 2.11 (34, 5) Lucius speaks of the 'ship of Venus' (*navigium Veneris*) in looking forward to his night of love with Photis. Cf. William R. Nethercut, *Classical Journal* 64 (1968), 112 f.

P. 271 *ad* p. 280, 19 f. *intra conseptum templi*.

Françoise Dunand, *Le Culte d'Isis dans le bassin orientale de la Méditer-ranée*, II (Leiden, 1973), 60, makes the plausible comment that in such details Apuleius is not necessarily following the exact details of a particular temple, such as that at Cenchreae, but is probably drawing on the traditional pattern of a temple of Isis.

P. 276 *ad* p. 282, 5-6 *notae dorsualis agnitiae*.

Cf. J. M. C. Toynbee, *Animals in Roman Life and Art* (London, 1973), 168.

P. 277 *ad* p. 282, 8 *candidum*.

Gertrude C. Drake, 'Candidus : A Unifying Theme in Apuleius' *Meta-morphoses*', *Classical Journal* 64 (1968), 102-109, finds a special revelatory significance in the name : 'the white horse, now called Candidus, or Gleaming White... is surprisingly returned to its regenerated owner' (p. 104). The argu-ment would be more forceful if the name occurred here for the first time; but it is rightly admitted that the horse is called *candidus* before this (in 7.2). Cf. William R. Nethercut, *Classical Journal* 64 (1968), 111.

P. 290 *ad* p. 284, 24 *decem... diebus*.

Cf. Eugen Fehrle, *Die kultische Keuschheit im Altertum*, 159 (a paragraph on 'Zehntägige Keuschheit'). He refers also to the conclusion reached by Hepding, *Attis*, 183, that the initiates of Attis and the Great Mother practised abstinence for nine days during the Spring Mysteries. Cf. Vermaseren in *The Crucible of Christianity*, ed. Arnold Toynbee, 256.

In a brilliantly argued study, 'Decem Illis Diebus', *Ex Orbe Religionum : Studia Geo Widengren* (Leiden, 1972), 332-46, Jan Bergman suggests that the ten days correspond to the ten months which were regarded in Egypt as the period of gestation; they are therefore the proper prelude in a process which leads the initiate to be reborn, *renatus*, in a new life produced by Isis, the All-Mother. An apt allusion to the ten-month period of gestation, in the purely physical sense, is quoted by Bergman from the Cyme Aretalogy (M 18) where Isis states : 'I have ordained for women that they should bring forth a ten-month child to the light.' Dieter Müller ad loc. explains this as a Greek reckoning based on the Greek lunar month of 28 days. In the Egyptian reckoning based on solar months nine is the total often given. Yet the Egyptian tradition seems to have varied somewhat, as F. Jonckheere shows in his article 'La durée de la gestation d'après les textes égyptiens', *Chronique d'Égypte* 30 (1955), 19-45. A text from Denderah which he quotes (pp. 41-2) speaks of placing the statue of Osiris on branches of sycamore for *seven* days, to symbolize *seven* months in the womb of Nut, goddess of the sycamore. Here, at any rate, is a symbolic equation of days and months. Jonckheere refers to texts of the Ptolemaic era concerned with the birth of Horus which denote nine months as the period. Yet Bergman can quote instances where ten months are implied. On the whole, however, a practical reason for the time-span is preferable—the ten-day week—especially as Apuleius, unlike the Denderah text cited by Jonckheere, gives no suggestion of a day-month correspondence. It should be added that Bergman proceeds to discuss the idea that Pythagorean influence may be present here, since ten was a perfect number in that system and the eating of meat was prohibited.

P. 299 : Underground Chambers.

It was only rarely, as at Ostia and Walbrook, London, that the geological conditions made underground chambers difficult or impossible in the building of Mithraea. At Santa Prisca in Rome the eventual plan of the Mithraeum included three lateral chapels used in special rites of initiation as well as an enlarged central chamber : see Vermaseren and Van Essen, *Santa Prisca*, 140 ff.; also Vermaseren, *Mithras, the Secret God*, 46 and *Mithriaca* I, 1 ff.; II, 5 ff.

P. 302 : The initiate subjected to cold, heat, and water.

Professor Vermaseren compares the finds in Room Z at the Mithraeum of Santa Prisca; see *Santa Prisca*, 142 ff. Both here and at Carrawburgh there is an arrangement which might involve 'alternating ordeals by heat and sudden cold' (Vermaseren, *Mithras, the Secret God*, 135). Rooms suitable for baptism with water are also known; cf. op. cit. 41 and 135.

P. 309 f. Nudity in the Rite.

Nudity in the ascent of the soul as portrayed by Empedocles, the Chaldaean Oracles, and Plotinus is discussed by Otto Geudtner, *Die Seelenlehre der chaldäischen Orakel* (Meisenheim am Glan, 1971), 69 f.; cf. E. Fehrle, *Die kultische Keuschheit*, 38 and the more extensive treatment by Joseph Hecken-bach, *De nudidate sacra sacrisque vinculis* (Giessen, 1911), 12 ff. where nudity is said to have been necessary in all the Mystery Cults. Heckenbach (p. 13) cites Aristophanes, *Nub.* 498 ff. with reference to the Orphic Mysteries : Strepsiades is made an *epoptes* and goes in naked. Yet in other religious situations nakedness was offensive; cf. Fehrle, loc. cit.

P. 312 *ad* p. 286, 1 *grypes Hyperborei.*

Cf. the griffons figured on the lid of a casket found in Walbrook : v. J. M. C. Toynbee, *A Silver Casket and Strainer from the Walbrook Mithraeum in the City of London* (Leiden, 1963), pls. 1-2 and the parallel adduced from the mosaic in the villa near Piazza Armerina in Sicily (pl. 15). Dr Toynbee explains the Walbrook scenes as related to hunting, but concedes that in this religious context the fight may allegorize the victory of good over evil. On p. 11 she quotes the dictum of Philostratus, *V. Apollonii*, 3.48, who says that griffons existed in India and were regarded as sacred to the Sun—a view that fits with the solar emphasis of our context. Cf. also Toynbee, *Animals in Roman Life and Art* (London, 1973), 29; 290; 291.

P. 314 *ad* p. 286, 3 *corona... palmae.*

Following a suggestion by H. St. J. Hart in *JTS* n.s. 3 (1952), 66-75 that the 'crown of thorns' as described in John 19.2-5 was a 'caricature of the radiate crown of the divine ruler' and was made from leaflets of the date palm (*Phoenix dactylifera*; 'strictly from the rachis of the leaf'), Campbell Bonner, *Harv. Theol. Rev.* 46 (1953), 47-8, compares the crown here described by Apuleius as being worn by the neophyte 'in the likeness of the Sun God'. Mockery, rather than torture, would then be implied by the 'crown of thorns'. Whereas the material of the crowns may be regarded as perhaps similar, it is not the divine ruler that is suggested by the crown of Lucius, but association with the Sun-god Rēᶜ, as Bonner rightly suggests; at the same time it is a 'crown of justification' conferred on the believer through the grace of Osiris.

P. 314 *ad* p. 286, 4 *ad instar Solis.*

G. H. Halsberghe, *The Cult of Sol Invictus* (Leiden, 1972), 3, unwisely includes this passage among the literary testimonies to the cult of Sol Invictus.

P. 317 : Apotheosis by drowning.

Following a tentative suggestion by Regina Salditt-Trappmann, Michel Malaise, *Les Conditions de pénétration et de diffusion des cultes égyptiens en Italie* (Leiden, 1972), 232, finds the idea of apotheosis by drowning present in the initiate's first rite of baptism in a bath, as described in ch. 23, by linking it with the concept of death and rebirth. There is, however, no hint of the idea in the description of the rite itself; nor is there any evidence that the idea was ever applied to any persons other than those actually drowned in the Nile. For the connection with the myth of Osiris, cf. J. Gwyn Griffiths, *Conflict*, 7.

P. 322 *ad* p. 286, 24 *luminas solem*.

On *luminas* as a neologism Julie Nováková in *Charisteria Francisco Novotoný* (Prague, 1962), 108, refers to the principle that in new coinages the new component can sometimes be a 'Null-Komponente' in the sense that an earlier component is omitted. She quotes as examples *effabilis* in relation to *ineffabilis*, and *luminas* here (presumably in relation to *illuminare*). She quotes the dictum of K. Janaček, 'The problem of the ἅπαξ λεγόμενα should always be solved... in connection with the author's whole vocabulary and his manner of expression.' Her own brief survey is a useful analysis of the kind of changes that produce neologisms, including those that occur only once.

P. 328 *ad* p. 287, 24-5 *fani quidem advena etc.*

See also Jan Bergman in *Temenos* 8 (1972), 22-3.

P. 331 *ad* p. 288, 12 *thyrsos et hederas*.

Cf. the remarks of Martin L. West on 'Graeco-Oriental Orphism' in *Summaries of Reports : the Sixth International Congress of Classical Studies* (Madrid, 1974), 36 ff.

P. 341 *ad* p. 291, 5-7 *deus deum magnorum potior etc.*

Cf. a locution in *The Complaints of a Peasant*, an Egyptian text of the Twelfth Dynasty (*c.* 1800 B.C.), where the peasant in his second complaint (B 1, 88 f.) addresses the high steward thus :
   O high steward, my lord, greatest of the great, richest of the rich, whose great ones include one greater, whose rich ones include one richer.
Cf. F. Vogelsang, *Kommentar zu den Klagen des Bauern* (Leipzig, 1913), 85 ff.; Alan H. Gardiner, *JEA* 9 (1923), 10 and R. O. Faulkner in *The Literature of Ancient Egypt* ed. W. K. Simpson (2nd ed., Yale U.P., 1973), 36; Gerhard Fecht, 'Zur zweiten Klage des "Bauern" ', *XXIXth International Congress of Orientalists : Abstracts of Papers* (Paris, 1973), 13.

P. 342 *ad* p. 291, 9 *visus est*.

The climatic vision of Osiris approaches the doctrine of *gnosis* as propounded in Plutarch's *De Iside et Osiride*. See the perceptive analysis by H. D. Betz. 'Eine seltsames mysterientheologisches System bei Plutarch', *Ex Orbe Religionum : Studia Geo Widengren* (Leiden, 1972), 347-354, with a discussion of Apuleius on pp. 351 f.

P. 343 *ad* p. 291, 14 *Syllae temporibus.*

Michel Malaise, *Les Conditions de pénétration et de diffusion des cultes égyptiens en Italie* (Leiden, 1972), 362-5, emphasises Sulla's religious eclecticism. In his previous volume, *Inventaire préliminaire des documents égyptiens découverts en Italie* (Leiden, 1972), 96, he rejects the attribution of the Nilotic mosaic at Praeneste to the time of Sulla, accepting D. Bonneau's argument that the Roman soldiers shown in the lower right-hand corner indicate an Augustan date. See Witt, *Isis Gr.-R.* pl. 8 and pp. 34-5, 289. The soldiers, however, may well be intended to represent the escort of a Ptolemy : see Castiglione, 'Isis Pharia', 44.

P. 345 (cf. p. 5) : Apuleius and Christianity.

Professor Vermaseren refers me to the recent discussion by Marcel Simon, 'Apulée et le christianisme', *Mélanges d'histoire des religions offerts à Henri-Charles Puech* (Paris, 1974), 299-305. After rejecting the idea that Apuleius in the *Apology* was really answering a charge of Christianity or philo-Christianity or that the wooden skeleton described in *Apol.* 61 and 63 was a crucifix, Simon considers the description of Aemilianus in *Apol.* 56 as a man who honours no religion; here he refers also to *Apol.* 18 : *Mihi etiam paupertatem opprobavit,* but it seems that Pudens rather than Aemilianus should be regarded as the subject here (so Vallette and Butler). One must agree with Simon, in any case, that no trace of Christianity emerges among the imputed qualities.

It is the description of the baker's wife in *Metam.* 9.14 that inspires Simon's best comments. He shows that the catalogue of vices belongs to a literary genre of which examples are found in Philo and the Pauline epistles, notably in Philo's *De sacrificiis Abelis et Caini,* 32 (a lengthy catalogue) and Paul's 1 Cor. 5.11 ('I now write that you must have nothing to do with any so-called Christian who leads a loose life, or is grasping, or idolatrous, a slanderer, a drunkard, or a swindler. You should not even eat with any such person.'). Simon sees five of the six adjectives having counterparts in epithets or phrases used by Apuleius. It is not impossible, it is argued, that Apuleius may have read Paul's work and may be here following the description in an attack on a Christian. Certainly the correspondence is striking, and both Pliny and Tacitus speak of the *flagitia* of Christians, as Simon remarks. Yet the doubt remains that the baker's wife may be thought of as Jewish rather than Christian; there is nothing distinctively Christian in the beliefs ascribed to her. At the same time the corresponding cameo of vices in 1 Cor. 5.11 goes some way to remove the doubt.

A SELECT BIBLIOGRAPHY OF WORKS CONSULTED

I. EDITIONS AND COMMENTARIES
(in chronological order)

Andreas De Buxis, Johannes. (Episcopus Aleriensis.) *Lucii Apuleii ... metamorphoseo liber*; *ac nonulla alia opuscula eiusdem* ... (Rome, 1469).

Andreas De Buxis, Johannes. (Eodem titulo.) (Vicenza, 1488).

Andreas de Buxis, Johannes. (Eodem titulo) (Venice, 1493).

Andreas De Buxis, Johannes. (Eodem titulo.) (Milan, 1497).

Beroaldus, Philippus. *Commentarii a Philippo Beroaldos conditi in Asinum Aureum Lucii Apuleii.* (Bologna, 1500).

Beroaldus, Philippus. (Eodem titulo.) (Venice, 1504).

Beroaldus, Philippus. *Apuleius cum commento Beroaldi : figuris noviter additis.* (Venice, 1516).

Philippus De Giunta. *L. Apuleii (Opera).* (Florence, 1512).

L. Apuleii Metamorphoseos, sive lusus Asini libri XI ... Venetiis in Aedibus Aldi e Andreae Soceri. (Venice, 1521).

(Bernardus Philomathes Pisanus). *L. Apuleii (Opera).* Florentiae per haeredes Philippi Iuntae. (Florence, 1522).

Beroaldus, Philippus. *Commentarii in Apuleij Asinum aureum.* The copy in the Bodleian Library, Oxford, lacks a title-page; the above title appears at the end, p. 1026. According to the Bodleian Catalogue its date may be 1570 (?).

Beroaldus, Philippus. *L. Apuleii ... Opera ... cum Philippi Beroaldi in Asinum aureum conditissimis Commentariis : recens. Godescalci Stevvechi Heusdani in L. Apuleii opera omnia quaestionibus et coniecturis ... adiectis* 2 Tom. (Leiden, 1587).

Colvius, Petrus. (Brugensis) *L. Apuleii ... Opera Omnia ... Emendata et aucta cura Petri Colvii Brugensis; cum eiusdem ... notis.* (Leiden, 1588).

Vulcanius, Bon. (Brugensis). *L. Apuleii ... Opera Omnia. ... post ultimam P. Colvii editionem.* (Leiden, 1594).

Hopperus, Marcus. *L. Apuleii ... Opera ... cum Philippi Beroaldi Commentariis et Godescalci Stevvechii ... Quaestionibus et Conjecturis.* Tom. 3. (Basel, 1597 (?)). [The third volume, devoted to the minor works, has not been seen.]

Vulcanius, Bon. (Brugensis). *L. Apuleii ... Opera Omnia* ... (Leiden, 1600).

Vulcanius, Bon. (Brugensis). *L. Apuleii ... Opera Omnia* ... (Paris, 1601).

Wower, Ioannes à. *L. Apuleii ... Opera.* Ioan. à Wower ... recensuit ... emendavit ... auxit. (Basel, 1606).

Vulcanius, Bonaventura et alii. *L. Apuleii ... Opera Omnia ... ad B. Vulcanii. P. Colvii, ac aliorum editiones, recognita et emendata.* (Raphelengii, 1610).

Beroaldus, Philippus. *L. Apuleii ... Opera ... G. Stevvechii ... quaestionibus et coniecturis ... adiectis . ... accesserunt I. Casauboni in Apologiam ... castigationes.* 2 Tom. (Leiden, 1614).

Beroaldus, Philippus. *L. Apuleii ... Opera ... Demum, Totus Apuleius ... cum vetustissimis Codicibus collatus ...* (Basel, 1620).

Elmenhorstius, Geverhartus, *Apuleii ... Opera Omnia. G. Elmenhorstius ... recensuit...* (Frankfurt, 1621).

Apuleii ... Opera Omnia ... serio emendata. Editio Nova. (Leiden, 1623).

Scriverius, Pet. *Apuleius ... serio castigatus. Ex musaeo Pet. Scriveri.* (Amsterdam, 1623), also 1624 and 1628).

Pricaeus, Ioannes. *L. Apuleii ... Metamorphoseos Libri XI, cum Notis et amplissimo Indice.* (Gouda, 1650).

Floridus, Julianus. *Lucii Apuleii ... Opera interpretatione et notis illustravit Julianus Floridus ... in usum ... Delphini.* 2 Tom. (Paris, 1688).

Lucii Apuleii ... Opera. (with variant readings and emendations culled from the commerntaries of Stewechius, Brantius, Puteanus and Elmenhorstius.) (Altenburg, 1778).

Oudendorpius, Franciscus van. *Appuleii Metamorphoseon Libri XI. cum notis integris Petri Colvii, Joannis Wowerii, Godeschalci Stewechil, Geverharti Elmenshorstii et aliorum, imprimis cum animadversionibus hucusque ineditis Francisci Oudendorpii.* (Leiden, 1786).
The book was republished in 1823 with two other volumes which presented the other works and an *Appendix Appuleiana* (vol. 3) with the commentaries of Beroaldus and Pricaeus.

L. Apuleii ... Opera, ad optimas editiones collata. Praemittitur notitia litteraria, studiis Societatis Bipontinae. 2 vols. (Deux-Ponts, 1788).

Apuleii Metamorphoseon Libri Undecim. Ex optimis exemplaribus emendati. 3 vols. (Paris, 1796).

Maury, J. A. *L'Ane d'Or d'Apulée, précédé du Démon de Socrate. Nouvelle Traduction.* (Latin and French.) 2 vols. (Paris, 1822).

Oudendorp, Franciscus van. *Apuleii Opera Omnia ex editione Oudendorpiana, cum notis et interpretatione in usum Delphini...* Curante et imprimente A. J. Valpy. 7 vols. (London, 1825).

Hildebrand, G. F. *L. Apuleii Opera Omnia.* 2 vols. (Leipzig, 1842).

Hildebrand, G. F. *L. Apuleii ... Opera Omnia. Editio Minor.* (Leipzig, 1843).

Eyssenhardt, Franciscus. *Apuleii Metamorphoseon Libri XI.* (Berlin, 1868).

Vliet, J. van der. *Lucii Apulei Metamorphoseon Libri XI.* (Leipzig, 1897).

Helm, Rudolfus. *Apuleii Opera Quae Supersunt.* Vol. I *Metamorphoseon Libri XI.* (Leipzig, 1907).
There were further editions in 1913 and 1931; the latter was reprinted with additions in 1955.

Helm, Rudolfus, *Apuleii Opera...* Vol. II, Fasc. 2. *Florida.* (The *Praefatio*, pp. v-lx, deals also with the *Metamorphoses*.) (Leipzig, 1910, repr. with additions, 1959).

Gaselee, S. *Apuleius, the Golden Ass. With an English translation by W. Adlington revised by S. Gaselee.* Loeb Classical Library. (London, 1915).

Médan, Pierre, *Apulée Métamorphoses Livre XI. Texte Latin... avec un commentaire critique et explicatif.* (Paris, 1925).

Carlesi, Ferdinando and Terzaghi, Nicola. *Apuleio, Gli XI Libri delle Metamorfosi. Traduzione di F. Carlesi. Texto critico riveduto da Nicola Terzaghi.* (Florence, 1954).

Robertson, D. S. and Vallette, Paul. *Texte établi par D. S. Robertson. Apulée, Les Métamorphoses.* Coll. Budé. 3 vols. (Paris, 1956).

Helm, Rudolf. *Apuleius Metamorphosen oder Der goldene Esel. Lateinisch und Deutsch.* Schriften und Quellen der alten Welt, 1. (1956, Ed. 5, Berlin, 1961).

Giarratano, Caesar, rev. Frassinetti, Paulus. *Apulei Metamorphoseon Libri XI.* Corpus Scriptorum Latinorum Paravianum. (Turin, 1960).

Brandt, Edward. *Apuleius, Der goldene Esel. Lateinisch und deutsch.* An appendix includes 'Lukios oder der Esel' (Griechisch und deutsch). (Ed. 2, Stuttgart, 1963).

II.   TRANSLATIONS AND STUDIES

Abt. Adam. *Die Apologie des Apuleius von Madaura und die antike Zauberei.* (RGVV 4, 2, Giessen, 1908, repr. Berlin, 1967).

——. 'Ein Bruchstück einer Sarapis-Aretalogie', *Arch. Rel.* 18 (1915), 257-68.

Adlington William. *The eleven Bookes of the Golden Asse.* (London, 1566). There were several later editions, as in 1596 (London).

Altheim, Franz. *Literatur und Gesellschaft im ausgehenden Altertum.* 2 vols. (Halle/Saale, 1948).

Amadasi, Maria Giulia Guzzo. *Le iscrizione Fenicie e Puniche delle colonie in occidente.* (Studi Semitici, 28. Rome, 1967).

Aly, Wolf. 'Novelle', *PW* (1937), 1171-1179.

Anderson, Walter. 'Das sogenannte Märchen vom Eselmenschen', *Zeitschrift für Volkskunde* 51 (1954), 215-236.

——. 'Nochmals : Das sogenannte Märchen vom Eselmenschen', *ibid.* 54 (1958), 121-125.

——. 'Zu Apuleius' Novelle vom Tode der Charite', *Philologus* 22 (1909), 537-549.

Angus, S. *The Mystery-Religions and Christianity.* (London, 1925).

ANON. *Les Metamorphoses ou L'Ane d'Or d'Apulée... traduits en François avec des Remarques.* 2 Tom. (Assigned by the B. M. Cat. to Compain de Saint Martin.) (Paris, 1707). There were several later editions.

ANON. *The New Metamorphosis : Or, pleasant Transformation of the Golden Ass of Lucius Apuleius of Medaura. Also the Golden Spy, ... written in Italian by Carlo Monte Socio.* 2 vols. (London, 1724).

Anrich, Gustav. *Das antike Mysterienwesen in seinem Einfluss auf Christentum.* (Göttingen, 1894).

Appel, Georg. *De Romanorum precationibus.* (RGVV 7, 2; Giessen, 1909).

Arbesmann, P. R. *Das Fasten bei den Griechen und Römern.* (RGVV 21, 1. Giessen, 1929).

Arnaldi, Francesco. 'L'episodio di Ifi nelle "Metamorfosi" di Ovidio (IX, 666 sgg.) e l'IX Libro di Apuleio', *Atti del Convegno Internazionale Ovidiano,* II (Rome, (1959), 371-375.

——, 'Vita letteraria a letteratura pagana d'Africa : Apuleio' in *Africa Romana* (Milan, 1935), 175-188.

Ausfeld, C. *De Graecorum precationibus quaestiones* (Diss. Leipzig, 1903).

Balogh, Joseph. 'Das "Gebetweinen"', *Arch. Rel.* 27 (1929), 365-8.

Barb. A. A. 'Diva Matrix' in *Journal of the Warburg and Courtauld Institutes* 16 (1953), 193-238.

Barnes, Timothy David. *Tertullian. A Historical and Literary Study.* (Oxford, 1971).

Barns, John Wintour Baldwin. 'Egypt and the Greek Romance', *Acta of the Eight Congress for Papyrology* (Vienna, 1956), 29-36.

Barr James. 'Which Language did Jesus Speak?—Some Remarks of a Semitist', *Bulletin of the John Rylands Library* 53 (1970), 9-29.

Beaujeu, J. 'Apulée helléniste', (resumé), *Rev. Ét. Lat.* 46 (1968), 11-13.

Becher, Ilse. 'Der Isiskult in Rom—ein Kult der Halbwelt?' *ZÄS* 96 (1970), 81-90.

Becker, Henricus. *Studia Apuleiana.* (Berlin, 1879).

Behr, C. A. *Aelius Aristides and the Sacred Tales.* (Amsterdam, 1968).

Bennett, Charles E. *Syntax of Early Latin.* 2 vols. (Boston, 1910, 1914).

Benz, Frank L. *Personal Names in the Phoenician and Punic Inscriptions.* (Studia Pohl, 8; Rome, 1972).

Berg, Paul-Louis van. *Étude critique des sources mythographiques grecques et latines (sauf de De Dea Syria). Corpus Cultus Deae Syriae (CCDS).* (ÉPRO 28. Leiden, 1972).

——. *Répertoire des sources grecques et latines* (sauf de *De Dea Syria*). Corpus Cultus Deae Syriae (*CCDS*). I, *Les sources littéraires.* Première partie. (ÉPRO 28. Leiden, 1972).

Bergman, Jan. 'Decem Illis Diebus: Zum Sinn der Enthaltsamkeit bei den Mysterien-weihen im Isisbuch des Apuleius,' *Ex Orbe Religionum: Studia Geo Widengren* (Leiden, 1972), 332-346.

——. *Ich bin Isis.* (Acta Univers. Upsal., Historia Religionum, 3; Uppsala, 1968).

——. '"I Overcome Fate, Fate Hearkens to Me"': Some Observations on Isis as a Goddess of Fate', in *Fatalistic Beliefs in Religion, Folklore and Literature*, ed. H. Ringgren (Scripta Inst. Donneriani Aboensis, II; Stockholm, 1967).

——. *Isis-Seele und Osiris-Ei.* (Acta Univers. Upsal, Historia Religionum, 4; Uppsala, 1970).

——. 'Zum "Mythus von der Nation" in den sog. hellenistischen Mysterienreligionen', *Temenos* 8 (1972), 7-28.

Bernand, Étienne. *Inscriptions Métriques de l'Égypte Gréco-Romaine.* (Annales litté-raires de l'univers. de Besançon, 98; Paris, 1969).

Bernhard, Max. *Der Stil des Apuleius von Madaura. Ein Beitrag zur Stilistik des Spät-lateins.* (Tübinger Beiträge zur Altertumswissenschaft, 2; Stuttgart, 1927; repr. Amsterdam, 1965).

——. Review of C. Giarratano, *Apulei Metam. Libri XI (1929), Gnomon* 7 (1931), 664-6.

——. Review of G. Wiman, *Textkritiska Studier till Apuleius (1927), Gnomon* 6 (1930), 205-311.

Berreth, Joseph. See Abbreviated Refs.

Bertram, G. 'Auferstehung, I (des Kultgottes)', *Reallexikon für Antike und Christentum* 1 (1950), 919-930.

Bétolaud, V. *Apulée : Traduction Nouvelle.* 4 Tom. (Paris, 1835).

——. *Œuvres Complètes d'Apulée traduites en français.* 2 Tom. (Paris, 1873; also 1883).

Betz, H. D. 'Ein seltsames mysterientheologisches System bei Plutarch', *Ex orbe Religionum : Studia Geo Widengren.* (Leiden, 1972).

Beyte, Fridericus. *Quaestiones Appuleianae.* (Diss. Leipzig, 1888).

Bianchi, Ugo. ed. *The Origins of Gnosticism.* (Colloquium of Messina, 1966; Leiden, 1967).

——. 'Il "Dio Cosmico" e i Culti "Cosmopolitici"' in *Mythos* (FS. Mario Untersteiner, Genoa, 1970), 97-106.

——. 'Seth, Osiris et l'ethnographie', *Rev. Hist. Rel.* 179/2 (1971), 113-135.

Bianco, Gerardo. *La fonte greca della metamorfosi di Apuleio.* (Antichità classica e cristiana, 10. Brescia, 1971).

Bilabel, F. *Die gräko-ägyptischen Feste.* (Neue Heidelberger Jahrbücher, 1929, 1-51; Heidelberg, 1929).

Binder, Gerhard and Merkelbach, Reinhold, ed. *Amor und Psyche.* (Wege der Forschung, 126; Darmstadt, 1968).

Birley, Anthony. *Septimius Severus.* The African Emperor. (London, 1971).

Birley, Anthony. 'Apuleius and Roman Provincial Life', *History Today* 18 (1968), 429-36.

——. *Septimius Severus.* The African Emperor. (London, 1971).

Bisi, Anna Maria. *Le Stele Puniche.* (Studi Semitici, 26; Rome, 1967).

Bissing, F. W. von. See Abbreviated Refs.

Blawatsky, W. and Kochelenko, G. *Le Culte de Mithra sur la côte septentrionale de mer noire.* (ÉPRO 8; Leiden, 1966).

Bleeker, C. J. 'Isis as a Saviour Goddess' in S. G. F. Brandon, ed. *The Saviour God* (Manchester, 1963), 1-16.

Blümner, H. 'Textkritisches zu Apuleius Metamorphosen', *Philologus* 55 (1896), 341-352.

——. 'Textkritisches zu Apuleius Metamorphosen' in *Mélanges Nicole* (Geneva, 1905), 23-38.

——. 'Zu Apuleius Metamorphosen', *Hermes* 29 (1894), 294-312.

Boeken, H. J. See Abbreviated Refs.

Bohn, H. G. (editor and publisher) *The Works of Apuleius... A New Translation.* (London, 1853).

Boiardo, Mattheo Maria. *Apulegio Volga Re.* (Venice, n.d.; 1518 acc. to Bodleian Cat.).

Boissier, Gaston. *L'Afrique Romaine.* (Paris, 1895).

Bonner, Campbell. 'Desired Haven', *Harv. Theol. Rev.* 34 (1941), 49-67.

——. 'The Crown of Thorns', *Harv. Theol. Rev.* 46 (1953), 47-48.

——. 'The Ship of the Soul on a Group of Grave-Stelae from Terenuthis', *Amer. Phil. Soc.* 85. 1 (1941), 84-91.

——. See also Abbreviated Refs.

Bonnet, Hans. See Abbreviated Refs.

Bornkamm, Günther. (tr. D. M. G. Stalker.) *Paul.* (London, 1971).

Bosticco, Sergio. *Musei Capitolini : I Monumenti Egizi ed Egittizzanti.* (Rome, 1952).

(Bothmer, Bernard V.) *Egyptian Sculpture of the Late Period.* (Brooklyn Museum, 1960).

Bouchier, E. S. *Life and Letters in Roman Africa.* (Oxford, 1913).

Bouthiere, George de la. *Metamorphose, autrement, L'Asne d'Or de L. Apulee de Madaure... Traduite de Latin en nostre Vulgaire...* (Lyon, 1553) .

Bowersock, G. W. *Greek Sophists in the Roman Empire.* (Oxford, 1969).

———. 'Zur Geschichte des römischen Thessaliens', *Rhein. Mus.* 108 (1965), 277-289.

Boyce, George K. See Abbreviated Refs.

Brady, Thomas Allan. See Abbreviated Refs.

Brakman, C. 'Apuleiana'. *Mnemosyne* 34 (1906), 345-360.

Branden, Alb. van den. *Grammaire Phénicienne.* (Beirut, 1969).

Brandon, S. G. F. 'Redemption in Ancient Egypt and Early Christianity' in *Types of Redemption*, ed. Werblowsky and Bleeker (Leiden, 1970), 36-45.

———. ed. *The Saviour God.* (FS. E. O. James; Manchester, 1963).

Braun, Martin, *History and Romance in Graeco-Oriental Literature.* (Oxford, 1938).

Breccia, Evaristo. See Abbreviated Refs.

Briem, O.E. (tr. from the Swedish by E. Guerre). *Les Sociétés Secrètes de Mystères.* (Paris, 1941).

———. 'Zur Frage nach dem Ursprung der hellenistischen Mysterien', *Acta Univers. Lund.* 24.5 (1928).

Broek, R. van den. *The Myth of the Phoenix.* (ÉPRO 24; Leiden, 1972).

Bruneau, Philippe. 'Isis Pélagia à Délos', *BCH* 85 (1961), 435-446.

———. 'Isis Pélagia à Délos (Compléments)', *BCH* 87 (1963), 301-308.

———. 'Illustrations Antiques du *Coq* et de l'*Âne* de Lucien', *BCH* 89 (1965), 349-357.

———, Review of Tran Tam Tinh, *Essai sur le culte d'Isis à Pompéi* (1964), *Rev. Ét. Grec.* 78 (1965), 439-441.

Brunner, Hellmut. *Grundzüge einer Geschichte der altägyptischen Literatur.* (Darmstadt, 1966).

Brunner-Traut, Emma. *Altägyptische Märchen.* (Die Märchen der Weltliteratur; ed. 2, Düsseldorf, 1965).

———. *Die altägyptischen Scherbenbilder* (*Bildostraka*) *der deutschen Museen und Sammlungen.* (Wiesbaden, 1957).

———. *Altägyptische Tiergeschichte und Fabel. Gestalt und Strahlkraft.* (Darmstadt, 1968).

Bürger, Carolus. *De Lucio Patrensi.* Diss. Berlin, 1887).

———. 'Zu Apuleius', *Hermes* 23 (1888), 489-498.

Bursian, C. 'Beiträge zur Kritik der Metamorphosen des Apuleius', *Sitzb. München*, 1881, Heft 1, 119-144.

Butler, H. E. *The Metamorphoses or Golden Ass of Apuleius of Madaura.* Translated with Introduction and brief notes. 2 vols. (Oxford, 1910).

——. with A. S. Owen. *Apulei Apologia*. With Introduction and Commentary. (Oxford, 1914).

Byrne, Francis D. *The Golden Ass of Apuleius*. Newly translated with Introduction and Notes. (London, 1904).

Callebat, Louis. 'L'archaïsme dans les *Métamorphoses* d'Apulée', *Rev. Ét. Lat.* 42 (1964), 346-361.

——. See also Abbreviated Refs.

Campbell, Leroy A. *Mithraic Iconography and Ideology*. (ÉPRO 11; Leiden, 1968).

Carcopino, Jérôme. *Aspects mystiques de la Rome païenne*. (Paris, 1942).

Carratello, Ugo. 'Apuleio morí nel 163-164?' *Giornale Italiano di Filologia* 16 (1963), 97-110.

Castiglione, L. 'Griechisch-Ägyptische Studien : Beiträge zur Deutung des Mosaiks von Präneste', *Acta Ant. Hung.* 5 (1957), 209-227.

——. 'Zur Frage der Sarapis-Kline', ibid. 9 (1961), 287-303.

——. See also Abbreviated Refs.

Castiglioni, L. 'Apuleiana III', *RIL* 71 (1938), 545-565.

Charpentier, Joannes-Petrus. *De Mystica Apuleii Doctrina*. (Diss. Paris, 1839).

Chassinat, Émile. *Le Mystère d'Osiris au mois de Khoiak*. 2 vols. (Cairo, 1966 and 1968).

Chodaczek, Ladislaus. 'Ad Apulei Metamorphoseon Libros Observationes Aliquot', *Eos* 34 (1932-33), 477-484.

——. 'Apuleianum', *Eos* 33 (1930-31), 534.

——. 'De Tribus Apulei Metamorphoseon Crucibus e notis antiquis ortis', *Eos* 33 (1930-31), 411-418.

Ciaffi, Vincenzo. *Petronio in Apuleio*. (Turin, 1960).

Clemen, Carl. See Abbreviated Refs.

Clouard, Henri. *Apulée l'Âne d'or ou Les Métamorphoses. Traduction nouvelle...* (Paris, n.d.; 1932 acc. to BM Cat.)

Cobb, Williams Henry. *A Criticism of Systems of Hebrew Metre*. (Oxford, 1905).

Cocchia, Enrico. *Romanzo e Realtà nella vita e nell'attività letteraria di Lucio Apuleio*. (Catania, 1915).

——. *Saggi Filologici*. Vol. V. *Le forme romantiche nella letteratura Romana dell'Impero : Petronio ed Apuleio, Curzio e Claudiano*. (Naples, 1915).

Colin, Jean. 'Apulée en Thessalie : fiction ou vérité?' *Latomus* 24 (1965), 330-345.

Cremaschi, Giovanni. 'Un codice dei "Metamorphoseon Libri" di Apuleio nella Biblioteca Comunale di Bergamo', *Aevum* 26 (1952), 369.

Cumont, Franz. 'Fatalisme astral et religions antiques', *Revue d'histoire et de la littérature religieuses* 3 (1912), 513-543.

——. *L'Égypte des Astrologues*. (Brussels, 1937).

——. See also Abbreviated Refs.

Damsté, P. H. 'Spicilegium criticum ad Apulei Metamorphoseon Libros' *Mnemosyne* 56 (1928), 1-28.

Daumas, F. 'La scène de la résurrection au tombeau de Pétosiris', *BIFAO* 59 (1960), 63-80.

Daux, Georges. 'Trois inscriptions de la Grèce du nord', *CRAIBL* 1972, 478-493.

Dee, Cornelius Henricus. *De ratione quae est inter Asinum Pseudo-Lucianeum Apuleique Metamorphoseon Libros.* (Leiden, 1891).

Del Corno, Darius. *Graecorum De Re Onirocritica Scriptorum Reliquiae.* (Testi e Documenti per lo studio dell'antichità, 26; Milan, 1969).

Della Corte, Matteo. *Iuventus.* (Arpino, 1924).

Del Re, Raffaello. *Apuleio, Sul Dio de Socrate.* (Scriptores Latini, 5; Rome, 1966).

Derchain, Ph. and Hubeaux, J. 'L'affaire du Marché d'Hypata dans la "Métamorphose" d'Apulée', *Ant. Class.* 27 (1958), 100-104.

Derchain, Ph. 'La couronne de la justification', *CdÉ* 30 (1955), 225-287.

——. 'The Egyptian World in the Age of the Ptolemies and Caesars' in P. Grimal, ed., *Hellenism and the Rise of Rome* (London, 1968), 207-241.

——. 'Snéfru et les rameuses', *Revue d'Égyptologie* 21 (1969), 19-25.

——. Review of J. Bergman, *Ich bin Isis (1968)*, ibid. 22 (1970), 212-214.

——. Review of Maria Münster, *Untersuchungen zur Göttin Isis (1968)*, *Bibl. Orient.* 27 (1970), 21-23.

Desertine, A. H. J. V. M. *De Apulei studiis Plautinis.* (Neomagi, 1898).

Dessau, H. 'Madauros', *PW* (1928), 201-202.

Deubner, Ludwig. 'ΠΛΟΙΑΦΕΣΙΑ', *Mitt. des Deutschen Arch. Inst. Athen. Abteilung* 37 (1912), 180-182.

——. *Attische Feste.* (Berlin, 1932).

Dey, Joseph. ΠΑΛΙΓΓΕΝΕΣΙΑ (Neutestamentliche Abh., 17, 5; Münster, 1937).

Dibelius, Martin. *Paul.* Edited and completed by W. G. Kümmel, tr. Frank Clarke. (London, 1953).

——. See also Abbreviated Refs.

Dieterich, B. C. 'The golden art of Apuleius', *Greece and Rome* 13 (1966), 189-206.

Dieterich, Dieter. 'Die Ausbreitung der alexandrinischen Mysteriengötter Isis, Osiris, Serapis und Horus in griechisch-römischer Zeit', *Das Altertum* 14 (1968), 201-211.

Dilthey, Carl. *Festrede.* (Göttingen, 1879).

Dölger, F. J. '*Esietus.* "Der Entrunkene oder der zum Osiris Gewordene" ', *Antike und Christentum* (Dölger) 1 (1929), 174-183.

Dornseiff, Franz. 'Lukios' und Apuleius' Metamorphosen', *Hermes* 73 (1938), 222-233.

Drake, Gertrude C. 'Candidus : A Unifiying Theme in Apuleius' *Metamorphoses*', *Classical Journal* 64 (1968), 102-109.

Drexler, W. 'Isis' in Roscher. *Lex. Myth.* II (1890-1894), 373-548.

——. *Mythologische Beiträge.* Heft 1. *Der Cultus der aegyptischen Gottheiten in den Donauländern.* (Leipzig, 1890).

Drioton, É. and Gabra, Sami. See Abbreviated Refs. (Gabra).

Dunand, Françoise. *Le Culte d'Isis dans le bassin oriental de la Méditerranée.* 3 vols. I. *Le Culte d'Isis et les Ptolémées.* II. *Le Culte d'Isis en Grèce.* III. *Le Culte d'Isis en Asie Mineure. Clergé et rituel des sanctuaires isiaques.* (ÉPRO 26. Leiden, 1973).

——. 'Une plainte de pastophores'. *CdÉ* 44 (1969), 301-312.

——. 'Sur une inscription Isiaque de Mégalépolis', *ZPE* 1 (1967), 219-224.

Duthoy, Robert. *The Taurobolium.* (ÉPRO 10; Leiden, 1969).

Ebel, Henry. 'Apuleius and the Present Time'. *Arethusa* 3 (1970), 155-175.

Edgar, C. C. *Greek Sculpture*. (CCG; Cairo, 1903).

——. *Greek Moulds*. (CCG; Cairo, 1903).

——. See also Abbreviated Refs.

Edson, Charles. 'Cults of Thessalonica', *Harv. Theol. Rev.* 41 (1948), 153-204

——. *Inscriptiones Graecae*. X 2, 1. *Inscriptiones Thessalonicae et Viciniae*. (Berlin, 1972).

Egger, Rudolf. 'Aus den Isismysterien'. (résumé) *Anzeiger der Österr. Akad. der Wissenschaften, Wien* 88 (1951), 1-2.

——. 'Zwei oberitalienische Mystensarkophage', *Mitt. des Deutschen Arch. Inst.* 4 (1951), 35-64.

Eicke, Wolfgang. *Stilunterschiede in den Metamorphosen des Apuleius von Madaura*. (Göttingen, 1956).

Eisler, Robert, *Orphisch-Dionysische Mysteriengedanken in der Christlichen Antike*. (Vorträge Bibliothek Warburg 2 (1922-23), 2. Teil, Leipzig, 1925).

Eitrem, S. 'Die vier Elemente in der Mysterienweihe', *Symbolae Osloenses* 4 (1926), 39-59 and 5 (1927), 39-59.

——. 'Vana'. *Symbolae Osloenses* 21 (1941), 125-128.

Engelmann, Helmut. *Die delische Sarapisaretalogie*. (Beiträge zur klassischen Philologie, 15; Meisenheim am Glan, 1964).

Erbse, Hartmut. 'Griechisches und Apuleianisches bei Apuleius', *Eranos* 48 (1950), 107-26, repr. in Binding and Merkelbach, *Amor und Psyche* (Darmstadt, 1968), 370-381.

Ericsson Harry, 'Sulla Felix, eine Wortstudie', *Eranos* 41 (1943), 77-89.

Erman, Adolf. *Die Religion der Ägypter*. (Berlin, 1934). See also Wild, Henri.

Fairman, H. W. 'A Scene of the Offering of Truth in the Temple of Edfu', *MDAIK* 16 (1958), 86-92.

——. *The Triumph of Horus*. (London, 1974).

Faulkner, R. O. 'The Bremner-Rhind Papyrus', *JEA* 22 (1936), 121-140.

——. *The Papyrus Bremner-Rhind*. (Bibl. Aegypt, 3; Brussels, 1933).

——. 'The Lamentations of Isis and Nephthys', *Mélanges Maspero*, I (Cairo, 1935), 337-348.

Fecht, Gerhard. *Literarische Zeugnisse zur 'Persönlichen Frommigkeit' in Ägypten*. (Abh. Heildeberg, 1965).

Fehrle, Eugen. *Die kultische Keuschheit im Altertum*. (RGVV 6; Giessen, 1910).

Feldbrugge, J. J. M. *Het schertsende Karakter van Apuleius' Metamorphosen*. (Utrecht, 1939).

Ferguson, John. 'Apuleius', *Greece and Rome* 8 (1961), 61-74.

Fernhout, J. M. H. See Abbreviated Refs.

Festugière, A.-J. 'À propos des Arétalogies d'Isis', *Harv. Theol. Rev.* 42 (1949), 209-234.

——. 'Les cinq sceaux de l'Aiôn Alexandrin', *Revue d'Égyptologie* 8 (1951), 63-70.

——. with Nock, A. D. *Corpus Hermeticum*. 4 vols. (Paris, 1945-54).

——. 'Les Mystères de Dionysos', *Rev. Biblique* 44 (1935), 192-211; 366-396.

——. *La Révélation d'Hermès Trismégiste*. 4 vols. (Paris, 1944-54).
——. 'Vraisemblance psychologique et forme littéraire chez les anciens', *Philologus* 102 (1958), 21-42.
——. See also Abbreviated Refs.
Fick, N. 'Du palais d'Éros à la robe olympienne de Lucius', *Rev. Ét. Lat.* 47 (1969), 378-396.
——. 'La symbolique végétale dans les *Métamorphoses* d'Apulée', *Latomus* 30 (1971), 328-344.
Firenzvola, Agnolo. *Apuleio dell'Asino d'Oro*. Tradotto. (Curiously it does not include Book XI.) (Vinegia, 1550).
Foucart, *Les Mystères d'Éleusis*. (Paris, 1914).
Fraser, P. M. 'Current Problems concerning the Early History of the Cult of Sarapis', *Opusc. Athen.* 7 (1967), 23-45.
——. *Ptolemaic Alexandria*. 3 vols. (Oxford, 1972).
——. See also Abbreviated Refs.
Frassinetti, Paolo. '*Cruces* Apuleiane (Metamorfosi)', *Athenaeum* 38 (1960), 118-131.
Freeman, Kathleen. 'Vincent, or the Donkey', *GR* 14 (1945), 33-41.
Friedrich, Johannes and Röllig, Wolfgang. *Phönizisch Punische-Grammatik*. (Ed. 2, Analecta Orientalia, 46; Rome, 1970).
Friesenhahn, Peter. *Hellenistische Wortzahlenmystik im Neuen Testament*. (Leipzig, 1935).
Fugier, Huguette. See Abbreviated Refs.

Gabra, Sami and Drioton, É. See Abbreviated Refs.
García y Bellido, A. 'Isis y el *Collegium Illychiniariorum* del *Pratum novum* (Conv. Cordubensis)' in *Hommages à W. Deonna* (Coll. Latomus, 28; Brussels, 1957), 238-244.
——. *Les religions orientales dans l'Espagne romaine*. (ÉPRO 15; Leiden, 1967).
Gardiner, Sir Alan. 'The Baptism of Pharaoh', *JEA* 36 (1950), 3-12.
Gargantini, Luisa. 'Ricerche intorno alla formazione dei temi nominali di Apuleio', *RIL* 97 (1963), 33-43.
Gasparro, Giulia Sfameni, *I Culti Orientali in Sicilia*. (ÉPRO 31; Leiden, 1973).
Gatti, Guglielmo. 'Topografia dell' Iseo Campense', *Rendiconti : Atti della Pontificia Accademia Romana di Archeologia* 20 (1943-44), 117-163.
Geisau, Johannes von. *Syntaktische Gräzismen bei Apulejus*. Sonderabdruck aus *Indogermanische Forschungen* 36 (1915).
——. See also Abbreviated Refs.
Geraci, Francesco. *Lucio Apuleio Madaurense, Oratore Avvocato e Conferenziere*. (Reggio Calabria, 1935).
Gerlitz, Peter. 'Fasten als Reinigungsritus', *Zeitschrift für Religions- und Geistesgeschichte* 20 (1968), 212-222.
Geudtner, Otto. *Die Seelenlehre der chaldäischen Orakel*. (Beiträge zur klassischen Philologie, 35. Meisenheim am Glan, 1971).
Giangrande, Giuseppe. 'On the origins of the Greek Romance', *Eranos* 60 (1962), 132-159

Giangrande, Lawrence. *The Use of* Spoudaiogeloion *in Greek and Roman Literature.* (Studies in Classical Literature, 6; The Hague, 1972).

Gilliam, Elizabeth H. 'The Archives of the Temple of Soknobraisis at Bacchias', *Yale Classical Studies* 10 (1947), 179-281.

Gilmore, A. ed. *Christian Baptism.* (London, 1959).

Gonzenbach, Victorine von. See Abbreviated Refs.

Goyon, Jean-Claude. 'Textes Mythologiques. I. "Le Livre de protéger la barque du dieu." ' *Kêmi* 19 (1969), 23-65.

Graham, Alexander. *Roman Africa.* (London, 1902).

Graindor, Paul. *Terres cuites de l'Égypte Gréco-Romaine.* (Antwerp, 1939).

Grant, Frederick C. *Hellenistic Religions.* (New York, 1953).

Graves, Robert. *The Transformations of Lucius, otherwise known as The Golden Ass.* Translated. (Penguin Books, 1950).

Gressmann, Hugo. *Die hellenistische Gestirnreligion.* (Beihefte zum "Alten Orient", Heft 5; Leipzig, 1925).

——. 'Die Umwandlung der orientalischen Religionen unter dem Einfluss hellenischen Geistes', *Vorträge Bibl. Warburg 1923-24*, pp. 170-195. (Leipzig, 1926).

——. See also Abbreviated Refs.

Griffith, John G. 'Apuleius, Metamorphoses 6, 29, 3', *Hermes* 96 (1968), 762.

Griffiths, D. R. 'Baptism in the Fourth Gospel and in the First Epistle of John' in A. Gilmore, ed. *Christian Baptism* (London, 1959), 149-170.

Griffiths, J. Gwyn. 'Allegory in Greece and Egypt', *JEA* 53 (1967), 79-102.

——. 'An Appeal to Nut in a Papyrus of the Roman Era', *JEA* 50 (1962), 182 f.

——. 'βασιλεὺς βασιλέων : Remarks on the History of a Title', *Class. Phil.* 48 (1953), 145-154.

——. 'The Death of Cleopatra VII', *JEA* (1961), 113-118.

——. 'The Flight of the Gods before Typhon ...', *Hermes* 88 (1960), 374-376.

——. 'The Horus-Seth Motif in the Daily Temple Liturgy', *Aegyptus* 38 (1958), 3-10.

——. 'The Isiac Jug from Southwark', *JEA* 59 (1973), 233-236.

——. 'Isis in Oxford', *CdÉ* 39 (1964), 67-71.

——. 'Luna and Ceres', *Class. Phil.* 63 (1968), 143-145.

——. *The Origins of Osiris.* (MÄR 9; Berlin, 1966).

——. ' "The Pregnancy of Isis" : a comment', *JEA* 56 (1970), 194 f.

——. 'Seth or Anubis?' *Journal of the Warburg and Courtauld Inst.* 22 (1959), 367.

——. 'A Translation from the Egyptian by Eudoxus', *CQ* 15 15 (1965), 75-78.

——. See also Abbreviated Refs.

Grimal, Pierre. 'A la recherche d'Apulée', *Rev. Ét. Lat.* 47 (1969), 94-99 (*ad* Scobie, *Aspects of the Ancient Romance*).

——. *Apulei Metamorphoses IV, 28 - VI, 24 : Le conte d'Amour et Psyché.* Édition, introduction et commentaire. (Paris, 1963).

——. 'Le calame égyptien d'Apulée', *REA* 73 (1971), 343-355.

Grimm, Günter and Haevernick, Th. E.' Die Überfangglasscherbe in Cameotechnik von Walldürn', *Jb. des römisch-germanischen Zentralmuseums Mainz* 10 (1963), 204-216.

Grimm, Günter. See also Abbreviated Refs.

Griset, Emanuele. 'Un Cristiano di Sabrata', *Rivista di Studi Classici* 5 (1957), 35-39.

Grundmann, Walter and Leipoldt, Johannes. *Umwelt des Urchristentums.* 3 vols. (Berlin, 1956-6; Ed. 2, 1967-70).

Gsell, Stéphane. *L'Algérie dans l'antiquité.* (Algiers, 1903).

——. 'Les cultes égyptiens dans le nord-ouest de l'Afrique sous l'empire romain', *Rev. Hist. Rel.* 59 (1909), 149-159.

——. with Joly, Charles Albert, *Khamissa, Mdaourouch, Announa.* 3 vols. Seconde Partie : *Mdaourouch* (Algiers, 1922).

Guaglianone, Antonio. 'A proposito di un nuovo codice frammentario di Apuleio', *Parola del Passato* 6 (1951), 451-456.

Guey, Julien. 'Au théâtre de Leptis Magna', *Rev. Ét. Lat.* 29 (1951), 307-317.

——. 'L'*Apologie* d'Apulée et les inscriptions de Tripolitaine', *Rev. Ét. Lat.* 22 (1954), 115-119.

Guilmot, Max. 'Le Sarapieion de Memphis: Étude Topographique', *Chronique d'Égypte* 27 (1962), 359-378.

Guimet, E. 'Le dieu d'Apulée', *Rev. Hist. Rel*, 32 (1895), 242-248.

Gullini, Giorgio. *I Mosaici di Palestrina.* (Rome, 1956).

Gundel, Hans Georg. *Weltbild und Astrologie in den griechischen Zauberpapyri.* (Münchener Beiträge zur Papyrusforschung usw., 53; Munich, 1968).

Gundel, Wilhelm. 'Heimarmene', *PW* (1912), 2622-2645.

Haight, Elizabeth Hazelton. *Apuleius and His Influence.* (Our Debt to Greece and Rome; London, 1927).

——. *Essays on Ancient Fiction.* (New York, 1936).

Halsberghe, Gaston H. *The Cult of Sol Invictus.* (ÉPRO 23; Leiden, 1972).

Hammond, Mason. 'Roman Africa', *Classical World* 53 (1959), 83-85.

Hanslik, R. 'Apuleius', *Lexikon der alten Welt* (Zürich, 1965), 232-233.

Harden, Donald. *The Phoenicians.* (Ancient Peoples and Places, 26; London, 1962).

Harris, Eve and John. *The Oriental Cults in Roman Britain.* (ÉPRO 6; Leiden, 1965).

Harris, Zellig S. *A Grammar of the Phoenician Language.* (American Oriental Series, 8; New Haven, 1936).

Harrison, Jane E. 'Mystica Vannus Iacchi', *JHS* 23 (1903), 292-324.

Haussleiter, Joh. 'Nacharistotelische Philosophen' (1931-36), Bursian, *Jahrsb.* 281 (1943), 151 ff.

Head, Sir George. *The Metamorphoses of Apuleius : A Romance of the Second Century.* Translated. (London, 1851).

Heckenbach, Joseph. *De nuditate sacra sacrisque vinculis.* (RGVV 9, 3. Giessen, 1911).

Heerma Van Voss, M. S. H. G. *Een Mysteriekist Ontsluierd.* (Leiden, 1969).

Heitsch, E. 'PSI VII, 844, ein Isishymnus' *Mus. Helv.* 17 (1960), 185-188.

Helck, W. See Abbreviated Refs.

Helm, Rudolf. 'Ceterum bei Apuleius', *Wiener Studien* 70 (1957), 131-147.

Henrichs, A. 'Textkritisches zur Isisinschrift von Megalopolis', *ZPE* 3 (1968), 109-110.

Hermann, Alfred. 'Sinuhe - ein ägypt. Schelmenroman?' *OLZ* 48 (1953), 101-109.

Herrmann, L. 'L'Ane d'Or et le christianisme', *Latomus* 12 (1953), 188-191.

——. 'Le dieu-roi d'Apulée', *Latomus* 18 (1959), 110-116.

Hesky, Richard. 'Zur Abfassungszeit der Metamorphosen des Apuleius', *Wiener Studien* 26 (1904), 71-80.

Hicter, Marcel. *Apulée Conteur Fantastique*. (Coll. Lebègue; Brussels, 1942).

——. 'L'autobiographie dans l'*Ane d'Or* d'Apulée', *Ant. Class.* 13 (1944), 95-111; 14 (1945), 61-68.

Hildebrand, G. F. *Commentationis de Vita et Scriptis Appuleii Epitome*. (Diss. Halle, 1835).

Höfler, Anton. *Der Sarapishymnus des Ailios Aristeides*. Tübinger Beiträge zur Altertumswissenschaft, Heft 27; Stuttgart, 1935).

Hopfner, Theodor. 'Mittel- und neugriechische Lekano-, Lychno-, Katoptro- und Onychomantien' in *Griffith Studies* (London, 1932), 218-232.

——. 'Mysterien, Die orientalisch-hellenistischen', *PW* (1935), 1315-1350.

——. *Plutarch über Isis und Osiris*. 2 vols. (Monographien des Archiv Orientální, 9; Prague, 1940-41).

——. See also Abbreviated Refs.

Hornbostel, Wilhelm. *Sarapis*. (ÉPRO 32; Leiden, 1973).

Hornung, Erik. *Das Amduat. Die Schrift des verborgenen Raumes*. 3 vols. (Ägyptologische Abh. 7 and 13; Wiesbaden, 1963 and 1967).

Hubaux, J. v. Derchain, Ph.

Hülsen, Chr. 'Porticus Divorum und Serapeum im Marsfelde', *MDAIR* (1903), 17-57.

Husson, Geneviève, *Lucien, Le Navire ou les Souhaits*. Introduction, texte et traduction. 2 vols. (Paris, 1970).

Iversen, Erik. *The Myth of Egypt and its Hieroglyphs*. In European Tradition. (Copenhagen, 1961).

Jahn, Otto. 'Die Cista Mystica', *Hermes* 3 (1869), 317-334.

Janssen, J. M. A. 'Notes on the Geographical Horizon of the Ancient Egyptians : Aethiopians and Haunebut', *Bibl. Orient.* 8 (1951), 213-217.

Jelínková-Reymond, E. *Les inscriptions de la statue guérisseuse de Djed-Ḥer-le-Sauveur*. (IFAO, BÉ 23; Cairo, 1956).

Jenning, Helmuth. *De Metamorphosibus L. Apuleii*. (Leipzig, 1867).

Jennison, George. *Animals for Show and Pleasure in Ancient Rome*. (Manchester, 1937).

Jéquier, Gustave. *Le livre de ce qu'il y a dans l'Hadès*. (Paris, 1894).

Jesi, Furio. 'Iside in figura di Kore?'. *Aegyptus* 41 (1961), 74-87.

——. *Letteratura e mito* (La ricerca letteraria. Serie critica, 4; Turin, 1968).

——. 'Sur les influences osiriaques', *Chronique d'Égypte* 35 (1960), 184-187.

——. *La vera terra*. (Turin, 1974).

Joly, Charles Albert. See Gsell, Stéphane.

Jonas, Hans. *Gnosis und spätantiker Geist*. (Ed. 3, Göttingen, 1964).

Jonckheere, Frans. 'La durée de la gestation d'après les textes égyptiens', *Chronique d'Égypte* 30 (1955), 19-45.

Jong, K. H. E. de. See Abbreviated Refs.

Jonge, B. J. de. *Ad Apulei Madaurensis Metamorphoseon Librum Secundum Commentarius Exegeticus.* (Groningen, 1941).

Junghanns, Paul. See Abbreviated Refs.

Junker, Heinrich. 'Über iranische Quellen der hellenistischen Aion-Vorstellung.' *Vorträge der Bibliothek Warburg 1921-22*, 124-178.

Junker, Hermann. See Abbreviated Refs.

Kádár, Zoltán. *Die kleinasiatisch-syrischen Kulte zur Römerzeit in Ungarn.* (ÉPRO 2; Leiden, 1962).

Kaibel, G. 'Apuleiana', *Hermes* 35 (1900), 202-204.

Kaiser, Martin. *Artemidor von Daldis : Traumbuch.* (Basel, 1965).

Kákosy, J. 'Gnosis und Ägyptische Religion', in *Le Origini dello Gnosticismo.* ed. U. Bianchi (Leiden, 1967), 238-247.

——. 'Osiris-Aion', *Oriens Antiquus* 3 (1967), 15-25.

——. 'Probleme der ägyptischen Jenseitsvorstellungen in der Ptolemäer- und Kaiserzeit' in *Rel. en Égypte*, ed. Derchain (Paris, 1969), 59-68.

——. 'Pythagoras hatás Apuleius Metamorphoses XI-ben?' *Antik Tanulmányok* (*Studia Antiqua*) 15 (1968), 243-245.

——. 'Zu einer Etymologie von Philä : "Insel der Zeit" ', *Acta Ant. Hung.* 16 (1968), 39-48.

Kamal, Ahmed Bey. *Stèles Ptolémaiques et Romaines.* 2 vols. (CCG; Cairo 1904-5).

Kater-Sibbes, G. J. F. *Preliminary Catalogue of Sarapis Monuments.* (ÉPRO 36; Leiden, 1973).

Kaufmann, Carl Maria. *Ägyptische Terrakotten der Griechisch-Römischen und Koptischen Epoche.* (Cairo, 1913).

——. *Graeco-Ägyptische Koroplastik.* (Ed. 2, Leipzig, 1915).

Kawczyński, M. 'Apulejusza "Metamorfozy" czyli powieśc o ztotym ośle', *Rozprawy Akademii Umiejetności*, II, 16 (Cracow, 1900), 165-274.

——. 'Ist Apuleius im Mittelalter bekannt gewesen?' in *Bausteine zur Romanischen Philologie* (FS. A. Mussafia, Halle, 1905), 193-210.

Keimer, Ludwig. 'Egyptian Formal Bouquets', *American Journal for Semitic Languages and Literature* 41 (1925), 145-161.

——. *Die Gartenpflanzen im alten Ägypten. Ägyptologische Studien.* I. Bd. (Hamburg, 1924).

——. 'La rose égyptienne' in his *Études d'Égyptologie*, 5. (Cairo, 1943).

Keller, Otto, *Die Antike Tierwelt.* (1909, repr. Hildesheim, 1963).

Kenny, Brendan. 'The Reader's Role in the *Golden Ass*', *Arethusa* 7 (1974), 187-209.

Kerényi, Karl. *Die Griechisch-Orientalische Romanliteratur in religionsgeschichtlicher Beleuchtung. Ein Versuch.* (Tübingen, 1927).

——. See also Abbreviated Refs.

Kiessling, Emil. 'Die Götter von Memphis in griechisch-römischer Zeit', *Arch. Pap.* 15 (1953), 7-45.

Kirchhoff, Alfredus. *De Apulei Clausularum Compositione et Arte.* (Diss. Leipzig, 1902).

Klasens, Adolf. *A Magical Statue Base (Socle Béhague) in the Museum of Antiquities at Leiden.* (Leiden, 1952).

Knox, Wilfred L. *Some Hellenistic Elements in Primitive Christianity.* (Schweich Lectures, 1942; London, 1944).

Kochelenko, G. See Blawatsky, W.

Köster, August. *Das antike Seewesen.* (Berlin, 1923).

Koziol, Heinrich. See Abbreviated Refs.

Kretschmann, H. *De Latinitate L. Apulei Madaurensis.* (Königsberg, 1865).

Kroll. W. 'Das afrikanische Latein', *Rhein. Mus.* 52 (1897), 569-590.

———. Rev. *W. S. Teuffels Geschichte der römischen Literatur*, III. (Ed. 6, Leipzig, 1913).

Kronenberg, A. J. 'Ad Apuleium', *CQ* 2 (1908), 304-312.

———. 'Ad Apuleium', *CR* 18 (1904), 442-447.

Labhardt, André. 'Curiositas, notes sur l'histoire d'un mot et d'une notion', *Mus. Helv.* 17 (1960), 206-224.

Lafaye, Georges. See Abbreviated Refs.

Lambrechts, P. *Augustus en de egyptische Godsdienst.* (Brussels, 1956).

———. 'Excavations at Pessinus (Turkey) by the University of Ghent', *Memo from Belgium* no. 97 (Brussels, 1968), 1-14.

Lancel, Serge, ' "Curiositas" et préoccupations spirituelles chez Apulée', *Rev. Hist. Rel.* 160 (1961), 25-46. Also tr. by Gerhard Binder in *Amor und Psyche* ed. Merkelbach and Binder (Darmstadt, 1968), 408-432.

Landström, Björn. *Ships of the Pharaohs.* (London, 1970).

Lanzone, R. V. *Le Domicile des Eprits. Papyrus du Musée de Turin publié en facsimile.* (Paris, 1879).

Latte, Kurt. *Die Religion der Römer und der Synkretismus der Kaiserzeit.* Religionsgeschichtliches Lesebuch, ed. A. Bertholet, 5; Tübingen, 1927).

———. See also Abbreviated Refs.

Lavagnini, Bruno. *Le origine del romanzo greco. Annali della r. scuola normale superiore universitaria di Pisa* 28 (1922), 7-104.

———, *Studi sul romanzo greco.* (Biblioteca di cultura contemporanea, 27; Messina, 1950).

———. Ch. 2, on Apuleius, was reprinted from *Annali ...* 29 (Pisa, 1923).

Leclant, Jean, 'En quête de l'Égyptomanie', *Revue de l'art* 5 (1969), 82-88.

———. *Enquêtes sur les sacerdoces et les sanctuaires égyptiens à l'époque dite 'éthiopienne'* (*XXVe Dynastie*). (IFAO, BÉ 17; Cairo, 1954).

———. 'Fouilles et travaux en Égypte et au Soudan', esp. the last section. 'Découvertes d'objets égyptiens hors d'Égypte' in a series of reports in *Orientalia* 30 (1961), ff.

———. With Gisèle Clerc : *Inventaire Bibliographique des Isiaca*, I-II. (ÉPRO 18; Leiden, 1972, 1974).

———. 'Notes sur la propagation des cultes et monuments égyptiens, en occident, à à l'époque impériale', *BIFAO* 55 (1955), 173-179.

———. 'Reflets de l'Égypte dans la littérature latin d'après quelques publications récentes' (Résumé), *Rev. Ét. Lat.* 36 (1958), 81-85.

———. See also Abbreviated Refs.

Lefebvre, Gustave. *Le Tombeau de Petosiris*. 3 vols. (Cairo, 1923-24).

Leglay, Marcel. *Les religions orientales dans l'Afrique ancienne*. (Algiers, 1956).

Lehner, Hans. 'Orientalische Mysterienkulte im römischen Rheinland', *Bonner Jahrbücher* 129 (1924), 36-91.

Lehnert, Georg. 'Bericht über die Literatur zu Apuleius...', Bursian, *Jahresbericht* 171 (1915), 147-176.

Leipoldt, Johannes. *Die Frau in der antiken Welt und im Urchristentum*. (Ed. 2, Leipzig, 1955, 74).

——. *Von den Mysterien zur Kirche*. Gesammelte Aufsätze. (Hamburg, 1962).

——. with Morenz, Siegfried. *Heilige Schriften*. (Leipzig, 1953).

——. with Regling, Kurt. 'Archäologisches zur Isisreligion', *Angelos* 1 (1925), 126-130.

——. See also Grundmann, Walter, and Abbreviated Refs.

Leky, Maximilianus. *De Syntaxi Apuleiana*. (Berne, 1908).

Lenormant, Fr. 'Cista Mystica', *Dar.-Sag.* (1877), 1205-1208.

Lersch, L. 'Isis und ihr heiliges Schiff', *Bonner Jahrbücher* 9 (1846), 100-115.

Lesky, Albin. 'Apuleius von Madaura und Lukios von Patrai', *Hermes* 76 (1941), 43-74; also in *Gesamm. Schr.* 549-579.

——. *Gesammelte Schriften*. (Bern, 1966).

Levi, Alda, 'L'Iside Barberini', *Monumenti Antichi* 28 (1922-23), col. 157-170.

Levi, Doro. *Antioch Mosaic Pavements*. 2 vols. (Princeton, 1947).

——. 'Mors Voluntaria : Mystery Cults on Mosaics from Antioch', *Berytus* 7 (1942), 19-55.

Lévy, Is. 'La légende d'Osiris et Isis chez Sénèque', *Latomus* 10 (1951), 147-162.

Lichtheim, Miriam. 'Situla No. 11395 and Some Remarks on Egyptian Situlae. Oriental Institute Museum Notes', *JNES* 6 (1947), 169-179.

Liebenam, W. *Städtverwaltung im römischen Kaiserreiche*. (Leipzig, 1900).

——. *Zur Geschichte und Organisation des römischen Vereinswesens*. (Leipzig, 1890).

Lindsay, Jack, *Daily Life in Roman Egypt*, (London, 1963).

——. *The Golden Ass of Apuleius* (New York, 1932 ; also London, 1960 and Indiana U.P. 1962).

——. *Leisure and Pleasure in Roman Egypt* (London, 1965).

——. *Men and Gods on the Roman Nile*. (London, 1968).

Löfstedt, Einar. *Late Latin*. (Inst. for Sammenlignende Kulturforskning, Ser. A, 25; Oslo, 1959).

——. *Spätlateinische Studien*. (Uppsala, 1908).

——. *Syntactica*. 2 vols. (Ed. 2, Lund, 1956).

Loew, E. A. See Lowe, E. A.

Loisy, Alfred. *Les mystères païens et le mystère Chrétien*. (Paris, 1919).

Longo, Vincenzo. *Aretalogie nel Mondo Greco. I. Epigrafi e Papiri*. (Genoa, 1969).

L'Orange, H. P. 'Das Geburtsritual der Pharaonen am römischen Kaiserhof', *Symb. Osl.* 21 (1941), 105-116.

Louueau, I. (d'Orleans). *Luc. Apulee De l'Ane Dore, XI Livres*. Traduit en François. (Paris, 1584).

Lowe, E. A. (= Loew in the first work listed).

———. *The Beneventan Script. A History of the South Italian Minuscule.* Oxford, 1914).

———. 'The Unique Manuscript of Apuleius' *Metamorphoses* (Laurentian. 68. 2) and its Oldest Transcript (Laurentian. 29.2)', *CQ* 14 (1920), 150-155.

Lübker, Friedrich. 'Apuleius' in *Reallexikon des klassischen Altertums* (Ed. 8, rev. J. Geffcken and E. Ziebarth, Leipzig, 1914), 89-91.

Lüddeckens, Erich. *Untersuchungen über religiösen Gehalt, Sprache und Form der ägyptischen Totenklagen, MDAIK* 11 (1943).

Luiselli, Bruno. *Tertulliani De Baptismo.* Ed. comm. (Corpus Scriptorum Latinorum Paravianum; Turin, 1969).

MacKay, L, A. 'The Sin of the Golden Ass', *Arion* 4 (1965), 474-480.

Macleod, M. D. *Lucian*, Vol. 8. esp. pp. 47-145 ('Lucius or the Ass'). (Loeb Classical Library, London 1967).

Magie, David. 'Egyptian Deities in Asia Minor in Inscriptions and on Coins', *AJA* 57 (1953), 163-187.

Malaise, Michel. *Inventaire préliminaire des documents égyptiens découverts en Italie.* (ÉPRO 21; Leiden, 1972).

———. *Les Conditions de pénétration et de diffusion des cultes égyptiens en Italie.* (ÉPRO 22; Leiden, 1972).

Mancini, Gioacchino. *Hadrian's Villa and Villa d'Este.* (Rome, 1950).

Mason, H. J. 'Lucius at Corinth', *Phoenix* 25 (1971), 160-165.

Matz, Friedrich. *ΔΙΟΝΥΣΙΑΚΗ-ΤΕΛΕΤΗ.* (Abh. Mainz, 1963. Wiesbaden, 1964).

Mau, August. 'Cista', *PW* (1899), 2591-2606.

———. tr. F. W. Kelsey. *Pompeii : Its Life and Art.* (New York, 1899).

Mazzarino, Antonio. *La Milesia e Apuleio.* (Turin, 1950).

McDermott, William Coffmann. *The Ape in Antiquity.* (John Hopkins University Studies in Archaeology, 27; Baltimore, 1938).

Médan, Pierre. *Le Livre XI des Métamorphoses d'Apulée. Ce qu'étaient les mystères d'Isis.* (Paris, 1927).

———. See also Abbreviated Refs.

Meier, C. A. tr. M. Curtis. *Ancient Incubation and Modern Psychotherapy.* (Studies from the C. G. Jung Institute, Zürich; Evanston, 1967).

Meiggs, Russell. *Roman Ostia.* (2nd ed. Oxford, 1973).

Mele, Salvatore. *Apuleio e l'Asino d'Oro. Saggio Critico.* (Turin, 1894).

Mensching, Gustav. *Das heilige Schweigen.* (RGVV 22, 2; Giessen, 1926).

Menzel, Hermannus. *De Lucio Patrensi sive quae inter Lucianeum librum qui ΛΟΥΚΙΟΣ Η ΟΝΟΣ inscribitur et Apulei Metamorphoseon libros intercedat ratio.*

Merkelbach, Reinhold. see Binder, Gerhard for *Amor und Psyche.*

———. 'Der Eid der Isismysten und die Zauberpapyri', résumé in *Annales Universitatis Saraviensis* (Saarbrücken) 8 (1959), 51-52.

———. 'Der Eid der Isismysten', *ZPE* 1 (1967), 54-73.

———. 'Ein Griechisch-Ägyptischer Priestereid und das Totenbuch' in *Rel. en Égypte,* ed. Ph. Derchain (Paris, 1969), 69-73.

———. 'Inhalt und Form in symbolischen Erzählungen der Antike' in *Eranos Jb.* 35 (1966), 145-175.

——. *Isisfeste in griechisch-römischer Zeit* : *Daten und Riten.* (Beiträge zur klassischen Philologie, 5; Meisenheim am Glan, 1963).

——. 'Der Isiskult in Pompei', *Latomus* 24 (1965), 144-149.

——. 'La nuovo pagina di Sisenna ed Apuleio', *Maia* 5 (1952), 234-241.

——. 'Das Osiris-Fest des 24./25. Dezember in Rom', *Aegyptus* 49 (1969), 89-91.

——. *Roman und Mysterium in der Antike.* (Munich, 1962).

——. 'Zwei Texte aus dem Serapeum zu Thessalonike', *ZPE* 10 (1973), 45-5 4.

Merzagora, Maria. 'La navigazione in Egitto nell'età greco-romana', *Aegyptus* 10 (1929), 105-148.

Mette, Hans Joachim, 'Curiositas', *FS. Bruno Snell* (Munich, 1956), 227-235.

Meulenaere, H. de. *Le Surnom égyptien à la basse époque.* (Uitgaven van het Nederlands Hist.-Arch. Inst. te Istanbul, 19. 1966).

Michel, Guill. *Lucius Apuleii de Lasne dore autrement dit de la Couronne Ceres ...* Tr. (Paris, 1522).

Milne, J. G. *Catalogue of Alexandrian Coins.* (Oxford, 1933).

Misch, Georg. *Geschichte der Autobiographie*, I, 2 (Ed. 3, Bern, 1950).

Mittelhaus, Karl. 'Kanopites', *PW* (1919), 1878-1881.

Molt, Margaretha. 'De vocabuli "Denique" apud Apuleium usu', *Mnemosyne* 11 (1943), 129-132. (By M. Helbers-Molt). See also Abbreviated Refs.

Monceaux, Paul. *Les Africains.* (Paris, 1894).

——. *Apulée. Roman et Magie.* (Paris, n.d.; before 1889).

Mordtmann, A. Jr. 'Monuments relatifs au culte d'Isis à Cyzique', *Rev. Arch.* N.S. 37 (1879), 257-262.

Morenz, Siegfried. 'Ägyptische Nationalreligion und sogenannte Isismission', *ZDMG* 111 (1961), 432-436.

——. *Altägyptischer Jenseitsführer. P. Berlin 3127.* (Leipzig, 1964).

——. *Die Begegnung Europas mit Ägypten.* (Sitzb. Leipzig,; Berlin, 1968).

——. with Dieter Müller : *Untersuchungen zur Rolle des Schicksals in der Ägyptischen Religion.* (Abh. Leipzig; Berlin, 1960).

——. 'Das Werden zu Osiris', *Forschungen und Berichte* I (Berlin, 1957), 52-70. See also Leipoldt, J. and Abbreviated Refs.

Moret, Alexandre. *Rois et dieux d'Égypte.* (Ed. 2, Paris, 1923).

——. *Sarcophages de l'époque bubastite à l'époque Saïte.* (CCG; Cairo, 1913).

Mosca, Bruno. *Apuleio : Apologia.* Tradotta e commentata. (Florence, 1939).

Moscati, S. *The World of the Phoenicians.* (London, 1965, repr. 1968).

[Moutlyard, J. de] *Les Metamorphoses ou l'Asne D'or de L'Apulée.* (Paris, 1648).

Movers, F. C. *Die Phönizier.* (Berlin, 1850).

Müller, Dieter. See Abbreviated Refs.

——. See Morenz, Siegfried (with) for *Unteruchungen zur Rolle des Schicksals usw.*

——. Review of J. Bergman, *Ich bin Isis* in *OLZ* 67 (1972), 118-130. (by Dieter Mueller).

Müller, Hans Wolfgang. See Abbreviated Refs.

——. *Der Isiskult im antiken Benevent und Katalog der Skulpturen aus den ägyptischen Heiligtümern im Museo del Sannio zu Benevent.* (MÄR 16; Berlin, 1969).

Münster, Maria. See Abbreviated Refs.

Mylonas, George E. *Eleusis and the Eleusinian Mysteries.* (Princeton, 1961).

Nägelsbach, Karl Friederich von. *Lateinische Stilistik.* (Ed. 9, Nürnberg, 1905; repr. Darmstadt, 1963).

Nehring, A. 'Don't monkey with the donkey!' *Classical Weekly* 45 (1952), 229-230.

Nethercut, William R. 'Apuleius' Literary Art : Resonance and Depth in the *Metamorphoses*', *Classical Journal* 64 (1968), 110-119.

Neue, Friedrich. *Formenlehre der Lateinischen Sprache.* Ed. 3, rev. C. Wagener. 4 vols. (Leipzig, 1902-).

Neumann, Ioannes. *De quinquennalibus coloniarum et municipiorum.* (Diss. Leipzig, 1892).

Nilsson, Martin P. 'The Bacchic Mysteries of the Roman Age', *Harv. Theol. Rev.* 46 (1953), 175-202.

——, 'Lampen und Kerzen im Kult der Antike', *Opuscula Archaeologica* 6 (1950), 96-111.

——. 'Studien zur Vorgeschichte des Weihnachtsfestes', *Arch. Rel.* 19 (1916-19), 50-150.

——. See also Abbreviated Refs.

Nisard, M. *Pétrone, Apulée, Aulu-Gelle, œuvres complètes avec la traduction en français.* (Paris, 1851; also 1875).

Nock, A. D. 'The Christian *Sacramentum* in Pliny and a Pagan Counterpart', *CR* 38 (1924), 58 f.

——. *Conversion.* (Oxford, 1933).

——. with Festugière, A.-J. *Corpus Hermeticum.* 4 vols. (Paris, 1945-54).

——. *Early Gentile Christianity and its Hellenistic Background.* (1928 and 1952 (in part); repr. New York, 1964).

——. See also Abbreviated Refs.

Norden, Eduard. *Agnostos Theos.* (Leipzig, 1923).

——. *Die antike Kunstprosa.* 2 vols. (Leipzig, 1898, repr. Darmstadt, 1958).

——. *Die Geburt des Kindes.* (Leipzig, 1924).

Norden, Fritz. *Apulejus von Madaura und das römische Privatrecht.* (Leipzig, 1912).

Norwood, Frances. 'The Magic Pilgrimage of Apuleius', *Phoenix* 10 (1956), 1-12.

Nováková, Julie. 'Die Apulejanische Wortzerlegung und ein ἅπαξ λεγόμενον', *Charisteria Francisco Novotný* (Prague, 1962), 107-109.

Oldfather, William Abbott. see Abbreviated Refs.

Otto, A. *Die Sprichwörter und sprichwörtlichen Redensarten der Römer.* (Leipzig, 1890, repr. Hildesheim, 1962).

Otto, Eberhard. *Das ägyptische Mundöffnungsritual.* 2 vols. (Ägyptologische Abh.; Wiesbaden, 1960).

——. 'Eine Darstellung der "Osiris-Mysterien" in Theben', *FS. Siegfried Schott*, ed. W. Helck (Wiesbaden, 1968), 99-105.

——. See also Abbreviated Refs.

Otto, Walter. *Ägyptische Priestersynoden in hellenistischer Zeit.* (Sitzb. Munich, 1926).

——. *Beiträge zur Hierodulie im hellenistischen Ägypten.* cur. Fr. Zucker. (Abh. Munich, 1950).

——. See also Abbreviated Refs.

Otto, Walter F. *Dionysos* : *Mythos und Kultus.* (Frankfurter Studien zur Rel. und Kultur der Antike, 4; Ed. 3, Frankfurt am Main, 1960).

Paardt, R. T. van der. See Abbreviated Refs.

Pagenstecher, Rudolf. *Die griechisch-ägyptische Sammlung Ernst von Sieglin.* I. *Malerei und Plastik.* A. (Expedition Ernst von Sieglin, Ausgrabungen in Alexandria, Bd. II; 1. Leipzig, 1923).

Panofsky, Erwin. ' "Canopus Deus" : the Iconography of a Non-Existent God', *Gazette des Beaux-Arts* 57 (1961), 193-216.

Paratore, Ettore. *La Novella in Apuleio.* (Ed. 2, Palermo, 1942).

——. 'La prosa di Apuleio', *Maia* 1 (1948), 33-47.

Parker, Richard A. *A Saïte Oracle Papyrus from Thebes.* with a chapter by J. Černý. (Brown Egyptological Studies, 4; Brown U. P., 1962).

Parlasca, Klaus. 'Osiris und Osirisglaube in der Kaiserzeit', *Les Syncrétismes dans les religions grecque et romaine* (Paris, 1973), 95-102.

——. *Repertorio d'Arte dell'Egitto Greco-Romano*, a cura du A. Adriani. Ser. B. Vol. I. (Palermo, 1969).

——. See also Abbreviated Refs.

Pascher, Joseph. *Η ΒΑΣΙΛΙΚΗ ΟΔΟΣ. Der Königsweg* zu Wiedergeburt und Vergottung bei Philon von Alexandreia. (Studien zur Geschichte und Kultur des Altertums, 17, 3-3; Paderborn, 1931).

Peek, Werner. *Griechische Grabgedichte.* (Schr. und Quellen der alten Welt, 7; Berlin, 1960).

——. See also Abbreviated Refs.

Pelekides, S. *ΑΠΟ ΤΗΝ ΠΟΛΙΤΕΙΑ ΚΑΙ ΤΗΝ ΚΟΙΝΩΝΙΑ ΤΗΣ ΑΡΧΑΙΑΣ ΘΕΣΣΑΛΟΝΙΚΗΣ.* (Thessalonikê, 1934).

Pepe, L. 'Lucio di Patrae o Aristide?' *Giornale Italiano di Filologia* 16 (1963), 111-142.

Perdrizet, Paul. 'Inscriptions de Philippes : Les Rosalies', *BCH* 24 (1900), 299-323.

——. 'Les représentations d'Anoubis dans l'imagerie gréco-égyptienne', *Revue Égyptologique* n.s. 1 (1919), 185-190.

——. See also Abbreviated Refs.

Peremans, W. and Van 't Dack, E. *Prosopographia Ptolemaica.* = *Studia Hellenistica* 6 (1950); 8 (1952); 9 (1953; *Prosopographica*); 11 (1956); 12 (1959); 13 (1963); 17 (1968; with L. Mooren and W. Swinnen).

Pernice, Erich. *Pavimente und figürliche Mosaiken.* (Die hellenistische Kunst in Pompeji, Bd. 6; Berlin, 1938).

Pesce, Gennaro. *Il tempio d'Iside in Sabratha.* (Monografie di Archeologia Libica, 4; Rome, 1953).

Perry, Ben Edwin. *The Ancient Romances.* (Sather Classical Lectures, 37; Berkeley, 1967).

—— 'An Interpretation of Apuleius' *Metamorphoses*', *TAPA* 57 (1926), 238-260.

——. *The Metamorphoses Ascribed to Lucius of Patrae. Its content, nature, and authorship*. (Lancaster, Pa. 1920).

——. 'Some Aspects of the Literary Art of Apuleius in the *Metamorphoses*', *TAPA* 54 (1923), 196-226.

——. Who was Lucius of Patrae?', *Classical Journal* 64 (1968), 97-101.

——. see also Oldfather, William Abbott.

Pettazzoni, Raffaele. *Essays in the History of Religions*. tr. H. J. Rose. (Leiden, 1954).

Pfister, Friedrich. Review of H. Riefstahl, *Der Roman des Apuleius* (1938), *Philologische Wochenschrift* 60 (1940), 533-541.

Picard, Charles, 'L'Anubis Alexandrin du Musée d'Alger', *Studi in Onore di A. Calderini e R. Paribeni*, III (Milan, 1956), 171-181.

Piechotta, Ioannes. *Curae Apuleianae*. (Diss. Bratislava, 1882).

Pietrangeli, Carlo. *Musei Capitolini : I Monumenti dei culti orientali*. (Rome, 1951.)

Places, Édouard des. 'Hymnes grecs au seuil de l'ère chrétienne', *Biblica* 38 (1957), 113-29.

Pietschmann, Richard. 'Anubis', *PW* (1894), 2645-2649.

Poland, Franz, *Geschichte des griechischen Vereinswesens*. (Leipzig, 1909).

Pollitt, J. J. 'The Egyptian Gods in Attica : Some Epigraphical Evidence', *Hesperia* 34 (1965), 125-130.

Poole, Reginald Stuart. *Cat. of the Greek Coins in the British Museum. Alexandria and the Nomes*. (London, 1892).

Posener, Georges. with Sauneron, S. and Yoyotte, Jean. *A Dictionary of Egyptian Civilisation*. (London, 1962).

Pouilloux, J. *La Forteresse de Rhamnoute*. (Paris, 1954).

Préaux, Claire. *La lune dans la pensée grecque*. (Acad. Roy. de Belgique. Mém. Lettres, 2e Série, 61, 4. Brussels, 1973).

Préaux, Jean-G. 'Deus Christianorum *Onocoetes*', *Hommages à Léon Hermann* (Coll. Latomus 44; Brussels, 1966), 639-654.

Preisendanz, Karl. ed. *Papyri Graecae Magicae*. 2 vols. (Leipzig, 1928 and 1931).

Du Prel, Carl. *Die Mystik der alten Griechen*. (Leipzig, 1888).

Purser, Louis C. See Abbreviated Refs.

Rachewiltz, Boris de. tr. R. H. Boothroyd. *Egyptian Art*. An Introduction. (London, 1960).

——. tr. R. H. Boothroyd. *An Introduction to Egyptian Art*. (London, 1966, repr. 1967).

——. 'Le Situle e la rigenerazione cosmica in Egitto e in Mesopotamia', *Archivio Internazionale di Etnografia e Preistoria* 1 (1958), 69-95.

Rademacher, Carl. 'Carnival', Hastings *ERE* 3 (1932), 225-229.

Rahner, Hugo. tr. B. Battershaw. *Greek Myths and Christian Mystery*. (London, 1963).

Ramage, Edwin S. See Scranton, Robert L.

Rattenbury, R. M. 'Romance : The Greek Novel' in *New Chapters in the History of Greek Literature*, III (ed. J. U. Powell, Oxford, 1933), 211-257.

Rayfield, J. R. *The Languages of a Bilingual Community*. (Janua Linguarum, Series Practica, 77; The Hague, 1970).

Reardon, B. P. 'The Greek Novel', *Phoenix* 23 (1969), 291-309.

——. *Courants littéraires grecs des IIe et IIIe siècles après J.-C.* (Annales littéraires de l'Université de Nantes, 3. Paris, 1971.)

Regen, Frank. *Apuleius philosophus Platonicus.* Untersuchungen zur antiken Literatur und Geschichte, 10. (Berlin, 1971).

Regling, Kurt. See Leipoldt, Johannes.

Rehm, A. 'Kanopos', *PW* (1919), 1881-1883.

Reich, Nathaniel Julius. 'An Abbreviated Demotic Book of the Dead', (P. BM 10072), *JEA* 17 (1931), 85-97.

Reitzenstein, R. 'Eros als Osiris', Nachr. Götttingen 1930, 396-399.

——. *Hellenistische Wundererzählungen* (Leipzig, 1906, repr. Stuttgart, 1963).

——. *Poimandres* .(Leipzig, 1904).

——. 'Zum Asclepius des Pseudo-Apuleius', *Arch. Rel.* 7 (1904), 393-411.

——. *Zwei religionsgeschichtliche Fragen.* (Strassburg, 1901).

——. See also Abbreviated Refs.

Richardson, N. J. *The Homeric Hymn to Demeter.* (Oxford, 1974).

Riefstahl, Hermann. *Der Roman des Apuleius.* Beitrag zur Romantheorie. (Frankfurter Studien zur Rel. und Kultur der Antike, 15; Frankfurt am Main, 1938).

Robertson, D. S. 'Lucius of Madaura : a Difficulty in Apuleius', *CQ* 4 (1910), 221-227.

——. 'The Assisi Fragments of the *Apologia* of Apuleius', *CQ* n.s. 6 (1956), 68-80.

Roeder, Günther. *Ägyptische Bronzewerke.* (Pelizaeus-Mus. zu Hildesheim, Wissensch. Veröffentlichung 3; Glückstadt, 1937).

——. 'Die Blumen der Isis von Philä', *ZÄS* 48 (1910), 115-122.

——. with Ippel, Albert : *Die Denkmäler des Pelizaeus-Museums zu Hildesheim.* (Berlin, 1921).

——. See also Abbreviated Refs.

Rölling, Wolfgang. see Friederich, Johannes.

Rohde, Erwin. *Der griechische Roman und seine Vorläufer.* (1873; Ed. 3, Leipzig, 1914; repr. Hildesheim, 1960).

——. *Ueber Lucians Schrift ΛΟΥΚΙΟΣ Η ΟΝΟΣ und ihrer Verhaltniss zu Lucius von Patrae und den Metamorphosen des Apulejus.* (Leipzig, 1869).

——. 'Zu Apuleius', *Kleine Schriften*, II (Tübingen, 1901), 43-74 (first in 1885).

Romanelli, Pietro. *Storia delle province Romane dell'Africa.* (Rome, 1959).

Roncaioli, C. 'Le accezioni di *bonus* nelle *Metamorfosi* di Apuleio', *Giornale Italiano di Filologia* 16 (1963), 229-237.

Roscher, W. H. See Abbreviated Refs.

Rose, H. J. See Abbreviated Refs.

Rougé, Jean, *Recherches sur l'organisation du commerce maritime en Méditerranée sous l'empire romain.* (École pratique des hautes études. — VIe Section. XXI; Paris, 1966).

Roullet, Anne. see Abbreviated Refs.

Roussel, Pierre. see Abbreviated Refs.

Rusch, A. *De Serapide et Iside in Graecia cultis.* (Berlin, 1906).

——. 'Lychnapsia', *PW* s.v. (1940, Suppl. 7), 420-423.

Ryle, Stephen Francis. see Abbreviated Refs.

Saint-Denis, E. de. 'Mare Clausum', *Rev. Ét. Lat.* 25 (1947), 196 -214.

Salač, Antonin, *Isis, Sarapis a Božstva Sdružená.* (Prague, 1915).

Saldit-Trappmann, Regina. See Abbreviated Refs.

Salem, M. S. 'The *Lychnapsia Philocaliana* and the birthday of Isis', *JRS* 27 (1937), 165-167.

———. See also Abbreviated Refs.

Samman-El, Achmet Ph. Αἱ Αἰγυπτιακαὶ Λατρεῖαι ἐν Ἑλλάδι. (Athens, 1965).

Samuel, Alan Edouard. *Ptolemaic Chronology.* (Münchener Beiträge zur Papyrus-forschung usw. 43; Munich, 1962).

———. Review of Merkelbach, *Isisfeste, Bibl. Orient.* 23 (1966), 38-43.

San Nicolò, Mariano. *Ägyptisches Vereinswesen zur Zeit der Ptolemäer und Römer.* 2 vols. (Munich, 1913).

Sandy, G. N. 'Knowledge and Curiosity in Apuleius' *Metamorphoses*', *Latomas* 31 (1972), 179-183.

Sauneron, Serge. *Les Fêtes Religieuses d'Esna aux derniers siècles du paganisme.* (IFAO, Esna V; Cairo, 1962).

———. 'Les songes et leur interprétation dans l'Égypte ancienne' in *Les Songes et leur Interprétation (Sources Orientales,* II, Paris, 1959), 17-61.

———. See also Abbreviated Refs.

Savignac, J. de. 'La rosée solaire de l'ancienne Égypte', *La Nouvelle Clio* 6 (Mél. R. Goossens, 1954), 345-353.

Schäfer, Heinrich. *Die Mysterien des Osiris in Abydos unter König Sesostris III.* (Untersuchungen, 4. 2; Leipzig, 1904).

———. See also Abbreviated Refs.

Schaller, Gualterus. *De Fabula Apuleiana quae est de Psycha et Cupidine.* (Leipzig, 1901).

Schanz. M.; Hosius, C.; Krüger, G. See Abbreviated Refs.

Schede, Martin. 'Isis-Prozession', *Angelos* 2 (1926), 60-61.

Schefold, Karl. 'Helena im Schutz der Isis', FS. D. M. Robinson, II (Saint Louis, 1953), 1096-1102.

———. *Orient, Hellas und Rom.* (Wissensch. Forschungsberichte, 15; Bern, 1949).

———. *La peinture pompéienne. Essai sur l'évolution de sa signification.* (Coll. Latomus, 108; Brussels, 1972).

———. *Pompejanische Malerei. Sinn und Ideengeschichte.* (Basel, 1952).

———. 'Zur hellenistischen Theologie Alexandrias', *Antidôron. Edgar Salin* (Tübingen, 1962), 167-181.

———. *Vergessenes Pompeji.* (Bern, 1962).

———. *Die Wände Pompejis. Topographisches Verzeichnis der Bildmotive.* (Berlin, 1957).

———. *Wort und Bild.* (Basel, 1975).

Schissel von Fleschenberg, Otmar. *Die Griechische Novelle.* (Halle, 1913).

Schlam, Carl C. 'The Curiosity of the Golden Ass', *Classical Journal* 64 (1968), 102-125.

———. 'Platonica in the *Metamorphoses* of Apuleius', *TAPA* 101 (1970), 477-487.

——. 'The Scholarship on Apuleius since 1938', *Classical World* 64 (1971), 285-309.

Schober, Ernestus. See Abbreviated Refs.

Schott, Siegfried. *Altägyptische Festdaten*. (Abh. Mainz, 1950).

——. *Die Reinigung Pharos in einem memphitischen Tempel* (Berlin P. 13242). (Nachr. Göttingen, 1957).

Schreiber, Theodor. *Die Nekropole von Kôm-esch-Schukâfa*. Expedition Sieglin, I. (Leipzig, 1908).

Schröeder, J. A. *De Amoris et Psyches Fabella A puleiana Nova Quadam Ratione Explicata*. (Amsterdam, 1916),

Schubart, W. 'Rom und die Ägypter nach dem Gnomon des Idios Logos', *ZÄS* 56 (1920), 80-95.

Schuman, Verne B. 'A Second-Century Treatise on Egyptian Priests and Temples', *Harv. Theol. Rev.* 53 (1960), 159-170.

Schwabe, L. von .'Apuleius von Madaura', *PW* (1896), 246-258.

Schwartz, Eduard. *Fünf Vorträge über den Griechischen Roman*. (Ed. 2, Berlin, 1945).

Scioppius, Casp. *Symbola Critica in L. Apuleji... Opera*. (Amsterdam, 1664).

Scobie, Alexander. *Aspects of the Ancient Romance and its Heritage*. (Beiträge zur klassischen Philologie, 30; Meisenheim am Glan, 1969).

——. *More Essays on the Ancient Romance and its Heritage*. (Beiträge usw. 46. Meisenheim am Glan, 1973).

Scranton, Robert L. 'Glass Pictures from the Sea', *Archaeology* 20 (1967), 163-173.

——. with Ramage, Edwin S. 'Investigations at Corinthian Kenchreai', *Hesperia* 36 (1967), 124-186.

——. with Ramage, Edwin S. 'Investigations at Kenchreai, 1963', *Hesperia* 33 (1964), 134-145.

Shore, A. F. 'A Drinking-Cup with Demotic Inscription', *British Museum Quarterly* 36 (1971), 16-19.

——. *Portrait Painting from Roman Egypt*. (London, 1962).

Sichtermann, H. 'Ganymed', *Encic. dell'Arte Antica Classica Orientale*, III. (Rome, 1960), 788-90.

Simon, Marcel. 'Apulée et le christianisme'. *Mélanges d'histoire des religions offerts à Henri-Charles Puech*. (Paris, 1974), 299-305.

Simpson, William Kelly, ed. *The Literature of Ancient Egypt*. (Yale U.P., 1972).

Sinko, Thaddeus. 'Apuleiana', *Eos* 18 (1912), 137-167.

Sittl, Karl. *Die lokalen Verschiedenheiten der lateinischen Sprache mit besonderer Berücksichtigung des afrikanischen Lateins*. (Erlangen, 1882).

Skemp. J. B. *The Greeks and the Gospel*. (London, 1964).

Smith, J. P. See Wagner, Günter.

Snowden, Frank M. Jr.. 'Ethiopians and the Isiac Worship', *Ant. Class.* 25 (1956), 112-116.

Sokolowski, Franciszek. *Lois sacrées de l'Asie mineure*. (École française d'Athènes, Trav. et Mém., 9; Paris, 1955, suppl. vol. Paris, 1962).

——. 'On the Rules regulating the celebration of the Eleusinian Mysteries', *Harv. Theol. Rev.* 22 (1959), 1-7.

Souter, A. ' "Zatchlas" in Apuleius', *JTS* 37 (1936), 80.

Spiegelberg, Wilhelm. 'Ein Denkstein auf den Tod einer heiligen Isiskuh', *ZÄS* 43 (1906), 129-135.

——. *Die Novelle im alten Aegypten. Ein litterar-historischer Essay.* (Strassburg, 1898).

Squarciapino, Maria Floriani. *I Culti Orientali ad Ostia.* (ÉPRO 3; Leiden, 1962).

Stambaugh, John E. *Sarapis under the Early Ptolemies.* (ÉPRO 25; Leiden, 1972).

Stemler, David. *Disputationem circularem de L. APULEJO MAD... proponit David Stemler Neustadiensis...* (H. Meyer (Leipzig ?), 1691).

Stephenson, William E. 'The Comedy of Evil in Apuleius', *Arion* 3 (1964), 87-93.

Stracmans, M. 'Osiris-Dionysos et les chants de harpistes égyptiens', *Le Muséon* 59 (1946), 207-214.

Strangeways, L. R. and Wood, R. S. *Stories from Apuleius.* (London, 1910).

Sullivan, J. P. *The Satyricon of Petronius.* (London, 1968).

Summers, Richard G. 'Apuleius' Juridicus', *Historia* 21 (1972), 120-126.

Szentléleky, Tihamér. 'Die Bedeutung des Iseums in Savaria', *Savaria Mus. Bull.* 3 (1965), 153-158.

——. *Das Isis-Heiligtum von Szombathely.* (Szombathely, 1965).

——. 'Architektonische Herausbildung und Entwicklung der Iseen in Ägypten, ihre Auswirkungen in Pannonien', *Anta Ant. Hung.* 15 (1967), 457-466.

Tatum, James. 'Apuleius and Metamorphosis', *American Journal of Philology* 93 (1972), 306-313.

Taylor, Lily Ross. *The Cults of Ostia.* (Bryn Mawr Coll. Monographs, 11; Bryn Mawr, 1912).

Taylor, Thomas. *The Metamorphosis, or Golden Ass, and Philosophical Works of Apuleius.* Translated. (London, 1822).

Teuffel, W. S. *Geschichte der römischen Literatur*, III. rev. W. Kroll and F. Skutsch (W. Kroll on Apuleius). (Ed. 6, Leipzig, 1913).

Thibau, R. 'Les Métamorphoses d'Apulée et la Théorie Platonicienne de l'Erôs', *Studia Philosophica Gandensia* 3 (Gent, 1965), 89-144.

Thiel, Helmut van. *Der Eselsroman.* I. *Untersuchungen.* II. *Synoptische Ausgabe.* (Zetemata, 54, 1-2; Munich 1971-2).

Thomas, Paul. 'Quelques notes sur les 'Métamorphoses' d'Apulée', Académie Royale de Belgique, Bull. 5e Série, Tome 14, pp. 214-221 (Brussels, 1928).

Todd, F. A. *Some Ancient Novels. Leucippe and Clitophon*; *Daphnis and Chloe*; *The Satiricon*; *The Golden Ass.* (Oxford, 1940).

Torr, Cecil. *Ancient Ships.* (Chicago, 1964).

Touny, A. D. and Wenig, Steffen. *Der Sport im alten Ägypten.* (Leipzig, 1969).

Toynbee, J. M. C. *Animals in Roman Life and Art.* (London, 1973).

——. *A Silver Casket and Strainer from the Walbrook Mithraeum in the City of London.* (ÉPRO 4; Leiden, 1963).

Tran Tam Tinh, V. *Le Culte des divinités orientales en Campanie.* (ÉPRO 17; Leiden, 1972).

——. With Labrecque, Yvette. *Isis Lactans.* (ÉPRO 37; Leiden, 1973).

——. 'Une statuette d'Isis-Ourania', *Rev. Arch.* (1970), 2, 283-96.

——. Le "Tibicen Magno Sarapi" ', *Rev. arch.* 1967, 101-112.

——. See also Abbreviated Refs.

Trencsény-Waldapfel, Imre. 'Ägyptische Motive in der lateinischen Poesie des goldenen Zeitalters', *Savaria* 3 (1965), 125-139. (The German summarizes a study in Hungarian.)

——. 'Das Rosenmotiv ausserhalb des Eselromans' in *Beiträge zur alten Geschichte und deren Nachleben* (FS. F. Altheim), 512-517. (Berlin, 1969).

——. *Untersuchungen zur Religionsgeschichte.* (Amsterdam, 1966).

Trenkner, Sophie. *The Greek Novella in the Classical Period.* (Cambridge, 1958).

Tschudin, Peter Friedrich. *Isis in Rom.* (Diss. Basel; Aarau, 1962).

Tudor, D. *Corpus Monumentorum Religionis Equitum Danuvinorum (CMRED).* I. *The Monuments.* (ÉPRO 30; Leiden, 1969).

Turcan, Robert. 'Le roman "initiatique": à propos d'un livre récent', *Rev. Hist. Rel.* 163 (1963), 149-199.

——. *Sénèque et les religions orientales.* (Coll. Latomus, 91; Brussels, 1967).

Turchi, Nicolaus. See Abbreviated Refs.

——. *La Religione di Roma Antica.* (Storia di Roma, 18; Bologna, 1939).

——. 'I quattro inni di Isidoro', *Studi e materiali di storia delle religioni* 22 (1949-50), 139-148.

Uxkull-Gyllenband, Woldemar Graf. *Der Gnomon des Idios Logos. BGU* V. 2 (Kommentar; Berlin, 1934).

Vandebeek, G. See Abbreviated Refs.

Van 't Dack, E. See Peremans, W.

Vanderlip, Vera Frederika. *The Four Greek Hymns of Isidorus and the Cult of Isis.* (Amer. Studies in Papyrology, 12; Toronto, 1972).

Vandier, Jacques. *Le Papyrus Jumilhac.* (Paris, 1962).

Vermaseren, M. J. *The Legend of Attis in Greek and Roman Art.* (ÉPRO 9; Leiden, 1966).

——. *Mithras, the Secret God.* (London, 1963). The Dutch original was published in Amsterdam, 1959. Cf. *Mithra ce dieu mystérieux* (Paris,1960) and *Mithras, Geschichte eines Kultes* (Stuttgart, 1959).

——. *De Mithradienst in Rome.* (Nijmegen, 1951).

——. *Mithriaca.* I. *The Mithraeum at S. Maria Capua Vetere.* (ÉPRO 16; Leiden, 1971).

——. *Mithriaca.* II. *The Mithraeum at Ponza.* (ÉPRO 16; Leiden, 1974).

——. 'Paganism's Death Struggle : Religions in competition with Christianity', *The Crucible of Christianity* ed. Arnold Toynbee. (London, 1969), 235-60.

——. See also Abbreviated Refs.

Veyne, Paul. 'Apulée a Cenchrées', *Rev. Phil* 39 (1965), 241-251.

Visser, Elizabeth. *Götter und Kulte im ptolemäischen Alexandrien.* (Amsterdam, 1938).

Vizani, Pompeo. *L'Asino d'Oro di Lucio Apuleio.* Tradotto... da motti dishonesti purgato. (Venice, 1612).

Vliet, J. van der. 'Die Vorrede der Apuleïschen Metamorphosen', *Hermes* 32 (1897), 79-85.

Vogt, Joseph. *Die alexandrinischen Münzen.* 2 vols. (Stuttgart, 1924).

——. See also Abbreviated Refs.

Vokes, F. E. 'Zeno of Verona, Apuleius and Africa', *Studia Patristica* 8. 2 (1966), 130-136.

Wagenvoort, H. *Studies in Roman Literature, Culture and Religion.* (Leiden, 1956).

Wagner, Günter. See Abbreviated Refs.

Wallert, Ingrid. *Die Palmen im alten Ägypten.* (MÄS 1; Berlin, 1962).

Walsh, P. G. 'Lucius Madaurensis', *Phoenix* 22 (1968), 143-157.

——. *The Roman Novel.* The 'Satyricon' of Petronius and the 'Metamorphoses' of Apuleius. (Cambridge, 1970).

——. 'Was Lucius a Roman?' *Classical Journal* 63 (1968), 264-5.

——. Review of L. Callebat, *Sermo Cotidianus dans les Métamorphoses d'Apulée.* *CR* 22 (1972), 128.

Watzinger, Carl. *Die griechisch-ägyptische Sammlung Ernst von Sieglin. I. Malerei und Plastik. B.* (Expedition Ernst von Sieglin. Ausgrabungen in Alexandria. Bd. II. 1; Leipzig, 1927).

Weber, Wilhelm. *Aegyptisch-Griechische Götter im Hellenismus.* (Groningen, 1912).

——. *Drei Untersuchungen zur ägyptisch-griechischen Religion.* (Heidelberg, 1911).

——. See also Abbreviated Refs.

Weinhold, K. 'Über das Märchen vom Eselmenschen', Sitzb. Berlin 26 (1893), 475-488.

Weinreich, Otto. *Antike Heilungswunder.* (RGVV 8, 1; Giessen, 1909).

——. *Ausgewählte Schriften*, I (1907-1921) ed. G. Wille. (Amsterdam, 1969).

——. 'Gebet und Wunder. Zwei Abhandlungen zur Religions- und Literatur-Geschichte. I. Primitiver Gebetsegoismus. II. Türöffnung...' in *Genethliakon Wilhelm Schmid* (Tübinger Beiträge zur Altertumswissenschaft, 5; Stuttgart, 1929).

——. *Der griechische Liebesroman.* (Zürich, 1950, repr. 1962).

——. *Triskaidekadische Studien.* (RGVV 16, 1; Giessen, 1916).

——. 'Zu Apuleius', *Hermes* 56 (1921), 333-334.

——. 'Zur hellenistisch-ägyptischen Religionsgeschichte', *Aegyptus* 11 (1931), 13-22.

——. See also Abbreviated Refs.

Weinstock, Stefan. 'Victor and Invictus', *Harv. Theol. Rev.* 50 (1957), 211-247.

Welles, C. Bradford. 'The Discovery of Sarapis and the Foundation of Alexandria', *Historia* 11 (1962), 271-298; also ibid. 12 (1963), 512.

Wenig, Steffen and Touny, A. D. *Der Sport im alten Ägypten.* (Leipzig, 1969).

——. tr. B. Fischer. *The Woman in Egyptian Art.* (Leipzig, 1969).

Werner, Hans. 'Zum ΛΟΥΚΙΟΣ Η ΟΝΟΣ, *Hermes* 53 (1918), 225-261.

Wessetzky, Vilmos. 'Neuere Belege zur Bedeutung des Isiskultes in Pannonien', *MDAIK* 25 (1969), 198-201.

——. 'Zur Wertung des ägyptischen Totenkultes in Pannonien', *Acta Ant. Hung.* 15 (1967), 451-456.

——. See also Abbreviated Refs.

West, Stephanie. 'An Alleged Pagan Use of *ΑΓΑΠΗ* in P. Oxy. 1380', *JTS* 18 (1967), 142-143; also ibid. 20 (1969), 228-230.

——. '*Joseph and Asenath* : A Neglected Greek Romance', *CQ* n.s. 24 (1974), 70-81.

——. 'Notes on P. Oxy. 1381', *ZPE* 3 (1968), 159-160.

——. 'Notes on Some Romance Papyri', *ZPE* 7 (1971), 95-6.

Westendorf, Wolfhart. See Abbreviated Refs.

Wilcken, Ulrich. *Urkunden der Ptolemäerzeit.* 2 vols. (Berlin, 1927-57).

Wild, Henri. translator of A. Erman, *La Religion des Égyptiens.* (Paris, 1952).

Wilson, Thomas. *St. Paul and Paganism.* (Edinburgh, 1927).

Wiman, Gerhard. *Textkritiska studier till Apuleius.* (Göteborg, 1927).

Winter, Erich. with Junker, Hermann. *Das Geburtshaus des Tempels. der Isis in Philä.* (Denkschr. Wien, 1965).

——. *Untersuchungen zu den ägyptischen Tempelreliefs der griechisch-römischen Zeit.* (Denkschr, der österreich. Akad. 98; Vienna, 1968).

Witt, R. E. 'The Importance of Isis for the Fathers', *Studia Patristica* 8 (Berlin, 1966), 133-145.

——. See also Abbreviated Refs.

Wittmann, Willi. See Abbreviated Refs.

Wlosok, Antonie. 'Zur Einheit der Metamorphosen des Apuleius', *Philologus* 113 (1969), 68-84.

Wölfflin, Eduard. 'Die ersten Spuren des afrikanischen Lateins', *Arch. Lat. Lex.* 6 (1889), 1-7.

——. 'Der Genetivus comparationis und die präpositionalen Umschreibungen', *Arch. Lat. Lex.* 7 (1892), 115-131.

Wolterstorff, G. 'Artikelbedeutung von *ille* bei Apuleius', *Glotta* 8 (1916), 197-226.

Würfel, Reingart. 'Die Ägyptische Fabel in Bildkunst und Literatur', *Wissenschaftliche Zeitschrift der Universität Leipzig* 3 (1952-53), 63-77.

Youtie, Herbert C. 'The Heidelberg Festival Papyrus : A Reinterpretation' in *Studies in Roman Economic and Social History in Honor of Allen Chester Johnson* (Princeton, 1951), 178-208.

——. 'The *Kline* of Sarapis', *Harv. Theol. Rev.* 41 (1948), 9-29. Also in *Scriptiunculae*, I. (Amsterdam, 1973), 487 ff.

Yoyotte, Jean. 'Le Jugement des Morts dans l'Égypte ancienne' in *Sources Orientales* 4 (Paris, 1961), 17-80.

Zandee, Jan. *Death as an Enemy according to ancient Egyptian Conceptions.* (Suppl. *Numen*, 5; Leiden, 1960).

——. 'The Book of Gates' in *Liber Amicorum... C. J. Bleeker* (Leiden, 1969), 282-324.

——. 'Prayers to the Sun-god from Theban Tombs', *JEOL* 16 (1964), 48-71.

Ziebarth, Erich. *Das griechische Vereinswesen.* (Leipzig, 1896).

Zimmermann, Friedrich. See Abbreviated Refs.

Zotović, Ljubica. *Les Cultes orientaux sur le territoire de la Mésie supérieure.* (ÉPRO 7; Leiden, 1966).

Zuntz, G. *Persephone : Three Essays on Religion and Thought in Magna Graecia.* (Oxford, 1971).

GENERAL INDEX

References are to pages, save when the text is referred to, in which case the chapter number is given with the paragraph and line in brackets. References to the text precede the others.

Abaton, 211
Ablative of present participle in -i, 234; Ablative Absolute, with subject unexpressed, 239; of neuter adjective, with Genitive, 247; irregular Ablative Absolute, 285
Ablution, customary, in baths, begins initiation, 23 (284, 20 f.); 286 f.
Abstinence, hard rules of, 19 (281, 7 f.); 273; from unhallowed and unlawful foods, 21 (283, 12 f.); 281; ten days of, 23 (284, 24 ff.); 290; 28 (289, 20 f.); 55; 335; 355 f.
Abstractions, 59; 64; 250; 251; 277; 326; 340
Abukir, 43; 197
Abundantia, in style, 157; 244
Abydos, 35; temple of Osiris in, 185; 216; 218; 222; nome-sign of, 226; 254; 274; 300; 312
Acarnania, 186
Accumulation, of divine epithets, 138
Accusative, in Greek construction, 193; 196; Acc. neuter of adjective after *in*, 240; after *similis*, 333
Acheron, darkness of, where Isis shines, 6 (271, 2); 165; 307
Acorn, brutish provender of, 2 (267, 5); 116
Acrocorinth, 17; 264
Actaeon, 29 f.; 152 f.
Adjective, pronominal, used for pronoun, 270; adjectives in -*bilis*, 279; 292
'Admiral', in cult of Isis, 46
Admonitions, kind, of Isis, 22 (284, 1)
Adoration, warmest, for Isis Campensis, 26 (287, 23); 53; 54; 319; 328
Adorned like sun, as initiate, 24 (286, 4 f.); 314 ff.
Adramyttium, 226
Adrasteia, 153
Advocate, speeches of in forum, in Latin, 28 (290, 3 f.); 3; 336 f.; 349
Aemilia Pudentilla, wife of Apuleius, 10; 49; 62

Aemilianus, 61; 359
Aeschylus, charge against, 292; See also Index of Authors and Works
Africa, and Apuleius, 11; 28; folk-tale in north-west, 22
Africa, Christianity in, 5
Africa, living Latin in, 56 f.
African accent, of Apuleius, 4; stylistic tendency, 64 ff.; 158; 164; 252; 257
Africans, call Isis Queen Isis, 5 (269, 20 ff.); 154 f.; in cult of Isis, 190 f.
Africitas, 56 f.; 128
Agatha, St., festival of, 210
Agathê Tychê, and Isis, 241; 242
Age, every, with initiated throngs, 10 (273, 15); 190 ff.
Agoracritus, statue by, 153
Agorius, Vettius, Praetextatus, 282
Aion, and Isis, 140; and Osiris, 140; rose sacred to, 161; 170; and Zervan, 243
Akhet-cow, 211
Alexander, 193; 200; 201; 330
Alexandreia, 202
Alexandria, and Isis Pelagia, 32; 42; statue by Bryaxis in, 127; oracle of Sarapis in, 139; theology of, 140; and Isis-Nemesis, 153; 199; 204; 212; and Agathê Tychê, 242; and Isis Pronoia, 253; statue of Sarapis in, 269; Serapeum, 271; and serpent forms, 311; 313; 314; 343
Alexandrian love-elegy, 21
Ali, changed into ass, 26
Allegorical approach, Egyptian, 28
Alliteration, 239; 244; 245; 250; 256; 270; 280; 281; 284; 296; 340; in triple sequence, 65; 235; 238; linked with assonance, 65; 112; 171; in prayer, 121; 123; 137; with five *r*-sounds, 168; three *f*-sounds, 235; and pleonasm, 261; of cognates, 268
All-powerful goddess (Isis), 16 (278, 6 f.); 256
Altar, high, carried by second in pro-

Forgiveness, of gods, prayed for, 23 (284, 21); 287; asked of Mithras, chief priest, 25 (287, 13 f.); 53; 325; 271
Form, sudden change of, 6 (270, 19 f.); 163
Fortis Fortuna, 241
Fortuna, 181; 241 ff.
Fortuna Nefaria, 24; 241
Fortuna Primigeneia, temple of, at Praeneste, 20; and Isis-Tychê, ibid.; 344
Fortuna Saeva, 24; 241
Fortune, 2 (267, 17); overcome by providence of Isis, 12 (275, 17); storms of, 15 (277, 4 f.); 241 ff.; blindness of, 15 (277, 9); 250; cruelty of, 15 (277, 11); wicked, 15 (277, 15); protection of a Fortune who is not blind, but sees (Isis), 15 (277, 15 f.); Lucius victorious over his Fortune, 15 (277, 20); 345; notable good fortune, 18 (280, 9); gales of, pacified by Isis, 25 (286, 22 f.); 322
Fortune, Good, and Isis, 147; 241 ff.
Fortune, modest, diminished by expenses of travel, 28 (289, 10 f.); 335
Forum, profit in, through advocate's speeches, 28 (290, 3 f.); 336 f.; 30 (291, 4 f.); fame and favour in the courts, 30 (291, 9 f.)
Fotis, see Photis
Four-footed form (of ass), 2 (267, 19)
Fourth, in procession, with emblem of justice, 10 (274, 8); 203 ff.; and small golden vessel, 10 (274, 11); 208 ff.
Fowler, part of, played, 8 (272, 11); 177
Fowling, 20; 177
Francis, St., Third Order of, 336
Freedom, result of, 15 (278, 2); 255 f.
Freemasonry, 302; 333
Freimaurer, 302
Freud, Sigmund, 10
Friends, help with expenses, 23 (284, 18); 286
Fringes, tasselled, of cloak of Isis, 3 (268, 16); 129 f.
Frost, followed by sunny day, 7 (271, 16 f.); 169
Funerary boat, and Isis, 37 ff.
Fussala, and Punic, 61
Future Indicative, with imperative meaning, 163

Gadara, swine of, 250
Gaetulia, 60
Gain, promise of, 20 (282, 7); 277

Galatea, Isis-priestess, funerary relief of, 130
Gales, of Fortune, pacified by Isis, 25 (286, 22 f.); 321 f.
Galli, and Attis, 175
Ganges, 144
Ganymede, and monkey, 179; 180; 353
Garlands, presented in temple of Isis, 17 (280, 2); 268
Garments, of goddess, stored in temple of province, 29 (290, 19 f.); 339
Gates, of hell, in power of Isis, 21 (283, 4 f.)
Geb = Cronus, 140; five children of, 204; 330
Gematen (Kawa), Isis in, 154
Genitive plural, shortened form, 145; double plural ending, 277, 325
Genitive, reflexive, 196; of description, 336; adverbial use, 270
Genitivus Inhaerentiae, 64; 273; 336
Geryones, 118
Gestation, period of, 355
Ghosts, repelled by Proserpina, 2 (267, 11 ff.); 117 f.
Gifts, presentation of, in dream, 20 (281, 18); of devotees, to Lucius, 23 (285, 23 f.)
Gil Blas, 23
Gladiator, part of, played, 8 (272, 7 f.); 176
Glory, of learning, destined for poor man from Madauros, 27 (289, 7 f.); 334
Glory, promised by Isis, 6 (270, 24); 164
Gnôsis, intuitive, 247; 358
Gnosticism, Valentinian, 243; and fate, 244
God, and Nous, 244
Goddesses of Song (Camenae), 9 (273, 9)
'God's Hand', 203; one-handed god, 207
Gods, above and below, approached and worshipped in initiation, 23 (285, 13 f.); 306; they honour Isis, 25 (286, 23 f.); 322; unexpected and marvellous commands of, 29 (290, 5 f.); 337; new and strange plan of, 29 (290, 8 f.); think Lucius worthy, 29 (290, 15); 339; generous providence of, 30 (291, 4); 341
Gods, father of, (Osiris), 27 (288, 7 f.); 329 f.
Gods, forgiveness of, prayed for, 23 (284, 21); 287
Gods, great, order Third Initiation, 29 (290, 23); 340

ary, 29 (290, 18); to be accepted with joyful heart at behest of great gods, 29 (290, 22 f.); equipment liberally procured for, 30 (291, 1 f.); 340

Instructions, secret, too holy to be uttered, 23 (284, 23 f.); 290; instruction to sell clothes, 28 (289, 16 ff.)

Integrity, of priests, questioned, 29 (290, 11 f.); 338

Interpretatio Aegyptiaca, 226

Interpretation, strict, of faith, 21 (282, 14)

Io, and Isis, 219; 221; 250

Iphis, Cretan, and Isis, 150; 237

Iranian thought, and fate, 244; and purification, 289; and light, 305

Iseo, Brescia, procession in, 207

Isermuthis, 128

Isidis Navigium, in Cenchreae, 15; 31 ff.; 111; 158; 178; 195; 245; 259 ff.; 275; 328; 350

Isis, in Acheron, shining in darkness, 6 (271, 2); 165 f.

Isis, admonitions of, 22 (284, 1)

Isis, adored in whole world, 5 (269, 14)

Isis, Aegyptia, 17; 18; 137; 264

Isis, to Africans Queen Isis, 5 (269, 20 ff.); 154 f.

Isis, and Agathê Tychê, 241

Isis, and Aion, 140

Isis, all-powerful goddess, 16 (278, 6 f.); 256

Isis, angry, 152

Isis, and Aphrodite, 142; 149; 150; 343

Isis, in Arabic legend, 132

Isis, and Artemis, 213

Isis, ass hateful to, 6 (270, 13 f.); 162; 6 (270, 18 f.); 24; 163

Isis, with ass, 26

Isis, and Athena, 147; cult in Athens, 149

Isis, august deity, beneficent grace of, 22 (284, 6 f.)

Isis, Augusta, 157

Isis, in Badalona, 195

Isis, on banqueting couch, with Sarapis, 319

Isis, and baptism, 288

Isis, and base of finest triangle, 204

Isis, beasts that roam the mountains in awe of, 25 (287, 3); 324

Isis, becomes bitch, 24

Isis, Bellona equated with, 5 (269, 18 f.); 152; 156

Isis, beneficent in helping mortal men, 25 (286, 18); 321

Isis, in Beneventum, 19; 223

Isis, birds in sky in awe of majesty of, 25 (287, 2); 324

Isis, birthday of, 184; 191

Isis, blessings of, 12 (275, 12); radiant blessing of, acclaimed, 13 (276, 13); 238; constant, 25 (286, 19 f.); 321

Isis, blindness inflicted by, 133; 237; 271

Isis, in boat, 34 ff.; in solar barque, 34; in funerary boat, 37

Isis, boys dedicated to, 186

Isis, breezes of sea and, 5 (269, 12 f.); 144 f.; favourable breeze for ship of, 16 (279, 6 f.); breezes blow by command of, 25 (287, 1); 323

Isis, buds grow by command of, 25 (287, 2); 324

Isis, in Busiris, 147

Isis, and Byblos, voyage to, 40

Isis, in Byzantium, 46

Isis Campensis, 26 (287, 23); 18; 54; 327 f.

Isis, care of, ever-watchful, 26 (288, 2); 329

Isis, carries bronze rattle, 4 (269, 1 f.); 132 f.

Isis, carries golden vessel, 4 (269, 4 ff.); 133 f.

Isis, in Carthage, 15

Isis, in Cenchreae, 15; 17. See Cenchreae.

Isis, Ceres to the Eleusinians, 5 (269, 18); 151; 156

Isis, chamber of, in temple, 17 (279, 13); 264

Isis, chaste, 29

Isis, in Cisalpine Gaul, 191

Isis, cloak of, black, 3 (268, 13 ff.); 128 f.; with knot, 3 (268, 15); 129; fringes, 3 (268, 16); 129 f.; stars and half-moon on, 4 (268, 17 ff.); 130 f.

Isis, in Cologne, 149; 167; 195

Isis, commands of, 5 (270, 4 f.); 157 f.; 6 (270, 17); 161; 7 (271, 10); 19 (281, 4); 272; 21 (283, 2 f.); 280; radiant commands in dark night, 22 (283, 18 f.); 281; divine commands, 22 (284, 9); breezes and rain-clouds by command of, 25 (287, 1); 323; seeds sprout, buds grow, ibid.

Isis, constellations move for, 25 (286, 25); 323

Isis, in Coptos, 211

Isis, in Corinth, 15; 17

Isis, and corn, 126; 151; 324

Isis, counsel of, by night, 19 (281, 3 f.); 272

Pluto, and Sarapis, 43; and Osiris, 142

Podium, for priests, 266

Poet, skilled, author of processional song, 9 (273, 10); 188

Poetical colouring, 65; 135; 168; 170; 193; 222; 256; 279; 280; 296; 351

Pollio, G. Asinius, 333

Pompeii, Iseum in, 19; shrine in villa at, 30; mural painting from Iseum, 41; statue of Isis in, 128; fresco with Isis-Fortuna, 131; house of Loreius Tibur-tinus, 152 f.; altar with 'Isis Augusta', 157; social origins of Isiacs, 191; 193; 194; boat-shaped lamps, 195; shrines, 196; situla, 209; *cista*, 223; Isis-Fortuna, 241; naval scene, 259 f.; 263; steps before temple, 269; Isea, size of, 271; altars near, 275; water system, 276; crypts, 284; lamps, 306; Isis znd Luna, 310; Harpocrates-Helius, 315; and incubation, 332; *decurio* at, 342; fresco, 349 f.

Pontianus, 49; 62; 272

Popidius Celsinus, N., 342

Popidius Florus, N., villa of, 223

Popular speech, 55 ff.; 157; 162; 163; 171; 183; 196; 207; 310; 335

Pornographic tradition, 2

Port, of Augustus, 26 (287, 19); 326

Poseidon, and Pallas Athene, 149; and Isis, 157; 262; 344

Position, in society, of no avail, 15 (277, 6 f.); 246 f.

Potaïssa, Dacia, 318

Potsdam, relief at, 214; 216; 229

Poverty, hard pressure of, 28 (289, 12); 335; not to be regretted, 28 (289, 19); 334 f.; 270

Pozzuoli, 195

Praeneste, temple of Fortuna Primigeneia at, 20; mosaic, 42; 344; 358 f.

Praises, of Isis, 25 (287, 4); 324 f.

Prayer, to moon-goddess, 2 (267, 4 ff.); 114 ff.; over ship of Isis, 16 (278, 15); 261; for fortunate sailing in new year's commerce, 16 (278, 18 f.); 262; prayers for prosperity of emperor, senate, knights, and whole Roman people, 17 (279, 17 ff.); 267; to adored image of Isis, 20 (281, 20 f.); 275; greatest prayer to be realised, 22 (283, 20); constant prayers for initiation, 22 (284, 8); for forgiveness of gods, 23 (284, 21); 57; 287; to Isis, 25 (286, 17 ff.); 320 f.

Predestination, 53; 253; 281

Preludes, musical, 9 (273, 11); 188

Preparations, for rite of initiation, 22 (284, 17); arranged on liberal scale, 23 (284, 17 ff.); 286; for Second Initiation, 28 (289, 20)

Present, and perfect tenses, 234; 327

Priene, 183

Priest, chief, utters prayers over ship of Isis, and purifies it, 16 (278, 15 ff.); 261; enters chamber of goddess, 17 (279, 11 ff.); 264; appears in visitation, 20 (281, 11); 273; entreated for initiation, 21 (282, 12); severe and strict, 21 (282, 14); 278; finishes address, 21 (283, 15); named Mithras, to be in charge of initiation, 22 (283, 21 ff.); 281 f.; greeted in lodging, 22 (284, 2 ff.); 284; blesses Lucius before initiation, 22 (284, 6 ff.); kindly old man, prepares with aid of sacred books, 22 (284, 10 ff.); carries out rites of First Initiation, 23 (284, 20 ff.); 286 f.; leads Lucius to heart of shrine, 23 (285, 5 f.); embraced and regarded as father, 25 (287, 11 f.); 325

Priest, goes round altars and pours libation, 20 (281, 21 ff.); 275

Priest, of initiation rites, chosen by fore-sight of Isis, 21 (282, 18 f.); 279

Priest, of Isis, addresses Lucius after transformation, 14 (277, 2 ff.); 240; excellent priest, then silent, 16 (278, 3 f.); 256; informed of divine vision by Lucius, 30 (290, 26); 340

Priest, Lector, 17 (279, 14); 265

Priestesses, of Isis, 182

Priests, comradeship of, 19 (281, 2); 272

Priests, of Isis, offer new barque, 5 (270, 7 f.); 158; priest in procession with crown of roses, 6 (270, 10 f.); 159; priest instructed by Isis, 6 (270, 15 ff.); 162; priests of ritual, 10 (273, 19); 193; priest with cow (= Isis) on shoulders, 11 (274, 19 f.); 221; brings with him destiny and salvation, 12 (275, 13); 233; carries sistrum and crown, 12 (275, 14 f.); 233; remembers vision by night, 13 (275, 22 f.); 234; holds out crown of roses, 13 (275, 25); provides linen garment for naked Lucius, 14 (276, 20); 239

Priests, two, advice of questioned, 29 (290, 10 f.); 338; also integrity, ibid.

Procession, 6 (270, 10, 12); religious and

179; and palm-branch, 201; 202; and
Ma'at, 205; and Anubis, 218; 222
Thousand, mouths and tongues, not
enough to express praise of Isis, 25
(287, 6 f.); 325
Threads, of fate, unravelled by hand of
Isis, 25 (286, 21 f.); 322
Three times, boon of initiation extended,
29 (290, 16); 337; meaningful number,
29 (290, 17); 339
Threefold countenance, of Proserpina, 2
(267, 11 f.); 117 f.
Throngs, of the initiated, 10 (273, 14 f.);
189 f.
Thurii, inscription from, 295
Thyrsus, 31; see also Wands (Bacchic)
Tiberius, 132; 148; 184; 246; 318; 327
Tikos (female deceased), and Osiris, 317
Time, first offspring of (Isis), 5 (269, 10);
141 f.
Titans, and Zagreus, 258
Tithorea, Phocis, temple of Isis in, 139;
272
Titianus, governor of Achaea, 13
Titus, 60
Tivoli, 'Canopus' of Hadrian in, 19
Tom Jones, 23
Tongue, incurs guilt through curiosity,
23 (285, 9); 293
Torch, used by priest in purifying ship
of Isis, 16 (278, 15); 261; carried in
right hand of initiate, 24 (286, 2 f.);
314; and Korê, 126
Torches, of magistrate, 8 (272, 9); 176;
carried in procession, 9 (273, 5 f.);
183 f.; 353
Touna el-Gebel, 205; 288; 292
Trajan, 199; 267; 326; 330
Trance, state of, in initiation, 297
Transformation, easy skill of Isis in,
13 (276, 12); 236 f.; Isis praised for,
16 (278, 6 f.); 256; name alluding to,
27 (289, 1 f.); 47; 235; 347; in after-
life, 298
Transitive use of intransitive verb, 169
Travel, expenses of, 28 (289, 10); 335
Travel tales, 20
Trees, revived in spring, 7 (271, 19 ff.);
170 f.
Triad, of goddesses, 118
Triadic structures, 58; 121; 138; 146; 244
Tricolon, 138
Trier, 207; Helen-mosaic from, 318
Trilingual, of Sicilians, 5 (269, 17); 150 f.

Trilingualism, of Apuleius, 62; 151; of
Sicilians, 150 f.; of Jesus, 352
Trivia, 118
Troubles, and joys, related, 19 (280, 18);
271
Tune, traditional to temple and deity, 9
(273, 12 f.); 189
Tunic of Isis, 3 (268, 10 ff.); 126 f.; white,
yellow, fiery, *ibid.*; snow-white festal
tunics of youths in choir, 9 (273, 8 f.);
187; linen tunic with sumptuous decor-
ations, worn by initiate, 24 (285, 21 f.);
310
Turin Stela (296), 246
Tut'ankhamûn, 159; 217; 220; 263
Tuthmosis III, 38
Twelve robes, of initiate, 24 (285, 18);
308 f.
Twelve Tables, and magic, 49
'Two Lands', of Egypt, 156
Tychê, and Nemesis, 153; 202; and Isis,
244; blind, 250
Tychê-Isis, 343 f.
Tympanum, 185
Typhon, repelled by sistrum, 133; soldier
of, 254
Typhonic crocodile, 129

Ulysses, blood of, 49; 246
Unbelievers, called to admit their mis-
take, 15 (277, 18 f.); 252
Unconquered, Osiris, 27 (288, 8); 330
Underworld, awful silences of, and Isis,
5 (269, 12 f.); 144 f.
Uninitiated, far removed, 23 (285, 4);
292; understanding of, 23 (285, 16)
Unio mystica, of believer with Isis, 53;
with Osiris, 307
Universe, mother of (Isis), 5 (269, 9;
140; mistress of (Isis), 7 (271, 18 f.);
170
Unvanquished deity (Isis), 7 (271, 7); 167
Uppsala, figure at, 229
Uraeus, of Wedjoyet, 125; 232 f.; 351
Uraei, and Isis, 125
Urania, 116
Uranus, 116
Uterus, and small vase in procession,
230 f.

Valentinus, Gnostic, 243
Variatio, 170; 234
Vase, small, of gold, image of highest
deity, 11 (275, 6 ff.); 227 ff.
Vegetarian diet, submitted to, 21 (283,

LINGUISTIC INDICES

LATIN

abstinentia, 273
Acheron, 30
ad istum modum, 123; 325; 334
adambulare, 58; 180
adfamen, 58; 170; 342
adfari, 270
adligere, 343
adluctor, 58; 233
adluvies, 171
adolere, 314
adorabilis, 58; 270
adsonare, 170
advena, 328
adytum, 284
aerumna, 58; 119
aerumnabilis, 119
aetatula, 247
Afer, 61
alioquin, 278; 325
aliquam, adv., 326
altiuscule, 58; 232
ambroseus, 135
amicimen, 58; 59; 182; 293
amphora, 45
ansa, 'handle', 231
antecantamentum, 58; 188
anteludium, 58
anteludia, 30; 32; 40; 172; 348
antistes sacrorum, 194
apertio templi, 55
ara, 245 f.
argutia, 28
aroma, 263
asellus = cinaedus, 27
asinarii, 5
aspis, 134
attollere, 217
aurea vannus, 31; 211 ff.
aureus, 212; 262
auspicari, 238; 239
auxilia, 13

balteus, 173
barba, 59
barbitium, 58; 59; 176
baxea, 58; 176
beatitudo, 250

beatus, 164; 257; 284
bella fabella, 7
bellule, 58; 341
beneficium, 50; 238; 320
bonae artes, 4
Bubastiacae, 181

caduceus, 198; 216
caelestis Venus, 116
calcare, 323
calvitium, 345
campestris, 153
canalis, 230
candidus, 277; 355
cantamen, 49
capreolatim, 58; 285
carchesium, 262
carne, vale, 172
carnelevarium, 172
carpentum, 326 f.
carrus navalis, 47
cataclista, 58; 187
cavere, 279
-ce, 169
Cecropeius, 149
censere, 272
cheniscus, 58; 263
cinaedus, 27
circumrorans, 58; 288
circumsecus, 58; 260
cista mystica, 31; 134; 135; 222 ff.; 250; 256; 293
cistophorus, 226
citrus, 263
cohors, 240; 286
commeator, 58; 216
comperior, 329
conceptus, 285
congerere, 'construct', 213
conradere, 58; 335
consequenter, 233
conservator, 181
conservatrix, 181
constrepere, 193
consulere, 338
consummatio, 319
contabulatio, 129

conversio, 252
coronamen, 58; 59; 182
corpus pausariorum, 259
crepides, 58; 174
crepitaculum *and* crepitare, 133
cubiculum, 284
curiositas, 25; 29 f.; 47 f.; 248 ff.; 294;
   354
curiosus, 249
currus navalis, 172
cymbium, aureum, 32; 133; 195 f.

de, 257; 331; 333
decurio quinquennalis, 342
delibutus, 268
demeare, 164
deorum, deum, 145
dependere, 133
deprecatus, 325
desiderium religiosum, 294
despoliare, 239
despondere, 334
deus deum magnorum potior, 65
Deus Invictus, 330
dexteram dare, 284; cf. 321 f.
dignatio, 281; 284; 339
disseminatio, 58; 342
distrahere, 276; 335; 337
diu denique, 325
diu diuque, 274
diva triformis, 118
divina disciplina, 48
doctrina, 'learning', 247
domina, 170; 280
dominus, 251
domuitio, 58
duumvir quinquennalis, 14

ebria bruma, 28
ecce ... et, 328
edicere, 188
effabilis, 358
effari, 240
effigiatus, 58; 232
elementa, 301 ff.; 323
eligere, 280 f.
elocutilis, 58; 123
Elysium, 30
emergere, 111
Enos Lases iuvate! 138
ergo igitur, 157; 281; 335
et ecce, 169
examussim, 58; 333
exanclare, 122 f.; 240

exercitius, adv., 58; 338
exuviae, 339

fabula ('comedy'), 7
fabula ('fiction'), 11
fabula Graecanica, 2; 27
fabulari, 58; 256
faces, 176
famosus, 278
fasces, 176
favens et propitia, 157
felix, 257; 284
festus asinorum, 26
fides, 257
fistulae, 184
flamina, 144 f.; 323
floride adv., 58; 310
fluctuare, 338
fui *for* eram, 169 f.

gaudialis, 58; 340
gaudium, 54
genialis, 183
gerere, 173
gloriosus, 164
grammateus, 265
gratias gerere, 325
guttatim, 58; 183

hactenus, 340
harundo, 177
hilaritas, 169
hilaritudo, 58; 169
historiae, 11
homo moriturus, 296

ignorabilis, 285
illae, Genit., 294
ille, 114
immo, 280
impaenitendus, 58; 335
incapistrare, 58; 276
incertare, 264
inclemens, 233
incubatio, 139
incunctanter, 58; 161; 342
indigena, 328
ineffabilis, 227; 358
inextricabiliter, 58; 322
inhumanus, 240
initia, 3 f.
initialis, 141
initiamentum Veneris, 9
initiare, 189
inlustrare, 330; 335; 340

innocentia, 257
inovans, 58; 252
inremunerabilis, 59; 320
instantia, 279
instar, 280; 339
insuper, 263
inter sacrum et saxum, 335
interpellare, 337
intritum; intrita, 263
invictus, 167; 330
invinius, 59; 291
Isia, 41
Isiaca, 181
Isidis Navigium, 15; 31 ff.
iste, 57; 157 f.; 250; 251; 284
iubere, 280
iugum, 255; 340
iuridicus provincialis, 12 f.

lacinia, 239
lares, 332
largiter, 270
largitus, 58; 340
legatus Augusti pro praetore, 13
limpidus, 192
longe longeque, 127 f.
lubricus, 247
lucerna, 46
luminare, 59; 358
lux, 280

magis aptior, 207
magis magisque, 277
magnificentia, 50
magus, 49
mane, 308
mare clausum, 45 f.
matronalis, 178
meatus, 322
meditullium, 310
metae Murtiae, 12
miles, 254 f.
Milesia, 2; 27
militia, 174
minuties, 59; 236
Miserere, 297
modificari, 279
moliri, 181
monitus, 158; 320
multiformis, 124
multinominis, 284
mundus, 322 f.
munerabundus, 59; 270

nactus, nanctus, 111

namque, 310
natalicium, 317
navigium Veneris, 355
necdum, 330
nefandus, 239
nefarius, 239
nefastus, 239
nimius = magnus, 238
nomen unicum, 144
nubilosus, 59; 171
nummorum nummi, 65
nuncupare, 262

obauratus, 59; 175
oblatio, 270
obliquus, 189
obpexus, 59; 183
obsequium, 255
observabilis, 279
obsibilare, 59; 171
omnipotens, 256
oppido, 58; 338
opus sectile, 19
orbis, 322; 323
orificium, 59; 232
ornatrix, 181; 183
osculabundus, 161
otiosus, 321

palla contabulata, 186
palma, 'victory', 137
palma victrix, 203
partim … partim, 286
pastophori, v. General Index
pater patrum, 282
pater sacrorum, 278; 283; 292
pator, 59; 196
patrocinium, 258; 336; 342
pauculus, 337; 341
pausarii, 259
pax deorum, 287
penitus, 58; 163
percolere, 116
percontare, 58; 273
perfluus, 59; 175
perhumanus, 240
peritia Aegyptiaca, 29
permixtus, 168
pervigilis, 59; 329
piissimus, 284
pompa circensis, 172
portus, 245 f.
post aliquam multum temporis, 58
potentia, 50
potentissimus, 194

unus Liber pater, 293
urnula, 42; 45; 227 ff.
utcumque, 239; 250
utique = ergo, 273
utut, 58; 274

vadimonium, 163; 258; 292
vannus, 211 f.
velle, 59
venatio, 174
venerabilis, 292
venia, 30; 53; 287

verba devorans, 320
vestigia, 269; 290
victrix, 167
vindicare, 251
viriculae, 59; 335
volentia, 59; 161
vota publica, 33; 172; 266 f.
votivus, 173
vultus, 123

xerophagia, 291

EGYPTIAN

'Imy Dw3t, 'He who is in the Underworld', 297
insw, inswty, 222
is, 'old', 142
it nṭrw, 'father of the gods', 330
itrt, 'shrine', 224

'3, 162
'fdt št3t, 'secret chest', 224
'nḫ-sign, 136; 209
'š3 rnw, 145

w'b, 'pure one', 251; 333
w't, 'unica', 145; 167
wpwty nsw, 'royal ambassador', 237
wnpt (of Nephthys), 269
wrt, 142
wḥm 'nḫ, 'repeating life', 258
wsr, 'mighty', 330
wš3it, 'the midnight one', 304
wšb, 'situla', 210; 222

b3, 244
bs, 'initiate', 189

p3 wšb i3d, of Osiris, 246; 321
p3 nṭr, of deceased, 316
p3 šdw, 'the saviour', 197
Pr-'3, 'Great House', 267
pr 'nḫ, 'House of Life', 284
pr md3t, 285

m3' ḫrw, 152; 164; 257; 317; 330
m3't, 206
mni, 'land, come ashore', 245

nbt, 156
nbt wi3, 34
nbt nṭrw, 142

nbt wš3w, 'Mistress of Midnight', 304
nfr, 164; 257
nis, 'chant', 186
nḥm, 'rescue', 246
nsw nswyw, 'King of Kings', 330
nsw nṭrw, 'King of the gods', 330
nswyt, 156
nṭr '3, 'Great God', 268; 329 f.
nd, 'he who saves', 197 f.
ndt, of Isis, 246

rḫ, and correct knowledge, 244

hn št3y, 'secret box', 222; 224

ḥnw-barque, 36
ḥnwt, 156
ḥnwt nṭrw, 142
Ḥr-m-'Inp, and Hermanubis, 200
ḥry sš3, 'guardian of the secret', 224
ḥk3t, 156
ḥtp, 'mercy', 246

ḫry-ḥbt, lector-priest, 265

sn t3, 'kissing the earth', 268
snṭri, 'that which makes divine', 316
sšmw iwf, 'Image of the flesh', 303
sšmw Wsir, 'Image of Osiris', 303
sšš, 'pluck papyrus', 133
sššt, 'sistrum', 133
sšt3, 'what is secret', 250

š3i, 'fate', 243

k3, and daemon, 243; 244
krḥt, 222

Dw3t, 288

ḏrt ỉmnt, 'Hidden Hand', 204
Ḏḥwty-ỉr-rḫ-sw, 'Thoth it is who knows him', 351

*Ḏd-ḥr-s, 'Horus says it', 351

GREEK

ἀγαθοδαίμονες, 135
ἀγάπη, 321
ἁγιασθείς, 308
ἅγιος, 321
ἀδελφοὶ εἰσποίητοι, 'adopted brothers', 328
ἀλλογενής, 328
ἀμφορεύς, 214
ἀνάγκη, 242; 323
ἀναγωγή, 300
ἀνίκητος, 330
ἄοινος, 291
ἀποθέωσις, 316
ἀποπομπή, 250
ἀπόρρητα, 331
Ἀρυώτης, 29
ἀρχιπαστοφόροι, 342

βαϊήθ, 202
βάϊς, 'palm-leaf', 202
βασίλεια, 114; 115
βασίλεια θεῶν, 142
βασιλεὺς βασιλέων, 341
βασίλισσα, 115
βαστάζειν, 217
βησάρτης, 350; 354
βοῶπις, 148

γνῶσις, 244; 247

δεσπότις, 148
δικαιοδότης, 13
δικαιοσύνη, 149; 153; 204
δός, 123
δρώμενον, 294

Ἐγώ εἰμι, 137 f.
εἱμαρμένη, 166 f.; 242; 244; 323
Εἷς Ζεὺς Σέραπις, 207; 246
ἐκθέωσις, 316
ἔκφρασις, 173
Ἐλέησον, 246
Ἐλέου βωμός, 246
ἐπιπομπή, 250
ἐπῳδαί, 49
ἐς κόρακας, 250
εὐδαίμων, 257
Εὔπλοια, 195
εὐπλόκαμος, 124

εὑρίσκειν, 324
εὐσεβείας ... δίδαγμα, 143
Ἐφέσια γράμματα, 268

ζυγόν, 255

ἤπιος, 321

θάλλος, 268
θαλλοφόροι, 268
θεὰ βασίλεια, 111
θεὰ μεγίστη, 198
θεοὶ σύνναοι, 150
θεὸς θεῶν, 341
θεραπευτής, 328

Ἰαῶ, 207
ἱερογραμματεύς, 265
ἱερός, 321
ἱερὸς λόγος, 294
ἱστορία, 20
ἱστορίαι, 11

κατάκλειστος, 187
κιβώτιον, 222; 232
κυμβίον, 133

λαμπαδεία, 183
λαμπτηροφόροι, 181; 183; 195
λάρναξ, 349
λινόστολος, 192
λυχνάπται, 195
λυχνάπτος, 353
λυχναπτρία, 183
λυχναψία, 350

μάκαρ, 164; 257
μαλακός, 175
μᾶλλον, 207
μαστίον, 210
μαστοί, of vases, 209 f.
μεγαλόθρονος, 152
μέγας, of gods, 238
Μέγας Βασιλεύς, 267; 330
μεγίστη, 148
μελανηφόρος, 128
μελανόστολος, 128
μεταμορφοῦσθαι, 342

μετάνοια, 252
μήτηρ θεῶν, 142; 148
μία, 145
μόνος--formula, 167
μυριόμορφος, 145
μυριώνυμος, 145
μυσταγωγός, 283

ναμοφόρον, 349
ναύαρχος, 46; 260 f.
νοῦς, 244; 246

ὄβριμος, 330
ὄλβιος, 257
ὄργια, 336
ὁρμίστρια, 'bringer to harbour', 245

παλιγγενεσία, 258
πάλιν γίγνεσθαι, 258
παντοκράτειρα, 141; 242
παράδοσις, 280
παραλαμβάνειν, 277
πασιφάεσσα, 116
παστός, 266
παστοφόριον, 344
περιεργία, 248
περιρραντήρια, 287
πεσσός, πεσσόν, 148
πίστις, 257
πλαγίαυλος, 188 f.
πλοιαφέσια, 31; 268
ὁ πλοῦς τῆς Ἴσιδος, 31
πολύμορφος, 145
πολυώνυμος, 145; 148; 284
πότνα, πότνια, 115
πρόνοια, 242; 323
προσήλυτος, 328

ῥοδόστερνος, 160

σεῖστρον and σείω, 133
σημεῖα, 50
σπονδαύλης, 210
σπονδεῖον, 210; 228; 276
στρατία (of Isis), 254
στρόφιον, 210
συνθήματα (of Mysteries), 57; 65; 294 f.
σῶς, 29
Σωταλᾶς, 29
σώτειρα, 148; 181
σώτειρ' ἀθανάτη, 238
σωτήρ, 181

ταυρῶπις, 148
τέθνηκα ἀνέζησα, 21
τελετή, 319
τρίμορφος, 152
τρίσμακαρ, 256
τρισόλβιος, 257
τριφνή, 147
τύραννος, 114

ὑψίστη, 198

Φαραώ, 267
φιλόστοργος, 321
φῶς, 280
φωτίζεσθαι, 330

ψαλτήριον, 185

ᾠδός, 186 ; 194 f.
ὡρολόγος, 276; 283
ὡροσκόπος, 276; 283

SEMITIC

אַל, with jussive, 163
אַל in Punic inscriptions, 341
אַל אֱלֹהִים, 341

לֹא, with imperfect, 163

מְרַר, 'dwelling', 60

פַּרְעֹה, 267

INDEX OF ANCIENT AUTHORS AND WORKS

Persius, *Sat.* (2.15 f.), 113; 168; (5.33), 129

Peter, Kerygma of, 252

Petronius, dialogue in, 56; and parataxis, 641; use of tenses, 234; erotic and magical themes in, 247; on Fortune, 253

Petronius, *Sat.*(37), 65; 341; (79), 239; (101.1), 253; (109), 177; (114.8), 251; (120), 171; (120.94), 253; fr. (49, 7 f.), 250

Petrus Chrysologus, 176

Philae, texts from, 132; 205

  Geburtshaus (65,12-15), 211; (105,10), 217; (265,11), 211; (268), 184; (308), 206; (326), 184; (358), 184; (359, 19 ff.), 184; (380), 201; (386), 184; (387,7 ff.), 184

  Der grosse Pylon (5,17 ff.), 341; (13,4), 170; (42,2-7), 210; (76,4-6), 166; (168,18-19), 323

Philo, *De sacrificiis Abelis et Caini* (32), 359

Philocalus, Calendar (March 5th), 31; 41; 268; (August 12th), 184; 350

Philostratus, *V. Apoll.* (2.20), 311; (3.48), 357; (4.18), 289

Photius, 1; 14; 153; *Bibl.* (129), 1; 14; (144 B), 154

Pindar, Fr. (129), 304; 309; *Ol.* (6.92 ff.), 151; (13.90 ff.), 180

Pithom Decree, 183

Plato, 48; 49; 53; 54; 141; 204; 207; 258; 351; *Phaedrus*, 53; *Phileb.* (61 C), 291; *Resp.* (518 D ff.), 252; *Symp.*, 53

Pseudo-Plato, *Axiochus*, 165; 309

Plautus, 56; 64; 123; 163; 165; 170; 171; 180; 198; 207; 238; 249; 256; 257; 329; 333; 338

  Amph. (1.3.43), 232
  Aul. (57), 269
  Bacch. (1068), 341
  Capt. (617), 335; (644), 208; (825), 342
  Cas. (704), 335; (848), 341
  Curc. (89), 157
  Men. (391), 176; (987), 208
  Merc. (558), 274
  Mil. (212), 169; (613), 208; (677), 169; (784), 270
  Most. (47), 158; (847), 157
  Pers. (111), 183; (226), 207
  Poen. (1188), 123
  Rud. (550), 338
  Trin. (756), 157

Pliny, Elder, 169; *HN* (praef. 6), 321; (2.4.22), 242; (2.55.142), 207; (5.5.1), 227; (5.8.43), 155; (5.12.65), 137; (7.2.11), 181; (9.56.14), 175; (10.70.136), 312; 313; (13.22.71 ff.), 28; (25.24.59), 273; (31.3.34), 113; (36.23.55), 263; (36.62.189), 344

Pliny (the Younger), 359; *Ep.* (3.3.4), 247

Plotinus, 356; (1.6.7), 309

Plutarch, 190
  Amat. (19), 116
  De fac. (28), 119
  De Iside et Osiride, 4; 6; (2), 247; (3), 127; 128; 176; 183; 192; 193; 203; 204; 264; 282; 317; 319; (4), 192; 193; 253; 290; (6), 291; (9), 142; 149; 170; (10), 113; (12), 282; 323; 330; 331; (13), 39; 42; 349; (14), 124; 218; (15), 40; 349; (16), 40; (18), 40; 225; (19), 219; 254; (20), 185; (21), 178; (27), 43; 142; 143; 151; 181; 254; (29), 162; (30), 162; (32), 140; 149; 324; (33), 331; (35), 186; 211; 258; 278; 331; (36), 194; 215; 225; 331; (37), 330; 331; (38), 151; (39), 39; 128; 183; 212; 219; 222; 223; 232; 278; (43), 111; 112; 125; 140; (44), 165; 216; (45), 253; (50), 40; (51), 179; 225; 313; (52), 128; 219; 298; (53), 140; 145; (56), 204; (61), 217; (63), 133; 301; (67), 253; (68), 205; 283; (72), 258; (75), 217; (77), 126 f.; 179; 313; 339; (78), 142; 143; 319; (80), 299
  De superst. (3), 113
  Fr. de an. (2), 296; 305
  Quaest. conv. (3.10), 117; (8.4), 136
  Quaest. Rom. (76), 119
  V. Alc. (34), 283
  V. Lyc. (15), 175
  V. Sull. (35), 343

Polybius (21,37), 175

Porphyry,
  De abst. (1.31), 309; (2.16), 288; (4.6), 293; (4.7), 287; 291; (4.8), 283; (4.9), 274
  De imag. 151

Proclus, 48; *Theol. Plat.* (4.9), 300

Propertius (2.3.14), 193; (2.28.62), 290; (2.33A.1-2), 290; (2.33.15 ff.), 181; (3.3.55), 331; (4.1.21), 234; (4.5.34), 181; (4.8.51), 168

Prudentius; *Peristef.* (5.293 f.), 342

Psellus; *Comm.* (1141 B), 300 f.

Pyramid Texts, 24; 218; 254; (490b), 34